EUROPEAN MODERNITY
AND BEYOND

EUROPEAN MODERNITY AND BEYOND

The Trajectory of European Societies, 1945–2000

Göran Therborn

SAGE Publications
London • Thousand Oaks • New Delhi

First published 1995

 SAGE Publications Ltd
6 Bonhill Street
London EC2A 4PU

SAGE Publications Inc
2455 Teller Road
Thousand Oaks, California 91320

SAGE Publications India Pvt Ltd
32, M-Block Market
Greater Kailash – I
New Delhi 110 048

British Library Cataloguing in Publication data

A catalogue record for this book is
available from the British Library.

ISBN 0 8039 8934 2
ISBN 0 8039 8935 0 (pbk)

Library of Congress catalog card number 94-74796

Typeset by Photoprint, Torquay, Devon
Printed in Great Britain by The Cromwell Press Ltd, Broughton Gifford, Melksham, Wiltshire

CONTENTS

LIST OF TABLES, FIGURES AND MAPS

Tables

Figures

Maps

FINS DE SIÈCLE

'At the watershed of two eras',[1] the great Dutch historian Jan Romein characterized Europe in 1900, in his 'integral history' of the continent. Without the benefit of hindsight, which Romein could use to guide his immense erudition, the same may also be said of Europe's second *fin de siècle*, the present turn of the century. The sense of a shift is more present today than last time. But between which eras?

In 1900 the 'going-to-the-dogs' feelings associated with the term *fin-de-siècle*, which originated from an obscure Parisian play in 1888,[2] were more of an artistic counterpoint to the main theme, which was that of a threshold. Stephen Kern has summed up the mood of those days: 'This [the 1900s] generation had a strong, confident sense of the future, tempered by a concern that things were rushing much too fast.'[3] Nobody would say that of the current generation of Europeans.

Ours is a much deeper, and mainly social and political, sense of ending, whether of the revolutionary era opened in 1789, of the 'short century' starting in August 1914, of industrial class society, of modernity, or even of history. In 1900, the expectation was rather a proximate end to 'the pre-history' of humankind, the pre-history of exploitation which the socialist labour movement set out to finish.

On the other hand, in terms of technology we now probably have a stronger sense of continuity. The video, the computer and nuclear energy look pretty modest if we compare them with the coming of electricity, the telephone, the radio, the cinema, the aeroplane and the car. Nevertheless, there is more drama ahead in genetic engineering, and the space ventures compare quite well with the polar, Central Asian and trans-Saharan expeditions a century ago.

'Post-modernism' being largely a halt of the caravans of modernity, we should not be surprised if its artistic and philosophical forms look more like yesterday's than did those of, say, Cubism, Nietzsche or the multiple realities held out by the 'perspectivism' of Ortega y Gasset. At least from among the trees, post-modernist culture and its overtaking of the avant-garde as a victory of mass culture resembles the rise of mass sports about a hundred years ago from the sport of 'gentlemen'.

Anyway, in contrast to the topics predominant among epochal interpretations, of the past, the present or the future, this work is not primarily concerned with art, technology or big power games. It is focused on the structure of societies rather than on high politics, on the spacing of the continent rather than on spatial conceptions, on the culture of populations rather than of artists, scientists or masses. It deals with trajectories during a period rather than with turning-points. It does, however, aim to bear upon epochal questions – of modernity, of Europe's place and future in the world; this implies also lifting one's eyes outside Europe, taking in the comparative contours of other continents.

This book is the emancipated offspring of two parent projects. One is the multi-volume 'history of Europe' broached by Perry Anderson, Maurice Aymard, Paul Bairoch and Walter Barberis, to the first volume of which, dealing with postwar Europe, I was invited to contribute a piece on 'the sociology of Western Europe',[4] which forms one part of the foundations. The second is a long-term research project, still in its early stages, on 'routes to and through modernity', which I hit upon when widening my 1970s studies of the history of suffrage for Robert Brenner's Center for Social Theory and Comparative History at UCLA in 1990.[5]

My work on the sociology of Europe was financially supported by the Swedish National Bank Tercentenary Fund, that on modernity by the latter and by the Swedish Humanities and Social Science Research Council. Most of the spadework I have done with my own hands, but I would like to acknowledge the competent research assistance of Dr Elisabeth Özdalga, and of graduate students Suzanne Grandin and Kristina Bartley.

Finally, as a middle-aged, post-Protestant workaholic, I think time is long due to thank my family, my wife, my mother, my two children, warmly and publicly, for their forbearance with my asocial struggling with this and with previous works.

Göran Therborn

Notes

1 *Op het breukvlak van twee eeuwen*, completed after his death, in 1962, by his widow, Annie Romein-Verschoor, also a historian, with the help of his friends and students. It was published in English in 1978 as J. Romein, *The Watershed of Two Eras*, Middletown, Conn. Wesleyan University Press, 1978. I have used the paperback edition of 1982.
2 M. Teich and R. Porter (eds), *Fin de siècle and Its Legacy*, Cambridge, Cambridge University Press, 1990, pp. 1–2.
3 S. Kern, *The Culture of Time and Space 1880–1918*, Cambridge, Mass., Harvard University Press, 1983, p. 107. Cf. Romein, *The Watershed*, pp. 25, 652–3.
4 It is published as 'Modernitá sociale in Europa (1950–1992)', in P. Anderson et al. (eds), *Storia d'Europa*, Vol. 1, Turin, Einaudi, 1993.
5 The published version appeared as part of a SCASSS project, 'The Right to Vote and the Four World Routes to/through Modernity', in R. Torstendahl (ed.), *State Theory and State History*, London, Sage, 1992.

PART I
THEORY AND HISTORY

1
STRUCTURE, CULTURE AND MODERNITY

A sociological history

'Europe' in this book is not the EC/EU of the early 1990s. It is 'the house' from the Atlantic to the Urals, from North Cape to Trafalgar during the second half of the twentieth century, viewed in the late afternoon glow of world modernity. This book is an attempt to grasp and to understand the world historical meaning of postwar Europe, East and West. It arises from a fascination with 'the present as history',[1] from the curiosity of an empirical comparativist, and from a minoritarian sociologist's commitment to a bridging of the humanistic and the scientific cultures which traverse, rend and – at least potentially – enrich his discipline.[2] It is an expression of the historical reflexivity of a social observer, of a peripheral participant writing right after the end of postwar Europe.

My enterprise is a *sociological history* – rather than a historical sociology, in spite of the scope of its ambitions.[3] Its overriding questions are of contemporary history: What does European society look like? How has it changed in the course of the second half of the century? Why? The intention is neither to expound a particular social theory in the course of a narrative nor to put a social theory to historical test. Rather than telling a story, the text will raise a number of questions, and will try to answer them in a systematic, and empirically conscientious, manner. The questions derive from a conception of sociology and of the main sociological dimensions of a society, but also from a view of the comparative history of modernity. The answers are fetched from empirical sources, with rather little extractions from the labour of historians.

The aim is neither an 'interpretative essay', where profound truths are pulled out of the writer's head, nor a handbook of existing knowledge, nor a report of runs of mathematical models, but a novel systematic synthesis, scholarly reliable – as far as the certainly not faultless reliability of serious scholarship goes – and accessible to a general interested public.

This ambition raises two major methodological issues and one minor one. The minor one relates to the mode of presentation, with the accepted goal of reaching beyond the walls of the lecture room. In spite of some editorial hints to the contrary, I have decided against telling the whole as a story, above all not as one story. Basically, I think, because the narrative form is not very suitable for putting forward the range of options and trajectories and the pattern of itineraries which the characters face and take. In a good story usually only one thing happens at the same time. Narration, then, is a suspect rhetoric for laying out an analytical argument, suspect in its single-minded view of the world. But my abstention from it may also very well be the self-recognition of a lack of the narrative skills of the great historians. Anyway, what I want to convey is not so much a story as a series of video installations or a set of exhibition exhibits, i.e. something more like recent Nam June Paik *oeuvres*, or the Beaubourg Paris/Berlin/Moscow/New York exhibitions, but set in the much more modest format available to a single sociologist. More prosaically, the task is to find a proper balance between empirical systematicity and reading accessibility.

The major methodological problems are conceptual and empirical. As the latter is amenable to a more succinct treatment, let us take that first: What is the proper empirical scope, and how should one gather trustworthy data for it?

The range of empirical issues is determined theoretically. What are the main dimensions of society according to macro-sociological theory? What are the main features of social – as distinguished from, say, aesthetic or epistemological – modernity? Those two questions, further specified below, have governed the empirical investigation. However, within that range a severe selection has been necessary, for reasons of time, space, stamina, research resources and competence. The criteria of selection have been the following:

The main questions raised by macro-sociology and by the theory of modernity, as I have understood them, have been empirically confronted, but a curiosity about late twentieth-century European societies has governed the book, rather than a concern with theory-testing. How deeply and how extensively to seek the answers has been decided quite pragmatically, by my interests, capacity, resources and access. This means that no claim to a total, or even full-scale, history is being made. The answers actually given have been made as systematic and as reliable as possible. Special efforts have been made to bring in data from both Eastern Europe and the EFTA countries, although I am, of course, quite aware of the fact that unrestrained research on Eastern Europe is only beginning. Therefore, I have often confined myself to indicating the direction into which currently available evidence is pointing, abstaining from any necessarily premature analysis.

New survey data have not been gathered, nor have archival excavations been made. The primary data are culled from many sources, but are mainly statistical, legal, discursive and polled opinion, supplemented by observations and by informants' interviews. The research of colleagues in a number of disciplines has also been amply used, ordinarily in forms different from the original.[4] My aim has been as far as possible to avoid a reproduction of existing forms of knowledge.[5]

There are three major conceptual problems. One is the conceptualization of modernity as an epoch, another is the place of Europe in a history of modernity, and the third is how to get a handle on the basic aspects of European society.

Why modernity? And what is it?

Having spent, largely in vain, a (short) course at a major department of a major US university trying to argue that modernity exists as a topic of social study, I know that the question 'Why modernity?' has to be taken very seriously indeed. To those who are prepared to listen, my argument is twofold. First, 'modernity' – and its relatives: modern, modernization, modernize – actually exists as a frequent topic of discourse, from literary criticism via the history of science to public policy and political programmes, and so do its targets – tradition, obsolescence, stagnation, sclerosis, un(der)development, reaction, fundamentalism – as well as its (partial) synonyms and companions – progress, development, growth, accumulation, flexibility, revolution, reform, etc. In other words, to deny or ignore it is simply to cut oneself off from much ongoing debate in a number of areas.

Secondly, the very generality of the concept of modernity is in some, not all, respects an advantage. In contrast to, say, 'industrial society' or 'capitalism', 'modernity' has a large number of connotations, which allow us, and which directly enable us, to look into their forms, or their lack, of interconnection. At present, there seems to be no epochal concept with a comparable cover of concerns.

Now, epochs are not fortresses of time, in which people can be shut up. They are expanses open at all ends. But even moving across the prairie you may notice the moving times of dawn and dusk. Epochal concepts are heuristic devices, like time zones. The object of this book is not modernity as such, but the historical meaning and significance of European modernity.

The actual existence of modernity as a topic does not mean that there is any consensus as to what it is. The claim I am making for the definition I am going to use is no more than that it seems to me to be the most fruitful, not that it *is* the most fruitful, let alone the most correct or the truest, nor even the most common one. Pertinent criteria appear to include the following. First of all, like any epochal concept for empirical use, modernity should be defined in a way which makes it possible to ascertain empirically · its beginning and its end. Secondly, it should be defined in a way which relates its beginning to some generally acknowledged major social or cultural change, other than its own criteria of definition. Even if logically arbitrary, historical period definitions should have some historical anchorage, i.e. be open to questioning of the location and the aptness of the grounding and of the stability of the moorings. Thirdly, the definition of the concept should have some relation to its etymological meaning, another aspect of avoiding idiosyncratic arbitrariness.

Modernity here will be defined culturally, as an *epoch turned to the future*, conceived as likely to be different from and possibly better than the present and the past. The contrast between the past and the future directs modernity's 'semantics of time',[6] or constitutes its 'binary code'. The present is 'valid only by the potentialities of the future, as the matrix of the future'.[7] The coming of modernity, then, is tantamount to the discovery of the future, of an open, this-worldly future, that is. This discovery is empirically verifiable/falsifiable, with regard to notions of knowledge, of politics and of other social affairs, and of art, for example. As such it is tied in with the rise of the idea of progress and the cumulation of knowledge,[8] with the Enlightenment, the opening up of a mundane time horizon[9] and the heralding of social evolution.[10] It is manifested in the loss of the previous, and etymological, retrospective meanings of the political concepts of reform and revolution, which instead turn into keys to the future.[11]

The second half of the eighteenth century appears as the period of the definite victory of modernity in Western Europe, with important vanguard forays in Francis Bacon's view of learning (from 1605) and in the French late seventeenth-century aesthetic *querelle des anciens et des modernes*. The rapid growth of commerce, the rise of industry, the scientific breakthroughs, the French Revolution, no doubt constitute the setting for this change. For all their creativity, the Re-naissance and the Re-formation, on the other hand, had their eyes on a golden past.

The complexity of the configuration of this breakthrough of modernity should be kept in mind as a warning against any facile interpretations of its demise. Not only the Renaissance, but also the Enlightenment, the Jacobin Revolution and the rulers of the British industrial Empire were also very much looking backwards, to models of Antiquity. However, as Marx said, 'the awakening of the dead' served in these cases 'to glorify the new struggles, not to parody the old ones, to exaggerate in phantasy the given tasks, not to flee back from their solution in reality'.[12]

The end of modernity, in the sense used here, has been well defined by Alain Touraine: 'we leave modernity when we cease to define a conduct or a form of social organization by its location on the axis of tradition–modernity or underdevelopment–development'.[13] When, we may add, the distinction between the past and the future loses its centrality in discourses on society and culture, when change into something different from the past and the present is no longer attractive or meaningful. Modernity ends when words like progress, advance, development, emancipation, liberation, growth, accumulation, enlightenment, embetterment, avant-garde, lose their attraction and their function as guides to social action.

Pre-modernity is looking back, over its shoulder, to the past, to the latter's example of wisdom, beauty, glory, and to the experiences of the past. Modernity looks at the future, hopes for it, plans for it, constructs it, builds it. Post-modernity has lost or thrown away any sense of time direction. The past as well as the future and the present have become 'virtual realities', or simultaneously combinable elements, as in post-modern architecture.

Modernity is, then, defined in terms of a prevailing concept of time, which is in consonance with the etymological meaning of the word, although it is true that the latter refers primarily to a distinction between the present and the past rather than to the future. While empirically traceable, the proposed concept of modernity does not contain any concrete institutional references, but leaves the latter as causes, effects or contingencies, for investigation. This seems to me a much better conceptual and research strategy than defining modernity in terms of certain concrete institutions and social conditions, a procedure which is very prone to stumbling into the pitfalls of institutional fetishism, into making certain specific institutional forms the hallmarks of a universal epoch.[14]

An institutional approach to modernity, which, of course, is not incompatible with a temporal definition of it, should focus on the dialectics of modernity, i.e. on its characteristic contradictions, dilemmas, tensions, conflicts.[15] Instead of counterposing, as in modernization theory, traditional and modern society, it appears to me, from post-classical hindsight, much more fruitful to specify institutionally different passes to and through modernity.

Routes to and through modernity

Positioning European society within a history of modernity means linking up with proto- and classical sociology, as well as with contemporary debates of epochal interpretation, about post-modernity or a new modernity, etc. The focal conceptualizations of the early sociologists centred on the transition to modernity: from Saint-Simon's proclamation that military society was giving way to industrial society or Comte's that the 'positive', scientific stage of social evolution was replacing the religious one, to Tönnies' distinction between *Gemeinschaft* and *Gesellschaft*, Durkheim's between mechanical and organic solidarity, or Weber's between the rational and the traditional.

However, neither early sociology nor latter-day modernization theory was systematically concerned with the possibility and the eventual character of different routes to and through modernity. The former should be forgiven, as they dealt with the emergence of a new type of society or civilization, but later unilinearism has less excuse.[16] As a starting-point, then, we shall use a global distinction of four major routes to and through modernity found in a study of the development of modern political rights.[17]

The distinction starts from the location of the forces for and against modernity, for progress or ancient customs, for reason or for the wisdom of forefathers and of ancient texts, once the issue of modernity arose. In the case of *Europe* both were internal, endogenous. This led to the particular European pattern of internal revolutions, of *civil war*, and of elaborate doctrinal -isms, ranging from legitimism and absolutism to socialism and communism, via nationalism, ultramontanism and liberalism. These internal cleavages of Europe either derived from or were overlayered with conflicts of *class*. The debate still goes on about the class or alternative origins and meanings of the great European revolutions,[18] hardly about the involvement and the consequence of class conflict. Class is a concept of internal division, and its importance to European modernity followed in part from the intra-European cleavages for and against modernity, in part from the relative weakness of kinship. Later, class was sustained by the unique significance which industrial capitalism and its polarized division of labour acquired along the European route through modernity.

Another pattern is that of the *New Worlds*, creations of overseas migrations on the eve of European modernity, represented primarily, but not exclusively, by the Americas, South as well as North. Here, the opponents of modernity were primarily on the other side of the ocean – in Britain in the case of the USA, in the Iberian peninsula in the case of Latin America – although the domestic modernists also drew heavily on European advances. Vice versa, the forward pushes of the New Worlds were important to the vanguards of the Old, from Lafayette and Tom Paine onwards. The enduring issues of modernity were, first of all, the effective application (or not) of the modern discourse of rights, and the question of who belongs to the people, the issue of 'race'. Ensuing political cleavages were ideologically pragmatic or syncretistic and socio-economically underdetermined. Struggles over, for example, gender and generational relations were also less principled, or rigid, and less pronounced than in Europe.[19]

A third route to and through modernity is that of the *Colonial Zone*, stretching from Northwestern Africa to Papua New Guinea and the South Pacific. To the Colonial Zone modernity arrived from the outside, literally out of the barrels of guns, while resistance to modernity was domestic, and crushed. Later on, colonial modernity involved the acculturation of part of the colonized, their learning the appropriate ideas of the colonizers – popular sovereignty, national self-determination, socio-economic development – and their turning them against the colonizer and the metropolitan masters. From this followed, *inter alia*, a deep cultural trauma – with a potential for extraordinarily creative new combinations to the extent that the trauma can be mastered – social fragmentization and the primacy of the national issue.

Finally, there was a group of countries, those of *Externally induced Modernization*, challenged and threatened by the new imperial powers of Europe and America, where a section of the ruling élite selectively imported features of the threatening polities in order to stave off colonial subjugation. In this way, citizens' rights as well as new concepts of enterprise and administration were introduced from above, gainst a more traditional populace. Japan is the most successful example of this group of countries. In the course through modernity the preserved pre-modern élite were allotted a particularly significant role, which was accompanied by a strong amount of popular deference and a variably successful but persistent blend of old domestic custom and universally competitive institutions.

The four routes are actually existing historical trajectories. But they may also be treated as Weberian ideal types, so that concrete historical experiences might include aspects of two or more ideal routes. Russia from Peter the Great onwards, for instance, contains features of the fourth road, as well as of Europe.[20] Those parts of the settled New Worlds where the indigenous population managed to survive and recover have also strong colonial traits. Southern Africa now seems finally to be seeing the end of the attempts to create a White New World and the beginning of the final round of de-colonization. 'Protectorates' like Egypt and Morocco have travelled both the third and the fourth road.

How much these structurally defined passes into and roads through modernity explain of modern history is so far an open question, about which my research project on routes to/through modernity is still in the pursuit of answers. In any case, I do not expect any far-reaching determinism. That is, the different passes of modernity affect the probabilities, forms and the outcomes rather than decide the occurrence of later events.

This problematic of modernity raises two major empirical questions. What has happened to *European* modernity, in comparison with other modernities? What has happened to European *modernity?* Is it still there, or has it been superseded by post-modernity?

Dimensions of society

Before we can go further into the issues of the place of Europe in modern social history, we have to lay out the fundamental dimensions of human society, or human social relations. We need a compass in order to orient ourselves among the myriad of social processes going on. We need a map to localize ourselves and other forces and events in the social world. We will also have urgent need for a manual, telling us basics about how the world operates and what aspect to look at in case of a problem or an interest in this or that. That is, we need handy and hardy instruments of everyday life, not pieces of art that one might take in on a Sunday afternoon at the gallery. On this side of the metaphor, we are here talking about simple, practical analytical tools for systematic empirical investigation. There will, then, be no lecture on social theory or methodology. However, the objective of accounting for postwar modernity in Europe has led me to reconsider even elementary formulations of the basics of sociology.

Sociology is, so far, a non-paradigmatic discipline, which means that there is no explicit, widely recognized sociological manual available. It can be argued, however, that a practical analytical handbook may be distilled from the actual practice of broadly defined mainstream sociology.[21] This would then entail looking at the social world from two fundamental vantage-points, from its *culture* and from its *structure*, while all the time seeing humans as *actors*. That is, human societies are made up of individual and collective actors, acting in and upon cultures and structures.

'Culture' refers to what is learnt and shared by some people, to their universe of meanings and symbols, to what provides an internal guide to their acting in society. 'Structure' here refers to a patterning of resources and constraints available to people as social actors. People act the way they do, sociologists assume, because they belong to a particular culture and/or because they are located in a particular place in the structure of resources and constraints. Because *cultural belonging* and *structural location* are taken to be the main explanations of action, cultural attachment and structural allocation – including detachment and diversion, respectively – are seen as the central consequences of social action.[22]

Without excursing into taxonomic detail, we may just list what appear to be the most important aspects or dimensions of structure and culture.

Structure involves above all:

1. a *boundary* of a social system and a regulation of its membership, of its population; and
2. a *situs pattern*[23] within the social system, as
   (a) an *institutionalized endowment* of resources and constraints; but sociologists have also come to emphasize
   (b) a *non-institutionalized*, 'informal', possibly 'deviant', but nevertheless *patterned access* or lack of access to resources of action; and, thirdly, a patterning of probable futures, of
   (c) a set of *chances*, of risks and of opportunities, over time.

The resources and constraints take a number of concrete forms, which may be summed up as *tasks, rights and means.*

The sceptical reader may very well ask, 'Why are people's tasks to be treated as their resources or constraints?' The simplest answer, with regard to current societies, might be to ask you to think of the set-up of tasks as a pattern of jobs, which any entrant to the labour market faces, and which is given by organizational legacy and by level of technology. The tasks, the division of labour, constitute a basic role script of any human society. As such, they make up at the same time resources and constraints of the members of the population, patterning what they are likely to be able or unable to do. The set of tasks comprises the basic set of obligations of any social system. The means, for their part, refer to distributional allocations and outcomes, of income, wealth, status, contacts, 'capital' of various sorts, which are means to social actors generally, and not only instruments to role-players for the fulfillment of their tasks.

Tasks and means constitute the mainstream classical heritage of social theory; Adam Smith, Emile Durkheim and Max Weber theorizing the former, followed by contemporary theorists of industrial and post-industrial society, or of Fordism and post-Fordism, of bureaucratic and post-bureaucratic society. Means, primarily conceived as an allocation of property and propertylessness, were the focus of Marx and Engels and the ensuing Marxist tradition, but are also part of otherwise founded allocational or distributive concerns.

Rights, on the other hand, have only very recently acquired a systematic attention in sociological theory.[24] T.H. Marshall's 1949 lectures on 'citizenship and social class'[25] did analyse rights from a sociological perspective but were subsumed under his citizenship concept and continued mainly in the Social Democratic orientation of welfare state studies. Law received great interest from the classical sociologists, such as Durkheim and Weber, but receded afterwards into a barely noticed background. Norms and obligations have, of course, been sociological stock in trade all the time, but largely severed from any anchorage in the legal system. However, law constitutes a major aspect of the social structure of resources and constraints, and legal rights appear to offer a sharper focus on the latter than legal norms.

There are two streams of widespread current discourse carrying issues of rights. One is political, the 'human rights' discourse embodied and given muscles by the US Carter administration, drawing upon an old American tradition of rights, and strengthened by the failures of more system-oriented conceptions of social justice. Another starts from individualist social theory, where individual rights, rather than social norms, occupy the centre-stage. That is the rationale of James Coleman, who as a Chicago sociologist of course draws upon the general North American rights tradition.

From an experience with welfare state studies one may also gain a third source of inspiration, social law, and, more clear-cut, the constitutional and jurisprudential implications and consequences of the welfare state. The latter has very much been a West German jurists' postwar preoccupation, following upon the formulation in the Bonn Constitution of 1949, that the Federal Republic of Germany is 'a democratic and a social federal state' (§20:1).[26]

Anyway, rights are actors' resources which derive from the recognition by others, first of all by a state. One set of rights are claims upon the state and its resources. Another consists of rights to act, *vis-à-vis* other members of the social system, including the state.[27] Like means, rights are involved in the structuration of tasks, but may also be defined and valid outside the division of labour.

'*Chance*' was part of Max Weber's radically probabilistic conceptualization, by which, for instance, a state consisted in the chance that a set of actors would act in a certain way.[28] That kind of probabilism has not found much following, although the more specific notion of 'life chances' has won posterior sociological burghership.

The recent discussion of *risk* actualizes anew the structuration of chances. In the late 1980s the highly charged issue of nuclear energy, and more generally an increasing environmental awareness, brought the concept of risk to the forefront of social thought, sixty years after its first major introduction into the social sciences, then as an interpretation and legitimation of profit.[29] (The concept had, of course, long since been part of the business world of insurance, which spread far and wide across Europe in the nineteenth century, and its accompanying actuarial field of knowledge. With the late nineteenth-century tackling of the social question by means of public insurance, 'social risks' became part of the discourse of social law.[30] But these contexts were all narrowly circumscribed.) The original German edition of Ulrich Beck's *Risk Society*[31] became a mass seller, and Beck's senior compatriot and colleague Niklas Luhmann has devoted a monograph to an elucidation of the risk concept.[32]

So far, the recent interest in risks has been bifurcated into two directions with little or no contact with each other. One is decision analysis, a highly formalized, even experimental, enterprise studying how individuals weigh and decide with regard to risks. The other is macro-social interpretation, the orientation spearheaded by Beck's book. But from the angle of sociological history, a third perspective emerges, which encompasses risk within a broader set of concepts and phenomena.

Risk is a temporal concept, referring to what might happen at some point in the future, to an actor or part, and to a system. In the language used here, risks refer to the structuration of resources and constraints over a period of time. As such, risk may be put alongside *opportunity*, as one significant set of empirical variables of how modern societies are structured. Opportunity is connected both with the events of life-course analysis,[33] and with the odds and outcomes of social mobility.[34] Social risks, life-course events and (inter-generational) mobility, while belonging to very different strands of thinking, usually ignoring each other, all refer to the structured probability of events occurring to a given population over time, contingent events dependent upon, but not determined by, prior decisions. From the vantage-point of structuration, chances consist of risks and opportunities.

Culture, would first of all include:

1   a sense of *identity*, a notion of an 'I' and of a 'we', which implies a boundary to the Other(s);
2   a kind of *cognition* or cognitive competence, a language in which to think and to communicate with the world, a vista, and a knowledge of the world;
3   a pattern of *evaluations* consisting of a set of values and norms, defining good or bad, what is and what is not to be done, and of a register of emotions expressing a specific mode of reactions to events of the world.

Cultures operate through *symbolic systems* by means of processes of *communication*.

This view of culture is not quite the textbook standard, no more than the conceptualization of structure and structuration was. Values and norms are, of course, standard mainstream concepts. But the two others have much weaker claims to any legitimate linear descent.

Cognition occupies a privileged place in the sociology of knowledge tradition, which, with Peter Berger and Thomas Luckmann's immensely influential work, stepped out of its Mannheimian footprints.[35] The sphere of cognition is here taken broadly enough to include the social semantics – in particular of early modernity – which Niklas Luhmann has brought to light in a series of works.[36] As an object of empirical study, cognition has flourished, above all, as sociologies of professions, of science and of language. In the form of *savoir-faire*, many of us have also encountered it in Pierre Bourdieu's unravelling of the cultural distinctions and the cultural 'capital' of the French.[37]

Interest in identity is currently riding on the crest of multiculturalism and ethnic conflict, but is, in fact, an unacknowledged 'bastard' of contemporary sociological theory. In the latest major handbook of sociology, not only is there no article on identity, but the concept does not even occur in the index.[38] In what is probably the discipline's internationally most used current textbook, there is no discussion of identity issues, save for a brief summary of Freud's conception of sexual identity. In an almost thirty-page long glossarium of 'basic concepts' and of 'important terms' there is no mention of identity. Nor does it appear in the index of what is arguably the most systematic recent more advanced theoretical textbook.[39] Furthermore, it has also proved possible to publish important recent collections on cultural sociology, neglecting issues of identity almost completely.[40]

The identity concept seems to harbour an enormous potential as a key concept of the 'sciences of humankind', being central to the psychology of personality formation and development and to the social psychology of groups, as well as bearing upon vast collective processes and issues known as class consciousness, professionalism, ethnicity, nationalism. Its pertinence to a sociological history of contemporary Europe appears rather evident.

Human populations and social systems exist in time and space. Time and space define the finiteness of life. The structure as well as the cultures of human populations, therefore, have *spatial and temporal dimensions*. Spatial aspects of social structures and cultures refer to territorial extensions, boundaries and territorial distributions or configurations of resources and constraints, and of identities, knowledge and values, respectively. Time also has extension, 'duration', boundaries, of ending and beginning, or of being in/out of step, and configurations, i.e. its sequences and its cadences. The features of temporality apply to cultures as well as to structures. Resources as well as, say, identities have their duration, their beginning and end in time, their location in a sequential order, and their rhythm, of monotony, regular beat or irregularity.

Space and time have their particular significance with regard to this study, a study of Europe and of modernity, that is, of a variously defined space in construction, and of an epoch whose current ending is being discussed. Time will here be especially treated with regard to social conceptions of time, and their possible change during the period under investigation, in other words with a view to the cultural cognition of time. Space will be approached from two angles: as a separate structural, primarily economic, spacing of the continent, and as territorially variably extended cultural layers. In the former case, the focus is on issues of integration, convergence or divergence; in the latter on the extension and the interlinkage of different cultural dimensions across current state boundaries.

At a level of general abstraction the dynamics of social systems might be formulated in terms of an asymmetrical relationship of elements, where a key element should be distinguished by independent variability and by predominant effects upon others. In the case of structuration, this role will befall to *means*, less institutionally inert than tasks and rights, available at the moment of decision, in contrast to the chances of the future. With regard to the relative variability and impact of cultural identity, cognition and values, my hypothesis is that *knowledge* is the most dynamic element. However, actual social dynamics is, it seems, largely driven by exogenous contingencies, pushing or pulling action and processes off tracks and onto new ones.

Before leaving our set of variables of investigation, we should make explicit their wider theoretical context. The structures of tasks, rights, means and risks and the cultures of identity, cognition and values which we are going to study may be taken as constituting the basic dimensions of *social systems*. Structurations and enculturations are systemic processes. But the social systems as such, the system-ness of the dimensions mentioned, and the systemic generation of the latter are not the focus of this study. That is, above all, because the social systemic character of the European state-bounded societies after World War II is subject to empirical investigation. To what extent were Eastern/Western societies part of one socialist/capitalist or Eastern/Western system? How far were they all modern European societies? Or something else?

The structural location and the cultural belonging of social actors, in turn, determine their *power*. The division of tasks, the allocation of rights, the access to means, the strength of identity, the amount of relevant cognition, all bear crucially upon the distribution of power. Here, however, the changing structural and cultural contexts and forms of the lives of postwar Europeans have been foregrounded, not the outcomes of their relative relations of power. Power may be regarded as a way to summarize a set of social relations or the resources and constraints of social actors. But here the emphasis is rather on what it is that might be summarized. What do structural and cultural conditions look like? What forms has social action taken? What have been the consequences for structures and cultures?

Structurations and enculturations give direction and shape to *social action*, collective and individual, the force of which is determined by the amount of power available, and by the use of the latter. Social action, in its turn, affects the social system, reproducing it or changing it, and its processes of structuration and enculturation. A part of this study will be devoted to some forms of collective action and their postwar history.

The structural and cultural effects of social action bear upon the maintenance, expansion, contraction or disappearance of social systems. And then we have closed the causal loop, returning to the social system governing the processes of structuration and enculturation. Figure 1.1 is intended to provide a brief overview of the theoretical context of this empirical study, shorn of the contingencies which turn models into reality.

Key: t1, t*n* = sucessive points in time

     ····· = implies, involves

     · — — = affects

Figure 1.1 *The theoretical sociological context of this empirical study*

At time 1, say 1945–50, the social system of European societies involves a particular set of structures and cultures and a particular set of spatial constellations, which we are here interested in getting a grasp of. In order to do that we shall also have reason to go back to time −1, before the war, including past power relations. At time *n*, the early 1990s, as well as at points in time between 1 and *n*, we shall again try to get a handle on what structurations, enculturations and spacing are in progress.

This study will concentrate on the structuring and enculturing outcomes of social action and of systemic processes. What do their trajectories look like? How can we account for them?

We shall finally also cast a glance at two kinds of social action of great interest to a sociologist or a historian of modernity, as they are both characteristic of the modern era. One is *collective action*, in particular organized and sustained collective action on the basis of a chosen collective identity. The other is *social steering*, attempts at deliberately guiding social processes over time in a certain direction. The current attempt at unifying Europe is obviously a major example of social steering in this context, and so was the Eastern European attempt to 'build socialism'. While any conclusion regarding the latter is most likely soon to turn out premature, some tentative reflections on it can hardly be avoided.

Social processes and historical trajectories

The cultural-structural manual, for all its prosaic lack of any conceptual ornamentation, provides us with some guidance to a systematic understanding of social development. Sociology also contains explanatory theories of structuration and of enculturation which might be put to the test. But the focus of this book is postwar Europe, rather than sociological theory, and there is no such theory at hand claiming to be able to explain a continental epoch. The theoretical lessons to be drawn from this theory-guided but not theory-focused study will only be touched upon at the end.

More pertinent, on the other hand, is to relate the conceptual scaffold to the epochal and continental questions. That is, what characterizes modern structuration and enculturation? Under what conditions could we talk about an end to modernity, about post-modernity? What is specific to the culture and structure of European modernity?

Answers to those questions will be attempted below. With regard to an eventual end of modernity, we have already defined it in terms of an end to the future-oriented conception of time. However, the macro-sociological perspective adopted here is not dependent upon that definition of modernity. It might, therefore, be warranted to hint at structural and cultural features associated with the historical epoch that many people, for different reasons, call modernity.

The modern processes of structuration have distinguished themselves generally by a rapid growth of resources – including resources to constrain others. This growth has not been linear, and has in fact included conjunctural oscillations down as well as up. An end to growth, beyond the variations of the business cycle, would mean an epochal change. At this general level, there is no very specific European form of modernity.

In modern times the structuration of tasks has involved, above all, a differentiation, or specialization, and a de-agrarianization, or a decline of food-procuring tasks. The European specificity has here been a relative prominence of industrial tasks in post-agrarian society.

Means in modern societies have grown enormously, and are generally more evenly distributed than in pre-modern agrarian societies, but exhibit large variations both across nations and over time.

Emancipation in terms of rights has been a characteristic of modernity, be it the emancipation of individuals, of citizens, of women, of workers, of nations, of humans *tout court*. A reversal in the growth of rights and the decline of duties would mean a major historical change.

Europe has been characterized, more than other areas of modernity, by a structuration of tasks, means and rights in terms of class, defined by clusters of economic tasks, and sustained by clusters of means and rights attached to groupings of economic tasks. This European mode of modern structuration has differed concretely more in contrast to ethnic and kinship than to individual bases of structuration.

The supply of risks follows most directly from the construction of human-made environments. Ever since the production of serious health risks by urbanization and working-class concentrations the importance and the unequal distribution of risks have been characteristic of modernity. A substitution of a general for a differentiated increase of life and health risks would mean a major change of the parameters of modernity. In the pre-1945 history of Europe there was no continental particularity in this respect.

Culturally, modernity has involved, first of all, change, variability between generations and cohorts, of identities, cognition and evaluations. An end to the context of modernity in this respect would mean the settlement of one stable pattern, alternatively random variation only.

The modern enculturation of identity has promoted identities of individuality and of chosen collectivities. At the same time, modern conceptions of identity have assumed the possibility of finding (in)authenticity of identities in the discovery of oneself and of the meaning of one's life, in the realization of one's interests and belonging, in standing up for one's convictions. A blurring of the line between authenticity and inauthenticity would entail a meaning of identity other than the one accompanying the rise of modernity.

More than other variants of modernity, the European one has been strung between the poles of clear-cut individuality and solidarily constructed collectivity, of association, class and nation-state, while in others either the former or the latter, or both, have tended to be less clearly differentiated.

Modern cognition is subject to continuous growth and cumulation, processes which need not be linear and which in fact have proceeded to a large extent through a purgatory of scepticism and criticism. Long-term stagnation of knowledge or a denial of knowledge's cumulativity would mean a cognitive rupture in modern culture. European modernity has included a particular autonomy of intellectual knowledge, more clearly autonomous of religion or traditional wisdom as well as of everyday know-how, an autonomy manifested in more demarcated institutions of science and scholarship.

With regard to values and norms, modernity has distinguished itself by its 'enlightenment', its attempt at grounding them in reason, rather than in divine prescription or in inherited tradition, and in its differentiation of values from cognition, and of different kinds of norms. An increasing recourse to authority and a de-differentiation of values and norms would reverse this process typical of modernity. The content of a European value system is utterly controversial and does not lend itself to serious brief summaries. At this point, however, we may say that the values of European modernity are largely shaped by the religious and state power mould in which the process of enlightenment developed.

Theoretical bearing, empirical grounding and systematic argumentation are claims of this work. Exhaustiveness is not. An understanding of late twentieth-century Europe and its place in world history on the basis of a systematic overview of major social structures, cultures and forms of collective action is my aim.

Notes

1 An expression I owe to the title of Paul Sweezy's collection of essays, *The Present as History*, New York, Monthly Review Press, 1953.
2 I think, then, that Wolf Lepenies' beautiful book on sociology between literature and science goes one number too high (in asserting a third, sociological culture): *Die drei Kulturen*, Munich and Vienna, Carl Hanser, 1985.
3 Although I have a quite different appreciation of the works of Barrington Moore, Perry Anderson, Immanuel Wallerstein, and Michael Mann than he, I do think that John Goldthorpe has pointed to some serious difficulties with 'grand historical sociology', which, however, I don't think apply to this work in the borderlands between sociology and history,

whatever its other limitations and weaknesses: J. Goldthorpe, 'The Uses of History in Sociology: Reflections on Some Recent Tendencies', *British Journal of Sociology* 42 (1991). In the ensuing debate, which comprised most of the March 1994 issue of the *BJS*, my own position is more similar to that of Nicos Mouzelis: 'In Defence of "Grand" Historical Sociology', *British Journal of Sociology* 45 (1994).

4 This includes access to the so far unpublished study known as the International Social Justice Project, to which David Mason has kindly given me access, and, above all, to the data files of the World Values Survey 1990–1991, directed by Ronald Inglehart (Institute for Social Research, University of Michigan). I am grateful for this kind collegial courtesy, and for the assistance of Dr Brantgärde at the Swedish Social Science Data Service in establishing the necessary contacts and rights.

5 Nor is it my intention to polemicize with preceding distinguished works. I would, however, like to signal a few among the more comprehensive contributions to our knowledge of contemporary Europe. Nearest in ambition are perhaps the economically focused economic and social history by Gerold Ambrosius and William Hubbard, *A Social and Economic History of Twentieth-Century Europe*, Cambridge, Mass., Harvard University Press, 1989; and the Western Europe-centred sociological work by Hartmut Kaelble, *Auf dem Weg zu einer europäischen Gesellschaft*, Munich, C.H. Beck, 1987. The important European studies by Max Haller are not yet complete, but have a similar range. EC-confined but also very informative are the collective work edited by Oscar Gabriel, *Die EG-Staaten im Vergleich*, Opladen, Westdeutscher Verlag, 1992; the handbook edited by François Féron and Armelle Thoraval, *L'Etat de l'Europe*, Paris, La Découverte, 1992; the older but still important collective efforts, M.S. Archer and S. Giner (eds), *Contemporary Europe: Class, Status and Power*, London, Weidenfeld and Nicolson, 1971, S. Giner and M.S. Archer (eds), *Contemporary Europe: Social Structures and Cultural Patterns*, London, Routledge & Kegan Paul, 1978. Less scholarly designed but also very EC-informative is Guy Mermet's compilation, *Euroscopie*, Paris, Larousse, 1991. Worth mentioning in this context also are the political science textbook by Jan-Erik Lane and Svante Ersson, *Politics and Society in Western Europe*, 2nd edn, London, Sage, 1991, and the more sociological overview edited by Joe Bailey, *Social Europe*, London, Longman, 1992. Highly relevant is also, of course, Eric Hobsbawm's *Age of Extremes*, London, Michael Joseph, 1994, which appeared too late to be considered here.

6 Cf. N. Luhmann, *Soziologie des Risikos*, Berlin, de Gruyter, 1991, p. 46.

7 R. Poggioli, *The Theory of the Avant-garde*, Cambridge, Mass., The Belknap Press, 1968, p. 73.

8 Cf. D. Spadafora, *The Idea of Progress in Eighteenth-Century Britain*, New Haven and London, Yale University Press, 1990.

9 R. Kosellek, *Futures Past*, Cambridge, Mass., MIT Press, 1985.

10 G. Therborn, *Science, Class and Society*, London, Verso, 1976, Ch. 4.

11 G. Therborn, 'Revolution and Reform: Reflexions on Their Linkages Through the Great French Revolution', in J. Bohlin et al. (eds), *Samhällsvetenskap, ekonomi, historia*, Göteborg, Daidalos, 1989, pp. 197–220.

12 K. Marx, 'Der achtzehnte Brumaire des Louis Bonaparte', *Marx–Engels Werke*, Berlin, Dietz, 1972, Vol. 8, p. 116.

13 A. Touraine, *Critique de la modernité*, Paris, Fayard, 1992, p. 208.

14 The high risk of such institutional fetishism is highlighted by the fact that even a major social theorist can fall into it. Piotr Sztompka, for example, in his otherwise sophisticated *The Sociology of Social Change* (Oxford, Blackwell, 1993, p. 137), characterizes the Eastern European Communist societies as representing a 'fake modernity', because they lacked, among other things, 'private ownership . . . the functioning market, . . . robust entrepreneurial elites and middle classes'. What my distinguished Polish colleague is saying here is no more than that non-capitalist societies are non-capitalist. Their lack of capitalist institutions and classes was not a fake, but a choice, maybe a wrong one, from this perspective or that. That modernity by definition has to include a capitalist economy hardly seems very illuminating.

15 Peter Wagner's *A Sociology of Modernity*. London and New York, Routledge, 1994, is an interesting effort in that direction, built around a discussion of liberty and discipline, although rather closely tied to a Western European experience and rather distant from empirical issues. Max Horkheimer's and Theodor Adorno's *Dialectic of the Enlightenment* (1944; English edn: New York, Herder and Herder, 1972) expressed a very special perspective in extreme form, but remains, as a work of pioneering thought, at the centre of interpretations of the negative dialectic of modernity. Cf. G. Therborn, 'Dialectics of Modernity: On Critical Theory and the Legacy of Twentieth-Century Marxism', in B. Turner (ed.), *A Companion to Social Theory*, Oxford, Blackwell, forthcoming.

16 See further G. Therborn, 'Routes to/through Modernity', in M. Featherstone et al. (eds), *Global Modernities*, London, Sage, 1995.

17 G. Therborn, 'The Right to Vote and the Four World Routes to/through Modernity', in R. Torstendahl (ed.), *State Theory and State History*, London, Sage, 1992, pp. 62–92.

18 The latest major thrust in this high-level polemic is Robert Brenner's *Merchants and Revolution*, Cambridge, Cambridge University Press, 1993. Brenner, a very distinguished American Marixst historian, is on the side of class, with new arguments.

19 G. Therborn, *Exits from Patriarchy and the Politics of Childhood*, forthcoming.

20 Cf. L. Greenfeld, *Nationalism*, Cambridge, Mass., Harvard University Press, 1992, Ch. 3.

21 See G. Therborn, 'Cultural Belonging and Structural Location, and Human Action', *Acta Sociologica* 34, 3 (1991); 'Sociology as a Discipline of Disagreements and as a Paradigm of Competing Explanations: Culture, Structure, and the Variability of Actors and Situations', in P. Sztompka (ed.), *Agency and Structure: Re-orienting Social Theory*, Philadelphia, Gordon & Breach, 1994.

22 The relative weight of 'culture' and 'structure' is an object of major controversy between idealist/culturalist and materialist/structuralist currents of social science. The relative importance of acting in cultures/structures versus acting upon them has also been the object of debate. In the 1970s–1980s the latter issue usually appeared under the name of the structure/agency problem.

23 In sociological parlance, 'situs', in contrast to the more common 'status', is not necessarily hierarchical.

24 In James Coleman's, *Foundations of Social Theory*, Cambridge, Mass., Belknap Press, 1990, Ch. 3.

25 They are included in T.H. Marshall's posthumous collection of essays, *Class, Citizenship, and Social Development*, Garden City, NY, Anchor Books 1965.

26 A key survey text is H.-H. Hartwich, *Sozialstaatspostulat und gesellschaftlicher status quo*, 3rd edn, Cologne, Westdeutscher Verlag, 1978. A legally oriented social policy study by the author is G. Therborn, 'The Politics of Childhood', in F. Castles (ed.), *Families of Nations*, Aldershot, Dartmouth, 1993.

27 This is heuristic distinction considered useful in this context, but no claim to its intrinsic superiority to other possible divisions is being made.

28 M. Weber, *Wirtschaft und Gesellschaft*, Cologne, Kiepenheuer & Witsch, 1964, Vol. 1, Ch. 2, §3 (p. 19).

29 By the American economist Frank Knight: *Risk, Uncertainty, and Profit*, Boston, Houghton Mifflin, 1921.

30 Cf. F. Ewald, *L'Etat de Providence*, Paris, Grasset, 1986; P. Köhler and H. Zacher, 'Einleitung', in idem (eds), *Ein Jahrhundert Sozialversicherung*, Berlin, Duncker & Humblot, 1980.

31 U. Beck, *Risikogesellschaft*, Frankfurt, Suhrkamp, 1986. English edition *Risk Society*, London, Sage, 1992.

32 Luhmann, *Soziologie des Risikos*.

33 Cf. K.U. Mayer (ed.), *Lebensverläufe und sozialer Wandel*, Kölner Zeitschrift für Soziologie und Sozialpsychologie Sonderheft 31/1990, Opladen, Westdeutscher Verlag, 1990.

34 For the current state of the art, see the major contribution by Robert Eriksson and John Goldthorpe, *The Constant Flux*, Oxford, Clarendon Press, 1992; and the review article from a competing perspective by H. Ganzeboom et al., 'Comparative Intergenerational

Stratification Research: Three Generations and Beyond', *Annual Review of Sociology* 17 (1991).

35 P. Berger and T. Luckmann, *The Social Construction of Reality*, Garden City, NY, Anchor Books, 1967 (1st edn, 1966).

36 See, e.g. N. Luhmann, *Gesellschaftsstruktur und Semantik*, Frankfurt, Suhrkamp, 1981, 2 vols; *Beobachtungen der Moderne*; Opladen, Westdeutscher Verlag, 1992.

37 P. Bourdieu, *La Distinction*, Paris, Minuit, 1979.

38 N. Smelser (ed.), *Handbook of Sociology*, Newbury Park, Sage, 1988.

39 R. Collins, *Theoretical Sociology*, San Diego and New York, Harcourt Brace Jovanovich, 1988.

40 J. Alexander and S. Seidman (eds), *Culture and Society*. Cambridge, Cambridge University Press, 1990; R. Wuthnow (ed.), *Vocabularies of Public Life*, London, Routledge, 1992.

2

EUROPE IN MODERN HISTORY

The ambiguous centre

First of all, even if a clear picture of the advanced pre-modern world, in the sense of 'modern' used here, still has to be drawn, there is no doubt, that Europe was the pioneer of modernity and the centre of it. Neither the Islamic, the Black African, the Hindu nor the East Asian Confucian world seems to have discovered the future as a new place, attainable but never visited before. Neither appears to have contained major arguments by mid-second millennium AD and ensuing centuries that the present was superior to the past.[1]

Europe became the undisputed centre of modernity in terms of knowledge as well as in terms of power. In the course of the seventeenth and eighteenth centuries Europe overtook both the Chinese and the Islamic civilizations in the production of knowledge, and it also developed an asymmetrical knowledge of the Other, of his/her language, customs and geography. Valid knowledge was overwhelmingly produced at home, although without rejecting raw materials from outside Europe (from Oriental languages to the Galapagos finches observed by Darwin). From the end of the fifteenth century, seafaring Europeans became the main conquerors of the world. European settlements spread around the globe in the ensuing four centuries. Capital investment in the world was mainly European, growing vigorously from the eighteenth century. European centrality was culturally reproduced by the Enlightenment, by nineteenth- and early twentieth-century Paris – 'the capital of the nineteenth century', as Walter Benjamin called it.[2] Paris was the city of liberty to political exiles from all over the world, the city of arts and the city of letters.[3]

Europe was the chief *organizer* of modernity, giving the latter its characteristic forms of vast seaborne empires, politically organized overseas settlements, intercontinental trade and investment, and deliberate diffusion of religious beliefs and techniques of rule. All this was linked to a system of increasingly national and secularized states at the centre, from which originated new technologies for the world and curious bodies of science and learning developing physics, astronomy and political economy, as well as Enlightenment, nationalism and orientalism.

The cultural flows of which Europe has been part in the course of modernity have not been one-sided, i.e. not exclusively from Europe to the rest of the world. They have been asymmetrical. Sporadically, the cultural élites, from Goethe to Picasso, and the upper classes of Europe have been attracted to and absorbed in features of extra-European cultures, such as Chinese and Japanese architecture, interior decoration and painting in the eighteenth century, and African sculpture and painting in the early twentieth century.[4] The 'mystique of the Orient' became generally very attractive to European élites in the nineteenth century, the 'Orient' variably located in North Africa, Egypt, India, China or in some exotic place. Ancient languages, like Sanskrit, ancient history and archaeology as well as contemporary non-European languages, religions and customs drew European men of learning, who often became *the* specialist of the field.[5] The flows in the other direction, outbound from Europe, came somewhat later and, most importantly, soon became (fairly broad) mass rather than élite phenomena, often reaching into the deeper regions of personal identity, in forms of European religious beliefs, European languages of ordinary communication, European norms of dress and housing, without ever creating viable new European cultures.

The location of Europe in the history of the world's material civilization is more complex. From the best estimates available, which must be taken with a considerable latitude of possible error, Europe, or even Western Europe, does not seem to ever have been (alone) the richest part of the world. From the beginning of the eighteenth century onwards that position seems to have been either shared with or held by the European settlements of North America, although the UK had the highest per capita income till the end of the nineteenth century.[6] China appears to have been ahead rather than behind Europe in per capita GNP by 1800, slightly after Western Europe, more tangibly in front of Eastern Europe. Japan and Asia as a whole probably had a product per inhabitant equivalent to that of Eastern Europe.[7] In terms of manufacturing output, China seems to have been a larger producer than Europe in the eighteenth century, clearly surpassed only in the second quarter of the nineteenth. Also the Indian subcontinent was on a par with the whole of Europe in the century of the Enlightenment.[8]

In other words, the definite breakthrough of modernity in Europe hardly followed from a unique economic take-off. Nor is it warranted to say that the economic expansion derived from a novel consciousness of modernity. Abstaining from any causal hypotheses, which would be outside the non-historian's competence, I would just like to point to an ambiguity of the *prima facie* evidence here and the complexity of the possible interrelationships between modernity as a cultural epoch and socio-economic structural transformations. The sociologist, no less than the social historian, is very reluctant to relinquish the suspicion that between the two there is a causal bond, but whatever it is it is neither simple nor straightforward.

The ambiguous location of Europe with regard to the world's wealth is underlined by the long, and increasingly massive, tradition of outward European *migration*. Between 1850 and 1930, when mass intercontinental emigration ceased about fifty million people left Europe (including Russia) for other continents.[9] The European organization of the world meant that Europe exported many of its paupers and criminals, its black sheep or simply cadet gentry, its persecuted populations as well as its enterprising poor, along with its military, administrative, economic and cultural conquerors.

The road of civil war

Like all major modern civilizations, the European has its ancient cultural and institutional structural roots, the most frequently hailed ones being Greek democracy, Roman law and Judaeo-Christian religion. However true, in principle, such invocations are incapable of accounting for the timing and the form of modernity, which clearly did not gradually evolve out of Christian Antiquity. Leaving aside, in this context, the famous question of 'Why European primacy?', we shall here emphasize the specific way in which modernity asserted itself, or was asserted, in Europe.

The European pass to modernity is civil war. By civil war I mean conflicts – usually but not necessarily always violent – for and against a particular social or cultural order within a given population, i.e. within a population with certain recognized connectiveness and boundaries. This dialectical form of change differs not only from evolution or growth, but also from imposition from above – with or without protest – and from exogenous propulsion, be it by diffusion-cum-adoption, imports-cum-imposition or by pressure and coercion.

From civil war comes what legal scholars regard as the modern European legal system, not evolving out of Roman law but established through the eleventh- and twelfth-century civil wars of European Christianity, between the Papacy on one side, and the Emperor and other secular princes on the other.[10] The current religious make-up of Europe and the secularism of modernity derives from a similar continental civil war, that is, from the Reformation and the Counter-Reformation, from the English Civil War of the seventeenth century, and from the French Revolution, with its ensuing intracontinental ideologized wars (1792–1815) and more than century-long aftermath of continent-wide national struggles over the place of the Church and of religion. Popular political rights and the constitutional binding of rulers asserted themselves in Europe also by revolution and civil war, again most importantly through the English Civil War and its sequel the Glorious Revolution of 1688 and through the French Revolution tail of revolutions and popular struggles against recalcitrant rulers.[11]

Charles Tilly has given us a panorama of revolutions in Europe since 1492.[12] His definition of a revolutionary situation is not identical with the meaning of civil war in this context. Wars of dynastic succession and ethnic wars or clashes created revolutionary situations, but would often not involve a socially pertinent civil war, for example. There is enough common ground, however, for a consideration of some of Tilly's results. What periods of

European history of the past half-millennium have been most revolutionary, that is, in the sense of periods of popularly supported competing exclusive claims for the control of a European state or a segment of it?

There are two such tides of internal war, it seems. One runs from the 1540s to the 1690s, with a peak in mid-seventeenth century; the other from 1792 to the 1840s. The consolidation of early modern states, whether absolutist dynastic states or, by crucial exception, a constitutional monarchy as in Britain, or even a bourgeois republic, as in the Netherlands, and the civil wars of religion are covered by the first period. The establishment of nation-states, of states as manifestations of the nation's sovereignty, rather than the dynasty's or the ruler's, was the most central, though not the exclusive, issue of the second era of European revolutionary situations.

The importance of civil war, and of other internal conflicts, stems most immediately from three conditions, governing internal conflict generally, which have been prominent features of Europe.

First is the absence, marginality or at most very distant threat of external conquest after the mid-sixteenth century – save for the brief moment of 1683 – Byzantium and the Balkans, conquered by the Ottomans, having already become peripheral by then. Issues of resistance to or collaboration with a powerful external force, of learning from the Other or rejecting him/her, have little bothered Europeans in recent centuries.

Second is the existence of clear boundaries demarcating the internal from the external, together with, thirdly, an internal connectivity, providing a pronounced interdependence of the demarcated population, and bringing internal conflicts to bear upon the organization of the whole. The Christian Church(es), the state system and the organization of absolutist states and even more of nation-states provided these boundaries and internal density to Europe on the threshold of modernity and before. The Church, particularly but not only the Catholic Church, demarcated and integrated Christianity in a way unrivalled by other major religions. The feudal maxim 'nulle terre sans seigneur' (no land without a lord) and the system of Renaissance and post-Renaissance states carved up all Europe, unevenly and a-rationally, but clearly, leaving virtually no room for simple segmented coexistence and for fuzzy sets of vague territorial claims of variable seriousness. The consolidation of these states and the spread of their judicial, fiscal and military networks enhanced the importance of the legitimacy and of the form of rule.

This work does not intend to explain the pioneering modernity of Europe. But, at least, civil war was the maelstrom in which and through which modernity struck its path in Europe. The relations of force and strength between, on one hand, reason, enlightenment, emancipation, progress, development, achievement, change, modernity, and, on the other, divine right and divine rules, ancient customs, the wisdom of the forefathers, heritage, birth, past experience, tradition, were largely and typically decided by civil war, by one form of internal conflict or another. So were alternative mechanisms of structuration such as inheritance, feudal contracts, markets and bureaucracy.

The cleavages of chosen collective identities and the consistency and persistence of value patterns have been particularly strong in Europe. One expression of this was the development of conflicting canons of interpretation of contemporary large-scale events, once more typified by the polemics around the English and the French revolutions, and of elaborate polemical doctrines and their followings – in brief, the development of '*-isms*'. Ultramontanism, Protestantism, legitimism, monarchism, conservatism, Fascism, liberalism, republicanism, socialism, Communism, anarchism, all, and some more, are of European origin and are or have been important features of European culture over the past two centuries. Probably the only major -ism of modern times not of European origin is fundamentalism, which has a North American (Protestant) pedigree, and is currently mostly applied to Islamic currents.[13] The phenomenon, if not the concept, is well covered by Catholic ultramontanism and by orthodox Protestantism.

The battles of -isms have been overlayered by or determined by another dialectic of particular significance in modern Europe, *class struggles*. Landowners, farmers, urban industrial or commercial bourgeoisies, urban petit-bourgeois, artisans, industrial workers and general labourers, more seldom agricultural workers, all have articulated and organized themselves in Europe, from the nineteenth century at least, beyond kinship, locality and occupation. In other words, class, loosely defined as a broad, exclusively socio-economic grouping, has constituted crucial lines of political and ideological cleavage and collective action in Europe.[14]

While the data are not yet in for a decisive empirical demonstration, I would argue that class conflict is another feature of modern social organization and action that has characterized European more than other societies. Skirting around the ongoing controversies about the pertinence of class to the English and French revolutions, we shall here only point to the nineteenth-century 'social question' or, alternatively, 'workers' question', to that century's notion of 'social movement';[15] to the line-ups of 1848; to the rise of the artisanal and the industrial labour movement, of farmers' parties and cooperatives, of employers' and landowners' organizations; to party systems and class voting; and, finally, to the Russian October Revolution and its repercussions.[16]

The specificity of the European class conflict, which European and Europeanized class theoreticians have long neglected to problematize, probably derives from three features, especially, of modern European history. The most basic appears to be the endogenous character of European modernization. In this context, one's relationship to external forces becomes irrelevant, something impossible outside Europe. True, Europe has had its ethnic conflicts too, and it has been the home of the world's only deliberate and systematic genocide, but even in the darkest hours of ethnic projections class remained pertinent. After all, in the end the only opponents to the Nazis' constitutional take-over of power were the explicitly working-class parties of Social Democrats and Communists.

Secondly, the salience of class in Europe must have been facilitated by the European kinship and family structure. At least after the end of the Germanic *Völkerwanderungen* (migrations), territorial rather than genealogical social organization and collective identity dominated Europe – the parish, the diocese, the city and the lord, rather than the clan, the lineage and the tribe.[17] The territorial organization was, of course, stronger in the ethnically more homogeneous Western parts of the continent. West of a line from Trieste to St Petersburg there also existed, already on the threshold of modernity, a distinctive family type, characterized by late marriages, a considerable number of people never married and nuclear family households.[18] Territorial divisions and loose family structures both facilitate – or at least, contrary to their opposites, do not raise obstacles to – internal socio-economic cleavages and internal socio-economic mobilization.

The uniquely comprehensive industrialization of Europe is a third factor favouring class consciousness, cleavage and conflict. Europe was not only a pioneer in manufacturing industry, but also the part of the world in which industry had its largest impact on the employment structure. Nowhere else did industrial employment become as large a part of the economically active population as in Europe, most importantly in Britain and Germany.[19] (We shall return more extensively to this point below, in Chapter 4.) Industrial relations of production and work further sever familial or pseudo-familial relationships, and a collective of workers with some skills – a widespread phenomenon in Europe with the connections between artisanal and industrial work – had some bases of autonomy from their boss.[20]

The topology of post-1945

From our vantage-point of comparative modernity we may say that Europe in 1945, on the eve of our sociological installations below, was facing two fundamental issues. One refers to its place in the world: What, if anything, can be done to the thoroughly undermined centrality of Europe in global modernity? How will, how should, the internal social dialectic of Europe unfurl?

The precarious position of Europe in the geo-economics and the geo-politics of the earth was not of very recent date. Economically, Europe had been clearly surpassed by the New Worlds by the turn of the century. In 1870 the GNP of the United Kingdom was about equal to that of the United States. By 1913, American GNP was 2.7 times larger than the British. Germany's national product was 42% of the American one in 1870, and 24% in 1913. French economic resources per year were four-fifths of the American in 1870, little more than a quarter in 1913.[21] Europe's share of the world's population culminated in the early twentieth century, at slightly more than a quarter.[22]

The American defeat of the Spanish in 1898 was less significant than the Japanese defeat of Russia in 1905. Spain had for long been on the decline, and the strength of the United States was known before. But that an Asian power could thrash a European one, a 'yellow' people a 'white' one, was something remarkable, in the heyday of imperialism, social Darwinism and generalized racism. It sent glimmers of non-European hope not only throughout Asia but also into North Africa.[23] The decisive geo-political event, though, was the US intervention in the European Great War of 1914–1918. In the wake of it, Europe received its first ever political directives from outside, in the Wilsonian principles of democracy and national self-determination.

To a significant section of the European avant-garde in the 1920s, the USA was seen as a beacon of progress, technically, socially and culturally (film, jazz music). One of the most penetrating reflections of this genre was written by an Italian Communist leader, Antonio Gramsci, distanced from day-to-day politics by the walls of a Fascist prison.[24]

However, Europe gained a respite. The USA withdrew from geo-political supremacy into what Wilson's successor called 'normalcy'. The formidable economic power of American capital was certainly present in postwar Europe[25] and central to the various 'plans' for stabilizing the German economy. But the gold standard, more than the house of Morgan, set the rules. And then came the Depression, which hit the USA harder and longer than Europe. From peak to trough the American economy contracted by almost one-third, the European only by one-tenth.[26] Only in 1939 did the US GNP catch up with the product of 1929. In comparison with the national product of 1913, USA had lost ground to Germany, and to a number of smaller Northwestern European countries, while gaining upon France and Britain only because of superior performance during the war and in the 1920s.[27]

The aftermath of World War I saw the first major modern anti-colonial movements: Arab nationalism, the Congress campaign in India with the martyrdom of Amritsar at its centre, the May Fourth Movement in China, the emergence of Panafricanism. But in the end all challenges to European colonial rule were successfully staved off. Indeed, the range of colonial power was even extended, with Britain and France taking possession of the major Arab parts of the sunk Ottoman Empire, Lebanon and Syria going to the French, Palestine and Iraq to the British. In the 1930s Spain and France finally subjugated the Moroccan Rif. Italy managed, with some effort, to seize Ethiopia. Europe was still expanding.

Culturally, centrality remained, by and large, little affected by the war. Ernest Hemingway and William Carlos Williams went to Paris, and Talcott Parsons to Heidelberg, rather than their European colleagues going to New York. 'They do things better in Europe', was a motto of the postwar American 'Lost Generation' of intellectuals.[28] True, some European actors and directors went to Los Angeles, to Hollywood. But it was the 1930s that saw the tide turn, and then by European push rather than by American pull.

Fascism and antisemitism then almost emptied central Europe of artistic, scientific and scholarly talent: the Bauhaus, the Expressionists, the Frankfurt School, Albert Einstein, Enrico Fermi and the other makers of the later Manhattan Project, Bertolt Brecht, Fritz Lang, Thomas Mann, Piet Mondrian and John von Neumann, the Prague Circle, psychoanalysis, the Surrealists, the Vienna Circle . . . , and so on.[29] This was probably the most successful cultural suicide ever attempted, well covered on its left flank by simultaneous rampant Stalinist terror in the USSR. During the new war, the vanguard of a major European art clearly set up tent outside Europe, painting in the New York of Abstract Expressionism.

World War II rocked the foundations of Europe's position of power in the world. Its leading economy was not only defeated but smashed. Even after recovering from the worst state of shock, the Italian economy was back at its level of 1927 or 1915–16 and the French at its level of 1913 (both in 1946), and the German national product had crawled back to 1913 by 1947. True, the British economy was above both prewar marks, but that meant about a half higher than in 1913, whereas the US economy was two and a half times as big as it was at that date.[30]

The heartland of the continent was occupied by foreign and by at least part-foreign troops. Although the RAF had shown an impressive capacity of urban destruction, in Dresden, in Hamburg and elsewhere, the obliteration of Hiroshima and Nagasaki demonstrated the arrival of a new military technology, heralding an era of an American airborne empire overtaking the old European naval ones.

The organization of the postwar world slipped out of European hands. With the Bretton Woods monetary system, the Marshall Plan, the Truman Doctrine and the New York-based United Nations, which succeeded the League of Nations in Geneva, American or American-controlled initiatives laid out the parameters of the new world order.

The big European retreat began, almost half a millennium after its expansion started. (The earlier retreat from the Americas had been well compensated for by new Asian and African conquests.) The British realized they could no longer keep the jewels of the imperial crown and relinquished India. US pressure forced the Dutch to stop fighting their colonial war and leave Indonesia. France managed to reconquer Vietnam, for a while, but had to give up its Ottoman spoils. In Africa European colonialism made no concessions, save for allowing Ethiopia back to independence from defeated Italy. The other ex-Italian colony, Libya, was occupied by Britain and France, for the time being.

The global centre position and the global organizer role were lost, largely, but not completely. After the war Paris, intellectually presided over by Sartre and his circle, remained the intercontinental cultural capital, if there was one anymore, although it now had to compete with New York and Los Angeles. The City of London kept its position as the financial hub of the world with less contestation. Paris and Geneva remained loci of interstate encounters.

Private property in question

The second issue of 1945 was the future of the European social dialectic, after the defeat of Fascism and after the destructions, the dislocations and the popular mobilizations of the war. The main issue was not, as after World War I, the organization of the state, republic or monarchy,[31] the suffrage, workers' councils or parliaments. It was rather the economic and social responsibility of the state, in the organization of the economy, with regard to citizens' social rights.

The Depression had been an indictment of liberalism, in the European sense. The defeat of Fascism emerged as an indictment of capitalism, and again of liberal conceptions of private enterprise. The February 1947 Ahlen programme of West German Christian Democracy (CDU), largely written by Konrad Adenauer,[32] expressed a widely held European opinion immediately after the war by stating:

> The capitalist economic system has not satisfied the vital state and social interests of the German people. ... The content and the goal of this [necessary fundamentally] new social and economic order can no longer be the capitalist striving for profits and power, but only the good life [Wohlergehen] of the people.[33]

Adenauer and his associates were trying to stave off the more radical version of contemporary Christian Democracy, led by Adenauer's main rival for all-German leadership, Jakob Kaiser, who stated in 1945 'The coming era . . . must . . . stand in the sign of a "socialist order"'.[34] The Ahlen programme was not equivalent to the Reading Resolution carried by the British Labour Party conference in 1944, however, calling for 'the transfer to public ownership of the land, large-scale building, heavy industry, and all forms of banking, transport and fuel and power'.[35]

Nevertheless, a new concept of property, open to nationalizations but above all emphasizing a publicly responsible and accountable mutation of private property, was occupying centre and centre-right opinion of the time. In Germany Adenauer and his friends, and the Ahlen Programme, referred to a 'gemeinwirtschaftliche Ordnung', a vague notion perhaps to be translated by 'a cooperative commonwealth'. The ideological leader of the French Christian Democrats (MRP), Henry Teitgen, a key author of the economic programme of the Resistance, was more outspoken about strengthening the position of the state in directing the economy, but the MRP also launched the idea of a 'nouvel aménagement de la propriété', a new organization of property.[36] Furthermore, the Dutch Catholics embryonically institutionalized the idea of a 'public law organization of enterprises' in the postwar period.[37]

This postwar anti-capitalist orientation was often given a European versus American draping. The British historian A.J.P. Taylor formulated it, in the wake of the British Labour Party electoral victory, with a self-assuredness more characteristic, perhaps, of the style of the British middle and upper classes before Suez than of the European majority, but hardly outside mainstream thought: 'Nobody in Europe believes in the American way of life', Taylor told listeners of the BBC in November 1945, '– that is, in private enterprise; or rather those who believe in it are a defeated party and a party which seems to have no more future than the Jacobites in England after 1688.'[38]

Also colouring the years around 1945 in Europe was a widespread, strong admiration for the Soviet Union. One example is the appreciation, at the end of the war, by the future leader of postwar Italian Christian Democracy, Alcide De Gasperi, of 'the immense, historical, and enduring [secolare] merit of the armies organized by the genius of Joseph Stalin'.[39]

The context was, first, the dawn after the Fascist nightmare, in the participation of which the part played by German, Italian and French big capital was well known, as was the latter's common prewar militant stance against workers and citizens' rights in general; secondly, the experience of collective and solidaristic wartime mobilization, either as a national war effort like in Britain, or as national resistance in occupied Europe; and, thirdly, the dreadful experience of the Depression, which had taken off any charm of warmed up 'back to normalcy' calls. In 1945 the wheel of the social dialectic appeared to have turned in a left-wing, a popular, direction.

The combination of gratitude to and distance from the USA in Western Europe was mirrored in the East with regard to the USSR. While socialism was widely perceived as the way out of poverty, ignorance and bigotry into a modernity of industrial prosperity and enlightenment, the new Communist leaders were in 1944–46 underlining again and again that their country was not going to follow the Soviet road of a 'dictatorship of the proletariat'. In Poland Gomulka asserted in November 1946, 'Our democracy is also not similar to Soviet democracy, just as our social system is not similar to the Soviet system.' Both in politics and property the 'people's democracies' originally distanced themselves from the Soviet model. 'Bulgaria will be a People's Republic' former Comintern head Georgij Dimitrov said, 'in which private property acquired by labour will be protected by the state authorities.'[40] This differentiation from the USSR should most probably be taken neither as tactical lying nor as expressions of independence from the latter. A gradualist conception of a socialist transformation was a conclusion drawn, by Soviet and Eastern European Communists alike, from the defeats after World War I and in the 1929–34 period. A fundamental loyalty to the CPSU characterized the Comintern generation of Communists, but among the cadres with firsthand experience of the Soviet Union this loyalty was often more masochistic than starry-eyed, and there was certainly a genuine hope of autonomy among them.[41]

Anyway, the hopes for a new European social system, a new European modernity, were soon dashed, in the West as well as in the East, albeit less violently in the Western half of Europe.

The ideological conjuncture after Stalingrad or after the fall of Berlin could also be interpreted as yet another moment in a *longue durée* of what Marxists called the increasingly *social character of the forces of production*, which might be translated as a tendency for optimal productivity being increasingly ensured by large-scale organization.[42] Public ownership and public regulation represent this trend; private cartels and trusts their seamy alternatives. Telecommunications, broadcasting, rail and air transport constituted the most clear-cut examples of the advantages of public enterprise for this reason, clearly established in Europe in the interwar period.[43]

Crucially involved was the *relationship between the enterprise and the market*. Socialist theory was predicated upon the tendential surpassing of the latter by the former. This was important, because an enterprise, and a state, can be collectively organized, in contrast to a market, the functioning of which requires just the opposite of a collective, a set of independent actors isolated from each other. The progress of industrial concentration and the extension of cartelization were manifestations of the aforementioned tendency, reinforced in the 1930s by the decline of world trade and the growth of state intervention. The 1930s were also the prime time of the Soviet Five-Year Plans, and of international admiration for them. The postwar call for, and official institutionalization of, public planning of the economy continued this trend, a tendency most articulated in France, the Netherlands and Norway.[44]

Globalization of the European civil war: the Cold War

After 1945 the intertwining of global geo-politics and the internal European dialectics of modernity took a new twist. Europe succeeded in remaining the central area of modernity in an ironic way, by becoming the main arena or battlefield of rival conceptions of progress and development, conceptions which both had their decisive striking capacity stationed outside the continent, beyond the Urals or on the other side of the North Atlantic. Briefly and crudely put, the European civil war was projected onto the global screen – in the form of the Cold (sometimes peripherally hot) War between the Western and the Communist blocs. European cleavages of class and crystallized ideological-isms were transmuted into a bipolar, ideologically highly charged worldwide state system in which the conflicts of civil society were reproduced globally.

Communism was an offshoot of the European working-class movement and the leftwing European intelligentsia, although its postwar Stalinist form was characterized by a number of specifically Russian traits, as well as by the brutality of a generation of militants formed by war and persecution. The personality cult, the labour camps, the mass deportations, were all of Czarist Russian origin, and so were *cordon sanitaire* and Balkan sphere of influence foreign policies, and the pomp of the Red Army. Anti-communism was first pushed vigorously in postwar Europe by the Americans, but the ensuing geo-political-cum-socio-ideological stance had no precedent in the New World or any extra-European state course. It had its only predecessors in Europe, most clearly in the alignments of 1792–1815 for or against revolutionary France, and in the earlier Protestant and Catholic blocs. Geopolitics aside, in Europe the postwar cleavage had a considerable continuity with that created ten years earlier by the Civil War in Spain.

The United States now assumed the leadership of one of the camps, after the exhaustion of Britain and France had become apparent by early 1947. However, although the Cold War was fought all over the world and the major battles took place in East Asia, Europe was still the centre-stage. A serious *faux pas* there, and only there, was regarded by both sides as fatal. The class and ideological conflicts of Europe thus became the fulcrum of a global state conflict.

How much and, in concrete terms, what the Cold War has meant are questions which cannot be answered here. What is clear, however, is that it did not absorb the internal dialectic of European modernity, nor did it determine the basic processes of structuration and culturation. The Cold War affected them, and was affected by them.

Our master questions below will be: What has happened to European modernity since World War II? Are we witnessing the maturation or the end of modernity, its acceleration, or another kind of turn? Have the societies of Europe become more similar to others on the globe? More distinctively European? More differentiated or more similar among themselves? Finally, what are the prospects of Europe after the decades of postwar change and after the end of the Cold War?

After this elaboration of how the scaffolding has been constructed, let us now look at the building of postwar European modernity.

Notes

1 These assertions will have to be fully documentally corroborated in the future. In the meantime, let me refer to scholarly accounts of the novelty involved in the encounters with European culture and its American off-shoots: on Black Africa: A. Boahen, *African Perspectives on Colonialism*, Baltimore, Johns Hopkins University Press, 1987; P. Curtin (ed.), *Africa and the West*, Madison, University of Wisconsin Press, 1972; R. July, *The Origins of Modern African Thought*, New York, Praeger, 1967; on the Arab and the Islamic world: A. Hourani, *Arabic Thought in the Liberal Age 1789–1939*, Cambridge, Cambridge University Press, 1983; B. Lewis, *The Muslim Discovery of Europe*, New York, Norton, 1982; H. Sharabi, *Arab Intellectuals and the West: The Formative Years, 1875–1914*, Baltimore, Johns Hopkins University Press, 1970; Asia: K.M. Panikkar, *Asia and Western Dominance*, London, George Allen & Unwin, 1953; China: Ssu-yü Teng and J. Fairbank (eds), *China's Reponse to the West. A Documentary Survey, 1839–1923*, Cambridge, Mass., Harvard University Press, 1954; J. Spence, *In Search of Modern China*, New York, Norton, 1990; on Japan: Centre for East Asian Cultural Studies *Meiji Japan through Contemporary Sources*, Tokyo, Centre for East Asian Cultural Studies, 1970; J.-P. Lehmann, *The Roots of Modern Japan*, Basingstoke, Macmillan, 1982; M. Miyoshi, *As We*

Saw Them: The First Japanese Embassy to the United States (1860), Berkeley, University of California Press, 1979; Southeast Asia: A. Reid and D. Marr (eds), *Perceptions of the Past in Southeast Asia*, Singapore, Heinemann, 1970.

2 The article in question is reproduced in the collection W. Benjamin, *Illuminationen*, Frankfurt, Suhrkamp, 1969, pp. 185–200.

3 Cf. the beautiful if not always systematic anthology directed by A. Kaspi and A. Marès, *Le Paris des étrangers*, Paris, Imprimerie nationale, 1989.

4 See further, e.g. D. Lach, *Asia in the Making of Europe*, Vol. 2, Chicago, University of Chicago Press, 1977, 2 vols; E. Said, *Culture and Imperialism*, London, Chatto & Windus, 1993.

5 Edward Said's acerbically polemical book *Orientalism* (New York, 1978; Vintage edn, 1979), provides the best general overview of orientalism, as well as being a fundamental frame of reference for contemporary non-European confrontations with European social and cultural knowledge.

6 P. Bairoch, 'The Main Trends in National Economic Disparities since the Industrial Revolution', in P. Bairoch and M. Lévy-Leboyer (eds), *Disparities in Economic Development since the Industrial Revolution*, London, Macmillan, 1981, pp. 4, 10, 12, 14. Note that the American figures for 1830 which Bairoch gives in Tables 1.4. and 1.6 are incompatible with each other. Cf. A. Maddison, *Phases of Capitalist Development*, Oxford, Oxford University Press, 1982, here used in the Dutch translation, *Ontwikkelingsfasen van het kapitalisme*, Utrecht/Antwerpen. Het Spectrum, pp. 20–21, whose figures put Western Europe and 'The Main Trends' close together.

7 Bairoch, 'The Main Trends', pp. 12 and 14. Rapid population growth indicates that also for China, the eighteenth century was a period of growth; cf. F. Braudel, *Civilisation matérielle, économie et capitalisme, XVe-XVIIIe siècle*, Vol.1, Paris, Armand Colin, 1979, pp. 27ff.

8 P. Bairoch, 'International Industrialization Levels from 1750 to 1980', *Journal of European Economic History*, 11, 2 (1982), p. 296. The estimates are based on calculations of the consumption of textiles and iron goods.

9 W. Woodruff, *Impact of Western Man*, London, Macmillan, 1966, pp. 104, 106. The figures are at the lower end of the best estimate. Woodruff (p. 107n) and others think that the Russian figures are too low. The tabulated number of emigrants 1850–1930 amounts to 48.7 million. The continental population estimate of 423 million for 1900 includes Asiatic Russia.

10 H. Berman, *Law and Revolution: The Formation of the Western Legal Tradition*, Cambridge, Mass., Harvard University Press, 1983.

11 See further G. Therborn, 'The Right to Vote and the Four World Routes to/through Modernity', in R. Torstendahl (ed.), *State Theory and State History*: London, Sage, 1992.

12 C. Tilly, *European Revolutions, 1492–1992*, Oxford, Blackwell, 1993. The years of revolutionary situations are given on p. 243, the definition of a revolutionary situation on p. 10. The Germanic lands, Italy and the Nordic countries are not included, while the European part of the Ottoman empire is.

13 N. Ammerman, 'North American Fundamentalism', in M. Marty and S. Appleby (eds), *Fundamentalisms Observed*, Chicago, University of Chicago Press, 1991.

14 Cf. the late Stein Rokkan's work on the historical and the social roots of political cleavages in Europe, e.g. his posthumously published article 'Eine Familie von Modellen für die vergleichende Geschichte Europas', *Zeitschrift für Soziologie* 9, 2 (1980); and 'Nation-Building, Cleavage Formation and the Structuring of Mass Politics', in S. Rokkan et al. (eds), *Citizens, Elections and Parties*, Oslo, Universitetsforlaget, 1970; and the monumental trilogy of nineteenth-century European history by Eric Hobsbawm, *The Age of Revolution 1789–1848* (1962), *The Age of Capital, 1848–1875* (1975), *The Age of Empire, 1875–1914* (1987), all London, Weidenfeld & Nicolson.

15 L. Stein, *Der Sozialismus und Communismus des heutigen Frankreichs*, Leipzig, 1842. In later editions titled *Sozialismus und soziale Bewegung*.

16 Whatever opinion may be held of Lenin and the Bolsheviks, the genuine working-class character of the overthrow of the Russian Provisional Government and the class lines of the

ensuing civil war are unmistakable. Cf. A. Rabinovitch, *The Bolsheviks Come to Power*, New York, Norton, 1976; English edn, NLB, 1979; M. Ferro, *La révolution de 1917*, Paris, Aubier, 1976, 2 vols.

17 J. Armstrong, *Nations before Nationalism*, Chapel Hill, NC, University of North Carolina Press, 1982.

18 J. Hajnal, 'European Marriage Patterns in Perspective', in D.V. Glass and D.E.C. Eversley (eds), *Population in History*, London, 1965. Cf. H. Kaelble, *Auf dem Weg zu einer europäischen Gesellschaft*, Munich, C.H. Beck, 1987, pp. 18ff.

19 P. Bairoch (ed.) *The Working Population and Its Structure*, Brussels, Editions de l'Institut de Sociologie de l'Universitie Libre de Bruxelles, 1968. See further below.

20 See further G. Therborn, 'Why Some Classes Are More Successful Than Others', *New Left Review* 138 (1983).

21 Calculations from Maddison; *Ontwikkelingsfasen*, p. 225.

22 Braudel, *Civilisation matérielle*, p. 26; Woodruff, *Impact of Western Man*, p. 103.

23 The Egyptian nationalist Mustafa Kamil, for instance, wrote a book on the occasion, *The Rising Sun*. See Hourani, *Arabic Thought*, p. 205.

24 A. Gramsci, 'Americanism and Fordism', in *Selections from the Prison Notebooks*, Q. Hoare and G.N. Smith (eds), London, Lawrence & Wishart, 1971.

25 Cf. Maier, *Recasting Bourgeois Europe*, Princeton, Princeton University Press, 1975, pp. 577ff.

26 A. Maddison, 'Economic Policy and Performance in Europe, 1913–1970', in C. Cipolla (ed.), *The Fontana Economic History of Europe* Vol. 5:2, London, Collins/Fontana, 1976, p. 457. The Austrian, Polish and Czechoslovak economies were hardest hit in Europe, and fell by one-fifth on the average. The German decline was one-sixth (ibid., p. 458).

27 Maddison, *Ontwikkelingsfasen*, op. cit. p. 232.

28 T. Wolfe, *From Bauhaus to Our House*, New York, Farrar Strauss Giroux, 1981, p. 9.

29 'Who stayed?', one may ask. Of established, first-rate intellectual talent, perhaps the most noteworthy examples are Picasso and Matisse, who quietly survived in occupied and collaborating France, and some German scientists, such as Werner Heisenberg. True, a number of *émigrés* found refuge in England, where they soon rose to recognized eminence. See P. Anderson, *English Questions*, London, Verso, 1992, pp. 61ff.

30 Maddison, *Ontwikkelingsfasen*, pp. 232–33.

31 True, in Italy and particularly in Belgium this was a major issue. But as such it was more related to that of collaboration with Fascism, of which both monarchies were, not quite unjustly, accused, rather than the form of the postwar state. Neither monarchy had had much power recently anyway.

32 H.-P. Schwarz, *Adenauer: Der Aufstieg 1876–1952*, 3rd edn, Stuttgart, Deutsche-Verlags-Anstalt, 1991, pp. 559ff.

33 'Das Ahlener Wirtschaftsprogramm der CDU für Nordrhein-Westfalen', from the documentary appendix to E.-U. Huster et al., *Determinanten der westdeutschen Restauration 1945–1949*, Frankfurt, Suhrkamp, 1972, p. 414.

34 T. Eschenburg, *Jahre der Besatzung, 1945–49*, Stuttgart and Wiesbaden, DVA and Brockhaus, 1983, p. 186.

35 P. Addison, *The Road to 1945*, London, Quartet Books, 1977, p. 256.

36 S. Nordengren, *Economic and Social Targets for Postwar France*, Lund, Institute of Economic History, 1972, pp. 82ff.

37 'Publiekrechetlijke Bedrijfs Organisatie'. See H.J.G. Verhallen et al. (eds), *Corporatisme in Nederland*, Alphen aan den Rijn, Samsom, 1980, esp. Chs 3 and 4.

38 Printed in the *Listener* (London), 22 November 1945, p. 576. The quote is here taken from Charles Maier's collection of essays, *In Search of Stability*, Cambridge, Cambridge University Press, 1987, p. 153.

39 E. Ragionieri, 'La storia politica e sociale', in R. Romato and C. Vivanti (eds), *Storia d'Italia*, Vol. 4, Turin, Einaudi, 1976, p. 2418.

40 Quoted from Z. Brzezinski, *The Soviet Bloc*, Cambridge, Mass., Harvard University Press, 1960, pp. 26 and 28n, respectively.

41 This combination of unshakeable loyalty, even when it is clearly inopportune, and of bitter criticism comes forth very clearly in the retrospective interviews made with Polish Communist leaders of the postwar period, J. Berman, H. Minc and others. See T. Toranska, *Oni*, Warsaw, 1982/1990, of which I have consulted the Swedish edition, *De ansvariga*, Stockholm, Brombergs, 1986. English edition, *Them*, New York, Harper & Row, 1987.

42 See further G. Therborn, 'States, Populations, and Productivity: Towards a Political Theory of Welfare States', in P. Lassman (ed.), *Politics and Social Theory*, London, Routledge, 1989, pp. 74ff.

43 R. Bloch, *L'entreprise remise en question*, Paris, Librairie générale de droit et de jurisprudence, 1964.

44 See further A. Shonfield, *Modern Capitalism*, London, Oxford University Press, 1965; P.J. Bjerve, *Planning in Norway, 1947–1956*, Amsterdam, North-Holland, 1959; and Nordengren, op. cit. We shall return to this topic below, in the last section of Chapter 6.

PART II

STRUCTURATIONS

The resources and constraints of social systems and of their actor-members are crystals of structuration processes. There is a certain logic of social construction in seeing the latter as running from delimiting societies with boundaries and inhabitants, via provision of the latter with tasks, rights and means, to patterning their chances of life and death.

3

THE BOUNDARIES AND THE PEOPLING OF EUROPE

The territoriality of Europe itself is a historical construct. From the Hellenistic period till the rise and challenge of Islam, what later became 'Europe' was the Mediterranean region, including Alexandria and other centres of south-shore civilization. The European space acquired its current extension only gradually, with the Christianizing of the North – completed only in the fourteenth century (Lithuania) – the Reconquista of the Iberian peninsula, the defeat of the Mongols in the East, the rise of Muscovy and the European turn of Russia under Peter the Great, and, finally, the retreat of the Ottomans and the nineteenth-century rise of European-oriented nationalism in the Balkans. In brief, current Europe is less than two hundred years old, since the first Serbian uprisings, the French-inspired 'Illyrian movement' and the Greek rebellion. The background was the weakening of the Ottoman empire, codified in 1700 in the peace treaty of Karlowitz (near today's Novi Sad in Voivodina); the Enlightenment, the luminescence of which radiated into the serail of the Sultan but even more onto his Balkan subjects; and the wars of the French Revolution, which brought Bonaparte's armies into the Ottoman area, disrupting its previous political order.[1]

Western Europe is older, about five hundred years. The 1490s are crucial: Granada was captured and the last remnants of the Islamic Andalucian civilization were destroyed; a Genoese in Castilian-Aragonese service opened up the Atlantic; the new Cape of Good Hope route circumvented the Mediterranean – where Byzantium had already disappeared and where

Venice was entering the serenity of irrevocable decline – to the spices of the East. Western Europe tilted to the Atlantic, and a century later to the North Atlantic. The Mediterranean became a border instead of a centre.

It is a geographical irony that the most clear-cut important European border today is the Mediterranean, now dividing the relatively prosperous regions of naturally declining populations and one set of politics on the north side from the pauperizing, rapidly growing populations under quite different political and religious systems to the south, while the same sea once held a common civilization together. The British Isles have until recently regarded themselves as anchored in Europe rather than as inhabiting it. The Urals are a cartographer's demarcation, hardly a natural physical border. Only the northern border, by North Cape, is 'natural'. In short, geographical Europe is a fuzzy set.

Delimitations

What has happened to the borders of Europe in the postwar era? The primary evidence is complex. First, take the effect of the loss of colonial empire. In one sense it has put Europe more on a par with the rest of the world, also consisting of sovereign independent states. On the other hand, the loss of 'overseas provinces' and other extra-continental possessions has made continental boundaries more clear, approximating geo-politics to topography. Secondly, the globalization of culture, sustained by satellite television, transistor radios and tape recorders has blurred all continental landmarks. However, while East Asian states have recently risen to challenge European or seemingly European-derived economic supremacy, economic and demographic developments have made Europe more, rather than less, distinctive in terms of resources than its immediate neighbours.

It is the southern, Mediterranean, border of modern Europe which is and which has become economically most clearly demarcated (see Table 3.1). In 1950 the (unweighted) GDP per capita of Egypt, Morocco and Turkey was 80% of Portugal's, in 1988 it was 46%. In 1965, the five most important southern neighbours of Europe had a GDP per head of about 65% of the Portuguese. By 1988 they had 49%. The Eastern–Southern border to Central Asia has also become more visible. The other borders are not very clear-cut, no more than that between Portugal and Spain, and have on the whole been stable. But there has been a postwar tendency towards differentiation in the Southeast. Also along the Atlantic frontier there has been a European strengthening since the war, including a reversal of relative prosperity in the Southwest.

The reflux of colonial migration has brought non-European cultures into Europe, most prominently Europe's classical adversary, Islam. On the other side, again, the internal process of unification and intercontinental processes of differentiation have given Europe more economic and political coherence than ever before in modern history.

In brief, the cultural boundaries of Europe have been blurred, while structural ones have rather become more clear-cut.

Table 3.1 *GDP per capita, 1950–1991 around Europe's borders*

Portugal = 100, and ratios, European border area/non-European border area.

Border	1950	1965	1988	1991
East–South[a]	*1.5, 1.4*[b]	*1.8, 1.7*[c]	–	*2.1, 1.5*
Russia	–	–	–	73
Central Asia[d]	–	–	–	34
Caucasus[e]	–	–	–	48
South–East	*1.3, 1.3*[f]	*1.8, 1.7*[f]	*–, 1.6*[f]	*1.3, 1.6*[f]
Balkans[g]	123.5	144	–	67
Greece	123	135	110	81
Turkey	95	81	68	51
Southern[a]	*2.7*[g]*, 3.3*	*3.3, 4.3*	*5.0, 7.5*	*6.0, 7.6*
Med. Europe[h]	217	215	241	289
Maghreb[i]	80[j]	65	48	48
Egypt	65	50	32	38
South–West[k]	*1.2, 0.6*	*1.5, 1.1*	*1.2, 1.8*	*1.8, 1.9*
Portugal	100	100	100	100
Brazil	86	65	83	55
Spain	159	176	139	134
Argentina	252	161	76	54
North–West	*0.6*	*0.6*	*0.6*	*0.7*
British Isles[l]	352	255	219	170
USA	614	412	345	234

Notes: [a] The first figure in the row refers to the difference between the European region in question and the first border area, the second between the former and the second non-European border area. [b] 1958, and refers to relative rouble income. [c] 1968, and refers to relative rouble income. [d] Kazakhstan, Kyrgyzstan, Tajikistan, Turkmenistan, Uzbekistan, unweighted averages. [e] Armenia, Azerbaijan, Georgia, unweighted averages. [f] Ratio of Greece: Turkey only. [g] Bulgaria and Greece, unweighted averages; [h] France, Italy and Spain, unweighted averages. [i] Algeria, Morocco and Tunisia, unweighted averages. [j] Morocco only. [k] The first ratio refers to Portugal and Brazil, the second to Spain and Argentina. [l] Population-weighted averages of the UK and Ireland.

Sources: Calculations from R. Summers and A. Heston, 'Improved International Comparisons of Real Product and Its Composition: 1950–1980', *The Review of Income and Wealth*, 30 (1984), pp. 220ff, adjusted GDP per capita (1950, 1965); idem, 'The Penn World Table (Mark 5): An Expanded Set of International Comparisons, 1950–1988', *The Quarterly Journal of Economics* CVI (May 1991), pp. 350ff. (1988); World Bank, *World Development Report 1993*, New York, Oxford University Press, 1993, Table 30 ('observed' estimates) (1991); K.von Beyme, *Ökonomie und Politik im Sozialismus*, Munich, Piper, 1977, Table 26 (USSR in 1958 and in 1968).

Demographies of modernity

The post-World War II period has seen the culmination, and break, of a trend, visible from the mid-1930s, towards *nuclear family domesticity*, with a high marriage rate, low mortality, little instability (immediate postwar break-ups apart), high frequency of full-time housewives (except in the reconstruction societies), and children kept with little intrusion within the poles of parental authority, neighbourhood and local school. The proportion of adults living alone reached a historical low and, correspondingly, living in marriage attained a historical high in Western Europe around 1970. Since then the crude marriage rate (per thousand population) had generally gone down in both East and West, although the spread of non-married cohabitation makes comparisons difficult.[2]

Before the war the proportion of never-married had been very high in some Western countries. At the end of their fertile cycle, at 45–54 years of age, 28% of Finnish women were single by 1940, and other high incidences of being single in the 1930s prevailed in Ireland (25% single), Sweden (22.5%), Norway (22%) and Scotland (21.5%). By 1970, corresponding Swedish and Norwegian figures were well below 10%, in Finland 12%, Scotland 15% and Ireland 19%. In Belgium, Denmark, England and Wales, and the Netherlands the celibacy rate was halved to about 8%. In France and Germany, with traditionally high marriages rates by Western European standards, the changes were small, from 11% to 9% and from 13% to 10%, respectively. Austria, Italy and Switzerland were in-between.[3]

The marriage boom meant, under prevailing gender norms, an early postwar tendency for the economic participation of women to decline in Western Europe.[4] But the extent of this decline is difficult to assess, because of the varying definitions and methods of counting helping family members (often from one census to the next within the same country). For Sweden, however, the picture can be shown with some precision. Excluding family helpers, however defined, the economically active female population declined in Sweden from 815,000 in 1930 to 795,000 in 1950, whereas the number of housewives – married to working men but themselves outside the labour market and not counted as greatly participating in the family farm or business – rose from 925,000 to 1,240,000.[5] Thereafter, the picture began to change, accelerating in the 1960s. (See further below, on the changes in patriarchy.)

The Eastern European postwar experience was in many ways different. Here, where almost everyone married, the new times meant female work outside the household, collective daycare and soon, after the 1950s liberalization of abortion, strongly reduced number of children. In these respects Eastern Europe may be seen as a forerunner of later developments in the West, particularly in Scandinavia. Communist egalitarian and contractarian family legislation did lead to a higher rate of divorce, but interestingly enough to a rate below that of the USA, with the USSR ultimately topping Europe, and Czechoslovakia and Hungary close to Scandinavia.[6]

In terms of birth rates a convergent lowering in Europe has occurred, leaving only Albania, with a crude birth rate of 25 live births per thousand population in 1989, as the single outstanding country. For the rest, East and West, the 10–15 promille band is enough, including Ukraine and, with an additional point, the Baltics. Russia under Communist government remained a bit difficult to squeeze in at 17 promille in 1987.[7] The demographically more sophisticated rates show that the population of Europe is no longer reproducing itself, naturally that is. West Germany stopped doing so in the 1960s, East Germany, France and the UK in the first half of the 1970s, and Italy in the second half of that decade. Many Western countries have seen a slight upturn in their natural population reproduction since the mid-1980s, but in 1990 only Iceland, Ireland and, just barely, Sweden were reproducing themselves. In Eastern Europe there was in several cases a temporary increase in fertility around the mid-1970s, and natural reproduction was generally maintained longer than in the West. However, by 1988–9 only Albania, Romania, the USSR and, almost, Poland were reproducing themselves.[8]

In the crisis ensuing upon the fall of Communism, Eastern Europe has entered into a demographic slump. In ex-GDR the latter has been dramatic, with the crude birth rate falling from 12.0 in 1989 to 5.3 in 1992, and the 'total fertility rate', which denotes the total number of live children likely to be born to a woman during her lifetime according to current age-specific fertility, falling to 0.8, while a rate of about 2.1 children per woman is needed for natural reproduction.[9] Romania and Russia have rapidly gone down to the reproductive level of Netherlands and Switzerland, Bulgaria to that still lower of Austria and West Germany.[10]

The major modern decline in birth rates in Europe occurred in the second half of the nineteenth century, whereafter they have undulated at a lower level. After the trough of the Depression, rates rose strongly after World War II, then flattened out, to fall again in the West in the 1970s and early 1980s. Whether the modest upturn in several Western countries after 1985 will maintain itself is open to doubt, while there seems to be no very good reason for excluding the possibility of a future, modest growth of the 'will to children'. However, taken as a whole, the development of European fertility in the past quarter of a century has made the continent more specific demographically.

The demographic distance to neighbouring Africa and Asia has become more pronounced. This occurred clearly within the USSR. Whereas Russian birth rates almost halved between 1940 and 1987, the Uzbek and the Tadjik rate actually increased, the Turkmen, the Kirghiz and, by and large, the Azeri stayed put, whereas the Kazakh declined by two-fifths.[11] Total fertility rates in Southeastern Europe (Yugoslavia, Albania, Greece, Romania, Bulgaria) have till 1989 on the whole fallen since 1970 slightly less than in Turkey,[12] while in Southwestern Europe they have somewhat more than in the Mahgreb.[13]

But the most pronounced demographic distance to Europe's neighbours emerges when we look at birth and death rates together (see Table 3.2).

Demographically, Europe is still an old world. More reproductive populations surround the continent, except in the empty Arctic seas to the north. The major changes are on the eastern borders of Europe, but distances have tended to grow along all borders, save in the Northwest. The situation reflects both current reproductive behaviour and age structures

Table 3.2 *Europe's demographic distance to its neighbours*

The rate of natural population growth (rates of birth minus death per thousand population) in European and non-European border areas, and border differentials, in 1950, 1970, and 1991.

Borders	1950	1970	1991
East–South[a]	−5.7, −7.8	−20.8, −11.2	−23.6, −13.7
Russia	12.4[b]	5.9	1.0
Central Asia[c]	18.1[b]	26.7	24.6
Caucasus[d]	20.2[b]	17.1	14.7
South–East	−	−15.2	−19.0
The Balkans[e]	−	8.8	2.0
Turkey	22.9	24.0	21.0
Southern[a]	−	−22.0, −14.7	−22.0, −21.0
Med. Europe[f]	8.9	8.3	2.0
Mahgreb[g]	−	30.3	24.0
Egypt	−	23.0	23.0
South–West	−	−15.0	−17.0
Portugal	12.1	10.0	1.0
Brazil		25.0	18.0
North–West	−5.5	−3.5	−3.8
British Isles[h]	6.8	4.5	3.2
USA	14.3	8.0	7.0

Notes: [a] The first figure refers to the differential between the European area and the first of the two border areas, the second to the differential to the second border region. [b] 1940. [c] Kazakhstan, Kyrgyzstan, Tajikistan, Turkmenistan, Uzbekistan, unweighted average. [d] Armenia, Azerbaijan, Georgia, unweighted average. [e] Bulgaria, Greece, Romania, Yugoslavia, unweighted averages. [f] France, Italy, Spain, unweighted averages. [g] Algeria, Morocco, Tunisia, unweighted averages. [h] Ireland and the UK, weighted by 1990 population.

Sources: Calculations from World Bank, *World Development Report 1993*, New York, Oxford University Press, 1993, Tables 1 and 27 (1970, 1991); OECD, *Demographic Trends, 1950–1990*, Paris, 1979, Tables 1–4 and 1–5 (OECD countries in 1950); and B.R. Pockney, *Soviet Statistics since 1950*, Aldershot, Dartmouth, 1991, Table 33 (ex-USSR 1940 and 1970).

derived from the past. Demographic regimes are not being evened out. Inside Europe, a very low rate of natural population growth has become a common trait, from the Russian steppes to the British Isles.

From colonialism and emigration to ex-colonial immigration

European colonialism achieved its last offensive victory just prior to World War II, when Fascist Italy conquered the only remaining indigenous independent state of Africa, Abyssinia (Ethiopia). By 1940, the colonial and more generally outward thrust of European modernity had reached its apogee. The whole of Africa was under European rule, either by settlement

(South Africa, Algeria) or by colonial or semi-colonial (Egypt, Morocco) rule. West Asia, except Turkey and the bulk of the Arabian peninsula, were under one form of indirect rule/'protection' or another. India was a 'jewel in the crown' of Europe. The Indochinese peninsula and the Southeast Asian archipelago were under firm colonial subjection. Shanghai and other coastal cities of China harboured European 'concessions'. European-type Bolshevism ruled Central Asia and, indirectly, Outer Mongolia. The Chinese Communists had become a major force, and were still largely steeped in the Moscow-based Comintern tradition.

The Americas were predominantly independent – although keeping a number of British, French and Dutch toeholds – largely settled by descendants of Europe, and culturally still looking up to the continent. The Spanish Civil War was the war of the American as well as of the European left. Japan had shown its teeth already in 1905, and the interior of China still remained too large to be colonized.

For the rest, there was not much that was really independent of Europe: Siam, about to begin calling itself Thailand; the Himalayan–Pamir region of mountains; the Arabian desert; Europeanizing Turkey, with its German army training, Swiss Civil Code, and English and French schools for the urban élite.

After the war, the losers of 1940, France, the Netherlands and Belgium managed to reconquer their colonies (unchallenged in the Belgian case). But Italy had to cede not only previously lost Abyssinia (Ethiopia) but also Eritrea, Somalia and Libya to the UN, and Britain relinquished the Indian subcontinent, Burma, Ceylon and Palestine, reluctantly but without armed resistance. In other areas, for example, Malacca and Kenya, however, the British held on with all the power of their guns. The Dutch were pressured by armed insurrection and by their Marshall Plan American paymasters to leave Indonesia in 1949.

A second, and final, wave of de-colonization began rolling with the Vietnamese victory over the French at Dien Bien Phu in 1954, completed only twenty years later with the Portuguese revolution yielding the 'overseas provinces' of Africa, or, in some sense, about forty years later when the countdown of European settler rule in South Africa started.

From 1500 to 1940 Europe was enjoying the world. Military might – originally based on naval gunnery and manifested in colonial conquests – economic power – achieved by eighteenth- and nineteenth-century industrialization[14] – and migration outlets for the locally disadvantaged or adventurous, were all globally concentrated in European hands. Even the English centre of global industry was an out-migration area, at its historical afternoon tea-time (see below). A conservative estimate is that about 50 million Europeans emigrated out of the continent in the period 1850–1930, which corresponds to about 12% of the continent's population in 1900.[15]

All European countries except France, the pioneer of popular birth control, were countries of (net) emigration, for longer or shorter periods (see Table 3.3).[16] The two major emigration areas were the British Isles and Italy.

Between 1850 and 1960 about half of the population of the British Isles in 1900 emigrated, and a good third of the Italian population in the same year.[17]

World War II did not in itself or immediately change the patterns of continental migration. Rather, the postwar period meant a resumption of the overall pre-Depression pattern. Migration poured out of the British Isles, of Ireland in particular, and in the Netherlands promotion of emigration continued to be official policy. Massive out-migration took place also from Italy, Greece, Portugal and Spain.

Colonial in-migration started before the war, into France in 1905–6. By the mid-1920s there were about 70,000 North Africans, most of them Algerians, in France. On the eve of the Franco-Algerian war, in 1954, the latter numbered officially 212,000, alongside much smaller contingents from the rest of the Maghreb and from Black Africa.[18] There was of old a tiny Black population in the former slave-trade ports of Britain, but numbers were small till the 1950s. In 1948, at the outset of postwar colonial in-migration, 547 migrants landed from Jamaica. Ten years later, by the time of the first racist riots in Britain, there were about 210,000 'coloured' colonial immigrants.[19] Also a significant number of South Moluccans retreated with the Royal Dutch East Indies Army from Indonesia into the Netherlands.

In the postwar period every single Western European country has had years of significant immigration, although in the Irish case this was confined to re-immigration in the 1970s. By 1990, only Ireland remains an emigration country. The importance of this immigration may be indicated by comparing West Germany and the United States. At its first peak (after the postwar settlement) in 1969–70 net immigration into West Germany was 0.9% a year of the resident population. That was equal to the American immigration in the top year of 1913.[20] In the *annus mirabilis* of 1989 net immigration into the Federal Republic amounted to 1.6% of the resident population.[21]

When did Europe as a continent become more of an arrival hall than a departure lounge for intercontinental migration? In the course of the first half of the 1960s. There were two processes involved: a decline of ancient overseas out-migration and a picking up of new inward migration from overseas.

After the postwar settlement, the major overseas emigration from Eastern Europe was virtually halted – and other emigration as well, of which Polish migration to Germany and France was important before the war. Exceptions were out of the GDR till the erection of the Wall, and after the acute crises in Hungary (1956), Czechoslovakia 1968–9, and Poland 1981–2.[22] Throughout the 1980s, emigration, most of it unofficial, using legal tourist passports, was nevertheless rather significant from Hungary and Poland, amounting net to 2–3 promille of the population annually, although the Hungarian figure is uncertain.[23]

From Northwestern Europe continental out-migration had mostly ceased to be significant by the Depression of the 1930s,[24] and from Central Europe that had occurred earlier. (Save for a brief period, 1948–52, Europeans had

Table 3.3 *Migration and migratory turns in Western Europe, 1814–1990*

Periods of significant net migration (at least one per thousand population) into or from Western European countries, 1814–1990. Before 1973 periods shorter than five years are not noted, nor are the two world wars.

Country	Emigration	Immigration
Austria[a]	1822–6, 1949–61, 1975	1965–73, 1980–1, 1986–90
Belgium	1847–66	1922–33, 1945–75, 1988–
Denmark	1866–1914, 1926–30	1985–7, 1990
Finland	1860s,[b] 1945–70	1981–3, 1989–90
France	–	1830–7, 1875–86, 1920–31, 1948–73, 1981, 1990
Germany[c]	1848–96	1947–73, 1978–81, 1985–
Greece[d]	1950–74	1975–84, 1988–90
Ireland[e]	1832–1970, 1982–90	1971–8
Italy[f]	1863–1971	1982–90
Netherlands[g]	1880–1913, 1946–57	1964–81, 1985–90
Norway	1849–1930	1981–2, 1985–8
Portugal[h]	1850–1973, 1976–9	1974–5, 1980–8
Spain[h]	1888–96, 1904–14, 1919–25, 1949–74, 1986	1976–7, 1980
Sweden	1830s, 1848–1930	1945–70, 1974–81, 1984–90
Switzerland[i]	1872–91, 1919–25, 1975–8	1892–1913, 1928–31, 1945–73, 1980–2, 1984–90
UK[j]	1901–31, 1965, 1980–2	1985–6
England & Wales[k]	1881–1926	1838–49, 1931–9, 1959–64

Notes: [a] The Republic from 1920 only. [b] Till 1989. Before World War II Finland had a pattern of migration oscillating strongly from year to year. [c] Data from 1842, territory of 1871–1937, after World War II Federal Republic. [d] Data from 1920. [e] From 1910, territory of the Republic only. [f] Data from 1863. [g] Data from 1841. [h] Data from 1850. [i] Data from 1872. [j] Data from 1901. [k] 1838–1975, migration within the UK included.

Sources: Unless otherwise stated, the primary data derive from official population statistics and include various forms of re-migration as well. Usually, this means that the migratory balance emerges as a residual after the registration of births and deaths. Till 1975, the main source is P. Flora (ed.), *State, Economy and Society in Western Europe, 1815–1975*, Vol. 2, Frankfurt, Campus, 1987, Ch. 6.1. After 1975, Council of Europe, *Recent Demographic Developments*, Strasburg, 1991, country tables. For 1975–9, and for Greece, Portugal and Spain for 1964–79, the main source is OECD, *Labour Force Statistics*, various volumes, National Table 1. For Greece, Portugal and Spain 1950–63: United Nations Economic Commission for Europe, *Labour Supply and Migration in Europe*, New York, 1979, Table II.9. Before 1950 for these three countries the calculations refer to the number of registered migrants related to population. See further G. Therborn, 'Migration and Western Europe: The Old World Turning New?', *Science* 237 (4.9.1987), p. 1188n. For countries with data for 1990 missing in the Council of Europe report, SOPEMI, *Trends in International Migration*, Paris, OECD, 1992, has been resorted to.

ceased to provide the majority of US immigrants during World War II.[25]) But the Greek, Italian, Portuguese and Spanish extra-European migration was vigorous in the 1950s.[26] Around 1960, it began to decline rapidly, however. In the Italian case, (gross) emigration became predominantly European in the second half of the 1950s.[27] Particularly in the Portuguese and Greek cases, the change basically meant a turn northeast, to Europe, whereas in the Italian and, above all, Spanish cases, net emigration as such started to ebb at that date.[28]

The other part of the turn was the inflow of extra-European immigrants. This had started on a significant scale, as planned labour imports, in France after World War II, with the bringing in of Algerian workers. From 1955 'women and children' were also allowed in. In the first years of the 1960s a Moroccan labour recruitment started again, and by mid-decade a Tunisian one followed. Maghrebin workers were also somewhat later recruited to Belgium and the Netherlands, and, later again, Moroccan workers entered Spain, largely unsolicited.

The extra-Europe-born population of Britain started to grow in the 1950s, mainly from the so-called New Commonwealth, i.e. of non-British descent, coming from the West Indies, India and Pakistan. But whereas the population born outside Europe in the Commonwealth increased by 344,000 people net in the ten years up to 1961, they added on another 327,000 in the five years thereafter.[29]

A major sender of immigrants into Europe has been Turkey. Two months after the rise of the Berlin Wall, the West German government signed a labour import agreement with the government of Turkey, continuing earlier recruitment deals with Italy (in 1955) and Greece and Spain (in 1960), to be followed by labour imports contracts with Portugal in 1964 and with Yugoslavia in 1968. The Turks responded very rapidly. By 1965 there were 133,000 Turkish workers in West Germany. Six years later, the Turks had overtaken the Italians as the most numerous group of foreigners in West Germany, making up a total registered population of 653,000.[30]

The climax of ethnic homogenization

A third long-term process of population structuring, after births and deaths and migration, is the shaping of the ethnic, however defined, composition. The rise of the modern nation-state has meant a major process of ethnic homogenization within state boundaries. The process was most marked in Eastern Europe, where the formation of modern nations and nation-states took place later than in the West. The change involved may be glimpsed by looking at the nineteenth-century or early twentieth-century ethnic composition of current national capitals in Eastern Europe (see Table 3.4).

In Table 3.4 the year refers, except in the case of Reval/Tallinn and Sofia, to the latest census that counted a minority of the ethnicity which later became the *Staatsvolk*, where this had ever occurred.[31] As a base of comparison, the capitals of the major multinational empires, from Ottoman

Table 3.4 _Early modern share of current national ethnicity of the population of the current national capital of Eastern European countries_

City	Year	% total pop.
Bratislava	1910	38[a]
Bucharest	c. 1850	c. 40
Budapest	1870	46
Chisinau	1926	40
Helsinki	1890	46
Istanbul	1878	62
Kiev	1926	42
Ljubljana	1880	c. 75[b]
Minsk	1926	42
Prague	1846	<36[c]
Riga	1913	42
St Petersburg	1910	89
Sofia	1866	c. 33
Tallinn	1871	52
Vienna	1910	85
Vilnius	1926	0[d]
Warsaw	1897	62
Zagreb	1910	75

Notes: [a] The secondary source used here, Glettler (1992, seebelow) actually gives a much lower figure of Slovaks, 14.9% (p. 302), as well as the data from which the above is calculated. Both are taken from official Hungarian statistics, but the one chosen here is from the contemporary source. [b] This is an estimate, from census data saying that the city had 23% Germans among its population. [c] This is a minimum, since the total, from which the Czech proportion is calculated, refers to 'the Christian population'. [d] The city was then under Polish rule, and the figure is that of the Polish census. In the 1897 Russian census Vilnius had 2% Lithuanians.

Sources: Slovaks in Bratislava: M. Glettler, 'The Slovaks in Budapest and Bratislava, 1850–1914', in M. Engman (ed.), _Ethnic Identity in Europe_, Aldershot, Dartmouth, 1991, pp. 301 and 307; Romanians in Bucharest: A. Schaser, 'Die Fürstentümer Moldau und Wallachia 1650–1850', in W. Fischer et al. (eds), _Handbuch der europäischen Wirtschafts- und Sozialgeschichte_, Vol. 4, Stuttgart, Klett-Cotta, 1993, pp. 986–7; Magyars in Budapest: J. Lukács, _Budapest 1900_, New York, Weidenfeld & Nicolson, 1988, p. 101; Moldavians (or Romanians) in Chisinau, Ukrainians in Kiev, Belorussians in Minsk, Lithuanians in Vilnius: C. Harris, 'The New Russian Minorities: A Statistical Overview', _Post-Soviet Geography_ 34, 1 (1993), pp. 18–19; Finnish-speakers in Helsinki: H. Pauninen, 'Finskan i Helsingfors', in _Helsingfors' två språk_, Helsinki, Meddelanden from Institutionen för nordiska språk och nordisk litteratur vid Helsingfors Universitet, 1980, p. 12; Turks in Istanbul: _Yurt Ansklopeditsti_, 'Istanbul', Istanbul, Agadolu Yanincilika, 1983, p. 3830; Slovenes in Ljubljana: A. Wandruska and P. Urbanitsch (eds), _Die Habsburgermonarchie, 1848–1918_, Vol. III: 1: _Die Völker des Reiches_, Vienna, Verl. d. öster. Ak. d. Wiss., 1980, p. 255; Czechs in Prague: G. Cohen, 'The German Minority of Prague, 1850–1918', in Engman _Ethnic Identity_, p. 268; Russian-speakers in St Petersburg: M. Engman, 'Finnar och svenskar i St Petersburg', in S. Carlsson and N.-Å. Nilsson (eds), _Sverige och St Petersburg_, Stockholm, Almqvist & Wiksell, 1989, p. 1989, p. 69; Bulgarians in Sofia: N.J.G. Pound, _An Historical Geography of Europe_, paperback edn, Cambridge, Cambridge University Press, 1988, p. 158; Estonians in Tallinn and Latvians in Riga: G. von Rauch, _Geschichte der baltischen Staaten_, Stuttgart, W. Kohlhammer, 1970, p. 19; Germans in Vienna: Wandruska and Urbanitsch, _Die Habsburgermonarchie_, Vol. 2, pp. 56–7; Poles in Warsaw: A. Kappeler, _Russland als Vielvölkerreich_, Munich, C.H. Beck, 1992, p. 327; Croats in Zagreb: Wandruska and Urbanitsch, _Die Habsburgermonarchie_, Vol. 2. The primary sources, the base of the categorizations, are those of official statistics, of Austrian, Hungarian, Russian, Polish, Ottoman and Romanian censuses. As a rule, the ethnic criterion is primary everyday language, but also religion, and in 1926 ethnic descent ('narodnost'): Kappeler _Russland_, pp. 233ff, referring to the Russian census of 1897; Harris 'The New Russian Minorities', p. 19n.

Istanbul to Czarist St Petersburg, are also included.[32] The transformation of
the later national capitals is the most remarkable ethnic change. But there is
also the ethnic restructuring of a number of port cities, once famous for their
variety of populations: Thessaloniki/Selânik/Soloun, Triest/e, Fiume/Rijeka,
Danzig/Gdansk, Vyborg/Viipuri. And there were ethnic cleansings of vast
land areas too.

Eastern European ethnic homogenization occurred in four waves, each
particularly related to one special cause of the original heterogeneity. The
first was set in motion in the last third of the nineteenth century, by peasant
emancipation, industrialization and new means of transport and communication, and manifested in massive rural–urban migration. In this way the
ethnic frontier between the German-Jewish (or Swedish, in the case of
Helsingfors/Helsinki) towns and the countryside of other ethnicities was
broken up, blurred or swamped. Nationalist institutions and policies of the
previously mainly rural ethnicities promoted new tongues and scripts.
Before the last turn of the century Budapest and Prague had become
predominantly Hungarian and Czech, respectively.

The break up of the old multi-ethnic empires at the end of World War I
and the creation of new nation-states led to various forms of forced ethnic
change. A major multi-ethnic force then broken up has been given a recent
Ehrenrettung (rehabilitation), namely the Habsburg army, which went down
without (recent) military glory, but which was genuinely committed to ethnic
blindness – Jews were vastly overrepresented among its reserve officers –
and mulitilingualism.[33]

A telling example of the new times was the fate of the multi-ethnic, largely
Jewish Ottoman city of Salonıkı, 'the bridgehead of modernity' in the
Ottoman empire, the base of a quatro-lingual labour movement, the cradle
of the Young Turk revolution, the residence of its positivist-sociological
ideologue Gökalp, the birthplace and military base of Mustafa Kemal, and
the original home turf of the rival ethnic armed bands – Bulgarian, Serb,
Greek – contesting the Macedonian issue. The city came to Greece in 1912
after the Balkan wars. In 1913 Saloniki had 158,000 inhabitants, of whom
the census counted 39% Jews (who had made up about half of the
population in the second half of the nineteenth century), speaking
djudezmo, a Jewish-Spanish vernacular, as well as 29% Turks and 25%
Greeks. It became a predominantly Greek city in the 1920s, when the Turks
were expelled and the Greek expatriates from Asia Minor arrived. The Jews
were then killed off (by the Germans) in the next wave, in 1943.[34] In early
1994, the city became notorious for the staging of militant chauvinist Greek
demonstrations against the Former Yugoslav Republic of Macedonia.

In the Baltics, Polish-ruled Wilna (Vilnius) counted a two-thirds Polish
majority in 1926, after having made up a third in 1897, and the Latvians
became the majority in Riga, 60% as against 45% in 1897.[35]

Eastern Europe had a very large Jewish population, mainly because of the
more tolerant policies of its rulers from late medieval times onwards, of the
Ottomans and of Poland and Lithuania in particular, compared to those

reigning in Western Europe. But with the urban massification of poverty and the rise of nationalism their position became difficult. Emigration was one way out. Then came the Nazis and the Holocaust. The virtual disappearance of the Jews was the third major wave of ethnic cleansing in Eastern European modernity.

Finally, the Germans' turn came, as a revenge for the horrors of Nazi German occupation. By 1948 about 10.7 million Germans had fled or been expelled from Eastern Europe. Of these, 40% landed in the Soviet Zone, where they constituted about a quarter of the total population.[36] In 1950 there were 8 million 'out-settlers' (*Aussiedler*) in West Germany, 16.4% of the inhabitants of the German Federal Republic.[37] In East Germany this phenomenon was played down, while it was for long played up in the West.

The economic success of the latter and the integrative political skills of postwar West German Christian Democracy (successfully Protestant as well as, basically, Catholic) ensured that in the course of the first half of the 1970s the direct political mouthpiece of the expellees in West Germany, the BHE (Bund der Heimatvertriebenen und Entrechteten, i.e. the league of people expelled from their homeland and deprived of their rights) disappeared from the political scene.[38]

But even after the postwar out-migration, there remained about 4 million Germans, or people claiming German descent, in Eastern Europe, in the USSR, in Poland, and in Romanian Siebenbürgen (Transsylvania) mainly. Those who were allowed to remain were granted specific minority rights, even during the period of high Stalinism, and in 1956 considerable overtures in their direction were made, from Poland to Romania.[39] By 1990 about half of them had gone to the Federal Republic.[40]

Related movements of postwar flight and expulsion also affected Italy (from Dalmatia and Istria) and Austria and Finland, which both received about 400,000 people, 6% and 10% of their populations, respectively. The Finnish case is very illustrative of the new significance of state boundaries. As noted above, hardly anybody left Finland for the Russians in 1809. The major out-settling population came from the main and decisive theatre of war in 1940 and in 1944, the Karelian isthmus, and Karelia north of the isthmus. In the pre-nationalist period the latter functioned as a meeting-ground of the Nordic and the Russian, where a number of Russian intellectuals and members of the upper classes had their summer dachas, and where the great Swedish-speaking Finnish poet Edith Södergran grew up, writing poetry in Russian and German as well as in Swedish, and as a lady, of course, also educated in French.[41]

The major ethnic cleansing operation took place in the construction of a new postwar Poland, from where 5 million Germans were expelled – according to an Allied agreement – and whose Ukrainian- and Belorussian-populated areas were ceded to the USSR. In Western Poland a concrete ground for the postwar settling operation had been laid by the Nazi occupiers, who had prepared a large-scale German colonization there.[42] 'For three years, Polish roads and railways were crammed with endless processions of refugees, deportees, transients, expellees, and internal migrants.'[43]

Hard data are hard to get at, but it seems that *around 1950 the states of Europe had achieved an unprecedented ethnic homogenization of their populations.* Vigorous policies and institutions of nation- and state-building, boundary changes, expulsions and repatriations had all contributed. Homogeneity should only be taken as a historically relative notion, however. Jaroslav Krejčí has counted sixty-nine different ethnic groups in Europe, which assures a certain constancy of heterogeneity.[44]

The statement does not quite fit the Western European experience, if we count only the displacement of foreign citizens (see below). Furthermore, three European states were clearly multi-ethnic, two of them explicitly so. The Swiss citizenry would in most contexts qualify as 'multi-ethnic', given its ancient and well-defined variety of linguistic-cultural communities. The Soviet Union and Yugoslavia had institutionalized multi-ethnicity in their forms of state. In both, the Communists built upon and may be said to have made a virtue of an inherited necessity, the multi-ethnicity of Czarist Russia and of prewar Yugoslavia. However, a *fin-de-siècle* historian is prone to stress the positive achievement of Leninist multinationalism, i.e. its capacity simultaneously to provide space for national cultures and identities and to keep different nationalities in peaceful coexistence.

The ethnic policy of the USSR in the 1920s was unique in its generosity. For forty-eight ethnicities written languages were created, for the first time. Illiteracy was eradicated by ethnic mother tongue schools, from Belorussian and Yiddish to Uzbek and Kirghiz. In the name of internationalism, seventy languages of the USSR were given a Latin script, which perhaps was not in the interests of Muslims and Buddhists, but which on the other hand went contrary to any Russo-centred view of the world.[45]

However, from the late 1930s the Cyrillic alphabet was imposed, and under Stalin, before the Revolution ironically the main Bolshevik spokes-man on it, nationality policy was subordinated to the centralist and chauvinist calculations of the dictator. But the principle of territorial national rights remained throughout the Soviet era, and became nationalist firewood with the disintegration of the union.

The successful postwar re-integration of the Czechs and the Slovaks – after the major Slovak party having sided with Hitler after Munich – and of the warring tribes of Yugoslavia, at each others' throats both before and during the war, was also one of the few still respectable outcomes of Communism.

Anyway, briefly put, mid-twentieth century saw an ethnic integration, by homogenization or through institutionalized multi-ethnicity, unique in European history. Both the processes which had brought it about were manifestations of European modernity. The former drew upon the Western Enlightenment and the French Revolution, the latter upon the Central Eastern Enlightenment, the tradition of Herder and the typical Central Eastern blend of Rationalism and Romanticism, out of which the Leninist conception of nationality also stemmed. The postwar boom, East and West, was to undo this outcome of decades of economically largely zero-sum political upheavals.

In the East a turn towards nationalism and new chauvinist divisions started earlier, however, with a paradoxical post-Stalinist disenchantment with Leninist enlightenment. From 1956 on, Eastern European Communist leaders started to play a nationalist card, directed above all against ethnic minorities under their thumb. The Romanians and the Bulgarians were first out, followed a decade later by Polish anti-semitism in 1968. By then, 'ethnonationalism' had begun to become a serious issue also in Yugo-slavia.[46]

Migrations and the new heterogeneity

Two major forces have reversed the historical trend towards ethnic levelling, which peaked around 1950. One has been labour scarcity in the novel boom economies, a scarcity for dirty jobs in particular, calling forth recruiting efforts, which in turn have had unintended family migration consequences. This has operated both East and West, though on a much smaller scale in Eastern Europe outside the USSR, and involving less extra-continental immigration, although there were a considerable number of Vietnamese recruited workers in the East as well as workers from Mozambique.[47] The now extremely sensitive issue of Russian, Belorussian and Ukrainian emigration into the Baltics, albeit with some special political features, appears to be part of a much broader continental pattern of migration.

Secondly, Europe has become an outlet for refugees and desperate people from other continents. The chickens of colonialism have come back to roost, so to speak. On a much more modest scale, this latter turn is, of course, no more than a reversal of the earlier pattern.

In Ibero-American relations, particularly, the turn might be seen as a displacement of the Eldorado, from Brazil and other parts of the Americas as the hope of dirt-poor Portuguese and Spanish migrants, to the new EC members perceived as offering wider opportunities, even to Argentinians and Brazilians, not to speak of Dominicans and other poor Americans. The Portuguese and the Spanish authorities have responded to this reversal of fortune by introducing expulsions of undesirably poor Latin Americans.[48]

The drying up of the (male) European labour market and the first immigration process started immediately after the war in France, Switzerland and Belgium, linking up with prewar practices in all three countries and swelled over all Central Northwestern Europe (save Ireland) in the brightest of the boom decades, the one preceding the oil crisis of late 1973. In spite of a number of serious attempts, the migration wave then turned out to be impossible to roll back – given the legal principles in existence – except in Switzerland and Austria.

The other immigration process began with de-colonization and its aftermath. It was sustained by the 1970s dictatorships of South America and their refugees, was strongly reinforced by the crises of the Middle East, the Islamic revolution in Iran, the invasion and wars in Lebanon, the break-up of Somalia etc., and given still another boost by the collapse in Eastern Europe.

Let us summarize the structural outcome of these processes by the end of the 1980s (see Table 3.5).

Table 3.5 *Foreign population in Western Europe, 1950–1990 (per cent foreigners among the resident population)*

Country	1950	1990
Austria	4.7	5.3
Belgium	4.3	9.1
Denmark	–	3.1
Finland	–	0.5
France	4.1	6.4
Germany	1.1	8.2
Italy	0.1	1.4
Netherlands	1.1	4.6
Norway	0.5	3.4
Sweden	1.8	5.6
Switzerland	6.1	16.3
UK	n.a.	3.3
UK[a]	3.2[b]	6.0[c]
UK[d]	0.4[b]	5.5

Notes: [a] Foreign-born. [b] 1951. [c] Born outside the British Isles. [d] 'Ethnic minorities' only, i.e. non-White population.

Sources: 1950: OECD, *The Future of Migration*, Paris, OECD, 1987, p. 40; 1990: SOPEMI, *Trends in International Migration*, Paris, OECD, 1992, p. 131; UK foreign-born 1951: S. Castles, *Here for Good*, London, Polity Press, 1984, p. 87; in 1990, R. Skellington, *'Race' in Britain Today*, London, Sage, 1992, p. 24; UK ethnic minorities: ibid., p. 37 (1951), and *Regional Trends 28*, CSO, London, HMSO, 1993, p. 43.

A longer-term perspective may be gained by bringing in earlier data from France and Germany. Foreigners made up 2.7% of France's population in 1881, 3.0% in 1911, 3.9% in 1921, and 6.5% in 1936. In the German Reich foreigners constituted 0.5% in 1871 and 1.9% in 1910. The overwhelming majority of these immigrants were Europeans, Italians and Poles and Austro-Hungarian citizens, respectively.[49]

The overall figures remain small, although they may be argued to be underestimating ethnic heterogeneity by not counting the *foreign-born*, who in Sweden, according to official statistics, made up about 9% of the population by the end of 1992, a situation similar to the French one by the beginning of the 1980s.[50] That is more than in the United States, with 8.3% of its registered population foreign-born in 1990, but less than Australia and Canada, with 20.8% and 15.6%, respectively, in 1986.[51]

As of 1 January 1991, only 2.8% of the EC population were non-EC citizens, and only 1.8% of non-European citizenship.[52] Among primary school children, however, foreigners made up 16.7% in Switzerland in 1988, 13.5% in Germany in 1987, 11.3% in Belgium, and 10.3% both in France and in Sweden in 1988.[53] Recent years have also seen a dramatic increase of Western European immigration, from between 1 and 1.2 million in 1985–7 to 2.5 million in 1991 and a good 3 million in 1992.[54] By July 1993, the break-up of former Yugoslavia had produced a good 750,000 refugees outside and almost 3.5 million inside the previous state of Communist multi-ethnicity.[55]

Immigrants are also very concentrated geographically, which creates a special local impact in some places. 'Foreigners' (excluding foreign-born citizens) constituted 16% of the resident population of Greater Paris in 1990, from 7% a century earlier. In Great Britain, the only European country in which 'race' and skin colour have entered legitimate public discourse and official statistics, 'whites' made up 94.5% of the total resident population, but 79.8% of the Greater London population, in 1991. In Amsterdam at the beginning of the 1990s 22% of the population were 'foreigners' – and half of the primary school population –, in Frankfurt about 25%, and in Brussels some 28%. In Paris in 1990 one-third of all youths below 17 live in a family of immigration. This matches well with the current proportion of foreign-born in New York City, a good fifth – or with Warsaw or Zagreb at the turn of the last century.[56]

Eastern European data are still more scarce. But, clearly, the postwar settlement migration movements were less extensive than in Western Europe, save inside the Soviet Union. We noted above how a quarter of the original GDR population were expellees from the East, which hardly contributed to endearing the ally of the Red Army in power to the GDR population. By the end of the socialist experiment in Germany, the GDR harboured foreigners, mainly Poles and Vietnamese, amounting to a good 1% of the population.[57] The total number of immigrant workers in the Comecon is not yet available, however.

In the USSR, census data of nationality show a continuous increase of local national identity (*nationalnost*) – i.e. the opposite of the Western European trend, however differently defined – between 1959 and 1989 in all the republican capitals, except Tallinn and Riga, where Russification was proceeding. The same exceptional development of two of the three Baltic capitals emerges from a comparison, in terms of language, between 1897 and 1989. The proportion of Estonian and Latvian speakers, respectively, was lower in 1989 than in 1897. The least national capitals of the now former USSR are Alma Ata and Bishkek, with less than a quarter Kazakhs and Kirghiz, respectively, in 1989.[58]

European modernity was *emigrant*, extra-European emigrant. How much decades of mass emigration meant to the class structuring of Europe is difficult to calculate, but what these decades meant is less unclear. Mass emigration diminished poverty and eased social pressure and conflict. Migration provided individual alternatives to collective action, on the one hand. On the other, it also led to less depressed labour markets and less social dependence, in other words better conditions of class organization for the majority who stayed. Furthermore, outbound migration maintained the relative ethnic homogeneity of the Western European states, a factor also favourable to class identification. France, alone, was never an emigration country, and indeed began to receive a first wave of immigration already in the 1830s. Switzerland, an old out-migration area, began to import and attract foreign labour *en masse* in the late nineteenth century, for railway construction and building in general. Belgium, meanwhile, imported miners after World War I. Certainly one of the major reasons why Switzerland, a heavily industrialized country, has only twice had a federal election in which the labour parties won above 30% of the vote, in 1917 and 1947, is because it has a large foreign and therefore disenfranchised working class.[59]

Labour scarcity in North Central Europe in the 1960s, the rapid development of Southern Europe in the 1960s and 1970s, the collapse of the Communist regimes in Eastern Europe, and the enlarged possibilities of intercontinental migration have turned Western Europe into an immigration area.[60] The change has been most dramatic in Germany. In 1968 and in 1969 net immigration into (West) Germany was the same as into the United States at the peak of intercontinental arrivals there in 1913, at 0.9% of the resident population. In 1988, German net immigration constituted 0.5% of the (1987) population with a special peak, at 1.6%, in 1989.[61] Gross inflows are generally much higher than net ones: in Germany in 1988 1.06% of the population, in Switzerland 1.42%, in Sweden 0.53%. In Austria and Belgium, however, gross immigration constituted 0.44% of the population, whereas in France the total was only 0.14%. By comparison, more narrowly defined immigration of registered permanent settlers and refugees into the old New World stood at the same time at 0.93% of the population into Australia, 0.63% into Canada and 0.26% into the USA.[62]

The shift from emigration to immigration represents an epochal change in European social history. Ethnic − and largely continental ethnic − conflict has substituted for intra-European nationalist rivalry. The socio-political effect has been to weaken class cleavages and politics in favour of ethnic and other non-class ones.

Xenophobic politics has established itself most firmly in France (Front National), but was in the late 1980s and early 1990s affecting discourse and social relations all over Europe, and also taking physically violent forms. At the same time, the smallness of the immigrant population, or their lack of political rights, makes virtually impossible in Europe − excepting some British areas with large, enfranchised ex-colonial populations − the ethnic coalition politics so important in the New Worlds.

Anyway, Europe's modern population history points further to the evolution of jobs, to rights of membership, and to the global distribution of means.

Notes

1 See further, e.g. G. Castellan, *Histoire des Balkans*, Paris, Fayard, 1991, Chs VIII–IX.
2 B.R. Mitchell, *European Historical Statistics 1750–1988*, 3rd edn., Basingstoke, Macmillan, 1992, pp. 109ff. The East German exception, according to Mitchell, is apparently an error. See J. Gysi, 'Familienformen in der DDR', *Jahrbuch für Soziologie und Sozialpolitik*, [East] Berlin, Akademie-Verlag, 1988, p. 513.
3 P. Flora (ed.), *State, Economy and Society in Western Europe 1815–1975*, Vol. 2, Frankfurt, Campus, 1987, pp. 214ff.
4 See P. Bairoch (ed.), *The Working Population and Its Structure*, Brussels, Editions de l'Institut de Sociologie de l'Université Libre de Bruxelles, 1968, Table A1. The British participation rate, less affected by family agriculture, was basically stable between 1931 and 1951, with a slight upward slope.
5 Calculations by the author from Swedish census data: G. Therborn, *Klasstrukturen i Sverige, 1930–1980*, Lund, Zenit, 1981, p. 138.
6 R. Philips, *Untying the Knot*, Canto edn, Cambridge, Cambridge University Press, 1991, pp. 211ff, 225; S. Sipos, 'Current and Structural Problems Affecting Children in Central and Eastern Europe', in G.A. Cornia and S. Sipos (eds), *Children and the Transition to the Market Economy*, Aldershot, Avebury, 1991, p. 18. Cf. F. Castles and M. Flood, 'Why Divorce Rates Differ: Law, Religious Belief and Modernity', in F. Castles (ed.), *Families of Nations*, Aldershot, Dartmouth, 1993; D. Lane, *Soviet Economy and Society*, Oxford, Basil Blackwell, 1985, pp. 122–3.
7 World Bank, *World Tables 1992*, Baltimore, Johns Hopkins University Press, 1992, country tables; B.R. Pockney, *Soviet Statistics since 1950*, Aldershot, Dartmouth, 1991, Table 3.3 (ex-USSR republics).
8 Council of Europe, *Recent Demographic Developments in Europe*, Strasburg, 1991, pp. 37, 41, 43, 44. Pre-1970 Western European information is culled from Flora, *State, Economy and Society*, Vol. 2, Ch. VI.
9 *Le Monde* 9.10.1993, p. 7.
10 *Le Monde* 9.11.1993, pp. 29 and 36, reporting from a recent issue of *Population et Sociétés*.
11 Pockney, *Soviet Statistics since 1950*, Table 33.
12 In 1970, the total fertility rate in the Balkans, except Albania, stood at 2.43 (child per woman) as against 5.05 in Turkey, and in 1989 at 1.84 to 3.64. In the European outlier Albania the rate went down from 5.16 to 2.96 in the same period: Council of Europe, *Recent Demographic Developments*, pp. 37 and 43.
13 Between 1970 and 1990, the (unweighted average) total fertility rate in France, Italy, Portugal and Spain went down from 2.63 to 1.48, and in Algeria, Morocco and Tunisia from 6.9 to 4.3: Ibid., p. 37, World Bank, *World Bank Tables 1992*, pp. 86–7, 426–7, 610–11.
14 For the last 50 years successfully challenged but not overwhelmed by the USA, however.
15 Calculated from W. Woodruff, *Impact of Western Man*, London, Macmillan, 1966, pp. 106, 104. The actual Woodruff figures yield a total of 48.7 million and 11.5% of the 1900 population (including Russia).
16 G. Therborn, 'Migration and Western Europe: The Old World Turning New?', *Science* 237 (4.9.1987), p. 1184; Woodruff, *Impact*, p. 106.
17 Calculations from Woodruff, *Impact*, pp. 104 and 106.
18 *Données Sociales 1981*, Paris, INSEE, 1981, pp. 46–7. Cf. O. Carlier, 'Aspects des rapports entre mouvement ouvrier émigré et migration maghrébine en France dans l'entre-deux-guerres', in N. Sraïeb (ed.), *Le mouvement ouvrier maghrébin*, Paris, CNRS, 1985, pp. 52, 55–6; J. Ruedy, *Modern Algeria*, Bloomington, Indiana University Press, 1992, pp. 99, 125; J.-P. N'Diaye et al., 'Les travailleurs noirs en France', *Réalités africaines* 5 (1963), pp. 79ff. By the end of the 1950s, there were about 15–20,000 Black African workers in France. Carlier's and Ruedy's estimates are higher than the official counts.
19 A. Briggs, *A Social History of England*, Harmondsworth, Penguin, 1983, p. 310.

20 Calculations from OECD, *Labour Force Statistics, 1964–1984*, Paris, 1986, p. 234, and *Historical Statistics of the United States*, Washington, DC, US Bureau of the Census, 1975, series A6–8 and C296–301.
21 Calculated from Council of Europe, *Recent Demographic Developments*, p. 105.
22 Austria, it has been claimed, received 200,000 Hungarians after 1956, 160,000 Czechoslovaks in 1968–9, and 120–150,000 Poles in 1980–81: H. Fassmann and R. Münz, 'Aufnahmefähig aber noch nicht aufnahmebereit', *Die Presse* 15/16.6.1991, p. 111. The 'Continuous Reporting System on Migration' of the OECD, SOPEMI, gives a much lower estimate for the Czechoslovak emigration after the end of the Prague Spring, at 90,000. SOPEMI, *Trends in International Migration*, Paris, OECD, 1992, p. 114.
23 The Hungarian figures referred to are taken from Council of Europe population data, *Recent Demographic Developments*, p. 120, while the SOPEMI report, after pointing to the unreliability of Hungarian migration statistics (*Trends*, p. 99) gives a table of very low flow estimates (p. 154). Polish data are previously classified flow calculations, reported by SOPEMI, *Trends*, pp. 106 and 107. Germany was the main recipient of Polish emigration.
24 Since the Depression, the Irish migration has gone mainly to the UK, instead of as previously to the USA: J. Sexton, 'Bilan de l'émigration irlandaise, de ses causes et de ses conséquences', OECD conference paper GD(93)49, Paris, OECD, 1993, p. 8. The Dutch postwar emigration went overseas.
25 *The Statistical History of the United States*, B. Wattenberg, New York, Basic Books, 1976, p. 105.
26 Cf. OECD, *The Future of Migration*, Paris. 1987, p. 270.
27 G. Rosoli, 'Italian Migration to European Countries from Political Unification to World War I', in D. Hoerder (ed.), *Labor Migration in the Atlantic Economies*, Westport, Conn., Greenwood Press, 1985, p. 97. In fact, Rosoli's article covers a longer timespan than that indicated by his title.
28 See further D. Kubat (ed.), *The Politics of Migration Policies*, New York, Centre for Migration Studies, 1979; United Nations Economic Commission for Europe, *Labour Supply and Migration in Europe*, New York, 1979, Tables II.8–II.10.
29 S. Castles, *Here for Good*, London, Pluto Press, 1984, p. 43.
30 U. Herbert, *Geschichte der Ausländerbeschäftigung in Deutschland, 1880 bis 1980*, Berlin and Bonn, J.W.H. Dietz Nachf., 1986, pp. 188–89, 193, 195.
31 A term from German constitutional law and political theory, meaning the people or ethnicity carrying or embodying the state. The Table does not take into account the postwar minorization of Latvians in Riga, due to Russian immigration (see further below).
32 The late figure for Vienna hides the Germanization of the city in the course of the nineteenth century. In his city guide of 1787, the Bavarian traveller Johann Pezzl emphasized that it was the 'mixture of so many nations' and the 'linguistic confusion [Sprachenverwirrung]' which 'above all characterizes Vienna among European places'. In a pre-nationalistic way Pezzl then had the following 'nations' in mind: 'Hungarians, Moravians, Transylvanians, Styrians, Tyrolians, Dutch, Italians, Frenchmen, Bavarians, Swabians, Silesians, Rhinelanders, Swiss, Westphalians, Lothringians etc. etc.' J. Pezzl, *Skizze von Wien*, 2nd edn, Graz, 1923, pp. 22–3; here cited from M. Czaky, 'Historische Reflexionen über das Problem einer österreichischen Identität', in H. Wolfram and W. Pohl (eds), *Probleme der Geschichte Österriechs und ihrer Darstellung*, Verlag der Österreichischen Akademie der Wissenschaften, 1991, p. 36.
33 See further I. Deák, *Beyond Nationalism*, New York, Oxford University Press, 1992.
34 See further G. Veinstein (ed.), *Salonique 1850–1918*, Paris, Ed. Autrement, 1992.
35 C. Harris, 'The New Russian Minorities: A Statistical Overview', *Post-Soviet Geography*, 34, 1, (1993), p. 18. Wilna, sometimes called the Eastern Jerusalem, still had a very significant Jewish population, officially 28%. Most of them were soon to perish.
36 Calculated from L. Niethammer, *Die volkseigene Erfahrung*, Berlin, Rowohlt, 1991, p. 303.
37 W. Benz, 'Fremde in der Heimat: Flucht – Vertreibung – Integration', in K. Bade (ed.), *Deutsche im Ausland – Fremde in Deutschland*, Munich, C.H. Beck, 1992, p. 382; Niethammer, *Die volkseigene Erfahrung*, p. 303.

38 Benz 'Fremde in der Heimat', p. 385.
39 *Der Spiegel* Vol. 10 (1956), no. 27, p. 29; no. 30, p.30; no. 31, p. 26.
40 Calculation from K. Bade, 'Fremde Deutsche: "Republikflüchtige" – Übersiedler – Aussiedler', in Bade, *Deutsche in Ausland*, pp. 404–5.
41 See further, P.-A. Bodin, 'Karelska Näset som mötesplats för nordiskt och ryskt', in S. Carlsson and N.Å. Nilsson, *Sverige och St Petersburg*, Stockholm, Almqvist and Wiksell, 1989.
42 Benz 'Fremde in der Heimat', pp. 376–7.
43 N. Davies, *God's Playground*, Vol. 2, Oxford, Clarendon Press, 1981, p. 562.
44 J. Krejčí, 'Ethnic Problems in Europe', in S. Giner and M. Archer (eds), *Contemporary Europe: Social Structures and Cultural Patterns*, London, Routledge, 1978, p. 129
45 A. Kappeler, *Russland als Vielvölkerreich*, Munich, C.H. Beck, 1992, p. 304.
46 See further R. Schönfeld (ed.), *Nationalitätenprobleme in Südosteuropa*, Munich, Oldenbourg, 1987; H. Poulton, *The Balkans*, London, Minority Rights Publications, 1991; D. Plestina, *Regional Development in Communist Yugoslavia*, Boulder, Col., Westview Press, 1992, pp. 161ff.
47 The GDR had a non-European population of about 85,000 or 0.5% of the total population in 1989, most of them Vietnamese: SOPEMI, *Trends*, 1992, p. 62. At the same, Bulgaria had about 40,000 non-European workers, also about 0.5% of the population: Poulton, *The Balkans*, p. 118.
48 *Frankfurter Allgemeine Zeitung*, 2.2.1993, p. 6; *El País*, 20.9.1992, p. 9.
49 G. Tapinos, *L'immigration étrangère en France*, Paris, Institut national d'études démographiques, 1973, pp. 4, 6; calculations from G. Marc, 'Les étrangers en France', in *Données Sociales 1987*, Paris, INSEE, 1987, p. 27; Herbert, *Geschichte der Ausländferbeschäftigung*, p. 25.
50 Marc, 'Les étrangers en France', p. 27. *Statistisk Årsbok 1993*, Stockholm, SCB, 1993, p. 63. The foreign-born and foreign citizens born in Sweden amounted together, after extraction from possible double counting, to 10.5% of the population by the end of 1992.
51 SOPEMI *Trends*, 1991, p. 28.
52 Eurostat, *Rapid Reports, no. 6: Population and Social Conditions* (1993).
53 SOPEMI, *Trends 1989*, p. 120.
54 *Financial Times*, 15.4.1993, p. 15, reporting research by Jonas Widgren.
55 *Die Zeit*, referring to UN sources, 6.9.1993, p. 5.
56 *Le Monde*, 11.5.1993, p. 17; Regional Trends 28, CSO, London, HMSO, 1993, Table 3.8; H. Molleman of the Dutch Ministry of the Interior in *Die Zeit*, 9.2.1990, p. 48; *Frankfurter Allgemeine Zeitung* 3.12.1991, p. 7; *Financial Times*, 14.4.1991, p. 7; *Le Monde*, 8.4.1994, p. 12, respectively.
57 Calculated from *Die Zeit*, 11.10.1991, p. 19.
58 Harris, 'The New Russian Minorities', pp. 18–19.
59 In 1917 the Swiss Social Democrats, an important part of the European labour movement at the beginning of the century, received 30.1% of the federal vote, in 1947 they and the Communists together got 31.3%: T. Mackie and R. Rose, *International Almanac of Electoral History*, 2nd edn, London, Macmillan, 1982, pp. 355ff.
60 For a general historical overview, see G. Therborn, 'Migration and Western Europe: The Old World Turning New?', *Science* 237 (4.9.1987).
61 Calculations from SOPEMI, *Trends*, 1989, pp. 128 and 133. Population figure from Eurostat, *Basic Statistics of the Community*, 27th edn, Luxemburg, 1990; and n.21 above.
62 SOPEMI, *Trends*, 1989, p. 8. Figures include asylum seekers, most of whom were likely to be kicked out again, but then be replaced by new hopefuls. Unregistered immigration should be relatively larger into the US than into the other countries.

4

TASKS: DIVISIONS OF LABOUR

A task from a sociological perspective is not just something you choose and set yourself. At whatever age you move around in the world you face a particularly structured supply of tasks. As an actor you are confronted with a social script, from which you may choose your part and your interpretation of it. The most common designation of the set-up of the *dramatis socialis personae* is the '*division of labour*'.

The division of labour had a central place in pre-modern social thought. It was part of a functionalist conception of society and legitimation of order in terms of the hierarchical interdependence between those who prayed, those who fought and those who cultivated the soil. The order between the first two could vary, as could the way traders and artisans were placed in the nourishing estate – exceptionally, as in Sweden–Finland, there might even be an official fourfold functionality, of nobility, clergy, burghers and peasantry. This functional, static, intrinsic division of labour was a central image within European feudalism.[1]

A modern conception of the division of labour emerged in the Scottish Enlightenment, in the lectures and writings of Adam Smith and of his disciple John Millar. Two ideas burst open the feudal mould into modernity. One introduced a temporal dimension. The division of labour was no longer timeless, and corresponding to the Trinity of the Christian God. Social tasks had evolved, from hunting, via pastoralism and agriculture, to commerce.

The other introduced a lateral open-endedness of the division of labour, no longer into three, or at most four, orders or estates, but into an infinite number of occupations and specializations, for instance of pin-making.[2] The latter idea was carried over into 'modernization theory', via Emile Durkheim's interest in the division of labour and Max Weber's focusing of the separation of the household and the enterprise, in the form of '*differentiation*'. The former, evolutionary conception branched out in two directions, into the Marxian one of a succession of complex socio-economic configurations, modes of production and their corresponding 'super-structures', and, much later, into Colin Clark's more strictly task-centred evolutionary perspective of agrarian, industrial and service societies.[3]

Trajectories of work, paid and unpaid

Here we shall stay in the more restricted division of labour tradition, paying attention to other aspects in other chapters, on rights, on means, on risks and opportunities. We shall stick to the historical conception of different systems of divisions of labour. But two new departures appear necessary.

One derives from the reflexivity of late modernity. We shall pay attention to the division between labour and leisure, and between paid and unpaid labour. The amount of work in relation to that of leisure, and the male–female division of tasks constitute two for a long time veiled expressions of the modern division of labour. Social science and social history are only beginning to explore both issues.

The other emerges from a globally comparative framework, in which the specificity of the European division of (paid) labour is highlighted.

Labour and leisure

Remunerated work occupied about a fifth of the year for the European working population around 1990, give or take a few per cent, with a higher figure above all in the East but also in Spain and Switzerland. Europeans, especially in the major countries and in Sweden, tend to work less than North Americans and Japanese. Sleeping, eating and similar personal basics occupy people about two-fifths of their time. Housework demands around 15 to 20% of people's time. The rest, on average between a fifth and a quarter is leisure, free time.[4] That is, in a year people spend as much, or more, time leisurely as on their job.

In a long-term perspective of industrial modernity, there have been two major periods of widespread reduction of working time. One was the period of strong eight-hour day demands, legislation and conflicts from 1913 to 1929, which in France and Italy continued into the 1930s as well. The other was the booming culmination of industrial society, i.e. from circa 1960 to the mid/late 1970s.[5]

Since 1980, most work reduction has taken the forms of early retirement and unemployment. But at the end of 1993 a renewed interest in working time reduction was noticeable, expressed in a lively full-scale, but ultimately non-committal, debate in the two houses of the French parliament on a 32-hour/four-day week,[6] and by the latter's realization at Volkswagen and Ruhrkohle.

There is a noteworthy class aspect of labour and leisure in contemporary Western Europe. Workers have more leisure than managers and employers. The 'leisure class' is acquiring a meaning different from that proposed by Thorstein Veblen a century ago.[7] Studies of Britain (from the 1970s), France (of the 1980s) and Sweden (in 1990–1) all point to manual workers having (somewhat) more leisure than 'the middle classes', employers and 'cadres', and than farmers/entrepreneurs and white collar employees ['tjänstemän'], respectively.[8] A Hungarian time budget survey of 1986–7, on the other hand, shows longer hours of work for manual workers than for managers and intellectuals.[9]

There are hardly any time series reliable enough to locate this turn of class relations chronologically, but it is probably a recent phenomenon. In the mid-1960s, at the time of the great cross-national time budget survey directed by Alexander Szalai (see below), no European country had 'high white-collar' workers with more free time than manual workers, although a small sample from Westphalian Osnabrück did indicate such a situation.

Seven Eastern European and three Western European countries participated. The most pronounced traditional-type class differences of leisure were found in Slovenian Maribor and in Serbian Kragajevac. In a national, though not very big, US sample, however, a weak tendency towards more leisure among employed skilled workers was found.[10]

But we may also look at the amount of work from another angle, from the *supply of remunerated tasks* in different societies at various points in time. Translated into empirical spadework, that means finding the number of people employed and the average number of hours worked per year, and then calculating the product of people times hours.

For two of the countries for which relatively reliable data exist, the UK and Sweden, we get the following picture of historical development. Since 1870 the social volume of work grew, in Sweden till the onslaught of the 1930s Depression, in the UK till World War II. There then occurred a moderate decline, but by 1973 more paid work was carried out in Sweden and in the UK than a hundred years earlier. (If 1870 = 100, in 1973 you get a figure of 116 for the UK and 108 for Sweden.) Without any seemingly exact figures, we can also safely conclude that in France there was, on the other hand, a significant decline in the volume of work during the same time.[11]

Since 1973, the general tendency in Western Europe has been a decrease in the societal amount of remunerated work, in contrast to the New Worlds and to Japan. But this is not without exceptions. Until the outbreak of the 1990s crisis, Sweden, for instance, experienced an increase in the volume of labour between 1973 and 1989 equal to that of Japan, a good 10%. Between 1973 and 1992 the volume of registered annual paid labour decreased from 100 to 91 in France, to 92 in West Germany in 1990, increased in Sweden to 103, and in the USA to 126. British data on annual hours worked by people in employment have not been supplied to the OECD, but for 1992 they should be in the range of 88 (assuming French reduction of hours) and 95 (US hours).[12]

The macro-socio-economic causes of these variable national paths of the volume of work are still little understood, or even noted. Most of the current international discussion of unemployment, and in West Germany of the 'work society' (*Arbeitsgesellschaft*) and its crisis or ending, has simply ignored this intriguing phenomenon.

Postwar Western Europe had for while a strange experience in the world history of capitalism – an almost perfect matching of the supply and the demand for remunerated tasks; in other words, *full employment*. What occurred was completely unanticipated by governments and economists alike. British welfare state planning, and 'high and stable employment' policies were unofficially based on a postwar target rate of unemployment at 8.5%. Keynes apparently thought a 6% level was the achievable maximum,[13] whereas in Sweden the later Nobel Prize Laureate Bertil Ohlin became notorious for having held in 1947–8 that 5% unemployment was about optimum.

By 1950, most Western European countries had a non-standardized unemployment rate of 2–3%, although West Germany and Italy constituted major exceptions, registering 7–8%. Full employment, by postwar standards, arrived in West Germany, Denmark and Austria in 1959–60, and in Belgium a couple of years later.[14] During the 1960s, only Greece, Ireland and Italy had unemployment persistently above 4%, around 5% in fact. North America's unemployment was then similar in size to that of the European countries with the highest unemployment, while the standardized rate of France and West Germany together was about the same as Japan's, i.e. slightly above 1%.[15]

Then, the mid-1970s crisis and the policy reaction to it put an end to full employment in most of the market economic part of the continent. Only Austria, Norway, Sweden and Switzerland stayed on, through a variety of measures, public and private.[16] The protracted 1980s boom demonstrated that high unemployment had again become permanent. Before rising again, the standardized rate of unemployment only dropped to 6.9% in Central and Western Europe (excluding Austria and Switzerland), and to 11.4% in Southern Europe (except Greece) in 1990. The international crisis of the early 1990s, aggravated by the de-regulations and speculations of the pre-ceding decade, then finished off full employment in the Nordic and in the Alpine countries.

Eastern Europe followed a similar trajectory to Norway and Sweden: full employment very soon after World War II, maintained throughout the vicissitudes of the ensuing four decades, then finally abandoned in the early 1990s, most likely for the rest of this millennium, maybe for ever.[17]

In December 1993, when the European Commission presented a White Paper on it, unemployment in the EU stood at 17 million, about 12% of the labour force. An original proposal of the Commission to commit the EU to halving the figure by the year 2000 was regarded as too ambitious by the national politicians. The heads of governments and their ministers of finance refused to embark upon any concerted European effort to reduce unemployment, while expressing their appreciation for the 'inspiration' of the White Paper.[18] (The unemployment situation in Europe has turned worse than in the USA, and much worse than in Japan, the latter since 1975, the former after 1980.)

Unemployment as a specific social problem was intellectually and politically discovered in the early 1890s, during the then Great Depression.[19] For twenty to thirty years – in Scandinavia and in Eastern Europe for more than forty years – after World War II, the problem appeared to have been solved. Now, a hundred years after its discovery, it seems to be in a process of being accepted as the final verdict of the court of capitalism.

Or, in the bulk of Western advice to the East, presented, *sotto voce*, as something which should be created as a normal part of a market economy.

The division of ages

One of the most profound social changes after World War II has been the social reconstruction of age. Human ageing was once a popular and widespread symbol of the pre-determined course of human life. In European pre- and early modernity, the vaulted life-staircase – first mounting to a peak at 30, 40 or 50, and then descending down to death – was the characteristic picture of the human life-course. Not until World War I was it to begin losing its attraction.[20]

Since about 1960 'old age' has been given quite a new meaning, quite new social implications. Linguistically it has been best captured in French, in the expression 'troisième âge', third age (after youth and maturity), as an age of a pension income, an age of leisure, positively freed from the confines of the work schedule.[21] You may find the best anecdotal evidence of the third age by looking at marriage and contact ads, nowadays containing a significant number of women and men above 60 announcing their appetite for life. Several of my mother's (b. 1907) widowed friends in rural conservative southeastern Sweden have acquired, or have been looking around for, new gentleman friends. A major problem, however, is the early dying out of the male species, which makes for very fierce competition at pensioners' dances.

Declining fertility and lowered child mortality have increased the share of old people in the population, to between one in eight, in Eastern Europe including USSR, and one in six, in Western Europe, being 65 and over.[22] Life expectancy at the age of 60, on the other hand, has had a very uneven development after 1950. Generally it has increased for women by three to four years in the 1950–80 period. Male life expectancy after 60 has on average increased by about one year, in France by 1.9 years. But in a couple of countries, in the Netherlands and in Norway, it has actually slightly declined, and in others the increase has been marginal – 0.2 years in Germany and Italy.[23]

There have been considerable increases, however, in the leisure, the chosen activity and, at least for many, health of older people. In 1950 more than half of all males above 65 in Finland, Ireland, and Switzerland were working, and in the poorer countries of Southern Europe (in Greece, Portugal and Spain) this figure was about two-thirds of elderly males, well above 50%. In the remaining countries of Europe a good third were working; in Germany a quarter.[24]

By 1985–6, only one male in twenty aged 65 and over belonged to the labour force in France and Germany, one in twelve in Italy, one in thirteen in the UK. Little more than a quarter of French males aged 60 and over remained in the labour force, while in Germany somewhat less than a third, and in Finland, Italy and the Netherlands somewhat more than a third, were still in the labour force at 60.[25]

Early retirement is primarily a working-class event, adding to the new class structure of leisure which we noted above for employed people. Sweden, for instance, has a normal retirement age of 65, but in the early 1990s only 5% of the members of the Metal Workers' Union aged between 60 and 65 were still working full-time.[26]

In postwar Eastern Europe, the age for a right to retirement – usually at 55 for women and at 60 for men, five years higher in the GDR and Poland, but at 45–50 after especially tough jobs[27] – was lower than in Western Europe, until the post-1974 massive *de facto* retirement there. On the other hand, under Communism these countries were chronically short of labour power, so pensioners were actively encouraged, with economic incentives and special work rights, to go on working.[28]

But in the end, the third age settled also in Eastern Europe. In the GDR by the early 1980s 13% of the population of retirement age were working, in Hungary in 1988 only 4%. Among males of 60 and older, Hungarian labour force participation decreased from 42% in 1949 and 39% in 1960 to 2% in 1984. In the Soviet Union labour force participation among people aged 55 and over actually increased between 1979 and 1989, but nevertheless only a quarter of the population (a third of males) aged 60 to 64 were still in the labour force.[29]

With on average about seventeen years more to live at the age of 60, a majority of European men are now living around one-third of their adult life outside the labour force. A rich life after the age of work is flourishing, resourceful – especially in the most developed parts of Western Europe –, leisurely and active, including erotically, if perhaps less often genitally, active.

Viewed historically, the coming of the third age represents a twist of the development curve of modernity. In terms of power, it means, under democratic conditions, a (partial) return of the weight of age, typically lost when the projects of the future started to count more than the experiences of the past. The nearest historical equivalent to the current pensioners, the *Rentner* of Northwestern Europe, provided for by public funds, were the *rentiers*, the men of 'independent means', of earlier modernity, the idle rich largely extinguished by World War II. The *rentiers* of yesterday have become the senior citizens of the welfare state.

This is a development which Western Europeans share with North Americans and Oceanians – who, however, have not followed the Central European pattern after 1975 of largely pensioning off people after 60 – but less so with the longer working Japanese. Although France and Sweden – due to low birth rates and, in the Swedish case massive emigration in the late nineteenth century – historically led the ageing of societies, it was in the United States that old age associations, leisure activities and consumption, as well as geriatric medicine first spread.[30] In other words, the ageing of the Old World makes it socially more similar to the New.[31]

The gendering of labour and leisure

The gendered division of labour has two main dimensions: the division of paid work between men and women (including the share of exclusion from paid work, i.e. of unemployment) and the division of unpaid household work. Both may then be further subdivided by examining how occupational and household tasks are divided.

The early modern gender system was characterized by a concentration of males in the market economy and women in the household economy, particularly upon marriage. This changed only marginally between 1910 and 1950, and in opposite directions among different countries.[32] For most countries of Western Europe, the cross-national pattern was one of trendless oscillation till the end of the 1960s, although Danish and Swedish women could leap onto the labour market from the mid-1960s. The cross-country variations of gendered labour force participation have remained quite substantial, as has the gender division inside each country, although a tendency towards more equality is discernible.[33]

The paid jobs of men and women are furthermore usually different from each other, with the more powerful, prestigious and the better remunerated positions occupied by the so-called 'stronger sex'. The amount of occupational segregation may be captured by an index of dissimilarity, which measures the proportion of the members of one sex who need to change tasks for there to be no segregation, assuming that the members of the other sex do not move. Equality in the labour force and equality of jobs do not hang together. Rather, there is a certain tendency to a trade-off between high female labour force participation and low occupational segregation (see Table 4.1).

Occupational segregation – the segregation of men and women into different occupations – has a cross-national configuration of its own. Greece, Italy, Japan and Portugal form a club among themselves, whereas the differences between the others are rather limited. The former is probably largely an expression of a still important economy of household enterprise, in agriculture, retail trade, and other services, but also of a wide use, particularly in Japan and in Portugal, of women in unskilled manufacturing labour, originally textiles, later also in electronics. Japan and Portugal are the only two countries where the proportion of women in manufacturing is about the same as their part in total employment.[34]

It is also noteworthy that the Nordic countries, except Sweden, tend to distinguish themselves by a greater degree of occupational sex segregation than in the continental EC countries. The 1980s saw some decline of occupational segregation in most EC countries.[35]

With regard to labour force participation, the north (high) pole is made up of Finland, Sweden and Denmark, and the southern one of Ireland, Spain and the Netherlands, i.e. a portion of a rich Protestant world versus a more modest and Catholic one, but no more than a portion. On the one hand, Norway is now actually both richer and more Protestant than its neighbours,

Table 4.1 *Gender divisions of paid labour in the OECD*

Labour Force: Female labour force participation as percentage of male, corrected for part-time employment; two part-time employed taken as equivalent to one full-time. *Circa* 1990.
Occupation[al Segregation]: Reversed Dissimilarity Index (100 − Index number) of single-digit occupational gender segregation. Ranges from 100 (no segregation) to 0. *Circa*. 1986. The values of the two variables are directly comparable to each other, ranging from full equality = 100 to absolute inequality = 0.

Country	Labour force	Occupation
Austria	62.2	55.6
Belgium	62.9	60.8
Denmark	71.6	59.5
Finland	87.5	57.0
France	67.1	61.7
Greece	55.2	75.6
Ireland	41.3	57.1
Italy	55.8	75.4
Netherlands	48.1	60.0
Norway	67.0	53.4
Portugal	69.3	74.9
Spain	47.3	63.1
Sweden	78.6	62.1
Switzerland	<63.0[a]	60.8
UK	62.0	55.6
W. Germany	56.8	62.2
Japan	60.0	76.9
USA	64.8	62.6

Notes: [a] Female labour market attachment would be 63% of the male rate where there was no difference in the amount of part-time employment between men and women in employment.

Sources: Labour force participation: calculated from OECD, *Employment Outlook 1991*, Paris, 1991, pp. 46 and 256. Occupational segregation: OECD, *Employment Outlook 1988*, Paris, 1988, p. 209.

and, on the other, Portugal is poorer and more Catholic than Spain, while the Dutch are still prosperous and about as Calvinist as they are Catholic.

Beneath the national variations in women's relationship to the labour market there are also wide regional differences. The percentage of women aged 15–64 years who are in the labour force ranged in 1986 in Portugal between 33% in the southern latifundia region to 50% in the northern minifundia and textile industrial region; in Spain, in the rather similar agrarian regions, this ranged between 18% in Extremadura and 38% in Galicia; in Italy between 24% in Sicily and 41% in Emilia-Romagna; between 30% in Corsica and 48% in central France; in Germany between 32% in traditional heavy industrial Saarland and 48% in West Berlin or 47% in newly industrialized Bavaria. British and other European regional differences are smaller, in Britain ranging, in 1991, from 47% in Northern Ireland to 55% in southeast England.[36]

The regional pattern indicates an economic rather than a cultural or national-institutional causation, although the impact of the latter is not to be excluded. Regions of heavy industry and of latifundian agriculture tend to have low rates of female labour force participation. On the other hand, the two most Catholic *Länder* of Germany, Saarland and Bavaria, constitute the two extremes of gendered labour markets in the old Federal Republic. While the more strongly Catholic southern Italy has a low participation rate, by national as well as by European standards, the deeply Catholic northern Portugal has a female labour force participation far above the EC average.

Data for *Eastern Europe* are more scanty, as usual. But changes in women's participation began earlier and occurred more rapidly than in the West. Female labour force participation was about 80% of the male rate by the end of the 1980s.[37] That is higher than in Western Europe, but not unique. It is lower than in Finland and about the same as in Sweden.

Unemployment became clearly feminized in the 1980s. For the decade as a whole female unemployment in OECD Europe (i.e. Western Europe plus Turkey) was 9.7% of the female labour force, while the male rate was 7.2%. In Belgium, France, Italy and, since the late 1980s, Netherlands and Spain too, the absolute number of unemployed women is significantly higher than that of men, in spite of the larger male labour force. The UK and Ireland are the exceptions, keeping unemployment a very predominantly male fate.[38]

Post-1989 Eastern Europe is following suit in this respect. The marketization of the East tends to hit women harder than men. Whereas in West Germany the female and male unemployment rates in 1993 were 8.4 and 8.0%, respectively, the corresponding rates in East Germany were 21 and 11%.[39] Polish statistics show a female majority among the unemployed, in spite of a male labour force majority.[40]

Still largely uncovered by regular statistical information gathering is the gendered participation in the *household labour force*, although irregular investigations by official statistical agencies have begun in the last decade. From the mid-1960s, however, we have a systematic and sophisticated cross-national time-use survey conducted by an international band of sociologists, directed by the Hungarian Alexander Szalai. It was symptomatic of the times that although the pertinent questions had been asked and the responses registered, the final report contains no special study of the gendered use of time. However, the tabulations allow us to make some summaries (see Table 4.2).

It should be noted that Table 4.2 compares men and women in the same situation with regard to paid work on the labour market and to marital status. A stark picture of a gendered division of the amount of household work emerges. There is a tendency for this division to be less pronounced in the East. The difference between East German Hoyerswerda (then a new-built mining and coking town) and West Germany is particularly striking. But as the primary data refer to individuals, not to households, we won't know how much of it is due to the ample Western supply of housewives, and how much

Table 4.2 *The gendering of household labour in the mid-1960s*

Married employed men's time spent on household work as a percentage of married employed women's.

Country	No children	With children
Belgium	10	8
Bulgaria	19	29
Czechoslovakia	21	21
France	18	14
E. Germany	17	24
W. Germany	5	7
Hungary	12	12
Poland	18	18
USSR	16	16
Yugoslavia	10	12
Peru	1	7
USA	17	12

Notes: The Belgian, West German and US data are from national samples, the French are from six cities, the Yugoslavian from two (one in Slovenia and one in Serbia), and the others in single local ones. All refer to non-agricultural populations aged between 18 and 65.
Source: Calculated from A. Szalai (ed.), *The Use of Time*, The Hague, Mouton, 1972, p. 643.

to a less inegalitarian division of labour among couples on the labour market.

Men put in longer hours outside the household than employed women did, in all the samples of the study. So to be fair, we should also compare the amount of leisure (see Table 4.3).

Table 4.3 *Gendered leisure in the mid-1960s*

Married employed women's amount of free time as a percentage of married employed men's.

Belgium	69
Bulgaria	81
Czechoslovakia	63
France	64
E. Germany	71
W. Germany	66
Hungary	62
Poland	67
USSR	57
Yugoslavia	61
Peru	64
USA	80

Source: Calculations from Szalai, *The Use of Time*, pp. 662ff.

Leisure is first of all a male prerogative. Married men have about 50% more free time than married women. The pattern is remarkably uniform cross-nationally. The United States is a more egalitarian outlier, as is Bulgarian Kazanlik. This time there is no reliable East–West divide in Europe. Indeed, the inegalitarian extreme was Slovenian Maribor, where women had only half the amount of leisure that men had.

Data quite comparable over time and place are rare in this field. The gender patterns of the 1960s persist, and it is difficult to say to what extent they have changed. The differences of leisure time seem to have decreased considerably, however. Averaging the crude results from seven Western European countries studied in the 1970s and 1980s, we find that women had 95% of men's amount of leisure. Hungarian studies show a narrowed but maintained leisure gap between men and women in all occupational groups between the mid-1970s and the mid-1980s. The changes in the distribution of unpaid housework appear more modest. As an overall average, Western European men put in a fifth of women's amount of housework.[41]

British surveys from 1992–3 tell us that among full-time employees women have two-thirds of men's leisure time, and part-time women nine-tenths of the leisure of full-time working males. Among full-time employees males put in half as much household labour as women, the care of own children uncounted.[42]

More precise Swedish data from 1990–1 showed that cohabiting (married or not) men with a partner working full-time did four-fifths of women's stint of household labour in childless couples and two-thirds in couples with children. Cohabiting women's leisure was about 95% of men's, except for one group of couples working full-time on the labour market, couples with children of school age, where women had 15% less free time than men.[43]

The high noon of industrial society

In a long-term world history of the social division of labour, two outstanding features of postwar Europe have been the compressed end of immemorial agrarian society in a climax of industrialism, followed by a rapid dismantling of industrial society.

In an overview of the precipitous decline of the agrarian classes a certain cavalier summariness with regard to their internal differentiation might be condoned. By the outbreak of the post-World War II peace, property-owning farmers were clearly the major stratum. But landowners were still significantly prominent in Hungary, Romania, parts of Poland, eastern Germany, southern and western Spain and southern Portugal – while, of course, also clearly to be seen at Ascot, Longchamps and other fashionable hang-outs of Western Europe – with their necessary retinue of agricultural workers, who were themselvers still also toiling for smaller-fry farmers.

Britain and, to a lesser extent, a Central–North corridor from Switzerland to Sweden apart, Europe on the eve of World War II was still a predominantly agrarian society (see Table 4.4).

Table 4.4 *Agrarian employment on the eve of World War II (per cent of the economically active population)*

Absolute majority	Trisectoral[a] plurality	Trisectoral[a] minority
Albania >80	Austria 39	Belgium 17
Bulgaria 80	Czechoslovakia 37	Denmark 29
Estonia 59	France 36	Germany 26
Finland 57	Ireland 48	Great Britain 6
Greece 54	Italy 48	Netherlands 21
Hungary 53	Norway 35	Sweden 29
Latvia 66	Portugal 49	Switzerland 21
Lithuania 79		
Poland 65	Japan 44	Argentina 26[b]
Romania 79		USA 16
Spain 52		
USSR 86[c]		
Yugoslavia 79		

Notes: [a] Agriculture, industry and services. [b] 1947. [c] 1928.

Sources: P. Bairoch (ed.), *The Working Population and Its Structure*, Brussels, Editions de l'Institute de Sociologie de l'Université Libre de Bruxelles, 1968, Table A2; G. von Rauch, *Geschichte der baltischen Staaten*, Stuttgart, Kohlhammer, 1970, p. 75 (the Baltic republics); P. Shoup, *The East European and Soviet Data Handbook*, New York, Columbia University Press, 1981, p. 397 (Albanian urban population in 1938).

When the second European world war broke out, European societies were more agrarian than industrial everywhere save the British Isles and West-Central Europe, i.e. Belgium, Germany, the Netherlands and Switzerland. East of the Leitha, the old divide of the Habsburg Dual Monarchy, and south of the Pyrenees the continent was overwhelmingly agricultural.

The USSR had embarked upon its forced 'de-kulakization', from which the country has so far recovered as little as the USA has from black slavery, but the Balkans, except Greece, and Lithuania were still in what may be called a primordial division of labour, with about 80% of the total labour force in agriculture. Central countries of early modern European history, like Italy, the home of the Renaissance, and France, the centre of the Enlightenment and the stage of the Great Revolution, were still predominantly agrarian societies.

The European development out of agriculture was for a long time very uneven. In Europe west of the USSR and north of the Balkans, 137 regions out of 465 still had more than half of their labour force in agriculture in 1950. In 1969 there were 72, and in 1970 15 of the latter.[44] The size of agricultural employment in the EC 12 in 1960, 21.1%, was reached by Britain in 1851 (by Belgium in 1920), and the 1989 EC figure of 6.9% was approximated by Britain (7.1) in 1921 (reached in 1964 by Belgium).

Right after the war, the agrarian sector was larger than the industrial one in France and Italy, till the early and the late 1950s, respectively.[45] In the early 1960s industrial employment overtook agricultural in Finland and Spain, followed in the late 1960s in Ireland, and in the late 1980s in Greece[46] (see Table 4.5).

Table 4.5 *Agrarian employment circa 1990 (per cent of the economically active population)*

Major employment	Significant employment	Marginal employment
Albania 55	Bulgaria 18	Austria 8
	Czechoslovakia 13	Belgium 2
	E. Germany 10	Denmark 5
	Estonia <13[a]	Finland 8
	Greece 22	France 5
	Hungary 18	W. Germany 3
	Ireland 13	Italy 8
	Latvia n.a.	Netherlands 4
	Lithuania 23	Norway 6
	Poland 28	Sweden 3
	Portugal 17	Switzerland 6
	Romania 29	UK 2
	Spain 10	
	USSR 19	Japan 7
	Yugoslavia 32[a]	USA 3
	Argentina 12	

Note: [a] 1980.

Sources: ILO, *Yearbook of Labour Statistics 1992*, Geneva, 1992, Table 2; P. Marer et al., *Historically Planned Economies: A Guide to the Data*, Washington, DC, World Bank, 1992, country tables (GDR and Yugoslavia); T. Raun, *Estonia and the Estonians*, Stanford, Hoover Institution Press, 1991, p. 197 (Estonia); G. Hernes and K. Knudsen, *Lithuania*, Oslo, Norwegian Trade Union Centre, 1991, p. 79 (Lithuania, survey data); A. Barbeito and R. LoVuolo, *La modernización excluyente*, Buenos Aires, Unicef/Criepp/Losada, 1992, p. 175.

While the recent trauma of the dispossessed farmers of the East and the misery of landless labourers of the East and the South have a legitimate claim on the memory of the historian, the agrarian question has at last been surpassed, by one means or another, in most, if not all countries. (Albania, Greece, Poland and the new republic of Moldavia still have more employment in agriculture than in manufacturing, however.)

The demise of the agrarian question is not peculiar to Europe. True, it lives on in the policy-making of the EC – as in the political concerns of Argentina, Japan, the USA – but as such it is now more a sectional 'trade' than a class issue. And the recent resurrection of agrarian property rights in post-Communist Eastern Europe seems to be more a matter of real estate, and of ideological principle, than of land. The break-up of the collective farms is a political intitiative from above, by the new political rulers and their economic advisers, rather than from below, by the farmers themselves.

It should be noted, however, that the current crisis of transition in Eastern Europe has in some countries led to a *re-agrarianization*. In Albania, Belorussia, Moldavia and Romania agrarian employment increased in absolute numbers between 1989 and 1991–2, while manufacturing employment fell significantly.[47]

One of the most important characteristics of European modernity has been Europe's unique moulding as an *industrial class society*. 'Industrial' in terms of the absolute and the relative size of industrial employment and of the proportion of the gross domestic product deriving from industrial production. 'Class' in the sense of class identity, class discourse and, most tangibly, class organization, of trade unions, employers' organizations, labour parties, farmers' parties. The two epithets are related, but not very closely. Cultural identities and collective action have a momentum of their own, as we shall have reason to underline further below. However, the strongly industrial socio-economic structure is unique to Europe, although not all Western European countries have had it. The explicit, articulated two- or three-class politics of most parts of Western Europe has no full equivalents, outside British-shaped Australia and New Zealand.

Europe was the only part of the world that took the path from an agrarian society to an industrial and then to a service society, defined in terms of the relative dominance of employment shares.[48] Britain was, of course, the first industrial country in this sense, already by 1821;[49] followed by Belgium, by the census of 1880, Switzerland by 1888, and Germany by 1907.

Around the turn of the last century another road was opened up, by Australia, New Zealand and by the Netherlands; a road asserting itself as a major alternative in the 1920s when taken also by the USA and Canada. That was the step directly from an agrarian to a service society, later followed by Chile by 1940, by Argentina at least by 1947, Japan between 1955 and 1960, and by South Korea in the 1980s.[50]

Industrialization continued in Europe after World War II, and industrial employment culminated in the twelve current EC countries in relative terms in the early, in absolute terms in the late, 1960s, at 40–1% of total civilian employment. Eastern Europe underwent a dramatic process of industrialization and became in the end the epitome of industrial society. This may be seen as a typical effect of Communist rule, the positive – i.e. non-repressive – aspects of which derived from the classical age of the labour movement, in whose vision industrialization, full employment, basic social security, workers' education and formal equality between men and women were all included.

To later social developments and demands, however, be they of income maintenance, actual gender division of labour or environmental protection, the ruling Communists were basically tone-deaf.

Table 4.6 *Historical industrial experience*

Periods of relative preponderance of industrial over agrarian and service employment; industrial employment (including mining, constructing and utilities) as per cent of civilian employment or total labour force (in peak year); per cent industrial employment in 1990. Periods are delimited by census or labour force survey years.

Country	Industrial period[a]	Peak % and year	% 1990
Albania	Never	25.7 (1980)	22.5
Austria	1951–66	42.8 (1973)	36.6
Belgium	1880–1965	49.1 (1947)	25.0
Bulgaria	1965–	46.4 (1987)	45.9[a]
Czechoslovakia	1961–	49.4 (1980)	49.4[b]
Denmark	Never	37.8 (1969–70)	27.4
Finland	Never	36.1 (1975)	30.9[c]
France	1954–9	39.5 (1973)	26.0[c]
Germany (FRG)	1907–75	48.5 (1970)	36.6
Ex-GDR	1946–90	50.2 (1970–4)	49.6[d]
Greece	Never	30.2 (1980)	26.8
Hungary	1963–before 1988	44.8 (1970)	36.7[c]
Ireland	Never	32.6 (1974)	23.6[a]
Italy	1960–5	39.7 (1971)	28.5
Netherlands	Never	41.1 (1965)	23.5[c]
Norway	Never	37.5 (1971)	23.2[c]
Poland	1974–91	38.9 (1980)	36.3[d]
Portugal	1982	37.5 (1982)	32.9
Romania	1976–	43.5 (1980)	43.0
Spain	Never	38.4 (1975)	31.4
Sweden	1940–59[c]	42.8 (1965)	27.5
Switzerland	1888–1970	48.8 (1963–4)	34.8
UK[e]	1821–1959	52.2 (1911)	27.1
USSR	1970(?)–73	39.0 (1980)	39.0[b]
Yugoslavia	Never	33.3 (1980)	33.3[b]
Argentina	Never	32.6 (1960)	c. 23
Japan	Never	37.1 (1973)	33.4
USA	Never	35.8 (1967)	26.4

Notes: [a] 1989. [b] 1980. [c] Census data show an industrial lead still a few years later, but we have here followed the definitions used by OECD labour force statistics. [d] 1988. [e] Before 1960 Great Britain.

Sources: Before 1960: Bairoch, *The Working Population,* Tables A2, and, for Britain in 1821, E.H. Hunt, *British Labour History, 1815–1914,* London, Weidenfeld, & Nicolson, p. 26; from 1960 on OECD, *Historical Statistics, 1960–1988,* Paris, 1991, Tables 2.9–2.12 and OECD, *Labour Force Statistics, 1965–1985,* Paris, 1987, Table 7.0 and national tables III A. When, as in the Belgian and Swiss cases, there is discrepancy between the comparative Table 7.0 and the national Table III A, the latter has been followed (OECD countries); Marer et al., *Historically Planned Economies,* national tables (ex-Communist countries, and GDR 1988). For 1990: ILO, *Yearbook of Labour Statistics 1992* and *1993,* Geneva, 1992 and 1993, national tables. For Argentina, 1960: Bairoch op. cit.; 1960–90: A Barbeito and R. LoVuolo, *La modernización excluyente,* p. 175.

Sixteen of the twenty-five European countries in Table 4.6 had a period of (relatively) predominant industrial employment. Outside Europe this has only happened in Taiwan, around 1980. To two of the four major countries of the continent, to Britain and Germany, it has been a long historical experience, whereas in France and the USSR dominant industrialism has been a rather brief interlude between an agrarian and a service economy. However, this way of presentation underestimates the specificity of European industrialism.

In Europe, industrial work often dominated the non-agrarian economy over a long period. That was the case in France since (at least) the 1840s, with a period of parity in the censuses of 1936 and 1946 with service activities. It was obviously the case with the Soviet Union, but also with Italy since 1871, Spain for 1860–1964, and Yugoslavia in the 1960s and 1970s. Indeed, of our twenty-five European countries, only the three seafaring nations of Greece, Netherlands and Norway never had a modern period of industrial dominance of their non-agrarian economy, though the equivalent periods in Denmark and Ireland were back in the nineteenth century.

In Argentina and in Japan this industrial lead of the non-agrarian economy never occurred. In the United States in the second half of the nineteenth century industry and services shared equally the non-agrarian part of the job structure, but by 1910 the services sectors were taking a lead. When the great German historian and sociologist Werner Sombart raised his famous question in 1905, 'Why is there no socialism in the United States?', the new historical path was not clearly visible. Sombart predicted instead that the American *Sonderweg* was drawing to a close and that in the future socialism would expand in the USA, perhaps even more widely than in Europe.[51]

Why that did not happen is outside the scope of this book. But why in the United States there is 'the working man' but no 'working class', 'organized labour' but no 'labour movement', is likely to be related to the non-European modern class structuration. That is, one going from an agrarian to a service economy without any comprehensive industrial mould casting occupations and trades into classes, and casting groups, interests and formal organizations into a movement.

Industrial activity never became overwhelmingly dominant, however. It is an important feature of modern class history that no national society ever became a factory writ large, nor similar to a company town. If we include transport, storage and communication, the latter of which has – or had, before media communication became significant – work relations relatively similar to the industrial sector, industrial and quasi-industrial employment constituted at most about 60% of the total in Britain in the 1910s. In 1965 it would have been 53–5% in Belgium, Britain, Germany and Switzerland, about 50% in Sweden, and around 45% in France and Italy. Also in Czechoslovakia and the GDR industry, storage and transport made up about 55% of the labour force in the 1970s and 1980s.

The intercontinentally unique industrialization of Europe spread and culminated after World War II. In Eastern Europe the change was particularly dramatic, highlighted by the new, gigantic industrial cities stamped out of the ground: Magnitogorsk in the Urals already before the war, Nowa Huta in southern Poland, Stalinstadt, later Eisenhüttenstadt, on the East German side of the Oder, among others. But an enormous industrial thrust also occurred in Finland, the Netherlands, Portugal and, after 1950, Spain. In the abstract world of social statistics, Europe was reaching its modern destiny.

The distribution of jobs within industry has, of course, changed greatly over time, and the distinctiveness of industrial work and working conditions has probably decreased. But their features have largely structured European social relations, putting people into large workplace units, with a clearly demarcated, collectively patterned division of labour, producing material commodities. This industrial society was the fertile ground of European class politics and class sociology.

However, our time has also seen the epochal tide turn. In Western Europe the range of industrialization peaked around 1970, at the end of the strongest and longest boom in history. Thereafter, de-industrialization has staged the drama. The industrial traits of Western Europe are now falling off. Since 1984, the share of industrial employment in Japan is larger than in the EC. In 1975, industrial employment in the European Community (of 12) was 9.1 percentage points higher than in the USA, a historical high water mark. By 1989–90, when EC industrial employment was 32.5%, the European lead was oscillating around six percentage points, about the same as in the 1960s.

The economic crisis of the 1970s constitutes a watershed in industrial history. The crisis definitely ended the extension of industrialism over the OECD area and opened an era of relative de-industrialization. The latter has been most pronounced in the oldest industrial countries, with industrial employment decreasing by 12.6 percentage points in the UK between 1974 and 1989, by 11.7 in Belgium, by 9.2 in Switzerland, and further by 13.7 in Luxemburg (the record), 9.3 in France and 6.9 percentage points in Germany and Italy.[52] Since the mid-1960s a particular industrial resilience has been visible in West-Central Europe, in West Germany and Austria in particular, less so in Switzerland.

This process has meant the closure of the whole or most parts of the pioneering branches of industrialization. First to go, from the 1950s and on, was coal mining, once providing the core of the British and Belgian labour movements, and also very significant in the social as well as the economic history of Germany, France and Spain. Then followed most of Northwest European textile industry, shipbuilding and, in a couple of waves, steel. In Britain in the 1970s these were joined by car production. Capital cities like Brussels, London and Paris have been emptied of industrial employment, but have found other outlets of activity. In the other industrial regions the capacity to adapt to a novel situation has varied, but de-industrialization has so far clearly created a number of long-term crisis areas of decline and desolation, with the earliest and longest-lasting in Wallonia, but also in major parts of northern England and in the English West Midlands, on Clydeside in Scotland, in the Basque Country, in Lorraine in France, Liguria in Italy, and Saarland and the Ruhr in Germany.[53]

In Eastern Europe, except in Hungary, de-industrialization will be part only of the capitalist restoration, which seems bound to ensure that the transformation will be about as cataclysmic as the postwar break-neck industrialization was. In the ex-GDR, which is of course a special case, one-third of all jobs disappeared between 1989 and 1992.[54]

Industrialization reached its zenith in the East in the 1980s, and outside East Germany the old coal mines, steelworks, textile mills and shipyards still have to be closed down. The East, on the eve of the war the most agrarian part of Europe, is currently among the most industrialized, together with the old but strongly modernized industrial centres of Lombardy and the Spanish East, with the postwar centres of Baden-Württemberg and, in particular, Bavaria (the producer of BMW and the postwar site of Siemens head-quarters), all having 40% or more of their employment in industry.[55]

Is there anything specifically European with regard to the coming *service society* and its occupational structuring of the population? In the course of the 1980s something did indeed become noteworthy, although it can hardly be taken as settled for a long time to come. That is the importance of public, government-provided services, of public service employment.

Given both the historical legacy as well as the current stereotypes about continental European bureaucracies and largely missing equivalents in the New World, one might have expected the difference to be clear and stark. In fact, there was *more* civilian public service employment in the USA than in Germany throughout the 1960s and the 1970s.[56] Since the late 1970s, however, the EC as a whole has had a somewhat – and increasingly – larger government service than the USA (in Germany since the mid-1980s). For the period 1980–90 general government provided 17.8% of total employment in the EC, as against 14.9% in the USA (1980–9), and 6.4% in Japan.

However, the figures above do not include non-bureaucratic public employment, i.e. marketed public services of any significance, such as postal and telecommunications services, railways and local transport. For a relatively small group of countries, comparable data on virtually all kinds of public employment are available. They give a clearer picture (see Table 4.7).

First of all, there is a Nordic pattern (Finland will not be far behind Norway),[57] a Nordic welfare state of public social service and public infrastructural services. But the extended data net also highlights the European service state in a clear contrast to the US and the Japanese bureaucratic-cum-educational apparatus. This pattern developed markedly after the onset of the crisis in the 1970s, both by a North American (and British) reduction of the public sector and by enlargement of the latter on the European continent. Privatization is far from a spent force, so it remains to be seen at what level this new difference of occupational structure will stabilize.

Socially, public sector employment tends to mean higher job security, better pay and working conditions for lower (sometimes also medium)

Table 4.7 *Total civilian public employment as a percentage of total employment in 1985*

Belgium[a]	24.4
Denmark[a]	37.4
France	25.7
Germany[b]	18.9
Norway[a]	34.3
Sweden	38.2
UK	26.2
Canada	17.9
USA	14.8

Notes: [a] 1984. [b] 1983.

Sources: T. Cussack et al., *Political-Economic Aspects of Public Employment*, Berlin, Wissenschaftszentrum FGG/dp 87-2, L987, p. 7 (public employment); OECD, *Historical Statistics, 1960–1989*, Table 2.14 (total employment).

ranked personnel, better conditions for unionization, and a political stake in the welfare state. In other words, the welfare state is an important feature of current occupational structuration. Furthermore, sectoral divisions of employment weigh heavily upon the chances of the most immediate forms of class organization emerging, namely in trade unions or equivalent associations of collective economic interest. After the now not very important domestic services, the distributive and the business services tend to be the least prone to collective employee action.

Inside Europe, the main service divide runs between Eastern and Western Europe, and, one may fairly add, not only in the quantity of employment but also in its quality. In the West, the public information employees and shop assistants of Madrid are justly notorious, but their Castilian boredom and arrogance would probably have been no match for the dictatorship of the insider proletariat governing shop, restaurant and other service encounters in the Communist East.

In the West commerce and catering, banking and other business services employed between a good fifth (West Germany, Sweden) and a small third (Japan, the USA, Switzerland) of total employment in 1990. In Eastern Europe normality was around a tenth, ranging from one-eighth in Hungary to one among fifteen Romanians.[58]

The size of the working classes

Class is 'the only independent [i.e. explanatory] variable of sociology', one of the latter's eminent practitioners sadly confided to me a late conference night a few years ago.[59] I don't think I quite agree with the statement, but that is another matter. Anyway, 'class' will be deployed here stripped of all theoretical *haute couture*.[60] It will be used heuristically – not because of any theoretical nihilism or cynicism but simply as a survival technique for an empirical sociologist in the face of an overwhelming mass of heteroclite data about half a century of a continent's social history. We shall encounter phenomena of class while looking at structurations of tasks with respect to working for oneself or for others, and among the latter with regard to the division between, on the one hand, the assistants of the employer, in managing and office work, and, on the other, the producers of the enterprise. Below we shall pay attention to the rights, the means, and the risks and opportunities of different classes of people.

Industrial employment has been used above not only as an interesting datum of socio-economic structuration, but also as an empirically manageable proxy for the development of the size of the working class (in singular), the only one of the modern classes for which the number of its members is a crucial variable.

If the industrialism indicator is not widely off the mark, there should be a certain correspondence with other indicators of class. That is, for Western Europe there should be a unique, early high point in Britain, a peak or at least a high plateau in the 1960s and early 1970s, and thereafter a rapid descent. For the British case the eminent labour historian Eric Hobsbawm has estimated the proportion of manual workers in the population at 75% in 1911, at 70% in 1931, 64% in 1961 and 55% in 1976.[61] The criteria are not made explicit, so the absolute figures should not be used for cross-national comparative purposes, but there is no reason to doubt the internal consistency of the calculation, and its pattern: about the same amount of change in the fifteen years after 1961 as in the fifty years since 1911.

In Belgium the number of workers in the economically active population was well above half from the turn of the century till before the war, and around half till the 1960s. Industrial workers were above 40% till 1947, slightly below in 1961. Workers according to the official German definition constituted 55% of the economically active in 1907 and just above 50% till the 1960s (including the 1961 census), then dropping down to slightly more than 40% in 1977. Manufacturing and artisanal workers made up a third of the gainfully active from the end of the Wilhelmine Reich well into the late 1970s, with a peak of 37% in 1961.

In the first third of this century France had a proportion of manual workers compared to the total adult population equal to that of Germany, i.e. one-third of all adults. But in contrast to Germany a decline began in France after the Depression. The share of non-agrarian manual workers in France in 1954 and 1962 was roughly on the same level as in 1926 and 1931, however, and the decrease remained small till 1968. In Sweden, non-agrarian manual workers and workers in industry and transport have their largest historical share both of the gainfully employed and of the total population aged 15–64 in 1950, with substantial change occurring only after 1975. Also in the other Nordic countries manual workers reached their broadest extension after World War II.[62]

Post-industrialism has meant a larger amount of tasks requiring educational qualifications. Keeping in mind the not always unwavering comparability of international statistics, we may catch a glimpse of the layers of agriculture, industrial labour and professionalism in the European occupational structure of the outgoing twentieth century from Table 4.8.

Table 4.8 *Agriculture, industrial labour and professionalism in the occupational structure of the 1990s*

Per cent of the labour force as agricultural workers, production and transport workers, professional, technical and managerial workers in 1990–2. National averages are unweighted.

Country	Agrarian	Industrial	Prof./Manag.
NW Europe	*4.9*	*29.3*	*19.8*
Austria	7.1	34.9	14.7
Belgium (1981)	2.9	32.1	15.7
Denmark	4.5	30.2	23.2
Finland	8.3	25.9	24.4
France (1982)	7.6	30.9	14.1[a]
Germany	3.4	30.2	16.1
Netherlands	4.5	22.2	23.2
Norway	5.2	24.6	23.7
Sweden	3.1	25.7	31.9
Switzerland (1981)	6.5	34.4	15.1
UK (1981)	1.3	30.8	15.9
SW Europe	*12.0*	*26.9*	*11.3*
Greece	12.5	23.2	12.1
Ireland	11.8	23.2	14.3
Italy (1982)	9.3	20.7	11.5
Portugal	17.0	31.8	8.5
Spain	9.4	35.5	10.1
E. Europe	*12.4*	*46.6*	*14.7*
Bulgaria (1981)	12.7	47.3	n.a.
Czechoslovakia (1970)	12.0	42.7	19.4
Hungary	6.0	51.4	14.7
Romania	19.5	55.4	9.2
Slovenia	11.7	36.3	15.3
Other			
Japan	6.2	34.2	11.5
USA	2.9	26.0	16.5

Notes: General: Please note that agrarian work is not synonymous with employment in agriculture, in Table 4.5. The latter may also employ professionals, transport and other non-agrarian workers, including industrial on collective farms. [a] 1989 18.2, calculated from *Données Sociales 1990*, Paris, INSEE, 1990, p. 27.

Sources: ILO, *Yearbook of Labour Statistics 1993*, Geneva, 1993, national tables 2B and 2C; and for missing countries the most recent ILO Yearbook.

In Western Europe, less than a third of the economically active population is engaged in industrial labour; this remains the largest single kind of work, however. The classical productive working class in Northwestern Europe and the USA is 1–2 percentage points fewer than the proportion of those working in industrial labour, who also comprise self-employed and family helpers. The equivalent figure for Mediterranean Europe and Japan is 5–8 percentage points fewer. Eastern Europe is clearly more industrial and working class. By the end of Communism it was the most industrial and working-class part of the world. The USA and Japan now clearly fall within the Western European range of variation.

The caring welfare states, the Nordic countries and the Netherlands, are the most knowledge-centred societies, offering the largest supply of professional and semi-professional jobs. Contrary to conventional presentations, the basis of the 'knowledge society' is the welfare state rather than the universities, the media and the self-employed professions. So far, Sweden is the only country in the world which has gone from being an industrial society, in the sense defined above, to a 'knowledge and information society', i.e. to having, in ILO-ese, more 'professional, technical and related workers' than 'production and related workers, transport equipment and labourers'. It should be noticed that 'bureaucrats' – as administrative and clerical workers – are in principle excluded from the professionals, as are sales service personnel.

Working for an employer has become the overwhelmingly dominant position in the economy, characterizing 80 to 90% of the economically active in most of Europe. In this sense, there is no difference between the two shores of Northeastern and Western Europe. The lines of differential proletarianization run within both Eastern and Western Europe.

Four forces seem to account for the pattern. The general level of development is one, expressed in the extent of agricultural work, differentiating above all between North- and Southwestern Europe. The internal organization of socialism was another, singling out Poland and Yugoslavia with their predominantly private agriculture in Eastern Europe. The third is the internal organization of capitalism, the mechanisms of which have been much less noted and studied, by which Greece, Italy and, outside Europe, Japan have come to keep an unusually large sector of self-employment, both in agriculture and outside. Finally, there is permanent mass unemployment with an adjunct black economy, which puts a sizeable number of the labour force in an 'unclassifiable' employment position, a force at work no longer only in the West, such as in Belgium, Italy and Spain, but now also registered in the recent Eastern European labour force surveys, e.g. the Romanian survey of December 1990.

However, we should note not only the spatial but also the temporal pattern. In the 1980s there was a turn in the long-term, albeit mostly very gradual, tendency towards 'proletarianization'. In a number of Western countries self-employment started to grow again. As previously in de-agrarianization, industrialization and de-industrialization, one may safely bet

Table 4.9 *Classes of employment in 1990 and in the 1980s*

Workers/employees as percentage of the labour force in 1990. Non-agricultural self-employment (excl. helping family members) as percentage of total civilian employment in 1979 and in 1990 in OECD countries, and of the total employment of Eastern European countries in 1990. For the OECD countries, the different ILO figures for non-agrarian self-employment are given as well, after the oblique (/).

Country	Workers/ employees	Non-agricultural self-employment 1979	Non-agricultural self-employment 1990
Austria	86.0	6.0[a]	6.4 / 5.9
Belgium	73.9	11.2	12.9
Bulgaria	98.2[a]	n.a.	0.2[a]
Czechoslovakia	91.2[b]	n.a.	0.1[b]
Denmark	88.8	9.2	7.2 / 6.4
Finland	85.5	5.2[c]	8.7 / 7.8
France	77.1[c]	10.6	10.3 / 8.5
E. Germany	98.3[d]	–	1.7[d]
W. Germany	90.2	7.2	7.7 / 6.8
Greece	50.6	32.0	27.2[e]/19.4
Hungary	80.2	n.a.	5.8
Ireland	77.0[f]	10.4	13.3 / 9.1
Italy	63.2	18.9	22.3 /17.8
Netherlands	81.9	8.3	7.2 / 6.8
Norway	84.2	6.6	6.1 / 5.4
Poland	75.1[g]	n.a.	2.8[g]
Portugal	67.4	17.0[h]	17.2 /12.9
Romania	73.0	n.a.	2.9
Spain	70.5	15.7	17.1 /12.7
Sweden	89.7	5.4	6.8 / 6.7
Switzerland	87.4[b]	n.a.	n.a.
UK	81.4	6.6	11.6 /12.1
Yugoslavia	65.7[c]	n.a.	2.3[c]
Japan	75.7	14.0	11.5 /10.4
USA	91.0	7.1	7.6 / 7.0

Notes: General: Please note that the percentages of columns 2 and 4 are calculated on different bases and therefore cannot be added. The difference between columns 2 and 4 can be made up by the self-employed in agriculture, by family workers in all sectors, and by people 'unclassifiable' in the given categories, most often unemployed with no prior labour market attachment or various precarious or informal positions. Because of the size of the last category, the proportion of the labour force is significantly smaller than in civilian employment in Greece (8%) and in Ireland, Italy and Spain (4–5.5%).
[a] 1985. [b] 1980. [c] 1981. [d] 1985, excl. 6.4% cooperative farmers. [e] 1989. [f] 1991. [g] 1983. [h] 1988.

Sources: ILO, *Yearbook of Labour Statistics*, 1984, 1985, 1988, 1991, 1992, Geneva, respective years, Tables 2A (workers and employees, and Eastern European self-employment); OECD, *Employment Outlook July 1992*, Paris, 1992, p. 158 (non-agricultural self-employment in OECD countries); OECD, *Labour Force Statistics, 1965–1985*, national tables (Swiss workers/employees and checks for times-series breaks in Finland, W. Germany, the Netherlands and Sweden); *Statistisches Jahrbuch der DDR 1987*, [East] Berlin, Staatsverlag der DDR, 1987.

that Western Europe is here showing the way for Eastern Europe. But the cross-national pattern will be heterogeneous, as it is already (see Table 4.9).

For the size of their national product, Greece, Italy and Japan have a distinctively petit-bourgeois flavour to their class structure. Looking more closely in the labour force data we find that there are almost nine (8.8) Greek self-employed and family workers for ten workers/employees, in contrast to only four Portuguese. In Italy there are four self-employed and family workers for every ten workers/employees, and in Japan three as against less than two in France (1.8) and in the UK (1.6), and about one in West Germany.

According to a calculation from sources other than those used in Table 4.9 the proportion of self-employed (and helping family members) amounted to 17.1% of total sectoral employment in Italian industry in 1987, in comparison with only 10.2% in the EC 10 as a whole (save Portugal and Spain). In Italian services 30.8% were self- or family-employed, as against 14.9% for the EC 10 as a whole.[63]

De-proletarianization, increasing non-agricultural self-employment, is a new tendency, which became widespread, albeit far from universal, in the 1980s. It is most noteworthy in the mass unemployment countries, Britain, Italy, Belgium, Ireland, Spain.[64] In other countries, such as in (then) Social Democratic full employment Sweden, it has so far manifested itself only as a quantitatively minor hitch in the long-term trend curve.

Work organizations

The social division of labour as well as the class relations of capital also have a dimension of work organization, with aspects of hierarchy versus collectivity and of different structurations of qualifications. The educational system, national social experiences, capital–labour power relations and labour market conditions seem to be the causal forces behind the wide variety of developed capitalist work organization.

Whether and if so to what extent there is a European type of work organization are questions which seem unanswerable at this stage, although, stretching my neck out, my suspicion is that there is no specifically European form, at least not as a blueprint. So far, the major models of work organization have been, first, American – 'Taylorism', 'Fordism' – and then Japanese – 'lean production', and 'flexible production', although the Italians have made a special contribution to the latter.[65] The Swedish auto corporation Volvo developed an original work organization concept in its Kalmar and Uddevalla plants, which have attracted international attention but which have hardly set a counter-standard. In the early 1990s, when Sören Gyll succeeded Pehr Gyllenhammar as the chief executive, the two novel plants received a death sentence.

Intra-European comparative research has given us a picture of typical industrial work organizations in the three most important countries of Western Europe, with France and Germany at either end of the spectrum and Britain in-between. Generally speaking, French enterprises were found to have more managers and supervisors than their German counterparts, more administration, more hierarchy, and sharper manual–non-manual differentials. This was found to be related to the higher skills and autonomy of the German *Facharbeiter*, the skilled worker formed by extensive apprenticeships; but not, interestingly enough, to managers and supervisors being relatively cheaper in France – in fact, the contrary is the case.[66]

Between East and West Germany there was, in 1990, an interesting difference in the skill structuration of the working class. Workers constituted 39% of the labour force in the GDR and 35% in the FRG, but the main difference was the proportion of skilled workers, of *Facharbeiter*. They constituted 27% of the total labour force in the GDR but only 14% in the FRG.[67]

For the rest and for the time being, we had better resign ourselves to the lack of larger-scale data on the organization of work in the Communist countries. From Michael Burawoy's excellent case studies we do know that late Communist industrial enterprises could, occasionally, be more efficient than capitalist ones, more concretely that a Hungarian machine shop could be more efficient than a US one.[68] And we also know, or think we know, that that was exceptional. It is in-between that our ignorance lies.

The Swedish concept, which derived from the costs of labour turnover and industrial labour unattractiveness in a prosperous egalitarian community, featured job enlargement and group autonomy, in contrast to the tightly managed group organization of the Japanese. However, the most productive plant of Volvo is its traditional Ghent one in Belgium, and at the time of writing the most original European work organization is about to close down.[69]

The study of *corporate cultures* pertains to the organization of work. Some of the most interesting studies in this field have been made by two Dutchmen working for multinational corporations, first Geert Hofstede working for IBM, and then Alfons Trompenaars working for Shell; also of note is a joint Dutch–English survey deriving from international management seminars.[70] Shed of consultancy jargon and jittery methods, the three converge in their findings on the corporate structuration of tasks, findings which also concord with the more anecdotal evidence culled by the author on business class flights in Europe and across the Northern Atlantic.

In terms of the hierarchy of tasks, there is a clear Germanic–Latin European divide, with the Latins, beginning with the Belgians, being much more hierarchical and correspondingly less collegial, much more anxious to distinguish the boss and his or her subordinates. There is less consensus as to how to fit the Americans into this schema. They are clearly more pushy than Germanic Europeans, but the style of US bosses tends to differ from that of Latin Europeans, less formal, more individualistic, which makes a task organization comparison more complicated.

What has happened over time to hierarchy and to work proletarianization, or, put differently, to the span of superordination and to a polarization between conception and execution? As no systematic cross-national overview of this once hotly debated issue seems to exist, I shall fall back upon one of my own studies of Sweden. It is based on census, industrial statistics and collective agreements data and covers, at least in part, the period from 1930 to the late 1970s; the results are most specific with regard to non-manual workers.

Between 1930 and 1950 in Sweden a clear proletarianization of the middle stata occurred, in the sense that not only the absolute numbers but also the proportion of non-manual employees having a clearly subordinate position increased from 18 to 27%. Then, in our period of study, there ensued a slow relative de-proletarianization, to 23% in 1975. Looking into more specific hierarchies after the war, it was found that in industry among technical personnel there was between 1947 and 1975 a basic stability between, on the one hand, managerial and independent positions, and, on the other, 'other', i.e. subordinate, positions. In the offices of industry, however, there was a decline of the share of subordinate positions, from 72% in 1947–52 to 55% in 1975. In the state bureaucracy, a continuous decline in the ratio of managers and clerks was found between 1957 and 1977. In health care there was also a decline in the ratio of physicians to nurses, 1:6.0 in 1930, via 1:5.0 in 1950, to 1:2.7 in 1975, while the proportion of auxiliaries increased continuously.[71] In brief, a picture opposite to that indicated by Harry Braverman was found.[72]

Labour market surveys may also contribute to our knowledge of work organization. From an OECD survey of temporary jobs we find that Western Europe divides into four categories. Spain is one, the worst for workers, with 26.6% of wage and salary employment in 1989 being temporary. Greece and Portugal form the next group, ranging from 17.2 to 18.7%, respectively. Then we have a set between 8.5% (France and the Netherlands) and 11.0% (Germany), comprising also Denmark and Ireland and, outside Europe, Japan. Finally, there are countries having only between 3.4% (Luxemburg) and 6.3% (Italy) in temporary jobs, including Belgium and the UK.[73] Much of this is due to the indirect effects of labour law. And the social division of labour is intimately related to the division of rights and obligations.

Notes

1 Cf. G. Duby, *Les trois ordres ou l'imaginaire du féodalisme*, Paris, Gallimard, 1978.

2 The classical works are, of course, A. Smith, *Lectures on Justice, Police, Revenue, and Arms*, ed. E. Cannan, Oxford, 1896; idem, *An Inquiry into the Nature and Causes of the Wealth of Nations*, 1776; (London, Methuen, 1970); J. Millar, *Observations Concerning the Distinction of Ranks in Society*, 3rd edn, 1771, reprinted in W. Lehmann, *John Millar of Glasgow*, Cambridge, Cambridge University Press, 1960. The secondary literature is immense. I would select a good Swedish work, B. Eriksson, *Samhällsvetenskapens uppkomst*, Uppsala, Sociologiska institutionen, 1988.

3 Cf. N. Luhmann (ed.), *Soziale Differenzierung: Zur Geschichte einer Idee*, Opladen, Westdeutscher Verlag, 1985; C. Clark, *The Conditions of Economic Progress*, London, Macmillan, 1957 (originally published 1940); S. Kozyr-Kowalski and A. Przestalski (eds), *On Social Differentiation*, Poznan, Adam Mickiewicz University Press, 1992, 3 vols.

4 This short paragraph tries to summarize a number of studies, cross-national and national. Annual working time (in the OECD area) is taken primarily from OECD, *Employment Outlook*, Paris, 1993, p. 186. Cross-national data of paid labour, housework and leisure have been put together by Jonathan Gershuny in several studies, e.g. 'Are We Running Out of Time?', *Futures* 24,1(1992); 'Emplois du temps', in F. Féron and A. Thoraval (eds), *L'Etat de l'Europe*, Paris, La Découverte, 1992, pp. 95–7, and 'La répartition du temps dans les sociétés post-industrielles', *Futuribles* 165–6 (1992). That issue is specially devoted to issues of labour time. G. Bosch, 'L'évolution du temps de travail en Allemagne', *Futuribles* 165–6, p. 94, provides a detailed effective labour-time comparison, for 1989 and 1990, between the then two states of Germany. Hungarian data have been collected and analysed by Rudolf Andorka et al. in their *Social Report*, Budapest, Tárki, 1992, Ch. 9. Statistics Sweden has made a useful time-use survey for 1990–1, reported in *Levnadsförhållanden Rapport nr 80*, Stockholm, SCB, 1992.

5 A. Maddison, *Ontwikkelingsfasen van het kapitalisme*, Utrecht, Het Spectrum, 1982, Table C9, p. 280; O. Marchand, 'Une comparaison internationale du temps de travail', *Futuribles* 165–6 (1992), pp. 30, 34.

6 *Le Monde*, 3.11.1993.

7 Thorstein Veblen's class *The Theory of the Leisure Class* was first published in 1899. It dealt with the rich of the 'gilded age' of US capitalism. A modern edition was put out by Mentor Books in New York in 1953.

8 Gershuny, 'La répartition', pp. 218ff; Marchand 'Une comparaison, p. 39; *Levnadsförhållanden*, pp. 80–1.

9 Andorka et al., *Social Report*, p. 133. To what extent that takes into account travel to and from work, included in the Swedish counting, is unclear, however.

10 A. Szalai (ed.), *The Use of Time*, The Hague, Mouton, 1972, pp. 658ff. Participating countries were Belgium (national sample), Bulgaria (Kazanlik), Czechoslovakia (Olomouc), France (six cities), East Germany (Hoyerswerda), West Germany (national sample plus Osnabrück), Hungary (Györ), Poland (Torún), USSR (Pskov), Yugoslavia (Kragajevac and Maribor), and Peru (Lima-Callao), and USA (national sample plus Jackson, Mich.). Interviewed were individuals aged 18 to 65 outside exclusively agricultural households.

11 I have taken my primary data from Maddison, *Ontwikkelingsfasen*, pp. 279–80, from OECD, *Employment Outlook 1986*, Paris, 1986, p. 142, and from Swedish labour market statistics, while checking the French case with Marchand, 'Une comparaison', p. 34. Swedish-reading readers are referred further to my article, 'Tar arbetet slut? och post-fordismens problem', in U. Björnberg and I. Hellberg (eds), *Sociologer ser på arbete*, Stockholm, Arbetslivscentrum, 1987.

12 Calculations on the basis of OECD data of the size of the population employed and on the average number of hours actually worked per year: OECD, *Labour Force Statistics, 1965–1985*, Paris, 1987, p. 24; *Employment Outlook, July 1992*, Paris, 1992, pp. 275, 277 (West German employment in 1990); *Employment Outlook July 1993*, Paris, 1993, pp. 5, 186.

13 A. Deacon, 'Unemployment and Politics in Britain since 1945', in B. Showler and A. Sinfield (eds), *The Workless State*, Oxford, Martin Robertson, 1981, pp. 63–4.

14 Maddison, *Ontwikkelingsfasen*, Table C6b, p. 276

15 OECD, *Historical Statistics, 1960–1990*, Paris, 1992, Tables 2.15 and 2.20.

16 See further G. Therborn, *Why Some Peoples Are More Unemployed than Others*, London, Verso, 1986.

17 The Czech Republic was still fully employed throughout 1993, although the number in employment had declined significantly. That is, the labour force had shrunk.

18 Commission of the European Communities, *Livre blanc sur la compétitivité, la croissance et l'emploi*, document O/93/355, Brussels, 1993. Cf. *Le Monde*, 14.12.1993, p. 21.

19 J. Garraty, *Unemployment in History*, New York, Harper & Row, 1978, pp. 121ff.

20 See further T. Cole and M. Winkler, ' "Unsere Tage zählen" ', in G. Göckenjan and H.-J.von Kondratowitz, *Alter und Alltag*, Frankfurt, Suhrkamp, 1988, pp. 46ff.

21 Cf. R. Lenoir, 'L'invention du troisième âge', *Actes de la recherche en sciences sociales* 26/27 (1979). Cf. A.-M. Guillemard, *Le déclin du social*, Paris, PUF, 1986, pp. 138ff, for the olitical context.

22 Calculated from United Nations. *World Economic Survey 1989*, New York, 1989, p. 222. The figures refer to 1990.
23 OECD, *Ageing Populations*, Paris, 1988, p. 14.
24 OECD, *Demographic Trends, 1950–1990*, Paris, 1979, p. 120. Belgium had an extremely low labour force participation, only 20%.
25 OECD, *Labour Force Statistics, 1965–1985*, Paris, 1987, pp. 480ff. Exact percentage figures of males 60–4 in the labour force were in 1986 for France 27.4, for Germany 31.8, for Italy in 1985 38.6, for the UK 53.4, for the Netherlands in 1985 36.4, and for Finland 35.5. Hungarian figures are taken from Andorka et al, *Social Report*, p. 65.
26 Sixty-one per cent were fully on early retirement, another 20% on partial retirement, 4% were sick, and 11% were unemployed. The union organizes more than 95% of the relevant workforce. The union report was presented in *Svenska Dagbladet*, 30.12.1993.
27 Institut für Soziologie und Sozialpolitik der AdW der DDR, 'Leistungen der Sozialversicherung europäischer sozialistischer Länder', [East] Berlin, 1988, pp. 17ff (unpublished paper). Cf. the more extensive but less systematic treatment in J. Dixon and D. Macarov (eds), *Social Welfare in Socialist Countries*, London, Routledge, 1992.
28 See, e.g. G. Edwards, *GDR Society and Social Institutions*, London, Macmillan, 1985, pp. 173, 187ff; [Czechoslovak] Federal Ministry of Labour and Social Affairs, 'Czechoslovakia', in Dixon and Macarov, *Social Welfare*, p. 87.
29 Edwards *GDR Society*, p. 192; *Statistical Pocket Book of Hungary*, Budapest, Statistical Publishing House, 1989, p. 27; Andorka et al., *Social Report*, p. 65; ILO, *Yearbook of Labour Statistics 1991*, Geneva, 1991, p. 50. Poland, with its backward private agriculture, had more than half of its men aged 60–4 still working in 1988 and a third of its males aged 65–9; ILO, *Yearbook*, 1991, p. 45.
30 P. Stearns, *Old Age in European Society*, London, Croom Helm, 1977, pp. 34ff, 108ff. Russian research was also advanced in this area.
31 Also in Argentina and Uruguay old age pensioners, 'jubilados', are developing important, autonomous social movements, occasionally referred to by far left political groupings as the 'vanguard' of social struggle. This is based on interviews, current press reports, and on flyers observed during a visit to Uruguay and Argentina in October–November 1992.
32 Maddison, *Ontwikkelingsfasen*, Table C2.
33 OECD, *Historical Statistics, 1960–1990*, Paris, 1992, p. 39. Cf. M. Schmidt, 'Gendered Labour Force Participation', in F. Castles (ed.), *Families of Nations*, Aldershot, Dartmouth, 1993.
34 ILO, *Yearbook*, 1991, Table 2A. Cf. H. Ishida et al., 'Intergenerational Class Mobility in Postwar Japan', *American Journal of Sociology* 96 (1991), pp. 985n and 986.
35 Commission of the European Communities, *The Position of Women on the Labour Market*, Women of Europe Supplements, no. 36, Table 8. The development in the 1970s lacked a uniform cross-national tendency: OECD, *The Integration of Women into the Economy*, Paris, 1985, p. 42.
36 Eurostat, *Regions Statistical Yearbook 1988*, Luxemburg, 1989, supplemented with national statistical yearbooks, and, for the UK, *Regional Trends 28*, CSO, London, 1993, p. 91. The regions are those of the OECD, *Employment Outlook 1989*, Paris, 1989.
37 ILO, *Yearbook*, 1991, Table 1, which covers Hungary, Poland and the USSR. GDR and Czechoslovak female participation was higher, and Albanian and Yugoslav lower: *Historically Planned Economies: A Guide to the Data*, World Bank, 1992. P. Marer et al., country tables.
38 OECD, *Historical Statistics*, Tables 2.15, 2.16, 2.17; OECD, *Employment Outlook 1993*, Tables J, M, N.
39 The annual report of the Bundesanstalt für Arbeit, summarized in *Frankfurter Allgemeine Zeitung*, 10.1.1994, p. 13.
40 *Unemployment in Poland, I–III Quarter 1993*, Glówny Urzad Statystyczny, Warsaw, 1993, Table 2.
41 Calculations from an overview by Jonathan Gershuny, 'Emplois du temps', p. 96; cf. idem 'La répartition du temps'. Countries included were Belgium, Denmark, France, Italy, Netherlands, the UK and West Germany: Andorka et al., *Social Report*, p. 133.

42 *Social Trends 24*, CSO, London, HMSO, 1994, Table 10.2.

43 Calculated from *Levnadsförhållanden*, Tables 14 and 16. Cohabitation without marriage has become very common in Sweden, and official statistical investigations usually treat all couples alike, wedded or not.

44 L. Neundörfer, *Atlas sozioökonomischer Regionen Europas*, 17th edn, Frankfurt, Soziogeographisches Institut a.d. J.W. Goethe-Universität, 1973.

45 P. Bairoch (ed.), *The Working Population and its Structure*, Brussels, Editions de L'Institut de Sociologie de l'Universitié Libre de Bruxelles, 1968, pp. 87,96, 98–9, 108, and OECD, *Historical Statistics, 1960–1989*, p. 40.

46 OECD, *Labour Force Statistics, 1965–1985* and *Labour Force Statistics, 1969–1989*, Paris, 1991, Table 7.0 in both cases.

47 ILO, *Yearbook of Labour Statistics 1993*, Geneva, 1993, Table 2A. Data for Russia and the Ukraine are missing.

48 'Industry', according to standard practice, then including mining, manufacturing, construction and utilities.

49 E.H. Hunt, *British Labour History, 1815–1914*, London, Weidenfield & Nicolson, 1981, p. 26.

50 Taiwan did have a brief period of relatively preponderant industrialism around 1980. In contrast to the trading city of Singapore, Hong Kong also developed as an industrial city-state. Neither had, of course, any agrarian background. OECD, *Employment Outlook 1991*, Paris, 1991, pp. 75–6. Historical data from Bairoch, *The Working Population*.

51 Sombart's analysis first appeared in a journal he edited with Max Weber, *Archiv für Sozialwissenschaft und Sozialpolitik*, and in 1906 in book form. An edited American version was put out in 1976 by M.E. Sharpe, White Plains NY: *Why Is There No Socialism in the United States?*

52 OECD, *Labour Force Statistics, 1969–1989*, Table 7.0.

53 Cf. *Regiones europeas de antigua industrialización*, Bilbao, SPRI, 1989. For Britain see also S. Fothergill and J. Vincent, *The State of the Nation*, London, Pan Books, 1985, pp. 32ff.

54 Calculations from *Die Zeit* 7.8.1992, p. 33, and *Frankfurter Allgemeine Zeitung* 14.1.1993, p. 11.

55 Marer, *Historically Planned Economies*, national tables; *Regional Trends 28*, Table 2.1.

56 OECD, *Historical Statistics, 1960–1990*, Paris, 1992, Table 2.13. The larger size of the American armed forces for most of that period is taken into account above: OECD, *Labour Force Statistics, 1965–1985*, pp. 88–9, 236–7.

58 See, A. Kruse, *Den offentliga sektorns effekter på sysselsätningen*, Stockholm, Nordiska Ministerrådet, 1984, p. 18. According to a somewhat less extensive system of calculation in the Nordic countries in 1981, public employment in Finland was 24% of the total, as compared with 25% in Norway.

58 ILO, *Yearbook of Labour Statistics 1984, 1988, 1991, 1992*, Table 2A. When recent census data or labour force surveys are not available, the ILO does not print them in their latest yearbook, which is why a bunch sometimes has to be consulted. No comparable data were found for Albania.

59 As the copyright has not been negotiated, I had better leave this, by no means non-controversial, statement anonymous.

60 The most recent Armani suit of class theory was offered by a US mathematical economist in the early 1980s, who became a cult figure among a small band of philosophers and would-be philosophers from Oslo to Southern California. While refraining from the outset from touching anything empirical about actually existing classes, the theory did originally claim to contribute some sort of explanation of the latter. Six years later, the designer told his still faithful readers that the theory was all about – morality. J. Roemer, *A General Theory of Exploitation and Class*, Cambridge, Mass., Harvard University Press, 1982; *Free to Lose*, London, Radius, 1988. A more empirically oriented and robust theory, although within the confines of treating classes as aggregates of single individuals only, is E.O. Wright's *Classes*, London, Verso, 1985. My own contribution to the industry has come to focus on the meaning and on the rhetoric of classes as social forces: 'Class Analysis: History and

Defence', in U. Himmelstrand (ed.), *Sociology from Crisis to Science?*, Vol. 1, London, Sage, 1986; 'Class and the Coming of Post-Industrial Society', in S. Kozyr-Kowalski and A. Przestalski (eds), *On Social Differentiation*, Vol. 1, Poznan, Adam Mickiewicz University Press, 1992.

61 E. Hobsbawm, 'The Forward March of Labour Halted?', in M. Jacques and F. Mulhern (eds), *The Forward March of Labour Halted?*, London, Verso, 1981, p. 3.

62 Several data sets have been used for this paragraph. One overview, calculated in terms of manual workers as part of the total adult population, is given in A. Przeworski and J. Sprague, *Paper Stones*, Chicago, University of Chicago Press, 1986, p. 35. For Belgium and Germany I have also used Bairoch, *The Working Population*, Tables B5 and C5; for Germany further J. Mooser, *Arbeiterleben in Deutschland, 1900–1970*, Frankfurt, Suhrkamp, 1984, p. 28; for France I have had kind access to the underlying basic tables for Przeworski's overview. A. Przeworski and E. Underhill, 'The Evolution of Class Structure in France 1901–1968', Chicago, University of Chicago Dept. of Political Science, 1978 (mimeographed); and for Sweden I have also taken recourse to my earlier work on Swedish censuses, *Klasstrukturen i Sverige, 1930–1980*, Lund, Zenit, 1981, p. 29.

63 Calculations from Eurostat, *Employment and Unemployment 1989*, Brussels and Luxemburg, 1989, pp. 104 and 108.

64 Absolute numbers have grown, so it is not just a relative effect due to the decline of employment. See further OECD, *Employment Outlook 1991*, Ch. 4.

65 Cf. M. Piore and S. Sabel, *The Second Industrial Divide*, New York, Basic Books, 1984, esp. Ch. 9; R. Boyer (ed.), *La flexibilité du travail en Europe*, Paris, La Découverte, 1986; OECD, *New Directions of Work Organization*, Paris 1992; S. Holland, *The European Imperative*, Nottingham, Spokesman, 1993.

66 The studies were made by LEST in Aix-en-Provence and the Institute for Social Research in Munich: M. Maurice et al., *The Social Foundations of Industrial Power*, London, MIT Press, 1986. For an overview which adds research on Britain, see C. Lane, *Management and Labour in Europe*, Aldershot, Edward Elgar, 1989. Cf. also the wage–salary relation reported by G. Mermet, *Euroscopie*, Paris, Larousse, 1991, p. 321.

67 *Das sozio-ökonomische Panel. Wochenbericht* 37/90, 1990, p. 520.

68 The American sociologist Burawoy had personally worked at and studied the two enterprises: M. Burawoy and J. Lukács, *The Radiant Past*, Chicago, University of Chigago Press, 1992, Part I.

69 Cf. C. Berggren, *Det nya bilarbetet*, Lund, Arkiv, 1990, and oral communication. I have also learnt, by my own way of interpretation, from conversations with Anders Boglind, now at Volvo, formerly at my department of sociology.

70 G. Hofstede, *Culture's Consequences*, London, Sage, 1980; A. Trompenaars, *Riding the Waves of Culture*, London, Economist Books, 1993; C. Hampden-Turner and A. Trompenaars, *The Seven Cultures of Capitalism*, New York, Doubleday, 1993.

71 Therborn, *Klasstrukturen*, pp. 68ff.

72 H. Braverman, *Labor and Monopoly Capital*, New York, Monthly Review Press, 1974. The Braverman thesis, it will be remembered, explicitly included white-collar work. Cf., as another empirical response to Braverman, who, incidentally, at least started from empirical experience: H. Kern and M. Schumann, *Das Ende der Arbeitsteilung?*, Munich, C.H. Beck, 1984.

73 OECD, *Employment Outlook 1991*, p. 50.

5

Rights to Claim: Membership and Welfare

Rights, and their obverse, obligations, differ from other resources, from means, by deriving directly from a recognition by others as belonging to the actor. Sets of rights and obligations make up social *institutions*, e.g. marriage, private property, social security. In the European, and European-settled, world, rights have long had a particular importance because of a unique differentiation of law, or the legal system, from religion, morality and power.[1] Such a differentiation has implied a differentiation of (legal) rights, has implied their invokability, and their, at least in principle, enforceability, with the help of the legal sanctions system, against the powers that be, and even against conceptions of religion and morality. It is this legal differentiation which provides the basis for the particular operation of rights: while deriving from their recognition by others, they belong to the actor, who can use them against others, because the former and the latter 'others' are differentiated from each other.

Neither in sociological theory[2] nor in social history nor in empirical sociology has there been much attention paid to rights. Sociologists have tended to be much more interested in obligations, or norms, than in rights. As always, one should be sceptical of one's own originality, however. There are several indications of a growing interest, outside the legal profession itself, in rights and in law.[3] But there remains a certain sense of loneliness, and therefore of caution, in sketching a postwar history of rights in Europe.

For our heuristic purposes here, at least, we may distinguish between two types of rights, *rights to claim and rights to act*. The early twentieth-century American legal theorist Wesley Hohfeld, to whom latter-day writers on rights are still endebted, actually distinguished four types of rights, but they may be grouped into two. Apart from claim rights, Hohfeld pointed to three legal action rights, the liberty to do x, the power to do x, and the immunity from x.[4] The boundary between them may be fuzzy, but that does not matter in this context.

The former type of right we may, for convenience's sake, call *entitlements*. They are recognized legitimate claims upon a society, usually upon its polity. Entitlements comprise, above all, rights to 'membership' of a state or of a community and, secondly, entitlements to service and economic support in case of need. T.H. Marshall thought, and has influenced a great number of others to think, of these issues in terms of 'citizenship', i.e. civil, political, and social.[5]

While Marshall, as an Englishman speaking in 1949, had good grounds to think so, his perspective stands up less well forty to fifty years later, for two reasons, in this context. At the time of British out-migration and domestic ethnic homogeneity, the issues of state membership and within-state difference could be kept latent, subsumed under the problematic of the claim rights of a *given* population. That is no longer the case. Secondly, from a non-Anglocentric view of the welfare state, the notion of 'social citizenship' is only one variant of social claim rights.

The history of entitlements can hardly be constrained within any evolutionary strait-jacket. If we allow for wide conjunctural oscillations as well as for area-variable sequences of sorts of entitlements – that judicial, political and social rights may be extended in variable order – we may however, say, that modernity has involved a tendential extension of entitlements, in particular of participation and social support rights. Europe and the European-settled New Worlds have been pioneers of this tendency, most clearly with regard to participation rights.[6]

Rights to act determine the radius of legitimate actions. They provide the institutionalization of social relations, they (together with corresponding duties) define social roles, they open and close legitimate opportunities. Three areas in particular have been subject to regulations of rights to act. One concerns the rights of what we may call *free adulthood*. It is a complex of various rights, from the time of the American and the French Revolutions often summarized under the rubric of the 'rights of man', but which historically involved the emancipation of slaves, serfs and women into human adulthood. It included answering the question of maturity: when and under what conditions a person acquires adult rights to act? From medieval Normandy and England and then from the French Revolution, male maturity was normally reached on the 21st birthday. Since 1972, the Council of Europe has recommended, and has been followed in, adopting 18 years of age as maturity for both women and men.[7] Free adulthood has come to contain freedom of expression and of peaceful organization, as well as rights of personal integrity and property *vis-à-vis* the legal authority.

The two other major areas of rights to act comprise two fundamental sets of social relations among adults. One is gender relations, concentrated around, without being reducible to, family law. The other refers to the economy and refers to class, i.e. in modern times, first of all the rights to act of property owners and of employed labour.

Membership

The importance of state membership was reinforced, after the post-mercantilist liberal interlude, by World War I and by interwar (more or less) zero-sum international relations. Since World War II, the issue has come to the fore with the new turn of migration into Europe.

The legal tradition contains two major criteria for state membership, for citizenship, namely 'soil' or 'blood', or, put in more solemn Latin, *ius soli* and *ius sanguinis*. Translated into everyday English, the former means that you acquire your citizenship by the place where you were born, and the latter that it depends on who your parents (or ancestors) were. By and large, settlement countries – the New Worlds – and empires, like the British and the French, have tended to opt for the soil, other European countries for the blood. In the French case, the weight of the imperial tradition is reinforced by the universalist claims of the Revolution and, more importantly, by the nineteenth-century military conscription demands of a uniquely early immigration country in Europe.[8]

In fact, the soil or blood distinction does not adequately capture post-World War II varieties in Europe and the trajectories of their general tendency towards restrictiveness. The UK has, since 1971, increasingly narrowed the gate for entrants from the non-White Commonwealth, while keeping, in spite of IRA terrorism, an open door to Irish immigration. Irish residents of the UK have the same rights as British citizens.

France has maintained its ambition of assimilation, and stunned a German audience in 1992 by bringing a Black junior minister into a Franco-German debate on migration. Its actual rate of naturalization in 1987 was, however, on par with the Dutch and considerably below the Swedish rate, and the French treatment of asylum-seekers is much more harsh than the German reception.[9]

Germany has been in many ways more restrictive. Labour imports were conceived as 'Gastarbeiter' (guest workers, as in Austria and Switzerland), and denied any rights to permanent residence. Until 1990, people unable to claim German descent had no right to citizenship, however long they had been in Germany. Citizenship was a grace that might be granted. Since that date, fifteen years of residence, or, in the case of youngsters aged 16 to 23, eight years of residence and six years of school, entitles a claim to citizenship.

On the other hand, blood rights have allowed a large number of Eastern Europeans to enter (West) Germany claiming German descent. The political asylum right, lodged in §16 of the Bonn Constitution, restricted in spring 1993, has also given membership of the Federal Republic another kind of openness. In 1991, for instance, France received, gross, 46,000 asylum-seekers, the UK 45,000, Italy 23,000 and Germany 256,000.[10]

Political rights of membership are most accessible in Britain and, since 1984, in Ireland. Commonwealth and Irish residents have full political rights in Britain, as have British citizens resident in Ireland since 1984.[11] Sweden gave foreign residents the right to vote in local elections in 1976, followed by Denmark and Norway, and by Iceland and Finland, but only with regard to other Nordic citizens. In the Swiss canton of Neuchâtel this has been a right since 1849 and in the new canton of Jura since 1980. For the rest, only the Netherlands have, since 1986, granted this right. In France, the Socialists have been toying with the idea, and in Germany the Social Democratic governments of Hamburg and Schleswig-Holstein proposed it in February 1989, but in the end it was turned down by the Constitutional Court.[12]

In Eastern Europe, postwar citizenship lost one of its otherwise most important accessories, the passport (note Vladimir Mayakovsky's proud and famous 'Poem about a Soviet Passport' to the contrary). With the exception of the Yugoslavs since the mid-1950s, the Hungarians since mid-1980s, and, to a more limited extent, the Poles since the 1970s, a passport was to Eastern Europeans not a right but a special privilege, earned by loyal service or by post-retirement age. On the other hand, Eastern European regimes, such as that of the USSR and the GDR, used their power to deprive citizens of their citizenship rights. Alexander Solzhenitsyn and Wolf Biermann were the most famous, or notorious, cases.

After the war, the individual right to *vote* was an issue only by exception. Now, at last, Balkan, Belgian, French and Italian women were also entitled to political membership, the right to vote. Greek women joined their Balkan sisters in 1952, after the settlement of the pro-Western authoritarian regime emerging victorious out of the postwar civil war. But Swiss women had to wait for recognition of their political maturity till 1971, and most Iberian women till the end of the dictatorships in the mid-1970s.[13]

Historically, the frontier regions of the Anglo-Saxon New Worlds had pioneered women's rights to membership in the political community. The political enfranchisement of women started in the New Worlds, in the USA west of the Mississippi, in New Zealand, and in outback Australia, before beginning at the northern periphery of Europe, in Finland (in 1906) and in Norway (in 1913).[14] At the end of World War I it spread throughout Central (excluding Switzerland), Northern, Northeastern Europe, stage-wise even onto the British Isles. The political distance between Finland and the Iberian peninsula, in terms of female enfranchisement, turned out to be about seventy years, between France and Norway somewhat above thirty years.

A special issue are *collective membership rights* within a state. That is, the rights of members of a religious, linguistic and/or territorial collectivity. Such rights were a constituent part of membership entitlements in the explicitly multinational states of Switzerland, the USSR and Yugoslavia. But they have also been granted, or conquered, in a number of other countries: Belgium (Flemings and Walloons), Czechoslovakia (Czechs and Slovaks), Denmark (German-speakers), Finland (Swedish-speakers, Laps), Germany (Danish-speakers, Sorbians), Greece (Thracian Turks), Italy (South Tyrolians, Val d'Aostans), Netherlands (Frisians), Norway (Laps), Spain (after Franco: the Basque Country, Catalonia, and other regions), Sweden (Laps), the UK (ancient Scottish institutions of Church, education, law, as well as Gaelic and the Welsh language).

On the whole, the postwar record of collective community rights has been rather positive, in the sense of achieving a fairly widespread, generally consensual accommodation. The issue has encompassed virtually all of Europe, with the possible exceptions of the Irish Republic, which has its external *irredenta*, and continental Portugal. France has more or less successfully tried to deny it, but not without challenge, most vigorously, perhaps, from Corsica. It is by no means solved or superseded, however, as the enduring violent conflicts in Northern Ireland (halted in the autumn of 1994) and the Basque Country demonstrate dramatically, and many other frictions testify. The Federalist Union of European Peoples, founded in 1949 and having its core in and around South Tyrol, currently claims more than seventy ethnic groups as members and is lobbying for a more extensive and systematic set of collective membership rights of autonomy.

Community rights have been hotly contested without reaching any stable solution in Bulgaria – with reference to Muslim and Turkish minorities – and Romania, with regard to German descendants, Hungarians, Gypsies. After the break-up of the multinational states of the East, first cheered on by the West, soon to be dismayed by the new nationalisms invoked, collective membership rights have become a hot bone of contention from Estonia to the Caucasus.

Social rights and welfare states

Social entitlements, rights to claim a certain level of income and access to health and social services, have become a distinctive part of European modernity. Their establishment as rights set them apart from old traditions of charity, handed out to the poor as the rich saw fit.

By the late 1940s the specificity of Europe in this respect was visible. Of the New World countries, only New Zealand had a national income commitment to social rights higher than the European average. All the others were below. On the other hand, the intercontinental difference was not that great. In 1949, sixteen Western European countries spent on average 8.8% of their national income on social benefits, while four New World countries (including Chile, but exclusive of the New Zealand outlier, at 14.4%) provided 6.5%.[15]

Extensive social entitlements have been generated by rich countries generally – even measured in *relative terms* – and by European countries in particular. On the basis of richness and Europeanness a certain political variation is also noticeable. In the early 1980s, Portugal and Yugoslavia, which spent a tenth of their GDP on social security, were the lowest-spending European countries in this respect out of twenty-five listed. Among thirty countries in the Americas, only four spent more than Yugoslavia (Canada, USA, Chile and Cuba), and one (Uruguay) as much. Only Canada was more generous than Switzerland, the second rearlight of Western Europe. Not a single African country provided 3% or more of its GDP for social security entitlements. Of the Asian and Pacific countries, from Turkey to New Zealand, only the latter was above the Swiss level, and only Australia and Israel were above that of Yugoslavia and Portugal. Another way of intercontinental comparison may be to look at the EC, Japan and the USA. In 1983 their social security commitment according to the ILO was 22, 11 and 13% of their GDP, respectively.[16]

The European welfare state first set out on its modern course in the 1880s, in Germany, after a set of abortive attempts during the French Revolution.[17] It emerged as a state response to the social risks and the political challenges of an industrial capitalist class society. Other kinds of large-scale modern social entitlements were conceivable, and one did in fact develop for a while, namely the claim rights of (Northern) American Civil War veterans and the advanced projects for mothers and children.[18] But in the end, the European was the only one that settled and grew.

Within the European pattern, two major subsets of social entitlements developed early. Neither was based on a principle of citizenship. By World War I, their core institutions were already established. The alternatives first settled with regard to pension rights. The continental variant, pioneered in Germany and Austria, tied public pension rights tightly to work record, including kind of work, and contributions made. The relationship of the state to the industrial working-class, with its rapidly growing movement, and to white-collar employees were central political concerns here.

The Anglo-Scandinavian alternative was first unfurled in Denmark in the 1890s. Here, pensions were primarily linked to age and income or wealth. Old people with meagre means were entitled to a pension. In Denmark this was originally a municipally administered old age relief, relieved of the stigma of the old poor relief. In Britain it became an immediately functioning, non-contributory means-tested pension system in 1908, whereas the Swedish parliament ultimately found the original proposal of excluding the well-off unnecessarily complicated, and in 1913, by default, introduced a universal contributory pensions scheme.[19]

Two considerations, in particular, seem to have led the Britons and the Scandinavians in a different direction than that pointed to by Bismarck. One was the weight of local poor relief concerns, crucial in Denmark and Britain, bringing in central state aid to municipal relief and de-stigmatizing old age poverty. The other was a pattern of class relations, expressed in political organization and leadership, characterized at the end of the nineteenth century by a considerable affinity between (smaller) propertied farmers and non-agrarian workers. This was of key importance in Denmark and Sweden. In 1884, the leader of the Swedish Yeoman Party persuaded parliament to incorporate consideration of provision for '[workers]' and with them equal persons' within the remit of the Workers' Insurance Investigation then being set up. The Investigation Committee then made a class analysis of Sweden and came to the conclusion, in 1888, that '94.25% of the whole population' were 'workers or with them equal persons'.[20] Since then, the idea of a wide extension of social entitlements has never left the centre-stage of Swedish politics.

The labour movement was decisive as a political challenge for the development of public social insurance. The German initiative was taken under the shadow of the Paris Commune.[21] When social income rights had been put on the political agenda, the labour movement developed its own distinctive conception of them.[22] However, the labour view has had an influence only within parameters set by stronger politico-economic forces.

After an early general proclamation of working-class principles of social security in the USSR, Soviet social policy came to develop piecemeal, adapted to considerations of labour allocation and political power, and strongly affected by the overall development of the economy. By the mid-1920s, social insurance for urban workers started to function more or less properly, at least with regard to temporary disability benefits. What resulted was a patchwork of special rights alongside no rights at all. Old age pensions were introduced only in 1929, and then only for manual workers in the mining, metal, electrical and textile industries, and in transport. Clerical staff were included in 1937, but at about the same time a new idea was introduced into public social insurance. As a disincentive against excessive labour turnover, insurance benefits came to depend on length of service in the same enterprise. Further differentiation set in after the war and wartime inflation, when 'basic categories' of workers and technicians in 'the leading branches of the national economy' received special entitlements.

In 1956 a certain kind of urban rationalization and equalization ensued, but only in 1964 did the surviving victims of agrarian collectivization obtain pension rights, and only in 1970 sickness and family benefits.[23] After the Soviet decree of 1929, old age in Communist countries arrived at a different age for men and women, usually five years earlier for the longer-living sex.

The new Communist regimes of Eastern Europe after the war extended existing social entitlements and, by and large, refrained from introducing the more idiosyncratic specificities of the Stalinist system. In Poland, the framework of prewar social legislation was even maintained, including special rights for white-collar employees (retained till the 1970s). The social law of the GDR also included many features of earlier German law. Everywhere, the continental system of work-related schemes was maintained. Cooperative farmers were gradually included into Eastern European social security and a uniformalization of rights took place, but certain special rights for certain categories remained the rule. Nor was social policy ever central to the Communist conception of socialism.[24]

In Western Europe, many states have come to enshrine social entitlements in their constitutions since the war, or later, after the fall of the remaining Fascist governments. Here we may find principles of social citizenship, but in fact the constitutional clauses have played at most a marginal part in the actual postwar development of welfare rights. Ironically, the most significant formula seems to have been the most innocuous one, §20:1 of the Bonner *Grundgesetz* which defines (West) Germany as 'a democratic and social federal state'.[25]

In the British Beveridge Report three traditions merged: the enlightened supersession of the Poor Law effort, represented above all by Beveridge himself; the working-class perspective of clear and uniform rights, expressed in the TUC call for what became the Report; and wartime national solidarity, which carried the proposals out of a sceptical Tory-dominated Cabinet into the country and among the troops. The Beveridge Report was, of course, the background to T.H. Marshall's hailing of social citizenship.

However, in spite of the inspiring postwar prestige of non-defeated Britain in general, and of the British Labour Party in particular – among left-of-centre people, that is – all the attempts to found new systems of social rights after the Gospel according to Sir William came almost to nothing in the rest of Western Europe. Part of the reason was that labour party people – whatever the name of the party – soon lost out in the postwar power game. Another part was that even powerful Beveridge fans, like the Swedish Social Democratic Minister for Social Affairs, Gustav Möller, ran into entrenched and different national institutions of social policy and into postwar economic squeezes.[26] In the end, the early twentieth-century division between Anglo-Scandinavia and the rest of Europe was reproduced, on a more generous footing, in spite of Beveridge and in spite of Yalta and Eastern Communism.

The defeat of Beveridgian ideas on the continent meant a defeat for the idea of social citizenship. Instead the prewar pattern of specific rights for specific social groups re-asserted itself. Only from about 1970 did important tendencies towards generalization and harmonization of the special regimes of social entitlements materialize.[27]

The expansion of the welfare state was a product neither of the war nor of the postwar settlement. It took place in the culminating boom years and their immediate aftermath. Around 1960, the issue was fought over and decided as to whether the boom meant that less social entitlements were needed or that more social entitlements were possible, and more just. By and large, it was the latter opinion that won, carried mainly by Social Democrats and by Christian Democrats. In Denmark and Sweden, the future of social policy was the main bone of contention of politically very polarized elections, and in Belgium it became part of the crisis policy issues of a major, militant working-class protest strike, about the turn of the year 1960–1.

As can be seen from Table 5.1, the ensuing growth of social entitlements was explosive, and it was primarily Western. The absolute figures for 1960 and 1980/1 in the Table are not comparable between groups of countries. The sources have been chosen with a view to getting the best time-series for groups of countries, rather than for minimum overall comparability. Definitions of social expenditure vary somewhat, and the denominator differs – GDP in the OECD, net material product in Eastern Europe. It is the *change* in the 1960s and 1970s which should be compared.

Here, Eastern Europe stands out in a surprisingly negative light if one is in favour of social entitlements; indeed, from a neo-liberal point of view the then Communist countries may appear as models of rectitude. In those two decades Western European social expenditure increased its share of – a growing – GDP more than in its previous history. The same held for Japan, whereas the rich New Worlds augmented very substantially, and the USA more so than during all its previous history. In this light, the Eastern

Table 5.1 *The expansion of social expenditure, 1960–1981*
(percentages of GDP/NMP, national averages are unweighted)

Country	Soc. expend.[a] 1960 %	Increase 1960–80/1 %
Western Europe[b]	*10.5*	*11.3*
Austria	15.9	8.0
Belgium	13.1	16.5
Denmark	9.8	15.9
Finland	8.7	11.0
France	13.4	10.4
W. Germany	18.1	8.2
Greece	6.8	4.2
Ireland	8.7	12.6
Italy	13.1	9.6
Netherlands	11.7	17.3
Norway	7.9	13.1
Portugal	4.4	9.0
Spain	(9.5)[c]	7.7
Sweden	10.8	16.0
Switzerland	4.9	9.6
UK	10.2	7.7
Eastern Europe	*11.0*	*4.3*
Bulgaria	10.7	1.5
Czechoslovakia	15.4	3.5[d]
E. Germany	12.7[e]	3.1[d]
Hungary	8.8	9.5
Poland	8.9	6.8[d]
Ukraine	9.1	6.4[d]
USSR	10.2	3.8[d]
Yugoslavia	12.2[f]	−0.1
New Worlds[f]	*8.4*	*6.1*
Japan	*4.0*	*8.5*

Notes: [a] Social insurance, assistance and services excl. education, but national variations of definition may occur. [b] Excl. Spain. [c] 1970. [d] 1980. [e] 1967. [f] 1965. [g] Australia, Canada, New Zealand and the USA.

Sources: Denmark: L.N. Johansen, 'Denmark', in P. Flora (ed.), *Growth to Limits*, Vol. 4, Berlin, de Gruyter, 1986, p. 234; Portugal: calculations from A. Bruto da Costa, 'A Despesa Pública em Portugal 1960–1983', Lisbon, unpublished paper, October 1986, pp. 38 and 50; Spain: I. Cruz Roche et al., *Política social y crisis económica*, Madrid, Siglo XXI, 1985, p. 76; other OECD countries: calculations from OECD, *Social Expenditure, 1960–1985*, Paris, 1985, Tables 1 and 3; Eastern Europe: ILO, *The Cost of Social Security*, Eleventh and Twelfth International Survey, Geneva, 1985 and 1988 respectively; in cases of discrepancy the more recent datum has been used.

expansion lacks lustre, and Yugoslavia positions itself in the non-European world by letting social expenditure stagnate.

The main thrust of the expansion has come from pension rights.[28] A new wave of welfare state expansion was introduced by the West Germans in

1957 and by the Swedes in 1958, with a new tier of public occupational pension systems. But the expansion came not only from the extension and the rise of pension entitlements, but also from the early maturation of old contributory schemes, and, not least, from a new system of indexation, which tied pension levels not to past contributions and past wages/salaries but, primarily, to the current growth of living standards.

The basic social prerequisite of old age as a third age of human activity, rather than as one of decay and waiting for death, was the establishment of pensions as a sufficient source of income for a decent standard of living. Although the phenomenon of pensions has been known in certain social groups in Europe for about two hundred and fifty years – the armed forces, the merchant marine, certain civilian public officials[29] – and although the first mass-targeted pension schemes in Europe go back to the Wilhelmine Reich, pensions providing an ordinary level of living for the bulk of retirees date back only to the post-World War II period, and mainly to the late 1950s. In 1950, pensions amounted only to 20–30 per cent of the average worker's wage in Europe. Only in Austria and in France were certain categories of employees entitled to pensions surpassing half a worker's wage, which at that time was not a high consumption income. In view of later developments, the low pensions in Scandinavia at that time are also worth noting.[30]

Then a process of rapid change took place, inaugurated by the German pensions reform of 1957, which tied pensions to the *current* income of the working population, and dramatized by the political struggle in Sweden (in 1957–60) over a general occupational pensions system. The latter was the object of the most heated political controversy in the history of social policy, the issue of one consultative referendum, one extraordinary parliamentary election, and the main focus of a second, regular parliamentary election.

The outcome was that the social question changed from being a 'workers' question' to an 'old age question'. By 1985 pensions alone amounted to almost half (46%) of public social expenditure (excluding education) in the OECD area. Health care for the elderly and pensions together made up almost two-thirds (62%) of welfare state spending.[31] The average pension level for the area was 58% of a worker's wage.[32]

The indexation of pensions was never adopted in Eastern Europe and is a main, if not the only, reason for the relative stagnation of social expenditure there. (Tighter control of health costs is another.) Pension levels were therefore much lower than in Western Europe, fairly measured in relation to the going national wage rates. Only the Hungarian levels were equivalent to those of Western Europe. In 1982 the average pension in the GDR was 30% of average income, in the USSR 35%, in Czechoslovakia 45%, and in Hungary 57%.[33]

At least three reasons may be distinguished as contributing to this East–West difference. Their relative weight is difficult to disentangle. One was the enduring labour scarcity in the East, which led to pensioners being entitled to draw both a pension and a wage, if they wanted to work. From that perspective, a generous pension system would have augmented the scarcity of labour. Another reason was the official ideology of fixed prices, which at least should have provided a threshold for indexation to enter the agenda. Thirdly, one might speculate about the effect of dictatorship. Pensioners do not have much economic clout, their main political resource is the vote. But under conditions of constantly rigged elections this does not amount to much power, and a cool social scientist should expect pensioners' interests to be low on the priorities of the powerful.[34]

But the issue is more complicated still. For most of this chapter we have been discussing social entitlements in the Western sense, including the ILO. This is a practical approach for a Western European scholar, and by now it may even have an aura of historical justification. From a more scientific angle, however, this perspective is biased. It does not take into account the different structuration of social rights.

In Eastern Europe subsidized low prices on basic everyday commodities were held as a fundamental social right. Attempts by the Polish government to diminish them, for example, immediately met with militant working-class protest, in 1956, in 1970, in 1976, and in 1980. Every time the Polish Communists backed down, but initially only after blood was shed. After 1989, unanimous expert Western opinion held that the abolition of those subsidies was a *sine qua non* for establishing a market economy. The subsidies were part of the Communist conception of social rights, and the way the social policy front line was drawn in Poland from 1956 to 1990 was both tragic and ironic. Anyway, the former were very substantial and costly. In the GDR, for instance, they amounted in 1987–8 to about half of Western-type social expenditure, taken broadly, i.e. including both education and housing. In fact, a third more was spent on price subsidies than on social security.[35]

How that priority should be judged will be left aside here. The point in this context is that the policy of heavily subsidizing basic needs provisions must have limited the resources available for other purposes.

Prevailing typologies of welfare states have stayed within the OECD world minus the poorer European members. Eastern Europe is always left out. If we want to bring in an all-European perspective on social entitlements and welfare state organization, however, three dimensions appear to be of special importance.

First is the organization of services and transfers. This variable ranges from supply by the state to a publicly regulated and more or less publicly financed but privately provided system of insurance and services. The three most heavy-weight concrete areas of variation in this respect are primary education, health care and pensions. Education and health care may be organized as a public supply or as a largely private provision subsidized by public insurance. Pension systems may be overwhelmingly provided by public social insurance, or they may be regulated private schemes, with some public minimum. In Table 5.2, the main weight will be put on health care and, secondly, pensions. Taking education more into account would complicate the demarcation between 'public subsidy/insurance' and 'mixed'

Table 5.2 *The pattern of European welfare states, second half of the 1980s*

Country	Organization	Rights	Size
Denmark	State supply	Universal	Big
Sweden	State supply	Universal	Big
Finland	State supply	Universal	Medium
Norway	State supply	Universal	Medium
Czechoslovakia	State supply	Particular	Medium
E. Germany	State supply	Particular	Medium
Hungary	State supply	Particular	Medium
Bulgaria[a]	State supply	Particular	Small
Poland	State supply	Particular	Small
Romania	State supply	Particular	Small
USSR	State supply	Particular	Small
Yugoslavia	State supply	Particular	Small
UK	Mixed	Universal	Medium
Ireland	Mixed	Particular	Medium
Italy	Mixed	Particular	Medium
Belgium	Publ. subs./insur.	Particular	Big
France	Publ. subs./insur.	Particular	Big
Netherlands	Publ. subs./insur.	Particular	Big
Austria	Publ. subs./insur.	Particular	Medium
W. Germany	Publ. subs./insur.	Particular	Medium
Greece[a]	Publ. subs./insur.	Particular	Small
Portugal	Publ. subs./insur.	Particular	Small
Spain	Publ. subs./insur.	Particular	Small
Switzerland	Publ. subs./insur.	Particular	Small

Note: [a] Close to 20%, not significantly different in size from Switzerland or the UK, just above.

Sources: The organization and entitlements data are assembled from a number of sources, national and cross-national. The latter include, for the Western countries: Flora, *Growth to Limits*, 4 vols, 1986–; D.C.H.M. Pieters and J.L.M. Schell, *Inleiding tot Het Sociale Zekerheidsrecht van de landen van de Europese Gemeenschap*, Delft, Commissie Onderzoek Sociale Zekerheid and Ministerie van Sociale Zaken en Werkgelegenheid, 1990; OECD, *Health Care Systems in Transition*, Paris, 1990; OECD, *Reforming Public Pensions*, Paris, 1988; for Eastern Europe: *Jahrbuch für Ostrecht*, XXIII, 1–2 (1982); G. Winkler, 'Leistungen der Sozialversicherung europäischer sozialistischer Länder', East Berlin, Institut für Soziologie und Sozialpolitik der Akademie der Wissenschaften der DDR, unpublished paper, March 1988; K. von Beyme, *Ökonomie und Politik im Sozialismus*, Munich, Piper, 1975. The size data, which include education, are for the Western countries from 1985 and are gathered from OECD, *Social Expenditure Trends and Demographic Developments*, mimeographed paper for meeting of the Manpower and Social Affairs Committee, 6–8 July 1988, Table 1; Polish welfare state size is taken from A. Wiktorow and P. Mierzevski, 'Promise or Peril?' Social Policy for Children during the Transition to the Market Economy in Poland', in G.A. Cornia and S. Sipos (eds), *Children and the Transition to the Market Economy*, Aldershot, Avebury, 1991, p. 211; Yugoslavia is estimated from the ILO, *The Cost of Social Security*, Geneva, 1988, Table 2, and the USSR therefrom and from the figure for the Ukraine in the following source; for the rest of Eastern Europe, quantitative data are taken from Unicef, *Public Policy and Social Conditions*, no. 1, Florence, 1993, p. 76.

systems somewhat, but it would, on the other hand, make the specificity of the Nordic, and the ex-Communist, countries even stronger, as private education is marginal in the former.

A second dimension is the patterning of social entitlements. Here the poles are, on the one hand, universalistic rights, entitling all citizens or residents to social services and income security, specified mainly by their position in the human life-cycle only. The other alternative is particularism, with a set of rights specific to occupational and other special social groups that are more needy, such as the poor and the destitute, or more deserving, such as war veterans, for instance. Pension rights here are top of the agenda.

Finally, there is the dimension of size or generosity of services and income transfers. For practical purposes, we may divide the size variable into three main values: 'big', meaning social expenditure (including education) of about a third of GDP (or above 30%); 'medium', around a quarter (between 20 and 30%); and 'small', less than a fifth.

If we trichotomize the three dimensions, we get the pattern of European welfare states shown in Table 5.2: East and West, North and South.

At the top we find the Nordic countries, all organized by a predominant state supply of services and income maintenance and with universalistic rights.[36] At the bottom we have the countries with small relative entitlements, particularistic rights and, significantly, if not exclusively, relying on publicly subsidized and regulated private provisions of services and benefits, especially particularistic Switzerland and the three latest developed countries of Western Europe.

The ex-socialist countries differ from the Nordic countries, not in their previous public provision, in East–Central Europe in some respects less extensive than in Sweden, but, primarily, in their particularistic social entitlements, for farmers, groups of intellectuals, political veterans, etc.

Universalistic systems of rights are exceptions rather than the rule. And not even in the universalistic area is citizenship very important. In fact, it is primarily *denizens*, legitimate residents, rather than citizens, who have rights to social claims on the state. This holds generally for social insurance and for publicly provided social services. Social assistance, and sometimes unemployment benefits, are usually guarded with restricted length of residence requirements, but it is rare that citizenship counts at all with respect to social entitlements.[37] In the era of immigration into Europe as well as of substantial intra-European migration, this disjuncture of political citizenship and social entitlements is too important to be sacrificed out of reverence for T.H. Marshall. But, while keeping in mind the European centrality of the welfare state, we have to move on to the contested areas of rights to act.

Notes

1 See further, H. Berman, *Law and Revolution: The Formation of the Western Legal Tradition*, Cambridge, Mass., Harvard University Press, 1983.

2 In Anthony Giddens' conception of modernity, which includes 'surveillance', rights are conspicuously absent: A. Giddens, *The Consequences of Modernity*, Stanford, Stanford University Press, 1990, p. 59. On the other hand, the classical work of Emile Durkheim does contain a substantial discussion of law with an eye to rights as well: *De la division du travail social*, livre premier, Paris, Quadrige/PUF, 1990.

3 A major theoretical turn is James Coleman's *Foundations of Social Theory*, Cambridge, Mass., Belknap Press, 1990, Ch. 3. Cf. also J. Habermas, *Faktizität und Geltung*, Frankfurt, Suhrkamp, 1992; N. Luhmann, *Legitimation durch Verfahren*, Frankfurt, Suhrkamp, 1983; W. Gephart, *Gesellschaftstheorie und Recht*, Frankfurt, Suhrkamp, 1993; G. Teubner (ed.), *Dilemmas of Law in the Welfare State*, Berlin, de Gruyter, 1986; idem (ed.), *Juridification of Social Spheres*, Berlin, de Gruyter, 1987; B. Turner, 'Outline of a Theory of Human Rights', *Sociology* 27, 3 (1993).

4 W. Hohfeld, *Fundamental Legal Conceptions*, New Haven, Yale University Press, 1964; 1st posthumous edn, 1919. Cf. R. Martin, *A System of Rights*, Oxford, Clarendon Press, 1993, Ch. 2; Coleman, *Foundations*, p. 49.

5 T.H. Marshall, 'Citizenship and Social Class', in idem, *Class, Citizenship and Social Development*, Garden City, NY, Anchor Books, 1965. (Lecture delivered in 1949.)

6 See further Therborn, 'The Right to Vote and the Four World Routes to/through Modernity', in R. Torstendahl (ed.), *State Theory and State History*, London, Sage, 1992.

7 G. Therborn, 'The Politics of Childhood', in F. Castles (ed.), *Families of Nations*, Aldershot, Dartmouth, 1993, p. 251.

8 T. Hammar, *Democracy and the Nation State*, Aldershot, Avebury, 1990, Ch. 5; *Le Monde*, 11.5.1993, p. 9, 3.7.1993, p. 7; *Die Zeit*, 6.8.1993, pp. 9–10. Cf. also R. Brubaker (ed.), *Immigration and the Politics of Citizenship in Europe and North America*, New York, University Press of America and German Marshall Fund of the United States, 1989, and J. Hollifield, *Immigrants, Markets, and States*, Cambridge, Mass., Harvard University Press, 1992, Chs. 8–9; and the interesting Franco-German historical discussion, between Jeanne and Pierre-Patrick Kaltenbach and Rudolf von Thadden organized by *Le Monde*, 3.7.1993, p. 7.

9 Hammar, *Democracy*, p. 77. Naturalizations constituted 5.0% of the Swedish foreign population in 1987, 3.3% of the French, 3.2% of the Dutch, 3.0% of the US, 1.2% of the Swiss, 0.3% of the German and of the Belgian. *Le Monde*, 6.2. 1993, p. 13; 17.11. 1993, p. 10.

10 *Libération*, 27.11.1992, p. 29. Cf. SOPEMI, *Trends in International Migration*, Paris, p. 122.

11 Hammar, *Democracy*, p. 151.

12 Ibid., pp. 152, 171.

13 Salazarist Portugal did acknowledge the right to vote for an educated minority of Portuguese women, and Franco Spain for female 'heads of households', i.e. to adult women in households without an adult male, but deprived other women of the voting rights they had under the Republic in 1933–39. See further D. Sternberger and A. Vogel (eds), *Die Wahl der Parlamente und andere Staatsorgane*, Berlin, de Gruyter, 1969.

14 See further, G. Therborn, 'The Rule of Capital and the Rise of Democracy', *New Left Review* 103 (1977), pp. 55ff.

15 ILO, *The Cost of Social Security, 1949–1957*, Geneva, 1961, Table 3.

16 All figures in this paragraph are taken or calculated from ILO, *The Cost of Social Security: Twelfth International Inquiry*, Geneva 1988, Table 2. The data refer to benefits as shares of GDP.

17 A. Forrest, *The French Revolution and the Poor*, Oxford, Basil Blackwell, 1981.

18 T. Skocpol, *Protecting Soldiers and Mothers*, Cambridge, Mass., Belknap Press, 1992.

19 The literature on the welfare state has become enormous, particularly with regard to Northwestern Europe. A standard work is P. Flora (ed.), *Growth to Limits*, Berlin, de Gruyter, 1986–, 4 vols, of which three have appeared so far. Cf. G. Esping-Andersen, *The Three Worlds of Welfare Capitalism*, Cambridge, Polity Press, 1990.

20 Arbetarförsäkringskommittén, *Betänkande*, Stockholm, 1888, p. 48.

21 W. Vogel, *Bismarcks Arbeiterversicherung*, Brunswick, G. Westermann, 1951.

22 The development of the working-class conception of social security is traced and documented in G. Therborn, 'Classes and States: Welfare State Developments, 1881–

1981', *Studies in Political Economy* 13 (Spring 1984). (Reprinted in W. Clement and R. Mahon (eds), *Swedish Social Democracy: A Model in Transition*, Toronto, Canadian Scholars' Press, 1994.)

23 The best secondary source I have found is A. Belinsky, 'Sozialrecht der UdSSR', in *Jahrbuch für Ostrecht*, XXIII, 1–2 (1982). A. Wiktorow, 'Soviet Union', in J. Dixon and D. Macarov (eds), *Social Welfare in Socialist Countries*, London, Routledge, 1992, gives a brief but not very profound overview. I have found it useful to consult some general works on Soviet socio-economic history: E.H. Carr and R.W. Davies, *Foundations of a Planned Economy*, Vol. 1, Harmondsworth, Pelican, Ch. 22; M. Dobb, *Soviet Economic Development since 1917*, 6th edn, London, Routledge, 1966, pp. 487ff; B. Deacon et al., *The New Eastern Europe*, London, Sage, 1992.

24 See further, *Jahrbuch für Ostrecht*, 1982; Dixon and Macarov, *Social Welfare*; Z. Ferge, *A Society in the Making*, Harmondsworth, Penguin, 1979; M. Matey 'La situation du travailleur en cas de maladie en droit Polonais', in *International Society for Labour Law and Social Security, 9th Congress*, Vol. II/2, Heidelberg, Verlagsgesellschaft Recht und Wirtschaft, 1978.

25 D.C.H.M. Pieters and J.L.M. Schell, *Inleiding tot Het Sociale Zekerheidsrecht van de landen van de Europese Gemeenschap*, Delft, Commissie Onderzoek Sociale Zekerheid/Ministerie van Sociale Zaken en Werkgelegenheid, 1990; H.H. Hartwich, *Sozialstaatspostulat und gesellschaftlicher status quo*, 3rd edn, Cologne, Westdeutscher Verlag, 1978.

26 See further, T. Berben et al. 'Stelsels van sociale zekerheid: na-oorlogse regelingen in West-Europa', *Res Publica* XXVIII, 1 (1986).

27 Cf. P. Laroque (ed.), *Les institutions sociales de la France*, Paris, La Documentation Française, 1980 pp. 905ff; M. Ferrara, 'Italy', in P. Flora (ed.), *Growth to Limits*, Vol. 2, Berlin, de Gruyter, 1986, pp. 390ff.

28 Cf. J. Palme, *Pension Rights in Welfare Capitalism*, Stockholm, Swedish Institute for Social Research, 1990; O. Kangas, *The Politics of Social Rights: Studies on the Dimensions of Sickness Insurance in OECD Countries*, Stockholm, Swedish Institute for Social Research, 1991.

29 J.-P. Gutton, *Naissance du viellard*, Paris, Aubier, 1980, Ch. IX.

30 Pensions amounted in 1950 to about a third of a worker's wage in Denmark, to one-fifth in Finland and Sweden, to around a sixth in Norway. Benefit levels have been calculated by Joakim Palme, *Pension Rights*, pp. 56ff.

31 Calculations from OECD, *Financing and Delivering Health Care*, Paris, 1987, p. 90, and OECD, 'Social Expenditure Trends and Demographic Developments', Paper for the meeting of the OECD Manpower and Social Affairs Committee, 6–8 July 1988, Tables 1 and 3 (mimeographed).

32 Palme, *Pension Rights*, p. 49.

33 K. von Beyme, 'Vetgleichende Analyse von Politikfeldern in sozialistischen Ländern', in M. Schmidt (ed.), *Staatstätigkeit*, Opladen, Leske & Budrich, 1989, p. 379. The USSR figure is taken from Wiktorow, 'Soviet Union', p. 196, as it seems that von Beyme's figure of 33.7 refers to 1980. In 1985 an average Soviet pension was 38.4% of the average gross wage.

34 I have elaborated on and documented these points in another context: G. Therborn, 'Staten och människornas välfärd', in B. Furuhagen (ed.), *Utsikt mot Europa*, Stockholm, Utbildningsradion, 1991. Cf. F. Castles, 'Whatever Happened to the Communist Welfare States?', *Studies in Comparative Communism*, XIX, 3/4 (Autumn/Winter 1986).

35 *Statistisches Jahrbuch der DDR*, here extracted from L. Lipschitz and D. McDonald, *German Unification*, Washington, IMF Occasional Paper No. 75, 1990, p. 156.

36 There are, as always, some qualifications to the state supply organization in the Nordic countries. Finland, for example, has a publicly legislated but privately supplied system of occupational pensions, alongside a major public pension scheme.

37 This conclusion follows from Council of Europe, *Comparative Tables of Social Security Schemes*, 5th edn, Strasburg, 1992; Pieters and Schell, *Inleding*; and from S. Roberts and H. Bolderson, 'How Closed Are Welfare States?', unpublished paper, Brunel University, July 1993.

6

RIGHTS TO ACT – POLITICS, SEX AND PROPERTY

After World War II, Western Europe was the first part of the world to establish a supra-state system of rights, which differs from international, or inter-state law, as well as from international declarations of rights. In the first case, but not in the latter, individuals can judicially invoke rights against states. It was one stream of the postwar efforts at European unification, that which issued into the Council of Europe, of 1949. In the autumn of 1950 a European Convention for the Protection of Human Rights and Fundamental Freedoms was adopted. It was inspired by the UN Declaration of Human Rights two years earlier, but with the crucial difference that in Europe a judicial machinery was set up, turning a rhetoric of declaration into a set of rights, a Commission and Court of Human Rights. True, it took some time – the European Court of Human Rights was established only in 1959, and it took till 1974 before such a major Western European country as France ratified the Convention. The Council of Europe system of rights covers basic human rights, of life, liberty and the collective as well as individual pursuit of happiness (rights of speech, assembly and association as well as freedom of conscience and of religion). Torture and the death penalty (in peacetime) are prohibited, and the right to judicial review is upheld. Individuals have, and make use of, the right of appeal to the Commission for Human Rights and to the Court. In 1988 1,000 appeals were registered.[1]

The dictatorships of Western Europe have not been allowed into the Council of Europe, but when Greece was captured by a military junta in 1967 an intervention by the Scandinavian countries was needed to get the junta to withdraw from the Council, which it did two years later. The then military government of Turkey was also called to court in 1982, which led to an agreement in 1985 about a more humane treatment of prisoners. After the fall of Communism, the Eastern European states have applied for and most have been accepted into the Council of Europe.

Also important to the socio-political process in Europe has been a non-binding, and for long not well heeded all-European declaration on human rights, namely the Helsinki Declaration, so called because it was the Final Act of the Helsinki-based Conference on Security and Cooperation in Europe in August 1975. The Declaration was significant at least in the sense that it provided a reference point, in a language whose legitimacy was near indisputable for people in states where human rights were clearly severely restricted. Its seventh section, on respect for human rights and fundamental freedoms, including the freedom of thought, conscience, religion or belief, was the price the Eastern European regimes had to pay for a recognition of the Yalta system of borders. The Helsinki Declaration provided a platform for much of the core intellectual dissidence in the USSR, Czechoslovakia, Poland and other Eastern European countries. Although not a binding treaty, it involved a periodical review process, which preserved it in a somewhat more endurable form than the sand in which solemn declarations are usually written.[2]

The extent of repression, East and West

One of the best ways to study rights is to look at the extent of their violation. The postwar Communist regimes of Eastern Europe paid an uneven attention to the right to life and little to the rights to liberty and to happiness by free choice. The full-scale terror of the Stalinist USSR was nowhere imitated in Eastern Europe, neither directly through liquidation nor indirectly in the collectivization of agriculture, or through starving neglect. But the record was bad enough. After the Polish civil war in 1944–6, which took about 30,000 lives on both sides together, around 2,000 people were killed by various forms of repression.[3] In Czechoslovakia, in spite of the bloody feuding among the Communists themselves (e.g. the Slánsky trial) the number of people killed was much lower, less than 300.[4] Only the years to come will reveal the full extent of the Communist oppression in Eastern Europe.[5]

Political suppression and surveillance were no Communist speciality in postwar Europe, however.[6] Portugal and Spain were right-wing dictator-ships till the mid-1970s, and so, for most of this period, was Greece. Northern Ireland was till the 1970s an ethno-religious majority dictatorship. The Cold War involved massive surveillance also of Western European citizens, including hundreds of thousands spied upon in neutral countries such as Sweden and Switzerland, and the Norwegian Parliament was bugged by its Labour government, according to a retired Labour Party top official, Ronald Bye. Communists were frequently discriminated against and often fired from their jobs, but only in West Germany was their party banned, from 1956 till the second half of the 1970s. Outside Greece and Spain no Communist was executed in the West after World War II.

While the hard comparative evidence about the amount of surveillance is not yet in, we do already have some bases for comparing the amount of repression. Our approach will be strictly sociological, bracketing all moral questions of innocence and guilt, of crime or injustice.

It should be remembered that part of the Stalinist revolution in the East was an anti-Fascist purge, which occurred on a large scale also in Western

Europe. In France, for instance, about 100,000 people were sentenced after Liberation, and between 2,500 and 3,500 people were executed. In Norway 92,000 people, 3% of the total population, were charged, of whom about 40,000 were punished. In the Netherlands, dossiers were compiled for 5% of the population, 3% were charged, and in the end 64,000 people (0.7% of the population) were sentenced, but only 35 Dutch Nazis were executed. Belgium charged about 4% of its population, 340,000 persons, of whom 58,000 were sentenced, and 241 executed.[7]

To my knowledge there are not yet available any corresponding data from Eastern Europe. But some comparisons may be made with Hungary. It appears that the direct anti-Fascist purge in Hungary was more limited than in the West. Till March 1948 there were 31,000 cases of trial, of whom 19,000 were sentenced, and 146 executed. Eight thousand cases were still pending trial.[8] On the other hand, under the gruesome years of late Stalinism, from 1950 to 1953, it has been estimated that *in toto* 650,000 trials and 380,000 convictions took place, in cases of all kinds, but most of them for economic or political 'sabotage'.[9] If we assume that the numbers refer to persons and were counted once only, which is not certain, that would mean about 7% of the population charged and 4% convicted. In other words, the number of victims of the repression of the Rákosi regime at its worst corresponds roughly to the number of people charged (but not of those convicted) for Nazi crimes and collaboration after World War II in the small formerly occupied countries of Western Europe.

Perestroika opened the archives of the late Soviet Union, which for the first time has made possible a scholarly analysis of the Stalinist repression.[10] The total number of executions from 1930 to 1953 appears to have been 786,000, of whom 682,000 were killed in the purges of 1937–8. In other words, the total number of direct Stalinist killings – not counting people who died in the camps, i.e. 1.05 million from 1934 to 1953 – amounted to about 13% of the number of Jews killed by the Nazis, not counting other people killed off by the latter, such as Slavs, Gypsies, anti-Fascists generally. The executed victims of the 1937–8 Stalinist purge constituted about 3.5 promille of the Soviet population, whereas the French anti-Fascist purge after Liberation took the lives of about 0.06–0.09 promille of the population. If we include the French settlement of Fascist accounts from 1944 to 1947, it seems that slightly less than 0.3 promille perished, about one-twelfth of the Soviet *Yezhovchina*.

By the death of Stalin, the Gulag and the labour colonies population amounted to about 2.5 million, to which number should be added about 300,000[11] prison inmates. That yields a total of 1.6 per cent of the population (in 1950). In Western, post-Fascist Europe there is no remote equivalent, but in the current USA there is. The custodial population of the USSR in 1953 was about equal to the proportion incarcerated among the Black population in the United States in 1990. Then 3.4% of the male Black population were in jail.[12]

Calculated on the basis of the total population, post-Stalinist Eastern Europe continued to have a larger custodial population than the West till the late 1980s. Then the USA overtook the USSR in the relative size of its population in jail – 426 per 100,000 in 1989 compared to 353 – and Poland became similar to Canada, at 107 and 111 per 100,000, respectively, while the UK led the Western European league of incarceration, at 90 per 100,000. Already in 1979, the Hungarian prison population was, in relative terms, only about half the US one.[13]

European jurisprudence

European law and the jurisprudence developed by the European Court of Justice are primarily concerned with rights to act, in particular of enterprises and of states in relation to enterprises. This kind of institutionalizing of a market, of embedding contracts in non-contractual elements, has been a classical perspective of sociology since the time of Emile Durkheim, a century ago. We shall return to the role of law in the process of Western European unification in the chapter on social steering. Here, however, we shall focus on the rights of genders and classes.

The structuration of rights to act is one very important feature of class as well as of gender relations. For the empirical comparativist, rights also offer the practical advantage of being more accessible and more manageable for systematization than many other aspects of social relations. Rights are, of course, no reliable proxy for, say, the division of labour or the distribution of means, but the latter we have paid attention to in other chapters. Legal rights are 'social facts', as Emile Durkheim would say, and as such of prime sociological concern.

There are at least two significant methodological problems involved in a comparative sociology of rights. One is how to cope with the different 'styles' of law. In the case of Europe, this is above all a question of the difference between the English common law and the civil law of the continent. The latter operates directly as a normative code, easily amenable to textual analysis. The former is largely implicit, indicated by procedural remedies more than by explicit rights, reversing the continental maxim of *ubi jus ibi remedium* into *ubi remedium ibi jus*.[14] While any serious student of law will distinguish the law of the books from the law of courts, taking notice of court practice, common law has to a large extent to be studied through court decisions. Below, I try to take the specificity of common law into account.

The second problem derives from possible national differences in the distance between legal rights and socially operative rights. With regard to postwar European family, property and labour law, the conclusion of this study has been that those differences are, with a few exceptions, negligible. That is, for the purposes of the comparisons made here.

Rights of women and patterns of patriarchy

Since time immemorial the lives of men and women have been vastly different. Gendered life-courses are still governing social life on the European as well as on other continents. But the post-World War II period has seen a very significant drooping of the ancient erection of male supremacy.

By World War II, the night of patriarchy was still engulfing Europe. In all Latin Europe, in the Balkans and in Switzerland, as we noted in the previous chapter, women were singled out politically as humans unfit to have a say in public affairs (to vote). In all Europe, except the Nordic countries and the USSR, male supremacy in marriage and parenthood was the official norm, backed up by family legislation.[15] Employers' rights to fire women upon marriage were valid everywhere save the USSR and, from 1939, Sweden.

In comparison with the rule of non-European civilizations, modern European women had more rights and freedoms. On the other hand, since colonial times Anglo-America had been ahead of Europe in individualizing social relations from the rule of the father/husband, and in creating, in the mid-nineteenth century, a women's movement. The French revolutions of 1789 and 1848 did not alter that, in spite of some brave attempts.[16]

In the course of the 1920s, the English Law Lords came to the conclusion that women were 'persons', first denied in 1923 when Lady Rhondda was denied a seat in the House of Lords, but then affirmed in 1929, when the Privy Council in London upheld that the Governor-General of Canada had the right to appoint women to the Canadian Senate.[17]

Wives and husbands

The pace-setting European family regulation by the French *Code Napoléon* (of 1804) was emancipatory in some respects – with regard to maturity, inheritance and divorce – but also repressive in other ways. The latter held particularly to the internal governance of the family, putting all powers into the hands of the husband and admonishing (§213) the wife to 'obedience'. In 1938 the Popular Front-dominated National Assembly replaced the obedience obligation with another formulation of male superiority: 'The husband is the head of the family.'[18]

The complexity of gender relations is difficult to grasp in a systematic, comparative way, comparative in both time and space. Law, however, offers a handle on the sets of values, norms and practices. The former is certainly not synonymous with the latter, but if we take the different styles of law and the different roles of the courts into account, we should be able to assume that the pattern of legal variation may stand as a proxy for the pattern of structuring gender relations.

European family law had by the last turn of the century developed *four conceptions of patriarchy*: two traditional and two modern. One form of traditional patriarchy derived directly and without mediation from Church law, as such strongly patriarchal. Another traditional conception was expressed in secular law, deriving from traditional male guardianship etc., prerogatives generally in process of erosion since the mid-nineteenth century. Modern patriarchy leant upon the legacy of the Enlightenment and constituted elaborate legal formulations of modernity. Within modern patriarchy we may distinguish two major types: one extreme of explicit declarations of male (husband/father) power and superiority, and one moderate, expressing norms of conjugal and parental partnership but legally giving the husband the decisive vote in cases of family disagreements. That legacy of the 1900s has largely shaped the development of family and gender relations in the twentieth century (see Table 6.1).

Table 6.1 *Forms of legal patriarchy in the early twentieth century (before 1914)*

Defined by legal and judicial stipulations of husband–wife and/or father–mother relations.[a]

Traditional		Modern	
Church law	Secular law	Moderate	Extreme
Albania[b]	British Isles[c]	Germany	Austria[d]
Bulgaria	Denmark	Hungary[e]	Belgium
Greece	Finland	Netherlands	France
Russia[f]	Norway	Switzerland	Italy
Serbia	Sweden		Portugal
			Romania
			Spain

Notes: [a] For definitions of the categories, see the text. [b] For the Muslim majority this was law according to the Hanefite school, i.e. the law of the Ottoman Empire. There was also local customary law, and the country was not yet legally unified. [c] UK and Ireland. [d] In terms of marriage the Austrian civil code while valid for all citizens was also religiously specified. [e] Alongside the new Marriage Act of 1894, traditional customary law, compiled in 1517, was also operative. [f] In a multiconfessional empire, Church law meant that family relations were governed by the stipulations of each religion.

Sources: A. Bergmann, *Internationales Ehe- und Kindschaftsrecht*, Vol. II, 1st edn, Berlin, Verlag des Reichsbundes der Standesbeamten Deutschlands, 1926; E. Loewenfeld and W. Lauterbach (eds), *Das Eherecht der europäischen und der aussereuropäischen Staaten*, Cologne, Carl Hegmann, 1963–72. See further G. Therborn, 'The Politics of Childhood', in F. Castles (ed.), *Families of Nations*, Aldershot, Dartmouth, 1993.

The pattern of official patriarchy is one of law and religion. Ecclesiastical law ruled in the Orthodox countries, with other religious jurisdictions coexisting in multireligious Russia. The traditional secular countries are the Protestant ones – the Nordic countries and the UK. The British Isles (excluding Scotland) has common law, the Nordic nations a distinctive variant of their own of continental civil law, the one least affected by the Roman inheritance.[19] To the right are the Catholic countries, but also the countries of pioneering legal modernity, France (1804) and Austria (1811).

The French Civil Code had a very important influence over Belgian, Italian, Luxemburgian, Portuguese, Romanian and Spanish civil law.

The three other Germanic civil law countries are all religiously rather evenly divided – currently with Catholic pluralities,[20] at the time of Table 6.1 with a politically dominant Protestantism – with their own legal traditions, and with turn of the century key formulations of family law. Germany received a new Civil Code in 1896, Switzerland in 1907, and the previously Napoleon-influenced Dutch put up a new piece of family legislation in 1901. Legal styles – the proneness to general normative admonitions in continental law – and legal temporality – the stamping of Napoleonic and Austrian legal thought in the generally more patriarchal mode of early modernity – have here had their impact, alongside religion.

The Catholic–Protestant divide is probably not theological to any great extent. Patriarchy has been prominent in Protestantism, and in the Netherlands the current most hostile to female rights was the orthodox Calvinist one, organized in the Anti-Revolutionary Party (so called because they were against the French Revolution, as well as, of course, all subsequent ones).[21] Crucial instead was the resilience of traditional religious tenets and of ecclesiastical authority. The Papacy ensured both in the Catholic world, and by 1900 patriarchy had been given a major boost by the encyclical *Rerum novarum* of 1891, otherwise best known for its social concerns, with its exultation of the power of the father. The bureaucratized, nation-state-attached Anglican, Lutheran and mainstream Dutch Calvinist (Hervormde) churches, on the other hand, were beginning to lose their grip on the population, while internally eroding in fundamentalist commitment.

In the second half of the nineteenth century, the rights of women began to expand, with regard to married women's rights, e.g. to property, and with regard to women's right to education, for example. The legally egalitarian family arrived in three big, widely staggered waves in Europe, one coming in the wake of World War I, the second following upon the next World War, and the third after '1968', i.e. the upheavals of the second half of the 1960s.

European marital egalitarianism after World War I was concentrated in the Nordic countries, from Finland to Iceland, and the Soviet Union. The new Eastern European states south of the Gulf of Finland were more cautious. The Baltic republics concentrated on undoing the previous confessional regulation, replacing it with a national one, valid for all Estonians/Latvians/ Lithuanians. Apart from this, the previous 'Livonian–Estonian–Kurlandish Private Law' was maintained in Estonia and (till 1937) in Latvia, with its modern moderate patriarchy, giving (in §197 in the revised Estonian law) the father the decisive vote in a communitarian family.[22]

In 1937 Latvia adopted a Civil Code of its own, §85 of which expressed male superiority in a peculiarly contorted way: 'In the regulation of their family life both spouses have the same rights. If they cannot agree, the vote of the husband decides; he decides among other things the domicile. The wife does not have to follow the arrangements of her husband, if he misuses his rights.'[23] Within the constitutional guarantees of religious freedom, interwar Lithuania kept the patriarchal religious marriage laws of Czarist Russia and of Congress Poland, plus German law in the Memel/Klaipeda area.[24]

Poland did not overcome the legal consequences of eighteenth-century partition before the new war. In western Poland, Poznan, Silesia, the German Civil Code of 1896 remained, with its modern moderate patriarchy. Southern Galicia (Crakow, Lvov) followed the older, more extreme Austrian Code, and central and eastern Poland (Warsaw, Lodz, Lublin) married according to confessional, canon or Mosaic, law. There were also areas in which the *Code Napoléon* was still venerated.[25]

The new Czechoslovak family legislation of 1919 was mainly concerned with securing the option between a secular and religious marriage. In the Czech lands of Austrian legislation this meant a secularization, while in Slovakia it meant a strengthening of the position of the Church in comparison with the Hungarian civil Marriage Act of 1894.[26]

The short-lived Hungarian Soviet Republic introduced secular and egalitarian family legislation, but it was immediately undone by the victorious counterrevolution. Yugoslavia was not legally united before World War II. Orthodox Church law governed Serbian and Montenegrin family relations. Croatia and Slovenia followed a confessional conception of the Austrian Civil Code, and Voivodina the Hungarian Marriage Act of 1894. Muslim citizens had their Shari'a law officially recognized. Romania's new possessions kept their own laws till 1943. That is, Transylvania and Bukovina had the Austrian Civil Code, and Bessarabia (current Moldavia) followed old Russian law, albeit without ecclesiastical jurisdiction. Albania received a Civil Code in 1928. In all these countries, patriarchy remained officially, legally endorsed.[27]

There have been three major forces of legal gender equality, and three historical waves of modern advance (see Table 6.2). One force was legal enlightenment, strongest in secularized Protestant milieux, and first successful in Scandinavia, but reaching out also to Japan via the US occupation army. The second was Marxism, which alone explains the vanguard role of Eastern Europe with regard to women's rights. The third is made up of feminist and pro-feminist movements, of major significance mainly since the late 1960s, although also present, active and influential in the nineteenth and early twentieth century in at least reining in unbridled patriarchy.

The crest of the first wave was Nordic and Bolshevik, and came out of a coordinated effort of Nordic jurists and of the October Revolution. First out were the Swedes, with their 1915 Marriage Act, followed by the Russian revolutionaries in 1918. The last were the Finns with theirs in 1929. The Nordic countries and the USSR took the torch of women's legal emancipation from the United States. In the latter, legal marriage equality was established in the majority of the (then) forty-eight states in the 1920s, but some, such as Ohio, kept their patriarchal codes well into the 1970s.[28]

After the Nordic reforms and the Bolshevik Revolution there was a long silence, and the end of World War II brought surprisingly little change in

Table 6.2 *The timing of legal equality between wife and husband*

First wave	Second wave		Third wave	
By 1929	By 1950	By 1960	By 1975	By 1985
Denmark	Albania	W. Germany	Austria	Belgium
Finland	Bulgaria		France	Greece
Iceland	Czechoslovakia		Ireland	Luxemburg
Norway	E. Germany		Italy	Netherlands
Sweden	Hungary		UK[a]	Portugal
(UK)[a]	Poland			Spain
USSR	Romania			Switzerland
	Yugoslavia			
USA[b]				Argentina
	Japan			

Note: [a] After the old male–female superordination had eroded, in divorce regulations in the 1920s, British common law neither proscribed nor prescribed marriage equality. Central judicial opinion seems to have harboured public anti-egalitarian opinions till the 1960s. [b] Most American states.

Sources: A. Bergmann, *Internationales Ehe- und Kindschaftsrecht*, Vol. I, 2nd edn, Berlin, Verlag für Standeswesen, 1938; A. Bergmann and M. Ferid (eds), *Internationales Ehe- und Kindschaftsrecht*, Frankfurt, Verlag für Standeswesen, 1955–, various vols; Loewenfeld and Lauterbach, *Das Eherecht*; I. Blom and A. Traberg (eds), *Nordisk lovoversikt*, Copenhagen, Nordisk Ministerråd, 1985; plus national legal sources and law commentaries, listed in Therborn, 'The Politics of Childhood'.

family and other legislations, except where Soviet and US power were decisive i.e. in the Soviet sphere of influence, in US-occupied Japan and in West Germany, after a decade's delay. The Eastern European Communists tolled the bell of legal patriarchy as soon as they had a rope to hang on. In Bulgaria, for instance, the equality of the sexes was proclaimed in October 1944.[29]

The postwar set-up of the German Federal Republic involved a new constitution, with a general equality clause, and a US-imported Constitutional Court. The former did not lead directly to any egalitarian family law, nor to legal gender equality outside the family,[30] but the latter did. In 1953 the misogynous legislation expired constitutionally, an event underlined by the Constitutional Court. But not before 1957 could the right-wing parliamentary majority bring itself to issue an 'Equal Rights Act' (*Gleichberechtigungsgesetz*) of family law. In 1959 the Constitutional Court declared it unconstitutional, because of the 'decisive vote' (*Stichentscheid*) still allotted to the husband. Only then was legal gender equality brought about in the Federal Republic.[31]

The equality clauses of the postwar French and Italian Constitutions, the Preamble of the 1946 and 1958 French ones and §3 of the Italian Constitution of 1947,[32] seem to have had no impact on official family norms.

The Napoleonic male 'head of the family' doctrine kept married women from exercising adult rights to act until the 1970s, in the Netherlands till

1956.[33] The French High Court of Appeal (Cour de Cassation) upheld in 1962 the right of a husband to prohibit his wife to practise a profession, and denied in 1969 the right of the wife of an adulterous husband, a wife who had been denied a divorce, to set up a separate domicile.[34] In 1970, the French government presented a bill to introduce into France, as a mitigation of the 'chef de famille'-clause, the male decisive vote formula, which the German Constitutional Court had rejected eleven years earlier. But this time Parliament reacted, rejected the bill, and instituted legal equality instead.[35] Italy, meanwhile, received an egalitarian family law only in 1975.

Ireland, which as an independent state grafted canon law and Catholic patriarchy onto its common law tradition, did away with legal inequality within marriage in a set of laws between 1957 and 1965. Its early mainstream position is somewhat bogus, however, since the country scrapped a regulation firing all women from public service upon marriage only after entry into the EC and upon the insistence of the EC Commission.[36]

The rearguard is made up of Greece, which Papandreou's Pasok government gave an egalitarian Civil Code in 1983; of the Netherlands, where the ultimate formal power of the husband and father, which had survived substantive alterations of the family law in 1969, was in the end discreetly discarded in August 1984; and of Switzerland, where in 1984 a major francophone (Protestant) contribution at long last tipped the referendum in favour of husband–wife equality.[37]

Married persons' rights to act also include rights to divorce. Originally severely restricted, for religious reasons, within Christianity – in particular within Catholicism, to which marriage is not, as Luther argued, 'a worldly thing' but a holy sacrament – divorce rights have been extended in the course of the twentieth century. In Western Europe, outside Scandinavia, the 1970s constituted a key period, widely allowing rights to divorce without having to prove a partner is at fault.[38]

Issues of discrimination and harassment

Gender equality and the disadvantaged position of women again became a major issue of modern societies with the social upheavals of the late 1960s. Like nineteenth-century feminists, the European women's movement of the last third of the twentieth century was originally much inspired by American thought and practice. The 1970s were also the years when gender discrimination generally was becoming socially indecent, or at least illegal. In that decade there was a spate of legislation explicitly directed against gender discrimination. In the United States the process had started somewhat earlier, with the Equal Pay Act of 1963 and the last-minute addition of sex to the anti-discrimination list of the 1964 Civil Rights Act.[39]

I shall not list the national variants here. However, the gender issue was institutionalized in the new mechanisms of European integration from their very beginning. Equal pay for the same work, whether done by men or by women, entered into (§119 of) the 1957 Treaty of Rome, because of French fears of German lower labour costs due to more far-reaching sexism, not because of any universalist French feminism.[40] Nevertheless, gender relations has been an area of persistent EC intervention. The most important effects have not been on pay[41] – which is very difficult to steer by legal interventions as a lot of factors and considerations weigh upon actual pay, and may protect going pay rates from legal steering – but in entitlements, to work, job security, social benefits.[42]

The centrepieces were the EC Directives (75/117) about equal pay – underlining the need as well as the obligation to take seriously §119 of the Treaty of Rome, formally in effect from 1962, and the ILO Convention no. 100 of 1951 – and, above all, 'the third directive' (76/207) of equal treatment of men and women, bearing primarily upon employment and social security rights. In the mid-1980s, I had the privilege of observing from the gallery how this directive forced a reluctant Christian Democratic–Liberal Dutch government to change its social entitlements.

In the East, Comecon was not concerned with gender rights, and as far as I have been able to discern, Eastern Europe saw no significant alteration of gender rights in this period. In the 1970s, natalist population policies constituted the main political output bearing on gender relations in the region. The early advance of these countries is no acceptable explanation, as the even earlier Scandinavian pioneers extended their equalization of gender rights and their commitment to actual gender equality considerably in this period.[43]

So far, we have dealt with legal gender rights. With regard to them, there has been a clear, historically outstanding tendency towards an equalization of rights, and in the case of divorce an extension of individual rights. But relations between men and women may also be looked at from a more explicitly sexual perspective. Two angles appear particularly pertinent here. One is women's rights to *sex*, in particular to non-marital sex.[44] The other is a restriction of men's rights to sexual assault, or, alternatively put, an affirmation of women's rights to say no, even to a husband or to a date. In both cases, the outgoing twentieth century has seen important changes.

It is noteworthy that the two sexual rights of women, to say *yes* and to say no, seem to correlate, and that Nordic countries, Sweden above all, have been among pioneers with regard to both. The new Swedish Criminal Code of 1962 did away with the assumption that rape could only take place outside marriage and put all contexts of sexual assault on the same footing. The legally pertinent background materials of the Code also made clear that the conduct of the woman prior to the rape was legally irrelevant.[45] Thirty years later, this unqualified criminalization of sexual assault still seems to be an exception in continental law.[46]

Common law has, of course, also held that marital rape is inconceivable.[47] In 1991 judicial opinion changed in England, however. A Court of Appeal upheld a (deserted) married man's sentence for rape of his wife, and the Law Commission presented a draft bill for abolishing the marital exemption from rape.[48]

In the 1970s sexual violence came out of the family closet. The London Chiswick Women's Aid for Battered Women opened in 1971, and became a European vanguard of protest.[49] The English Domestic Violence and Matrimonial Proceedings Act of 1976 brought domestic violence into the legal limelight. In Scandinavia, wife-battering was brought under 'public prosecution', i.e. became liable to prosecution even without the wife making a legal complaint.[50]

Sexual harassment became visible and punishable about a decade later than discrimination and violence. Again, the USA made up the vanguard, more concretely the Federal courts of appeal, which in 1977 and in 1981 ruled that sexual harassment was sex discrimination and thereby an offence under the Civil Rights Act. While all the Anglo-Saxon New World soon followed suit in explicitly, by law or by judicial decision, making sexual harassment an offence, not all European countries have done so. By 1991, Belgium, France, Ireland, Spain, Sweden, Switzerland and the UK had. Belgium and Sweden have legislated on affirmative action, on sex and gender relations, as well.[51]

De facto gender disadvantages, discrimination and sexual harassment never became officially recognized issues in Communist Europe, although a few Feminist voices were raised in the very last years. Late Communist officialdom had a strong smell of male sexism, clearly noticeable even to the occasional Eastern traveller. A considerable amount of anecdotal evidence indicates also a significant amount of sexual exploitation and harassment from Soviet males in authority, including universities and research institutes.

Rights of property and labour rights

Methods for systematizing and for comparing cross-nationally capital–labour or state–labour relations are still not developed enough to provide us with any ready-made handle, not to speak of comparing capital–labour with state–labour relations.[52] The interwoven social relations of property, of workplace organization, the distribution of knowledge and skills, accumulation patterns, collective interest organization – what in English is generally known as 'industrial relations' – labour law and labour markets are usually carved up between different disciplines and networks of specialists.

Capitalism has never been of one piece, and penetrating comparative analyses of different variants began before the waning of explicitly socialist alternatives. However, a masterly work such as Andrew Shonfield's *Modern Capitalism*[53] did not galvanize a comparative research industry. And in particular, the field of capital–labour and capital–society relations has largely been left in the dark between bright illuminations of business–government relations[54] and of industrial relations.[55] With regard to capital–labour, capital–society relations, we still have to grope for analytical dimensions and for their available indicators.[56] Comparative state–labour relations under socialist regimes are in an even more embryonic stage of study, largely due to their limited accessibility under Communist rule.[57]

The problematic of capital–labour/state–labour relations may be approached from either side of the relation. From the capital/state side we may look at the *extension* and the *absoluteness of property*. The two dimensions can vary freely against each other. Narrowly circumscribed or wide-ranging property may both be either absolute or severely qualified. On a high level of generality, we may say that the three poles of contemporary high capitalism exhibit three different such combinations. Private property is most extensive and absolute in the USA, whereas it is considerably less both in extension and absoluteness in Western Europe. In Japan, private property is also very extensive, but much less absolute than in the USA.[58] The limits of private absolutism are not only labour rights, however, but appear also in the form of awards conferred upon core employees of big enterprise.[59]

Command rights and livelihood rights

In this section we shall focus on the *absoluteness of property*. Generally speaking, the absoluteness of property refers to the degree to which the owner of something can freely use it, draw benefit from it, and dispose of it. Capitalism will have reached its moment of maximum triumph when all social phenomena can be appropriated as private property, and when the power of the proprietor is unlimited, which would mean that everything in the social world can be bought and sold, or discarded by its owner. Then everything social will be subject to *commodification*. That is, to paraphrase Oscar Wilde, everything will have a price, and nothing any intrinsic value.

The corresponding absoluteness of statism – since most socialist projects have had the goal of (ultimately) abolishing the state, it would be improper to call absolute state property 'socialist' – may be called, in modern times, *politicization*. All social phenomena can be appropriated and disposed of by the rulers of the state, for their political goals.

Both commodification (as a dimension of property) and politicization may contain arbitrary proprietal despotism or squandering,[60] as well as systemic rationality. The absoluteness of capitalist property is cut into whenever any benefit can be got from the owner without profitable exchange or payment. That of state property whenever anything can be got without political exchange or payment.

A modern market enterprise may be either a bundle of commodities, i.e. of assets, activities and products to be bought and sold, or an organization carrying out certain tasks. The poles are ideal types, and actually existing capitalist enterprise tends to contain aspects of both, but in visibly different doses. A commodified enterprise can be freely purchased, disposed of, carved up, and closed down, even against the wishes of everyone active in it. The key actor on the enterprise commodity market, 'the corporate raider', became a prominent figure in the USA in the 1980s. Enterprise commodification in this sense is, so far, primarily an American and possibly an Anglo-

Saxon variant of capitalist relations. On the European continent, there are a number of vested rights restricting it, from extensive family ownership to trade union rights. In Central and Northern Europe social rights and considerations of various sorts are more important, further south the barriers to enterprise commodification are more familistic.[61]

The activity of market enterprise may also be either a commodity of capital accumulation or the carrying out of certain social tasks. Michel Albert, himself an insurance executive, presents a stark contrast between commodi-fied Anglo-Saxon insurance and what he calls the 'Alpine model', to be found in Switzerland, Austria, Germany and Italy. In the latter case insurance is viewed as a mutuality between insurer and insuree. There is one automobile insurance tariff, and the activities of the insurance companies are normatively regulated. The insurance business is private property under competition, but property rights are severely circumscribed.[62] The informal relations between the state and big business in Japan and in the heyday of Social Democratic Sweden represent other examples of a certain de-commodification of enterprise activity.

The managers' questionnaires of Hampden-Turner and Trompenaars, whatever their representativeness, show a clear difference between Ameri-can and continental European managers with regard to their view of profit as the only goal of corporations. Britons and Canadians were in the middle, while the Japanese were the least single-minded of all with regard to profit.[63]

A job in an enterprise on the market (or in any other kind of organization) may be either a pure instrument of the enterprise owner, or, at the other end, an entitlement of the job-holder. The latter case emerged in the public service, but bits and pieces of it have spread into capitalist enterprise, even within the United States. In the mid-1960s the 'ownership of jobs' became the subject of a book-length study.[64] In the course of the 1970s, beginning with the Italian Workers' Statute of 1970, a spurt of labour legislation and basic collective agreements extended job rights in Europe. In the ensuing decade, however, job entitlements became the target of 'flexibility' campaigns.[65]

Legally, the power of property may be restricted by claim rights[66] of non-owners, of workers, of citizens. Sociologically, the power relations between labour, on one hand, and capital or the state, on the other, also depend on their relative economic capacities.

From our chosen perspective, of class upon rights, the intersection between the *command rights of property* and the *livelihood rights of labour* is the focus of analysis, not the institution of property *per se*, nor the general status of labour, which contains many other aspects, in part treated elsewhere in this book. While easily conflictual, it should be noticed that the one is not simply the reverse of the other. They do refer to two different dimensions of class relations. The command rights of property comprise above all the owners' rights to determine how their enterprises are run and to direct their employees, once employed and while employed. Against the command rights of property have been posed rights of working cooperation, e.g. rights of information, consultation, bargaining, of co-determination, or to respectful treatment (non-harassment, non-discrimination).

Labour rights to livelihood involve, first of all, access to jobs and safety and security of employment, given the modern division of property-owners and propertyless. This refers to the regulations and practices of hiring and firing. The parallel with the women's issue in common law should be noted. Labour rights concern whether workers are persons or just 'production factors', whether commodities in capitalism or physical inputs in authoritarian planning.

The centrality of class within European modernity has put the rights of property and of labour at the centre of the agenda of domestic conflict and policy. However, class rights do not constitute a corpus of academic research. What we are interested in in this chapter will therefore have to be excavated from three different kinds of sources: from labour law, which also deals with the relevant property rights; from the study of 'industrial relations' as it is called in the English-speaking world, i.e. studies of collective labour and employer relations drawn from disciplines of history, political science, sociology or some other discipline; and from comparative studies of organization and management, pertinent to the actual operation of property rights.

The 'rights' we are concerned with are in fact of three, possibly four, sorts. One is, of course, substantive legal rights. They seem to have developed most extensively in the civil law countries where guild traditions were carried over into industrial capitalism – the Germanic countries of central Western Europe, Iberia and Italy[67] – and/or where and when weak unions had powerful political friends, such as in Greece and in France in the first half of the 1980s.

Anglo-Saxon common law, also spilling over into Ireland, rather than declaring positive rights has largely taken another road. Instead, labour law has largely developed as legal 'immunities' of workers' actions from the torts according to contract and property rights.[68] On the whole, that was the way in which labour's rights of collective organization in the interests of their livelihood emerged. That is, not as rights to form trade unions, but as immunities from sanctions against economic interest associations.[69]

Thirdly, besides legal rights and immunities, there are rights by collective agreement, the importance of which reflects the autonomy and relative power of class organizations. The forerunner here was Denmark, where 'the September Compromise' of 1899 between the confederated unions and the central employers' association provided the constitution of the twentieth-century Danish labour market. Backed up by Parliament, the collective agreement further gave rise, in 1910, to a 'Permanent Arbitration Court' ('faste voldgiftsret'), consisting of two representatives each of the unions and of the employers plus an independent jurist.[70] In the 1930s, Norway, Switzerland and Sweden followed suit in settling basic labour rights of organization, bargaining and due process by collective agreement.

Finally, there are the implicit, *de facto* rights and immunities, to which we shall also pay attention as far as they are discernible. An important immunity in a non-juridical sense is immunity from 'employer law liability', i.e. from unemployment and misery. In capitalist countries, in spite of the rhetoric of some constitutions and of progressive politicians, there is no right to work in any strict sense. But what developed in major parts of postwar Western Europe for a considerable amount of time was an immunity from unemployment, in some countries politically institutionalized, with the rise of relatively stable full employment economies.

The postwar rise of labour

At the start of our story important labour movements with *de facto* rights of association and of collective bargaining existed only in the northwestern corner of Europe: in the British Isles, in the Low Countries – although some major enterprises like Philips still successfully refused to bargain – in Switzerland, and in Scandinavia. The once powerful German and Austrian movements had been smashed by the Nazis, and labour relations had increasingly been geared to mobilization for war. The victors over the labour movement were also ruling in Italy, and in Iberia. French employers had explicitly rescinded the 1936 agreement with labour and opted for open confrontation. In the 'Successor States' – following upon the fallen Romanov and Habsburg empires – from Finland to Hungary unions usually existed but were weak and isolated and as a rule, except in the Czech lands, without any possibility of collective bargaining. In the Balkans the ghettoization of what here may well be called by the American term 'organized labour' was even worse. In the USSR the workers who made the October Revolution were largely killed off in the Civil and Intervention Wars, and an iron-fisted accumulation drive to turn peasants into industrial workers accelerated in the 1930s.[71]

On the eve of World War II, the command rights of property were hardly restrained anywhere, neither in the Stalinist management of the USSR nor in Western capitalism. At the end of World War I, challenges had been mounted East, West and Centre by shop stewards and by workers' councils, but almost everywhere a 'return to normalcy' had soon set in. The threat of social revolution in Central Europe had left an important institutional legacy of some (modest) co-determination rights in Austria (the Works Councils Act of 1919) and Germany (the Works Councils Act of 1920), but the revolutionary ebb, the Depression and the victory of Fascism had explicitly restored the 'Führer Principle' in the running of enterprises.

While local considerations might be wisely taken, owners and their representatives reigned supreme. Beneath the institutional carapace and/or the crust of decisive power, reality was, of course, not quite the same. Skilled workers could hardly be bossed around at will outside times of depression, particularly not in Britain and in Scandinavia. But the rights workers might have had tended to be reactive and defensive, 'restrictive practices' as their enemies called them. The exclusive managerial prerogatives of ownership were still institutionalized, East and West, North and South.

With regard to workers' livelihood rights, on the other hand, important changes had already occurred. On the eve of World War I, the employer's liability for job safety, either directly or indirectly through public accident insurance, had been established across virtually all Europe, laggards such as Bulgaria and Spain following very soon after the war.[72] The eight-hour day conquered industrial Europe after World War I, and paid vacation for workers had been introduced in some countries as a legal right, in Western and Central Europe first in Norway (in 1919) and then in Poland (in 1922).[73]

Where trade union and collective bargaining rights were not recognized, they sometimes had their 'functional alternatives' with respect to livelihood rights. The 'corporatist' doctrine of the Fascist countries, from Germany to Portugal, had led to an institutionalization of employers' socio-economic responsibility. Stalinist USSR, which had abolished the right to labour mobility, for its part, did provide an effective right to a job.

Set against this sombre background the advances of labour during the three or four decades after 1945 were very significant, and constituted an important aspect of postwar sociological history. It would not be off the mark to characterize postwar developments in terms of *the rise of the working class*. In Eastern Europe it was proclaimed the 'ruling class', something which at least a cultural sociologist, or a cultural historian – both in high current esteem – should take very seriously, though not necessarily *ad notam*.[74]

With much less pomp something similar was clearly taking place in the classical vanguard of European modernity, Britain, in the second half of the 1940s. In peripheral but rich Sweden and Norway what proudly called itself 'the workers' movement' was hegemonic in party politics till the 1970s, and has remained a very significant force ever since. In Austria, it has had the upper hand in a consensual polity since 1970. In more diluted forms, (West) Germany, France, Belgium, Finland, the Netherlands, Spain, Portugal and Greece for the first time in their history had consolidated governments, in which the dominant force claimed to represent, above anybody else, the working class. East and West, both claims had to adapt to hostile external economic constraint, and both had largely to rely on the class representativity of the political government.

Beleaguered and/or short-lived labour governments had emerged in the interwar period, but only in the Scandinavian countries did they achieve any measure of stability and recognized legitimacy. Before World War II the rise of the Soviet Union, 'the workers' fatherland', did of course, justly or injustly, have a considerable international impact, one comparable only to the French Revolution. But before Stalingrad the USSR was even more beleaguered and disdained by 'respectable' opinion than the Western labour governments, and among the working-class it was a hotly divisive issue between Communist believers and Social Democratic accusers.

The immediate aftermath of the last war saw in Western class relations, as well as in gender relations, new constitutional clauses of parity and some institutional changes, in the former case the official recognition of trade unions and of collective bargaining everywhere and the installation of some kind of workers' consultative representation in all continental Europe. But under the aegis of the Marshall Plan, the changes of power relations between classes were successfully reined in, as were those of gender relations in demobilized Europe.

The two most ambitious early attempts at postwar change of Western European property rights were undertaken in the Netherlands and in West Germany. The Dutch concept of a 'public law enterprise organization' ('publiekrechtelijke bedrijfsorganisatie') derived largely from Catholic corporatist doctrine, but was given a special force by its *de facto* convergence with Social Democratic notions. From both angles, the absolutism of private property was questioned. In the end, however, Dutch democratic corporatism recognized labour rights of representation and of livelihood – concretized in institutions of 'social partnership' and of social insurance – but without infringing upon the managerial rights of property.[75]

The other thrust forward was undertaken in West Germany, as a compromise manoeuvre to avoid more far-reaching challenges to property rather than as a principled concept of change as was the case in 1920. The American military authorities stopped any radical diminution of private property rights, but the representatives of the British Labour government promoted, for quite pragmatic reasons, workers' representation in iron and steel enterprises.[76] The coal, iron and steel industry – classically the core of German employerdom, and the economic sector most favoured by the Nazi war drive – which was the target of powerful demands for socialization, and to begin with also *démontage* (dismantling), acquired parity between capital and labour representations on the board of directors in 1951. The following year, laws were passed establishing works councils, separate from the unions, and minoritarian employee representation on the supervisory boards of the two-tier governing structure of German enterprises.

For the rest of Western Europe it took till the 1970s, in France and Greece till the 1980s, before any substantial change of the command rights of owners occurred.

What the eight-hour-day was in 1918–19, full employment was in 1945, i.e. *the* central labour demand. The outcome of the latter was more uneven, not surprisingly given the much more intricate issue of full employment. In the end, full employment was institutionalized in Norway, Sweden and Switzerland – later, in the years around 1960 also in Austria – as a fundamental right of labour and/or as an overriding goal of public policy. In the rest of Western Europe, including Britain, the home country of 'Keynesianism', it remained a pious wish, with little institutionalized underpinning.[77]

However, postwar modernity in Europe has also put an end to the common law principle of 'employment at will', and to its continental equivalents, constraining employers' rights to act with regards to hiring and firing. In this respect, too, West Germany was the trail-blazer with its Protection against Dismissals Act of 1950. Subsequently, important collective agreements were made in some countries in the 1960s, and in the 1970s and early 1980s important legislated labour rights ensued.[78]

After the full employment commitment was abandoned in Norway and Sweden around 1990 and only partly and precariously maintained in Austria and Switzerland, at the expense of contractable feminine and foreign labour supply, the best current indicator of labour rights is perhaps the regulation of dismissals. From the point of view of 'flexible' employer rights, it has been the focus of a number of recent comparative labour market studies.[79] In order to get a current profile of labour and property rights in Western Europe, we shall try to combine the, by no means conclusive or consensual, results of these studies of labour pliability with an indicator of the managerial prerogatives of property.

Table 6.3 *Property and labour rights in Western Europe in the early 1990s*

Labour rights	Property rights		
	Weak	*Medium*	*Strong*
Strong	Austria	Greece Italy Netherlands Portugal	Spain
Medium	Finland Germany Norway Sweden	Belgium France	Switzerland
Weak	Denmark	Ireland	UK

Note: Weak property rights are defined as legal employee representation on the board of enterprises, strong as its absence, and a medium position as certain employee rights with regard to the supreme authority of ownership, e.g. of attendance, of advance notice, or of representation in some kinds of enterprise. Labour rights are defined in terms of the cost and difficulty of an employer's dismissal, as assessed by the EC and by the OECD.

Sources: Labour Rights: Commission of the European Communities, *Employment in Europe 1993*, Brussels, 1993, pp. 176, 184; OECD, *Employment Outlook, July 1993*, Paris, 1993, pp. 96–7; H.-D. Harder, 'Allgemeiner Kündigungsschutz in ausgewählten europäischen Ländern', *Jahrbuch für Sozialwissenschaft* 44, 1 (1993), p. 89; Property Rights: T. Hamani and J. Monat, 'Employee Participation in the Workshop, in the Office, and in the Enterprise', in R. Blanpain (ed.), *Comparative Labour Law and Industrial Relations*, 2nd edn, Deventer, Kluwer, 1985, pp. 266ff; M. Ellis and P. Storm (eds), *Business Law in Europe*, Deventer, Kluwer, 1990–, country reports; OECD, *Employment Outlook*, July 1994, Paris, 1994, pp. 149 ff. (The 1994 outlook excludes the cost aspect of employment protection.)

The classification in Table 6.3 is of necessity rather crude. The stipulations of laws and collective agreements are here, as always, nationally very specific. The weighting of the different clauses, e.g. the longer severance pay of Germany and the more extensive coverage of the French rights of labour, for instance, remains a discretionary decision. While I would be rather cautious about the exact location of the two partition lines, I do think that the combination of sources used gives the best possible ranking of countries (while not forgetting the alphabetical order used in the Table).

The classical countries of collective agreement rights, Britain, Ireland (derived from Britain), and Denmark, now rank at the bottom in terms of labour rights. While Thatcherism has certainly established this in the UK, the placement of Denmark might be open to some argument. Pre-capitalist corporatist traditions there still weigh upon the relative de-commodification of labour at the end of the twentieth century.

The poles of the diagonals in Table 6.3 are interesting: Austria and the UK, Denmark and Spain. Austria maintained a pre-capitalist tradition of economic regulation (through chambers of professions and of branches of industry), faced the challenge of a possible Socialist revolution (in 1919), had a spell of domestic corporatism (Austrofascism), an exposed postwar experience of class collaboration and, in the 1970s, a strong Social Democratic government, which in 1974 launched a Works Constitution Act, replacing the 1919 Act. The UK did away with pre-capitalist restrictions, evaded any deadly serious threats of both workers and Fascists, and after some weak Labour governments in the 1970s got a tough, albeit electorally minoritarian, right-wing, anti-union government from 1979.

On the other diagonal is Denmark, with ancient, strong, state-autonomous trade unions, with a long history of democracy, interrupted only by Nazi German occupation, and with an important Social Democratic party, though one never able, in a system of proportional representation, to gain a parliamentary majority. In Spain, which has never had any strong trade union movements, and where instead powerful anti-democratic forces have focused on the (authoritarian) de-commodification of labour, pro-labour forces have recently held political power.

Eastern Europe between accumulation and working-class rule

By Western standards, late Communist Eastern Europe may be justly described as combining very strong labour rights with weak or very weak property rights. Although not impossible – the Soviet courts had 4,000 cases of claims for reinstatement before them in 1975[80] – dismissal of labour was extremely difficult. Special rules ensured that enterprises had to accept a certain proportion (in the USSR 2%) of handicapped.[81] The principle of self-management, originally a Yugoslav heresy, was generally accepted just before the end. The Yugoslavs had enshrined an elaborate conception of self-management in their 1974 constitution, but its rights always coexisted both with massive unemployment and with massive labour out-migration. From 1987 Soviet top managers were to be elected by the employees. In Hungary the same principle worked from 1985. It had cropped up again and again during or in the immediate aftermath of political crises of Eastern Europe, in 1956, in 1968, in 1981.[82]

From a naive socialist point of view, that is, of course, what was to be expected. Naive socialists may not be in very high demand these days, but the times are such that the above could very well be taken as an indictment – soft on labour, neglecting property rights. Whatever your inclination of interpretation, already the intermittent history of self-management in Eastern Europe should suggest to you its contingent rather than intrinsic location in the postwar history of property and labour rights in Eastern Europe.

Enterprises and the rights of property and labour were caught in the dilemma between the two major objectives of the Communist revolutions, working-class rule and accelerated economic development. In a longer-term perspective of, say, one or a few decades, the objectives were not incompatible. The economic development under the rule of the vanguard of the working-class could lay a more solid foundation for the rule of the latter. *De facto*, the project was full of inherent conflicts.

Accelerated development meant accumulation, speed-up, more rather than less managerial control over labour, deferred consumption. Early postwar Eastern European conceptions of co-management were soon rescinded. In the Soviet Zone of Germany, for instance, the Weimar tradition of works councils (*Betriebsräte*) was abolished in 1948.[83] There followed immediate conflicts with the moral economy of labour. Those conflicts were aggravated by the socialist politicization of the target. Not just any development was at stake, but the politically planned, the politically correct one. (That politicization made it possible for the very bourgeois forces of West Germany to get away with their expropriation of an East German workers' uprising against speed-up and accumulation in 1953, celebrating it as 'The Day of German Unity'.)

The goal of working-class rule involved the issue of representation. Although the Communist rulers never doubted that they represented the working-class, at least the latter's long-term interests, the claim was never taken lightly. All the ruling CPs were till the very end very concerned about the composition of their recruitment, about their presence at all the major sites of production, and all felt they had to pay ritual tribute to the working-class. At the same time the CP was the force of government and accumulation. The issue of representation could never be laid to rest.

The accumulationist conception of state property meant an assertion of property rights by means of criminalization. Absenteeism and unwanted labour turnover were submitted to a whole arsenal of punitive sanctions by a Soviet decree of December 1938, imitated in Eastern Europe after the war, until the former's abolition by the Soviets in 1956.[84] The Plan had a mandatory status equivalent to a law. A mixture of a juridification of economic relations following from a statist conception of property and political paranoia led to a vast indictment of economic mismanagement, non-conscientious labour and pilfering as 'economic sabotage'. Again, the de-Stalinization congress of the CPSU in 1956 brought a major change.[85]

However, the characteristic way of running a state socialist enterprise was not by martial law. Instead, it was by the *management–workforce contract* about how to implement the Plan. This kind of collective contract, a major break with capitalist forms of management, had been introduced in the USSR after the October Revolution. Under High Stalinism, more concretely between 1935 and 1947, the enterprise contract was done away with, but it returned and was exported to the new Communist countries.[86]

More important, perhaps, was that this right of the enterprise workforce to bargain with the management about the work to be done, as well as about its fringe benefits – basic rates of remuneration were originally set higher up – was strongly sustained by the actual operation of socialist enterprises. This material basis constantly undermined the 'Leninist' principle of single management. State socialist enterprises had to meet an externally given target with a (largely) given labour supply and under erratic conditions of non-labour supply. Under those conditions, managers tended to become dependent upon well-functioning relations with their labour force.[87]

Now, under conditions of enterprise autonomy from the plan, a product of the late-Communist economic reforms, a new game could be entered into. Labour rights of employment remained guaranteed, but labour remuneration might vary widely. Under those conditions, it was possible to set up high-productivity wage systems, while maintaining the basic labour right to remunerated employment. In Hungary, in fact, enterprises could be more productive than in the USA.[88]

The politicization of the workplace came not only from a statist conception of property, but also from the programme of working-class rule. That meant a crucial party presence at every workplace, political sloganeering – 'My workplace – battleground for peace', for example – and a whole set of political distinctions, i.e. honorary titles, both individual and collective, medals, etc., which were within the reach of ordinary people, in contrast to the British 'Honours list'. Above all in the GDR, it meant organizing of 'socialist collectives' in the workplace, with their elaborate norms of how to 'work in a socialist manner, learn in a socialist manner, live in a socialist manner'.[89]

What became triumphant in 1989–90, however, were neither the rights nor the norms of labour, but the perceived opportunities of the consumer. The lack of resistance to the abolition or marginalization of workplace democracy is what appears most noteworthy. To what extent the socialist experience has left any evaluative inheritance is a question to which we shall return below.

From nationalization to privatization

Future historians will certainly take note of the strikingly parallel developments in postwar Europe, East and West, despite all obvious differences of political system and ideology, developments naturally lost to most people living on one or the other side of the postwar iron divide. However, these parallels – at least the ones this study finds significant – do not follow the lines highlighted by theories of modernization and of industrial society, vistas confined within a singular conception of modernity.[90] We have already noted the pan-European specificity of industrial society. In this section we shall deal with what most theorists, ideologues and militants of class – any modern class – regarded as the key issue: the extension of private and public property.

Until the late 1970s the twentieth century saw a long-term tendency towards public property, of the so-called infrastructure of transport and communications most clearly but also towards public property or other kinds of supra-enterprise regulation in basic commodity industries, whereas, on the other hand, agriculture tended in the direction of the family farm. In other words, while capitalist market economies were expanding with manufacturing, opposite forces were also gathering strength.

Requirements of coordination, capital needs, low private profitability under existing conditions, perceived conservative national interest, all pushed in the direction of public property or at least of inter-enterprise regulation, 'cartelization'. In the eyes of posterity, perhaps the most remarkable aspect of this tendency, which Marx once had predicted as 'the increasingly social character of the productive forces' – meaning the widening of the organizational parameters of optimal productivity – was its fundamentally non-ideological character. That is, the tendency cut its path through variable ideological terrain. The London Passenger Transport Act of 1933 was one its high water marks, the municipalization of the Paris Métro in 1949 another. Post, telephone and telegraph, local mass transit, railways, broadcasting, air transport, all tended towards public ownership in Europe.[91] The interwar international cartels, for instance in steel, may be seen as another side of the same process.[92] The Depression led to the state bailing out bankrupt private enterprises in a number of countries, from Fascist Italy to pre-Social Democratic Sweden.

Then, after the war, came major nationalizations in Austria, Britain, France and Eastern Europe. Vigorous public enterprise also started and developed in several other countries, from Finland to Spain (here launched during the war). The trend culminated in the decade from the early 1970s to the early 1980s, with the last nationalization drives in Eastern Europe,[93] with the Portuguese revolution, with the Swedish 'wage-earners' funds' project, and with the French Socialist 'rupture with capitalism' and its industrial nationalizations in 1981–2.

Thereafter the pendulum swung in the opposite direction, spearheaded by Britain under the premiership of Mrs Thatcher, with privatizations in the West, openings for private enterprise in Hungary and other Eastern countries, and finally the surrender of Communism.[94] In a 1984 interview the great Hungarian writer and dissident George Konrád pointed to 'socialist embourgeoisement' as the single most important recent event in Hungary.[95] In early 1988 a stock exchange re-opened in Budapest.

Polish Solidarity in 1980–1 was, we now know in retrospect, the last socialist opposition in Eastern Europe. In the course of its repression in the ensuing years and under strong US influence a shift took place. Programmatically, the explicit turn from social to private ownership occurred in 1989, right after the formation of the (non-Communist) Mazowiecki government.[96]

The amount of public ownership was never uniform, neither in the East nor in the West, and a number of national reasons and forces were always involved. For the East we may look back at Table 4.9 on classes of employment, since almost everybody who was a worker or employee was employed by some public institution. In terms of employment, then, the Eastern European public sector ranged under late Communism from 98% of the labour force (in Bulgaria) to 66% in Yugoslavia, via 91% in Czechoslovakia and, from the other end, 75% in Poland and 80% in Hungary.

By comparison, total public employment in Denmark and Sweden was 37–8% in the mid-1980s, in Britain and France 26%, and in West Germany 19%.[97] In the West, however, and particularly in Scandinavia, public jobs are in social services. The Austrian public holding company, ÖIAG, dominates the country's industry more than any other set of public enterprises has ever done in postwar Western Europe (except, perhaps, in Portugal during the Revolution). It accounted for one-tenth of total employment in mining and manufacturing in 1986.[98]

However, in the face of all this diversity the question remains: is the parallelism in time trajectories just a coincidence? A social scientist is reluctant to admit that it might be. I would like to hypothesize that two general forces, interrelated but irreducible one to the other, have governed the development of property relations, or structured the options of political leaders. One has to do with the social *organization of productivity*,[99] with the character of the productive forces as Marx would have put it, the other with class power, or more specifically with the *power* relationship between private property and private propertylessness.

The former we may approach by looking at the relative capacities of enterprises, markets and states. Other things being equal, the larger the market is in relation to the enterprises and to the state, the more productive relative to other forms of enterprise is a set of autonomous units, and vice versa. The enterprise–market relation is largely governed by a competition–monopoly argument, namely a market which is much larger than the sales of any enterprise within which it tends to be competitive. When one or a few enterprises dominate the market, a strong case can be made for public ownership or public regulation to ensure the interests of customers. This case is the stronger the more important an egalitarian access to products and services is considered, in particular extra-monetary equality, as for instance between inhabitants located in different areas or with different mobility for age and health reasons. And it is stronger the more open to feedback the public system is.[100]

The state–market relation derives its importance from a dependency argument. The less the state is dependent on external markets, the more leeway it has to organize the economy and society. But there is a trade-off here: autarky decreases dependency in the short run, but may very well increase it in the longer term, because of the costs of protection from competitive pressure to innovate.

Under given market conditions, the larger the state in relation to a set of enterprises, the more effectively the state can regulate enterprise performance.

'Size' here refers to economically pertinent resources, in the case of markets primarily to the size of effective demand and supply. In the case of the enterprise it refers to output and capital, and with regard to the state the tax base and other financial resources. For all three institutions the size of knowledge is also important, the spread of relevant information among market actors, the amount of knowledge in the enterprise and in the state apparatus.

This third part of the hypothesis is a capacity argument, capacity to undertake given tasks. A financially resourceful state may be able to undertake investments and set up enterprises held too big, too risky or too long-term by relatively small private enterprises or entrepreneurs. But not only finance counts. Crucial also is the distribution of knowledge and of rationality. The constructive capacity[101] of the state vis-à-vis private enterprise is the greater the more skilled and the more committed to collective rationality the personnel of the state apparatus is.

In other words, while certainly important, 'rivalry' and 'budget constraints' are far from the whole story of modern property relations.[102]

The absolute magnitude of the variables pointed to above may be extremely difficult to measure, but that does not really matter, as long as directions of change are discernible. My theory fragment aims at explaining effects upon property relations by changes in the relative size of enterprises, states and markets. In this slice of explanatory hypotheses we are assuming that the changes in the relative size of market, state and enterprise are exogenously determined, i.e. primarily affected by forces other than the markets, states and enterprises we are looking at. These forces are probably primarily technological determinants of (dis)economies of scale and the political economy of the world (or pertinent supra-state) system.

The drive towards public ownership in the first half of the twentieth century mainly covered three areas.[103] Infrastructural transport and communications were one, started by private enterprise but soon running into situations of one or a few enterprises and a bounded state or municipal market. Another consisted of basic industries, usually providing important inputs to other enterprises, facing inelastic demand and/or special exposure to depressive cycles. Mining and crude steel production are major industrial examples, banks in depressive crises an important service sector. The third consists of new large-scale enterprises in fields not or only feebly entered into by local private enterprise, the German mass production car company Volkswagen being perhaps the most famous example in Western Europe. But big public enterprise in Finland, Italy and Spain also fits into this pattern, as does public ownership industrialization in Eastern Europe, regardless of the issues of power and ideology involved there.

Those experiences all fit very well into our enterprise–market–state grid. But in the second half of the century the trend has been in the direction of relative market growth. From the end of 'La Belle Epoque' (in 1914) till the late 1940s the state/market ratio was increasing. The share of exports in the national product was declining for Western Europe as a whole. In the postwar period the trend was reversed, but only around 1970 did the export/product ratio surpass that of 1913. The relative decline of foreign trade was greater in Eastern Europe, including the prewar non-Communist East, than in the West, and the postwar reversal occurred there too.[104]

In the 1980s supra-national financial and currency markets began to dwarf national states. By the end of the decade the British currency trade was reportedly sixty-nine times larger than the country's trade in products and services, and Sweden's currency trade twenty-three times larger than its ordinary trade.[105] These figures may be compared with total public expenditure, which in Britain is about 80% of the total export/import trade and in Sweden about 120%.

Technological developments in communications have made the latter outgrow any politically bounded territory, and have opened up a new global market. Private capital accumulation in Western Europe has reached such proportions as to make credible – albeit not necessarily true – the argument that even large European states like Britain and Germany will have to rely on private capital to ensure their postal and related services of the future.[106]

Industrial development and then de-industrialization have tended to reduce economies of scale, and have rendered the former basic industries no longer basic, at times even superfluous. The satisfaction of elementary consumer needs by the postwar economic growth also implies diseconomies of enterprise scale in the face of an increasingly diverse demand.

In Europe private enterprise organization was in early industrial modernity often modelled after or at least in part inspired by knowledge assembled in the military, administrative and judicial apparatuses of the state. While French business has continued after the war to recruit executives from the public sector, I think it is a warranted impression that in this period the development of managerial expertise and routines have mainly taken place in private business, thus tilting the state–enterprise distribution of organizational knowledge.

In brief, *the postwar changes in the relative size of markets, states and enterprises should lead us to expect pressures against public ownership and public regulation to mount at the close of this century.*

But nationalizations and privatizations are both also issues of power, at the same time manifestations of power and means to more power. After 1945 it was the question of breaking the power of 'private monopolies', of the economic rulers of the Depression, and of the financiers, the collaborators and the appeasers of Fascism, or of now defeated Germany regardless of its Fascist regime. In 1980s Britain, in the Tory vanguard, privatization was a crucial means to defeat the labour unions, still formidable in the 1974 miners' strike but a declining force in the rapid de-industrialization after 1974.[107] In the rest of Western Europe this question of class revenge seems to have been of minor significance, if any.[108] However, the ending of industrial society tends to weaken and divide the labour movement, which should tend to give more weight to forces of privatization.

In Eastern Europe privatization is now of course largely seen as a means to dismantle Communist power, but tendencies towards *sub rosa* private appropriation could also be expected to arise from the thinning out of the militant wartime and prewar persecuted generation of Communists.

Obviously different in many respects, the sociological history of Eastern and Western Europe in the second half of the twentieth century has also in many ways run parallel. We shall find something similar in the next chapter.

Notes

1 B. Arvidsson, *Europarådet 40 år*, Stockholm, UD, 1989, p. 21. See further A.H. Robertson and J.G. Merrills, *Human Rights in Europe*, 3rd edn, Manchester, Manchester University Press, 1993.

2 The text of the Helsinki Declaration may be found in *Human Rights and International Law*, Strasburg, 1992, Ch. IV, which also contains follow-up documents. A modest sketch of the context is given by W. Brinton, 'The Helsinki Final Act and Other International Covenants Supporting Freedom and Human Rights', in W. Brinton and A. Rinzler (eds), *Without Force or Lies*, San Francisco, Mercury House, 1990.

3 Dr Andrzej Werblan, Warsaw, oral communication. Dr Werblan, a former high Communist official turned historian, has written a history of Polish Stalinism.

4 Professor Ivan Mozny, Prague, oral communication.

5 A brief, but spine-chillingly concrete account of the coming of the revolutionary pressure and intimidation in Hungary is given non-Magyar readers by the Hungarian sociologist, Elemér Hankiss in a penetrating study somewhat misleadingly called *East European Alternatives*, Oxford, Clarendon Press, 1990, Ch. 1.

6 Before the war, repression had, of course, been an anti-Communist trait in Europe west of the USSR.

7 My sources for the figures on France, the Netherlands and Norway are the national contributions by H. Rousso, P. Romijn and G. Hirschfeld, and S.U. Larsen, respectively, to K.-D. Henke and H. Woller (eds), *Politische Sauberung in Europa*, Munich, dtv, 1991. Belgian data are from J. Fitzmaurice, *The Politics of Belgium*, London, Hurst & Co., 1983, p. 45.

8 M. Szöllösi-Janze, ' "Pfeilkreuzler, Landesverräter und andere Volksfeinde" Generalabrechnung in Ungarn', in Henke and Woller, *Politische Säuberung*, pp. 331–2. By October 1946 60,000 public employees had also been fired, in a process part purge, part finacially motivated. A large part of these firings were soon retracted. Ibid., pp. 343–4.

9 Hankiss, *East European Alternatives*, p. 40. Hankiss cites B. Magyar, *Dunaapáti, 1944–1958*, Budapest, 1986.

10 The number of the victims of Stalinist repression below are taken from J.A. Getty et al., 'Victims of the Soviet Penal System in the Pre-war Years: A First Approach on the Basis of Archival Evidence', *American Historical Review* 58 (1993), pp. 1017–49. Population figures are from other Western publications of official census data. For the sources regarding anti-Fascist purges, see above.

11 That is the figure for 1945–8, Getty et al., 'Victims', p. 1049. Figures for 1953 are still missing.

12 N. Christie, *Crime Control as Industry*, London, Routledge, 1993, p. 119. If we make the strong assumptions that no Black women were imprisoned and that the gender ratio

among US Blacks is unity, then 1.7% of the total Black population was imprisoned in the United States in 1990.

13 Ibid., pp. 28–9.

14 Cf., e.g. S.M. Cretney and J.M. Masson, *Principles of Family Law*, 5th edn, London, Sweet & Maxwell, 1991, p. 186.

15 Continental and Irish family law explicitly put wives under the thumb of their husbands, and leading British judges held similar views, although common law did not include the detailed juridification of family relations characteristic of the civil codes: A. Sachs and J. Hoff Wilson, *Sexism and the Law*, Oxford, Martin Robertson, 1978, pp. 141–2.

16 See further, e.g. R. Evans, *The Feminists*, London, Croom Helm, 1979, and Sachs and Hoff Wilson, *Sexism and the Law*.

17 Sachs and Hoff Wilson, *Sexism and the Law*, pp. 33ff, 38ff. Legal texts referred to 'persons', with certain qualifications having certain rights or possibilities. The judicial issue was then whether women were 'persons' or not. It took about half a century before it was settled positively.

18 Cf. O. Dhavernas, *Droit des femmes, pouvoir des hommes*, Paris, Seuil, 1978, pp. 89ff.

19 Scotland has its own legal system, related to civil law but under strong common law influence. On different legal traditions, see further K. Zweigert and R. Kötz, *Introduction to Comparative Law*, 2nd edn, Oxford, Clarendon Press, 1987, 2 vols. Finland and Iceland were not sovereign states at the time, and Norway became one only in 1905. However, all three of them had got their own legislation in the course of the nineteenth century. For a survey of pertinent Nordic legislation since 1810, see I. Blom and A. Traberg (eds), *Nordisk lovoversikt*, Copenhagen, Nordisk Ministerråd, 1985.

20 M. Clévenot (ed.), *L'État des réligions dans le monde*, Paris, La Découverte/Le Cerf, 1987, pp. 339, 350, 356; *Der Fischer Weltalmanach*, Frankfurt, Fischer, 1989, p. 136. Re-unified Germany has a Protestant majority.

21 See S. Stuurman, *Verzuiling, kapitalisme en patriarchaat*, Nijmegen, SUN, 1983, pp. 231ff.

22 A. Bergmann (ed.), *Internationales Ehe- und Kindschaftsrecht*, Vol. II, 1st edn, Berlin, Verlag des Reichsbundes der Standesbeamten Deutschlands, 1926, pp. 132ff, 287ff, 304, 309–10.

23 The text of the family code is given in A. Bergmann (ed.), *Internationales Ehe- und Kindschaftsrecht*, Vol. I, 2nd edn, Berlin, Verlag für Standeswesen, 1938, p. 358. The last sentence is basically identical with §1354 of the then valid German Civil Code, and is probably taken from there.

24 Ibid., pp. 378–9.

25 S.M. Grzybowski, 'Das Eherecht der VR Polen', in E. Loewenfeld and W. Lauterbach (eds), *Das Eherecht der europaischen und der aussereuropäischer Staaten*, Cologne, Carl Hegmann, 1963–72, pp. 9–10; Bergmann (ed.), *Internationales Ehe- und Kindschaftsrecht*, Vol. I, 2nd edn, pp. 44ff.

26 V. Knapp and J. Elis, 'Das Eherecht der Tschechoslowakischen sozialistischen Republik', in E. Loewenbeld and W. Lauterbach *Das Eherecht*, pp. 127ff; Bergmann, *Internationales Ehe- und Kindschaftsrecht*, Vol. II, 2nd edn, pp. 681ff.

27 T. Pap, 'Das Eherecht der Ungarischen Volksrepublik', in Loewenfeld and Lauterbach, *Das Eherecht*, pp. 690ff; B. Blagojevic, 'Das Eherecht der Föderativen Volksrepublik Jugoslawien', in ibid., pp. 65ff; T. Popescu and M. Eliescu, 'Das Eherecht der sozialistischen Republik Rumänien', in ibid., pp. 625ff; K. Begeja, 'Das Eherecht der Volksrepublik Albanien', in ibid., p. 841; Bergmann, *Internationales Ehe- und Kindschaftsrecht*, vols I and II, 1st edn, pp. 697ff, 260ff, 537ff, 7ff, respectively; vols I an II, 2nd edn, pp. 794ff, 352ff, 594 and 15, respectively.

28 *Fordham Law Review*, 'Comments' [1936], reprinted in *Selected Essays on Family Law*, compiled and edited by a committee of the Association of American Law Schools, Brooklyn, Foundation Press, pp. 607–14; M.A. Glendon, *State, Law and Family*, Amsterdam, North-Holland, 1977, p. 183n.

29 F. Milkova, 'Le droit de famille en Bulgarie contemporaine', in R. Ganghofer (ed.), *Le droit de famille en Europe*, Strasburg, Presses Universitaires de Strasbourg, 1992, p. 163. See

further, more obliquely, M. Miklasz, 'La famille en Pologne et ses problèmes depuis 1945', in ibid., pp. 151–53, and H. Scott *Kan socialismen befria krinnan?*, Stockholm, Liber, 1978 (orig. edn *Does Socialism Liberate Women?* 1974). Ch. 4.

30 Originally a constitutional equality of women was voted down in the preparatory parliamentary committee, by the Christian Democrats and the Liberals. Only after the issue was brought to public debate was gender equality accepted into the West German constitution of 1949. The 1950 provisional Civil Service Act (*Bundespersonalgesetz*) of 1950 explicitly allowed for the right of the employer to dismiss a female civil servant whose 'economic provision [wirtschaftliche Versorgung] is secured', i.e. by being married to an economically secure husband. The Compensation Act for Nazi Injustice also excepted female civil servants who had been dismissed because of their gender from the compensation which only was to be allotted for dismissals because of race, faith and worldview. A. Vogel, 'Frauen und Frauenbewegung', in W. Benz (ed.), *Die Geschichte der Bundesrepublik Deutschland*, Vol. 3, Frankfurt, Fischer, 1989, pp. 162ff.

31 See, e.g. ibid., pp. 168–9 and Glendon, *State, Law and Family*, p. 119.

32 A. Rieg, 'Traits fondamentaux de l'évolution du droit des régimes matrimoniaux dans l'Europe du XXe siècle', in Ganghofer, *Le droit de famille en Europe*, p. 429; F. Boulanger, *Droit civil de la famille*, Vol. 1, Paris, Economica, 1990, pp. 42–3.

33 Then Dutch married women were granted the rights of mature adulthood: Boulanger, *Droit civil de la famille*, pp. 44, 279.

34 Dhavernas, *Droits des femmes*, pp. 103 and 114, where the primary sources of the verdicts are indicated.

35 Ibid., pp. 107ff. Belgium had adopted a law on the husband's decisive vote in family affairs in 1965: L. Lohlé-Tart, 'Law and Fertility in Belgium', in M. Kirk et al. (eds), *Law and Fertility in Europe*, Vol. 1, Dolhain, Ordina, 1975, p. 152. But only by 1985 was full equality instituted: Rieg, 'Traits fondamentaux', p. 429.

36 M. Kirk, 'Law and Fertility in Ireland', in Kirk et al., *Law and Fertility in Europe*, Vol. 2, pp. 416ff.

37 J.M. Grtossen, 'Switzerland: Further Steps Towards Equality', *Journal of Family Law* 25 (1986), pp. 255ff.

38 See further, F. Castles and M. Flood, 'Why Divorce Rates Differ: Law, Religious Belief, and Modernity', in F. Castles (ed.), *Families of Nations*, Aldershot, Dartmouth, 1993.

39 French courts had also by the early 1960s made clear that clauses of female celibacy were invalid, and Italy made dismissal upon marriage illegal by statute in 1963. In Britain this had to wait until the Industrial Relations Act of 1971, and by the mid-1970s the egalitarian clause of the West German Constitution had not been tested with regard to discrimination of married women. See further F. Schmidt, 'Discrimination because of Sex', in F. Schmidt (ed.), *Discrimination and Employment: A Study of Six Countries by the Comparative Labour Law Group*, Stockholm, Almqvist & Wiksell, 1978, pp. 154ff.

40 Cf. E. Haas, *The Uniting of Europe*, Stanford, Stanford University Press, 1958, pp.515–19.

41 §119 did provide a rallying focus for an important women's strike in Liège in Belgium in 1966, though: Cf. S. Andresen (ed.), *Frauenbewegungen in der Welt* Vol. 1, West Berlin, Argument, 1988.

42 Cf. S. Mazey, 'European Community Action on Behalf of Women: The Limits of Legislation', *Journal of Common Market Studies*, XXVII, 1 (Sept. 1988).

43 Blom and Traberg, *Nordiskl Lovoversikt*, pp. 68–9, 100–1, 181, 203–4. Finland seems to have been a laggard here.

44 Male rights to pre-marital sex have rarely been seriously contested, although the theory of Church officialdom has not admitted them. According to dictionaries in my possession, admittedly not a rock-solid basis of knowledge, there is no special English word for male chastity, i.e. corresponding to female virginity. In Swedish there is – 'svendom'.

45 This was before the recent women's movement, and the move seems to have been produced by forces of legal enlightenment. The background to the Code (Brottsbalken) is given in *Nytt Juridiskt Arkiv* 87 (1962), pp. 170ff.

46 At least it is missing in countries which in the course of the last two decades have had series of family and gender reform legislation, such as Austria and France: C. Bernd and E. Schlatter, 'Domestic Violence in Austria: The Institutional Response', in E. Viano (ed.), *Intimate Violence: Interdisciplinary Perspectives*, Washington DC, Hemisphere Publishing Corporation, 1992, p. 243; G. Deveze, 'Viol conjugal: comme tous les viols un crime', *Nouvelles questions féministes* 16–18 (1991), p. 215.

47 Cretney and Masson, *Principles of Family Law*, pp. 183–4.

48 E. Hearthfield (ed.), *Halsbury's Laws of England 1991*, London, Butterworths, 1992, p. 186.

49 The Norwegian Annika Snare is a good witness: 'Den private volden: om hustrumishandling', in C. Høigård and A. Snare (eds), *Kvinners skyld*, Oslo, Pax, 1983, p. 224.

50 Ibid., pp. 230ff.

51 R. Husbands, 'Sexual Harassment Law in Employment: An International Perspective', *International Labour Review* 131,6 (1992), pp. 540, 549.

52 Michael Burawoy, in particular, has made a very important contribution, however: *The Politics of Production*, London, Verso, 1985; M. Burawoy and J. Lukács, *The Radiant Past*, Chicago, University of Chicago Press, 1992.

53 A. Shonfield, *Modern Capitalism*, London, Oxford University Press, 1959.

54 Which was, by the way, the main focus of Shonfield. See further, e.g. P. Katzenstein, *Small States in World Markets*, Ithaca NY, Cornell University Press, 1985; S. Strange, *States and Markets*, New York, Blackwell, 1988; J. Zysman, *Governments, Markets, and Growth*, Ithaca, NY, Cornell University Press, 1983.

55 See, among the best, e.g. C. Crouch, *Industrial Relations and European State Traditions*, Oxford, Clarendon Press, 1993; H. Slomp, *Labor Relations in Europe*, New York, Greenwood Press, 1990; G. Baglioni and C. Crouch (eds), *European Industrial Relations*, London, Sage, 1990; R. Boyer (ed.), *La flexibilité du travail en Europe*, Paris, La Découverte, 1986; P. Schmitter and G. Lehmbruch (eds), *Trends Towards Corporatist Intermediation*, London, Sage, 1979; K. Sisson, *The Management of Collective Bargaining*, Oxford, Blackwell, 1987.

56 There are some works to consider in this context, however. A recent, interesting contribution is M. Albert, *Capitalisme contre capitalisme*, Paris, Seuil, 1991. Unfortunately, Albert, an insurance executive, is more interested in writing a mass seller than in systematizing his insider's knowledge of business institutions in a number of countries. Two British sociologists, Scott Lash and John Urry, have followed what they perceive as the change from organized to disorganized capitalism in a broad-brushed comparative manner: *The End of Organized Capitalism*, Cambridge, Polity Press, 1987. Walter Korpi, a Swedish sociologist, has made a comparative study of class power and class conflict from an organized labour point of view: *The Democratic Class Struggle*, London, Routledge & Kegan Paul, 1983. The welfare state and its articulations with capitalism is the fulcrum of Gøsta Esping-Andersen's *The Three Worlds of Welfare Capitalism*, Cambridge, Polity Press, 1990.

57 Beginnings were made however before the fall of the regimes. See, e.g. V. Nee and D. Stark (eds), *Remaking the Economic Institutions of Socialism: China and Eastern Europe*, Stanford, Stanford University Press, 1989.

58 Please consider our findings below about the extent of the welfare state and the sources of household income. See further A. Heidenheimer et al., *Comparative Public Policy*, 2nd edn, p. 134 and 3rd edn, pp. 145ff, New York, St Martin's Press, 1983 and 1990, respectively. A particular aspect of the qualified character of private property in Japan is corporate responsibility for more or less full employment. See G. Therborn, *Why Some Peoples Are More Unemployed Than Others*, London, Verso, 1986.

59 Cf. K. Dohse et al. (eds), *Statussicherung im Industriebetrieb*, Frankfurt, Campus, 1982; Lord Wedderburn, *Employment Rights in Britain and in Europe*, London, Lawrence and Wishart, 1991.

60 Here there is, of course, a contradiction between the absolutism of private property, which entails the legitimacy of squandering it and of using it for any purpose, however irrational

or value-rational, and the absolutism of the market, with its universalistic cost-benefit rationality.

61 See, e.g. the overview in the *Economist*, 30.11.1991, pp. 67–8, 'Europe's Corporate Castles Begin to Crack', i.e. are beginning to become no more than commodities. Cf. Albert, *Capitalisme contre capitalisme*, Ch. 3 and passim.
62 Albert, *Capitalisme contre capitalisme*, Ch. 4.
63 C. Hampden-Turner and A. Trompenaars, *The Seven Cultures of Capitalism*, New York, Doubleday, 1993, p. 32.
64 F. Meyers, *Ownership of Jobs: A Comparative Study*, Los Angeles, UCLA, Institute of Industrial Relations, 1964.
65 See further Boyer, *La flexibilité* and Baglioni and Crouch, *European Industrial Relations*.
66 Cf. A. Okun, *Equality and Efficiency*, Washington, DC, Brookings Institution, 1975, Ch.1.
67 In his monumental work, *Industrial Relations and European State Traditions*, Oxford, Clarendon Press, 1993, Colin Crouch has drawn our attention to the importance of the guild traditions in the non-Germanic lands, e.g. p. 311. However, in my opinion, Crouch, in his brief treatment of the matter, is much too dismissive of the importance of the corporatist legacy of democratic Italy, Portugal and Spain. The stringent employment security clauses in Spain and Portugal have their background in the corporatist official de-commodification of labour. The postwar Italian codification of the rights of labour appears to have a legal style not qualitatively different from that of corporatism. However, Crouch's prime concern is not with class rights but with industrial relations.
68 Cf. Wedderburn, *Employment Rights*, Ch. 4.
69 Lord Wedderburn 'Discrimination in the Right to Organize and the Right to Be a Non-Unionist', in Schmidt *Discrimination in Employment*, pp. 373, 378, 383, 386, referring to Sweden, Germany, France and Italy.
70 See further I Dübeck, 'Hvordan skabtes arbejdsretten i Danmark?', in *Rättsvetenskap och lagstiftning i Norden*, Stockholm, Juristförlaget, 1982.
71 This is based on a large variety of sources, but a good general overview is given by Slomp, *Labor Relations in Europe*. Cf. Crouch, *Industrial Relations*, pp. 158ff.
72 ILO, *International Survey of Social Services*, Geneva, 1933.
73 G. Ambrosius and W. Hubbard, *A Social and Economic History of Twentieth Century Europe*, Cambridge, Mass., Harvard University Press, 1989, p. 53.
74 Even the once staunchly anti-cultural sociologist Michael Burawoy learnt in Hungary the significance of ritual and ideology, of 'painting socialism': Burawoy and Lukács, *The Radiant Past*, pp. 139ff.
75 See further, H.J.G. Verhallen et al. (eds), *Corporatisme in Nederland*, Alphen aan den Rijn, Samson, 1980.
76 H.-H. Hartwich, *Sozialstaatspostulat und gesellschaftlicher status quo*, 3rd edn, Cologne, Westdeutscher Verlag, 1978, pp. 85ff.
77 This thesis is substantiated in Therborn, *Why Some Peoples Are More Unemployed Than Others*, Ch. III.5.
78 B. Hepple, 'Security of Employment', in R. Blanpain (ed.), *Comparative Labour and Industrial Relations*, 2nd edn, Deventer, Kluwer, 1985, pp. 495ff.
79 Commission of the European Communities, *Employment in Europe 1993*, Brussels, 1993, Ch. 7; OECD, *Employment Outlook, July 1993*, Paris, 1993, pp. 95ff; H.-D. Harder, 'Allgemeiner Kündigungsschutz in ausgewählten europäischen Ländern', *Jahrbuch für Sozialwissenschaft*, 44,1 (1993), esp. pp. 89ff.
80 N. Lampert, *Whistleblowing in the Soviet Union*, London, Macmillan, 1985, p. 152.
81 R. Berner, *Rysk arbetare*, Stockholm, Författarförlaget, 1976, p. 98.
82 A. Tyomkina, 'The Problem of Advancing Industrial Democracy in a Post-Socialist Society', *Economic and Industrial Democracy* 14, Supplement (Nov. 1993), p. 30; J. Kornai, 'The Hungarian Reform Process: Visions, Hopes, and Reality', Nee and Stark (eds), *Remaking the Economic Institutions of Socialism*, p. 40; M. Myant, *Transforming Socialist Economies*, Aldershot, Edward Elgar, 1993, pp. 35ff.
83 L. Niethammer, *Die volkseigene Erfahrung*, Berlin, Rowohlt, pp. 57, 89.

84 I. Deutscher, *Soviet Trade Unions*, Oxford, Oxford University Press, 1950, pp. 90ff; H. Berman, *Justice in the USSR*, rev. edn, Cambridge, Mass., Harvard University Press, 1963, p. 350.

85 See, e.g. Hankiss *East European Alternatives*, pp. 27–8; I. Morzol and M. Ogórek, 'Shadow Justice', in J. Wedel (ed.), *The Unplanned Society*, New York, Columbia University Press, 1992, pp. 64ff.

86 Berman, *Justice in the USSR*, pp. 353–9; C. Klessmann and G. Wagner (eds), *Das gespaltene Land*, Munich, C.H. Beck, 1993, pp. 386ff.

87 Burawoy and Lukács, *The Radiant Past*, 1992, p. 76; D. Stark, 'Coexisting Organizational Forms in Hungary's Emerging Mixed Economy', in Nee and Stark, *Remaking the Economic Institutions of Socialism*, p. 146; Klessmann and Wagner *Das gespaltene Land*, p. 422.

88 Burawoy and Lukács, *The Radiant Past*, pp. 66ff.

89 Cf. Berner, *Rysk arbetare*, pp. 76ff; Niethammer, *Die volkseigene Erfahrung*, pp. 372–3; Klessmann and Wagner, *Das gespaltene Land*, pp. 372–3.

90 For a brief, critical introduction, from a different perspective, into the pertinent derivations from modernization theory, see the editors' first chapter to Nee and Stark, *Remaking the Economic Institutions of Socialism*.

91 See further R. Bloch, *L'entreprise remise en question*, Paris, Librairie générale de droit et de jurisprudence, 1964; G. Therborn, 'States, Populations and Productivity: Towards a Political Theory of Welfare States', in P. Lassman (ed.), *Politics and Social Theory*, London, Routledge, 1989.

92 D. Jacobs, 'Gereguleerd Staal', Nijmegen, Katholieke Universiteit, PhD thesis, 1988, Part III.

93 P. Shoup, *The East European and Soviet Data Handbook*, New York, Columbia University Press, 1981, tables E-36, E-37.

94 Cf. C. Derbasch (ed.), *Les privatisations en Europe*, Paris, Ed. du CNRS, 1989.

95 Here quoted from his friend Ivan Szelenyi, who made a very interesting study of the rural side of the phenomenon, *Socialist Entrepreneurs*, Madison., University of Wisconsin Press, 1988, p. 50.

96 For an English introduction to the property conceptions of Solidarity in 1980–1 see D.M. Nuti, 'Theses on Poland' *New Left Review* 130 (1981); and T. Garton Ash, *The Polish Revolution*, London, Granta Books, 1991 (originally published 1983), pp. 235ff. On later developments I am indebted to the Polish economist Dr T. Kowalik, whom I interviewed in Budapest 22 September 1991. In the spring of 1993 the *Financial Times* (6.4.1993, p. 2) reported a recent survey among Polish state sector industrial workers: 14% thought that their workplace should be privatized, while 51% held on to state ownership and 25% wanted workers' ownership. But Polish workers had little say, except 'No' in extreme situations, under Communism, and they have not got more under the transition to capitalism.

97 Calculated from T. Cussack et al., *Political-Economic Aspects of Public Employment*, Berlin, Wissenschaftszentrum FGG/dp 87–2, L987 p. 7 (public employment); OECD, *Historical Statistics, 1960–1989*, Paris, 1991, Table 2.14 (total employment).

98 *Austria: Facts and Figures*, Vienna, Federal Press Service, 1987, p. 82 and OECD, *Labour Force Statistics 1968–1989*, Paris, 1991. See further P. Saunders and F. Klau, 'The Role of the Public Sector', *OECD Economic Studies* 4 (Spring 1985), p. 78 and passim.

99 See further, G. Therborn, 'States, Populations and Productivity'.

100 My sociological historical explanation is not couched in terms of functional optimality, so it is not necessary for public ownership or regulation to be optimal, only that they would be more likely to meet satisfying criteria for policy-making under conditions of small markets/ big enterprises than in the opposite cases.

101 A capacity which may very well be surpassed by its repressive and destructive capacity.

102 This is not meant to question the brilliance of the Hungarian economist János Kornai, who has given us the important concepts of 'soft' and 'hard' 'budget constraints', which underly his analysis of *The Economics of Shortage*, Amsterdam, North-Holland, 1980. Nor the

liberal argument about rivalry and competition, well analysed by Don Lavoie in *Rivalry and Central Planning*, Cambridge, Cambridge University Press, 1985.

103 The short-lived French nationalizations of 1981 included a fourth one, some dominant national enterprises held to be central to future national development. But these national champions were also big in relation to their domestic market.

104 Ambrosius and Hubbard, *A Social and Economic History of Twentieth-Century Europe*, p. 209, and calculations from relating their Table 3.1. to their Figure 3.15.

105 These data come from business journalism, *Svenska Dagbladet*, 14.3.1993, supplement *Näringslivet* p. 1. In the Finnish National Bank operations in support of the Finnish mark in November 1991 currencies to a value of 17% of the Finnish GDP or 80% of annual Finnish trade were sold, in vain: *Die Zeit*, 18.6.1993, p. 28.

106 See the overview of official argumentation in the *Financial Times*, 10.12.1992, p. 14 (Britain) and *Die Zeit*, 4.12.1993 (Germany).

107 See the thorough case study by D. Swann, *The Retreat of the State*, Hemel Hempstead, Harvester Wheatsheaf, 1988, Ch. 7.

108 Cf. Derbasch, *Les privatisations en Europe*.

7

MEANS: 'THE GLORIOUS YEARS'

The most eloquent economic history of postwar Europe has been written by
a Frenchman, unsurprisingly. The title is untranslatable, but the opening
message is understandable enough. It contrasts two villages. One was
underdeveloped, overwhelmingly agrarian (80% of the population) had a
life expectancy of 62 years, houses that were largely without indoor toilets
and central heating, and in which buying a kilo of butter cost seven hours of
work. The other was highly developed, predominantly into services, having
recruited two-thirds of its inhabitants from outside, giving a life expectancy at
birth of 75 years, with most houses having indoor plumbing and a car, half of
them central heating, and in which a kilo of butter required one hour and
twenty-five minutes of work.

In fact, Jean Fourastié compares the same French village, Douelle en
Quercy, in 1946 and in 1975.[1] He then moves on to contrast 'the two
Frances': the stagnant rural France of 1946, and of the century or centuries
before; and the prosperous urban France of 1975, produced by the
accelerated development after World War II.

The common boom of European capitalism and socialism

The post-World War II period has been an unprecedented period of
economic growth in all parts of Europe, of income rises, of a widening of
material resources. We can compile a table demonstrating this (see Table
7.1), less aesthetically pleasing than a growth curve but containing more
precise information than a graph.

The figures in Table 7.1 should be taken as estimates with a considerable
margin of error for each country.[2] They are, however, robust enough to
draw a reliable picture of historical development. By mid-century the
annually available economic resources of Europeans were about the double
of what they had been in 1913. That meant an annual growth rate of about
1.8%, which was a remarkable achievement for a period containing two
major wars, two waves of revolution, and one big depression – inflated, it is
true, by small lucky countries counting as much as larger, less lucky ones.
Before the rise of industrial capitalism, long-term growth rates were well
below 1% a year. True, the growth between 1820 and 1913 was somewhat
higher, at about 2.1%.[3] But between 1950 and 1990 the most developed

Table 7.1   *Economic resources in Europe, 1870–1990*
Index figures of GDP. 1913 = 100. Boundaries of 1970/1980.

Country	1870	1938	1950	1965	1990
Austria	36	103	110	242	550
Belgium	43	125	146	251	534
Bulgaria	–	157	219	579	–
Czechoslovakia	–	150[a]	156	282	–
Denmark	32	187	248	438	798
Finland	31	198	243	498	1,205
France	49	121	145	299	672
W. Germany	30	169	177	480	866
Greece	–	219	168	438	1,148
Hungary	–	134	128	247	–
Ireland	–	109	124	177	488
Italy	54	148	170	385	934
Netherlands	41	172	243	480	1,003
Norway	41	208	292	521	1,264
Poland	–	105[b]	–	–	–
Portugal	–	145	196	394	1,112
Romania	–	178[b]	–	–	–
Spain	–	142[c]	123	309	787
Sweden	31	193	279	504	893
Switzerland	41	163	210	425	732
UK	45	133	161	247	431
USSR	35	198	253	630	–
Yugoslavia	–	156	181	418	–
Europe[d]	*39*	*157*	*189*	*393*	*839*
Western Europe	*39*	*160*	*202*	*398*	*824*

Notes: [a] 1937. [b] Manufacturing production only. [c] 1935. [d] Unweighted. [e] Excl. Greece, Ireland, Portugal and Spain.

Sources: Total volumes 1870–1965: A. Maddison, *Ontwikkelingsfasen van het kapitalisme*, Utrecht, Het Spectrum, 1982, pp. 230ff; and idem, 'Economic Policy and Performance in Europe, 1913–1970', in C. Cipolla (ed.), *The Fontana Economic History of Europe*, Vol. 5:2, London, Collins/Fontana, 1976, Appendix B, for countries not included in the former source, i.e. Eastern Europe and poor Western Europe; for USSR/Russia in 1870: A. Maddison, *Economic Growth in Japan and the USSR*, London, George Allen & Unwin, 1969, p. 155. Manufacturing in Poland and Romania: I. Svennilson, *Growth and Stagnation in the European Economy*, Geneva, UN Economic Commission for Europe, 1954, pp. 304–5; 1990: calculations from OECD, *Historical Statistics, 1960–1990*, Paris, 1992, Table 3.1, p. 48 taking Maddison's *Ontwikkelingsfasen* 1960 figures as the base year.

Western European economies were growing by 3.6% annually, as can be calculated from Table 7.1.

Now, annual rates of economic growth are more apt as economic policy indicators, and as goalposts in ideological economic polemics, than as pointers to long-term historical trends, because they don't take the size of growth into account. Therefore, Table 7.1 is arranged so as to emphasize the magnitudes involved. One way of reading it is that between 1950 and 1990 Western European economic resources expanded by six times those available at the end of the so-called Belle Epoque. Or, with another baseline, by three times the resources available in 1950.

In terms of national patterns, leaving aside for a moment the thorny issue of the economic record of Communist Eastern Europe, we can say that over the long haul, since 1870, the Nordic countries have pushed themselves forward most strongly. This holds in particular for Finland, increasing its national product by about forty times between 1870 and 1990, Norway and Sweden doing so around thirty times, and Denmark – the most developed Scandinavian country at the outset – by about twenty-five times. After 1950, Greece and Portugal have given Finland and Norway a good match.

Also for Eastern Europeans the postwar period meant an enormous widening of opportunities, an unprecedented soaring of the level of living. Exactly how much is considerably less certain, however, and still less the concrete trajectories of investment and consumption. The fall of the Communist regimes has opened up the data archives, and once the new ideological dust settles better historical series will certainly come forward. For a non-specialist to enter that fray now is unwise. Since even OECD economic figures often don't survive more than one annual of OECD statistics, we should not expect anyone yet to have very reliable growth rates or per capita income figures for Eastern Europe. Comparisons with other countries may only be made with considerable margins of error. But all this does not seriously undermine the available evidence that Communist Europe underwent significant, if by no means unique, economic growth.

The most ambitious, respectable historical estimate available is that Eastern European GNP per capita was about 60 per cent of the Western European in 1913, falling after World War I to 55% on the eve of the Depression, then moving up again to about two-thirds in 1938. By 1950 the Eastern national product had decreased somewhat, then to bend upwards to a good two-thirds again by 1960.[4]

Most of the recent controversy about Eastern European economic development has concentrated on the last decades of the previous regime, on what Gorbachev and his associates called 'the period of stagnation'. To offset this Table 7.2 takes 1965 as the year of assessment.

Even at the lower end of postwar Eastern advance, the average annual growth of the Czechoslovak and Hungarian economies, of 4.3%, is well worth the respect of economic historians, and it has a considerable margin of revision before it would lose it. The main impression is surely that, Communist or capitalist, it is an all-European growth pattern we see at work.

This is corroborated by the estimates of Summers and Heston (see Table 7.3), used already in Table 3.1 above, and which we shall utilize again.

In 1945–50 the USA was at the pinnacle of its world power and relative affluence. Since then, the economic distance to the rest of the world has diminished, save for the poorest countries. By 1950 most of the direct wartime destructions had been overcome in Europe. The national product

Table 7.2 *Economic growth in Eastern and Western Europe, 1950–1965 (1965 GDP as a multiple of that of 1950)*

Poor Western Europe[a]	2.31
Poor Eastern Europe[b]	2.48
Medium Western Europe[c]	2.23
Medium Eastern Europe[d]	1.87

Notes: [a] Greece and Portugal. [b] Bulgaria, USSR, Yugoslavia. [c] Austria and Italy. [d] Czechoslovakia and Hungary.

Sources: As Table 7.1

Table 7.3 *European growth in intercontinental perspective*

Index of GDP per capita. USA = 100. Continental averages unweighted.

Area	1950	1965	1980
Western Europe[a]	44	58	69
Eastern Europe[b]	29	41	48
Rich New World[c]	69	74	76
Latin America[d]	25	27	32
Africa[e]	17	18	22
South Asia[f]	8	8	7
Japan	17	43	72
Asian Tigers[g]	10	14	28
Turkey	15	19	26
Israel	17	46	51

Notes: [a] Austria, Belgium, Denmark, Finland, France, Germany, Greece, Ireland, Italy, the Netherlands, Norway, Portugal, Spain, Sweden, Switzerland, UK. [b] Bulgaria, Czechoslovakia, the GDR, Hungary, Poland, Romania, the USSR, Yugoslavia. [c] Australia, Canada, New Zealand. [d] Argentina, Brazil, Chile, Mexico. [e] Egypt, Nigeria, South Africa. [f] India, Pakistan. [g] South Korea (from 1953) and Taiwan.

Source: Calculations from R. Summers and A. Heston, 'Improved International Comparisons of Real Product and Its Composition: 1950–1980', *The Review of Income and Wealth* 30 (1984) pp. 220–1, 259–60.

per inhabitant of the three then developed big European countries – Britain, France and Germany – was then on the average about 48% of that in the USA. In 1929, at the peak of jazzing 1920s, it had been 55%. (In 1989 the corresponding figure was 71%, for the EC 65%.[5])

The remarkable postwar all-European economic growth is, then, hardly characterizable as a recovery from the ravages of war. It is a new economic dynamic, common to Communist and capitalist Europe alike. As such it has an equivalent in the first two decades after World War II only in two other countries in the whole world, in Japan, and in the new state of Israel.

This common European dynamic has so far been barely noted in comparison with another novelty of the post-1945 world: the emergence of a tripolar economically developed world, with the Japanese GDP/capita 13% higher than that of the European Community in 1990. Japan surpassed the EC in this respect in the course of 1981.[6]

What might account for this European success, common to Communist socialism – at least for a couple of decades – as well as to all varieties of European capitalism?

To my knowledge, the question has hardly been raised by economic historians yet, and to answer it properly is clearly beyond my competence. But a hypothesis might be advanced. The postwar boom of European socialism and capitalism got a particular impetus from the war, from its destruction and from its socio-economic lessons.[7] We should also expect to find this special war effect, if there is one, in Japan and, after a certain delay, in Korea and in the new Guomindang Taiwan, in Southeast Asia generally. (Israel is a special case, as a new New World, yet also formed through war.)

Within Europe, the war effect should differentiate between those countries not ravaged by war and occupation, i.e. Ireland, Portugal, Sweden, Switzerland and the UK, and the rest, although we should expect there to be some spill-over into the former because of Marshall Aid, Nato, and other intra-European and Euro-American links. Prima facie evidence here gives partial support for the hypothesis. The UK and the two poor non-ravaged countries, Ireland and Portugal, did have a slower growth from 1950 to 1965 than the European average, but not the two rich neutrals, Sweden and Switzerland. The latter were, of course, very much economically integrated into the rest of Europe, as open, export-oriented economies, and should have benefited more strongly from the all-European dynamism than the three other countries outside the war zones.

It stands at least as a very plausible hypothesis that postwar European modernity has been very significantly shaped by the socio-economic dynamics unleashed by the contingency of World War II. Below we shall also see, however, strong evidence of the enormous cultural loss postwar Europe has suffered from the temporary victory of Fascism.

Let us return to the economic record. Another way of questioning the conventional East–West divide is to make use of a statistical technique, cluster analysis, for dividing units into groups, so that the within-group differences are as small and the between-groups differences as large as possible. If we divide Europe into four groups with respect to their GDP per capita (see Table 7.4), what clusters of countries do we then find? The electronics of computer statistics may be seen as a contemporary sister to the blindfolded goddess of Justice.

There were no downwardly mobile countries in Europe between 1950 and 1980. Denmark, Sweden and Switzerland stayed in the rich, the Netherlands and the UK in the upper middle, and Romania in the poor group. All the other eighteen countries moved upwards, i.e. the European economies became more skewed towards their richer pole. Austria, France, East Germany, West Germany and Italy moved two steps on the intra-European ladder of four. The others one step.

**Table 7.4   *Clusters of European countries with regard to GDP/capita,
1950–1980***

Cluster	1950	1965	1980
Rich	Denmark Sweden Switzerland	Denmark Sweden Switzerland	Austria Belgium Denmark France West Germany Norway Sweden Switzerland
Upper middle	Belgium Netherlands Norway UK	Austria Belgium Finland France West Germany Netherlands Norway UK Czechoslovakia East Germany	Finland Italy Netherlands UK Czechoslovakia East Germany
Lower middle	Austria Finland France West Germany Czechoslovakia	Ireland Italy Spain Bulgaria Hungary Poland USSR	Greece Ireland Portugal Spain Bulgaria Hungary Poland USSR Yugoslavia
Poor	Greece Ireland Italy Portugal Spain Bulgaria East Germany Hungary Poland USSR Yugoslavia	Greece Portugal Romania Yugoslavia	Romania

Source: Calculations from Summers and Heston, 'Improved International Comparisons'.

For the last years of the disappeared Communist regimes we now have
high-powered external estimates which may give us a glimpse of the relative
extent of stagnation (see Table 7.5).

Table 7.5 *Economic growth, East and West, 1970–1988*

GDP at domestic market prices of 1987; 1980 as multiple of 1970; 1988 as multiple of 1980.

Country	GDP 1980/1970	GDP 1988/1980
Austria	1.43	1.14
Greece	1.58	1.12
Italy	1.44	1.18
Portugal	1.60	1.20
Albania	n.a.	1.14
Bulgaria	n.a.	1.33
Czechoslovakia	n.a.	1.13
Hungary	1.61	1.16
Poland	n.a.	1.11
Romania	n.a.	1.19
USSR	1.70	1.35
Yugoslavia	1.80	1.02

Source: Ex-Communist countries: P. Marer et al., *Historically Planned Economies: A Guide to the Data*, New York, World Bank, 1992, country tables; other countries: World Bank, *World Tables 1992*, Baltimore and London, Johns Hopkins University Press, 1992, country tables.

If the World Bank economists are to be believed, it is difficult to pin the blame for the fall of Communism on non-capitalist economics having reached a dead end. With the exception of Yugoslavia there was no spectacular economic failure in the last decade.

That modest conclusion is not, it should be added, incompatible with a growing economic dissatisfaction among the population, both with regard to specific difficulties of provision and in relationship to levels of aspiration, raised highly in the 1980s by the reception of Western television and of much other information from the West. We shall come back to the East European experience of economic development in the last section of Chapter 15.

The rise and modelling of consumer societies

From a sociological point of view, one of the most important implications of this postwar economic growth period was that it gave birth to the mass consumer, Europe-wide. In other words, the development of mass markets for consumer goods, following upon the emergence of market options to the masses, whose incomes now had outgrown basic necessities. In the history of class societies, this is a new, late modern phenomenon. In classical class analysis, classes are defined as different kinds of producers and as non-producers appropriating and consuming products of the producing classes. From that baseline, the rise of mass consumption may be seen either as a blurring of class divisions, or as an extension of class divisions into consumption patterns.

Spanish household surveys provide a telling example of the new process. In 1958, on average 60% of the expenditure of Spanish households was spent on food and housing. In 1968 expenditure on these necessities had decreased to 55% of annual spending, in 1973/4 to 48%, in 1985 to 44%, and in 1988 to 42%. The decline of the share of food was even more striking, from 55% in 1958 to 44% in 1968, and to 27% in 1988.[8] In the late 1980s, food (excluding alcohol and tobacco, which in the British Isles amounted to more than half of solid food expenditure), housing and heating took up between one-third and two-fifths of Western European consumers' money, except in Greece and Portugal, where they still required almost half of total expenditure.[9]

Two features of the new mass consumption stand out as particularly important determinants of people's everyday life, the television set and the automobile. In Europe both became items of the masses at the same time, in the course of the 1960s, with some lag in Southern Europe. It is one of the fastest processes of social mutation and diffusion in modern times.

It had its precursors, however, in the radio and in the pre-mass distribution of cars. Let us first look at the patterning of the embryos of the later consumer society (see Table 7.6).

On these two items of consumption Europeans tended to groups themselves into four clusters on the eve of World War II. At the bottom were the Balkan, the Appenine and the Iberian peninsulas together with Poland and, we may safely assume, the USSR; in brief, the southeastern rim of Europe. Top consumers, on the other hand, were the British and the French, followed by Germans, Swiss and Scandinavians, and the inhabitants of the Low Countries. A lower-middle group was formed by Austria, Finland, Czechoslovakia, Hungary and Ireland, the latter with a remarkable Anglo-inspired car density, however. The USA was very far ahead, while Japan in this respect resembled Hungary.

Let us now look into the development of mass consumption society, as indicated by the purchase of significant consumer durables (see Table 7.7).

Around 1960 there were about 3 persons per household in Europe,[10] so a good 300 cars or TV sets per thousand population would have meant that virtually every household had one. A hundred promille would mean mass ownership. For instance, by 1965, at 131/1000 above, slightly more than half of all French working-class households had a TV.[11] European mass consumption in this, somewhat special, sense starts in Sweden and Britain in the late 1950s, rolls over most of the Western continent in the 1960s, and finally reaches Spain in the 1970s, and Greece and Portugal in the 1980s.

The most dramatic jump to mass consumerism took place in Sweden between 1955 and 1960, and Sweden led European consumerism in the 1960s and 1970s, then to be overtaken by West Germany. In car consumption France made even by the end of the 1980s, whereas Switzerland and, most worth noting, Italy surpassed the rich arctic welfare state in this sort of private consumer urge.

Let us now make a comparison with Eastern Europe. Did mass consumption reach the citizens of Communist socialism? The answer, according to Table 7.8, is yes. The general diffusion of television started earlier and

Table 7.6 *Radios in Europe, Japan and the USA, 1938–1960; cars in 1937 (passenger cars and radio receivers per thousand inhabitants)*

Country	Radios 1938	Radios 1950	Radios 1960	Cars 1937
Albania	n.a.	7	33	n.a.
Austria	101	190	279	5
Belgium	135	179	289	17
Bulgaria	8	31	182	n.a.
Czechoslovakia	72[a]	195	259	6
Denmark	178	283	332	27
Finland	81	180	276	7
France	114	165	241	48[b]
W. Germany	172	180	287	16
E. Germany	172	190	323	16
Greece	3	22	94	1
Hungary	44	66	222	3
Ireland	51	100	174	17
Italy	(23)[c]	68	162	6
Netherlands	129	195	272	11
Norway	125	241	285	16
Poland	27	59	177	1
Portugal	11	27	95	4
Romania	17	19	109	1
Spain	11[d]	32	90	3[e]
Sweden	196	307	367	21
Switzerland	131	221	270	17
UK	182	244	289	40[f]
USSR	n.a.	61	205	n.a.
Yugoslavia	9	21	84	1
Japan	58	93[g]	n.a.	0.5
USA	310–20[h]	590[h]	n.a.	197

Notes: [a] 1937. [b] 1939 and the figure includes also small vans. [c] Licences, excl. free licences, and a single licence may cover more than one receiver. This figure is probably incomparably low. [d] 1940. [e] 1948. [f] Great Britain only. [g] 1949. [h] Estimates of sets in use.

Sources: Radios in 1938: calculations from United Nations, *Statistical Yearbook 1951*, New York, 1951, Tables 178 and 1 (population of 1937); the population figures have been checked with those of P. Flora (ed.), *State, Economy and Society in Western Europe, 1815–1975*, Vol. 2, Frankfurt, Campus, 1987, Ch. 1, and in the French and German cases of discrepancy the latter source has been used. Radios in 1950 and 1960: *Unesco Statistical Yearbook 1963*, Paris, 1964, pp. 451ff. Cars in 1937: calculations from United Nations, *Statistical Yearbook 1951*, Tables 136 and 1, and Flora, *State, Economy and Society*, Ch. 1.

went further than in the poorest countries of Western Europe, i.e. than in Portugal and Greece. Also the private car got rolling, although a decade later than in the West. Czechoslovakia and the GDR were in the end on par with Ireland and Spain. The supply of passenger cars to Bulgarians, Hungarians, Poles and Yugoslavs was about equal to that available to Greeks and Portuguese. The quality of the goods – e.g. the comfort of the cars, the

Table 7.7 *The spread of the car and the TV in postwar Western Europe, Japan and the USA (units per thousand population)*

Country	1950 Car	1950 TV	1960 Car	1960 TV	1965 Car	1965 TV	1970 Car	1970 TV	1975 Car	1975 TV	1989 Car	1989 TV
Austria	7	–	57	27	109	98	162	192	192	254	366	328
Belgium	32	–	82	68	142	163	213	216	267	252	335	447
Denmark	28	–	89	119	156	228	218	266	289	308	282	528
Finland	7	–	41	21	99	159	152	221	n.a.	n.a.	303	488
France	37[a]	–	121	41	196	131	252	201	290	235	340	402
W. Germany	13	–	81	83	158	200	227	272	289	305	412	506
Greece	1	–	5	n.a.	12	n.a.	26	10	49	106	116	195
Ireland	31	–	62	17	99	89	134	172	165	178	222	271
Italy	7	–	40	43	106	117	192	181	270	213	459	423
Netherlands	14	–	45	69	104	172	192	223	254	259	362	485
Norway	20	–	63	13	125	131	193	220	n.a.	n.a.	369	423
Portugal	7	–	18	5	35	20	60	38	84	66	159	176
Spain	3	–	9	8	26	55	70	174	119	174	229	389
Sweden	36	–	160	156	232	270	285	312	336	354	369	471
Switzerland	31	–	95	24	155	104	221	203	285	n.a.	394	406
UK	46	11	105	211	165	248	209	293	249	315	366	434
Japan[b]	0.3	–	5	145	n.a.	n.a.	65	220	132	237	285	610
USA	266	n.a.	347	n.a.	387	289	436	321	495	571	589	814

Notes: [a] 1948. [b] 1949 instead of 1950.

Sources: A.S. Deaton, 'The Structure of Demand in Europe, 1920–1970', in C. Cipolla (ed.), *The Fontana Economic History of Europe*, Vol. 5:1, London, Collins/Fontana, 1976, pp. 124–5 (Europe 1950–70); Eurostat, *Review 1975–1984*, Luxemburg, 1986, p. 110 (1975); Eurostat, *Basic Statistics of the Community*, 29th edn, Luxemburg 1992, p. 295 (TV 1989); United Nations, *Statistical Yearbook 1988/89*, New York, 1992, Table 112 (cars in use in Austria, Ireland, the Netherlands and the UK in 1989); World Bank, *World Tables 1992*, country tables (population figures for the countries of the previous source); *Statistisches Jahrbuch der Schweiz 1992*, Zurich, Verlag Neue Zürcher Zeitung, 1991, p. 220; *Japan Statistical Yearbook 1991*, Mainichi Shinbusha, Tokyo, 1991, p. 687; *Statistical Handbook of Japan 1988*, Tokyo, Statistics Bureau, 1988, Tables 5 and 41; *The Statistical History of the United States*, ed. B. Wattenberg, New York, Basic Books, 1976, pp. 10 and 716 (US cars, 1950–70); *Statistical Abstract of the United States 1989*, Washington, DC, Dept of Commerce, 1989, pp. 7, 596 (US cars); US TV diffusion in 1970 and 1975 is calculated from rounded-off data in *Statistical Abstract of the United States 1990*, Washington, DC, Dept. of Commerce, 1990, p. 550.

colour of TV sets – is not captured in Table 7.8, but the differences are known and systematic, in Western favour. Nor, perhaps more importantly, does the Table show the erratic shortages arising from a malfunctioning centralization of retailing.[12] Nevertheless, the main picture is a common mass consumption society, the internal differentiation of which does not follow the postwar political border of demarcation.

The historical development of configurations of the consumption of durables is apparent if we combine the data of the three previous tables and submit them to a cluster analysis (see Table 7.9).

By the end of Eastern European Communism, the major durables consumption divide of the northern latitudes did not run geo-politically,

Table 7.8   *Passenger cars and TV sets in Eastern Europe, 1960–1989 (cars and receivers per thousand inhabitants)*

Country	1960 Cars	1960 TV	1975 Cars[a]	1975 TV	1989 Cars	1989 TV
Albania	–	–	–	2	–	83
Bulgaria	–	0.6	–	225	140[a]	249
Czechoslovakia	20	58	100	337	200	410
E. Germany	18	60	110	(465)[b]	234	413[b]
Estonia	–	–	–	–	109[c]	349[c]
Hungary	4	10	55	271	164	409
Poland	4	14	30	209	120[d]	292
Romania	1	3	–	139	50[a]	194
USSR	–	22	30[e]	217	58	323
Yugoslavia	3	1.4	70	159	131[d]	197

Notes: [a] Rounded off, approximate figures. [b] The Unesco-reported GDR figures for 1975 and for 1989 (779) are unbelievably high. They may be due to some error in the Unesco statistics production. A recalculation from East German statistics would yield a 1988 figure of 413. Part of the high figure may be due to demographic and social policy factors, the larger part of it is most likely due to error. The two former possibilities would derive from an aged population of small households, and from old age pensioners not having to pay a television licence (G. Edwards, *GDR Society and Social Institutions*, London, Macmillan, 1985, p. 176). My recalculation is based on the conservative assumption that the 95.7% of all GDR households with a TV set had only one. Counting colour TV receivers only in the same way would give us a figure of 224 per thousand. [c] 1985. [d] 1988. [e] 1978.

Sources: TV receivers: United Nations, *Statistical Yearbook 1970*, New York, 1971, Table 212; Unesco, *Statistical Yearbook 1991*, Paris, 1991, Table 9.2; Cars: Deaton, 'The Structure of Demand', p. 124; calculations from United Nations, *Statistical Yearbook 1987* and *1988/89*, New York, 1990 and 1992, Tables 133 and 112, respectively (cars), and population figures from the World Bank, *World Tables 1992*, Marer et al., *Historically Planned Economies*, country tables (1975 and Bulgaria and Romania 1989); calculations from G. Fischbach (ed.), *DDR-Almanach '90*, Landsberg, Bonn-Aktuell, 1990, pp. 24, 45, 93 (GDR cars and TVs in 1988); Eurostat, *Basic Statistics of the Community*, 29th edn, p. 309 (USSR 1989). Estonia: M. Rywkin, *Soviet Society Today*, New York, M.E. Sharpe, 1989, p. 125.

between 'East' and 'West', but between North America and Europe.[13] The late 1980s difference in the diffusion of cars between, say, the USA and the UK was larger than that between the latter and former East Germany, and the gap between Canada and Denmark wider than that between Denmark and Czechoslovakia. Japanese per capita consumption of cars was in quantitative terms closer to the East German than to the West German pattern, although the two Germanies were closer to each other.

Between the four clusters of consumption, there was only one clear case of downward mobility and that was outside Europe: Argentina. (Denmark has had less of an automobile expansion than might have been expected, opting for a more TV-concentrated pattern of consumption. Whether that should be regarded as a relative climbdown is at least open to argument.)

Table 7.9 *Intercontinental clusters of mass consumption in 1938 and in 1989–1990*

Four clusters of similar distributions of radios and cars in 1938, of TV sets and cars in 1989–90. Europe, Argentina, Japan and the USA.

1938	1989–90
Cluster 1: Highest consumption USA	*Cluster 1: Highest consumption* USA
Cluster 2: Next highest consumption Belgium Denmark Germany Netherlands Norway Sweden Switzerland UK	*Cluster 2: Car-driven*[a] Austria Belgium Czechoslovakia Finland France East Germany West Germany Hungary Italy Netherlands Norway Spain Sweden Switzerland UK
Cluster 3 Argentina Austria Czechoslovakia Finland France	*Cluster 3: TV-driven*[a] Denmark Japan
Cluster 4: Lowest consumption Albania Bulgaria Greece Hungary Ireland Italy Japan Poland Portugal Romania Spain Yugoslavia	*Cluster 4: Lowest consumption* Albania Argentina Bulgaria Greece Poland Portugal Romania USSR Yugoslavia

Note: [a] Cluster 2 is held together by high car ownership (average 327 per thousand) and by relatively lower TV ownership (429 per thousand), whereas cluster 3 is characterized the other way around (with average TV ownership at 569 per thousand and car ownership at 284).

Sources: Tables 7.6, 7.7 and 7.8 above.

No Eastern European country fell back in relative mass consumption under Communism. Hungary actually jumped upwards, together with Ireland, Italy, Japan and Spain. Czechoslovakia climbed one step, together with Austria, Finland and France.

Both because of its historical origins and because of its socially structuring effects the rise of consumer society may well be called an *Americanization of Europe.*

As an object of mass consumption (as well as of mass production), the car is an American invention. Already in 1929 there were 190 cars per thousand Americans,[14] a figure not reached by any European country until after 1960.[15] But relatively little of the special American auto culture, from car models to city planning, seems to have been imported into Europe. It is further noteworthy that the Japanese apparently are more eager producers than consumers of cars. They have, of course, *inter alia*, good spatial reasons for that.

Television is a postwar phenomenon on both sides of the Atlantic, apart from experimental broadcasting, which also occurred on both shores. But it started somewhat earlier and spread more rapidly in the USA, from the Northeast. By 1952 37% of American homes had a TV set.[16] (We shall return to the phenomenon of mass culture below.)

The mass consumer emerged in the USA, and many of the preset standards of mass choice derive from there, with regard not only to consumer durables, but also to non-durables, such as jeans, Coca/Pepsi Cola and fast food. McDonald's went abroad only as late as 1970, starting in Canada and opening in Australia and Japan prior to doing so in Western Europe. Beginning in the Netherlands and in Germany in 1971, American hamburgers captured a significant mass market in Europe in the course of the 1970s.[17] In Eastern Europe they reached a segment of the upscale food market just before Communism expired. The self-service shop and the 'supermarket' also spread across Europe in our period from its American home-base. The department store, however, is an invention of the French Second Empire and the retail chain is of late Victorian British origin.[18]

Mass consumption is pertinent to class structuration of culture and social action in several, albeit rarely unambiguous, ways. The use of the two core symbols of mass consumption, the car and the TV, both tend to favour the walled-off individual/family rather than the collective circle and public dialogue, even if Scandinavia has shown, so far, that the individual and the family and the collective circle and public dialogue may also be combined in strong forms of both.

Although consumption patterns tend to have a considerable class imprint, the development of discretionary consumption possibilities for the whole population enlarges the possibility of chosen life-styles and chosen consumption identities. In the 1980s a considerable international literature, rhetoric and amount of research on life-styles developed, as topics of journalism, as targets of advertising and marketing, and as foci of sociological and political analysis. The whole scale of positions from class-determined distinctions to economically independent consumption patterns was represented, and a large number of styles have been discovered and subjected to competitive labelling. But, on the whole, the prevailing tendency has been to combine economic position, age, sometimes gender, and cultural choice into different configurations of life conduct.[19]

We shall leave, for the time being, the ongoing controversy about how to interpret the meaning and the implications of new modes of consumption. Discretionary mass consumption has clearly added something to classical class structuration. On the other hand, life-styles are not chosen at random socially.

Configurations of Western capital

Class is also capital, in forms and in power. The structure of Western European big enterprise turned out, in the end, to have been relatively little affected by the ravages of war and by the aspirations of the postwar settlements. Only in Austria, due to fear of Soviet intervention in the economy, and in France were there enduring restructurations, which here took the form of nationalizations. Public enterprise tended to expand immediately after the war in most countries, as we noted at the end of Chapter 6, and some of them were to ride the ensuing boom, in Finland, Italy, Spain, for example. But prewar constellations of big private capital, including business dynasties, remained, or re-asserted themselves. The permanence of the Agnellis (of Fiat) and the return of the Krupps, till the final economic crisis of German steel, are only the most spectacular cases. West Germany came gradually to represent a considerable rupture in German cultural history, as we shall examine in Part IV below. But after some early attempts by the Allies and by the anti-Fascist left to the contrary, most of the prewar German capital structure re-emerged out of the ruins.

In this section we shall abstain from entering into the field of postwar business history. Instead we shall confine ourselves to taking stock of Western European variations, around 1990, in the configurations and the weight of capital.

Western Europe has a large number of very big industrial corporations. Among the world's top 100 in 1990, 45 companies were European, 33 American, and 16 Japanese, while 6 were based in the rest of the world. In comparison with the American and the Japanese company structure, the European one is top-heavy, with a larger proportion of its 168 of the world's 500 largest industrial enterprises concentrated in the first quintile, than USA of its 164 and Japan of its 110.

On the other hand, few European corporations are world-leading. Among 26 industrial branches singled out by the editors of *Fortune*, US companies were the biggest in 13, Europe in 7 and Japan in 6. In one or two cases the European placement probably means little more than having the largest sales figure within a not very distinctively defined industrial branch: for example, Spanish INI in 'mining, crude oil production' and, perhaps slightly less dubiously, Italian IRI in 'metals'. If that argument is accepted, there would be only four cases of European world leadership among twenty-four industrial branches. The champions are French Saint-Gobain in building materials, Swiss-Swedish Asea-Brown Boveri in industrial and farm equipment, Dutch AKZO in metal products, British-Dutch Shell in petroleum refining, and British BAT in tobacco. The industrial classification is not beyond dispute, but, nevertheless, the absence of any German firm is noteworthy.[20]

Fortune magazine has also compiled a list of the world's 500 largest service corporations out of eight different sublists of service activities. According to this list 199 are European, 150 American and 106 are Japanese. Their distribution across the sublists varies strongly. Nine Japanese trading houses top the list of the 100 largest 'diversified service companies', followed by the American ATT and the German Veba. Five Japanese banks head a ranking of the 100 largest commercial banks (by assets, but also, with few modifications, by deposits), followed by three French banks, another Japanese, Deutsche Bank and Barclay's Bank. The world of finance is further represented by two other groupings, of fifty, which are hardly independent of the set-up of the banks. The 'fifty largest diversified financial companies' (by assets) list is led by the French Cie. de Suez, followed by American Express. The fifty largest savings institutions are headed by two British building societies, and include also seven Spanish Caixas. The Japanese savers absent themselves from that league, however.[21] The largest life insurance companies are Japanese and American, followed by British Prudential and German Allianz.

The three largest retailing companies are American, but twenty-one of the fifty are European, with German Tengelmann and French E. Leclerc as the largest. The largest utilities corporations are publicly owned. In terms of revenue it is Nippon Telegraph and Telephone, in terms of assets Electricité de France. The world's two largest transportation companies (in revenue terms) in 1990 were the government-owned French and German railway companies, followed by the private American United Parcel Service, and by Air France. But if the private Franco-Belgian diversified leisure Cie. International des Wagons-Lits had been allowed to run in the transportation class, it would have won.

Crudely summarized, we may say that in the service world the Japanese dominate finance and wholesale trading, the Americans have a clear lead in retail trade, and American Time-Warner is the biggest entertainment corporation on the lists. The Europeans are particularly prominent in transport and in utilities, the two branches with the largest component of public service.[22]

The weight of capital and big enterprise is unevenly distributed across Europe. A good source concerning the former here is the *Financial Times* top 500 list of the largest European corporations according to their market capitalization. This is a pertinent measure of capitalist power, as it includes both financial and industrial corporations according to their worth on the stock market, *the* capitalist criterion of value. The drawback is that firms owned by individuals or families outside the stock market are not counted.

In a sense, then, the FT 500 is a measure of *impersonal capitalism*. With that qualification, we should expect that, *ceteris paribus*, the larger and the more concentrated capital is in a country, the bigger is the power of capital in the class structure. 'Power' here means capacity to act, not necessarily a zero-sum share of control over others. The power of labour is most immediately gauged as the rate of trade union organization, and not as an absence of big capital. Therefore it is possible for combinations like strong capital plus strong labour, or weak capital plus weak labour to exist. (Cf. the section on the rights of property and labour in Chapter 6 above, and that on class action and class organization in Chapter 15 below.)

The *Fortune* Industrial and Service 500s, by comparison, express the weight of big enterprise, some of which is in fact publicly owned. In cases where the publicly owned enterprise is important, it will be highlighted in the text. Together, the three measures of Table 7.10, properly qualified, should give us a reasonably systematic brief overview of capitalist enterprise in Europe.

The ranking between individual countries has a certain market volatility and may change from one year to another, but there is also a more basic pattern. With regard to capitalization, Swiss capital is in a category of its own, followed by the UK and, rather surprisingly for some perhaps, by Sweden. A calculation for capital values in 1993 of the fifty largest companies in Europe confirmed the unique position of Switzerland ($21,600 per capita), the second rank of the UK ($6,600), but placed the Netherlands ($5,100) before Sweden ($3,500). Germany ($1,500), France ($1,300), Spain ($600) and Italy ($500) were well behind, and no other country made it into the top fifty. (Belgium had two in the 51–100 division.[23])

Little-developed capital markets, family capitalism and, particularly in Austria, France and Italy, little-capitalized big state enterprise bring the capital score down in France, Austria and in Southern Europe. Privatizations are now gradually changing this, above all in Latin Europe. Germany has further kept into high modernity an important set of personally owned enterprises. Capital shares are much less spread in Germany and France than in Britain and in the Nordic countries. Switzerland and Belgium also have a very concentrated ownership of shares.[24] London alone has almost half of the EU equity market (44% in 1992), Germany and Paris having 15% each. Still, the London stock market is smaller than that of New York and Tokyo.[25]

The heavy weight of capitalist enterprise in Switzerland, Sweden and Britain is underlined again in the industrial sales and in the service assets and sales columns, although in new variations upon the theme. Germany scores rather mediocrely on all three indicators of the size of individual enterprises. Italy stays consistently low for a large country, in spite of its big state enterprises. Its banks and financial institutions put it somewhat higher up among the services list than on the industrial one. Spain's savings institutions

Table 7.10 *The weight of capital and of big enterprise in Western Europe in 1990*

The sum total of market capitalization per country and per capita by Europe's 500 largest corporation by market capitalization. 1990/1, dollars per inhabitant; the number of companies among the world's 500 largest industrial corporations; the number of companies among the world's 500 largest service companies.

Country	Capital	Industry	Service
Switzerland	18,063	10.5	13
UK	13,800	44	49
Sweden	9,248	17.5	12.4
Netherlands	6,076	8	10.5
Denmark	4,669	0	1.3
Belgium	4,198	4	5.5
Germany	4,058	30	41
France	4,045	30	33
Norway	3,220	8	1
Spain	2,161	4	14
Ireland	1,746	0	0
Italy	1,393	7	14
Luxemburg	1,231	1	0
Finland	1,147	8	1
Austria	945	1	2
Portugal	93	1	1
Iceland	0	0	0
Greece	0	0	0

Note: Corporations with a double national base, such as Shell, Unilever, Asea-Brown Boveri and the Eurotunnel Group, have been divided up half and half. The Scandinavian airline SAS has been allocated 40% to Sweden and 30% each to Denmark and Norway, which is a rough decimal translation of the division of shares, 3/7 to Sweden, 2/7 each to the others. The German per capita calculation refers to the population of the FRG.

Sources: Financial Times, 'European 500', special supplement, 13.1.1992, p. 2; Eurostat, *Demographic Statistics 1990*, Luxemburg, 1990, p. 101, and OECD, *Historical Statistics, 1960–1989*, p. 22 (national populations in 1989); *Fortune*, 29.7.1991, p. 85; *Fortune*, 26.8.1991, p. 133.

do the same. Finnish business has the opposite structure, about 1.5 big industrial enterprise per million inhabitants, but only one services listing.

But among the 25 largest employers in Western Europe in 1993, 9 were German, including the 2 clearly largest, Daimler Benz and Siemens, 6 were French, 4 were British, 2 each were Dutch and Italian, 1.5 were Swiss, and 0.5 was Swedish.[26] Capitalization and industrial muscle are not the same.

The power of financial capital seems to have taken a leap in the 1980s, with the globalization of de-regulated national markets for all kinds of speculation, and with the invention of new instruments of trading, so-called derivatives.[27] At the end of Chapter 6 we noted the enormous expansion of the trade in foreign currency, of which London is the world centre. Future economic historians might find another event in the late 1980s representing a manifestation of a major change of capitalism. In 1986 transnational capital transactions exceeded foreign trade with respect to West Germany. By 1993, capital transactions were already five times larger than trade.[28]

The configurations of capital vary both over time and across countries. Contrary to official Eastern European belief, a 'normal' capitalism is something elusive.

Issues of distribution

The distribution of income is actually a tangle of issues, even to non-philosophers and to non-statisticians. We may get a certain handle on them by focusing on two dimensions: Distribution among whom? Distribution according to what (criteria of concern)? On each we have as analysts several options, and as comparative observers we can note several in actual use.

'Distribution among whom?' may refer either to the population as an aggregate of individuals (and/or households), or to the distribution among meaningful parts of the population. The former may be seen as a statistical summary of all variants of the latter. Its measures may be taken as the best summary obtainable, but a good summary does not necessarily make the most interesting chapter.

As far as sections of the population are concerned, four kinds have received most attention. Classes, or 'socio-economic groups', as Statistics Sweden, probably the most class-conscious of current statistical bureaux, usually calls them, constitute one. Demographic categories, gender, age-groups, family types, constitute another. Thirdly, there are territorial divisions of the population, like city–countryside, different provinces, different cities. Fourthly, different ethnicities or 'races' may be distinguished. While this is long-established and official in (parts of) the New Worlds, e.g. in the USA, it is only emerging in Europe, after the previous ethnic cleansings have partly been undone.

The axis of 'distribution according to what?' refers to conceptions of distributive justice, implied or explicit. Here, we shall approach it not from the angle of theory but from the field of public discourse. In Northwestern Europe, three such discourses of distributive criteria have developed in the postwar period, two with strong prewar roots, one with more tenuous ones.

There is a British, and an ex-British rich New World focus on *poverty*, on the exclusion and the distanciation of a part of the population from the 'normal' or prevailing 'minimum' standard of living. This kind of discourse may derive from the formidable, because national and elaborate, English Poor Law, and latter-day attempts to reform it, including the important tradition of philanthropic investigation established by Mayhew, Booth and Rowntree. There are certainly other reasons too. The point I wish to make is that in my opinion the reason why British postwar social reformers, from Richard Titmuss to Brian Abel-Smith, Peter Townsend and others, are so concerned with poverty is not because there is more poverty in the UK than in other parts of Europe.[29]

In the Netherlands, and also in Belgium, Austria and Germany, the main focus of distributive discourse has not centred on poverty, but rather on 'justice' (*rechtvaardigheid*), security of existence (*bestaanszekerheid*), or, translated into professional English, income maintenance, on solidarity versus exclusion. This goes back to the search for Christian ethical and legal foundations for public intervention *vis-à-vis* market outcomes,[30] and to the centrality of social insurance to continental European social policy. To the extent that Southern Europe, including France, is to be captured by the criteria of distribution singled out here, it should be within this set of *justice, security, integration*. (The French Socialist government of the 1980s spoke also about 'inequalities', and poverty was discovered, but the characteristic concepts of social protection, exclusion/integration and solidarity were still reproduced.[31])

Swedish, and, to a somewhat lesser extent, Nordic, distributive discourse has since the late 1960s centred on *equality*. A few years after the Johnson administration had declared the American 'War on Poverty', and the British 'poverty lobby' began their action against 'child poverty', the Swedish labour movement and Social Democratic government issued the slogan 'More equality'.[32]

Overall equality is regarded as the supreme norm of distributive justice, not without contestation, true, but also without any remotely successful rival. This norm of equality is 'tous azimuts', as the French would put it, that is, it aims at all directions, statistical aggregates, classes, genders, age-groups, ethnicities, territories. Most immediately, the equality discourse took off from the late 1960s radicalization-cum-political success of Swedish Social Democracy, but it may claim an ancestral base in a free peasant society.

In pre-revolutionary Russia there had developed a unique tradition of family budget statistics, which was given a strong official boost after the Bolshevik Revolution, as a means to monitor issues of distribution and minimum subsistence. With the accumulationist drive of the Five-Year Plans and the establishment of Stalin's concept of power, distributive data became classified. Only in the mid-1950s, under Khrushchev, could distributive issues begin to be discussed again. But the latter continued to be highly sensitive, and recurrently barred from public debate, till the very last years of Communist rule in Eastern Europe.[33]

The official Communist Eastern European distributive conception was *functional*. That is, it based policies of distribution upon considerations of incentives to the proper functioning of the economic and the political system. As it was put, with characteristic GDR woodenness, in a dictionary on social policy, where distribution appears as 'Distribution according to work performance', which is called a 'specific economic law of socialism': '[Distribution] must strengthen the efforts of the working people to high work results, to a correct economic allocation of the labour force, and to the rise of qualifications.'[34] In other words, a socialist plan mirror of the market discourse on distribution for incentives preached by the bulk of Western economists, by liberal politicians and capitalist forces.

In brief, there are many ways in which this section may be written. Some aspects are dealt with elsewhere. Income security, the object of a bulky welfare state literature, was dealt with in Chapter 5, on welfare claim rights. Territorial distributions are treated in Chapter 10. Here we shall focus on the class and demographic dimensions of (in)equality and poverty.

The history of modernity is an uneven process of equalization, varying widely in time and place. It is also a story of the reproduction of poverty in an ever richer world.

Around the turn of the last century, Western Europe was more inegalitarian than the United States. That pattern began to change, with lesser shares going to the European upper classes since the late nineteenth century and with larger shares going to the top earners in the USA up till 1929. The 1930s and 1940s were years of massive Depression and wartime redistribution, ebbing out in the postwar boom.

After the war, there were minor equalizing tendencies in West Germany in the late 1950s and in the first half of the 1970s, with corresponding unequalizing tendencies in the 1960s. For the UK there was overall stability till about the 1970s, then somewhat stronger equalizing tendencies for that decade, to be sharply reversed thereafter. In 1981–2 income inequality (after tax) was slightly higher than in 1949. Amidst general boomtime distributive stability, Switzerland and Finland had a clear tendency towards a more uneven distribution, but starting from a distribution more egalitarian than that of most other countries.[35]

A good comparable cross-national data set on income distribution is now being compiled, the Luxemburg Income Survey, while the Eastern European situation, at the end of the Communist era, has been much clarified by the impressive work of Anthony Atkinson and John Micklewright. The most usual way of summarizing the income distribution is by the so-called Gini coefficient, which ranges from 0, complete equality, to 100 (or 1), maximum inequality (see Table 7.11).

We should allow for a margin of error when considering the figures in Table 7.11 as they are the result of sample surveys. But there is also a difference of methodology which overestimates inequality in the East, or, alternatively, underestimates it in the West. The Eastern surveys report the distribution of household per capita income, which means that the income of a four-member household is simply divided by four. The Western surveys try to take into account the economies of scale of a household by introducing the notion of 'equivalent income', of which a variety exist. According to the equivalence scale used in the first major Luxemburg Income Survey report, the income of a family of four would be divided by 2.5, and according to the OECD scale by 2.7.

The effect of the equivalence scales is to reduce the inequality coefficient. By how much depends on the household composition, but for Finland and the UK in the 1980s the effect has been calculated to 3–3.5 points on the Gini coefficient.[36] In other words, to be comparable the Eastern inequality measure should probably be reduced by about three units.

Table 7.11 *The distribution of net income in the East and in the West in the second half of the 1980s[a] (Gini coefficients)*

Eastern Europe	Western Europe	New World
Belorussia 23.8	Finland 20.0	Australia 28.7
Czechoslovakia 20.1	France 29.0	Canada 26.9
Hungary 24.4	W. Germany 24.5	USA 31.8
Latvia 27.4	Netherlands 26.2	
Lithuania 27.8	Norway 22.2	
Poland 26.8	Sweden 21.1	
Russia 27.8	Switzerland 33.6	
Ukraine 23.5	UK 27.8/26.5/29.3[b]	
USSR 28.9		

Note: [a] Eastern data from 1989, save in Hungary (1987) and Czechoslovakia (1988). Western data from 1985–7 except from France and Germany (1984), and from Norway (1979) and Switzerland (1980). Eastern data are per capita incomes, whereas the Western weight household members by an 'equivalence scale'. The data therefore systematically overestimate Eastern inequality. See further in the text below. [b] The first figure is the one most comparable with the other Western data, taken from the Luxemburg Income Survey; the last is calculated in the same way as the Eastern European data; the one in-between is a re-calculation from the same data base as the third figure, but according to the way Gini coefficients are currently calculated in the West.

Sources: Eastern Europe and UK the two last figures: A. Atkinson and J. Micklewright, *Economic Transformation in Eastern Europe and the Distribution of Income*, Cambridge, Cambridge University Press, 1992, p. 137, Table B13; Finland: B. Gustafsson and H. Uusitalo, 'Income Distribution and Redistribution during Two Decades: Experiences from Finland and Sweden', in I. Persson (ed.), *Generating Equality in the Welfare State*, Oslo, Norwegian University Press, 1990, p. 85; Switzerland; D. Mitchell, 'Comparative Income Transfer Systems: Is Australia the Poor Relation?', in F. Castles (ed.), *Australia Compared*, London, Allen & Unwin, 1991, p. 178. The rest: D. Mitchell, 'Taxation and Income Redistribution: The "Tax Revolt" of the 1980s Revisited', paper presented to the ISA Research Committee on Welfare Conference in Oxford, September 1993, Table B2.2; the Norwegian mid-1980s figure there had been subject to some computing error and is not used above.

With the above qualifications, three conclusions may be drawn from the table. *First*, Europe has a more egalitarian income distribution than the (developed) New World, due to the contributions of Northwestern and Eastern Europe. Southern Europe would blur the line, and the remarkable economic inequality of the Swiss, in part due to cantonal cleavages, should be noted. In 1987, after tax and transfers – neither of which, it should be said, is very important in Switzerland – per capita income of the five richest cantons was 80% higher than that of the five poorest.[37]

Secondly, Eastern Europe is, or was, on the whole more equal than Western Europe. Earnings data show this also with regard to Eastern and Western Germany.[38]

Thirdly, radical economic equality does not necessarily require a Communist revolution. Finland, and perhaps also Norway and Sweden, were in the end no less egalitarian than Hungary, and more so than Poland. Czechoslovakia, before the coming of Václavs Havel and Klaus, appears to have been the overall most egalitarian developed country in the world. As we shall see shortly, however, that summary egalitarianism contained a stark element of inequality as well.

Comparisons of *wealth* distribution are less developed, and reliable data more scanty. But the available evidence suggests a cross-national shape irreducible to that of income distribution. Britain, for instance, has a more uneven wealth distribution than other Western European countries, including France, which in this respect appears relatively little inegalitarian. Sweden comes out the least inegalitarian again, and the USA does not clearly distance itself from the European pattern.[39]

We shall approach *class aspects of inequality* by glancing at relative income shares and at the relative importance of different sources of income.

The wage (and salary) shares of economy in the EU and the USA have been basically the same for the three decades of 1960–90. The Japanese share was higher in 1960, became equal for the 1960s as a whole, but has since been significantly higher. Within the current EU 12, Greece and Ireland have been significantly above the average all the time. Somewhat below you find the Dutch and the Germans.[40]

With regard to gross profits as proportion of value added, the Japanese top the league for 1960–90, followed by the Finns and the Dutch in manufacturing, by the oil and gas-rich Dutch and Norwegians, and generally by the Canadians in industry-cum-transport and communication. US profit shares, net and gross, manufacturing or industry et al., are among the lowest in the OECD, as are, a little more even, those of the UK. The latter rose under Thatcher, but without reaching medal levels.[41]

The class division of labour and class organization (cf. Chapter 4 above and Chapter 15 below) apparently do not directly determine the class distribution of shares, whether of the value added in manufacturing (as in the OECD study) or of the economic pie as a whole (as in the EC figures). The structure of industry and its technological parameters seem to play a significant part. Only in some such way do the leading profit share of Finland and Canada (in terms of net operating surplus as part of gross value added in manufacturing) among the OECD countries, or the uniquely high wage share in Greece amidst the EC countries (followed by that of the Irish), seem to make sense.

Consultants, banks and business papers present a variety of comparative studies, of very variable reliability, of executives and managerial pay. But at least one pattern seems clearly established when relating the former to OECD or EU wage statistics. Spanish, French and Italian executives earn disproportionately more than the relative wages of their workers would warrant. In other words, class differences of income in big enterprises are particularly significant in Latin Europe. The Scandinavian executives'– workers' pay structure is the opposite of the Southern European one.[42] That Latin–Nordic divide corresponds to related ones of work organization and corporate culture, as well as of unionization.

Of old, the manual–non-manual divide has been sharper in Europe than in the New World.[43] Income data from the 1970s confirm that pattern again, particularly in the differentials between skilled workers and ordinary white-collar employees, both male and female. Whereas in France and Germany all white-collar categories had a higher income than an apprenticed skilled worker, in the USA the latter's income surpassed that of all lower non-manual groups.[44]

The Eastern European income patterning between the manual working-class and the non-managerial white-collar strata was closer to the US than to the Western European pattern. But it was not of one piece. In the USSR manual workers in the postwar period had considerably higher wages than office workers. Calculated on all non-manual/all manual, Bulgaria, Czecho-slovakia, Poland and Romania all had much lower ratios than Western European countries, represented by Belgium, West Germany and the UK. The Eastern average was 114:100, and the Western was 154:100. Hungary, however, had a ratio of 162.[45]

With the expansion of the welfare state since the 1960s, income distribution has become crucially affected by the size and by the structure of the latter, by its mode of finance and its pattern of entitlements. The welfare state has become a major source of income, comparable, in developed capitalist countries, to income from capital and entrepreneurship. While wage and profit shares of the total economy or of value added are affected by industrial structure and accumulation patterns, a look at the sources of household income may give a more concrete sense of class distribution.

We may get the most comprehensive overview of household income from the national accounts, available for most OECD countries, and lately beginning to appear for ex-Communist countries. The major source of household income apart from social and property income (see Table 7.12) is remuneration from work (including for executive and managerial work), although there are also private transfers, which in traditionally emigrant countries may be of some significance.

To the extent that the Eastern European data are reliable and comparable with the Western they are yet another nail in the coffin of 'totalitarianism'. Property income in 'socialist' Poland and Yugoslavia was more important to the national households not only than in the Nordic countries, but in the Polish case also than in Switzerland. There is in any case no clear systemic divide of relative sources of household income.

The share of property income is biggest in the least developed, the least proletarianized countries. But only in Greece is it larger than labour income.[46] In advanced capitalist countries, profits, interest, rent and entrepreneurship normally account for between a fifth and a quarter of household income. This is clearly a socially complex kind of capitalism, in the USA and Japan as well as in Europe.

In three countries the welfare state has become more important than private property as a source of household income. Public transfers of social insurance and social assistance surpass income from property and entrepre-

Table 7.12 *The importance of social and of property income*

Public transfers[a] to households, and income from property and entrepreneurship[b] as percentage of total household receipts. Averages 1985–9.

Country	Social income	Property income
Austria	17.2	19.1
Belgium[c]	20.4	26.2
Finland	15.5	18.1
France	20.0	20.8
Greece	15.2	42.3
Italy[c]	17.1	36.9
Netherlands	25.9	20.5
Norway	19.7	17.1
Portugal[c]	9.9	36.1
Spain[c]	15.7	32.3
Sweden	19.8	14.7
Switzerland	14.6	20.9
UK	13.9	23.1
W. Germany	15.5	23.6
Average W. Europe	*17.2*	*22.3*
Bulgaria[d]	19.6	n.a.
Czechoslovakia[e]	25.4	3.4
Poland[f]	20.7	25.2
Russia	14.4	n.a.
Yugoslavia[f]	13.3	20.2
Japan	12.7	23.4
USA	10.9	22.4

Notes: [a] Defined as the sum of what the national accounts statistics call 'social security benefits', 'social assistance grants' and 'transfers from general government'. Only 'pensions and allowances' and 'scholarships' are counted among the transfers, not those from 'the financial system' nor 'other income'. [b] Defined as the sum of 'operating surplus of private unincorporated enterprise' and 'property and entrepreneurial income'. [c] 1985–8. [d] 1980 and 1989 average.

Sources: Calculations from, OECD: OECD, *National Accounts 1969–1989*, Vol. 2, Paris, 1991, national tables 8; Bulgaria: I. Chernozemski, 'Children and the Transition to Market Economy in Bulgaria: "Shock Therapy" with a Difference?' in G.A. Cornia and S. Sipos (eds), *Children and the Transition to the Market Economy*, Aldershot, Avebury, 1991, p. 129. Russia: World Bank, *Statistical Handbook 1993: States of the Former USSR*, Washington, DC, 1993, p. 551. Rest of Eastern Europe: data from B. Milanovic, 'Income Distribution in Late Socialism', paper referred to by T. Smeeding et al. 'Poverty in Eastern Europe: Lessons for Crossnational Income Comparisons from LIS', in *Poverty Measurement for Economies in Transition in Eastern European Countries*, Warsaw, Polish Statistical Association and Central Statistical Office, 1992, p. 349.

neurship in the Netherlands, in Norway and in Sweden. In France the two income categories are about equal. It should be noted that the wages and salaries of public employees are not included among transfers, and, secondly, that Table 7.12 refers to the booming second half of the 1980s, when property-holders were enjoying themselves more than usual. (To eliminate arbitrary effects of annual oscillations, the proportions of Table 7.12 have been calculated as five-year averages.)

Tendencies in this remarkable direction, of public social insurance surpassing income from private property, could first be discerned in Western Europe in the Netherlands and in Sweden at the beginning of the 1970s. The possibilities of systemic combinations and the range of political-economic options are underlined by the fact that the Netherlands and Sweden are, with Belgium, among Europe's most open economies, both having world competitive big capitalist enterprise, as we saw in the previous section. Vigorous capital accumulation may be used for massive public redistributions of income, as well as mainly for the benefit of property-owners.[47]

While bearing upon class relations, the contemporary welfare state is, as we found in Chapter 5 above, above all a *demographic* institution, coping with retirement and with services for the aged. Distributive (in)equality may also be looked at according to demographic categories.

The overall income distribution of a country is strongly affected by the household composition, in terms of the number of household members who are economically active or inactive. A recent, unusually penetrating study of income distribution in Finland found household composition more important than class in determining disposable income, even among households headed by prime age adults (25–64). Class determined no more than 15% of the variation in individual income after tax and transfers, but household composition – one or two income-earners, children, etc. – determined 25%.[48] The comparison of class and demography did not take into account the life-course, however. That is, that members of all classes in the course of their lives tend to go through a series of household compositions, with and without children, with one or two income-earners, part- or full-time. Uusitalo's study concretizes the distributive importance of social demography, but it cannot, in the end, tell us exactly how important it is. Nor, to my knowledge, has any other study been able to do so.

With regard to the demography of (in)equality we shall here touch upon one demographic category only: *gender*. Whereas gender equality before the law finally was established all over Europe in the 1980s, economic inequality between men and women is universal (see Table 7.13). It is true, however, that some women are more unequal than others.

The three top female wage positions shown in Table 7.13 are all Scandinavian, with Finland somewhat behind, ranking seventh. The salary data are patchy, but they confirm Sweden's top rank in female remuneration, and show a relatively respectable but far from brilliant performance by the other Nordic nations. The New World does not in any sense distinguish itself with respect to gender economics. Japan is remuneratively the most misogynous, and in Western Europe the UK and Switzerland form the rear.

The gender earnings gap may be seen as a product of two different forces, of which only one derives from sexism and the disadvantaged social position

Table 7.13 *Economic differentials between men and women in the OECD (female position as percentage of male)*

Wage: Female hourly wage as percentage of male in manufacturing, about 1988.
Sal[ary] I and II: Monthly earnings of full-time employed women as percentage of male employees, about 1980 (Belgium, Ireland, Italy, the Netherlands in 1974); I in retail trade, II in government service.

Country	Wage	Sal. I	Sal. II
Austria	n.a.	69.5[a]	83.9
Belgium	74.5	71.1	n.a.
Denmark	84.6	72.6	n.a.
Finland	76.8	79.3	74.0
France	79.5	67.5	83.9
Greece	78.0	n.a.	n.a.
Ireland	68.9	58.5	n.a.
Italy	n.a.	85.8	n.a.
Netherlands	78.0	61.2	n.a.
Norway	85.5	80.6	76.3
Portugal	n.a.	n.a.	n.a.
Spain	n.a.	n.a.	n.a.
Sweden	89.5	92.2	92.5
Switzerland	67.5	63.0	78.8
UK	68.4	56.1	n.a.
W. Germany	72.8	67.9	n.a.
Australia	79.6	79.6	n.a.
Japan	48.9	n.a.	n.a.
New Zealand	75.3	n.a.	n.a.
USA	n.a.	60.0	n.a.

Note: [a] All private employees.

Sources: Wages: OECD, *Employment Outlook 1991*, Paris, 1991, p. 58. Salaries: OECD, *The Integration of Women into the Economy*, Paris 1985, p. 84.

of women. The other causal variable is the general pattern of income inequality. At any given level of female discrimination the gender earnings gap will vary with the overall system of income differentials. If the latter are small, the gender gap will, *ceteris paribus*, be smaller than in a society with wide differentials. North American, British and Austrian women should suffer from large, and recently widened, differentials, while Dutch, Italian and Swedish, women, for example, should draw advantages of less general earnings dispersion.[49]

A longer-term picture is that the economic gender gap has declined in Western Europe in the postwar period, except with regard to earnings in Switzerland, where only marginal changes have occurred. Income equalization generally got going from the mid-1960s. The Nordic countries were already in 1955 treating their working women slightly better than other countries, but the difference then was rather small.[50]

Outside Europe, USA actually had a widening gender gap (measured in annual earnings of full-time workers) in the 1950s, then stabilized in the 1960s and most of the 1970s, coming back to the 1953 distance only in 1981. Japan has also kept its women much lower paid, increasing the distance to male hourly earnings after 1973.

In Czechoslovakia the average female wage seems to have been two-thirds of the male one throughout the postwar period. It was 68% for manual workers in 1946 and 64% in the civil service. In 1959 women full-time workers in the whole state sector earned 66% of men's earnings, in 1988 68–9%.[51] It should be added that the Czechoslovak amount of gender discrimination was at a level that British women attained only in the second half of the 1980s, starting from median earnings in 1967 little more than half those of males.[52]

The misogynous egalitarianism of Czechoslovakia was rather specific to that country. The other Eastern European societies had both smaller gender differences and more overall inequality. But no one had much gender income equality to show. Average or median earnings for full-time women workers ranged between 70–5% of male earnings in the mid- or late 1980s, in Bulgaria, Hungary, Poland and the USSR. Therefore, Eastern European women were relatively somewhat better off than their sisters in Britain or in West Germany.[53] ('All workers' being a much more heterogeneous category than those used in Table 7.13 above, these earnings ratios exaggerate Eastern gender inequality in comparison with Western table figures.)

We may conclude that the gender earnings gap in Eastern Europe was rather similar to, albeit slightly smaller than, that in the Western part of the continent, but in the end larger than the Scandinavian ones.

Poverty has not disappeared from the rich countries of advanced modernity, at least not in the sense of a part of the population excluded from the normal standard of living of the majority. It has rightly become a matter of concern to the European Commission, which has promoted several studies of it.

It was not abolished by Communism. Even according to official sources, of the late *glasnost* era, households falling below the (low) national poverty line constituted 7.5% of the population in Czechoslovakia, between 10 and 15% in Hungary and the USSR, and between 10 and 25% in Poland. Pensioners, and pensioned farmers in particular, were the ones most exposed to poverty. The mid-1980s saw an increase in poverty in Hungary and, above all, in Poland, whereas in Czechoslovakia there was a free fall.[54]

The postwar boom and the rapid socio-economic transformations, East and West, put an end to most traditional poverty, rural, unskilled or marginal urban poverty, and for a long while to the poverty of unemployment. Even the abysmal rural poverty in the USSR and the Balkans, for long neglected by the new rulers, began to be eradicated after the end of Stalinism.

The expanding welfare state gradually drained most, but rarely all, of the poverty of old age and long-term sickness. Old age was never very well dealt with in Eastern Europe, although Hungary made considerable progress in the 1980s. Among the most developed parts of Western Europe, the persistence of a significant amount of old-age poverty in Britain and in Switzerland is noteworthy.[55]

But hardly had the processes of industrialization, urbanization, welfare expansion, economic boom and public growth policies reached their maximum effects, by the 1970s (about a decade later in the South of postwar Fascism), than the tide turned. New poverty-producing currents came pouring in.

Piecing together different national sources, a recent study has found that relative poverty – defined as an income below half of the average disposable income of the country corrected for household size – increased in the European Community in the years of crisis from 38.6 million around 1975 to 43.9 million people in 1985, i.e. 13.9% of the EC population. The highest nationally relative poverty rate was found in the poorest countries, in Greece, Ireland, Portugal and Spain, comprising between a fifth and a quarter of the population. Above average poverty was noted also in France and Denmark.[56]

There are several reasons for this increase in poverty. First, after 1974 most countries of Western Europe, one after another, have dropped the idea of full employment, and the evidence so far, of twenty years, is that once abandoned full employment does not return, even in heated booms. A new kind of permanent mass unemployment is being created.

Secondly, more unstable family patterns, together with tough labour markets, and, usually inadequate child-care facilities, have produced single parenthood with risks of poverty. Although facing much better prospects in Europe than in the (rich) New World, between a fifth and a sixth of single-parent families lived in (relative) poverty in the early 1980s in Britain, France and Switzerland, and a tenth in Germany.[57]

Thirdly, the economic transformations in the wake of de-industrialization, with the new labour market, have made many of the once invited 'guest workers', and their descendants, redundant. There is now emerging in Europe something well-known and well-established in the USA, an ethnic production of poverty.

Finally, in the early 1990s a large-scale process of impoverishment has started in Eastern Europe, as the price which old people and a good part of the former industrial working-class have to pay for the restoration of capitalism. How far it will go and how long it will continue nobody knows. But in the former Soviet Union it has already reached macabre proportions. We shall return to this subject in the following chapter.

Notes

1 J. Fourastié, *Les Trente Glorieuses*, Paris, Fayard, 1979. The title, 'the thirty glorious ones', refers to the three postwar decades, but is also a pun on the 'three glorious [days],' 27–9 July 1830, i.e. the July Revolution.

2 The OECD readjusts its statistics retroactively on and off, and for the same countries there are also some differences between the three texts by Maddison.

3 A. Maddison, *Ontwikkelingsfasen van het kapitalisme*, Utrecht, Het Spectrum, 1982, pp. 19 and 68. Maddison's averages have been recalculated, excluding non-European countries.

4 Calculated from P. Bairoch, 'The Main Trends in National Economic Disparities since the Industrial Revolution', in P. Bairoch and M. Lévy-Leboyer (eds), *Disparities in Economic Development since the Industrial Revolution*, London, Macmillan, 1981, p. 12.

5 Calculated from ibid., p. 10 (1929), and OECD, *Historical Statistics, 1960–1989*, Paris, 1991, pp. 18 and 21 (1989). The latter ratio refers to GDP per capita at purchasing power parities.

6 OECD, *National Accounts, 1960–1990*, Vol. 1, Paris, 1992, p. 147. The GDP comparisons are made in terms of purchasing power parities.

7 This would be an extension of the thesis for capitalist democracies put forward by Mancur Olson in his *The Rise and Decline of Nations*, New Haven, Conn., Yale University Press, 1982.

8 *Encuesta continua de presupuestos familiares: Año 1988*, Madrid, Instituto Nacional de Estadistica, 1989, p. 221.

9 A good overview, largely based on national official statistics is given by Euromonitor, *European Consumer Expenditure*, London, 1987. Cf. also A.S. Deaton, 'The Structure of Demand in Europe, 1920–1970', in C. Cipolla (ed.), *The Fontana Economic History of Europe*, Vol. 5:1, London, Collins/Fontana, 1976, pp. 100ff.

10 Council of Europe, *Household Structures in Europe*, Strasburg, 1990. The number has gone down since then, to about 2.5.

11 *Annuaire rétrospectif de la France, 1948–1988*, Paris, INSEE, 1990, p.154.

12 For instance, in the late 1980s, according to the city's director of trade, only 75–80% of the official consumption norm could be supplied to the population of the major industrial city of Magnitogorsk: Nikolai Gurzhii interviewed by S. Kotkin, *Steeltown, USSR*, Berkeley, University of California Press, 1991, p. 3.

13 In other respects, more closely related to features of marketing, one can, of course talk about an East–West line, with regard to brand numbers, packaging, etc.

14 *The Statistical History of the United States* ed. B. Wattenberg, New York, Basic Books, 1976, pp. 10 and 716. In the Depression the number of cars in the US went down considerably, from 23.1 million in 1929 to 20.7 in 1933. The 1929 consumption of cars was surpassed again in 1936.

15 The European countries with the highest automobile density before World War II were France, the UK and Denmark, with 41.9, 38.7 and 29.4 passenger cars per thousand inhabitants, respectively: I. Svennilson, *Growth and Stagnation in the European Economy*, Geneva, UN Economic Commission for Europe, 1954, p. 280.

16 L. Bogart, *The Age of Television*, 2nd edn, New York, Frederick Ungar, 1958, p.10.

17 J. Love, *McDonald's*, Stockholm, Svenska Dagbladet, 1987.

18 D. Davis, *A History of Shopping*, London, Routledge & Kegan Paul, 1966, pp. 283ff

19 Cf. H.-P. Müller, 'Lebensstile: Ein neues Paradigma der Differenzierungs- und Ungleich-heitsforschung?', *Kölner Zeitschrift für Soziologie* 41 (1989).

20 The above is a set of calculations and summaries from the US business magazine *Fortune*, 29.7.1991, pp. 66ff.

21 In terms of deposits, the largest building society, Abbey National, would have ranked 49 among the commercial banks.

22 The above information is culled from *Fortune*, 26.8.1991, pp. 130ff.

23 Calculations from the *Financial Times*, 20.1.1994, supplement 'The FT 500', p. 7, and from Eurostat, *Basic Statistics of the Community*, 29th edn, Luxemburg, 1992, p. 107 (population). A check of all the 500 showed that Dutch capital had just surpassed Swedish in that grouping too.

24 *International Herald Tribune* 3–4.10.1992, p. 19, reporting an international overview by Pro Share.

25 *Financial Times*, 4.3.1994, p. 8.

26 *Financial Times*, 20.1.94, supplement 'The FT 500', p. 6. Unilever and Shell are shared out among the British and the Dutch, ABB among the Swedes and the Swiss.

27 See further the 'Derivatives' supplement of the *Financial Times*, 20.10.1993.
28 *Die Zeit*, 6.5.1994, p. 28, reporting data from the Bundesbank.
29 See further, e.g. R. Walker, et al. (eds), *Responses to Poverty: Lessons from Europe*, London, Heinemann, 1984. The core of the British 'poverty lobby' is the Child Poverty Action Group, launched in 1965: see M. McCarthy, *Campaigning for the Poor: CPAG and the Politics of Welfare*, London, Croom Helm, 1986.
30 Cf. G.M.J. Veldkamp et al., *Inleiding tot de sociale zekerheid*, Deventer, Kluwer, 1978, 2 vols.
31 Cf. L. Ménière (ed.), *Bilan de la France, 1981–1993*, Paris, Hachette, 1993, Part III. On Continental Europe generally, see Walker et al. *Responses to Poverty*; A. de Vries, *Effecten van sociale zekerheid: onderzoek, theorie, methode*, Vol. 3: *Armoede onderzocht*, Tilburg, Katholieke Universitet IVA, 1986.
32 See further G. Therborn, 'Swedish Social Democracy and the Transition from Industrial to Postindustrial Politics', in F. Fox Piven (ed.), *Labor Parties in Postindustrial Societies*, Cambridge, Polity Press, 1991, pp. 108ff.
33 M. Mathews, *Poverty in the Soviet Union*, Cambridge, Cambridge University Press, 1986, Ch. 1; A. Atkinson and J. Micklewright, *Economic Transformation in Eastern Europe and the Distribution of Income*, Cambridge, Cambridge University Press, 1992, Ch. 7.
34 G. Winkler (ed.), *Lexikon der Sozialpolitik*, Berlin, Akademie-Verlag, 1987, p. 406.
35 F. Kraus, 'The Historical Development of Income Inequality in Western Europe and the United States', in P. Flora and A. Heidenheimer (eds), *The Development of Welfare States in Europe and America*, New Brunswick, NJ, and London, Transaction Books, 1981. On postwar West Germany, I have relied on J. Alber, 'Germany', in P. Flora (ed.), *Growth to Limits*, Vol. 2, Berlin, de Gruyter, 1986, p. 66; for UK on R. Parry, 'United Kingdom', in ibid., p. 198.
36 T. Smeeding et al., *Poverty, Inequality and Income Distribution in Comparable Perspective*, Hemel Hempstead, Harvester Wheatsheaf, 1990, p. 12; Atkinson and Micklewright, *Economic Transformation in Eastern Europe*, pp. 137–41; H. Uusitalo, *Income Distribution in Finland*, Helsinki, Central Statistical Office, 1989, p. 32.
37 Calculated from OECD, *Regional Problems in Switzerland*, Paris, 1991, p. 30.
38 OECD, *Economic Surveys of Germany*, Paris, 1991, p. 22.
39 A. Pålsson, 'Economic Policy and the Distribution of Wealth', in I. Persson (ed.), *Generating Equality in the Welfare State*, Oslo, Norwegian University Press, 1990, p. 85; the rest: p.127.
40 *Economie européenne* 46 (1990), p. 253. The shares are corrected for the proportion of employers and self-employed.
41 OECD, *Historical Statistics, 1960–1990*, Paris, 1992, pp. 78–9.
42 E.g. *Financial Times*, 16.9.1987, p. 15; 12.10.1990, p. 1; 24.5.1991, p. 1; 15.10.1991, p. 2; 1.11.1991, p. 1; G. Mermet, *Euroscopie*, Paris, Larousse, 1991, p. 322
43 Cf. J. Kocka, *Angestellten zwischen Faschismus und Demokratie*, Göttingen, Vandenhoeck & Ruprecht, 1977.
44 M. Haller, *Klassenstruktur und Mobilität in fortgeschrittenen Gesellschaften*, Frankfurt, Campus, 1989, pp. 208–9.
45 D. Lane, *Soviet Economy and Society*, Oxford, Blackwell, 1985, p. 179, and T. Boeri and M. Keese, 'Labour Markets and the Transition in Central and Eastern Europe', *OECD Economic Studies* 18 (1992), p. 143, respectively.
46 It should then be borne in mind that by 1990 the proportion of employers/self-employed/family workers to wage and salary employees was 88%. ILO, *Yearbook of Labour Statistics 1993*, Geneva, 1993, p. 200.
47 The extraordinarily high proportion of public transfers in the Netherlands is due to a low rate of employment and a unique amount of permanent unemployment disguised and compensated for as 'disability'.
48 Individual income, refers to the variation of income among individuals after adjustment for the household consumption unit where they live. If the comparison had been between the income of households, the composition of the latter would have determined 60% of the

variation: Uusitalo, *Income Distribution in Finland*, p. 71. 'Class' consisted of these categories: self-employed in agriculture, other self-employed, upper white-collar, lower white-collar, workers, economically inactive.

49 Cf. F.D. Blau and L.M. Kahn, *The Gender Earnings Gap: Some International Evidence*, Urbana-Champaign, University of Illinois, 1991, reported in the *Financial Times*, 13.1.1992, p. 4. Two recent EC studies have found Britain to have the largest pay gap between women and men, and the largest amount of very low-paid workers. One-fifth of all full-time UK employees earn less than two-thirds of the median wage: *Financial Times*, 25.9.1991, p. 9, and 17.12.1991, p. 2, respectively. On wage-dispersion in the OECD somewhat earlier see further P. Hedström and R. Swedberg, 'The Power of Working Class Organizations and the Inter-Industrial Wage Structure', *International Journal of Comparative Sociology*, XXVI, 1–2 (1985).

50 OECD, *Employment Outlook 1988*, Paris, 1988, pp. 152–3, 212.

51 J. Vecernik, 'Earnings Distribution in Czechoslovakia: Intertemporal Changes and International Comparison', *European Sociological Review* 7 (1991), pp. 244–5, 250. The author gives 68 as the 1988 percentage, the data in his table imply 69.

52 Atkinson and Micklewright, *Economic Transformation in Eastern Europe*, p. 96.

53 Ibid., p. 97; Boeri and Keese, 'Labour Markets and the Transition in Central and Eastern Europe', p. 143.

54 Atkinson and Micklewright, *Economic Transformation in Eastern Europe*, pp. 222ff.

55 In the early 1980s 19% of single aged persons in Switzerland and 16% in Britain had an adjusted income less than half of the median household income per capita, after tax transfers: D. Mitchell, 'Comparative Income Systems: Is Australia the Poor Relation?', in F. Castles (ed.), *Australia Compared*, London: Allen & Unwin, 1991, p. 176.

56 The study was carried out for the EC Commission by M. O'Higgins and S. Jenkins, 'Poverty in Europe: Estimates for the Numbers in Poverty in 1975, 1980, 1985', seminar paper 1989. It is here summarized from G. Room, *'New Poverty' in the European Community*, London, Macmillan, 1990, pp. 55ff. That volume is also sponsored by the EC Commission.

57 In the USA it was almost half, in Australia and Canada about two-fifths. The data are from the Luxemburg Income Survey: Mitchell, 'Comparative Income Systems', p. 176.

8

RISKS AND OPPORTUNITIES

Between conceiving modernity in terms of opportunity, of achievement or performance in contrast to ascription, and viewing it as a risk society, a certain amount of experience and reflection has occurred.

Opportunity, and the equality of it, is an ancient concern of liberal modernity. Conceived as intergenerational mobility it is also a longstanding concern of sociology, dating back, if not exactly to the classics, at least to the 1920s.[1] An interest in the opposite of opportunity, in risk, is of much more recent date. True, risk is an old stock-in-trade of insurance actuaries, at least since the nineteenth century, and it is an established concept of twentieth-century continental social law, but the centre-stage of social thought was not open to actuaries and insurance lawyers.

A general attention to risks is a post-World War II phenomenon, beginning with apprehensions of the risk of mutually all-destructive nuclear war, and then broadened into an awareness of the possibility of peacefully produced disasters, from environmental pollution generally and from nuclear energy in particular. In other words, the low probability of huge human-made disaster put 'risk' on the social, political and theoretical agenda.

Risk arrived on sociological Broadway in the mid-1980s. In 1986, a rapidly fashionable West German sociologist named Ulrich Beck published *Risikogesellschaft*, which started out from nuclear energy concerns. In France, and among Francophiles, François Evald made the welfare state a hot item of general theory by positioning the old social insurance and law notion of risk at the centre of a Foucauldian philosophical discourse. Less influential but more professional was the anthropologist Mary Douglas's reflections on risk a year before. To date, the most penetrating analysis of the concept is by sociology's recently emerited specialist in profundity, Niklas Luhmann.[2]

However separated by contexts of favourable ideological reception, the discourses of opportunity and risk are fundamentally the same. Both pertain to the probabilities of events over time. Both also refer to the consequences of decisions. Opportunity, social mobility, express an unreflected faith in modernity, whereas risk conveys a critical, though not necessarily hostile, reflection of the latter.

Between the belief in opportunity and the concern with risk, an Anglophile German scholar, Sir Ralf Dahrendorf, proposed the concept of life chances as enabling a more reflective approach to modernity. But instead of elaborating the useful Weberian concept into something covering both opportunity and risk, Dahrendorf gave it a special twist by connecting the possibility of choice with the need for social 'ligatures' or social bonds, or, more prosaically, for English-type traditions.[3]

With its face to the future, risk is very much a modern concept, and, as Beck has emphasized, one of reflexive modernity, of a modernity reflecting upon itself, and not only projecting its aspirations into the future. The possibilities of its assessment, of its being taken into account, of being 'managed', make up a thin but sharp line of demarcation between risk and one of the three major tropes of conservative or reactionary thought, 'jeopardy'; that is, the argument that (further) change will jeopardize existing valuables, a rhetoric that might be more conservatively modern than anti-modern reactionary.[4]

So far, risk and opportunity have not been treated side by side. They belong to different sides of the coin of modernity, and prevailing social science has not yet found a way of taking both into account. Here, however, we shall make an attempt at paying attention to both, within the confines of a synoptic empirical study.

Risks of death

Death is the ultimate risk, and in this section we shall look at some facets of it.

In Europe as elsewhere the chances of survival of children born alive have increased enormously since World War II. But how has the diminishing of risks at entry into life been distributed? Let us divide Europe into four groups with regard to the infant mortality rates in 1937 and in 1990 and let the statistics of cluster analysis determine what country sets we come up with (see Table 8.1).

Infant mortality rates may be taken as indicators of the capacity of social organization, of couples as well as of communities. They are affected by public hygiene, economic resources and birth control. The data are among the least unreliable of all across countries and periods, but they are not perfect. There is general underreporting in some countries, and there are varying definitions of what constitutes a live birth, with regard to premature and underweight babies. To this day most of Eastern Europe, except Czechoslovakia and Hungary, has a more restricted conception of what is a live birth, something which tends to lower the infant mortality rate, but hardly very significantly.[5]

With respect to the cross-national pattern it is, perhaps, first of all noteworthy that all the future Communist countries are in the two right-hand columns, of the lowest survival chances of infants – except Estonia and Latvia. The former were not alone, however, but were part of a risky Southeastern area.

Table 8.1 *European infant mortality rates in 1937 (four clusters: cluster means per thousand)*

Very low: 43	Low: 73	High: 124	Very high: 159
Netherlands	Austria	Albania[a]	Bulgaria
Norway	Belgium	Czechoslovakia	Portugal
Sweden	Denmark	Greece	Romania
Switzerland	Estonia	Hungary	USSR[b]
	Finland	Italy	
	France	Lithuania	
	Germany	Poland	
	Ireland	Spain[c]	
	Latvia	Yugoslavia	
	UK		

Notes: [a] 1951. [b] 1928. [c] 1935.

Sources: League of Nations, *Statistical Yearbook of the League of Nations 1937/38*, Geneva 1939, Table 5; B.R. Mitchell, *International Historical Statistics: Europe, 1750–1988*, 3rd edn, Basingstoke, Macmillan, 1992, Table A6 (Albania and USSR).

Outside Europe, the USA and the Antipodes could have entered the first cluster, and Argentina (94) the second. Japan was a big military power, but still socially underdeveloped, and belonged to the third cluster (106).

Table 8.2 *European infant mortality rates in 1990 (four clusters: cluster means per thousand)*

Very low: 7.7	Low: 11.8	High: 15.0	Very high: 23.5
Austria	Bulgaria	Estonia[a]	Albania
Belgium	Czechoslovakia	Hungary	Romania
Denmark	Greece	Poland	USSR
Finland	Latvia[a]		Yugoslavia
France	Lithuania[a]		
E. Germany	Portugal		
W. Germany			
Ireland			
Italy			
Netherlands			
Norway			
Spain			
Sweden			
Switzerland			
UK			

Note: [a] 1987.

Sources: World Bank, *World Tables 1992*, Baltimore and London, Johns Hopkins University Press, 1992, country tables; B.R. Pockney (ed.), *Soviet Statistics since 1950*, Aldershot, Dartmouth, 1991, Table 37 (republics of the former USSR); P. Marer et al., *Historically Planned Economies: A Guide to the Data*, Washington, DC, World Bank, 1992, pp. 99, 147.

When we compare the situation in 1990 (see Table 8.2) the overwhelming picture is one of vastly augmented chances of survival everywhere. The picture is also characterized by skewed cross-national convergence. In comparison with that of 1937, the 1990 Table has tilted to the left. If we enter non-European countries, Japan would rank in the first group, the USA in the second and Argentina in the fourth. The Eastern European countries have done very well in relation to the New Worlds, with Albania and Romania clearly surpassing Argentina, and East Germany the USA, which in turn would be sharing a cluster with Bulgaria, Czechoslovakia and two of the Baltics.

But after initial advances in the 1950s Eastern Europe has hardly distinguished itself in comparison with Western Europe over the full course of their history. In the light of current ideologies one should add that they have certainly not lost. The biggest winners in postwar Europe, however, have been Italian and Spanish children, whereas Japanese babies emerge as the major winners over all Europeans.

The remarkable stagnation of the infant mortality rates of the former Soviet Union from the mid-1960s (27.2 promille in 1965, 25.4 in 1987) is due, above all, to a macabre development in Central Asia, with a *rise* of the mortality rate in the 1970s, spectacular (and perhaps in part a statistical artefact) in Uzbekistan, significant in Kazakhstan, Turkmenistan and Tajikistan, and noticeable also in Azerbaijan, Armenia and Georgia. In Kyrgyzstan and in the European USSR, except in Moldavia where there was a dramatic increase of infant deaths in the 1970s, the decline continued, most vigorously in Lithuania, Latvia and Belorussia.[6] The Tajik (48.9) and the Uzbek (45.9) infant mortality rates are nevertheless still apparently lower than the Turkish one, at 65.0 promille in 1987, although the foundations of comparability are admittedly shaky.[7]

The interrelationship of risk and opportunity is indicated by the other side of death risk, by life expectancy. An important part of the postwar increase of opportunities is their prolongation, i.e. the longer life expectancy at birth (see Table 8.3).

Between 1930 and 1965 there is not only a general rise in life expectancy, but also a significant inter-country rapprochement. The spread narrows from 21 years to 9, with catching up taking place in both Western and Eastern Europe. On the other hand, there is little equalization between 1965 and 1990, the spread going down to 8 years. The reason for that is mainly the slowing down of social change in Eastern Europe, here more clearly visible than in figures of the economy.

The seven Communist countries increased life expectancy at birth by on the average three years between 1965 and 1990, Hungary by one year, whereas the sixteen capitalist states of Europe prolonged it by five years. The discrepancy between economic growth and human well-being was most pronounced for Hungarian males, whose life expectancy at 40 declined in the 1970s and 1980s[8] while the economy was expanding. Late-

Table 8.3 *Life expectancy at birth in Eastern and Western Europe, 1930–1990 (years, female and male; unweighted national averages)*

Country	Around 1930	1965	1990
E. Europe[a]	49	69	71
W. Europe[b]	59	71	77

Notes: [a] Bulgaria, Czechoslovakia, Hungary, Poland, Romania, the USSR, Yugoslavia. [b] Austria, Belgium, Denmark, Finland, France, West Germany, Greece, Ireland, Italy, the Netherlands, Norway, Portugal, Spain, Sweden, Switzerland, the UK.

Sources: 1930: League of Nations, *Statistical Yearbook of the League of Nations 1937/38*, Geneva 1939, Table 11, and P. Flora (ed.), *State, Economy, and Society in Western Europe, 1815–1975*, Vol. 2, Frankfurt, Campus, 1987, pp. 96ff; 1965: World Bank, *World Development Report 1990*, New York, Oxford University Press, 1990, pp. 241 and 244; 1990: World Bank, *World Tables 1992*, country tables.

Communist Hungary was known as 'the jolliest barrack in the camp', but the relative fun the Hungarians might have had was apparently not very healthy. Two countries blur the East–West risk border between 1965 and 1980: Denmark, increasing life expectancy only from 73 to 75 years, and Yugoslavia, from 66 to 72.

In Argentina, Brazil and Chile life expectancy augmented by nine years on average between 1965 and 1990. Thereby life expectancy was brought up to Romanian and Soviet standards, i.e. 70 years, which, incidentally, is the same as that of South Korea.[9]

For reasons which have still not been unravelled, Communist Europe failed to match the progress of Western Europe in the 1970s and 1980s. A unique increase in deaths from cardiovascular diseases was the most specific feature.[10] Health development was most negative by far in Hungary but the other Eastern European countries had an increase of male age-standardized death rates as well, albeit less dramatically. The only Western European countries similar in this dark respect to the best Eastern ones, East Germany and Yugoslavia, were Denmark and (in the 1970s) Sweden, which makes the picture even more intriguing. In Russia after the mid-1980s there ensued a more expected turn to the better.[11]

Perhaps the best illustration of the East–West death risk/life expectancy pattern is conveyed by looking at East and West Germany. In 1970, East German male life expectancy at birth was 68 years, and the West German one 67 years. Due to East German stagnation, followed by a slow increase in the 1980s, the West Germans overtook their Eastern comrades in 1977. Infant mortality was considerably higher in the West till about 1975, but from 1980 it was slightly lower. At the age of 65 German males had the same likely number of years ahead of them in the early 1970s, but then the Westerners began to live longer. By the end of the GDR, older West German males lived two years longer than their East German counterparts.[12]

The ideologues of the present as well as of the past were mistaken. Communist Europe was not always and in all respects a failure, nor was it ever a particular success. Something went wrong with the physical life chances of the population in the 1970s and 1980s, but we do not yet know why, nor even exactly when, due to the possibility of still unknown time lags.[13] And the ideologues have been equally mistaken about the consequences of the end of Communism.

In Russia, the costs of the destruction of Communism amount to about a half a million dead in two years. They have, of course, not been killed by anti-Communist repression, and the figure should be compared not with the dead of the Gulag but with the havoc of the agricultural collectivization. (By that sinister standard the process of privatization still fares quite well, although the Belorussian mortality increase of 1930–33 was lower than the Russian one of 1991–3.) The figure refers to the number of excess deaths in Russia in 1992 and 1993, after the break-up of the USSR, as compared to 1991.[14]

Upward bends in the human death curves after the end of Communism took place all over Eastern Europe – manifesting the human cost of radical social change, in whatever direction – most weakly and least durably in the Czech Republic and in Slovakia, most strongly in Russia (and probably the rest of the ex-USSR).

Behind the national averages there are amazing variations in the exposure to mortal risk. A good deal of such variation is class-specific, for which I have not been able to find any comprehensive cross-national data, however. Instead, due to a large, English-centred medical investigation for the EC Commission we have a good descriptive map of regional Western European mortality rates, standardized for the age of the population (see Table 8.4). Why it looks the way it does is another matter, which the medical team, working from other questions of interest, left unanswered.

There seem to be at least three different causal forces at work behind the death pattern in Table 8.4. One lethal force will derive from old, concentrated industrialization and mining, such as the high-mortality industrial belts from the Scottish Clydeside to the English Midlands, from the Ruhr to Belgium-Luxemburg and northeastern France, and from Turin to Milan. Another, more erratic force appears to imperil life in big urban conglomerations, in London, Copenhagen, Berlin, Hamburg, Naples. But not always; not in Amsterdam, Athens, Paris and Rome. Thirdly, there must be some killing forces in certain rural areas (whisky?) *not* related to the overall standard of living, thus accounting for the high rates throughout Ireland and Scotland (including the Highlands), and some preservatives contributing to the below average rates in central France, on Corsica, in most of southern Italy and Greece.

The cited medical researchers were primarily interested in finding patterns of 'avoidable death', referring by that to causes of death by causes manageable either by proper medical cure and care, by proper life-style (like death from lung cancer and liver cirrhosis) or by proper regulation (traffic accidents). The list of illnesses and diseases defined as avoidable causes of death used is medically precise and apparently drawn up in an extensive

Table 8.4 *The risk geography of death in the EC 10
(age-standardized mortality rates for the whole population, 1974–8;
index EC 10 = 100)*

Above average EC mortality
Belgium   108, all regions
Germany   104, all regions except Hessen and Baden-Württemberg
Ireland   117, all regions
Luxemburg   114
UK: Northern Ireland   118
      Scotland   115, all regions
      England and Wales   104, all OECD regions except East Anglia,
      Southeast and Southwest; the southern subregions of London and Kent are
        above EC average
Danish region of Copenhagen (103)
French regions of Alsace-Lorraine, Picardy-Normandy, Nord-Pas-de-Calais
   (113.6), Brittany
Greek region of Thrace   (102)
Italian regions of Lombardy   (103.6), Piedmont and the Northwest   (102.4),
   Friuli-Venezia Giulia, Naples   (107)

Below average EC mortality
Denmark   95, except the capital region
France   96, except regions mentioned above
Greece   88, all regions except Thrace
Italy   96, except regions mentioned above
Netherlands   91, all regions

Source: W.W. Holland (ed.), *European Community Atlas of 'Avoidable Death'*, Oxford, Oxford
University Press, 1988, pp. 255ff.

collective effort among specialists. How far the death cause statistics are cross-
regionally reliable is another matter, whereupon this writer has no opinion.

Avoidable deaths account normally for 3–5% of all deaths, except in
southern Italy: in Naples the former were found to constitute 12.9% of the
latter; in Caserta (also in the region of Campania) 12.3%; in Bari, Taranto
and Catanzaro 10% or more. By and large, albeit with considerable
variation, avoidable deaths tend to form a pattern similar to that of all deaths.
Southern Italy is the major exception, high on the former, low on the latter.

Insofar as the data are reliable, the relative disparities in rates of avoidable
mortality are absolutely staggering. Still taking the EC 10 rate as equal to
100, Belgian provinces range from 20 in East Flanders to 183 in Wallonian
Hainaut; on the German *Länder* level from 52 in Hamburg to 509 in West
Berlin; from 83 in the city of Copenhagen to 10 in the county of
Copenhagen; among French departments from 0 in Tarn and Alpes-
Maritimes to 389 in the North and 326 in Pas-de-Calais; in Greece from 24
in Thessaly to 377 in Thrace; in Italy from 16 in Ravenna to 944 (!) in Naples;
in Ireland from 86 in the Northwest to 224 in Midi-West; in the Netherlands
from 0 in six of eleven provinces (!) to 15 in Friesland; in the UK from 0 in

Bromley and 1 in Oxfordshire in southeastern England to 384 (!) in Greater Glasgow.[15] Nothing is more unequal than the chance of avoidable death.

If we recalculate the index figures into rates for the somewhat more comparable OECD regions and try to get a quick grasp of cross-national differences in regional disparities of avoidable deaths, we may get the following. Among the four bigger countries the distance from the highest to the lowest region is: 606 (percentage points of the EC average) in Italy, 457 in Germany, 362 in France and 179 in the UK. In the smaller countries, the difference is 91 in Greece, 89 in Belgium, 12 in Denmark and 5 in the Netherlands. (Cf. Chapter 10 below, on the economics of Western European regions.)

The risk of *AIDS* has, so far, been primarily North American and African. By mid-1993 the World Health Organization had registered 719,000 cases of declared AIDS in the world: 40% of the total in the USA; 33% in Africa; 13% in Europe; 11.5% in the rest of the Americas; and 1% in Asia and Oceania. Current estimates guess that a good two-thirds of all *de facto* cases are in Africa, one eighth in the USA, and one-twentieth in Europe. Asia, still only marginally affected by the intercontinental sex trade – in the Asian locations of which the disease is reported to be rapidly spreading – , is also estimated to harbour only 1% of the world's diseased.

The reasons for this very special disease geography, in which the world's richest and poorest countries are isomorphic, are still enigmatic. So also is the European distribution (see Table 8.5).

Table 8.5 *The distribution of AIDS in Europe by 31 March 1993*

Country	Cases declared	Cases per 100,000 population
Austria	943	12
Belgium	1,364	14
Denmark	1,182	23
France	24,226	42
Germany	9,697	12
Great Britain	7,341	13
Italy	16,860	30
Netherlands	2,575	17
Portugal	1,255	13
Romania	2,353	10
Sweden	817	9
Switzerland	3,028	44

Sources: WHO, as reported in *Le Monde*, 1.12.1993, p. 11; Eurostat, *Basic Statistics of the Community*, 30th edn, Luxemburg, 1993, Table 3.1 (population in 1992); Marer et al., *Historically Planned Economies*, p. 197 (Romanian population, extrapolated to 1991).

The US figure is in the class of 110–20 per 100,000 population. The Communist countries were hardly affected, with the exception of Romania, where the main explanation seems to have been the widespread provision of blood transfusions to institutionalized children, under little-controlled hygienic conditions.

If we compare AIDS with traffic deaths, we find that among European countries only in Switzerland, France and Italy are there more cases of AIDS accumulated till spring 1993 than the *annual* toll of European traffic. The most dangerous roads are to be found in Portugal and Belgium, with 25 and 20 deaths per 100,000 inhabitants, respectively, in 1990; the safest in Norway, with 8 deaths, and Sweden and the UK, both with 9 deaths per 100,000.[16]

The main immediate causal complexes behind AIDS are known: unprotected male homosexual practices, the injection of drugs with infected needles, the transfusion of contaminated blood. But how and why they coalesce into particular national configurations are still beyond grasp. Particularly noteworthy, and puzzling, are the differences between Sweden and Austria, on the one hand, at the low end of tragedy, and Switzerland, on the other, or between Britain and France.

The sudden emergence in the 1980s of the new disease AIDS, or the nuclear plant disaster at Chernobyl in 1986, help to explain the wide receptivity of the risk society idea. However, paradoxically, while the potential of human-made accidental death may have increased, and while the theorization of it has surged, the actual occurrence of accidental death has in fact declined, even if we include the new killer of motor traffic (see Table 8.6).

Table 8.6 *The historical development of accidental and violent death (age-standardized rates per 100,000)*

	1881	1931	1951	1964
England & Wales				
Males	118	66	33	29
Females	42	37	15	16
France				
Males	n.a.	82[a]	70	82
Females	n.a.	24[a]	23	28
W. Germany				
Males	n.a.	n.a.	n.a.	90
Females	n.a.	n.a.	n.a.	32
Italy				
Males	n.a.	65	n.a.	61
Females	n.a.	22	n.a.	17
Sweden				
Males	n.a.	75[b]	62	67
Females	n.a.	21[b]	20	24

Notes: [a] 1936. [b] 1940.

Source: S. Preston et al., *Causes of Death*, New York and London, Sewin Press, 1972.

Another long-term time series, on accidental and violent deaths in Sweden, including suicide, shows a decline of the male rate of death between 1911 and 1921, and stability thereafter till 1985, and an increase for females of the risk of violent and accidental death in the 1920s, 1930s, 1950s, 1960s, with a slight decline thereafter. In 1911 the male death rate of accidents and violence was 102 per 100,000, in 1921 79 and in 1985 77. Women's risk increased from 22 to a maximum of 47 in 1971, then falling back to 42 in 1985.[17]

Career and property opportunities

Nineteenth-century Europe has been held to have been characterized by less occupational mobility than the USA.[18] Post-World War II sociological opinion, however, has tended to emphasize the basic similarity of social mobility among developed industrial societies, although placing the USA at the upper end of the continuum or characterizing it as especially open in some respects.[19]

The study of intergenerational social mobility has become technically quite intricate – as well as analytically sophisticated – but here we shall refrain from entering into any technicalities. Given the extensive and elaborate literature we can also be brief, but we shall seek an answer to the question: Is there anything special about European social mobility?

One particularity derives from Europe's particularly distinctive socio-economic history, which was touched upon above: that is, the sequence from agrarian to industrial and then to service society. Other things being equal there should be more manual/non-manual mobility and, perhaps less strongly, more overall mobility in the New Worlds and in Japan, which from agrarian dominance went straight to service sector relative dominance.

The mobility studies do tend to show such a pattern for the twentieth century, i.e. less manual/non-manual mobility in Western Europe than in the New Worlds and in Japan, but the differences are not large.[20] It should be pointed out, however, that here as well as below we are primarily talking about relative mobility, i.e. the relative odds of the sons or daughters of fathers in different classes or occupational sets moving into one or the other class position or occupational destination. In contrast to absolute mobility rate, the relative rate is independent of any change of the class structure itself, from fathers' to children's generation.

However, some European countries do match the New Worlds and Japan, while clearly belonging to the European pattern of industrial development, namely the now ex-Communist Eastern Europe and, at the time of writing, ex-Social Democratic Sweden, but the data were collected mainly in the first half of the 1970s and refer to mobility experiences of the second and, above all, the third quarter of this century. From a book by the leading social mobility researchers of the 1980s, John Goldthorpe and

Robert Eriksson, we get the list of social openness or, as the authors call it, 'social fluidity' shown in Table 8.7.

Table 8.7 *Overall social fluidity in the highly developed world*

β values. The cross-national average is set to zero. Positive values mean less fluidity or class openness than the average, negative values mean more fluidity/openness.

England	0.09
France	0.16
Germany	0.13
Ireland	0.16
Italy	0.12
Netherlands	0.16
Scotland	0.19
Sweden	−0.17
Czechoslovakia	−0.23
Hungary	0.02
Poland	−0.18
Australia	−0.23
Japan	−0.20
USA	−0.20

Source: R. Eriksson and J. Goldthorpe, *The Constant Flux: A Study of Class Mobility in Industrial Societies*, Oxford, Clarendon Press, 1992, p. 381.

What emerges from the Table is a very homogeneous Western European pattern of social fluidity, with one exception, Sweden. (Data for the other Nordic countries are lacking.) The three Central-Eastern European countries all deviate from Western Europe into more social openness, but Hungary turns out to be the unique representative of average relative social mobility in the highly developed world.

Another mode of calculation yields a similar result. Expressed in the odds ratios of sons of ending up in the same set of occupations as their manual or non-manual fathers, the geometrical means referring to circa 1970 was 3.8 for the New Worlds (Australia, Canada, New Zealand, the USA), 3.9 for Communist Europe (Czechoslovakia, Hungary, Poland) and 5.3 for Capitalist Europe (Austria, Belgium, Denmark, England and Wales, Finland, France, West Germany, Italy, the Netherlands, Norway and Sweden). For long-term Social Democratic Europe (Norway and Sweden) the geometric mean was 4.2. Sweden alone had an odds ratio of 3.4.[21]

A Habsburgian comparison with reference to the first half of the 1980s also supports the general tendency, the exact strength of which is difficult and risky to pin down: intergenerational mobility was lower in Austria than in the Czech Republic, Slovakia and Hungary, but the differences were far from staggering.[22]

Communism has increased equality of opportunity, but only compared to what might have been expected from European capitalism.

Behind the overall mobility measures lie a number of intergenerational trajectories, which are combined in nationally more or less specific ways. A detailed comparison of US and English mobility by Eriksson and Goldthorpe yielded the interesting conclusion that the somewhat higher overall US mobility is largely due to less occupational inheritance among farmers and (mostly small) proprietors, and at most only unevenly and marginally due to more upper-middle-class openness. Contrary to both myth and recent sociological opinion in the USA, the data showed no better chances in the USA than in England for sons of manual workers, themselves starting out as manual workers later in life to move into managerial or professional positions.[23]

Within Europe, a comparison by Antonio Cobalti, using the same basic data set as Goldthorpe and Eriksson, has measured occupational inheritance into the professional-managerial-administrative class. Below average inheritance, or more than average openness, was found in Sweden, West Germany and Hungary. Clearly more closed were, first, Italy and, secondly, France.[24] A study around 1970 of the recruitment of upper civil servants found the USA and Britain equally high in intergenerational opportunity, closely followed by Sweden, and leaving Italy and West Germany far behind.[25]

In terms of ruling élites, Communism certainly signified a radical sociological break with the past. But there ensued a new closure, a social one, not the obvious political one. A study by Max Haller, Tamás Kolosi and Péter Róbert, using huge national data sets from 1982–6, found, *inter alia*, the postwar pattern of bureaucratic and managerial élite recruitment in East–Central Europe illustrated in Table 8.8.

Table 8.8 *Postwar élite recruitment patterns in Austria, Czech Republic, Hungary and Slovakia*

Percentage of sons, by age at the time of study, in higher bureaucratic or managerial positions having fathers in the same kind of positions. Data from 1982–6.

Age-group	Austria	Czech Republic	Hungary	Slovakia
18–35	27	36	41	29
36–50	28	24	20	12
51–65	25	15	11	9

Source: M. Haller et al., 'Soziale Mobilität in Österreich, in der Tschechoslovakei und in Ungarn', *Journal für Sozialforschung* 30 (1990), p. 66.

Three things, in particular, emerge from the table: first, the basically unchanged pattern of élite access in postwar Austria; secondly, the strong original impact of the Communist revolutions – on the assumption that the prewar Hungarian and Czechoslovak regimes were not significantly more equal that the Austrian – , indicated by the low proportion of sons of higher bureaucrats and managers in the oldest age-group, who reached their positions in the earlier part of the postwar period; and, thirdly, the ensuing process of closure of the Czechoslovak and the Hungarian élites, with the new managerial stratum reproducing itself very successfully, especially since about the mid-1970s.

To open intergenerational opportunities is clearly a difficult and erratic process. There seem to be at least three different roads to some relative success: New World liberal capitalism, Communism and Nordic Social Democracy.

A fascinating topic for future sociological historians will be a special kind of inequality of opportunity. That is, the way in which persons or the descendants of persons of property and/or of high culture manage to reproduce it through periods of adversity. Perhaps the first researcher to draw attention to how capitalist or petty commodity entrepreneurship could revive after a Communist hibernation was Ivan Szelenyi, writing about Hungary in the 1980s, who discovered 'a strong positive correlation between a family's pre-socialist entrepreneurial orientation and current entrepreneurship.'[26]

The background of the new Eastern European 'robber barons' still has to be tracked. But a safe bet is that they have a disproportionately high connection with previously resourceful classes. More uncertain is how much of the resources were gathered during the Communist period alone, and how much dates back to previous capitalism. The restoration and inheritance principle of privatization, which a number of Eastern countries have adopted, after the German example, will, of course, bring the old property-owning families back without effort. But the return of the *Junker* landowners was excluded from the East German *Anschluss* treaty, and the actual return of the old ruling class is patchy.

The Czech Republic has so far been most receptive, in spite of its recalcitrance regarding unlimited property restoration. Václav Havel set the example, by making a Habsburgian Prince, von Schwartzenberg, his Head of Staff, and the return of the Bata family of shoemaking is probably the most important literal restoration of ancient capitalism in Eastern Europe.

Portugal offers another interesting European example of the survival capacity of capitalists. Since the mid-1980s the old economically ruling families of Portugal – dislocated by the revolution of 1974–5 – are returning, invited, carrying new wealth with them: the Champalimaud, the Espirito Santo, the Mello.[27] Something similar is occurring in China (from Hong Kong and Taiwan), and might occur tomorrow in Cuba.

Apparently, there is something to the allocation and transmittance of cultural and social skills – or 'capital', as it is supposed to be called in academic Chicago (Becker, Coleman) and Paris (Bourdieu) – which can circumvent enormous economic and political upheavals. Borrowing a word from a now defunct type of regime, there is a *cultural nomenklatura* which sociologists and social historians had better look out for.

Notes

1 A pathbreaking work was P. Sorokin, *Social Mobility*, Glencoe, Ill. Free Press, 1927.

2 An overview of recent risk research is given by Mary Douglas, *Risk Acceptability According to the Social Sciences*, London, Routledge & Kegan Paul, 1986, pp. 7ff. Ulrich Beck's, *Risikogesellschaft*, first appeared in German: Frankfurt, Suhrkamp, 1986; English edn: *Risk Society*, London, Sage, 1992. François Ewald, *L'Etat de Providence*, Paris, Grasset, 1986. See further Niklas Luhmann, *Soziologie des Risikos*, Berlin, de Gruyter, 1991.

3 R. Dahrendorf, *Life Chances*, Chicago, University of Chicago Press, 1979.

4 Albert Hirschmann, who has given the brilliant analysis *The Rhetoric of Reaction*, Cambridge, Mass., Harvard University Press, 1991, did not explicitly see it that way, however. The two other figures of reactionary rhetoric singled out by Hirschmann are futility and perversity.

5 Unicef, *Public Policy and Social Conditions*, no. 1, Florence, 1993, p. 16.

6 B.R. Pockney (ed.), *Soviet Statistics since 1950*, Aldershot, Dartmouth, 1991, p. 78.

7 The Turkish figure is from World Bank, *World Tables 1992*, Baltimore and London, Johns Hopkins University Press, p. 615. On the Tajik and Uzbek data see the previous note.

8 *Social Indicators Research* 23, 1–2 (1990), p. 190 (Rudolf Andorka).

9 Actually it is 72 years in Chile, 71 in Argentina and 66 in Brazil, but 70 in South Korea: World Bank, *World Tables 1992*.

10 WHO, *Evaluation of the Strategy for Health for All by the Year 2000*, vol. 5, Copenhagen, 1986, pp. 226 ff.

11 H. Janecková and H. Hnilicová, 'The Health Status of the Czechoslovak Population: Its Social and Ecological Determinants', *International Journal of Health Sciences* 3 (1992), p. 148; E. Mezentseva and N. Rimachevskaya, 'The Health of the Populations in the Republics of the Former Soviet Union', *International Journal of Health Sciences* 3 (1992), p. 134.

12 J.U. Niehoff et. al., 'Reflections on the Health Policy of the Former German Democratic Republic', *International Journal of Health Sciences* 3 (1992), pp. 207–8.

13 Neither the specialists of the special, cited issue of *International Journal of Health Sciences* 3 (1992) nor those of C. Marmand and P. Vaughan (eds), *Europe without Frontiers: The Implications for Health*, Chichester, John Wiley & Sons, 1993, have any explanations on offer.

14 The crude death rate is taken from the Unicef publication *Central and Eastern Europe in Transition. Public Policy and Social Conditions*, no. 2, pp. 46 and 90. 'Excess mortality', disregarding ageing effects, caused 526,000 dead in Russia in 1992 and 1993. Unicef, op. cit., p. 42.

15 W.W. Holland (ed.), *European Community Atlas of 'Avoidable Death'*, Oxford, Oxford University Press, 1988, pp. 311ff.

16 Calculations from Eurostat, *Basic Statistics of the Community* 30th edn, Luxemburg, 1993, Tables 7.11 and 3.1.The figures are not quite to the point, as they do not take foreign traffic and population density into account. The death rate may also be affected by the quality of the ambulance and hospital services. But the high risks of Portuguese and Belgian traffic stand out also when compared with similar countries, with Spain (18 deaths), Italy (11) and the Netherlands (9).

17 *Hälsa i Sverige*, Stockholm, SCB, 1988, p. 138.

18 Cf. S. Thernstrom, 'Working-Class Social Mobility in Industrial America', in M. Richter (ed.), *Essays in Theory and History*, Cambridge, Mass., Harvard University Press, 1970; H. Kaelble, *Auf dem Weg zu einer europäischen Gesellschaft*, Munich, C.H. Beck, 1987, pp. 34ff.

19 See, e.g. S.M. Lipset and R. Bendix, *Social Mobility in Industrial Society*, Berkeley, University of California Press, 1959; P.M. Blau and O.D. Duncan, *The American Occupational Structure*, New York, Wiley, 1967.
20 For an overview of pertinent mobility studies, see H. Ganzeboom et al., 'Intergenerational Class Mobility in Comparative Perspective', *Research on Social Stratification and Mobility* 9 (1989).
21 Re-calculated from W. Uitee et al., *Sociologie*, Groningen, Wolters-Noordhoff, 1992, p. 540. (The lower the odds of ending up in the same occupational category as your father, the more social mobility.)
22 M. Haller et al., 'Soziale Mobilität in Österreich, in der Tschechoslowakei und in Ungarn', *Journal für Sozialforschung* 30 (1990).
23 R. Eriksson and J. Goldthorpe, 'Are American Rates of Social Mobility Exceptionally High? New Evidence on an Old Issue', *European Sociological Review* 1 (May 1985), pp. 8, 10, 13.
24 A. Cobalti, 'Italian Socal Mobility in an International Perspective', Trieste, Dipartimento di scienze dell'uomo, Universitá degli studi di Trieste, 1991, p.17.
25 B. Putnam, 'The Political Attitudes of Senior Civil Servants in Britain, Germany, and Italy', in M. Dogan (ed.), *The Mandarins of Western Europe*, Beverly Hills, Sage, 1975, pp. 96–7.
26 I. Szelenyi, *Socialist Entrepreneurs*, Madison, University of Wisconsin Press, 1988, p. 210.
27 *Financial Times*, 22.4.1994, p. 3.

PART III

SPACING

Looking at space and spatial ordering from the perspective of European modernity will involve taking space both as an 'independent' and as a 'dependent' variable, to use the jargon of sociological analysis. That is, spatiality – demarcations, proximities, distances, connections in space – is, on the one hand, a historical legacy, of importance to the contemporary sociology of the continent, and, on the other, the target of a particular postwar effort of world historical significance, at Western European supra-state integration.[1]

Spatial ordering, territorial delimitations, differ primarily from divisions (of resources and constraints, of rights and obligations, cultural identities and other cultural divides) on the basis of genealogy or descent – of family, clan, tribe, ethnicity – or in terms of religion (or any value community). As such, space and territory have always been central to the heartlands of Europe. This derives from a sedentary as opposed to a nomadic tradition, the latter of which has always been strong in the Islamic civilizations,[2] but also from a weaker position of ancestry in the European traditions of religion and ethics, in comparison with the also sedentary Asian high cultures.[3]

In the ancient Greek *polis*, with its city-bounded body of citizens, native-born males were equals on the expanse of the *agora*, a pattern reproduced, *mutatis mutandis*, in the self-governing medieval cities. The Roman Empire developed an elaborate territorial organization, the tradition and even sometimes the concrete forms of which long survived the Empire itself. Medieval Europe managed to absorb the Germanic, the Slavic and the Magyar tribes into a territorial world, although more precariously in Eastern than in Western Europe.

The Christian Church, with the imperial model before its eyes, laid the whole continent under a territorial grid. The settlement of the civil wars of Christianity, of the Reformation and Counter-Reformation, rested on a territorial principle, 'cuius regio, eius religio' (whose realm, his religion). The dark side of that coin was the establishment of a sort of totalitarian religious territoriality in Western Europe, save for the Netherlands. The Eastern Europe of the Ottomans and, in part, of Poland-Lithuania developed a more tolerant pattern of religious coexistence.

While not reducible to it, the territorial and the genealogical principles of structuration clearly derive a good part of their relative force from the physical character of the territory. Deserts and steppes promote nomadism and thereby genealogy, and humid plains favour sedentary agriculture and territorial delimitations.

Physical geography impinges upon social relations and social practices in a number of ways. Mountainous regions favour patriarchal autonomy, while the power of landowners and rulers rests over plains, both of which may be explained by the more general sociological argument about the effects of the variable possibilities of concentrating resources of violence in a delimited area, being low in the high mountains and high on the low plains.

Furthermore, there is the influence of the climate and the soil on the production and consumption of food and drink, continually reproduced as habits and preferences long after the marginalization of agricultural production. That is, the production/consumption of potatoes or cereals, of butter or olive oil, of citrus fruits, of spirits, beer or wine, for example.[4] The industrial importance of the occurrence of coal as well as the effect of waterways on the connection of sites and populations we shall touch upon below.

Physically, Europe may be structured according to three major climatic zones: a Mediterranean, a maritime North Atlantic and an inland continental one. To these three zones, the high mountain regions should be added as a fourth special area. But here, social man-made space is our concern.

Notes

1 By comparison, the Eastern European Comecon, as it is usually called in the West, was always much less ambitious in its integrative ambition, and was not confined to Europe. Some attention will be paid to it, but its limited significance and the, arguably even more limited, competence of this author have led to its marginal treatment here.

2 This contrast is elaborated by John Armstrong, *Nations before Nationalism*, Chapel Hill, NC, University of North Carolina Press, 1982.

3 Cf. Max Weber, 'Die Stadt', *Archiv für Sozialwissenschaft und Sozialpolitik*, 61 (1921).

4 Cf. F. Braudel, *La Méditerranée et le monde méditerranéen à l'époque de Philippe II*, Vol. 2, Part 1, 5th edn, Paris, Armand Colin, 1982. See also V. Scardigli, *L'Europe des modes de vie*, Paris, Ed. du CNRS, 1987, pp. 60–1.

9

CITIES AND STATES

The interaction of cities and states in shaping modern Europe historically has been a major theme of the works of Stein Rokkan and Charles Tilly.[1] Here the rubric will cover a brief overview of two aspects of the postwar spatial ordering of Europe.

From a geographical theory of central locations (*zentrale Orte*) – in terms of trade, transport and administration – and their circumference (the areas of their centrality), the German geographer Walter Christaller has proposed a spatial order of mid-twentieth-century Europe, which is probably the best strictly spatial structuration of the continent, unrivalled by latter-day atlas-makers. It exhibits a beautiful topological symmetry. Its exclusion of the USSR/Russia from the European grid proper, making European Russia the Western part of a Eurasian territorial patterning, is postulated rather than argued.[2] Anyhow, Map 9.1 includes Russia.

Without trying to, Christaller's 1950 spatial vision of Europe implicitly locates the actual postwar centre of all-European efforts, economic and political, i.e. in the 'CC region', albeit with a slightly westward bend, towards the Lower Rhine, from Frankfurt to Amsterdam. The division of postwar Germany explains this westward tilt.

The Nordic region, which is singled out, has developed its coherence in the postwar period, and after the cessation of Portugal's pretensions to being an overseas power, the Iberian peninsula is beginning to do likewise. The break-up of the European Soviet Union follows roughly the geographical grid of 1950. Significant political and cultural deviations from Christaller's European space structure appear only with regard to his Centre-East and South-East regions.

In the postwar era the Danube-centred Centre-East region, running from Bohemia to Romania, with Bratislava as its 'ideal' and Vienna as its *de facto* historical metropolis, has been turned westwards, including Slovenia and, possibly, Croatia, rather than Romania. Geographically, Thessaloniki should be the metropolis of the South-Eastern, Balkan region. We all know that this has not happened, Istanbul, Athens and Belgrade have each pulled more weight. On the other hand, Macedonia, the Greek part of which is headed by Saloniki, is again becoming a centre of competing Balkan ambitions, like it was about a hundred years ago.

Christaller's theory, in spite of his empirical awareness, does not bring out the current central nodes of the continent, however. Based on their top

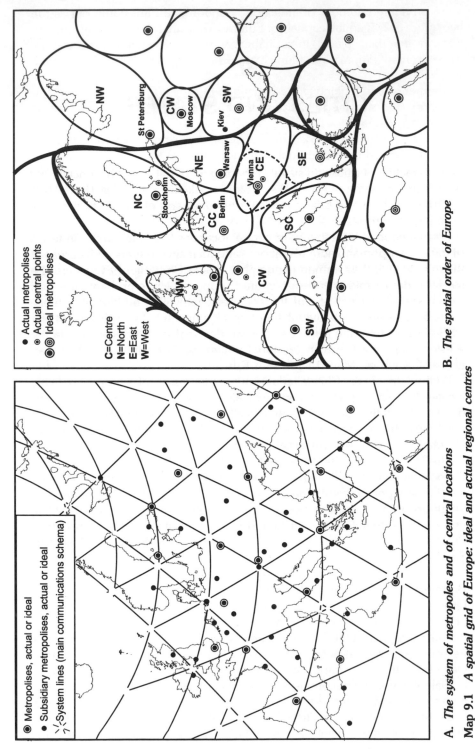

A. The system of metropoles and of central locations

B. The spatial order of Europe

Map 9.1 A spatial grid of Europe: ideal and actual regional centres

Source: Adapted from W. Christaller, 'Das Grundgerüst der räumlichen Ordnung in Europa', *Frankfurter Geographische Hefte* 24, 1 (1950), pp. 98–9.

score on a large number of indicators, London and Paris come out as the two, more or less equal, capitals of Europe. They are followed by Milan, and then in the third place, in alphabetical order, Amsterdam, Barcelona, Brussels, Frankfurt, Madrid, Munich and Rome. The fourth rank begins with Vienna.[3]

Another way of looking at the spacing of Europe is to search for core and periphery. We shall here juxtapose three mappings of the core of Europe (see Map 9.2).

One was presented in 1929, by R. Delaisi, and expressed a conception of centrality derived from industrial capitalism taken as an explanatory power: coal plus capital plus science. The second, by D. Seers from 1979, defines centrality in what might well be called post-industrial terms of its movement effects, of its attractiveness to migrants and of its capacity to send tourists.[4] The third is similar to the second, but more exclusive in its criteria of centrality. It is a mapping of urban networks in the EC, developed by Roger Brunet and the RECLUS/DATAR group of French researchers, which provides a composite view of centrality in terms of communications and of a number of aspects of site attractiveness.

Between the industrial and the fifty years younger post-industrial map, there is a striking similarity. The central core has moved westwards on its eastern flank, with the postwar system of industrial socialism in Eastern Europe, and eastwards on its western side, taking some notice of the decline of the old industrial heartland of the English Northwest. The RECLUS/ DATAR 'urban tissue' map gives the most thoroughly researched formulation of the EC 'banana', the bent, drawn-out economic and cultural centre region stretching from Lombardy and Milan to the Greater London area. The basic stretch of the 'banana' is the medieval city belt of Europe, along the North–South trade routes from Germany to Italy, with a bend towards the modern imperial City of London.

A major contrast with the maps of Delaisi and Seers is the conferral of peripheral status to a large part of France, as well as to northern Germany, the northern Netherlands and Denmark. The nineteenth-century division of developed and less developed France went from St Malo to Geneva, separating the Northeast from the Southwest, respectively, whereas the 1970 economy was found to run more straightly North–South, from Caen to Marseilles.[5]

The RECLUS study further points to the rise (again) of a northwest-shore Mediterranean region from Livorno to Valencia, perhaps linking up with Madrid, very attractive as a residential area to prosperous old people, housing a considerable amount of late modern industry and commercial horti- and agriculture, and investing heavily in science and higher education.[6]

Historically speaking, the postwar period, 1945–90, represented not only an East–West division of Europe, but a drawing apart of the continent, not taken into account by the non-political maps of Delaisi and Seers. Western Europe leant over westwards, with the peripherialization of Berlin and

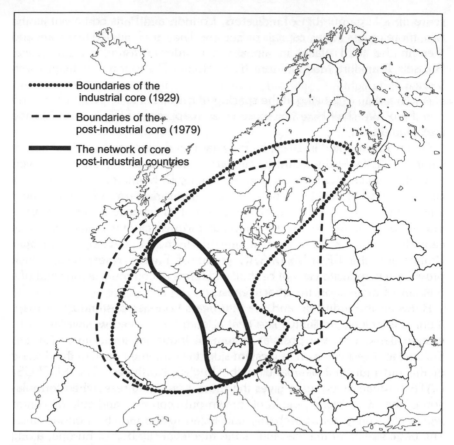

Map 9.2   *Figurations of the core of Europe*

Sources: S. Rokkan and D. Urwin, *Economy, Territory, Identity*, London, Sage, 1983, p. 43; RECLUS/DATAR, *Les villes 'européenes'*, Paris, La documentation française, 1989, p. 79.

Vienna, with the Easternization of Prussia and part of the Habsburg Crown Lands. Eastern Europe became more Eastern, both with the strong Russian influence and orientation and with the (earlier) post-revolutionary move of the Soviet capital from Petrograd to Moscow.

Urbanism and postwar European modernity

It was only after World War II that Europe, together with the Americas but a couple of decades after North America, made urbanism the dominant way of life. From medieval times till 1800 the urbanites made up a tenth of Europe's population. By 1900 they constituted almost a third, by 1950 about a good two-fifths. But in 1980, two-thirds of all Europeans were urban.[7]

The definitions of urbanization vary, so one data set is not necessarily quite comparable with another. Urbanism can be measured according to an international standard, or according to individual national definitions. Despite this, clearly rural right after the war was all Eastern Europe, (excepting the GDR and Czechoslovakia) all the Nordic countries, and Ireland, Portugal and Greece. The urbanity of Austria, Spain, and Switzerland might be contested; nevertheless, both there and in France and Italy, the urban–rural division was about even.[8]

It should be noted that rurality was not synonymous with traditonalism or underdevelopment. Denmark, Sweden and Switzerland, as we saw above in Chapter 7, were the richest countries of the continent in 1950. At least Sweden and Denmark might be argued to be among the least traditional countries, having been very significantly affected by the labour movement and by leftwing liberalism. The rural population also differed enormously, from the prosperous farmers of Denmark and southern Sweden, with their often unionized workers, to the dirt-poor *kolkhozniks* of the Stalinist USSR or the land-less and rights-less labourers of Alentejo, Andalusia or Vallachia. There is a positive correlation between urbanity and modernity, but it has always been far from perfect.

By the beginning of the 1990s, even the old peasant nations of Europe had become two-thirds or more urban: Finland, Lithuania, Poland, Belorussia, Ukraine, Bulgaria. Only Albania and, interestingly enough, Portugal are still mainly rural.[9] The countryside has become only a weekend or holiday resort to most Europeans. A constructed townscape is what shapes most of our everyday life.

The postwar surge of urbanization and population concentration was broken in the 1970s in most parts of Western Europe, save in Ireland and Portugal. A certain tendency towards counter-urbanization became visible in Britain, France, Germany and the other rich countries of the northwest, no doubt related to the dramatic process of de-industrialization in the wake of the 1973–4 crisis. But urban de-concentration appears not to have been longlived, except in West Germany.[10]

The controlled growth of European urbanization has come to stand out in contrast to the rest of the world. Between 1950 and 1980 the population of Greater London was stagnant, while that of the Parisian agglomeration increased by somewhat less than half. Moscow, the continent's third city in 1950, grew by 70%, in spite of special administrative migration regulations. Only Madrid (almost trebling) and Rome among Europe's big cities (globally defined) at least doubled their population, although Athens and Milan nearly did so. Outside Europe, New York increased by half, while Tokyo and Los Angeles more than quadrupled.[11]

According to another, slightly different way of calculation which included the Rhine–Ruhr area as a metropolitan agglomeration, in 1950 thirteen of the world's thirty-five largest conurbations were European, including numbers two (London), four (Rhine–Ruhr), and seven (Paris). In 1985 seven were European, starting from rank twelve (London).[12]

One feature of the relationship between states and cities is the extent of uniqueness and dominance – political, economic and cultural – of the

Table 9.1 *States and capitals in Europe*

Dominant capital[a]	Monocephalous[b]	Contested monocephalous[c]	Polycephalous[d]
Albania	Belorussia	Belgium	W. Germany
Austria	Bosnia-Herzegovina	Spain	Italy
Croatia	Bulgaria		Ne●.erlands
Denmark	Czech Rep.		Switzerland
Estonia	Finland		
France	E. Germany		
Greece	Lithuania		
Hungary	Norway		
Ireland	Poland		
Latvia	Portugal		
Macedonia	Russia		
Moldavia	Slovakia		
Romania	Sweden		
Serbia	Ukraine		
UK			

Notes: [a] Its urban agglomeration having at least three times the population of the next city, and no major functions shared with another city. [b] That is, single-headed, the capital city not sharing any major political, economic or cultural functions with another city, but less than three times the size of the second conurbation. [c] Where the second city has and/or claims certain special rights as the capital of a major subnational division. [d] That is, multi-headed, major functions shared between different cities.

Sources: Pieced together from official population statistics, from national political, economic and cultural data, and from P. Cheshire and D. Hay, *Urban Problems in Western Europe*, London, Unwin Hyman, 1989, Table A12.

capital city. This is a major manifestation of a spatial configuration of power (see Table 9.1).

Multi-capitaled countries may be found in the old city belt of Europe, where the political capitals Rome, Berne, Bonn and the Hague, and the future capital Berlin, have to accept the superior economic and cultural weight of Milan, Zurich, Frankfurt and a couple of other cities, and of Amsterdam et al., respectively. The overwhelming capitals are spread all over the continent, the outcomes of very different histories. Between forty-five and seventy-five years of Communism do not seem to have had any specific impact on the quantitative history of European urbanization. The Communists were an urban lot and promoted urbanization, but the amount of postwar urbanization, according to national definitions, was not significantly higher in Bulgaria, Poland or Romania than in Greece or Portugal.[13]

The German social historian Hartmut Kaelble has argued that the European city offers a particular quality of life, of the middle-sized city, due to controlled growth and urban planning.[14] Kaelble is one of the many writers, one among the very best, to whom 'Europe' equals Western Europe. That is also the perspective of Arnold Heidenheimer et al., who in

their deservedly successful *Comparative Public Policy* also argue for the
superiority of European urban planning.[15]

From a Scandinavian perspective that is a perspective very easy to concur
with. The sizeable economic resources (of taxation), the political clout, and
the progressive visions of Nordic local politicians have led to a large number
of functionally well-planned small and medium-sized cities with a rich supply
of public social and cultural services, as well as relatively well-integrated
capital cities. The power of urban planners in Europe, West and East, in
comparison with that of their colleagues in the rest of the world is striking.
Here, all Europe is clearly building upon exceptionally consensual aspects of
a long history of modernity.

Part of the legacy may be squandered, however. The early pattern of
upper-middle-class suburbanization has in Britain led to a postwar social
implosion of the big city centres, comparing little better than the trajectory of
US cities. The Thatcherite distrust of civil bodies intervening between the
Cabinet and market agents, which led to the abolition of metropolitan
organs of representation and elected authority, has not favoured urban
planning. Brussels, meanwhile, is splintered between nineteen municipalities, and has become a victim of constructed urban deserts – in connection
with the World Exhibition in 1958 and with its EC/EU capital aspirations –
interfoliated with areas of speculative decay.

The axis of urban planning runs as much North–South as East–West.
North–South there are dimensions of the extension of public services, of
local political honesty, of environmental concerns and pollution control. The
extent of public regulation in Western Europe, and in the north in particular,
meant that the different property systems East and West did not matter that
much. There was, in fact, in the 1960s and 1970s, more owner-occupied
housing in Bulgaria, Czechoslovakia and Yugoslavia, than in, say, West
Germany, Italy or Sweden.[16]

Ironically, the most successful efforts at postwar Communist urban
planning were directed towards restoration, e.g. of the old centre of Warsaw,
or of the Buda Hill – efforts hardly imaginable under the rule of the market.
Restoration apart, any positive, specifically Communist, features of urban
planning are hard to find. Following after Magnitogorsk, which relied a good
deal on American planning in the 1930s, the new socialist industrial cities,
like Halle-Neustadt, Hoyerswerda, Eisenhüttenstadt, Nowa Huta and others,
are hardly remembered with veneration, except perhaps the first.[17] True, the
Moscow underground, a monument of high Stalinism, was a wonder of
cleanliness and safety compared to the New York subway, and also
compared very favourably with the London underground and the Paris
Métro. Late-twentieth-century *flâneurs* should appreciate the physical safety
of the big Eastern European cities even late at night before the collapse of
Communism. But the latter was due more to social control than to urban
planning foresight.

The national traditions and the collective ideals vaunted by postwar
Communist planners were in the end completely subordinated to the power

monumentality and the parade ground spatiality of the new rulers, from the Stalin/Karl Marx Allee in East Berlin to the Victories Avenue and Palace of the People in Bucharest. The drab, windy vacuousness of power space, the dearth of cafés, restaurants and shops, and the appalling scarcity and overcrowding of housing in Communist Eastern Europe severely diminished, though did not negate, the advantage of urban living in Europe in comparison with, say, Detroit or Tokyo. The Eastern European big cities, from Warsaw to Sofia, did keep a good deal of their historical charm, in spite of everything, at low rent and night safety. But industrial pollution was reined in, if at all, less and later than in Northwestern Europe.

The new traditionality of the postwar state ordering

The division of postwar Europe was, of course, as after every war, drawn up by the victors, at Yalta, Potsdam and elsewhere. On the whole, the new boundaries followed old European divisions. The USSR got back what Russia had lost in 1918–20, minus Finland but plus Vyborg, and the other conquests of the 1721 Nystad peace with Sweden, minus central Poland but plus East Galicia (Lvov area) and northern Bukowina (with Paul Celan's Czernowitz), and Kant's Königsberg.[18] (In the agony of the Soviet Union these new Western territories later became prime centres of anti-Soviet and anti-Russian agitation and movements: the Baltics, Western Ukraine [as former East Galicia is now known as], Moldavia [ex-Bessarabia].)

The lands of the landowners of the second serfdom, east of the Elbe and the Leitha and north of the Danube, the late hard core of the European *anciens régimes*, gendarmed in the nineteenth century by the Czarist armies, plus the early Russian-protected former Ottoman Balkan states were allocated to the Soviet sphere of influence. Ambiguous cases of previous history like Finland – since 1809 much more autonomous than the Baltics and Bessarabia, and always with a free but stateless peasantry – , the Czech lands and Austria proper west of Leitha were left ambiguous, for a while. In the end, the strong local Communists took Czechoslovakia to the East,[19] no holds barred, while strong non-Communists cautiously steered Austria and Finland in a western direction. In Greece, clearly on the Western side of Yalta Europe, the militarily victorious anti-Communists, generously aided by British troops and US money and arms, gave no pardon.

By and large, the Yalta division fell back upon the Elbe–Leitha line which in the ninth century constituted the Eastern limit of the Carolingian Empire (see Map 9.3).[20]

The ideological division of post-World War II Europe also had its historical precedent, in the line-up of the continent *pro et contra* the French Revolution. In both cases, there was the trail-blazing fatherland of the 'patriots' or of 'the workers', of 'freedom' or of 'socialism'; the blend of missionary zeal and big power arrogance of the leaders, soldiers and civilian agents of this fatherland; embattled revolutionary minorities in allied parts of Europe; bold but not always popular measures of social change; nationalist

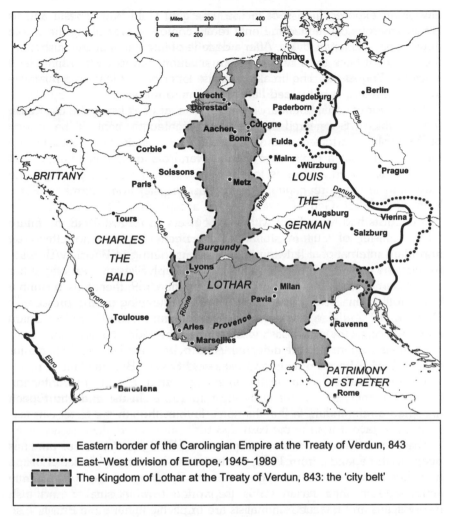

Map 9.3 *East–West divisions of Central Europe, 843–1945/1989*

Sources: Adapted from G. Holmes (ed.), *The Oxford Illustrated History of Medieval Europe*, Oxford, Oxford University Press, 1988, p. 98, and modern atlases.

mobilizations of counter-revolution; cautiously manoeuvring neutrals; and a safe and powerful extra-continental centre of counter-revolution – Britain in the case of the 1789 revolution, the United States and, as a poor second, Britain, in the case of the 1917 revolution. The major difference between the structurations for and against Jacobin/Napoleonic France and Stalinist USSR – apart from the involvement of the USA in the latter – was the caution of Stalin and his successors, which made possible four decades of Cold War stabilization.

But the postwar settlement also included a number of other sensitive issues. While West Berlin, an island in the Soviet zone of Germany, was always an exposed 'hot' spot in the emerging Cold War, Trieste and its Istrian environs constituted the only really contested area along the whole new cross-continental divide. After a decade of international administration, the city went back to its prewar Italian situation, but its eastern hinterland stayed in Yugoslavia. The break-up of the latter has, at least in a relatively low-key fashion, re-actualized Italy's borders to the east.[21]

The major national boundary change was that of Poland. The old Polish realm which disappeared in the late eighteenth century had been precariously resurrected after World War I and again obliterated by the Hitler–Stalin Pact in 1939. After the new war, Poland not only returned, but was literally moved westwards, losing to the east to the USSR, gaining to the west, and in the north-central (former East Prussia) from Germany. For a long time West Germany refused to accept this. The East German Communists had to, but not with a light heart. In August 1948 the future GDR Minister of Culture, Johannes R. Becher, refused to attend an important international leftwing intellectual gathering in Wroclaw/Breslau, because he could not bring himself to visit a 'Polish Silesia'.[22] As long as the Social Democrats were kept out of office, i.e. till 1969, there was in Bonn a high-profile Minister of Expellees in charge of keeping up the pressure.[23] Only in 1972 did a slender Social Democratic–Liberal parliamentary majority accept the new Polish west frontier, the Oder–Neisse line.

On their western side the defeated 'Axis' powers agreed with little demur to give back Alsace-Lorraine and Nice and Savoy. But Saarland a major steel region, remained, as in the interwar period, a bone of contention between France and Germany till the mid-1950s. In the end, the French accepted a referendum in the German's favour, though the result was less strongly in favour than in the Nazi 1930s.[24]

The Saar settlement was a crucial part of the EEC deal. Since Saarland has been off the agenda, from 1956, the interstate borders of Western Europe have been uncontested, although the South Tyrolians have only reluctantly acquiesced in their Italian status (separated from Austria),[25] and Irish Republicans and Basque Nationalists are implicitly fighting the British–Irish and the Spanish–French border, respectively.

Although certain stirrings among the Sudeten Germans, expelled from Czechoslovakia after the war, and since the war the protégés of Bavarian Christian Socials, are notable and have been reacted to with strong irritation by the ultra-occidentalist regime in Prague in 1993–4, the old East–West border is basically stable. Even the Italian motions around Istria should probably not be taken too seriously.

Apart from the post-Communistically fragmented multinational states, the USSR, Yugoslavia and Czechoslovakia, each with its own specific internal dynamic of *ressentiments*, sometimes peaceful sometimes violent, the most sensitive borders of postwar Europe have remained, or have in the end become, the Albanian, Greek and Hungarian ones.

Albania proclaimed its independence from the moribund Ottoman Empire in 1912, and was immediately drawn into the maelstrom of rival Balkan nationalisms. Serbia seized Kossovo, while Montenegrin and Greek demands were staved off by Great Power recognition. The Versailles powers re-confirmed Albania's borders, but the issues remained. They were revived when Fascist Italy occupied Albania and made Albanian demands on Greece and Yugoslavia Italian. During the Resistance, the superior strength of the Yugoslav comrades forced the Albanian ones to recognize the right of the former to ethnically mainly Albanian Kossovo.

The thawing of the Cold War has also unfrozen the Serbian–Albanian issue over Kossovo, and the Greek–Albanian one over Gjirokaster/Northern Epirus. The latter is an Albanian province with a Greek minority. The Greek conflict with the former Yugoslav republic of Macedonia is symbolic – over the legitimate inheritance of the name 'Macedonia' and of the more than two thousand year old symbols of Philip II and Alexander the Great – rather than territorial. But the border might become a victim of the rivalry of the relics.

Hungary suffered heavy retribution for having lost World War I and, having sided with the ultimately losing side again, ended up no better off after World War II. The problem was that significant Hungarian populations were confined on the side of hostile neighbours: Romania, Yugoslavia, Czechoslovakia – lands where Hungary had ruled heavy-handedly before 1918. At the time of writing (autumn 1994) there are no signs of any impending open conflict, but the fuel for one is there, in the ethnic pressures of the Romanian, Serbian and Slovak states and in the presence of overtly irredentist forces in Hungary.

State boundaries reached their highest historical significance in Europe from about 1950 till around 1980. Before World War II, a number of the new states were never legally unified, as we noticed in Chapter 6: Czechoslovakia, Lithuania, Poland, Romania, Yugoslavia.[26] Afterwards they were. It is true, however, that the age of the passport began after the first of the world wars.

The new demarcation of two politico-economic systems followed state boundaries, with the creation of two German states. And even though the Americans kept watch over Western Europe, and the Russians more heavy-handedly intervened in the East,[27] the different states of both camps kept their specificities. As his dramatic break with the Yugoslavs demonstrated, Stalin was always very suspicious against any Eastern European integration, other than bilateral, i.e. state-to-state, relations wth the USSR. Even the sinister machinations of the Soviet secret services at the height of late Stalinist terror had very different national outcomes.[28]

The importance of states began to decline in the 1980s, when capitalist states began to drift in the high seas of global financial markets, when the EC gathered momentum in the second half of the decade. The change was consummated in the early 1990s, when the multinational states of the USSR and Yugoslavia broke up into chaos, as well as into new, fragile states, and when private financial operators brought down the monetary system of Western European states.

In pre-modern Europe, territorial boundaries were often provincial or city boundaries, rather than borders of sovereign states. Legal and political systems, for example, were more often than not provincial or local, and they usually remained across the vicissitudes of warfare. The new seventeenth-century big power Sweden even made it an official policy not to incorporate the new territories around the Baltic into the political and legal system of the realm, which was just becoming within its old borders the most unified state of Europe. Only after a nearly successful attempt by the Danes to recapture Scania was a vigorous policy of Swedification introduced there, in spite of a renewed peace treaty stipulation to the contrary.[29] On the European periphery, this relationship of state and province borders survived into the age of modernity. When Russia conquered Estonia and Livonia from Sweden in 1721 or Finland in 1809, the Tsar promised, and by and large kept his promise, to respect not only the religion but also the laws and the institutions of the land. Into the twentieth century, the pattern was, that rulers came and went but the population and their laws and customs stayed.[30]

The next two chapters will look into contemporary transgressions of state boundaries.

Notes

1 For example S. Rokkan, 'Cities, States, and Nations: A Dimensional Model for the Study of Contrasts in Development', in S.N. Eisenstadt and S. Rokkan (eds), *Building States and Nations*, Vol. 1, Beverly Hills and London, Sage, 1973; C. Tilly, *Co-ercion, Capital, and European States, AD 990–1990*, Oxford, Blackwell, rev. paperback edn, 1992.

2 W. Christaller, 'Das Grundgerüst der räumlichen Ordnung in Europa', *Frankfurter Geographische Hefte* 24, 1 (1950), pp. 15–16.

3 RECLUS/DATAR, *Les villes 'Européenes'*, Paris, La Documentation Française, 1989, p. 52.

4 R. Delaisi, *Les deux Europes*, Paris, Payot, 1929; D. Seers, 'The Periphery in Europe', in D. Seers et al. (eds), *Underdeveloped Europe*, Brighton, Harvester Press, 1979. Both are summarized in S. Rokkan and D. Urwin, *Economy, Territory, Identity*, London, Sage, 1983, pp. 42ff.

5 Rokkan and Urwin, *Economy, Territory, Identity*, p. 195n. They are primarily referring to a doctoral thesis by M. Quellenec, 'Analyse structurale de dévéloppment économique des régions françaises, 1864–1970', Paris, Université de Paris, 1972.

6 See further, R. Laffont, *La nation, l'Etat, les regions*, Paris, Berg International, 1993, pp. 106ff.

7 P. Bairoch, *Cities and Economic Development*, London, Mansell Publishing, 1988, pp. 302–495.

8 Eastern Europe: D. Turnock, *The Human Geography of Eastern Europe*, London, Routledge, 1989, p. 156; P. Shoup, *The East European and Soviet Data Handbook*, New York, Columbia University Press, 1989, p. 382; Nordic Countries: S. Swedberg, *Våra grannländers näringsliv*, Stockholm, Rabén & Sjögren, 1959, p. 18; *Historisk Statistik för Sverige*, 2nd edn, Stockholm, SCB, 1969, p. 48; More general: OECD Urban Affairs Programme, 'Urban Statistics in OECD Countries', Paris, 1988 (mimeographed), p. 13; A.G. Champion, 'Geographical Distribution and Urbanization', in D. Noin and R. Woods (eds), *The Changing Population of Europe*, Oxford, Blackwell, 1993, pp. 28–9; P. Flora (ed.), *State, Economy, and Society in Western Europe, 1815–1975*, Vol. 2, Frankfurt, Campus, 1987, Ch. 3.

9 World Bank, *World Development Report 1993*, New York, Oxford University Press, 1993, Table 31. My statement about Albania is an extrapolation from the 1980 figure of Turnock, *Human Geography*, p. 156.

10 A.G. Champion, 'Geographical Distribution and Urbanization', in Noin and Woods, *Changing Population*, pp. 30ff; *Stadsregioner i Europa*, Stockholm, SOU, 1990: 34, pp.28ff.

11 Bairoch, *Cities and Economic Development*, p. 309.

12 M. Dogan and J. Kasarda (eds), *The Metropolis Era: A World of Giant Cities*, Vol. l, London, Sage, 1988, pp. 14–15.

13 Shoup, *East European and Soviet Data Handbook*, Tables H13–21; Champion 'Geographical Distribution', p. 28.

14 H. Kaelble, *Auf dem Weg zu einer europäischen Gesellschaft*, Munich, C.H. Beck, 1957, Ch. II.6.

15 A. Heidenheimer et al., *Comparative Public Policy*, 3rd edn, New York, St Martin's Press, Ch. 8.

16 K. von Beyme, 'Reconstruction in the German Democratic Republic', in J. Diefendorf (ed.), *Rebuilding Europe's Bombed Cities*, Basingstoke, Macmillan, 1990, p. 204.

17 Ibid., p. 192.

18 Cf. the serenely melancholic reportage by Verena Dohrn, *Reise nach Galizien*, Frankfurt, Fischer, 1992.

19 However ugly in its rather immediate sequels in the era of late Stalinism, the so-called Prague Coup was nevertheless a sort of unbloody Communist revolution, in which popular mobilization rather than the Soviet Army played the significant role. See further, e.g. J. Bloomfield, *Passive Revolution*, London, Allison & Busby, 1979.

20 Cf. J. Szücs, *Die drei historichen Regionen Europas*, Frankfurt, Neue Kritik, 1990, pp. 13, 15.

21 On this last point, see *Le Monde*, 14.2.1992 p. 2; *Frankfurter Allgemeine Zeitung*, 27.7.1993 p. 3. The sad history of the once multicultural Habsburg freeport city of Trieste, at the meeting-point of the three major cultures of Europe, in alphabetical order, the Germanic, the Latin and the Slav, is fascinatingly narrated by A. Ara and C. Magris, *Trieste: Une identité de frontière*, Paris, Seuil, 1982.

22 W. Schwiedrzlk, *Träume der ersten Stunde*, Berlin, Siedler, 1991, p. 87.

23 See further W. Benz, 'Fremde in der Heimat: Flucht – Vertreibung – Integration', in K. Bade (ed.), *Deutsche im Ausland – Fremde in Deutschland*, Munich, C.H. Beck, 1992

24 In 1935 more than 90% voted for *Anschluss* to Nazi Germany. Twenty years later 68% voted to reunite with Christian Democratic Germany. Cf., from a German perspective, H.-P. Schwartz, *Adenauer: Der Staatsmann, 1952–1967*, Stuttgart, Deutsche-Verlags-Anstalt, 1991, p. 233.

25 The upheavals in Eastern Europe gave a brief push to the Tyrolian minority movement: *Frankfurter Allgemeine Zeitung*, 2., 4., 5., 16., 17.9.1991.

26 Also Spain had its regional family rules and customs, and Austria had a religiously divided family law. See further, A. Bergmann, *Internationales Ehe- und Kindschaftsrecht*, 2nd. edn, Berlin, Verlag für Standeswesen, 1938.

27 The Soviet ambassador to Sofia apparently attended meetings of the Bulgarian Politburo in the early 1960s, under Jivkov: G. Horn, *Freiheit die ich meine*, Hamburg, Hoffmann und Campe, 1991, p. 149.

28 The East German and the Polish equivalents to Rájk and Slánsky and their Hungarian and Czechoslovak comrades, Ackermann, Dahlem, Gomulka, etc; were put on ice, and not liquidated. In Romania the purge of 1952 turned out to clear the way for a nationalist Communism.

29 J. Rosén, *Det karolinska skedet*, Lund, Gleerups, 1963, pp. 67ff, 214ff. For comparative perspectives, see further P. Sahlins, *Boundaries*, Berkeley, University of California Press, 1989, pp. 113ff, and G. Therborn, *Borgarklass och byråkrati i Sverige*, Lund, Arkiv, 1989, Part 1.

30 Some noblemen, intellectuals and politicians might go, and after the Partitions of Poland they were many enough to set up a Polish Legion in the French Italian campaigns, as well as, more easily at hand, in the Grande Armée to Moscow in 1812.

10

THE EUROPEAN ECONOMIC SPACE

The city belt and the European Community

In his conceptual mapping of Europe – developed for purposes of explaining national political variations and, to my knowledge, never applied to the unification of Europe – the late Stein Rokkan used two geo-political variables of European history, which together formed an East–West dimension, centre formation and city network. The 'seaward peripheries' in the West, from Norway to Brittany, were weak in both. By contrast, the 'seaward empire nations', from Denmark to Spain and Portugal via England and France, were strong on both. In the east, the 'landward buffers', from Finland to Hungary, were weak in both centre formation and in urban network, whereas the 'landward empire nations', from Sweden to Austria, via Prussia, developed strong centres but weak city networks.

Between 'seaward' and 'landward' Europe ran a territory which Rokkan sometimes called the 'backbone' (*épine dorsale*)[1] of Europe, but more often the 'city belt'. This European backbone is characterized by weak centre formation and a strong network of cities. It runs North–South along old trade routes, bridging the cultural divides between Latin and Germanic Europe, between Catholic and Protestant Europe. From the Hanseatic cities on the Baltic, down through the Rhineland, what is now the Netherlands, Belgium, and Luxemburg, old Lothringia, Switzerland, across the Alps down onto the Italian peninsula.[2] By and large, the city belt corresponds to the short-lived Kingdom of Lothar of the Treaty of Verdun, 843 (see Map 9.3 above).

In terms of the two master variables, which Charles Tilly has used for explaining processes of state formation in Europe, the city belt was characterized by accumulation and concentration of capital, rather than by a concentration of coercive means.[3]

After the end in 1945 of the historically rather brief Prussian centre domination of Germany, the gravity of Germany shifted back to the city belt, with its absence of a monocentric territorial structure. And unified Italy is still in many ways polycephalous. In other words, after a millennium, the European city belt is still visible on the politico-economico-cultural map. The weak, or, better, non-exclusive nation-state attachments of the city belt have been decisive both for the original launching of the European unification project and for gearing it into a new momentum later. The Dutch, the Belgians and the Italians have provided both the federalist crack troops and the key negotiators, from Spaak to Lubbers. From the Rhineland came the decisive political leaders at the outset, Robert Schumann and Konrad Adenauer, and the most important politician behind the economic union project of the 1990s, Helmut Kohl.[4]

The European Community in construction is also in itself a city belt writ large, a loosely coupled entity, without any strong and mighty centre, a network of largely sovereign units, connected, above all, by trade and by commercial law. In the historical structuration of power and states in Europe, the EC constitutes a bend in a long-term curve, with intra-European power and polity formation developing mainly along the route of capital concentration.

This little or un-noticed geo-political backbone of the EC is essential to an understanding of the rise of the latter, but it is, of course, not meant as an explanation on its own. Much more recent history was crucial in bringing France, in a sense the first developed nation-state in Europe, into a supra-national network, and in keeping the Swiss from assuming their old role in the trading belt of Europe. In the former case, it is worth noting, however, that the other EC members have always had to pay a special price of homage to French nationalism, giving the French an officious role of political and cultural leadership of the EC.

Integration without convergence?

At first sight it may appear that territorial distributions are what European integration is about. However, on further consideration the reader will no doubt realize that territorial convergence and similarity are not synonymous with the constitution of a society. State-bounded societies sometimes exhibit vast territorial disparities – and other socio-economic inequalities – and tendencies of polarization or divergence as well as of convergence.

An overall summary of what has happened to the territorial pattern of economic resources in Western Europe is that the European territories have become more similar in the course of the post-World War II period, that this is due primarily to the economic boom and modernization, and that the EC has contributed nothing visible to territorial convergence or assimilation. Table 10.1 gives a first overview.

The smaller the coefficient of variation (which can range from 0 to 1), the less variation or dissimilarity there is. The 1960s clearly was the period of most convergence, as well as the time of fastest growth. The process then slowed down, and came to a halt with the recession. Between 1970 and 1973 the OECD coefficient of variation decreased from 0.285 to 0.252, by 0.033 in three years. For the remaining seven years till 1980 the decrease was 0.019. During the second oil shock recession, disparity actually rose, to 0.246 in 1985.

The 1950–70 period was that of de-agrarianization, industrialization and internal migration. By 1950 all western France from Normandy to the

Table 10.1 *Postwar economic convergence in Western Europe[a]*
(coefficient of variation of GDP per capita, and poor European[b]
average as percentage of the all-Western Europe average)

	All-Western variation		Poor Western average	
Year	S–H[c]	OECD[d]	S–H[c]	OECD[d]
1950	0.36	–	53.7	–
1960	0.32	–	53.5	–
1970	0.26	0.28	62.1	59.7
1980	0.23	0.23	65.9	63.4
1989	–	0.23	–	63.9

Notes: [a] Sixteen countries, exclusive of Iceland and Luxemburg, not population-weighted.
[b] Unweighted average of Greece, Ireland, Portugal and Spain. [c] Summers and Heston, see
below. [d] OECD, *Historical Statistics,* see below.

Sources: Calculations from R. Summers and A. Heston, 'Improved International Comparisons
of Real Product and Its Composition: 1950–1980', *The Review of Income and Wealth,* 30
(1984), data tables (1950–1980); OECD, *National Accounts 1960–1987,* Vol. 1, Paris 1989;
Historical Statistics, 1960–1989, Paris, pp. 18ff. The OECD data refer to GDP per capita at
purchasing power parities.

Pyrénées had more than half of all its employment in agriculture. So had
southern Italy and the whole eastern part of the peninsula up to the border
of Lombardy. Bavaria, Rhineland-Palatinate, Lower Saxony and Schleswig-
Holstein had more than 30% of their employment in agriculture.[5]

The Eastern European pattern is strikingly similar to that of Western
Europe. For the eight countries there (Albania missing), the coefficient of
variation of the GDP per capita according to the Summers and Heston
estimates was 0.35 in 1950, 0.33 in 1960, 0.26 in 1970 and 0.22 in 1980.
Here too the 1960s was a period of growth, with the poor (Balkan) countries
catching up with the rest of Europe.

For the twelve countries which currently make up the EC/EU we can put
together another time series (see Table 10.2).

The most striking aspect of Table 10.2 above is that *all convergence
between the current EC 12 took place before they had come together in the
EC.* The twelve countries became more similar at the time when the then
EEC had only six members, i.e. till 1973. The original EC members, for their
part, were set on a course of convergence before the Treaty of Rome started
to operate, which then continued under the Treaty.

Noteworthy, also, though much less surprising, is that the postwar
experience has been that boom times decrease disparities within Western
Europe, while recession times increase them, albeit not dramatically.[6]

The effects of EC membership on relatively poor countries may be
gauged by looking at Ireland (member since 1973) and Greece (member
since 1981). In 1972 Irish GDP per inhabitant was 61.4% of that of the EC
12 (OECD data), in 1990 the corresponding figure was 67.3% (EC data).
The Greek experience has so far been less positive, going from 58.2% of EC

Table 10.2 *Economic disparity between the EC countries 1950–1990 (coefficient of variation of GDP per capita, 1960–1990, at purchasing power parities)*

Year series	EC 5[a] 1950–90 series	EC 12 1960–85 series	EC 12 1980–90
1950	0.19	–	–
1958	0.23	–	–
1960	–	0.27	–
1965	–	0.23	–
1970	–	0.19	–
1973	0.08	0.17	–
1980	–	0.18	0.168
1985	–	0.19	0.175
1990	0.06	–	0.162

Note: [a] Belgium, France, West Germany, Italy, the Netherlands. Luxemburg excluded.

Sources: 1950–90 series: calculations from A. Maddison, *Ontwikkelingsfasen van het kapitalisme*, Utrecht, Het Spectrum, 1982, pp. 21, 225, 234, 252, and OECD, *National Accounts, 1960–1990*, Vol. 1, Paris, 1992; 1960–85 series: Commission of the European Communities, *The Regions of the Enlarged Community*, Brussels and Luxemburg, 1987, p. 128; 1980–1990 series, idem, *De regio's in de jaren negentig*, Brussels–Luxemburg, 1991, p. 86.

GDP in 1980 to 53.0% in 1990 after a decade in the Community. In other words, there is no clear effect of EC membership.

The GDP range of EC countries in 1990 is considerable: 2.43:1, if we take Luxemburg as the richest country; 2.14:1, if we think that Luxemburg is so small to be special and take Germany. (Greece is the poorest, closely followed by Portugal, until 1989 poorer than Greece.)

But Yugoslavia harboured larger differences within its, now ripped apart, state boundaries. In 1988 the GMP (gross material product) per capita of Slovenia in relation to that of Macedonia was 3.22:1, in relation to that of Kosovo, 7.52:1.[7] In the former USSR, inter-republican disparity in per capita GDP in 1990 was 3.6:1 between Estonia and Tajikistan. Within European USSR the range between Estonia and Moldavia was 1.75:1, i.e. significantly less than in the EC.[8]

The United States also has much smaller territorial differences than the EC. The maximum range between states there is 1.82:1 – between Connecticut and Mississippi in 1986[9] – and the population-weighted coefficient of variation was only 0.124 (in 1983),[10] as compared to 0.175–0.19 in the EC. The EC inter-country variation in the 1980s is about the same as that of the USA inter-state pattern in the 1950s.[11]

The autonomous dynamics of trade

Trade, a Common, and most recently a 'Single', Market, has constituted the core of the process of Western European unification. How far has this effort actually gone in linking member states through trade?

Table 10.3 *The development of intra-EU trade, 1956–1992 (EU share in per cent of national exports)*

The first figure in every cell refers to export to the original six EEC member states, the second to the twelve EC members of 1992.

Country	1956	1973	1980	1992
Belg.–Lux.	44, 57	64, 75	57, 73	57, 75
Denmark	26, 62	22, 45	30, 51	36, 55
France	22, 34	38, 61	31, 56	32, 63
Germany	26, 37	34, 51	33, 51	31, 54
Greece	37, 58	38, 56	34, 48	36, 54
Ireland	9, 93	19, 78	23, 76	35, 74
Italy	26, 34	45, 55	41, 52	42, 58
Netherlands	40, 52	59, 72	57, 72	55, 76
Portugal	21, 41	21, 51	34, 58	44, 75
Spain	n.a.	34, 52	34, 52	44, 71
UK	14, 20	24, 35	26, 46	40, 56
Sweden	41, 58	40, 51	34, 51	39, 56
Switzerland	n.a.	29, 50	36, 53	39, 59

Sources: Calculations from United Nations, *Commodity Trade Statistics*, New York, Series D (1956–1980); OECD, *Monthly Statistics of Foreign Trade*, October 1993 (1992).

From Table 10.3 we see that there is an increasing intra-European trade, which is accentuated by the fact that foreign trade has risen more rapidly than the national product in the postwar era. In 1960 exports accounted for 19.4% of the GDP of the current EU states, in 1990 28.3%.[12] But the pattern and the possible impact of the Common Market are uneven.

The very development of extra-national trade itself has been very differentiated. Whereas, for instance, the export share of Belgian GDP rose from 38.4% per cent in 1960 to 74.3% in 1990, the German changed only from 19.0 to 32.0%, or the French from 14.6 to 22.5%.

If the Common Market has governed European exports, we should expect to see in Table 10.3 a markedly higher growth of trade between 1956 and 1973 among the original six EEC members than among the rest. Decoding the figures of the table, we should expect two trends from comparing the first two columns. First, that for the six member states, the intra-EEC (the first set of figures in each cell) share should rise more than the broader European one, including those countries not yet members (the second set of figures in each cell). Secondly, that the growth of exports to the six original members should be slower from non-member states.

The actual pattern does not support that hypothesis. The founding EEC members expanded their exports as much to the not-yet members as to the members. Indeed, the two most powerful economies, Germany and France, oriented their export offensives rather more outside than inside the EEC, but still within Western Europe. On the other hand, to non-member states the

EEC market did increase more slowly, if at all. Rather than by trade integration, the 1956–73 period seems to be characterized by a broad European export orientation, sustained by a continental pattern of economic vitality, having as its centre the inner EEC couple, France and Germany.

After 1973 intra-EU trade has stagnated relatively as far as the original members are concerned, even receding between 1973 and 1980. The new members do increase their EU trade, but there is no trend bend upon joining, Spain and, to an extent, Denmark excepted. Non-member Switzerland has become more integrated with the EC than Germany, and the Swedish export orientation is basically similar to that of Greece.

By way of summary, *the trade orientation and trade integration effects of twenty-five years of the Common Market have been marginal.* The international trade of Western European countries has been driven by a dynamic largely beyond Community efforts.

How much effect '1992' will have, i.e. the establishment of the so-called Single Market of people, goods, capital and services, the successfully mobilizing goal of the EC in the late 1980s, remains to be seen. The prospects for the Cecchini Report coming true look dim, although the unspecified 'medium term' of benefits from the Single Market makes the Report difficult to falsify. (In other words, difficult to discuss seriously.)

It is certain, however, that the EC economy did not receive the predicted 'supply-side shock' in 1993. When the long-announced date, 1 January 1993, finally arrived, it was quite undramatic, little noticed by the citizens of the area. Only in Spain did a significant number of major enterprises notice advantages arising from it by early 1994: 42% of Spanish executives polled, compared with 23% of British, 12% of German and 9% of French executives.[13]

The Single Market's first year of functioning was lacklustre, characterized by recession, and certainly not by any of the envisaged accelerated economic growth. The member states could not agree on doing away with passport control. Coping with different VAT rates and other national regulations still made a significant difference between national and EC trade. Corporation policies of keeping national markets segmented and prohibiting wholesalers from re-exporting to the other EC countries add extra weight to maintaining existing divisions.

Further, the Single Market 'medium-term', of an extra addition of 4–5% to GDP and of 1.8 million more jobs,[14] hardly started very auspiciously. In 1993, the EC economy actually declined, by −0.3% according to an OECD December 1993 estimate. The number of jobs fell, to a greater extent than ever before in EEC history, by more than 2.5 million. In terms of growth the EC fared slightly better in the recession than Japan, slightly worse than non-EC Europe, and much worse than the USA. With regard to employment loss the new Single Market was *sui generis* among all the major markets, although some small countries outside did even worse.[15]

Markets, in plural, are likely to keep their own dynamics, and the Single Market is unlikely to come to resemble the floor of a stock exchange.

On the other hand, the new rules set by the EC and its Court constitute an impressive legal framework, which the market players and the citizens will certainly take into account. The new élite networks, whose growth is now much promoted, not only of businessmen, top politicians and bureaucrats but also of rank and file politicians, trade unionists, academics and students, are also likely to become increasingly important supports of a united Europe.

The Europe of the regions

The general regional pattern is roughly the same as the national one. From 1950 to 1973 there was a marked decline of regional disparities, after that oscillations around a basic stability. The increase of regional disparities within the EC in the 1980s was somewhat more marked than the cross-country one. For 174 regions the population-weighted coefficient of variation increased from 0.261 in 1980 to 0.279 in 1986, whereafter a slight downward bow began. Between Hamburg and the Northern Aegean islands the economic disparity stood in the late 1980s at 4.58:1, to the Portuguese North it is 4.36:1.[16]

Unemployment figures diverge much more than GDP. Within the EC for 1988–90, the ratio between the most and the least unemployed region, Andalusia and Luxemburg, respectively, is 15.63:1, and the regional coefficient of variation is 0.512.[17]

Regional and national disparities are not fully comparable. Available regional data are mainly GDP ones, which do not take transfers into account. Such transfers are, of course, more important between regions within a state than between states, even within the EC. The fit between regional product and the income of the inhabitants of the region is not perfect.

In the never-perfect world of social science, however, the fit is not that bad. For Finland it has been possible to gather both regional product and disposable income (after tax and transfers) data.[18] The correlation between the two is 0.86, which means that from the GDP data we can account for 74% of the regional variation of disposable income.

Convergence in the past was also somewhat different between regions within a country and between countries. Migration from poor regions to prosperous ones played a major part in intra-national inter-regional convergence of GDP per head in the 1950–70 period. Only in the 1960s did employment migration contribute to inter-country convergence. The rest was achieved by catching-up patterns of economic growth.[19]

With the above qualifications we may then make some comparisons between inter-country and inter-regional distributions (see Table 10.4). Of the total of GDP per capita differences between regions within the EC, about one half (47% in 1985) is due to inter-country disparities and another half to intra-national regional ones.[20] Intra-nation-state territorial differences are, in fact, quite large in Western Europe.

Table 10.4 *Regional economic differences within Western European countries, in the EC, and in Yugoslavia (coefficients of variation of GDP per capita in 1985)*

Area	Coefficient of variation
Germany	0.187
France[a]	0.251
Italy	0.247
UK	0.182
Belgium	0.176
Netherlands[b]	0.134
Denmark	0.128
Greece	0.086
EC 10	0.260 (0.143)[c]
Spain	0.187
EC 12	0.285 (0.187)[c]
Finland[d]	0.200
Switzerland[e]	0.184
Yugoslavia	0.520 (1988)

Notes: [a] Exclusive of Corsica. [b] Exclusive of Groningen. [c] Figure within parenthesis refers to inter-country variation. [d] 1986. [e] 1980.

Sources: Commission of the European Communities, *Regions of the Enlarged Community*, p. 27; (calculation from) *Statistisk Årsbok för Finland 1987, 1990*, Helsinki, Statistiska Centralbyrån, 1987 and 1990, pp. 39 and 318, respectively, OECD, *Regional Problems in Switzerland*, Paris, 1991, p. 35; calculation from D. Plestina, *Regional Development in Communist Yugoslavia*, Boulder, Col., Westview Press, 1992, p. 180 (for the six republics and the two then autonomous regions of Yugoslavia).

France and Italy have the largest intra-national disparities in Western Europe, although the latter pale aside the chasms of ex-Yugoslavia.[21] Furthermore, regional differences within France and Italy are almost as large as those between all the regions of the EC exclusive of the Iberian peninsula (the EC 10). Intra-country disparities in both the EC 12 and the EC 10 are considerably smaller than those between French or Italian regions.

In comparison with the situation in the United States (coefficient of variation 0.124 it will be recalled), the regional gaps in Latin Europe are large. Switzerland seems to be the only country in Western Europe in which regional disparities are larger in the 1980s than in 1950.[22] The remarkably even territorial distribution in Greece should also be noted.

The territorial patterning of the production of economic resources within the EC should provide a good ground for a supra-state integration, rather little different as it is from that of the larger European states. On the other hand, we have also seen that so far the EC has hardly had any converging impact.

Regions across states: re-dividing Western Europe

Hitherto we have only spoken about the regions of the EC, not of Western Europe as a whole. But the OECD has developed a somewhat more standardized regional division, by which we may bring in the EFTA countries and their regions onto the same plane as the EC.[23] For all of Western Europe's 101 regions in the OECD mapping, except one (the Azores and Madeira), we have pieced together regional GDP data. These data have then been submitted to the statistical procedure of cluster analysis with the aim of finding the units with the smallest intra-unit variation and the largest inter-unit variation. Put in another language, we have constructed twelve new 'countries' in Europe which are as regionally homogeneous as possible. How far will these 'countries' differ from the existing ones? To what extent is the economic situation of regions in different states similar? To what extent do regional differences within states overtake disparities between states? Table 10.5 will give an answer.

The new regional economic geography of Europe according to the regional production of economic resources redraws the state maps almost completely. On one hand, it singles out regions of prosperity (Hamburg, Ile-de-France, in 1990 also Brussels) and poverty (the Portuguese North, and some further parts of Portugal and Greece). On the other, it draws politically and territorially widely apart regions together, like Iceland and Emilia-Romagna, Lazio and northern Norway, southeastern Austria and Lisbon, Mediterranean France and Scotland, Lower Saxony and southwestern Finland.

The regions above all have a certain political and/or administrative reality, which is both an advantage and a disadvantage in this context. It is an advantage in comparison with the mapping of existing state boundaries. It is a disadvantage in some economic comparisons, because the criteria of politico-administrative divisions differ cross-nationally. At the upper end, for instance, a certain upgrading is given to compact city-states like Hamburg and Bremen in relation to broader regions, such as southeastern England and Lombardy.[24] Greater London as a region has a GDP per capita of 136[25] (if the EC average is set to 100) which is somewhat higher than the product of southeastern UK, at 125.5, and would put London in the 'prosperous' cluster of the former.

The structural potential of regional realignments in Europe is apparently quite large. None of the sixteen states of Western Europe consisting of more than one region[26] has all of its regions in the same cluster, and only Greece, with three regions, has all of them in two adjacent clusters. The spread is quite wide. German regions fan out between clusters 1 and 7, French between 2 and 9, Italian between 4 and 10, British between 5 and 9, Austrian between 6 and 9, Belgian between 2 and 8, Danish between 4 and 7, Dutch between 5 and 8, Finnish between 4 and 8, Greek between 9 and 10, Irish between 9 and 11, Norwegian between 3 and 6, Spanish between 8 and 11, Swedish between 4 and 6, and Swiss between 3 and 6.

Table 10.5 *The twelve most regionally homogeneous countries of Western Europe constructed*

Results of regional cluster analysis of GDP per capita at purchasing power parities in 1986. Figures are cluster averages and index numbers, EC = 100.

1. The super rich 183.2
Hamburg

2. The very rich 165.5
Ile-de-France

3. The wealthy 149.5
Southern Norway
Bremen
Brussels
Northern Switzerland (Zurich, Basle, etc.)

4. The Prosperous 138.3
Eastern Norway (Oslo etc.)
Stockholm
Uusimaa (Helsinki etc.)
Danish capital region
Western Switzerland (Geneva etc.)
Lombardy

5. The upper middle class 124.9
Iceland
Western Norway
Southeast England
Hessen
Baden-Württemberg
West Berlin
Northern Netherlands
Luxemburg
Central Switzerland
Northwestern Italy
Emilia Romagna

6. The solid middle class 112.9
Northern Norway
Central Norway
Northern Sweden
Middle Sweden
Western Sweden
Southern Sweden
Denmark west of Storebaelt (Jutland etc.)
North Rhine Westphalia
Bavaria
Western Netherlands
Rhône-Alpes
Southern Switzerland
Danubiana (Vienna etc.)
Northeastern Italy
Central Italy (Tuscany etc.)
Lazio

7. The very middle 99.9
Southwestern Finland
Yorkshire and Humberside
East Midlands
East Anglia
Southwest England
West Midlands
Northwest England
Scotland
Denmark east of Storebaelt (excl. the capital)
Schleswig-Holstein
Lower Saxony
Rhineland-Palatinate

8. The lower middle class 87.7
Northern Finland
Central Finland
Northern England
Wales
Eastern Netherlands
Wallonia
Nord-Pas-de-Calais
Western France
Auvergne-Limousin
Abruzzi-Molise
Basque Country
Southern Netherlands
Madrid

Table 10.5 *continued*

Saarland
Flanders
Normandy-Picardy
Central France
Eastern France
Southwestern France
Mediterranean France
Western Austria

9. The lower class 74.4
Eastern Ireland (Dublin etc.)
Northern Ireland (UK)
Corsica
Southeastern Austria
Puglia
Sicily
Sardinia
Asturias-Cantabria
Aragon
Eastern Spain (Catalonia, Valencia)
Castilla-Leon
Canary Islands
Lisbon

10. The poor 60.5
Central Ireland
Southern Ireland
Campania (Naples etc.)
Basilicata-Calabria
Galicia
Castilla-La Mancha
Murcia-Andalusia
Central Greece (Athens etc.)

11. The very poor 49.2
Northwestern Ireland
Extremadura
Central Portugal
Southern Portugal
Northern Greece
Eastern Greece (incl. islands)

12. The extremely poor 41.4
Northern Portugal

Note: Within each cluster regions are listed not according to GDP, but according to the OECD definitional order, which, basically, runs from north to south. The following qualifications apply to the data: Swedish and Irish regional GDP figures do not exist, therefore the regional distribution of household gross income has been used as a proxy, applied to the national GDP per capita. Swiss data are calculated on the basis of the distribution of cantonal national income (Kantonale Volkseinkommen/Revenu cantonal), then applied to the national GDP per capita. The Corsican figure refers to 1984. The Austrian regional division is that of 1985, applied to the GDP of 1986.

Sources: The regional divisions are taken from OECD, *Employment Outlook 1989*, Paris, 1989, Annex 3A. Whenever necessary GDP statistics have always been regrouped in accordance with that division. National and regional GDP data are primarily taken from Eurostat, *Basic Statistics of the Community*, 27th edn, Luxemburg 1990, pp. 38 and 50ff; when lacking for 1986, earlier editions have been searched. For Iceland, OECD, *National Accounts, 1960–1988*, Vol. 1, Paris, 1991, p. 145 has been used. For Austria, Finland, Ireland, Norway, Sweden and Switzerland, the following national sources have been utilized: *Statistisches Handbuch für die Republik Österreich 1990*, Vienna, 1990, pp. 13 and 224; *Statistisk Årsbok för Finland 1987, 1990*, pp. 39 and 318, respectively; *Household Budget Survey*, Dublin, Central Statistical Office, 1989 (1987 regional distribution of household gross income); *Nasjonalrekenskaperne fylkesvis 1986*, Oslo, Statistisk Sentralbyrå, 1989; *Statistisk Årsbok 1989*, Stockholm, SCB, 1989, p. 208; *Annuaire statistique de la Suisse 1991*, Zurich, Neue Zürcher Zeitung, 1990, pp. 28 and 115.

In the course of the 1980s, most of French, Greek – Attica especially – and German regions lost relatively, with exceptions such as, for instance, Ile-de-France and Bavaria. Most of Spain – except Catilla-León and the Northwest – on the other hand, gained, in particular Madrid, Catalonia and the Valencia region. Central Italy lost ground, whereas Lazio (around Rome) and northern Italy advanced. The UK advanced in the South, in Wales and in East Anglia, while more or less staying put for the rest. The two heaviest losers were the provinces of Alentejo in southern Portugal, paying dearly for the reinstated forces of socio-economic conservatism after the revolution of the landless labourers in 1974–5, and Sterea Ellada in central Greece.[27]

Culture is no more confinable within state borders than economics.

Notes

1 S. Rokkan, 'Eine Familie von Modellen für die vergleichende Geschichte Europas', *Zeitschrift für Sociologie*, 9, 2 (1980), p. 123n.

2 See, e.g. ibid., pp. 123–4; S. Rokkan and D. Urwin, *Economy, Territory, Identity*, London, Sage, 1983, pp. 30ff.

3 C. Tilly, *Coercion, Capital, and European States, AD 990–1990*, Oxford, Blackwell, 1992.

4 See further the proceedings of the three Strasburg colloquia of historians, R. Poidevin (ed.), *Histoire des débuts de l'unification européenne*, Brussels, Milan, Paris and Baden-Baden, Bruylant, Giuffré, LGDJ and Nomos, 1986; K. Schwabe (ed.), *Die Anfänge des Schuman-Plans 1950/51*, publication details as above, 1988; E. Serra (ed.), *Il rilancio dell'Europa e i trattativi di Roma*, publication details as above, 1989.

5 W. Molle, *Regional Disparity and Economic Development in the European Community*, Farnborough, Saxon House, 1980, pp. 55ff.

6 The US record is in that sense more dramatic, but it has the same features as the European one, a convergent long-term trend and a reversal effect of the post-1973 recession: R. Barro and X. Sala-I- Martin, 'Convergence across States and Regions', *Brookings Papers on Economic Activity* 1 (1991), esp. p. 141.

7 D. Plestina, *Regional Development in Communist Yugoslavia*, Boulder, Col., Westview Press, 1992, p. 180.

8 World Bank, *Statistical Handbook 1993: States of the Former USSR*, Washington DC, 1993, pp. 10–11.

9 *Statistical Abstract of the United States 1990*, Washington DC, Dept. of Commerce 1990, Tables 26 and 702. Resource-rich, sparsely populated Alaska is here excluded. If Alaska is taken as the richest state, then the range would have been 3.04:1.

10 Commission of the European Communities, *The Regions of the Enlarged Community*, Brussels and Luxemburg, 1987, Annex, p. 23. The figure is calculated for the fifty states of the USA.

11 0.182 for 1950–61: J.G. Williamson, 'Regional Inequality and the Process of National Development: A Description of the Patterns', *Economic Development and Cultural Change*, XIII (1965), p. 12.

12 OECD, *Historical Statistics, 1960–1990*, Paris, 1992, p. 71.

13 *Die Zeit*, 25.2.1994, p. 27.

14 P. Cecchini, *The European Challenge 1992*, Aldershot, Wildwood House, 1988, p. 97.

15 OECD, *Economic Outlook 54*, Paris, December 1993, pp. 126 and 142.

16 Molle, *Regional Disparity*, p. 80; Commission of the EC, *Regions of the Enlarged Community*, p. 59; idem, *De regio's in de jaren negentig*, Brussels and Luxembourg, 1991, pp. 87, 109, 111.

17 Commission of the EC, *De regio's in de jaren negentig*, pp. 89 and 109ff. The extra-European provinces of France and Spain have then been excluded.

18 Regional GDP per capita calculated from *Statistik Årsbok för Finland 1990*, p. 318 (GDP), and *1987*, p. 39 (population), Helsinki, Statistika Centralbyrån, 1990 and 1987, respectively; disposable income from H. Uusitalo, *Income Distribution in Finland*, Helsinki, Central Statistical Office, p. 62. GDP refers to 1986 and disposable income to 1985.
19 Molle, *Regional Disparity*, pp. 82ff.
20 Commission of the EC, *Regions of the Enlarged Community*, p. 24.
21 Yugoslav disparities were similar to those of China. Measured, like the Yugoslav ones, before transfers and in terms of material product, the Chinese regional coefficient of variation was 0.34 in 1952, 0.69 in 1960, and 0.57 in 1985: Kai Yuan Tsui, 'Regional Inequality 1952–1985', *Journal of Comparative Economies* 15,1 (1991), p. 9. The Yugoslav variation coefficient increased in the postwar period, from 0.39 in 1953.
22 OECD, *Regional Problems in Switzerland*, Paris, 1991, p. 35. The population-weighted cantonal coefficient of variation was 0.168 in 1950 and 0.146 in 1960, as compared to 0.184 in 1980. Against an unweighted 1950 coefficient of 0.191 in 1950 stands one for 1987 of 0.240.
23 OECD, *Employment Outlook 1989*, Paris, 1989, pp. 115ff.
24 For those and other reasons, our regional study is not comparable to patterning of European cities or urban regions. Concerning the latter, there are, e.g. P. Cheshire and D. Hay, *Urban Problems in Western Europe*, London, Unwin Hyman, 1989, and RECLUS/DATAR, *Les villes 'européennes'*, Paris, La Documentation Française, 1989. In their analysis of urban problems in the 1970s and early 1980s, the former placed the Frankfurt region in a specially favourable position, followed at some distance by Venice, Düsseldorf and Brussels.
25 Calculated from *Regional Trends 28*, CSO, London, HMSO, 1993, p. 132. As in the Table this figure refers to 1986. Eurostat apparently uses a different delimitation of 'Greater London' than do British statisticians, offering London figures similar to those for Ile-de-France, i.e. for the region around Paris: Commission of the European Communities, *De regio's in de jaren negentig*, p. 111.
26 Iceland and Luxemburg are here considered as consisting of only one region each. With the Northern Aegean Islands of Greece, Portuguese Alentejo is the poorest province of the EU, at 34–5% of the EU GDP per capita. Alentejo went down from 49 in 1980 to 35 in 1990.
27 Eurostat, *Rapid Reports*, no. 1: *Regions* (1993).

11

EUROPE'S CULTURAL SPACE

Europe is not just a continent of nations in a process of possible economico-political and cultural unification or convergence. The population of a state-bounded territory does not necessarily make up an unproblematic cultural unit. The latter may be overarched by supra-national linkages and undermined by territorial and/or functional divisions of the state-bounded population. Nor is the continent to be treated as a given cultural entity, which through time has been provided with different meanings. Rather, Europe should be seen as an area with a geology of spatially distributed sediments of cultural history, layered upon, cross-cutting or under-cutting, partly overlapping with and clashing and combining with each other.

The cultural space of Europe may be seen as shaped by a set of cultural systems, providing and reproducing identities, knowledge and norms and values. We can discern a small number of cultural systems which have formed contemporary European culture and its specific territorial unity and divisions, its centres and peripheries. While not denying the possible significance of others, I would argue that this set of cultural systems gives us the basic elements of a historical-cultural geography of Europe. But before looking into them, we shall pay notice to a few other ways of viewing the cultural space of Europe.

The social-scientifically most ambitious mapping of Europe was developed by the already mentioned late Norwegian political scientist Stein Rokkan. He operated with a geo-political-cum-geo-economic East–West axis and a geo-cultural North–South dimension, both historical, with a view to explaining contemporary political cleavages. The geo-cultural dimension was religious, running from supreme Protestantism in the North via mixed areas and areas of 'National Catholicism' in the middle to Counter-Reformation Catholicism in the South. From West to East ran the rural maritime peripheries (from Iceland and Norway to Brittany via Scotland and Wales), the seaward empire-nations (England, France, Denmark, Portugal, Spain), the city belt (from the Baltic Hansa to Italy), the rural landward states (Sweden, Prussia, Bavaria, Austria) and the 'continental buffer states' from Finland to Hungary, or Yugoslavia. Russia and the Balkans were usually left out of this schema.

The North–South differentiation of Europe was, of course, first the line between Mediterranean civilization and barbarism, between the Roman Empire and the Germanic tribes, the latter line crystallized in a lasting linguistic divide between the Romance and the Germanic languages. Added to that since the Middle Ages were legal systems differing in their penetration by, their preservation of, Roman law. While the frontiers do not quite coincide, the North–South cultural differences of ancient history, language, religion and law do tend to superimpose themselves upon each other.

However, apart from the century of Reformation–Counter-Reformation, the major conflicts in Europe have run East–West, rather than North–South. That is, they have been related more to rival state formations, than to cultural differences. The French crown was for centuries the centre of conflict, fighting the English monarchy in the West and the Habsburgs in the East, at times also the Prussians and under Napoleon even the Russians. The unification of Germany made the new Reich the centre of Europe, and of European war-making, taking on the Russians in the East and the French and the British in the West.

Rokkan's aim with his 'conceptual mapping' was to summarize the history of European state-making with a view to explaining twentieth-century parliamentary political systems.[1] While capturing in compact form a very important slice of European history, Rokkan never succeeded in making it a popular theory. The verdict of a later great student of European history is severe:

> It left a muddled idea of the actual social processes connecting these changes [among rulers, neighbouring powers, dominant classes, and religious institutions] with alternative state trajectories. It is hard to see how Rokkan could have gotten much farther without laying aside his maps and concentrating on the analysis of the mechanisms of state formation.[2]

However, Rokkan's problematic is not reducible to Charles Tilly's state formation, and consequently Tilly's judgement is unduly curt. Within his limits Rokkan went rather far, and is still illuminating the spacing of Europe.

A bold, interesting, but overdone mapping of Europe has been developed by the French demographer Emmanuel Todd.[3] Here, Europe is divided according to its rural family patterns, primarily late nineteenth-century/ twentieth-century patterns. By crossing two variables, the rules of inheritance and the co-residence or not of two generations of adults, Todd creates four family types.

The 'absolute nuclear family' comprises only one generation of adults and has no egalitarian rules of inheritance. Todd finds it mainly in most of England and Denmark, in Brittany, save for the westernmost tip, in the western Netherlands, and southeastern Norway. The 'egalitarian nuclear family' differs from the former in having egalitarian succession rules. It dominated most of Spain, save Andalusia, Aragon and the Northwest, central Portugal, southern and northwestern Italy, French Provence, the Paris Bassin and most of northern France. The 'stem [souche]' family combines intergenerational adult co-residence with non-egalitarian inheritance. It was found to be preponderant in most of Norway and Sweden, southwestern Finland, the eastern Netherlands, most of western Germany, Austria, Switzerland, the western parts of England, Ireland and Brittany, the Scottish Highlands, southwestern France, northwestern Spain and northern Portugal. Finally, there is the 'communitarian family', co-residential and egalitarian, which has been rare in Western Europe. Todd finds it in central Italy, however, in central-western France, and as the 'traditional' family in central and eastern Finland.

These patterns include certain features of temporal and spatial cleansing, or standardization, which are far from immune from scholarly criticism.[4] But most controversial is Todd's argument that each type of rural family generates its own specific set of modern ideologies, its own form of socialism, nationalism and religious reaction. In spite of an impressive amount of work, neither the variables nor the causal mechanism is sufficiently elaborated for this writer to be convinced. Noteworthy, in any case, is that these features of traditional family rules by no means coincide with national frontiers, nor even with contiguous areas. At least in that sense traditional family sociology contributes significantly to demonstrating the multi-layered spacing of Europe.

A simpler, more widely accepted, but also much less ambitious division of Europe according to family values has been proposed by Josef Hajnal. Hajnal draws a line from Trieste to St Petersburg, dividing, on the west side, late marriages, high celibacy and relatively low birth rates from its opposites in the East.[5] Another variant counterposes a nuclear family, married late, preponderant since early modernity in North-Central/Western Europe (Scandinavia, Britain, the Low Countries, Germany, Austria, Switzerland and northern France) to a more extended family with earlier marriages in both the Mediterranean and in Eastern Europe.[6]

Outside the compound of scholarly specialists, the most important recent discussion of European cultural spatiality has focused on 'Central Europe' or 'East-Central Europe', as opposed to Western and Eastern Europe, i.e. to the USSR/Russia. While argued by historians,[7] it was primarily an expression of Czech (Milan Kundera) and Hungarian (György Konrád) dissidence in the last decade of Communism.[8] Its main edge was against the Yalta division of East and West, and its basis earlier delineations of power in Central-Eastern Europe. Clearly, the history of Russia is very different from that of the Czech lands or of Hungary. Post-Communist history has also emphasized that we should take heed of the differentiation within Eastern Europe, but where the main lines run has hardly yet been settled.

We shall start our journey into Europe's cultural space by following *radiations of power*. Power should be treated theoretically as an effect of structuration and enculturation – and also of spacing and timing. However, the promiscuity of power makes its offspring a convenient ordering principle, patterning identities, cognitions, norms and values, through its monuments, remnants and memories. Power has borne upon all the specific cultural systems forming the continent. Of these we shall pay some attention to: *religion, language, law and audio-visual communication.*

The nation, certainly a very important cultural system in European history, will here be seen as located within the above-mentioned coordinates of European culture. While abstaining from entering the fray about the determinants of nations, we shall treat the latter as situated within European cultural history rather than as the producers of the former. Issues of postwar national identity will be dealt with below, in the next chapter.

The interaction between the dimensions of cultural geography is asymmetrical. Power and the experience of power bear more upon religion than vice versa, likewise religion bears more on language, language more on law, and law more on audio-visual communication than the other way around. The asymmetry of the above-mentioned determinants of contemporary culture is also one of duration. The force of each of them is recurrent, none is a one-shot hit. But power, in this case, is older and more enduring in its effects than religion, which in turn is older and more enduring than language, and so on.[9] With a broader, more complex and less political perspective, this historical mapping of Europe diverges from some existing ones.

Radiations of power

The experience of power creates legacies of institutions and contacts, leaves memories and gives lessons, provides connotations and associations of thought, which all weigh upon later generations. The first major such experience of relevance to contemporary European history was Athenian democracy, which made popular and electoral rule a conceivable form of collective organization, relayed onto modern times by the Roman Republic, the Church and the medieval towns of the city belt. On the eve of modernity, the two highest potentates of Europe, the Pope and the Emperor, were both elected accorded to fixed rules. On the other hand, while the memory of ancient democracy was an important part of European high culture, popularized in the iconography of the French Revolution, there was hardly any direct link between the former and modern forms of politics.[10]

The Roman Empire left more direct and tangible effects. Its extension in Europe largely defined (the core of) modern Western Europe, leaving out the continent east of the Elbe and (by and large) of the Danube, and, except for brief forays, north of the Rhine. The Roman defeat, in AD 9, in the Teutoburger Forest is still part of the national folklore of Lower Saxony (invoked in the provincial hymn). Its frontiers with Scotland and Ireland have become less important, but they still exist.

The East–West divide of Europe was reproduced in the Middle Ages, with the Carolingian Empire and its successor kingdoms, and in early modern times with feudalism, urban growth and later peasant emancipation in the West, stronger, agrarian-based patrimonialism in the East, followed, in the early modern period, by the 'second serfdom'. (The Italian Mezzogiorno today still largely follows the extension of the medieval kingdoms of Sicily and Naples, and their successor, the two Sicilies.)

Northern Europe set itself apart again by the Viking society of a free and armed peasantry.[11] An autonomous farming society never subdued in Finland, Norway and Sweden, and surviving at least as a resurrectable tradition in landowners' Denmark, was strong enough to characterize a good part of Nordic politics from the mid-nineteenth to the mid-twentieth century. It is visible even in the 1990s, in the still important post-agrarian 'centre' parties of Finland, Norway and Sweden, and in the (by now for quite some time fairly right-wing) 'left' party in Denmark.

The power and glory of the Arabs have left persistent effects in European culture, many of which run so deep that their origin has been forgotten. At the peak of their reign in Europe, in the ninth century AD (the third century AH) the Arabs governed most of what is now Spain and Portugal, southern France, from Aquitaine to the western Alps, Corsica, Sardinia, Sicily, and Calabria and Apulia in southern Italy.

It was from Arab mathematicians – who had learnt from India – that Leonard of Pisa learnt and in the early thirteenth century brought to Europe the much more practical and sophisticated number system that slowly replaced the use of clumsy Roman numerals. A considerable amount of common European words are of Arab origin, from alcohol to coffee and lemonade, from orange to rice. Through the Christian purges the Spanish language, in particular, has preserved a considerable Arabic heritage, most easily recognizable in non-Latin words beginning with 'al'.[12]

The Arab conquest has left its unforgettable architectural imprints on the Iberian peninsula, not only the Alhambra of Granada and the Mosque of Cordoba, but also in the art of building and exterior house decoration up to reconquered Aragon, in northern Spain.[13] The Reconquista is still the object of a popular festival in Spain.

The rule of the Mongol and Tatar Golden Horde cut off Russia from the European High Middle Ages and Renaissance, and contributed after its end to the iconography and, arguably, the conception of power of the Muscovite Tsars. The obligation of general service to the state, inscribed in the Code of Genghis Khan, was carried over into Russian and Soviet law.[14]

Southeastern Europe, for its part, has been significantly shaped by the near half-millennial rule of the House of Osman. The complexity of the Ottoman heritage needs emphasis, without any attempt being made here to assess the relative weight of its components. One element, largely destroyed recently, is religious tolerance, which provided persecuted Jews from Spain a haven in the Ottoman Empire and left a mosaic of Christian, Muslim and Jewish communities in contemporary Albania, Bosnia-Hercegovina, Bulgaria, Greece and Serbia.

Ottoman Thessaloniki was, as we saw in Chapter 3, a shining example of vibrant multiculturalism. The echoes of Ottoman tolerance are still audible in the autobiography of Elias Canetti, from now Bulgarian Ruse on the Danube, and in the verse of Abdullah Sidran of Sarajevo, a contemporary Muslim poet and film scriptwriter. Sidran writes in Serbo-Croat, but his poem in memory of the Sephardim of the Jewish graveyard also has lines in Spanish.[15]

Erratic, occasionally despotic power largely unbound by rules, economic and intellectual languor, and long social decay are also Ottoman legacies, however. It is the heritage of an empire that long outlived itself, helplessly suspended between Southern Europe and West Asia, its roots loosening on both sides, and kept alive largely by the rivalry of its enemies.

Furthermore, not to be forgotten, the Ottomans also bequeathed an anti-Ottoman tradition, of the military frontier of the Habsburg Empire, the Kraijina, the breeding-place of most of the most ferocious fighters of the Serbo-Croat and the Bosnian wars at the break-up of Yugoslavia; and of the anti-Turk nationalism, which the late Communist rulers of Bulgaria were appealing to in the second half of the 1980s, forcing the Muslim minority to adopt 'Bulgarian' names.

In modern times the most important moments in the geo-politics of popular culture are the French Revolution and the world wars of the twentieth century, both periods taken in their immediate aftermath as well as in their trajectory. About the former, we should remember Eric Hobsbawm's conclusion that 'it can be said with little exaggeration that no important Continental state west of Russia and Turkey and south of Scandinavia emerged from these two decades with its domestic institutions wholly unaffected by the expansion or the imitation of the French Revolution'.[16]

It would be fully in line with Hobsbawm's analysis to qualify the extension of the area of the French Revolution by pointing out that the Austrian Empire and the kingdom of Prussia, though severely beaten by Napoleon, brought about their adaptations to a revolutionary age by themselves, in their own way. In other words, there was what we may call Napoleonic Europe – France, the Low Countries, Western Germany, Switzerland, the Appenine and the Iberian peninsulas – and what is now more or less Poland, Croatia and Slovenia – an area largely coinciding with the Western European part of the Roman Empire (save Britain, but plus Poland). Outside it were the Germanic heartlands of Prussia and Austria, Hungary, the Ottoman Balkans, Russia, the British Isles and Scandinavia. The latter countries embarked upon a road of profound endogenous social reform in the late 1780s–90s, simultaneous with the revolutionary upheavals in France and its vicinity.[17]

The two world wars and their outcome drew the old East–West borderline anew, created the Franco-German trauma which gave impetus to the EC process, and re-affirmed the success of neutrality to the Swiss and the Swedes, while, in the second round, demonstrating its futility to the Dutch, the Danes and the Norwegians.

Culturally, the outcome of World War II tore Europe apart. In the East, the Communists in power danced to the bells of the Kremlin and tried, with ever less success, to bring their recalcitrant societies with them in adopting Soviet Russian institutions, monumentation and rituals, including gigantic statues of

Stalin, which had to be hauled down after the 20th Party Congress of the CPSU. In the West, the great powerhood of Germany and Italy had been quashed and that of Britain and France was fading fast. Instead, the USA had drawn nearer, having become in the eyes of the anti-Communists an honorary member of Europe, the major force of Nato, the key Western player in all conferences on European security, the major magnet of 'Western culture', high and low.

The geography of experience remains even after the crumbling of institutions. 'Socialism' and 'Socialist' have a different meaning in 1990s Western Latin Europe than in the East. Moreover, '1968' has rather diametrically opposed political connotations in Eastern and Western Europe. A widespread, though by no means universal, Eastern European experience of the year was conveyed to this writer by a young Serbian sociologist in June 1991, who said, referring to Yugoslavia: 'After 1968 no intelligent person could believe in Communism any more.'

In the East, 1968 meant the antisemitic campaign in Poland, the police crackdown on the students in Belgrade, the invasion of Czechoslovakia and the ensuing cultural freeze all over that part of continent. In the West, however, 1968 created a generation of left-wingers, many of whom became Communists, of one variety or the other. Their wisdom has always been controversial, but the intelligence of their prominent figures rarely disputed. In Western Europe, 1968 meant opposition to the American war in Vietnam, student rebellion, the May events in France and the prospects of revolutionary social change, the discovery of Marxism, the Maoist Cultural Revolution and national liberation movements in the Third World.[18]

The divisions of a Christian continent

Religion, Christianity, was the first European cultural allegiance, something which produced a conscious affinity between the many different lordships of the continent and among their subjects, pitting Christian Europe against Dar-ul-Islam.

From the very beginning, structural institutions underpinned the conception of Europe as the continent of Christendom: the Papacy and the conception of a Christian Empire from Constantine and, anew, from Charlemagne on; the language of the Church, Latin in the West, and Greek or Slavonic in the East. In some countries – Spain, Portugal, Poland, Austria, Serbia – the religious frontier became a crucial aspect of national culture.

After having been the first unifier of Europe, religion also became the first and the major divider of the continent, from 1054 between East and West, from 1517 between North and South (of Western Europe). Both religious divorces had far-reaching sociopolitical implications, which can only be hinted at here. Roughly put, Eastern Christendom stayed tied to political power and separated from intellectual pursuits, whereas the Western Church took the opposite road, always asserting/struggling for independence from secular powers while linking itself to scholarship and intellectual efforts.

The split between Reformation and Counter-Reformation was not only one of theology. It was also one of alliance with or autonomy from secular political power, of using and unifying national languages or of sticking to international Latin, of promoting (biblical) literacy or not – without here entering into the controversies around the Max Weber thesis of a relationship between the Protestant ethic and the 'spirit of capitalism'. Stein Rokkan judged the outcome of the Reformation effort to be *the* (North–South) cultural divide of Europe.[19]

The religious division of Europe largely follows the ancient power divisions. Catholic Europe is the Western Roman Empire, minus Britain, plus early medieval Ireland and high- and late-medieval Poland and Lithuania. Orthodoxy covers the Europe of the Eastern Empire and the Byzantine missionary area among the Slavs. Protestantism succeeded on the northern part of the continent, in Germany and in the Low Countries north and east of the *limes*, and in Britain (see Map 11.1).

That large-scale division should not, however, lead us to overlook the many imbrications of religious majorities and minorities emerging from the sixteenth- and seventeenth-century wars of religion. England had enough Catholics to make Catholic emancipation an issue of state and academia well into the nineteenth century. The British colonization of Ireland has left an embattled Protestant population in Ulster. French Protestantism was crushed, but minorities have managed to survive: some prominent, such as the nineteenth- till prewar twentieth-century 'Haute Banque Protestante' of high finance; some peripheral, as in the Cevennes. In southern Germany, Württemberg is a major Protestant province. Furthermore, the Netherlands reproduced sizeable Catholic communities 'north of the big rivers'.

The three centuries of Swiss religious wars usually ended in a draw, which gradually taught a *modus vivendi*, although Catholic emancipation at the federal level only ensued after World War I. Hungary has perhaps the continent's largest religious minority, between a fifth and a quarter Protestants (mainly but not all Calvinists) in a Catholic country, asserted by armed struggle against the Habsburg Counter-Reformation. The smaller Protestant minorities of Transylvania and of Slovakia are largely part of the pattern of their former Hungarian rulers. In Bohemia and Moravia the Hussite movement and the forces of Reformation were violently defeated, but Catholicism has been a rather superficial layer over the Czech lands ever since.

With the fall of Communism, the religious map of Europe has acquired a new importance. One of the new areas of conflict resurging derives from old relations between Orthodoxy and Catholicism. Byzantium under pressure from the Ottomans and a Pope under conciliar pressure found themselves in a concilium of *rapprochement* at Florence in 1439, recognized by, among others, the metropolitan of Kiev. The re-union met with strong opposition within Orthodoxy, and after the fall of Constantinople the project petered out. But the idea never died. When most of the Ukraine, including Kiev, had

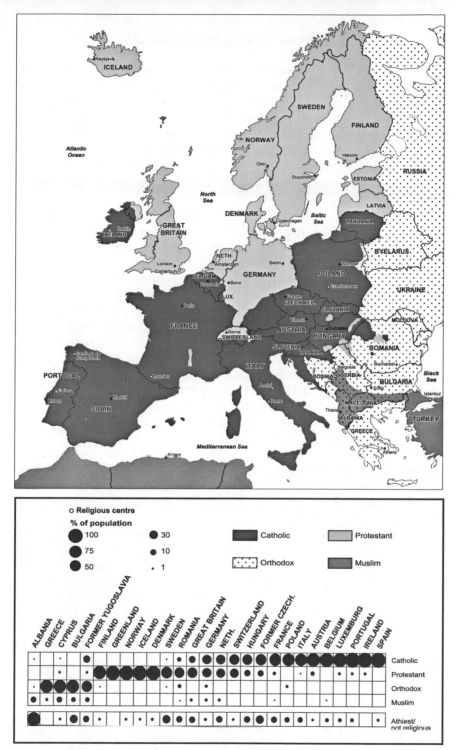

Map 11.1 *The major religions of Europe*

Source: Adapted from M. Clévenot (ed.), *L'Etat des religions dans le monde*,
Paris, La Découverte/Le Cerf, 1987, pp. 334–5.

come under Polish-Lithuanian rule, it got the backing of power. The Council of Brest in 1596 led to a separate Uniate Church, of Byzantine liturgy and Papal allegiance. Under Hungarian auspices a similar Church emerged in Ruthenia, which is now also Ukraine. About a century later Hungarian, now Romanian, Transylvania also acquired an Eastern Catholic Church. Under postwar Communism, in the Ukraine from 1946, in Romania from 1948, these Western Churches were suppressed, in favour of national Orthodoxy. Their recent re-emergence has been characterized by great friction with the latter.[20]

The distribution of Judaism largely followed the late-medieval till sixteenth-century distribution of bigot powers: absent/expelled from the intolerant West, except for the commercial republics, the Netherlands and Venice; present/attracted to the more tolerant East, whether Catholic Polish or Islamic Ottoman. However, one of the features of postwar European cultural history has been the much diminished role of Jews in it.

The major cause is, of course, the Holocaust, which hit Eastern Europe primarily, as did the Nazi terror generally. It was a general genocide, but its major postwar cultural effect was probably the extinction of preponderantly Jewish intellectual milieux. To all the Central-Eastern European capitals, from Berlin and eastwards, this meant a tangible cultural impoverishment, most strongly, perhaps, in Vienna. Another consequence has been mobility, social or geographical. The latter has meant the disappearance of a Jewish working-class, before the war a distinctive component of labour in Eastern Europe, in Amsterdam, and in London.

The number of Jews in contemporary Europe is unknown, and the criteria for counting are ambiguous – religious, ethnic or what? Only in France, re-invigorated by an influx of post-colonial North African Jewry, and Britain in the West and in the ex-USSR and Hungary in the East do they amount to about 1% of the population.

Islam was firmly implanted in Europe by the long Ottoman rule of the Balkans and by the Mongols in Russia. Sizeable old Islamic populations exist in Albania, Bosnia-Hercegovina, Bulgaria, Kossovo, Macedonia, Russia (the Tatars) and Serbia. Currently it is the major religion of Albania and Bosnia-Hercegovina, and of a significant minority in Macedonia, the remains of Yugoslavia and Bulgaria (*ca.* 10%). Good 1% minorities exist in Greece and Romania. After the war, European industrial labour scarcity led to an organized import of a second round of Muslims, of Turks into Germany and Belgium, of Maghrebins into France and the Low Countries.[21]

We shall return to the religious aspects of the new multicultural Europe below.

Linguistic links and demarcations

The language pattern of Europe is a fascinating recording of the histories of power and religion onto a new medium.[22] The Roman Empire, the *Völkerwanderungen* (mass migrations) and the outcomes of their armed battles cast a basic mould. Processes of state formation, the Reformation and the printed translated Bible set distinctive standards to continua of dialects. But neither complex of determinants has always left a neat linguistic cut.

The Western frontier between the Romance and the Germanic languages, for example, has been remarkably stable for more than a thousand years, but it has rarely run along the most important political borderlines of the area. Nor does it correspond to a religious divide, nor even to any natural landmarks. It unfolded west of the Rhine, in what is now French Alsace, through, or, more adequately, tearing apart, what is now Belgium.[23]

The unique trisection of the Germanic, the Romance and the Slavic languages, on the other hand, has largely been encased by the vicissitudes of twentieth-century political power. Its cultural possibilities seem to be little more than a nostalgia for what Trieste once was, or might have become.[24]

The modern linguistic map of Europe was drawn largely by nineteenth-century nationalists. A number of new languages were invented, from Norwegian to Serbo-Croat. In contrast to the classical orientation of the Arab Renaissance (*Nahda*), the European nationalist intellectuals did not, where they might have, fall back upon classical languages, like ancient Greek, Latin or Church Slavonic, but built their inventions on popular dialects, elaborated and standardized.[25]

The dedication with which late nineteenth-century cohorts of intellectuals set out to learn their new languages, with a view to lifting and mobilizing their peoples, is amazing. Swedish-educated and normally Swedish-speaking Finnish intellectuals embarked upon learning Finnish, Italian-educated and -speaking Croatians set themselves to learn Croatian, etc. In this light, the conspicuous failure of the Celtification of Ireland appears as an enigma, which I have not had the competence to solve.

The creativity of these intellectuals is perhaps most vividly illustrated in the invention of Serbo-Croat, one language with two alphabets, as a strategic calculation in the face of what was perceived as a common enemy, the Austro-Hungarian Empire, and common threatening high cultures, German and Italian in particular. Similar power constellations led to the establishment of the Czechoslovak language. Both languages are now falling apart, due to new gravitations of power.

Above (Chapter 3) we took note of the effects of power and language in a dramatic linguistic turn of virtually all the current Eastern European capitals, from Helsinki to Sofia. Language became a marker and a demarcation of state power.

But now we shall concentrate on a couple of contemporary aspects of the linguistic set-up in Europe, in particular with regard to supra-national relations. One concerns the commonality of language across the borders of nation-states.

Western Europe has several such commonalities. Britain and Ireland are linked by a common English; Germany, Austria and the major part of Switzerland speak German; France, Wallonia-Brussels and western Switzerland have French in common; the Dutch and the Flemings have Dutch.[26]

The Eastern European pattern is interestingly different. There you have linguistic diasporas and minorities. That is, language traces of bygone heterolinguistic states: Swedish-speakers in Finland, Russian-speakers in the Baltics, and so on till Turkish-speakers in Greek Thrace. But there are no language communities, rather the break-up of previous ones – Czecho-Slovak, Serbo-Croat, perhaps also Russian-Belorussian.

The very sensitive, though *de facto* close, Anglo-Irish relations aside, these Western linguistic commonalities are institutionally underpinned by supra-national associations, networks and cultural exchange, cooperation and distribution channels. There is, for instance, an association of francophone sociologists and there are occasional congresses of German-speaking and of Dutch-Flemish sociologists. A German quality weekly like *Die Zeit* presents regularly every week an overview of what is on German-speaking theatre stages in the three countries. In the west-central triangle of the continent the newspapers have for a long time regularly listed prominently what is offered on Dutch and Flemish or on French-speaking television from across the border. Between the three German-speaking countries there is now also developing a tradition of an annual meeting of their economic ministers.

Close linguistic affinity, without commonality, may also contribute to creating cultural bonds. The Romance languages seem to have some potential for relatively unrestrained inter-communication,[27] but it does not appear to have developed very far.

Inter-lingual communication is very well established among the Nordic countries, however. Many things bring the Nordic countries together: a common sociopolitical history, the Reformation, a common relative geo-political isolation from the major culture and power centres of the continent, a relatively equal (small) size of population. But one of the more important is also the proximity of their languages. In the inter-parliamentary Nordic Council, or in the Nordic Sociological Association, Swedes, Norwegians and Finland-Swedes speak their native tongue. The Danes use their native language too but often with a Scandinavianized pronunciation (to facilitate understanding), while the Finns and Icelanders speak the language of their former rulers, i.e. Swedish and Danish, respectively.

However, cultural integration of Europe is hampered by *linguistic imbalance*. In spite of considerable public efforts,[28] rather few Germans know French, and even fewer Frenchmen know German. To the people of the two key countries of the EC it is not the other's language which is the first foreign language, but English. Apart from the German-speaking countries, only in the Netherlands and in Denmark is there a widespread knowledge of German, about equal to that of English. French is clearly the first foreign language only in Italy, but there only about a quarter of the population claim to be able to speak it.[29]

Unesco statistics on book translations provides some hard evidence on current language relations (see Table 11.1). In the mid-1980s, English was the original language (translated from) in almost half, 46.8%, of all the world's translations. Nine other languages provided the source for at least

Table 11.1 *Book translations by country of publication in Western Europe, Japan and the USA*

Total number and major languages translated from. Average absolute annual number and per cent of total translations from each language 1983–5

Country	Total	English	French	German	Italian	Spanish	Scandinavian
Austria	387	59.3	11.1	6.4	4.7	3.9	0.8
Belgium	724	57.8	10.1	19.9	2.3	2.7	1.0
Denmark	1,591	54.4	6.9	9.4	1.1	1.2	19.8
Finland	1,386	55.1	5.4	9.2	0.9	15.3	0.8
France	3,979	65.0	3.3	10.0	5.4	2.6	1.3
Greece	181[a]	39.8	26.5	13.8	5.5	1.1	1.7
Iceland	573[b]	49.7	10.0	6.0	0.5	1.3	28.3
Ireland	6.5[c]	7.7	23.1	7.7	15.4	15.4	0
Italy	1,107	44.8	23.2	15.5	0.9	3.3	0.6
Luxemburg	5[d]	40	20	0	0	0	0
Netherlands	4,286[a]	56.8	18.0	15.1	1.3	1.1	2.4
Norway	901	64.4	2.8	6.5	0.7	0.3	19.6
Portugal	754	47.6	29.1	6.9	5.6	4.4	1.8
Spain	7,711	50.1	20.0	10.6	6.3	–	1.9
Sweden	1,937	65.5	5.5	6.5	0.7	1.3	12.5
Switzerland	1,096	46.2	16.2	15.7	3.8	0.9	1.1
UK	1,139	4.0	23.2	25.7	6.8	3.1	6.2
W. Germany	6,676	60.7	11.9	3.4	3.2	1.9	3.9
Japan	2,696	78.3	7.9	7.5	1.2	0.7	0.5
USA	606	0.3	21.8	23.8	5.2	6.1	4.5

Notes: [a] 1985 only. [b] 1983 and 1984. [c] 1984 and 1985. [d] 1983 only.

Source: Calculations from Unesco, *Statistical Yearbook 1991*, Paris, 1991, Table 7.11.

1% of the world's translations:[30] French 10.8%, German 8.4%, Russian 3.8%, Italian 2.9%, Swedish 1.8%, Spanish 1.5%, Hungarian 1.2%, Latin 1.1% and Danish 1.1%. The neglect of other major languages is remarkable: Japanese is the source of 0.4% of the world's translations, Arabic of 0.7% and Chinese of 0.3%.[31]

The reason why Swedish and Danish appear among the world's major literary source languages is largely the Scandinavian cultural family. About a third of all translations from Swedish, Danish or Norwegian go into the other Scandinavian languages, and 61.2% are translations into the other Nordic languages (the three Scandinavian ones, Finnish and Icelandic).[32] The also perhaps surprisingly large number of translations from Hungarian, on the other hand, is mainly into English and German.

The Nordic countries and Spain are the main translators, in relation to their population. Iceland is *sui generis*, with one foreign book translation annually per *circa* 410 inhabitants. The English-speaking nations, by contrast, translate very little; Ireland, with a population not much smaller than Norway's, translating hardly anything. With a population about a

Table 11.2 *Book translations by country of publication in Eastern Europe*
Total number and major languages translated from. Average absolute annual number and per cent of total translations from each language, 1983–5.

	Total	Russian	English	French	German	Italian/Spanish
Albania	86	4.3	2.7	3.5	6.6	1.2
Bulgaria	740	32.5	14.0	8.5	9.6	4.2
Czechoslovakia	1,251	24.9	10.6	6.1	8.0	3.7
E. Germany	776	35.1	16.3	9.8	–	5.5
Hungary	1,279	11.6	14.9	5.6	10.0	2.3
Poland	675	14.8	22.0	9.8	10.0	5.2
Romania	550	3.7	10.6	11.5	5.4	5.1
USSR	7,747	54.8	9.2	3.3	4.2	1.3

Source: As Table 11.1.

thousand times larger, the United States publishes about the same number of translations as Iceland.

Translations from English dominate strongly everywhere, with some modification in Greece and Portugal. In Europe, but after Japan, Sweden and Norway are the most English-oriented literary cultures among the smaller languages. The French take only a tenth of their translations from German, and the Germans just over a tenth of theirs from French.

There is a certain Romance pattern, within the overall English domination, visible in the translations of Italy, Portugal and Spain, but hardly reciprocated by the French. The strong inter-Nordic links have no equivalent, however. Only 4.4% of Portuguese translations are from Spanish, and in the not very likely case that all translations from Portuguese into Spanish were made in Spain, only 1.0% of Spanish translations were from Portuguese.[33] There is little of an all-Germanic affinity in the world of translations, albeit German culture has a somewhat less weak reception in Scandinavia than French. (Translations from Russian in the West were of any significance only in Greece, the UK and the USA, with 6.1%, 8.4% and 7.2% of all translations, respectively.)

Let us now look at late-Communist Eastern Europe and its linkages of translations (see Table 11.2).

The East Germans and the Bulgarians were the most Russian-oriented, more so than the politically rather even more orthodox Czechoslovak regime, the dissenting Balkan states the least. English was the relatively dominant source of translations into Polish and Hungarian, while the Latin connection was kept alive by Ceauşescu's Romania. Translations from Scandinavian languages played a certain part in East Germany (3.3% of translations) and Poland (2.4%). ('Other languages', not in the table above, were mainly other Eastern European ones.)

Families of law

The fourth major cultural tradition linking nations into informal unions has been much less noted by non-specialists: law. While legislation is national –and sometimes sub-national, as we shall touch on below – or internationally treaty-made, there are supra-national traditions of legal conceptualization and reasoning, and of the proper part of the courts in the functioning of law. On such bases, scholars of comparative law distinguish systems or 'styles' of law.[34] In modern Western European law, these families of law differ mainly in their mode of legal reasoning, in the sources of law which they recognize, and in specific legal concepts or institutions.

Legally there are two lineages in Western Europe: the Anglo-Saxon common law in the British Isles (excluding Scotland), with the special importance it assigns to case law and judicial precedent, and codified continental civil law. The latter, in turn, may be grouped into three, or, at least from the late 1940s to the late 1980s, four, families of modern civil law. There is the Napoleonic family, deriving from the French Civil Code of 1804, comprising France, Belgium, Luxemburg, arguably also the Netherlands (influenced too by its eastern neighbour), Spain, Portugal and Italy – as well as Quebec and Louisiana in North America and other non-European areas. Secondly, a legal affinity links a Germanic family, of Austria, Germany and Switzerland, together with Greece, although Greek family law kept its Orthodox ecclesiastical footing till the 1980s.[35] Thirdly, there is a Nordic family of law, which alone has also developed institutional forms of international legal cooperation.[36]

Before World War II, Eastern Europe west of the USSR was, as we saw in Chapter 6 above in the section on gender rights, a legal patchwork, reminiscent of the pre-1919 empires, including the Ottoman and its Hanafi school of Muslim jurisprudence. Russian law derived from Roman law, as did other systems of modern European law, but it was long intellectually underdeveloped, unsustained by legal scholarship and a consolidated judiciary. Old Russian traditions carried over into Soviet law, and, we may add, into post-Soviet law, such as the blurred distinction between a decree and a law, the institution of the procuracy, and the Mongol notion of obligatory service in case of need.

After the war, a national legal unification of Eastern countries took place, for the first time in their history. Communist socialism created a legal family of its own, which should not be reduced to what post-Stalinism called 'violations of socialist legality', to arbitrary policies. A socialist family of law developed, the distinctiveness of which may be derived from new notions of property and contract, and new conceptions of family relations, from new institutions of arbitration between enterprises, and of lay courts.[37] However, we also noted above how prewar conceptions of social entitlements were kept, modified or resurrected in Communist Europe.

Although the Napoleonic Code was first spread by the guns of the Napoleonic armies, its retention after Waterloo, or its influence upon the late nineteenth-century codifications in Italy, Spain, and Portugal, testifies to a cultural influence, irreducible to military power, or even to the experience and the memory of it. It also remained the base of civil law in the German Rhineland and in Baden till the legal unification of the Reich, in the *Bürgerliches Gesetzbuch* of 1896. Austria acquired its modern code in 1811, deriving from the Josephine Enlightenment, and Prussia kept its own monument of absolutist *Grundlichkeit* in its General Land Law of 1794 with its 17,000 paragraphs (actually meant to promote public accessibility of the law). The Swiss cantons were legally very divided before the process of unification began in 1874: the three original cantons, Basel and a couple of others had no codified private law; Berne, Lucerne and others were under Austrian legal influence; the French- and Italian-speaking cantons had versions of the *Code Napoleon*; while, fourthly, Zurich had developed a code of its own, which had also affected some other cantons.[38] In 1907 a liberal Zurich jurist, Eugen Huber, got his Swiss Civil Code accepted by his compatriots.

Inter-Nordic legal cooperation and coordination, through commissions of jurists, began in 1872, i.e. before any similar endeavour started between the Swiss cantons (1874) or between the states of the USA (1892).[39] Commercial law was the first common Nordic undertaking, followed by family law. The latter was arguably the most important joint Nordic legal endeavour, adopted by the national legislatures in the course of the 1920s. But Nordic legal family contacts have continued rather regularly throughout this century.

Legal integration is now a very significant part of the European integration process. The key actor is the EC Court of Justice, the powers of which seem closer to, though less than, that of the US Supreme Court than to those of the national European judiciaries.[40] On the basis of the Community treaties and drawing upon the national legal systems, the Court has developed certain general principles of law for its jurisdiction. French and German law appear to have been the most influential sources, but the Court has developed into a strong, self-conscious supra-national institution, which has also been able to integrate common law Britain. In the integration process, the primacy of Community law over national law, and its 'direct effect' (*l'applicabilité directe*), or 'self-executing character' in legal English, within the national jurisdictions have been successfully asserted, since the Van Gend en Loos case of 1963.[41]

The process is complex, however, and no general unification is in sight. Rather, a European family of law may be seen in the making, with a whole set of relations between Community and national law, sometimes summarized as substitution, harmonization, coordination and coexistence.[42] Probably one should add to the set a series of national legal and judicial adjustments to the changing normative order of Europe.[43]

Audio-visual Americanization

The four previously mentioned dimensions of the European cultural space have mainly delimited it internally, bringing nations culturally together and apart. The dimension of audio-visual communication is important on its own, primarily because of the ways in which it relates European to non-European culture. With a somewhat caricatural formulation one may say that the predominant pattern of international audio-visual communication tends to turn Europe into a cultural satellite, circulating in the orbit around North American – and, to some extent, more generally Anglo-Saxon – mass culture.

In so far as twentieth-century mass culture has been international, it has, by and large, been American (and sometimes British). On the European continent the new signs appeared after World War I, with jazz, American dance music, and Hollywood films. They accelerated after World War II, particularly with the coming of rock music and television.

The breakdown in the 1980s of the concept of public service television, under the weight of new productive forces of telecommunication (satellites, cables) as well as under ideological pressure, has taken the process onto a new, and higher, stage. Till then, the legally regulated public monopoly service had given European broadcasting a common European national character, sometimes bent into a governmental direction, more often into a civil servant's sense of objectivity and a public school teacher's idea of cultural education.[44]

While specialized anti-Communist radio stations like Radio Free Europe and Radio Liberty certainly reached some audience in the East, it was the diffusion of television which in the 1980s made visible another world than the domestic one. East Germans tended to see more West than East German television, Estonians watched Finnish TV, and Romanians often preferred Bulgarian or Yugoslav stations to the national ones. Audio visual mass communication perforated the so-called 'Iron Curtain'.[45]

According to a survey in 1988, at most two-thirds of television programmes viewed in Luxemburg, Italy, Ireland, Spain, Portugal and France were of European origin, i.e. either national or imported from another European country. For a medium reaching into your private living-room, that is a remarkable extra-European exposure. Britain, the Netherlands and Belgium had about 70% European television, Denmark 75% and Greece and Germany around 80%. Of the total programme offer of the around seventy supra-local TV networks in Western Europe, two-thirds by one criterion, below 60% in the French media definition, was of European origin. Of the twenty private chains only three offered 50% (or more) European programmes.[46] An EC study of 1987 found a major import of European programmes only into the public Belgian TV and into the Luxemburg-based but mainly Belgian-owned private RTL.[47]

American films dominated virtually all Western European markets in the early 1990s, with sales shares around two-thirds.[48] French film has lost heavily in recent years, but has fought back several times, with some success. In 1993 the French also led the forces of European film protection in the GATT negotiations, and not in vain.

The top-level Blum–Byrnes agreement of 1946 which opened the French film market to Hollywood met with strong resistance in France, and was replaced by a more protectionist treaty. From almost half of the French cinema market in the late 1940s the American share went down to a fifth by the early 1970s, then to rise again, at an accelerating speed.[49] In the second half of the 1980s France was the only Western European country where a plurality of films was of either domestic or other European national origin.[50]

The *music* market appears more American-British than American-dominated. Recorded music has become a major part of late modern mass culture. For some reason, this is less so in Italy and France than in Germany and Britain, in Austria than in Switzerland, in Belgium than in the Netherlands. Per capita the most avid buyers of music in Europe are the British, with 3.8 albums per capita in 1988, followed by the Swiss at 3.6, the (West) Germans with 3.1, the Dutch with 2.8, the Swedes 2.7, the Finns and the Norwegians 2.6, the Danes 2.3. The Italians bought no more than 0.8 album per inhabitant, the Austrians 1.6, the Belgians 1.7 and the French 1.9.[51]

Between 90 and 95% of albums sold are rock or light music, between 5 and 10% are classical music. The higher figure holds for Austria and France, and, in 1990, also for Britain, the lower for countries such as the USA, the Netherlands and Sweden, with Germany in-between.[52] Foreign pop music accounts for 60–5% of sales in Sweden and the Netherlands, the overwhelming part of which is British or American. The picture is probably somewhat different in Germany, but the conclusion seems warranted that mass music is either domestic or Anglo-Saxon, only rarely other European. Again, the French are trying to resist, having, for instance, a domestic music TV channel, trying to compete with worldwide American MTV, and with other protective devices around their *chansons*.

The patterns of audio-visual communication constitute a basic dimension of contemporary culture. They have a distinctive configuration, very different from other cultural aspects and forms. To the internal cultural delimitations of Europe, by experiences of power, religion, language and law, the audio-visual dimension adds an extra-continental cultural centre of contemporary Europe. The orientation of television, radio, cinema and music should be expected to affect their audiences' view of the world, even though we still know little about how and how much.

But it does not seem far-fetched to think that this stratum of European culture is related to the results of a large Western European consumer survey in the spring of 1991, according to which in Britain, France, Germany and Italy more people said that if they had to live abroad, they would prefer the USA, Canada or Australia to any European country. Among the six nations interviewed, there was a preference for Europe only in the Netherlands and in Spain. With young people (16–24), the predilection for the Anglo-Saxon New World was particularly strong.[53] Europe is not a meaningful concept of current youth culture. In the Swedish referendum in November 1994 the youngest voters were the only age-group negative to the European Union.

Notes

1 The last map, published posthumously, was S. Rokkan, 'Eine Familie von Modellen für die vergleichende Geschichte Europas', *Zeitschrift für Soziologie* 9, 2 (1980), p. 123. There is also the larger posthumous work, finished by Derek Urwin: S. Rokkan and D. Urwin, *Economy, Territory, Identity*, London, Sage, 1983, pp. 30ff; cf. S. Rokkan, 'Cities, States, and Nations: A Dimensional Model for the Study of Contrasts in Development', in S.N. Eisenstadt and S. Rokkan (eds), *Building States and Nations*, Vol. 1, Beverly Hills and London , Sage, 1973, p. 86.

2 C. Tilly, *Coercion, Capital, and European States* AD *990–1990*, Oxford, Blackwell, paperback edn, 1992, pp. 12–13.

3 E. Todd, *L'invention de l'Europe*, Paris, Seuil, 1990.

4 Cf. the more complicated picture coming out of J. Goody et al. (eds), *Family and Inheritance*, Cambridge, Cambridge University Press, 1976.

5 J. Hajnal, 'European Marriage Patterns in Perspective', in D.V. Glass and D.E.C. Eversley (eds), *Population in History*, London, 1965. As you see when you draw a pencil line on a map of Europe from Trieste to St Petersburg, the major parts of Estonia and Latvia, but not of Lithuania, are west of it. That also corresponds to prewar family patterns: cf. W. Schlau, 'Der Wandel in der sozialen Struktur der baltischen Länder', in B. Meissner (ed.), *Die baltischen Nationen*, 2nd edn, Cologne, Markus Verlag, 1991, pp. 365–6.

6 J. Goody, *The Development of the Family and Marriage in Europe*, Cambridge, Cambridge University Press, 1983; R. Wall et al. (eds), *Family Forms in Historic Europe*, Cambridge, Cambridge University Press, 1983.

7 J. Szücs, *Die drei historischen Regionen Europas*, Frankfurt, Neue Kritik, 1990. Szücs was a Hungarian historian, very much inspired by another Hungarian social and historical writer, István Bibó.

8 For later discussions, as well as references to the original texts, see G. Schöpflin and N. Wood (eds), *In Search of Central Europe*, Cambridge, Polity Press, 1989; S. Graubard (ed.), *Eastern Europe   Central Europe , , , Europe*, Boulder, Col., Westview Press, 1991.

9 This is no power theory of culture. It is an empirical generalization of European history. I am more uncertain about the location of value systems in the chain.

10 See further G. Therborn, 'The Right to Vote and the Four Routes to/through Modernity', in R. Torstendahl (ed.), *The State in Theory and History*, London, Sage, 1992.

11 See further, P. Anderson, *Passages from Antiquity to Feudalism, and Lineages of the Absolutist State*, both London, NLB, 1974.

11 See further S. Hunke, *Allahs Sonne über dem Abendland*, Stuttgart, Deutsche-Verlags-Anstalt, 1960.

13 As the visitor to the 'Spanish village' in Barcelona learns. On the monumental legacy see G. Godwin, *Islamic Spain*, London, Viking, 1990.

14 I have learnt much about the cultural history of Russia from P.-A. Bodin, *Ryssland och Europa*, Stockholm, Natur och Kultur, 1993. On the iconographic inspiration from the Khan of the Horde, see pp. 67ff. On the legacy of Mongol public law, see H. Berman, *Justice in the USSR*, Rev. edn, Cambridge, Mass., Harvard University Press, pp. 194ff.

15 Abroad Sidran is perhaps best known as the screenwriter of the film *Time of the Gypsies*. The poem mentioned was published in German translation in *Die Zeit*, 3.12.1993, p. 60. His latest collection of poems has the title *Sarajevski tabut* ('Sarajevan coffin').

16 E. Hobsbawm, *The Age of Revolution, 1789–1848*, New York, Mentor Books, 1964, p. 116.

17 This, so far little remarked, coincidence is discussed somewhat in G. Therborn, 'Revolution and Reform: Reflexions on Their Linkages Through the Great French Revolution', in J. Bohlin et al. (eds), *Samhällsvetenskap, ekonomi, historia*, Göteborg, Daidalos, 1989.

18 We shall return to the 1968 movement in the West below, in Chapter 15.

19 The last formulations of Rokkan's 'conceptual maps' of Europe are his book with Derek Urwin, posthumously published, *Economy, Territory, Identity*, esp. Ch. 1, and a lecture also published posthumously (by Peter Flora) as an article, 'Eine Familie von Modellen'.

20 Further reading may begin with M. Clévenot (ed.), *L'Etat des religions dans le monde*, Paris, La Découverte/Le Cerf, 1987; D. Martin, 'The Religious Condition of Europe', in S. Giner and M. Archer (eds), *Contemporary Europe: Social Structures and Cultural Patterns*, London, Routledge & Kegan Paul, 1978; and, as a historical background, G.R. Elton, *Reformation Europe, 1517–1559*, London, Fontana/Collins, 1963.

21 Clévenot, *L'Etat des religions*, pp. 331ff.

22 See further the exquisite study by John Armstrong, *Nations before Nationalism*, Chapel Hill, NC, University of North Carolina Press, 1982. Ch. 8; and the penetrating analysis by Stein Rokkan and Derek Urwin, *Economy, Territory, Identity*.

23 Armstrong, *Nations before Nationalism*, pp. 25 and 281.

24 See further, A. Ara and C. Magris, *Trieste: Une identité de frontière*, Paris, Seuil, 1982.

25 Cf. E. Hobsbawm, *Nations and Nationalism since 1780*, Canto edn, Cambridge, Cambridge University Press, 1991, pp. 54ff. My comparison with the Arab nationalist Renaissance is indebted to the linguistic expertise of my Göteborg colleague Jan Retsö, Professor of Arabic.

26 The list stops short of much more asymmetrical commonalities, such as the common language of Italy and Ticino, of the Swedes and the Finland Swedes, and by the still more special cases of trans-frontier language minorities, such as the Danes on the German side of the border and the Germans on the Danish side, the German speakers in South Tyrol, etc.

27 This is based on a personal experience in Barcelona some time in the late 1970s, of a large intellectual gathering, where speakers spoke Italian, French, Catalan, Castilian and Portuguese and appeared to be received with understanding.

28 A good illustration from Ludwigsburg, Colmar and Strasburg is given in the *Frankfurter Algemeine Zeitung*, 13.4.1991, p. 4.

29 M. Maggiore, *Audiovisual Production in the Single Market*, Luxemburg, EC, 1990, p. 60. Italian academia is rapidly becoming Americanized, however.

30 Not counting translations from Russian or Czech within the then USSR or Czechoslovakia into other languages of the same country.

31 All percentages are averages for the three years of 1983–5: Unesco, *Statistical Yearbook 1991*, Paris, 1991, Table 7.10.

32 Calculations from ibid., Tables 7.10 and 7.11.

33 In contrast to the interrelated trade pattern of the Nordic countries, trade between Portugal and Spain has also been very insignificant, until recently, when it has begun to pick up after the two joining the EC. There is now also an annual political summit between the two Iberian neighbours.

34 See the excellent overview by K. Zweigert and H. Kötz, *Introduction to Comparative Law*, Vol. 1, 2nd edn, Oxford, Clarendon Press, 1987.

35 The Irish Republic grafted canonical family law upon the British-derived common law.

36 The family tree above relies largely upon the authority of Zweigert and Kötz, *Introduction to Comparative Law*. For an empirical analysis of how legal families of nations weigh upon cross-national normative patterns and their development in the course of the twentieth century, see, e.g. G. Therborn, 'The Politics of Childhood', in F. Castles (ed.), *Families of Nations*, Aldershot, Dartmouth, 1993.

37 See further H. Berman, *Justice in the USSR*, Cambridge, Mass., Harvard University Press, 1963, and Zweigert and Kötz, *Introduction to Comparative Law*, Part V.

38 E. Huber, *System und Geschichte des schweizerischens Privatrechts*, Vol. 1, Basel, Dekoffs Buchhandlung, 1896, 2 vols, pp. 50ff.

39 W.E. von Eyben, 'Inter-Nordic Legislative Cooperation', *Scandinavian Studies in Law* 6 (1962); F. Schmidt, 'The Prospective Law of Marriage', *Scandinavian Studies in Law* 15 (1971).

40 Cf. J. Martens, 'Die rechtsstaatliche Struktur der Europäischen Wirtschaftsgemeinschaft', *Europarecht* 5 (1970). See further, more generally, T.C. Hartley, *The Foundations of European Community Law*, Oxford, Clarendon Press, 1983; J. Boulouis, *Droit institutionnel des communautés européennes*, Paris, Montchrestien, 1991.

41 This, the most famous case of European jurisprudence, was originally a customs duty conflict between a private firm and the Dutch state, where the former invoked community law, and the latter referred the matter to the European Court, which ruled that §12 of the EEC Treaty, against new or increased customs duties, had 'direct effect', overruling Dutch law and courts. Cf. Hartley *The Foundations of European Community Law*, pp. 187ff. For a discussion of the issues facing Britain in the face of Community law, see J.D.B. Mitchell, 'British Law and British Membership', *Europarecht* 6 (1971).

42 E.g. by Boulouis, *Droit institutionnel*, pp. 209ff.

43 Labour law and social law are not (yet) very developed on the EC level, but national consequences of various sorts are already visible and discussible. Cf. R. Birk, 'Die Folgewirkungen des europäischen Gemeinshaftsrechts für das nationale Arbeitsrechtr, *Europarecht* 25 (1990); B. Schulte, 'Europäisches und nationales Sozialrecht', *Europarecht* 25 (1990).

44 See further H. Kleinsteuber et al. (eds), *Electronic Media and Politics in Western Europe*, Frankfurt Campus, 1986; F. Balle, *Médias et sociétés*, 5th edn, Paris, Montchrestien, 1990, pp. 317–440, 501ff.

45 This is largely based on informants' interviews, but for the hard GDR data the reader is referred to C. Lemke, *Die Ursachen des Umbruchs 1989*, Opladen, Westdeutscher Verlag, 1991, p. 190.

46 Balle *Médias et sociétés*, p. 515.

47 Maggiore, *Audiovisual Production*, p. 50.

48 *Svenska Dagbladet*, 25.11.1993, p. 27. American films also cover about half of Japanese film viewing: *Die Zeit*, 22.10 1993, p. 25.

49 Léon Blum was the Socialist French Prime Minister, James Byrnes was the US Foreign Minister: M. Boujut (ed.), *Europe–Hollywood et retour*, Paris, Autrement, 1986, pp. 91ff, 139.

50 Maggiore, *Audiovisual Production*, p. 59. The data refer to 1985.

51 Calculated from Euromonitor, *Consumer Europe 1989/90*, London, 1989, pp. 476–7. The raw data are rounded off millions of LP and EP records, compact discs and pre-recorded cassettes sold in 1988.

52 These and other music data are culled from 'A Survey of the Music Business', *The Economist* Supplement, 21.12.1991, and from interviews with staff of the Dutch and the Swedish phonogram producers' associations, NVPI and GLF, respectively.

53 Henley Centre, *Frontiers: Planning for Consumer Change in Europe*, London, 1991, as reported in the *Financial Times*, 19.9.1991, p. 8.

PART IV

ENCULTURATIONS

One of the most basic premises of sociology is that human beings do not have 'stable preferences', deductible from the imagination of any tenured economist. On the contrary, one of the sociologically most fascinating aspects of humans is that they belong to different cultures, embrace different identities, have different kinds of knowledge – not just 'incomplete information' – and heed different values and norms.

These identities, cognitions and values and norms, like their structural counterparts, boundaries, tasks, rights, means and risks and opportunities, should be viewed as effects of always ongoing processes – of change as well as of reproduction. That is why we are talking of enculturations, rather than of cultures.

The disciplinary recognition of the basic issues of culture is very uneven. Values and norms are basic stock in trade. The sociology of knowledge, of explicit interwar origin but with early twentieth-century Durkheimian roots, has by now acquired a classical patina. In recent years, language and other cultural codes, symbolic forms, communicative action and symbolic competition and hierarchies have come into the limelight.

On identity, however, there has been a stunning silence, as we noted in Chapter 1, remarkable not only because of identity's importance but even more because of its current prominence, in the politics and ideologies of multiculturalism, in the new assertions of religious or national identity, 'fundamentalism', nationalism.[1]

Note

1 The literature on nationalism and ethnicity is enormous, most of it by historians, anthropologists and political scientists. Not to be missed are B. Anderson, *Imagined Communities*, London, Verso, 1983; J. Armstrong, *Nations before Nationalism*, Chapel Hill, NC, University of North Carolina Press, 1982; E. Gellner, *Nations and Nationalism*, Oxford, Blackwell, 1983; E. Hobsbawm, *Nations and Nationalism since 1780*, Canto edn, Cambridge, Cambridge University Press, Anthony Smith, *The Ethnic Origin of Nations*, Oxford, Blackwell, 1986.

12

ISSUES OF IDENTITY

This is an empirical monograph and not a theoretical treatise. However, given the state of sociological theory on the subject of identity, a few words of general introduction may be called for. It is a fascinating phenomenon, reaching from individual child or development psychology to historical macro-sociology. Here we shall, of course, confine ourselves to the latter, while pointing out at the outset the enormous interdisciplinary potency of the concept.

'We' and 'the Others'

Identity is post-classical Latin and means sameness. As such it is operative only dialectically, i.e. in connection with its opposite, otherness. Because of this dialectic we may say that there is a primacy of otherness over sameness in the making of identity. The great Norwegian anthropologist Fredrik Barth taught us that a quarter of century ago, when he suggested that ethnic studies should focus on the *'boundary* that defines the group'.[1] Alter is primary to Ego. The 'self' also typically means 'not anybody else'.

The process of identity formation may be seen as composed of three crucial moments: by differentiation, by the settlement of self-reference or self-image, and by the recognition by others.

Differentiation refers to the separation of the potential 'me' or 'us' from the environment. In this process of differentiation there are two aspects: experiences of an other, and discoveries of a self.

Differentiation is a social construction, of a boundary. While inscribed in the dynamics of personality formation, it has no intrinsic basis within a system of social interaction. Rather, in modern societies it should be seen as the outcome of competition among possible demarcations. The latter include not only the delineation of different collectivities, but also deciding the issue: group/community or individuals/aggregates? Like other constructions, collective identities have their architects, their entrepreneurs and their builders, who vary in their competitiveness on the imperfect identity market.

In situations of unusual uncertainty or adversity, entrepreneurs of mistrust, of more narrow boundaries of identity, should, *ceteris paribus*, be expected to be more successful than proponents of trust and open boundaries.

Other things being equal, we should also assume, in spite of the inherently constructed bases of collective identities, that the more clearly the others can be seen, and the more different they appear, the earlier and the stronger a separate identity should emerge. That the turn of Europe from a continent of emigration to one of immigration should lead to more ethnic awareness in Europe should come as no surprise.

On the other hand, since we are referring to experiences, the other relation also holds, namely the more clear the self, other things being equal, the more clear the difference to the other. It is because of the latter that the socio-economically relatively speaking most egalitarian Nordic countries exhibit the strongest sense of class identity in Europe.[2]

The experience of the Otherness of the Other is intimately related, but irreducible, to the discovery and the making of the self. The cutting loose from close others is a feature of self-making. Apart from the experience of others, this self-assertion process appears to be driven by the growth of internal resources, be it of the individual, of a set of occupational practitioners, or of a historical potential community. That is, other things being equal, the more resourceful, the greater the demand for a separate autonomy. This holds, I think, in personality dynamics, and it holds, by and large, for the history of professions and for that of nation-states, most recently manifested in the vanguard of the Baltics and of Slovenia and Croatia in breaking up the USSR and Yugoslavia.

Differentiation is a very uneven process over time. It involves certain ruptural moments and stable, durable sediments of self–other perceptions in-between. In the field of collective identities, the most dramatic and important ruptural moments of identification are wars and the breakdown of a given state order.

Secondly, identity should not be conceived as just a blank negation of the Other. Identity is also, normally, something positive, an identification *with* somebody or something, after an awareness of separateness, that is. With a bow to the great sociologist Robert Merton and his theory of reference groups,[3] we might refer to this second aspect of identity formation as *the settlement of a self-reference* or self-image (including the possibility of several). 'Settlement' is used to cover the outcome of the process, whether by deliberate self-selection, deliberate other-socialization or by some subconscious process of adaptation. We should think of this process as temporally very uneven, as one marked by a small number of decisive events with very enduring effects.

Here the epoch, the *Zeitgeist* or spirit of the times, comes in, as a patterning of the supply of pertinent selves. Channels of communication are very important.

In the consolidation and reproduction of collective identities, *rituals* play a main part. Rituals revive memory and meaning, organize and visualize togetherness, and express a mutual re-affirmation, re-assurance of the collectivity. Hence rituals constitute an important empirical means of entry into the collective identities of a population.

In the making of collective identities, this self-reference or -image may be constructed as an *origin* common to the potential collective, as a common *competence* or task – be it of speaking the same language, of doing wage-work or of having a particular education or a special insight, for example – and/or as holding certain *values* – Christian, Muslim, socialist, liberal or other.

Empirically, it is identities of common origin or ancestry that have been most powerful. They more than others have mobilized people to kill and to be killed. In European history, that overtowering national identity is known as 'the ideas of 1914'. Why bonds of common origin should exert such a powerful hold is a perennial question of the nationalism literature. The sociological theory underpinning this study has at least a couple of hypotheses to offer on this issue.

We should expect identities based on ideologies of inclusion/exclusion to be more antagonistic than identities deriving from positional differentiations within a division of labour. That is, that ethnic and religious identities should clash more violently, if they collide, than class or professional identities.[4] Secondly, it may be that it is not national or ethnic identity that is supremely powerful, but power itself. The sociology of this work would assume that the most effective collective identities would be those most effectively backed up by power. In modern times, states are the most important sites of power, insofar as power has any site. The enthusiastic soldiers of 1914 identified with their states, rather than with their nations. Until the waves of massive defeat came rolling in, the soldiers of the different nations of the Habsburg Empire, for instance, fought for their Kaiser and his state.[5]

A national or ethnic identity also has a crucial *temporal dimension*. Affirming an ethnic identity amounts to discounting the present and the future for the past, to thinking and saying that the past is more important than the present. (Whatever there is to ethnicity/national belonging, it is inherited from the past. Who your parents were is more important than what you do, think or might become.) So, the less value the present appears to provide, the more important the past, the more important ethnicity, other things being equal.

Eastern European nationalism grew, first, on the weakening of the multinational/officially internationalist Other, and then on the discounting of the present and the future. To the extent that the liberal occidentalist sirens will deliver their promised goods to the majority of the population, we should expect Eastern European nationalisms to recede, if not necessarily to disappear. In the, apparently more likely, case of non-delivery in the foreseeable future, recurrent nationalist reactions are to be expected.

Finally, self-identity depends upon the Other, not only in separating from him/her, but also upon being recognized. *Recognition* is the third crucial process of identity formation.

Chronology is not implied here. Recognition by others may precede differentiation. Discriminatory recognition may provide the impetus to collective identity. Antisemitism and the defeats of universalist projects have spawned Zionism and other forms of Jewish ethnic identity, for instance.

In current controversies about ethnic and sexual identities a 'politics of recognition' has come to centre-stage.[6] So also in the current sociological theory of professions, in which the state recognition of the identity of a particular category of people as the only legitimate possessors of a certain kind of knowledge is taken as crucial. It is less prominent in development psychology, socialization theory and consciousness conceptions, and it is just postulated in role theory.

A very important, implicit politics of recognition is made up by the territorial boundaries, even for purely administrative purposes, of a potentially multinational state at the onset of nationalist agitation. Again, in the Europe of the former USSR and in Yugoslavia the same fetishism of boundaries repeats itself as in the Americas about two centuries ago, or in Africa a generation back. However contingent and recent, the pre-national boundaries delimit *at least* the sacred territory of the father/motherland, which may, of course, include non-liberated territory across the border. True, in the Americas and in Africa those administrative and judicial divisions were, on the whole, used quite pragmatically for nation- and state-building. In Nagorno-Karabakh, in Croatia and in Bosnia-Hercegovina, however, they have led to vicious wars, and about Crimea to a basic political conflict, which might issue into war.

A theory of identity formation, then, should look out for key moments of differentiation, for the supply and demand of reference images, and for positive and negative recognition.

Sociologically, identity has three main sorts of effects. What or whom you identify with is an important *source of your norms and values*. From your identity follows, by and large, your evaluative standards, your 'style', and your ethics. Secondly, identity determines the *scope of rationality*. The meaning of a pursuit of rational self-interest depends on who this 'self' is – myself only? my parents and me? my husband and me? my children and me? my parents, my husband, my children, my siblings and me? my class fellows and me? my family, my clan and me? my tribe or ethnie and me? etc.

A recent example is the 1993 GATT negotiations between the EU and the USA. 'According to the French view', a collaborator of the right-wing liberal German newspaper *Frankfurter Allgemeine Zeitung* wrote critically, 'the European Union has to secure a "European identity." ' The Socialist ex-Minister of Industry and Foreign Trade, Dominique Strauss-Kahn, expressed this French view in dramatic terms at about the same time: 'at stake, finally, [in the GATT negotiations on international trade] is the very existence of Europe.'[7] As far as it is effective, a collective identity affects the scope of rationality. The French are arguing that there is a European identity at issue, whereas the Frankfurt 'newspaper for Germany' takes that stance as a manifestation of an irrational 'fortress mentality'.

Before the official unification of the European language after Maastricht, the different conceptions of identity and rationality with regard to Western Europe were well captured by the difference between, on the one hand, the continental conception of a 'European Community' (Europäische Gemeinschaft, Communauté Européenne) and the standard British designation of the same phenomenon as 'the Common Market'. You may identify yourself with a community but hardly with a market, even if 'common'.

Thirdly, very importantly, identity determines the *range of valid norms*. Within the range of identification, killing is a sort of suicide, refusal to help is a sort of self-denial, is scabbing, fouling one's own nest. Outside it, in relation to the Other, it may be legitimate, even a duty, a sign of uprightness and honesty. The Other may be defined in any terms of non-identity, family, tribe, ethnicity, class, religion and so on. It is not the Serbs who identify with Bosnia who are shelling Sarajevo, nor the Croats identifying with it who are attacking Mostar, but Serbs who identify themselves as Serbs and Croats as Croats.

The narrow European range of norms became clear already at the end of World War II, when politicians and officers who had claimed to be fighting for democracy and independence against Fascism, demonstrated that democracy and even elementary civil rights were not for French, Belgian and Dutch colonials, and while possibly for Indians and some others, certainly not for all subjects of His British Majesty. After armed challenges, this European delimitation of human rights and norms had to be given up, the early 1960s being the period of a formal acceptance of universalism.

In what follows we shall look at two kinds of identities, at European identities and at the identities of Europeans. In both cases we have to deal with historically evolved social constructions. Identities are contingent, not essential. Any given identifier may have an indeterminate number of identities that he/she adopts/recognizes, which is why European identities are not identical with identities of Europeans. The latter may have a number of identities, of which the one with Europe is one possibility.

European identities here refers to identifications with Europe, which we shall compare with other territorial identifications. But the possible identities of Europeans are infinite. In this context we shall concentrate on their most important collective identities, as manifested in rituals and celebrations. There we shall find the history of Europe, rather than Europe itself, as the locus of commemoration.

European days of commemoration

'It is above all at Christmas that one feels a stranger', i.e. a European, a woman resident of Algiers said.[8] A collective identity is not just an identity held in common in their souls by an aggregate of individuals. As a rule, it is also a public thing, manifested in and sustained by public rituals. A look at collective identities should therefore start by eyeing around for any celebrations and ceremonies of the collective.

In this perspective, the collective identity of Europeans is still more than anything else a religious, a *Christian* identity. The latter is not so much expressed in an embrace of Christian theology as in participating in the great

Christian holidays – and in Christian family rites, such as baptisms and burials. To be a European is to celebrate Christmas and Easter, perhaps also Whitsuntide in common with almost everybody else around. There are Christians in other parts of the world, most of whom have, incidentally, now even adopted Sunday as the normal weekly day off, but only in Europe and, by and large, in the European-settled New Worlds does the social year largely follow the year of the Christian Church.

The Bolsheviks abolished Christmas, but the new New Year celebration had no sharp *de facto* demarcations from the Christmas of the Orthodox calendar. The Orthodox Church had already merged New Year and Christmas, as well as pagan customs with Christian ones. When Soviet rituals were revived in the 1960s, their managers always took into consideration the dates of the Christian calendar, and in Central Asia of the Islamic one.[9]

Christendom has for a long, long time been multicultural: between Sinter Klaas bringing Dutch children their presents on the 6 December to the arrival of the Reyes Magos to the Spanish there is a month. The relative importance of Christmas and Easter is also variable, the latter more so by the Orthodox and by the Spanish Catholics than among the Protestants.

As a European you are also likely to react with a feeling of different identities upon learning that Al Qods, suddenly appearing in an otherwise familiar-looking French or English text in, say, a Moroccan or an Egyptian newspaper, refers to what you are used to calling Jerusalem. Or, you may find it strange to be referred to as a 'Messian', an adherent of Messias – as in contemporary Arabic, alternatively as a Nazarene, in the language of the Qu'ran – when you think of yourself as a Christian.

This Christian character of the European calendar is not likely to be much affected by the recent settlement of significant Islamic communities in Europe. The European Muslims are likely to celebrate Ramadan and other Islamic holidays in the interstices of the over-arching Christian calendar, as Christians have long been celebrating theirs in the Islamic world. A more radical threat comes from the zealots of Mammon and their pharisees.

The *Economist* lamented editorially over the British Christmas of 1993 for taking too many days away from 'trading' and 'do[ing] business'. 'Public holidays should be abolished', the paper argued. They are 'economically damaging and no fun'. I guess that is about as radical a formulation of individualist commodity fetishism that you could get.[10] Its success is perhaps open to some doubt.

As a poor second to their diluted religion, Europeans have their great and horrible *wars* in common. Like their Christian holidays and the high moments of the latter, memories of the same wars vary in time, form and relative importance, but in contrast to Christianity also in meaning, across the continent. In the UK and in France, 11 November began to be celebrated in 1919, not as a day of victory but rather as a day of mourning, in memory of the fallen of the World War. In 1918, 11 November was Armistice Day, ending World War I. The British introduced two minutes of silence at 11 a.m. throughout their empire. Since World War II, 11 November, or rather the Sunday closest to it, has become a day of memory and mourning the dead of both European 'world wars'.

But to begin with the Italians celebrated their victory – after the Habsburg army had collapsed – at Vittorio Veneto, and the defeated powers were not celebrating at all. In Belgium, the *Ijzer Bedevaart* (Pilgrimage) was not only in memory and mourning of the fallen at the Ijzer front and generally in World War I, but also a manifestation of Flemishness, with a sacral intonation – 'Everything for Flanders, Flanders for Christ', as the Ijzer Monument has it –, but also with far right jarrings.

The date of the Kaiser's abdication, 9 November, has a special, and specific, ring in Germany: it is also the date of the first Nazi putsch in 1923, the date of the big Nazi pogrom in 1938, and the date of the breakthrough of the Berlin Wall. However, in 1931 the Social Democratic Prussian government inaugurated a monument, located in the early nineteenth-century nationalist New Watch (*Neue Wache*) in Berlin, to the fallen of the world war. After the fall of the Nazi regime the tradition was taken up again by the GDR, broadened to the victims of militarism and Fascism. In November 1993, it was incorporated into the new National Day of Mourning (*Volkstrauertag*) of the Federal Republic.

The Dutch, who were spared World War I, celebrate their liberation from German occupation in World War II on 5 May, mourning the victims of the latter in the evening of the previous day. Italy remembers 25 April (1945), as the Day of Liberation (from Fascism), because of the final call of the Resistance for insurrection. In France, President Giscard d'Estaing abolished 8 May (1945) as a national holiday, as a gesture of reconciliation both with Germany and with Vichy France. It was not a very popular decision, and 8 May returned as a day of war memory with the Presidency of Mitterrand.

The Soviets fêted 9 May as the day of victory. To them, World War II was the 'Great Patriotic War', and the strength of nationalism was indicated by the more local and family character of Victory Day – as a day of memory – as opposed to Mayday and the anniversary of the Revolution.[11] Victory Day is likely to survive the discredit of proletarian internationalism and of revolution. Under Communism, the other Eastern European countries celebrated the end of Nazi rule, which tended to coincide with the entry of the Red Army.

Stretching from July (the proclamation of the Polish Committee of National Liberation in 1944) to May, though concentrated in the early days of November and of May, celebrating the end of the two world wars is a major collective ritual of Europeans. In most countries, however, its intrinsic meaning is probably more indifferent to the late-born generations than the message of the birth, death and resurrection of Christ.[12]

After Christianity and war there comes, again at a distance, a third focus of collective identity among Europeans: *class*. Although also in process of fading and abandonment, Mayday, or some day near to 1 May, is still a common European holiday. A recent attempt by the class-conscious anti-labour government in Britain to abolish it appears to have been abandoned.[13]

True, the origin of Mayday is North American and the aim of it is universal. However, Mayday is, above all, a European holiday. The American Federation of Labor investment in 1 May 1890 was overshadowed in the USA almost from the beginning by a non-class celebration of Labor Day in September. Outside Europe and, later on, the Soviet-affiliated states, Mayday has not been institutionalized as a day of working-class solidarity and demand. In Latin America, where it started in Buenos Aires and Havana already in 1890, the tradition has been very intermittent, due to the political vicissitudes of the area, though it was incorporated in the official traditions of Argentine Peronism, Brazilian Populism and the Mexican Revolution. Also in Oceania, where the eight-hour day was won early, Mayday demonstrations tended to dry up during the Cold War. In Japan, however, they were revived after World War II.

Before World War II only three countries had made 1 May a national holiday. First, the USSR, of course, where the labour movement already in 1917 switched to the Western calendar in order to celebrate Mayday on the same day as their class comrades in the rest of Europe. Secondly in Germany, where, however, the 1919 law failed to gather a parliamentary majority for renewal in 1920, and then only lived on in a few *Länder*, such as Saxony and Hamburg. It was Hitler who, in 1933, made 1 May 'a Day of Celebration of National Labour', a tradition which curiously enough was later carried over into German-occupied Europe, such as in the Netherlands. The third country was Sweden, whose Social Democratic government in 1938 made 1 May Sweden's first non-religious holiday. (Sweden has no proper national holiday.)

Since World War II, Mayday has become a major working-class holiday in most countries of Europe, although very unevenly in space and over time. In Franco Spain it was the day of St Joseph the Labourer. In the Communist countries it was a day of parades of power, including army units marching, which makes the day's post-Communist future problematic. The day never got really rooted in the British labour movement, which stuck to local events, such as the Durham miners' gala, but in 1978 a Labour government made Mayday a day off from work. In the Netherlands it was always overshadowed by the Queen's Day on 30 April and Liberation Day on 5 May.

In France, Mayday celebration followed closely the political conjunctures. In the mid-1940s the attraction of 1 May was such that the Gaullists organized their alternative gathering, in Paris in Bois de Boulogne, to the demonstrations of the labour parties. Drawn into the controversy about French ownership of Algeria, Mayday demonstrations were forbidden between 1955 and 1967. After an ensuing ten to fifteen years of revival, the celebration of Mayday virtually petered out in the late 1980s, leaving the 'Fête de l'Humanité' the only major labour festival.[14]

The strongest and most stable Mayday traditions developed in the Nordic countries, in Austria, Belgium, Italy, Germany, and parts of Switzerland, in Basel, Zurich and Ticino especially.[15]

From the sale of Mayday badges by Swedish Social Democrats we can obtain a long time series of the support for Mayday, from the 1920s to the 1990s (see Figure 12.1).[16] At its own high level the shape of the graph will quite accurately capture the extent of Western class identities over time. They strengthened in the 1930s, with the experience of the Depression. They rose again after the war with the hopes for a new society, but were enfeebled in the 1950s and 1960s by the unexpected openings of individual discretionary consumption and by the Cold War divisions. Then ensued a new rise from around 1970, with labour movements invigorated by full employment, and now including a new internationalism of anti-imperialist students and of immigrant workers. From the mid-1980s came a rapid decline with the combined effects of post-industrial labour division and the disillusions of left-wing internationalism.

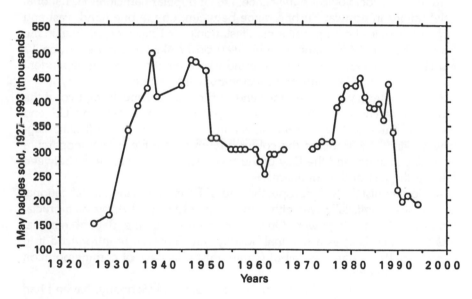

Figure 12.1 *Mayday badges sold in Sweden, 1927–1994 (thousands)*

Sources: SAP Annual Reports, 1916–1992; Inger Mähler, SAP Party Executive, oral communication.

The future of Mayday will probably depend upon the extent to which it can be wedded to a new and forceful internationalist multiculturalism. The tendency of Mayday to turn from a day of class solidarity and class internationalism to multi-ethnic radicalism has been visible all over Western Europe, with immigrant workers, students and militants mounting contingents. But whether it will be strong enough to offset the decline of class is at least open to doubt.

Class organizations – trade unions, labour parties, class-specific cultural organizations – and also the welfare state may be seen as functionally equivalents to class rituals, as manifestations of a socio-economically based collective solidarity. In that sense, Europe is an eminently class-conscious continent (cf. Chapters 5 and 15). Survey data also convey that the identification with socio-economic class position is stronger in (Western) Europe than in the (Anglo-Saxon) New World.[17]

National celebrations in Europe exhibit a wide range of variation, in their national significance as well as in their objects of commemoration. Constitutions and national independence are the two most common reasons for national commemoration, but the latter may also include the death of a poet (the Portuguese Luis de Camões, in 1580), a royal birth (of ex-Queen Juliana of the Netherlands, born in 1909), a navigational exploit (by Columbus, the Genoese remembered in Spain, and in Spanish America), a saint (St Patrick, in Ireland) or a revolution (in France and in the former USSR).

In terms of sociological significance, i.e. of popular participation, national celebrations in postwar Europe range between, on the one hand, vast and large-scale official-cum-popular manifestations – in France on 14 July, in the Soviet Union on 7 November, in Norway on 17 May, and in Ireland on 17 March. The masses have rallied around two revolutions, one independent constitution (of 1814), and one missionary saint, respectively.

On the other hand, at the other end of the national spectrum, two of the oldest monarchies of Europe have no proper national day: the UK and Sweden. They do have a poor substitute, of a royalist and officially flag-waving kind: the 'trooping the colour' march before the British monarch a Saturday in June, and the Day of the Swedish Flag on 6 June. In-between falls all the rest of the continent.

In Communist Eastern Europe, the end of Fascism was the official national day, which unofficially was either the entry of the Red Army or a crucial Communist bid for power. Only in Romania was the day of national independence kept as a national holiday, till Jaruzelski re-introduced it in Poland in 1987. After the fall of Communism, its days of commemoration are being forgotten.

The late big nations of Western Europe, Italy and Germany, haven't had much to celebrate consensually, with their convulsive internal history. Neither nation has a popular national day. Italy officially celebrates 25 April (1945), the launching of the general anti-Fascist insurrection, and 2 June (1946), the day of the referendum abolishing the monarchy. Neither with much enthusiasm.

The West Germans were polled in 1965 about a suitable day of national celebration. One third each opted for Soldier's (November) Sunday, commemorating the fallen of the world wars, and 17 June, in memory of the uprising in East Germany in 1953. Between a quarter and a fifth suggested Europe Day (9 May), one-sixth the foundation of the Federal Republic of Germany, and one-eighth 20 July, the day of the failed anti-

Hitler coup of 1944.[18] The scant attachment to the actual West German state is remarkable.

Officially, West Germany celebrated a working-class uprising in East Germany, on 17 June 1953, as the Day of German Unity, and after the end of East Germany (3 October 1990) as the Day of Re-unification. How long and how much of 3 October will survive is open to doubt, though, as there is already serious discussion about transferring it to the following Sunday, as a contribution to the finance of long-term care of the elderly.[19]

The amount and the depth of nostalgia in national rituals also vary. Some of them are curiously necrophiliac, like the current Serbian veneration of a catastrophic defeat in 1389, or, until recently, the Swedish predilection for paying homage to the death of their great warrior kings. Till about 1960 Swedish school pupils marched in memory of the death in combat of Gustavus II Adolphus (on 6 November 1632), while the somewhat mysterious killing of Charles XII besieging Fredrikshald in Norway (on 30 November 1718) was the object of a much more selective right-wing manifestation.

Some national celebrations express a deep religious commitment, to St Patrick or, now after Communism, to *Svataja Rus* (Holy Russia). Others celebrate a bygone national splendour – 'the heroes of the sea' in the Portuguese national hymn, the Spanish discovery of America, the *Glanz* (glory) of the Habsburgs unofficially very vividly remembered in contemporary Austria. Other national memories are more rationally fastened onto pertinent events, be they revolutions, dynastic occurrences, constitutions or achievements of national independence.

We may also discern a pattern of variable pomp in national celebrations. The European prize for national pomposity has in the postwar period been shared by the two countries celebrating universalistic revolutions, France and the Soviet Union. In the cool jargon of sociology, national pomposity is here defined as an official celebration of the nation's history with, among other things, military parades. After the end of the USSR, of Yugoslavia, and Communist partisan Albania, and of the borrowed lights of the former, France remains as the ultimate bastion and champion of ritual armed national glory on the European continent.

National rivalry, state dissent and hyphenated identities

With the end of the Cold War celebrations in West Germany, and of controversial partisan takeovers in Eastern Europe, internationally contentious commemorations, fêting the victory of one over the other, have, by and large, become obsolete. The Ulster Protestants are still celebrating, with great popular fanfare, the final victory of William of Orange (i.e. the Netherlands) over James Stuart on 12 July 1691, but that is why they appear so out of place in current Western Europe.

In the heyday of mass nationalism in Europe, i.e. the last third of the nineteenth and the first third of the twentieth century, this competitive commemoration was more common. In the German Empire a popular day of celebration was the Day of Sedan, i.e. the Prussian victory over the French at Sedan on 2 September 1870.[20] This was also the time when the anthem 'Die Wacht am Rhein' ('The Watch on the Rhine'), that is, against the French, was a central ritual of German identity.

However, the fall of Communism has resurrected nationalism in parts of the European periphery, and not only among the former multinational Communist states, the USSR and Yugoslavia. It has also, for example, ignited Greek nationalism.

Greece has revived 'the Macedonian question' of the early twentieth century, not without help from Skopje, true. The once multi-ethnic city of Saloniki (see Chapter 3 above) has become the parade ground of Hellenism, shepherded by an amazing alliance of 'Socialist' cadres and Orthodox priests. With the same impetus, the Greek Parliament in February 1994 declared 19 May a national day of mourning – remembering the exodus of the Black Sea Pontian Greeks after World War I –, the day which to the modern enemies of the Greeks, the Turks, is the Day of Youth, commemorating Mustafa Kemal's launching of the Turkish 'War of Liberation' in 1919 (against the Greeks, among others).[21]

However peaceful, postwar Western Europe has not been a haven of harmony of nations and states. By state dissent or non-state political identity we shall refer to political affiliations based either on a territory other than that of the given state, or on a language other than the predominant one of the given state. Western Europe had by the early 1990s four major patterns of dissenting identities in this sense.

First of all, in Western Europe there have been two particularly problematic nation-states, Austria and Belgium. After having smashed the Habsburg Empire in World War I, the victorious Allies prohibited rump Austria from calling itself German Austria, but in the end they were unable to prevent *Anschluss* to Germany, hailed even by anti-Fascist Austrians as a final encounter with destiny. Even before World War I, German Austrians had increasingly asserted their Germanhood, by singing 'Die Wacht am Rhein', by celebrating the Day of Sedan, and in many other ways.

By 1945 Austrians were more ambivalent about their Germanhood, which had ultimately brought them little benefit. But a sense of an Austrian nation still required some time to sink in. In 1957, i.e. after Austria had regained its full independence in 1955, the third 'libertarian' party of the country, the Freiheitliche Partei Österreichs (FPO), the heir of earlier Pan-Germanism, programmatically reaffirmed 'Austrians' belonging to the German nation'. Only in the latter half of the 1960s did a majority of Austrians believe that Austrians constituted a nation.[22]

Currently *sui generis* is Belgium, which does not have a single national party. All political parties have, since the mid-1960s, been based on sub-state linguistic and territorial identities – Flemish and francophone Christian

Democrats, Socialists, Liberals, Ecologists, and some pure non-Belgian nationalists. 'I am not Belgian', Belgium's greatest living writer, Hugo Claus, recently told the Spanish newspaper *El País*, except when football is on.[23] Right after the war a Walloon congress opted to take the Walloon half of Belgium to France. No attempt at implementation was made, however, and the decision was soon rescinded by its authors. The early 1990s Walloon Movement for the Return to France is a fringe grouping, but its very existence, with some marginal French support, underlines the peculiar precariousness of the Belgian state.[24]

From a general historical or sociological vantage-point, one should expect this to reflect a situation on the eve of a civil war or at least of a state break-up. The former seems to stand little chance, and the latter looks more unlikely than likely, however, although Belgium is becoming more of a confederation than a unitary state.

In a second group we find states in which non-national parties govern part of the country. Germany provides the oldest case in Bavaria, never ruled in the period of postwar democracy by a national German party. It was joined in the last decade or so by Catalonia and the Basque Country in Spain. In spite of persistent Basque ETA violence, the main pattern is one of peaceful coexistence. A coexistence which does not preclude friction, however. Like in Belgium – or Canada – the language issue in Catalonia has become sensitive. What are the legitimate rights of the Spanish in Catalonia?

Thirdly, there are minority nationalisms, minoritarian on their own home turf, more or less militant in their demands on the existing state. All the three peripheral parts of the United Kingdom have this sort of political identity, of the Plaid Cymru in Wales, the SNP in Scotland, and all the political parties of Northern Ireland (none of which is currently allowed to govern). Italy has recently acquired some proto-party political movements of this sort, such as the Lega Nord, in 1994 part of the Berlusconi government. There are also subnational parties in Switzerland.

Finally, there are national minority representations in a number of countries – of Turks in Greek Thrace, of South Tyrolians and Val d'Aostians in Italy, of Germans in Belgium and Denmark, of Danes in Germany, and Swedes in Finland.

In post-Communist countries this has also become a phenomenon of some significance, above all in Bulgaria, where the party of the Turkish minority constitutes the third party of the country. The status of national minorities is a very sensitive issue in the Baltics, above all in Estonia and Latvia, with their large Russian populations. It is also a focus of conflict in Romania and Slovakia. The break-up of Yugoslavia brought most of the new state borders to battlefields of armed confrontation.

From this rapid overview, two conclusions emerge. One is the widely spread phenomenon of political identities having a base which is differently delimited than the existing state. During the second half of the twentieth century, only Sweden, Portugal and Norway have consistently lacked any significant expression of dissent from the constitution of the state. Secondly, in spite of the low-intensity war in Northern Ireland, the recurring violence in the Basque Country, and a few other occasional outbursts, the relative success after World War II of Western European nations in coping peacefully with these different identities is striking. The contrast with the current violence of ex-Yugoslavia and of the Caucasus region, as well as the persistent tension between Romania and Hungary, Hungary and Slovakia, Greece and Albania are noteworthy.

The dramatic wave of immigration in the late 1980s and early 1990s has not passed by without effects on Western European nationalism. Among young people, a resurgent salience of national symbols – the flag, the anthem, etc. – is clearly discernible. More sinisterly, there is also a notable tendency towards xenophobia and xenophobic violence, reaching even normally very peaceful countries like the Netherlands and Sweden.

However, the most likely short- or medium-term outcome of the new cultural heterogeneity of Western European states is not state dissent or warring nationalisms, in the earlier European tradition, but a New World pattern of ethnical relations within the state. Among second- and third-generation new immigrants in Europe we can already discern the development of *hyphenated national identities*: Turkish-German, Moroccan-French, Chilean-Swedish, etc. Special days or festivals remembering and celebrating the culture of the country of origin are already visible. Music bands and youth gangs form on the basis of these new hyphenated identities.

Ethnic competition, ethnic stratification and occasional ethnic violence are likely to accompany the European societies of tomorrow. The latter may at times be related to ethnically delimited local turfs. But on the whole, this New World ethnicity is much less dangerous (to peace and freedom) than the rival nationalisms of the Europe of yesterday and their mutually exclusive calls for identification.

In Chapter 14 below we shall return to the question of nationalism as a value. Though related, it is not quite the same thing as the issue of the nation as an object of identity.

European and other attachments

Like national or ethnic identity, Europeanism is a historically constructed, historically variable, historically moulded chosen collective identity. A European identification in this latter sense does not in any substantive sense differ from, say, a British, Irish, Polish or Swedish identification. In talking about Europeanism and European identity, we are talking about something which might as well be called nationalism, nationality and/or ethnicity. Whether Europe will ever become a nation-state is an uncertain question, upon which few people would be prepared to bet heavily. But however defined, it is not only less populous but also less culturally – e.g. religiously and linguistically – diverse than one established nation-state of the world, than India.

The Others of 'Europe'

Like all collective identities, European identity formation has faced two kinds of Others: one outside, beyond the range of the (potential) collective, the second inside, dividing the self to be made. A persistent problem of Europeanism, albeit variable to a degree, has been that the unifying Other outside has been distant, weak or nebulous, and therefore largely irrelevant to most people of the continent, whereas the divisive Other within has been close and strong, in many cases stronger and closer than in other parts of the world.

Arguably, the earliest and strongest form of a modern European identity developed in the cosmopolitan colonial cities, or urban areas, in, say, Alexandria – 'almost a European country', according to Flaubert,[25] – Cape Town, Casablanca – and the other new cities of 'protected' Morocco, such as Rabat or new Fès, built as European cities by Hubert Lyautey and his architect Henri Prost[26] – Colombo and Tangiers,[27] from the mid-nineteenth to the mid-twentieth century. Compared to the visible presence of the Others to the settlers of the colonial edge, the Ottoman Empire was too far off to most Europeans, and its threat too asymmetrical. In fact, both the Sublime Porte and the other proximate Muslim power, Morocco, were also drawn into the power game of the European players.

The existence and the significance of the external Other should not be lost within Whiggish presentations of European unification. In late modern times the external Others have been the USSR, the USA and, most recently, Japan. None has been ideal, from the point of view of identity formation, that is. The USSR was in several ways a good candidate – close, clearly different, powerful, threatening. And it did play a positive role in furthering Western European integration: the US–Soviet *détente* of 1955 was quite important in spurring Adenauer along the road to Western European integration, and into the Treaty of Rome.[28] On the other hand, it could be argued that the USSR this side of the Urals was part of Europe, or, alternatively, that the Soviet 'sphere of influence' in Eastern Europe was, *in toto* or in parts, part of 'Europe', that Yalta had carved up Europe, rather than drawn its Eastern boundary. In brief, the best external Other was perhaps also dividing Europe as much as uniting it.

The USA was geographically easier, and its marketeering 'flexibility' was an important competitor at the time of European Single Act (in the 1980s), as its impressive wartime mobilization was to Jean Monnet and his generation. On the other hand, the USA was also the rescuer of Europe, i.e. ensuring victory to the latter's Western powers in both world wars, and after World War II the provider of Marshall Aid and of a nuclear shield against the Russians.

Although already at the turn of the twentieth century Kaiser Wilhelm II talked about the 'Yellow Peril', East Asia emerged as a significant Other to Europe only in the 1970s, and then only as an economic competitor. While market rivals may function as significant Others for the building of competitive corporate identities, it is much more difficult to catapult a market rival into a significant Other of a continental population.

While the American, Russian, West and East Asian Others have played a part, contemporary European identity is most of all differentiated from the *nation-state*. Since the nation-state is a European invention – articulated during the French Revolution and during the German resistance to Napoleonic France – the main Other of current European identity is the *past of Europe*. That ruptural conception of history, nowadays often neglected in pious pilgrimages to histories of the 'European idea', gives the original Europeanist project a clearly modernist edge.

National identities in Europe have twice challenged evolutionary conceptions of modernity. First, with their rise, concomitant with what the pioneering sociologists[29] saw as the transition from warring military to peaceful industrial societies. Secondly, by declining precipitously after World War II.

In Europe after World War II, the tide of national identity, which began rising with the French Revolution and the Napoleonic wars – which generated German nationalism – ebbed. European nationalism reached its paroxysmic climax in the new thirty years' war of 1914–1945, or, rather, in 'the spirit of 1914', in the 1918–20 'national self-determination' settlement, and in the 1930s' mobilization for national revenge.

The final coming of the war of revenge also marked the turn. Indeed, at the height of the war, European unification was a slogan of all the warring forces, of the anti-Fascist Resistance, of the ruling Fascists, of Hitler for example, and of the ruled and collaborating Fascists, for instance of Vichy France.[30] Until, in the face of approaching total defeat, it became a desperate call to fight, the Fascist notion was, of course, primarily an elaboration of a German-dominated continent, a project which was shattered in 1945.

The German war machine had defeated most of the nation-states of the continent, but in so doing had unleashed both a non-state Resistance, which was more anti-Nazi German than nationalist, and an enemy global alliance of supra-national and largely non-European forces: the British Empire, the USSR and the USA.

The postwar settlement meant a marginalization of the Resistance, the main bearer of a non-hegemonic European identity. But what was established was not so much the national states as a system of *socio-economic states*. That is, political carvings of Europe primarily geared to economic reconstruction, social integration and economic growth. This socio-economic state, of which competing variants were on offer, largely replaced the prewar divisions between a national (right-wing), a (left-wing) class and, in Catholic or religiously heterogeneous countries, a religious political project.

As long as it delivers, this socio-economic state is not very vulnerable to low values on traditional forms of national loyalty, of national pride, of willingness to fight for one's nation. On the other hand, when the prospects of economic growth and/or of social advance grow dim, perhaps even black, then other identities become more attractive. The most noteworthy of the latter is native identity, which had a first breakthrough in France in 1983–84, after the stalling of the left socio-economic project, then in West Germany, Europe's major country of immigration, in the late 1980s.

In the 1990s, nativism is spreading throughout Europe, largely as poor young people's response to the end of the Socialist and the Communist labour movement vision of a different future. The élites of the Social Democracies and the trade unions are abandoning the socio-economic welfare state project in a Europeanist direction, first in Iberia in the mid-1980s, then taken up in the Nordic and Austrian Social Democracies in the early 1990s.

The new socio-economic states, driven by their new internal dynamics, surrendered their *overseas empires* – another precondition of a domestic European identity – certainly not voluntarily but with less bloodshed and resistance than might have been expected. The countdown started when the British left their Indian 'jewel in the crown' in 1947 without a fight. On occasions – in Malacca and in Kenya for instance – the British did fight, with success for a while, and the French, the Dutch and the Portuguese fought quite bitterly and ferociously. However, only the poor, semi-Fascist Portuguese regime was prepared to slug it out to the end. The process of de-colonization became decisive after the defeats of the French at Dien Bien Phu (in 1954) and, above all, of the French and the British at Suez in 1956, a crucial background to the Treaty of Rome.

The leadership of French Social and Christian Democracy clung to Algeria, but the national hero, de Gaulle, realized the senselessness of the Algerian war. European de-colonization ended, for all practical purposes, in 1974, with the Portuguese Revolution and relinquishing of the 'overseas provinces'. Having lost their empires, France, Britain and Portugal, in that order, were prepared to identify themselves primarily as parts of Europe, rather than as European powers extended onto the world.

The special otherness from which Europe primarily differentiated itself – the previous European nation-state and nation-empire – has meant that a European identity has always been a feature of élite culture, although it is true that the need to avoid another national war in Europe is generally acknowledged. The postwar rise of the welfare state brought the nation-state much closer to the population than ever before. Europeanism has all the time been an identity primarily of a set of national politicians, with an entourage of some intellectuals, bureaucrats, and, for a long time quite few, businessmen.

As an élite identity in a democratic age, where a dedicated band of servants – like the multiculturally loyal Habsburg officer corps – is no longer sufficient, the relative success of Europeanism is above all due to its insertion into a process of political steering, to which we shall come later below.

In the East, heavy-handed Soviet bilateral hegemony barred most of any positive Eastern European identity, and the Comecon never became a focus of identification comparable to the EEC/EC/EU. But there too, the Communist variant of the socio-economic state kept nationalism at bay, till the Ceauşescu dissent in Romania (after 1965) and the late-1980s stirrings among (anti-)Yugoslav, (anti-)Soviet and Bulgarian Communist leaders and intellectuals.

Continental allegiances

Loosely defined, without any concrete specifications, Western European unification has had a wide public support. Since the first surveys of the early 1950s, more than 70% of the West German public has held European unification to be a good thing. In Italy more than 60%, and from 1970 75–80% of interviewees have been in favour of a united Europe. French figures started out similar to the Italian ones, but dipped briefly after the rejection in 1954 by the French National Assembly of a European Defence Union. Since the mid-1970s French opinion has become similar to West German and Italian. After the Treaty of Rome, British opinion has been clearly less European than Franco-Italian opinion, but with the British entry into EC a majority of British opinion is declaring itself in favour of European unification.[31]

But that support is not necessarily committed, and it exhibits a pattern which might be interpreted as largely an adaptation to national policy. The answer to another question, to the reaction if the EC was scrapped, is probably more reliable and revealing (see Table 12.1).

Indifference, not hostility, has been and is the major alternative to a European commitment. But the European unity idea is stably embraced by at least a good 40% of the inhabitants of the EC, which should be taken as a success of its proponents. After the euphoria at the time of the first enlargement of the EC ensued a disenchantment during the recession. After the Single Europe Act commitment increased again, to be followed by an after-Maastricht hangover (see Table 12.2).

The West Germans, and not the Beneluxians or the Italians, first developed a widespread commitment to the European Community. Denmark and the UK are the only countries which have ever had a plurality looking forward to leaving the EC with relief. While Danish opinion has been oscillating back and forth, the British were generally more hostile than positive until 1987. Among the other countries, only in Greece and in Ireland has there ever been any significant minority hostile to the EC. So far, that has been an initial reaction which soon petered out.

Faced with the issues of the Maastricht summit in December 1991 – monetary union and common currency, common foreign policy, common defence policy, extended rights to the European Parliament – the Italians were consistently the most pro-European, and the Danes the most sceptical. Denmark was the only country with a clear majority against a common currency and against a common foreign policy. In Britain opinion on the former was about even, with 40% in favour, 42% against.

Table 12.1 *Reactions to an abandonment of the European Community, 1971–1993 (per cent of interviewees)*

European Community	Regret	Relief	Indiff./NA
Eur. 6			
1971	40	5	55
1974	56	4	40.5
1981	43	5	52
1984	43.5	4	52.5
1988	48	5.5	46.5
1990	52.5	4.5	42.5
Eur. 10			
1973	41	10	49
1974	48.5	13	38.5
1981	37.5	14	48.5
1984	38.5	10	51.5
1988	43	9	48
1990	51.5	8	45.5
Eur. 12			
1985	42	9	49
1988	42.5	9	48.5
1990	48.5	7	44.5
1993	42	11	47

Sources: *Eurobarometer, Trend Variables, 1974–1990*, March 1991, Table B7; *Eurobarometer* 39, June 1993, Luxemburg, p. A16.

With those exceptions, European opinion was clearly in favour of more unity, although it may be noted that in the traditional strong currency countries of the EC, Germany and the Netherlands, a third of the public was against a common European currency.[32] A survey in late 1990 found strong and above EC average support for Community, instead of national, decision-making on a dozen issues in Italy, the Netherlands, Belgium and France, about average (majority) support in Germany, and lower in the other countries.[33]

The identification with Europe has become significant, but how meaningful it is to the people of Europe is open to debate. In 1981 a broad survey by the European Values System Study Group, comprising the EC except Portugal and Greece, found little identity with Europe. Given five choices of territorial identification, 47% identified first of all with their locality, 27% with their country, 15% with their region, 9% with the world as a whole and 4% with Europe.[34] But in the autumn of 1986 the *Eurobarometer* interviewers noticed a considerable number of people who 'often' considered themselves a 'citizen of Europe'. A total of 19% of all EC respondents did so, 27% in France, 26% in Luxemburg, 24% in Greece,

Table 12.2 Reactions to an abandonment of the EC among the EC nations, 1971–1993 (per cent)[a]

Country	Regret	Relief
Belgium:		
1971	25	4
1993	37	5
Denmark:		
1973	30	29
1993	42	18
France:		
1971	31	5
1993	39	14
Greece:		
1981	30	18
1993	50	5
Ireland:		
1973	37	17
1993	56	5
Italy:		
1971	35	3
1993	55	5
Luxemburg:		
1971	36	6
1993	58	5
Netherlands:		
1971	40	10
1993	47	5
Portugal:		
1985	25	8
1993	41	7
Spain:		
1985	35	6
1993	39	8
UK:		
1973	23	41
1993	28	24
W. Germany:		
1971	52	7
1993[b]	45	9

Notes: [a] Annual averages in cases of more than one *Eurobarometer* survey in the same year. [b] West Germany; East German support weaker, 37–9, respectively.

Sources: As in Table 12.1.

21% in Spain, 20% in Germany and in Italy, 19% in Denmark, 18% in Holland, 17% in Belgium, 16% in Portugal, 14% in Ireland and 11% in the UK. Only in Britain (67%) and in Ireland (58%) was there an absolute majority who said they never felt being a citizen of Europe.[35]

An interesting, though somewhat oblique, answer to the question of the reasons for feeling a European citizenship was given by a *Eurobarometer* of 1989. The question was: What shows most strongly the existence of a citizens' Europe? The most frequent answer was: unhampered travelling (51%), followed by young people's possibilities to study in other EC countries (44%), and the possibility of buying foreign products without having to pay customs (42%).[36]

The referenda on Europe in 1992, in Denmark and France on the Maastricht Treaty, and in Switzerland on the EC–EFTA European Economic Area Agreement, showed a considerable popular resistance to Europe. The narrow victory in France, 50.8% in favour and 49.2% against in European (metropolitian) France, and the narrow defeat followed by a narrow victory in Denmark highlighted a fragility of Europeanness, not captured by the *Eurobarometers*. A strong hostility to participation in European unification was also manifested in the Norwegian popular rejection of the EC in 1972, still largely maintained among the Norwegian people. Who, then, are the anti- and who are the pro-Europeans?

The French results were summarized by *Le Monde*. For Maastricht there was a 'rich and urban' population, and against there was 'rural and working-class France', of the north, the centre south of Paris, and of the Mediterranean provinces.[37] A similar pattern is discernible in the other parts of Europe put to test most clearly in the membership referenda in Finland, Norway and Sweden in October to November 1994.[38] People in positions of political, cultural, economic and spatial centrality tend to support the European Union, people in the periphery tend to be sceptical. The EC/EU project remains an élite one. As such it is also primarily a male project, receiving considerably more male than female support.[39] In Switzerland, there was also an ethnic division, with the francophone cantons voting in favour, the German-speaking and Italian-speaking against.[40]

A comparative view from the outside is often very illuminating. Do Europeans identify themselves more continentally than people of other continents? The answer is: not to any significant extent (see Table 12.3).

Within Western Europe a certain unification effect may be ascertained. But for the rest, there is not more of a European than a Latin American or an African identity.

Local and regional identities, in relation to national ones, tend to be stronger in Europe than elsewhere. Only in four of twenty-five European countries was there a plurality of national, over local or regional, identification – in Czechoslovakia, Finland, Iceland and Poland. But it was the case in eight out twelve non-European countries in the same survey – in Canada, Chile, India, Japan, Nigeria, South Africa, South Korea and Turkey.

Table 12.3 *Continental identifications*

Per cent choosing a continental identification as a
first or a second choice of territorial identification, in
1990–91. Unweighted national averages.

Western Europe in EU	16
Western Europe not in EU	9
Eastern Europe	15
North America	10
Latin America	14
Africa	22
Asia	5

Note: EU: all countries except Greece and
Luxemburg. Non-EU Western Europe: Austria,
Finland, Iceland, Norway, Sweden. Eastern Europe:
Belorussia, Bulgaria, Czechoslovakia, Estonia, GDR,
Hungary, Latvia, Lithuania, Poland, Russia. North
America: Canada, USA. Latin America: Brazil, Chile,
Mexico. Africa: Nigeria, South Africa. Asia: China,
Japan.

Source: World Values Survey 1990–1991 (directed
by R. Inglehart), Institute for Social Research,
University of Michigan (data file), variable 320.

The globalization of youth

The arrival of a 'third age' situation of active old age (see Chapter 4 above)
coincided with the beginning of an international, permanent youth culture,
centred on rock music. Its beginning may, perhaps, be dated to 1956, when
Elvis Presley's first hit was released, 'Heartbreak Hotel'. Except for Britain,
Europe has largely been at the receiving end of this new culture, radiating
from the USA. By and large, Britain has kept a central international position
in it even after the 1960s, of the Beatles, the Rolling Stones, and the fashion
of Carnaby Street (cf. Chapter 11 above), whereas Paris has again become
little more than a place to visit, after the extinguishing of the fireworks of the
May 1968 'événements' which for a moment provided the brightest beacon
of rebellion. True, there have occasionally been some local stars of
international glitz, like the Swedish pop group Abba, but on the whole it is
the long-term reproduction of US centrality that is remarkable. The
Eurovision Song Contest, which also started in 1956, has remained a
second-rate protection product, for instance.

From a sociological perspective, the most important aspect is, probably,
the establishment of *an international – largely global – generational culture
which maintains itself from one youth cohort to the next*, with its specific
processes of identifying what it is to be young. The centre of it, insofar as
there is one, is at present probably MTV, broadcasting video music around
almost the whole globe. This is a world of historical novelty, hardly possible

before the electronic media, while on the other hand being a direct effect neither of the gramophone, film, radio, nor of television. The international simultaneity and the reproductive capacity are new.

New also is the amount of money involved. Youth has become big business, and young megastars, not only in music but also in professional sports, general entertainment and fashion design, have become some of the highest income-receivers on earth. Stars are not new. Theatre, ballet, film, produced them too. What *is* new is their number and their wealth, which makes it a rational pursuit for hundreds of thousands of young people to try to become a rock musician or a professional sportsman/woman.

Youth cultures go back to pre-industrial Europe, but before current times they were overwhelmingly local – *qua* cultural orientations, if not in their structural parameters – with some national, and occasional even cross-national, streaks from the culture of wandering journeymen, like the original Tour de France.[41] Explicit youth movements developed in the aftermath of the French Revolution, and of the July Revolution. Mazzini's Young Italy movement and Young Europe aspirations came to set an international model of patriotic, anti-traditionalist youth movements.

The '1968 generation' may be seen as one in a rather small set of especially formative 'historical generations'. Others include the early-nineteenth-century Young Europe; the post-Victorian turn-of-the-century generation of mass organizations like the Scouts, and the Wandervögel; Socialist and religious youth mobilizations; the Spanish generation of 1898; the 1930s Depression generation; and of a new wave of youth mobilization: Fascist and anti-Fascist, Social Democratic and rural in Scandinavia.[42]

Of more enduring importance than the 1968 generation, however, is this global, US-(UK-)centred culture of cohort upon cohort of young people. It spread through Eastern Europe as well, and was partly incorporated into the repertoire of Communist youth supply, partly, and much more significantly, the rallying cry of dissidence, such as of the Václav Havel circle and Charter '77. In Communist Czechoslovakia the music of the Velvet Underground acquired the political qualities of mid-nineteenth-century Verdi operas.

Contemporary youth culture is, of course, not homogeneous. It is structured by class, gender and ethnicity, and its concrete manifestations tend to operate like fashion cycles. But the phenomenon as such remains persistent. The combination of global media exposure and relatively loose local attachments – to families and jobs – is a powerful force of enculturation. It is expanding not only in space, but also in time. International music styles are now being embraced by, for instance, Swedish daycare kids, and probably also by more lonely pre-school MTV watchers in many other countries.

The material infrastructure of this youth world consists primarily of communications media, the prolonged system of education and the loosening grip of parents. The expansion of education was even more drastic than that of the welfare state and the pension system. Most dramatic was the change, and its consequences, in France and Italy (see the next chapter).

In a more low-key sense, Western Europe has of old had a longer youth period than other parts of the world. That is part of the *(West) European family pattern*, of late marriages (and relatively high rates of never marrying), and, especially after the war, of more frequent leaving of the parental home before marriage.[43] In other words, the narrower European systems of higher education than in the USA and Japan (see below) are, in a way, compensated for by another age structuration providing youth with a space of its own: a space of individual living, untied by family responsibilities. After a secular decline till 1975, the average age of first marriage has bent upwards again in Europe, to 24.6 years for women at their first marriage and 27.1 for men in the EC.[44]

Now, youth is not only a subject of identity. It is also an object of systems of education, an important part of cognitive enculturation.

Notes

1 F. Barth (ed.), *Ethnic Groups and Boundaries*, Boston, Little, Brown & Co., 1969, p. 15.
2 See the next section and the section on class voting in Chapter 14.
3 R. Merton, *Social Theory and Social Structure*, rev. and enl. edn, Glencoe, Ill., Free Press, 1957, Chs VIII and IX.
4 Cf. G. Therborn, *The Ideology of Power and the Power of Ideologies*, London, NLB/Verso, 1980, pp. 22ff.
5 E. Hobsbawm, *Nations and Nationalism since 1780*, Canto edn, Cambridge, Cambridge University Press, 1991, pp. 127–8.
6 The explicit analytical awareness of the importance of recognition varies widely across the subfields of identity formation. It is central in the Hegelian philosophy of history, recently resurrected by Francis Fukuyama, to whom 'history' is a 'struggle for recognition': F. Fukuyama, *The End of History*, New York, Free Press, 1992, Part III. Cf. C. Taylor et al., *Multiculturalism and 'The Politics of Recognition'*, Princeton, Princeton University Press, 1992.
7 *Frankfurter Allgemeine Zeitung*, 25.11.93, p. 15; *Le Monde*, 19.11.93. p. 2.
8 *Le Monde*, 26–27.12.1993, p. 7.
9 Cf. C. Lane, *The Rites of Rulers*, Cambridge, Cambridge University Press, 1981, Ch. 8.
10 *The Economist*, 25.12.1993–7.1.1994, p. 16.
11 Lane, *Rites of Rulers*, pp. 143ff.
12 The literature on collective European rituals and ceremonies is overwhelmed by the monumentality of the work by Pierre Nora (ed.), *Les lieux de mémoires*, Paris, Gallimard, 1984–93, 7 vols. A European follow-up is presented in *le débat* 78 (janvier–février 1994). Also bewilderingly rich and without a sharp focus is Ralph Samuel (ed.), *Patriotism: The Making and Unmaking of British Identity*, London, Routledge, 1989, 3 vols. To my knowledge there is little of any compact, systematic comparability. More pictorially –'imagologically'– oriented is H. Dyserinck and K.U. Syndram (eds), *Europa und das nationale Selbstverständnis*, Bonn, Bouvier, 1988. Focused but selective and largely hooked up in the immediate postwar years is G. Namer, *La commémoration en France de 1945 à nos jours*, Paris, SPAG, 1983. The national overviews above and below have been pieced together from a number of sources, including the current national press. A certain skeleton of national dates of memory and ceremony can be found in A. Fierro, *L'Europe des différences*, Paris, Bonneton, 1991; and D. Visser, *Flaggen, Wappen, Hymnen*, Augsburg, Battenberg, 1991. (The latter contains a bit more than its title suggests.)

13 *Financial Times*, 17.12.1993, p. 9.
14 The 'Fête de l'Humanité' has as one of its purposes to collect money for the Communist paper of that name. In spite of the increasing isolation of the French CP, the Festival has maintained a good part of its popular character.
15 There is no proper international history of Mayday. But there are two richly illustrated catalogue books, originally made for exhibitions, which have a universal scope. The most scholarly, but the one least useful for our purposes because it covers mainly the first decades, is A. Panaccione (ed.), *The Memory of May Day*, Venice, Marsilio, 1989. The other has a better time coverage, but the individual contributions are very uneven. Many are largely miniatures of political history, from a Communist Party point of view, rather than proper analyses of Mayday celebrations: A. Achten et al. (eds), *Mein Vaterland ist International*, Oberhausen, Asso, 1986. Eric Hobsbawm has lent a scholarly hand with 'Mass-Producing Traditions: Europe, 1870–1914', in E. Hobsbawm and T. Ranger, (eds), *The Invention of Tradition*, Cambridge, Cambridge University Press, 1983 from where I learnt about Russia in 1917. Jens Flemming, 'Der I. Mai und die deutsche Arbeiterbewegung', in U. Schultz (ed.), *Das Fest*, Munich, C.H. Beck, 1988, treats the pre-World War II German case. An odd mixture of historiography and Communist pamphlet is Philip Foner's *May Day*, New York, International Publishers, 1986. For the rest I have relied on participant observation and national newspapers. I also want to acknowledge my debt to a so far unpublished study of the Finnish Mayday tradition by my friend and colleague Risto Alapuro.
16 The absolute relationship of the number of badges sold to the number of demonstrators is impossible to ascertain. Badges are sold prior to 1 May as well as at the demonstrations. Not every demonstrator has a badge, not every buyer of badge takes part in the rallies. Some badges are no doubt commissioned and accounted for by activists, but never sold to individual users. Nevertheless, there is little reason to suppose that anything of this should substantially alter the significance of the indicator over time.
17 This holds not only with regard to the US but also, for instance, with regard to Australia: G. Evans, 'Class Conflict and Inequality', in R. Jowell et al. (eds), *International Social Attitudes: The 10th BSA Report*, Aldershot, Dartmouth, 1993, p. 126. Cf. E.O. Wright, 'The Comparative Project on Class Structure and Class Consciousness: An Overview', *Acta Sociologica* 32,1 (1989), p. 13.
18 E. Noëlle and E.P. Neumann (eds), *The Germans: Public Opinion Polls*, 1947–1966, Westport, Conn., Greenwood, 1981, p. 178.
19 Both Christian Social Bavarian and leading Social Democratic *Länder* politicians have declared themselves for an instrumentally pragmatic approach to national celebration in the above-mentioned direction: *Frankfurter Allgemeine Zeitung*, 15.4.1994, p. 4.
20 P.-C. Witt, 'Die Gründung des Deutschen Reiches von 1871 oder dreimal Kaiserfest', in Schultz, *Das Fest*, pp. 313ff.
21 *Turkish Daily News*, 26.2.1994, p. 1.
22 M. Czaky, 'Historische Reflexionen über das Problem einer österreichischen Identität', in H. Wolfram and W. Pohl (eds), *Probleme der Geschichte Österreichs und ihrer Darstellung*, Vienna, Verlag der Österreichischen Alademie der Wissenschaften, 1991, quote on p. 31; E. Brockmüller, 'The National Identity of the Austrians', in M. Teich and R. Porter (eds), *The National Question in Europe in Historical Context*, Cambridge, Cambridge University Press, 1993, p. 199.
23 *El País*, 2.10.1993, p. 6.
24 On the Walloon movement of the 1990s I have learnt from *De Standaard*, 18–19.12.1993, p. 4.
25 A.G. Minet (ed.), *Les Lettres d'Egypte de Gustave Flaubert*, Paris, 1965, p. 119, here cited from J. Lagoudis Pinchion, *Alexandra Still*, Cairo, American University in Cairo Press, 1989, p. 25.
26 Cf. P. Rabinow, *French Modern*, Cambridge, Mass., MIT Press, 1989, pp. 288ff
27 Colonial Shanghai, by contrast, seems to have been more 'foreign', i.e. non-Chinese, than 'European', given its significant Japanese and American presence.

28 H.P. Schwarz, *Adenauer: Der Staatsmann, 1952–1967*, Stuttgart, Deutsche-Verlags-Anstalt, 1991, p. 296.

29 Saint-Simon, Comte, Spencer.

30 W. Lipgens, *Europa-Föderationspläne der Widerstandsbewegungen, 1940–45*, Munich, Oldenburg, 1968. Cf. F. Bédarida, 'Frankreich und Europe – von gestern bis heute', in W. Mommsen (ed.), *Der lange Weg nach Europa*, Berlin, edition q, 1992, pp. 5ff.

31 R. Inglehart, *Culture Shift in Advanced Industrial Society*, Princeton, Princeton University Press, 1990, p. 418.

32 *Eurobarometer* 36, here cited from *Frankfurter Allgemeine Zeitung*, 9.12.1991, p. 11.

33 *Eurobarometer* 34, December 1990, Figure 2.5.

34 And 4% did not know: S. Harding et al., *Contrasting Values in Western Europe*, London, Macmillan, 1986, appendix, question 346a.

35 *Eurobarometer*, December 1986, here quoted from *Journal für Sozialforschung* 27 (1987), Meinungsprofile pp. 373ff.

36 *Journal für Sozialforschung* 30, 1 (1990), Meinungsprofile, pp. 74ff.

37 *Le Monde*, 22.9.1992, pp. 2–4, 9.

38 Workers and women were generally skeptical of EU, and the worker populations of the northern parts of the three countries were particularly negative. Norwegien opinion was the one most polarized, both attitudinally and territorially. In the capital, Oslo, 66.5% wanted to join the EU, whereas 53.5% of the national electorate said no, and more than 71% of the voters of the three northernmost provinces of Norway voted no. *Svenska Dagbladet*, 27.11.1994, p. 13; *Dagens Nyheter*, 15.11.1994, p. A9. On Denmark, see further K. Siune et al., *Det blev et nei*, Copenhagen, Politiken, 1992; *Dagens Nyheter*, 6.9.1993, p. 2.

39 *Eurobarometer* 39, June 1993, p. A18.

40 *Le Monde*, 8.12.1992, p. 4.

41 Cf. J. Gillis, *Youth and History*, expanded edn, Orlando, Fla., Academic Press, 1981; M. Mitterauer, *Sozialgeschichte der Jugend*, Frankfurt, Suhrkamp, 1986.

42 Cf. R. Braungart, 'Historical Generations and Youth Movements', in R. Ratcliff (ed.), *Research in Social Movements: Conflicts and Change*, Greenwich, Conn., JAI Press, 1984.

43 Cf. H. Kaelble, *Auf dem Weg zu einer europäischen Gesellschaft*, Munich, C.H. Beck, 1987, pp. 18ff.

44 Eurostat, *Demographic Statistics*, Luxemburg, 1990, p. 186.

13

HORIZONS OF KNOWLEDGE AND TIMES OF BELIEF

Postwar Europe saw the final arrival of general and extended formal education, even into the Eastern and the Southern parts, although doubts about the universality of functional literacy have continued to persist in many countries. Secondary and tertiary education became mass phenomena, Europe here catching up with the United States.

The coming of *television* changed the scope of everyday knowledge, as well as the forms of leisure, in ways that still have to be ascertained.[1] It came from the USA into Britain and Sweden in the 1950s, rapidly spreading across the continent, reaching the masses of Spain and of most of Eastern Europe in the 1970s, those of Greece and Portugal, Romania and Yugoslavia in the 1980s (Chapter 7 above).

While it seems obvious that cross-border television contributed to the corrosion of the Communist ideological armour in the East, there appear to be no tangible effects demonstrated. Nevertheless, between 1985 and 1988 West German television became the majoritarian medium of young people in the GDR.[2] As we shall see in the next chapter, this at least correlates with a mounting distanciation from the East German regime.

A reasonable hypothesis is that the effects of television are most important in shaping people's world and life perspectives in countries with weak literary mass cultures and weak associations. The Southern countries in the EU, for instance, have small newspaper circulations, have until recently had an illiterate section of the population, and – in the cases of Spain and Portugal in 1990 – devote an unusually large amount of time to TV-watching.[3]

The rise of commercial television in Europe in the course of the 1980s and 1990s, with the lightest entertainment as a major weapon of competition, is reproducing in new forms a division between élite and mass knowledge, a longstanding division characteristic of the British press, but one not as pronounced on the continent.

The first breakthrough of TV politics in Europe came in the spring of 1994 with Italy's media mogul Berlusconi succeeding in catapulting himself into the Premiership. That took place only after the collapse of the postwar political system, but it may very well inaugurate a new era of imaginary politics.

The corpus of scientific and technological knowledge has expanded enormously. Our period under review opened in the shadow of the *science of death*, with the German industrial perfection of Auschwitz and the American scientific jumps into nuclear and hydrogen bombs. The peculiar stability of the ensuing Cold War was due to an equilibrium of annihilation capacity.

But while high politics has had to look to 'mutually assured destruction', socially most important has probably been the widening of the horizon of the *life sciences*, from the early diffusion of penicillin to the unlocking of the genetic code (in 1953) and the recent beginnings of genetic engineering, via the contraceptive pill, which spread in the 1960s. Most spectacular were excursions into *space*, an offshoot of Cold War rivalry and military technology, pioneered by the Russians, who sent the Sputnik into space in 1957.

Cognition and the production of knowledge are being transformed by the *computer* revolution, of computer-aided design and manufacturing and of the introduction of the personal computer into ordinary knowledge production, a phenomenon, in the more developed countries, of the 1980s and on.

How the tempo of cognition has developed in the postwar period is still hard to discern, and to distinguish from the dramatic rise of the number of scientific papers produced and published. In terms of technological innovations, including the intervention of scientific instruments, the postwar period as such has not distinguished itself. There appears to be a certain consensus that for the first three-quarters of this century the most innovative period in the above sense was the years just before the war, in 1935–9[4] – the geography of the production of novel scientific knowledge changed dramatically in the postwar era, away from Europe, and from Western Europe in particular.

Postwar Europe was turned towards the future, a new future to be constructed. As such it was overwhelmingly modernist, in the West as well as in the East. But hopes in revolution, in democracy or national self-determination were tempered in comparison with post-World War I expectations. The Depression, Fascism and the new, even more destructive war had taught a certain amount of modesty in the face of the forces of evil.

When Jean-Paul Sartre presented Europe's arguably most significant postwar intellectual journal, *Les Temps Modernes*, a title inspired by Chaplin's prewar movie, in August 1945, he said nothing about modernity or 'modern times'. His focus was on 'total man. Totally committed and totally free.'[5] Post-World War II modernity was low key, but it was omnipresent, from poetry to political rhetoric, from architecture to social engineering.

In the 1970s the modern times were a-changing. A new disbelief in the future raised its head, questioning the very meaning of modernity, aesthetically, economically and politically. In the 1980s, the notion of 'post-modernity' set arguments on fire.

This chapter will deal with only a few of its possible topics, primarily reflecting the limitations of the writer, perhaps also to some extent those of his discipline. (And some practical mishaps, which make a systematic approach to the organization of knowledge, professional or otherwise, practically impossible.)

Systems of mass education

It was only after the war that basic illiteracy ceased being reproduced in Europe, with all children going to school. In Albania this occurred some time after 1965, in Portugal and, by and large, in Yugoslavia just after 1970, in Spain in the 1960s, in Italy in the 1950s, and in Greece and the rest of Eastern Europe in the 1950s or late 1940s. Around 1960, half of all Greeks and Bulgarians above 65 years of age were illiterate, a third of all Spaniards, and a quarter of all Italians of that age.[6]

The general level of education has risen, and the sharp demarcations between illiterates, people who leave after primary school, and an educated élite have been replaced by more gradual differentiations. But there seems to have been no general trend of equalizing educational opportunities among youth of different social backgrounds. Class structuration still operates, but at a higher educational level, which is what we found above with regard to occupational mobility. Nor has Communism produced any strong and consistent systemic effects on education.

The class quota rules for access to higher education, which the Eastern European countries were operating for at least about a decade after the war, have had measurable effects, but unevenly and temporarily. In Poland and Hungary this policy led to considerably more equal life chances, but in Czechoslovakia no effect was found in comparing Communist and pre-Communist age cohorts. In Poland a tendency back to a *de facto* more socially closed educational system appears to have set in in the 1970s. (With regard to élite recruitment we noted in Chapter 8 above the same kind of reversal in Czechoslovakia and in Hungary.) Only the Netherlands and Sweden show persistent trends of equalizing access to education in the course of the twentieth century.[7]

The ratios of the high education odds of children of higher white-collar strata and those of working-class children are less in Poland and Hungary than in Western Europe, but are hardly different from those in Sweden. (Comparable data for Czechoslovakia and the GDR are not available.) France stands out as having a particularly élitist system. The earlier US lead in educational opportunity seems to have been overtaken by Sweden for the cohorts born after 1950 (1950–64).[8]

Implied, or sometimes explicit, in the results of the educational mobility studies is that there seems to be no strong, persistent effect of the primary and secondary educational system as such upon educational opportunity. There is a tendency for comprehensive school systems, like those in the Nordic countries, Scotland and Communist Eastern Europe, to have egalitarian effects. But apparently they can be counteracted or compensated for by other mechanisms.

The break-up of the comprehensive school in East Germany and its replacement with the tripartite division of post-primary education dominant in West Germany will provide an interesting test. So far (April 1994), the appreciation of the educational changes by the East Germans has been negative. Out of a representative adult sample, 36% thought that education in schools had deteriorated after re-unification, while 22% thought that it had improved.[9]

One of the findings of Walter Müller and his associates working on education and class mobility in Europe has been that countries differ less in their degree of access into higher education or into occupational destinations than in the *relationship between educational qualification and occupational destination*.[10]

'Credentialism', the requirement of formal educational credentials, is most developed in Germany, Hungary, Sweden and, at the top, in France, and least in the British Isles. Müller explains the difference primarily by the historical role of the state in the shaping of the professional-managerial class, a major state role leading to high credentialism.

According to Walter Müller's analysis, which refers mainly to the situation before the educational expansion of the 1960s and 1970s, below the top occupational positions, the educational qualifications of European classes tended to form a tripartite national pattern. France constituted one pole, with the least educated white-collar, petit-bourgeois, farming, and working classes, and Germany the other, with the most educated. In-between France and Germany were the other countries, differing insignificantly among themselves.[11]

This pattern derives from the very extensive system of organized vocational training in Germany, and the particularly restrictive French system of higher education, coupled with very little special vocational education.

However, since the 1960s and 1970s, the French set-up, more than most, has changed considerably (see below). In the EC labour force survey of 1989, 74% of the French reported having acquired some vocational training, a figure below the German one of 87%, on par with the Danish (of 76%), and above the Community average of 66%. The fewest skilled people were found in the UK (48%) and in Ireland and Portugal (both 50%).[12]

A massive expansion of education has been a general postwar phenomenon, but even with the expansion and a catching-up the relative narrowness of the road of higher education has been maintained in Western Europe, and even more so in Eastern Europe (see Table 13.1).

Between 1960 and 1970 the number of students in higher education trebled or more in France and in the Nordic countries, and almost trebled in Italy and Belgium. Little wonder that the educational system burst asunder. The absolute numbers involved alone made the latter into a significant societal crisis. The national pattern is not uniform, however. England and

Table 13.1 *The expansion of higher education in Western Europe,*
1960–1975 (university and other tertiary education; thousands and per
cent of population aged 20–4)

Country	1960 Thous.	1960 %	1965 %	1970 %	1975 Thous.	1975 %
England/Wales	103	3.6	5.5	6.1	237	8.9
France	250	8.7	16.4	17.7	752	22.9
Italy	190	4.9	8.6	13.6	562	18.8
Austria[a]	23	4.9	5.9	10.7[b]	56[b]	16.0
Belgium	41	7.3	13.2	16.4	118	18.2
Denmark	19	6.1	9.4	15.6	64	21.9
Finland[a]	18	5.8	8.8	12.8	58	18.1
Ireland[a]	11	6.9	9.1	9.9[b]	21[b]	9.9
Netherlands	63	7.9	9.9	13.2	159	18.8
Norway	9	4.3	7.5	9.4	29	13.0
Sweden	32[c]	7.0[c]	10.3[d]	16.8[e]	114[e]	19.3
Switzerland[f]	34[g]	7.6[g]	7.8[h]	9.5[i]	43[i]	10.0[j]
Scotland	26	7.7	10.8	11.0	44	13.8
W. Germany	261	5.6	7.7	11.5	428	17.4

Notes: [a] Universities only. [b] 1971. [c] 1959. [d] 1964. [e] 1969. [f] Percentage calculated on the 15–19 population. [g] 1961. [h] 1967. [i] 1972. [j] 1974.

Source: P. Flora (ed.), *State, Economy, and Society in Western Europe, 1815–1975*, Vol. 1, Frankfurt, Campus, 1983, Ch. 10.

Wales – the United Kingdom is not quite united as far as its educational system goes – Ireland, and, in particular, Switzerland kept a much more narrow system, and the main expansion in Germany, the Netherlands and Austria took place somewhat later, in the early 1970s.

The USA pioneered higher mass education. In 1950 one-fifth of American 20-to-24-year-olds were enrolled in higher education, in 1960 almost one-third.[13] The North Atlantic gap has decreased since then, but it has not disappeared.

The Eastern European countries, which expanded higher education after the war and introduced social quotas – class, rather than gender and ethnic ones – were more cautious in letting higher education grow. In the end they stayed clearly behind Western Europe in the supply of tertiary education. According to the admittedly crude Unesco measure of tertiary education students per 100,000 population, there were in 1989 2,431 students in Western Europe and in Eastern Europe 1,415, in both cases unweighted averages.[14] Portugal, with 1,525 students per 100,000 population, was the only Western country crossing the Eastern border. East Germany, with 2,683 in 1988, the only one trespassing in the Western direction. After the GDR, it was the USSR which had the highest number of third-degree students in Eastern Europe, at 1,846 per 100.000 in 1989.

That clear-cut East–West division is of recent date, however, an outcome of Eastern retrenchment in the 1980s. In 1980, the Soviet Union had more students per population than Austria, Greece, Ireland, Portugal, Spain, Switzerland and the UK, and virtually as many as France and Italy. Also Poland then had a relatively larger student population than Switzerland, the UK and the poor Western countries.

Table 13.2 *The proportion of youth obtaining a first university degree or equivalent qualification in the OECD countries in 1987 (per thousand 22 to 23-year olds, or 23 to 24-year-olds)*

Austria	72
Belgium	146
Denmark	129
Finland	124
France	159
Greece	117
Italy	76
Netherlands	80
Spain	96
UK	148
W. Germany	128
New World[a]	*229*
Japan	223
USA	241

Note: [a] Unweighted average for Australia, Canada and the USA.

Source: OECD, *Education in the OECD Countries*, 1987–88, Paris, 1990, p. 113.

The (more or less) Anglo-Saxon New World in general, not just the United States, provides more higher education than Western Europe (see Table 13.2). Again, as in the trajectory of occupational structure, in welfare state building and in social mobility, we find the Japanese, in their own way, taking a route of contemporary development more similar to that of North America than to the European. In other cultural respects we shall find it rather the other way around. In any case, 'development' is not a single road, nor is modernity a one-room flat.

It is now about a century since *women* began to be allowed into higher education. The current gender structure of higher education exhibits considerable international variation. By the late 1980s, most parts of Eastern Europe, a good part of Western Europe, and of the New Worlds had reached an equal gender distribution or even in several cases a female over-representation. But there are also significant exceptions to equality.

A curious Central European pattern of keeping women at bay emerges from Table 13.3, a pattern linking Austria, West Germany and Switzerland – once a pioneer of openings for women's education, attracting several

Table 13.3 *Misogny in the tertiary education of developed countries (female students as percentage of male students in 1988, in countries of pronounced inequality)*

Western Europe	
Austria	44
Ireland	44
Italy	46
Netherlands	43
Portugal	40[a]
Switzerland	32
UK	46
W. Germany	40
Eastern Europe	
Czechoslovakia	41
Outside Europe	
Japan	38

Note: [a] 1989.

Source: Calculations from Unesco, *Statistical Yearbook 1991*, Paris, 1991, Table 3.10.

resourceful women from the Russian Empire – with Czechoslovakia, whose sexist incomes policies we encountered above in Chapter 7.

An EC labour force survey in 1989 concerning vocational skills found 70% of the men and 59% of the women in the dependent labour force reporting trained vocational skills. In four countries the skilled/unskilled division was roughly gender-equal, in Ireland, with a slight female lead in skills, in Belgium, Greece and Italy. Germany, Portugal and Spain were on the EC average. A larger than average gender gap of skills was found in France (16 percentage points, as against the average 11), and in the UK (18 percentage points gender differential).[15]

Science goes west

Adolf Hitler is very much part of postwar European cultural history, although he took his life among the ruins of Berlin on 30 April 1945, in a late, exceptional moment of good taste. His killing off of most of the Jews devastated the European cultural landscape, and his blend of Fascism and antisemitism destroyed the major part of European science. If not yet millennial, both effects have proved much more long-lived than his twelve-year 'Thousand Years Reich'.

The Nobel Prizes should not be taken as verdicts of history. Behind them is the usual wrangling social scientists should expect. However, while not perfect, they do provide us with an unrivalled roll-call of scientific merit.

Over a long time, and over large areas, they may be taken as fairly representative of international scientific opinion.

It is in this sense, as an indicator of the frontier of scientific knowledge, that the Nobel Prizes of science and economics are of interest here. As can be seen from Table 13.4, World War II constituted a watershed.

Table 13.4 *Nobel Prizes in science and in economics 1901–1993 (by country of residence)*

Country	1901–45	1946–93
France	15	10
UK	26	42
W. Germany	34	26
Other Europe	38	49
Eastern Europe[a]	2	10[b]
All Europe	113	127
USA	24	173
Other New World	2	7
(Ex-)Colonial Zone	1	0
EIM[c]	0	3
Total	140	310

Note: [a] Postwar Communist Europe, included in 'Other Europe'. [b] Excl. East Germany, which received one prize. [c] Countries of Externally Induced Modernization (but never fully colonized): Japan, China, Thailand, Iran, Iraq, Saudi Arabia, Turkey, Egypt, Morocco, Ethiopia et al. Cf. Chapter 1 above.

Source: Calculated from data kindly provided by Nobelstiftelsen, in Stockholm.

The postwar period has seen a spectacular European desertion of the front lines of scientific knowledge in favour of the USA. But from a global perspective, it is at least as striking that almost the whole élite series of scientific knowledge seems to be a game between Western Europe and the USA. Within Europe there is an enormous concentration in Western Europe. However, if Communism had any effect on the attainment of Nobel Prizes, it was positive, increasing the Eastern European proportion of Laureates.

After Sputnik – the first human satellite dispatched into space, by the Soviets in the autumn of 1957 – world public opinion held that 'Russia' was going to lead the world of science. In a Gallup poll in 1960, this was the predominant opinion in Western Europe (Britain, France, West Germany, Holland and Norway), in Uruguay, and in India. The Greeks were split evenly. Only the Americans believed in the USA.[16]

If we divide the Laureates by country of birth, or by education, the US domination decreases significantly, but not decisively. Of the 24 US Laureates in 1901–45, 16 were born in the USA, and 129 of 173 after the war. That is, in 1901–45, 11% of all the Laureates were born in USA, and in

1946–91 42%. Eastern Europe fares better in terms of education. Twenty-two of the post-1945 Laureates were educated in Eastern Europe.

The US domination is spread fairly evenly across the disciplines. After 1945 the United States have conquered 22 of 34 prizes in economics, 51 of 93 in physics, 36 of 75 in chemistry, and 64 of 108 in medicine and physiology.

The absence of the Japanese is striking, capturing only 3 of 310 postwar Nobel Prizes. Any informed social scientist would underwrite the surprising modesty also of Japanese 'human sciences'. How much of this is due to their having something to be modest about, and how much is due to the language barrier and to an abstention from participating in the international exchange of scholars is anybody's guess.

The computer revolution has been directed from the USA, by IBM, by Microsoft, Intel, Motorola, Apple and others. In contrast to their successes in the radio, TV and video areas and elsewhere, the Japanese have (so far) not been able to make it big. The Europeans have hardly even tried, although Sinclair in the UK and Nixdorf in West Germany, for example, have been quite innovative, and even though there are still a few European players in the field.

Table 13.5 *Computers per thousand inhabitants in 1993*

USA	265
Australia	175
Canada	162
UK	134
Singapore	116
France	111
West Germany	104
Japan	84
Italy	57
South Korea	33
Hungary	24
Mexico	13
Ex-USSR	4
India	1
China	1

Source: Die Zeit 11 (1994), p. 11.

Now, the cognitive importance of the spread of computers (see Table 13.5) should not be taken strictly *ad figuram*. Many are just entertainment gadgets. So also are a large amount of the mobile telephones around. Here, however, the old Nordic, and basically Swedish, strength of telephony has asserted itself again. In July 1993, about twice as large a share of the Swedish population as the American one had a mobile phone. After the Swedish lead followed, closely, Finland and Norway (Danish data lacking), then Singapore and the USA neck and neck, and, at some distance, the UK, and still later Germany, Italy, Japan and France.[17]

The *Financial Times* has made a very interesting estimate of the cognitive frontiers from a commercial point of view. While no definite truth to believe in, it seems to be a better recent guess than most. The FT distinguishes six areas of frontier technology. European prospects are held to be 'poor' in personal computers, 'fair' in gene splicing, in high-temperature super-conductivity, neural networks and in communications satellites. Europe is held to be 'good' only in magnetic resonance imaging.[18]

A serious sociologist, not working in the field, should be cautious in commenting. But two things might be added, one amateur and one professional. The former would underline the continuing centrality of a few European centres of natural and medical science, for instance the Geneva centre of particle physics, CERN, the Heidelberg centre of molecular biology, and the Paris Institut Pasteur, which finally won the trans-Atlantic AIDS dispute.

With regard to the broad area covered by the French expression 'sciences de l'homme', including both the humanities and the social sciences, I may claim at least a part-professional competence. Here, I think, without going into details, one can discern a historical trajectory. The Americans taught the Europeans a lot from the late 1940s till the 1960s. Paul Lazarsfeld, originally Austrian, coming to Oslo in 1948 on an American scholarship and teaching the first generation of Norwegian sociologists, is one example. Theodor Adorno, the musician, musical critic, philosopher turned sociologist, who could be invoked as a keynote speaker on empirical sociology, learnt in American exile, among German postwar sociologists, is another one.[19] Thereafter, I think it's fair to say that a Western European orientation asserted itself and was even exported to the USA. It becomes a matter of taste where you locate the leading lights. The most prestigious journals still tend to be American in a number of disciplines, however.[20] But in the humanities and in the social sciences many of the intellectual signposts are now Western European rather than North American. In the wide and vaguely drawn field of 'social theory' there is probably only one American, John Rawls, who has had a recent intercontinental influence comparable to that of Pierre Bourdieu, Michel Foucault, Anthony Giddens and Jürgen Habermas.

While world literature is consolidating globally, with the ex-empires 'writing back', science and scholarship are still amazingly provincial. Their most influential contributors still come from and produce their work in only a couple of provinces of the earth.

The future dims: moments of post-modernity

Early postwar Europe was hardly characterized by a straightforward belief in progress, or even a starry-eyed view of the future. The two World Wars, the Depression and the Stalinist trauma had left their imprint. To young people on the left the dawn was certainly rising. Like later volunteers in Cuba,

Nicaragua or Guinea-Bissau, young people from many countries went contributing to the construction of the new Eastern Europe – a railway in Yugoslavia, a stadium in Bucharest, etc. But most intellectuals and politicians of the time were aware of the dialectic of the Enlightenment, even if they hadn't read it.[21]

The French journal *Les Temps Modernes* started, as we noted above, without any fanfare of modernity or of the future. Several of the postwar Communist leaders had seen the evil in their own camp close at hand, without having been numbed and dumbed, although they kept silent – men like Dimitrov, Gomulka and Togliatti. Hugh Dalton may have had a 'song in his heart', when he presented his British budget in November 1945, and British workers were standing tall after a century of deference, but their leader Attlee, with the charisma of an average building society manager (according to Hobsbawm), did not have 'much idea about destiny'.[22]

German anti-Fascist intellectuals saw themselves as an embattled 'democratic élite' hoping for a Christian Socialism, standing on a heap of ruins above the pit of Nazi crimes, surrounded by beaten, resentful, Nazi-seduced masses, precariously protected from the latter, belittled and humiliated by the occupation powers.[23] In Sweden Social Democratic party ideologues were celebrating 'harvest time', but among intellectuals the jubilant modernist mood of the 1930s had given way to predominant experiences of despair and disorientation, well expressed by the key collection of poems, Erik Lindegren's *mannen utan väg* (literally 'man of no way'), and most accessible to non-Swedish readers in the posthumous translations of Stig Dagerman's prose.

On the other hand, it was in the 1950s and the 1960s that people learnt to expect that their economic resources next year would be larger than this and last year's. Since the early 1950s, 'growth' has been a standard goal of all mainstream politics. In left-wing politics, all roads, be they national or universal, however long, were still leading 'to socialism'.

In the realm of art, no new vanguardism asserted itself, but prewar modernism could, for a while, ride on the waves of defeated anti-modernist Fascism. And, *sotto voce*, new vanguard institutions were built, with West Germany offering the most important bases: Darmstadt for music and Kassel (through Documenta) for painting and sculpture.

Modernity's 'will to the future', as Oswald Spengler called it, was later sapped by three different, largely unconnected movements. Together, however, they attacked three of the four main pillars of modernity.

The first was aesthetic and largely North American in origin, although soon spreading to Western Europe. It was a questioning of avant-garde art, of an aesthetics for the future. Instead, it proposed a monumentalization of the present, of commercial mass culture, from the architecture of Las Vegas to the copies of Madison Avenue. It was post-modern architecture and pop art emerging out of the maturing postwar American boom, the lesson of Robert Venturi[24] and the message of Andy Warhol.[25]

Secondly, the meaning of capital accumulation and economic growth was questioned by the Club of Rome, a select global grouping of maverick businessmen and concerned scientists, founded in 1968 by an Italian businessman, Aurelio Peccei, and a Scottish scientist and civil servant, Anthony King. They commissioned a report, by an American research team at MIT, which became a manifesto to the world, *The Limits to Growth*. It appeared in 1972, just before the UN environmental conference in Stockholm, and little more than a year before the oil shock shook the self-confidence of the Western economy. The book is reported to have sold about 10 million copies and spearheaded a new ecological movement of conserving the present (and the past), rather than constructing a new future.[26]

Finally, the bell tolled for left-wing politics and its 'grand narratives' of progress, emancipation, socialism, etc. Thereby the new phrase 'post-modernism' finally stuck. It was a French achievement. Jean-François Lyotard's *La condition postmoderne* appeared in 1979. The author had an impeccable leftist background, being a long-time member of the 'Socialism or Barbarism' (1949–65) group of dissident Trotskysts and linked to the first May '68 movement, the *anarchisant* 22 March Movement. Lyotard's obituary of modernity was part of a series of French farewells. A year later the leftist sociologist Alain Touraine proclaimed 'post-socialism', and the radical journalist and philosopher André Gorz bid solemnly 'adieux' to the proletariat.[27]

The background was also very French. To a matchless extent, the French intelligentsia was of predominantly Marxist persuasion for the first three decades after the war. It was also, more importantly, involved in an increasingly unhappy love affair with Communism, either with the exceptionally crude local keeper of Orthodoxy, with a number of local dissidences, or with the Maoist heresy. The May events of 1968 deepened the rift between the PCF and the dissidents and the heretics, and seemingly strengthened the latter two against the former. When the Maoist 'New Resistance' began to wane in the 1970s, the stage was set for one *coup de théâtre* or other.

First it was the Gulag. The Soviet expulsion of Alexander Solzhenitsyn and the publication in Paris (but in Russian by an *émigré* house) of the first part of *The Gulag Archipelago* immediately became the centrepiece of vintage Parisian polemics. In its frontal attack on the Marxist conception of the Enlightenment tradition, it prepared the ground for what came later. However, in the short run, 'the New Philosophers' were confined to a much enlarged, but still embattled anti-Communist terrain, in danger of being outflanked by the new spectre of 'Eurocommunism', a proudly Western European variant, appealing with considerable success to left Latin European opinion in the mid-1970s.[28]

In France, it seemed from polls and local elections in 1976 and early 1977 that the new Socialist–Communist alliance was going to win the parliamentary elections of 1978. Then, in the autumn of 1977, the alliance soured, and in the end it was, narrowly, defeated in March the following year.

That defeat was the immediate cause of post-modernism, post-socialism and the abandonment of the working-class. All the latter were, of course, eloquently argued and well received by the media arbiters of taste.

For a while there might have been some consternation, because the French left won the Presidential elections of 1981, but when its government got bogged down in the international recession, the verdicts of 1979–80 appeared vindicated again. (There were also other elections, it should fairly be added, which fitted into the Parisian ex-left-wing mood of 1979–80, the rise of Thatcher and Reagan, the ignominious falling apart of the left-of-centre coalition in West Germany.)

Post-leftist post-modernism could also point to the coming of post-industrial society (cf. Chapter 4 above), with its effects upon the industrial working-class's capacity to guide humanity into the future.[29] Then the evaporation of Communism in 1989–91 destroyed the ramshackle bridge to the future that actually existed. And it was not replaced by any other belief in a radiant future. 'Normalcy', a 'normal economy', a 'normal state', 'back to Europe', were the post-Communist slogans. Warren Harding was post-humously rehabilitated.[30]

Avant-garde art, liberal economics and ideology, socialist politics and ideology have been three pillars of modernity. The fourth one has been science. There, there has not been any significant challenge to modernity, i.e. challenging the possibility and the desirability of knowledge accumulation. No respectable body of scientists has yet issued a call for a limit to the growth of knowledge. In the interpretative disciplines which continental Europeans include among the sciences, something called post-modernism has certainly had an impact, but even there there are strong and highly placed defenders of modernity.[31]

True, Helga Nowotny, the distinguished Austrian sociologist of science, has presented a critique, inspired by the aristocratic Finnish philosopher Georg Henrik von Wright and by ecology, of the scientific future concept, in favour of a 'prolonged presence', distinguished by a re-discovery of cyclical time, but integrated into future-oriented perspectives.[32] However, I think it proper to conclude that Nowotny's position, or at least the scientific turns she is referring to, belong to a critical reflexivity of modernity, questioning the naïvetés of straightforward progressivism, rather than to an undermining of the cumulativity of science.

The future has been subjected to scientific investigations, or 'conjectures'. 'Future studies' have since the 1960s become an institutionalized intellectual enterprise – mainly in the USA, Western Europe and Australia – not quite respectable by university standards but sponsored by several governments and corporations. They are big enough to include different schools and rival professional societies, but at present not intellectually vibrant enough to contribute much to a general modernist orientation.[33]

Between the two Universal Expositions in Europe, which this author has visited, in Brussels in 1958 and in Seville in 1992, a clear shift of time frame took place. The Brussels exposition was proudly futuristic, centred on technology, in particular the peaceful use of the atom, as it was then called. Therein it differed from the more backward-looking European performance at the 1939 New York World Fair, where only the Soviet Union managed to match the American sense of modernity.[34] Thirty-four years later, the most central themes were historical – commemorating Columbus in 1492 – and conservationist/environmentalist.

The cultural definition of social modernity adopted in this book makes sociologically important the ideological shifts indicated above. To put it bluntly, one need not have any sympathies with the postures of post-modernism to take seriously their challenge to modernity. Something important in the history of modernity is happening.

But a cautious empirical sociologist or historian ought to refrain from proclaiming the arrival of a new age. The artistic avant-garde may be dead, or at least absent for the time being. The socialist vanguards have disappeared, or gone into hibernation. Currently, the centre-stage of protest is occupied by restorationist movements, religious or nationalist. But the liberal growth view of the world survives, under fairly limited ecological attack. In Europe, the futuristic unification project is still there, uncompleted. Science is still predominantly turned expectantly to the future. There seems to be no compelling reason for excluding a rise of new future-oriented movements. The present gives many people little reason for contentment.

A tiny bit of global circumspection also reveals the provincial character of the post-modernist discourse. Without reflection the latter was trumpeted to the world about the same time as the Chinese leadership was calling for the 'Four Modernizations' of China, of industry, agriculture, science and technology, and defence.

Modernity has come under siege, in Western Europe and in the New Worlds. But it has not surrendered. The possibility of it resuming its march can hardly be denied.

A glimpse of the world outlook of modernity is indicated by the (1990–91) answers to the World Values Survey question about the value of old and new ideas (see Table 13.6).

Scandinavia, Chile and Turkey emerge as the most modernist countries in 1990–1. Taking countries singularly, Chile and Sweden constitute the modernist vanguard. Turkey was the most divided of all, statistically indicated by having the largest standard deviation of all countries in the sample. The historical routes to/through modernity give little guidance here, and there is wide variation within Western Europe, for instance. But, clearly, in spite of all modernizations, achieved or called for, Confucian East Asia (China, Japan, South Korea) appears as the most traditionalist part of the world. The weariness of modernity demonstrated in the USA, quite different from the rest of the New Worlds (including Canada, at 5.3), is also worth noting.

Table 13.6 *The world's belief in old and new ideas in 1990–1991*

Average national scores on a ten-point scale, where the value of 1 indicates the fullest agreement with the statement 'Ideas that have stood the test of time are generally better', and 10 with 'New ideas are generally better than old ones'. In brief, *the higher the score, the more modernist.*

Western Europe[a]	*5.3*
Austria	4.8
Belgium	5.2
Britain	5.2
Denmark	5.6
Finland	5.0
France	5.0
W. Germany	5.0
Ireland	5.0
Italy	5.2
Netherlands	5.7
Norway	5.7
Portugal	5.7
Spain	5.5
Sweden	5.9
Eastern Europe[a]	*5.1*
Belorussia	4.9
Bulgaria	5.6
Czechoslovakia	5.2
E. Germany	5.2
Estonia	5.4
Hungary	4.5
Latvia	4.8
Lithuania	4.9
Poland	5.5
Russia	4.5
New Worlds[b]	*5.3*
USA	4.9
China	*3.5*
Japan	*4.1*
South Korea	*3.9*
Turkey	*5.7*
Ex-Col Zone[c]	*4.9*

Notes: [a] Unweighted averages of countries below. [b] Unweighted averages of Brazil, Canada, Chile, Mexico and the USA. [c] India (4.4) and Nigeria (5.4).

Source: World Values Survey 1990–1991, (directed by R. Inglehart), Institute for Social Research, University of Michigan (data file), variable 324.

The edge of modernity, as indicated by the belief in new ideas, is far from overwhelming. But it is still ahead in Europe, in contrast to the USA, and, above all, Asia. How far this European specificity turns up in current evaluations will be the topic of our next chapter.

Notes

1 It is, of course, possible to draw ideal types, for instance contrasting the 'logosphere', the 'the graphosphere', and the 'videosphere' and their societies, as did Régis Debray, *L'Etat séducteur*, Paris, Gallimard, 1993, pp. 74–5.

2 C. Lemke, *Die Ursachen des Umbruchs 1989*, Opladen, Westdeutscher Verlag, 1991, p. 190.

3 G. Mermet, *Euroscopie*, Paris, Larousse, 1991, pp. 346, 353–4. On their weak associative culture see below Chapter 15.

4 Volker Bornschier summarizes four such calculations, which all point to 1935–9, in his grandiose study *Westliche Gesellschaft im Wandel*, Frankfurt, Campus, 1988, p. 97.

5 J.-P. Sartre, 'Présentation', *Les Temps Modernes* 1 (October 1945). Quotation from p. 19.

6 The sources of this paragraph are: *Unesco Statistical Yearbook 1973*, Paris, 1974, Table 1.4, pp. 71ff; World Bank, *World Development Report 1990*, Oxford and New York, Oxford University Press, pp. 241, 244–5 (Portugal, Albania, Eastern Europe generally); World Bank, *World Tables 1992*, Baltimore and London, Johns Hopkins University Press, 1992, pp. 498, 654 (Portugal, Yugoslavia). So-called 'functional illiteracy', the incapacity to cope adequately with reading and writing in everyday life, has turned out more difficult to eradicate.

7 J. Peschar (ed.), *Social Reproduction in Eastern and Western Europe*, Nijmegen, Institute for Applied Social Sciences, 1990, esp. pp. 131–2, 166, 250ff; Y. Shavit and H.-P. Blossfeld, as reported in R. Eriksson and J. Jonsson, *Ursprung och utbildning*, Stockholm, SOU:1993:85, 1993, p. 355. The countries compared were Czechoslovakia, Hungary, and Poland; England and Wales, Italy, the Netherlands, Sweden, Switzerland; USA; Japan and Taiwan.

8 Eriksson and Jonsson, *Ursprung*, Ch. 10. Eriksson and Jonsson also refer to special reports written for their public investigation by Y. Shavit and H.-P. Blossfeld, and Walter Müller.

9 *Frankfurter Allgemeine Zeitung*, 13.4.1994, p. 5.

10 W. Müller et al., 'Class and Education in Industrial Nations', in M. Haller (ed.), *Class Structure in Europe*, Amonk, NY, M.E. Sharpe, 1990.

11 W. Müller, 'Education and Class Position in European Nations', paper presented at the Conference 'European Society or European Societies? Social Mobility and Social Structure', Gausdal, Norway, 24–7 November 1991, Figures 1–4.

12 *European Economy* 47 (March 1991), p. 25. Self-definitions of vocational training may differ across the nations, but there is no reason to assume that the French position should not have changed radically since the time of mobility surveys. Cf. *Données sociales 1990*, Paris, INSEE, 1990, p. 39. British labour force surveys, for their part, show a lower proportion of non-skilled than the EC study: 32.3% in 1989: *Employment Gazette*, October 1991 (London), p. 561.

13 OECD, *Policy and Planning for Post-Secondary Education: A European Overview*, Paris, 1971, p. 80; idem, *Education in the OECD Countries, 1987–88*, Paris, 1990, p. 109.

14 Unesco, *Statistical Yearbook 1991*, Paris, 1991, Table 3.10.

15 Denmark and Luxemburg are not reported: *European Economy* 47, pp. 25–27.

16 G.H. Gallup, *The Gallup Poll*, Vol. 3, New York, Random House, 1972, 3 vols, p. 1653.

17 *Financial Times*, 11.2.1994, p. 12.

18 *Financial Times*, 2.3.1994, p. 9.

19 R. Wiggershaus, *Die Frankfurter Schule*, Munich, Carl Hanser, 1986, pp. 501ff.

20 In the two disciplines I know of first hand, political science and sociology, this is clearly the case. It also holds for economics, as far as I can see.

21 Max Horkheimer's and Theodor W. Adorno's bitter aphoristical masterpiece *Dialektik der Aufklärung* (*Dialectic of the Enlightenment*) was written mainly at the end of the war, but became more generally available only in 1969, in German (Frankfurt, Suhrkamp), and in 1972, in English, in New York by Herder and Herder.

22 P. Hennessy, *Never Again*, London, Vintage, 1993, Ch. 3.

23 See further W. Schwiedrzik, *Träume der ersten Stunde*, Berlin, Siedler, 1991.

24 R. Venturi et al., *Learning from Las Vegas*, Cambridge, Mass., MIT Press, 1972.

25 Cf. A. Huyssen, *After the Great Divide*, Bloomington, Indiana University Press, 1986, part III.

26 D.H. Meadows et al., *The Limits to Growth: A Report for the Club of Rome's Project on the Predicament of Mankind*, London, Pan/New York, Universe Books, 1972. Cf. P. Moll, 'The Discreet Charm of the Club of Rome', *Futures* 25 (1993).

27 J.-F. Lyotard, *La condition post-moderne*, Paris, Ed. de Minuit, 1979 (*The Post-modern Condition*, Minneapolis, University of Minnesota Press, 1984). Cf. idem, *Peregrinations*, New York, Columbia University Press, 1988. The journal of the group was called *Socialisme ou Barbarie*. A. Gorz, *Adieux au prolétariat*, Paris, Galilée, 1980 (*Farewell to the Working Class*, London, Pluto Press, 1982); A. Touraine, *L'après-socialisme*, Paris, Grasset, 1980.

28 The Parisian eruption of Solzhenitsyn's *Gulag Archipelago*, which nobody could read at first, is vividly narrated by one of its key actors, Jean Daniel, chief editor of the left-of-centre anti-Communist weekly *Le Nouvel Observateur: L'ère des ruptures*, Paris, Grasset, 1979, pp. 184ff. The Eurocommunist possibility is very well conveyed by the introduction of two French scholars to a selection of Eurocommunist documents, M. Bosi and H. Portelli (eds), *Les PC espagnol, français et italien face au pouvoir*, Paris, Christian Bourgeois, 1976.

29 With a Parisian intellectual intuition Alain Touraine had written about post-industrial society at the crest of European industrialism, just before the turn, *La société post-industrielle*, Paris, Denoël, 1969 (*The Post-industrial Society*, New York, Random House, 1971).

30 Some European readers might appreciate a reminder of who Warren Harding was: on the basis of a 'back to normalcy' campaign Harding won the US Presidential election in 1920. Those of us who remember him often think of him as a monument of mercantile mediocrity.

31 Cf. P.M. Rosenau, *Post-modernism and the Social Sciences*, Princeton, Princeton University Press, 1992; J. Habermas, *Die Moderne – ein unvollendetes Projekt*, Leipzig, Reclam, 1992; U. Beck et al., *Reflexive Modernization*, Cambridge, Polity, 1994.

32 H. Nowotny, *Eigenzeit*, Frankfurt, Suhrkamp, 1989, Ch. 2.

33 Cf. R. Homann and P.H. Moll, 'An Overview of Western Futures Organizations', *Futures* 25 (1993); the Editorial of *Futures* 1,1 (1968); the first issue of *Futuribles* 1–2 (1975).

34 D. Nye, 'European Self-Representations at the New York World's Fair of 1939', in R. Krues et al. (eds), *Cultural Transmissions and Receptions*, Amsterdam, VU University Press, 1993, pp. 60, 63–4.

14
VALUES OF CONTEMPORARY MODERNITY

The value patterns of European modernity are first of all those of Christian religion and its secularization, of the nation-state and its citizenship, and of individualism and class. All three refer to dilemmas, conflicts, rivalries, inherent in the European road through modernity.

Then there is also the new issue raised by multiculturalism, with the coexistence of segmented cultures alongside each other; an issue once thought to be solved by a secularization of the state and the assimilation of its inhabitants, by national self-determination, and by individual equality, or, alternatively, by ethnic cleansing and genocide.

This chapter shall try to indicate a few constellations and trajectories on this vast field.

The sceptical continent

The post-World War II period has, until recently, seen two major changes in the religious landscape of Western Europe. One is primarily an outcome of the war and its immediate political effects. The other refers to a new phase in a long-term historical trend. The altered *relationship of Catholicism to the state* is the former, new levels of *secularization* constitute the latter.

As a supra-national organization, moreover one long linked to the medieval socio-political order, the Catholic Church ran into conflict with modern nationalism and liberalism, with the modern state. (Among Catholic populations without any developed political structure of their own, but ruled by rulers of another denomination, however, the Catholic Church could, and did, become a rallying-point of modern nationalism. Ireland and Poland are the best cases.)

In most Catholic countries, nationalists and liberals won the fierce political struggles of the nineteenth and early twentieth century, Belgium being the most clear-cut exception. The result was a relative national, political and administrative marginalization of the true believers. The process of reconciliation and re-integration did begin after World War I – importantly underlined by the 1929 Concordat between the Vatican and Fascist Italy – but was consummated and stabilized only after the World War II.[1]

In this period, explicitly Catholic politicians have become the leaders of a number of modern Western nations, of the Italian state, which the Papacy for more than half a century held anathema, of formerly Protestant-run countries like Germany and the Netherlands. Political Catholicism became part of the state-carrying 'third force' in postwar France, before imploding. In Switzerland Catholics had become re-integrated already after World War I. Portugal and Spain maintained their interwar authoritarian regimes of Counter-Reformation. But when democracy returned, in the second half of the 1970s, both clericalism and anti-clericalism had become irrelevant, not giving rise to any significant Christian Democracy.

In Eastern Europe, the Iberian continuity was broken. The more or less Fascist regimes, in Croatia, Hungary, Slovakia and prewar Poland, with which the Catholic Church had been intimately allied, all fell or were thrown into the dustbin. Little conciliatory spirit was shown on any side.

The heavily compromised Croatian Primate, Cardinal Stepinac, was confirmed in his position by the Vatican, and continued a militantly right-wing posture. His colleague in Hungary, Mindszenty, also chose an uncompromising stand against the postwar social changes. In Czecho-slovakia and Poland, the Church was less intransigent. The Communists, who had the state power, responded with arrests and trials.[2] In the 1950s a sort of Catholic–Communist *modus vivendi* was established in Eastern Europe. But only in intensely Catholic Poland did the Church succeed in continuing to spiritually shepherd its flock.

In largely Protestant East Germany, the success of Communist seculariza-tion was both striking and persistent, in spite of the role that the Lutheran Church played as a shelter for opposition movements in the last years of agony. According to official figures, the proportion of people not professing any religion increased from 7.6% in 1950 to 63.5% in 1989.[3] But the outcome is perhaps best illuminated by the post-*Anschluss* maintenance of the secular youth *rite de passage*, the *Jugendweihe*, a ceremony deriving from the classical German labour movement and very much promoted by the Communist regime. In 1994, about half of all East German 14-year-olds passed the *Jugendweihe*. In East Berlin, the ratio of this secular ceremony to the religious communion was 7.5:1.[4]

The effects of the Second Vatican Council in 1965 were, above all, internal to Catholicism, opening it to the people of the modern world. In the short run, at least, the permeability of the Church to secular influences increased thereby, something which John Paul II is now trying to counteract.

The second major postwar change is *secularization*. This has been most dramatic in the Netherlands, where political, cultural, social and to some extent also economic life had become organized in confessional 'pillars' (*zuilen*), the Calvinist (in turn subdivided into different varieties), the Catholic, the Social Democratic and, more weakly, the Liberal. There were associations of 'Roman Catholic Studs Breeders' and of 'Protestant-Christian Gardeners', as well as employers' and charity organizations, and Social Democratic and Liberal insurance companies, etc. One way of highlighting Dutch secularization is to spot its political expression.

In the twelve parliamentary elections from 1918 to 1963, the Dutch religious parties won between 52 and 58% of the vote. In 1967 the countdown began – 47.5%, then in 1971 41.0%, and to 36.0% in 1972, whereupon the confessional electorate settled around a third of the vote, now captured mainly by an inter-denominational Christian Democracy.[5] In the 3 May 1994 parliamentary elections, the religious Dutch parties caught only slightly more than a quarter of the vote, the inter-confessional CDA receiving 22.2% and the three allied fundamentalist Calvinist parties, SGP, RPF and GPV, together mustering 4.8%.

Though general and generally setting in anew from the late 1960s, secularization has been an uneven process. It has affected the major Protestant Churches more strongly than the Catholic Church, and more fundamentalist brands of Protestantism least. Together with differential fertility this has led to the fact that in the 1980s West Germany, the Netherlands and Switzerland all had Catholic pluralities.[6] Where the Church has been linked with recent national formation, religious beliefs and practices have maintained themselves much better than in other countries. In Europe, such is the case with Ireland and Poland. The relatively strong Orthodoxy in Greece and Romania falls into the same pattern.[7]

On the whole, Europe, West and East, emerges as the continent of secularization (see Table 14.1). The religious distance of Europe to the New Worlds as well as to the ex-Colonial Zone is striking. Within Europe, each half contains one very religious exception to the rule, Ireland and Poland, both Catholic. The Dutch are polarized, having both a strong contingent of non-believers and, on the other side, an even larger community of frequent church-goers. The Nordic countries, like in several other respects, turn out rather similar to Eastern Europe, in particular to the non-Catholic parts of the latter. But even more, the former cluster together with France, the centre of Western European struggles for and against modernity.

It may be seen as an aspect of the secularization process that the remaining cultural influence of religion has become less institutional, more disembodied, more 'purely cultural'. The Catholic Church is still a powerful supra-national institution, but with the modern separation of Church and state, the *de facto* influence of the Pope and the Vatican upon the Catholic nations, even with regard to religiously very sensitive current issues, such as patriarchy, divorce, abortion, is diffuse and indirect, rather than exercised in institutional rulings or formal negotiations.

The Protestant Churches, for their part, are all national, in Germany even provincial, institutions, but for a long time without any special access to the polity and policy-making of their nation. Protestantism, and its subdivisions into Lutheranism and Calvinism, forms a specific inherited cultural resonance to the discussions of contemporary issues in the Protestant countries. Apart from linkages through other contexts, such as the World Council of Churches and the regional-territorial links between the Nordic countries, there appears to be little cooperation between the national

Table 14.1 *Patterns of (ir)religiosity in the early 1990s (per cent)*

Region/Country	Belief in God	Service attendance at least once a month
Western Europe	*75*	*33*
Austria	87	44
Belgium	73	35
Britain	83	25
Denmark	64	11
Finland	76	11
France	62	17
W. Germany	78	33
Ireland	98	88
Italy	85	51
Netherlands	65	31
Norway	65	13
Portugal	89	48
Spain	85	40
Sweden	45	10
Eastern Europe	*55*	*24*
Belorussia	43	6
Bulgaria	40	9
Czechoslovakia	n.a.	21
E. Germany	36	20
Hungary	65	34
Latvia	58	9
Poland	97	85
Russia	44	6
New Worlds[a]	*94*	*52*
USA	*96*	*59*
Ex-Col. Zone[b]	*98*	*80*
EIM[c]	–	*(24)*
Japan	65	14

Notes: [a] Brazil, Canada, Chile, Mexico, USA. Unweighted average, like all others. [b] India and Nigeria. [c] China (1% attending service), Japan (14%), South Korea (64%) and Turkey (38%).

Source: World Values Survey 1990–1991 (directed by R. Inglehart), Institute for Social Research, University of Michigan (data file), variables 147 and 166.

manifestations of the same Protestant faith. There seems to be more interest in broader ecumenical contacts, than in international Lutherdom or Calvinism. True, there has been, since 1973, a Concordat between a large number of Lutheran and Calvinist Churches in Western Europe, now signed by about eighty denominations, but its real effects appear to be very limited. The significant Nordic Lutheran state Churches have not joined.[8]

Table 14.2 *Belief in science*

Dominance scores: per cent of people believing that scientific advances will be of help to humanity minus per cent believing they will be of harm,[a] 1990–1. Unweighted averages and regional ranges.

Region/Country	Average	Range
Western Europe[b]	20.1	0.9–32.2
Eastern Europe[c]	44.7	30.0–66.2
North America[d]	44.1	40.5 47.6
Latin America[e]	27.2	17.0–38.3
Ex-Col. Zone[f]	55.3	42.4–68.2
Japan	18.2	–
Other EIM[g]	53.9	37.3–67.0

Notes: [a] The interviewees could also give more ambiguous answers. The latter are taken into account by the dominance score. [b] Austria, Belgium, Britain, Denmark, Finland, France, Ireland, Italy, the Netherlands, Norway, Portugal, Spain, Sweden, West Germany. [c] Belorussia, Bulgaria, Czechoslovakia, East Germany, Estonia, Hungary, Latvia, Lithuania, Poland, Russia. [d] Canada, USA. [e] Brazil, Chile, Mexico. [f] India, Nigeria. [g] Countries of Externally Induced Modernization, other than Japan, are China, South Korea and Turkey.

Source: World Values Survey 1990–1991, variable 271.

Western Europe is the sceptical continent, with the weakest beliefs in both God and science (see Table 14.2). Its smallest country, Iceland, is the positive outlier (with a pro-science dominance score of 41.2%, not included above). Western Europe ranges between two Nordic countries: between the most sceptical Norwegians, among whom the believers and the disbelievers in science are almost equal – 0.9% being the plurality of believers in science, followed by the Austrians (6.8%) and the Dutch (8.0%) – and Norway's western neighbour, Iceland, or, if discounted, Norway's closest, eastern, neighbour, Sweden (32.2%).

Whereas the Catholic Irish have a Western European scepticism towards science (dominance pro-science score 15.2%), their Polish brethren and sisters are enthusiastic, holding the European record of scientism, 66.6%.

Taking beliefs in God and science together, Europeans and Japanese emerge as the sceptics of the world, delimited from the believers in the New Worlds, in the ex-Colonial Zone, and in a Muslim country of Externally Induced Modernization, like Turkey.

... and the challenges of multiculturalism

It would be wrong, however, to end this discussion on a note of cool complacency. Scepticism and supra-ideological assimilation are recent phenomena as predominant Western European features, and their very foundations are being challenged in new ways.

The capital of Western Europe, Brussels, is very much at the centre of these challenges, with more than a quarter of its population being foreign, drawn apart by intra-Belgian conflicts, bewildered by dramatic post-industrialization, polarized between privileged Eurocrats with their hangers-on and poor Muslim immigrants who try to make use of the traditional religious rights accorded Catholics, and fragmented by nineteen different municipalities. So far, nobody in his or her right mind could say that the capital of the EU has stood level to the challenges.[9]

In Chapter 3 we found that ethnic, and thereby largely cultural, homogeneity culminated in Europe in the 1950s, after which the picture began to change, with the historical reversal, in the early 1960s, of five centuries of continental out-migration turning into immigration.

Antisemitism did not die with Hitler. It was clearly kept alive in the final period of Stalin's reign, most sinisterly in the concocted 'Doctors' Plot' of his last days. It was always a sensitive issue in Communist Eastern Europe, because Jews had traditionally, and also after the war, been more attracted to Communism, Communist politics and Communist intellectual life than other ethnicities. On the basis of a persistent, latent popular antisemitism, Jew-baiting could always be used in opportunistic in-fighting among the rulers. The worst post-Stalinist case was Poland in 1967–8.

In West Germany antisemitism receded slowly. While somewhat less than half of the population had no opinion, a clear majority of the West Germans who had one thought at the end of 1952 that a Germany without Jews would be a better Germany. Only in the mid-1950s was this distribution of opinion reversed. The first recorded reversal is dated April 1956. In March 1960 a majority of those who had any opinion would *not* agree to 'a very able' Jew becoming a Federal Chancellor. That rejection was common to Christian Democrats, Social Democrats and Free Democrats but the rejection of a Jew was most pronounced among the supporters of the liberal Free Democrats. A year later a majority of the population was still unreservedly against marrying a Jew(ess).[10]

If a new wave of anti-ideology should emerge in Europe, it is more likely to be anti-Islamic than anti-Jewish, if for no other reason than that Muslims are more recent, therefore more different, and now becoming more numerous.

While everywhere a tiny minority, the arrival of new religious communities – mainly Muslim, but in Britain also Hindu and Sikh – poses new challenges to secularized states and historical religious compromises.

The first major mosques in Europe, outside the ex-Ottoman area, were built in the 1920s. One in Berlin, primarily catering to diplomats and guest students, the other in Paris, expressing the particular character of French colonial power over North Africa. Since the mid-1960s there has been a spectacular growth of Islamic places of worship in France, from 68 in 1975 to 912 in 1985.[11] Islam has become a significant minority in Europe.

The number of Muslims is not exactly known. There seem to be about 3 million in France, 2 million in Germany and 1 million in Britain, and you find them also in the of old homogeneously Lutheran Nordic countries.[12]

Indeed, Europe is becoming increasingly central to Islam and Islamic debate. This is mainly due to the wider freedom of expression in Europe in contrast to the heartlands of Islam.[13] But the new Islamic centrality of Europe also has its ugly side. The persecution of Salman Rushdie was instigated from the South Asian Islamic community of Bradford, England, and its two most representative victims, so far, have been the imam and the vice-imam of the Brussels Muslims, both killed.

The building of mosques, the raising of Islamic demands for education – e.g. in Brussels in 1989 Muslim demands for the application to Islam of the state–Catholic Church compromise on public support for confessional education, the wearing of 'Islamic dress' to school, a concern with morality in public education, the establishing, in France, of a Muslim university, etc., all natural demands of a religious community familiar from continental European history, have led to cultural friction, challenging secularization and Christianity alike.[14]

For about twenty years a largely religious 'low-intensity' war has been going on in a part of Western Europe, in Northern Ireland between Catholics and Protestants, with no end in sight till the end of 1994. The break-up of Communism has already cleared the deck for religious, or religion-reinforced, conflicts in the Balkans, the Ukraine, in Caucasus and in Central Asia. Greek Orthodoxy, Catholicism, (different tendencies of) Islam and, perhaps, American Protestantism are major competitors for the vast new markets of souls in Eastern Europe and in the area east of Europe's borders.

At the moment of writing there is no firm basis for predictions regarding the European periphery, neither of peaceful competition nor of religious wars and new religious conflicts. But the process of secularization has been stopped there, for the time being, and it is being questioned in centres of the continent.

If there is a peaceful solution, it will hardly be either secularization/assimilation or the shining path of the correct belief, but a re-establishment of consciously multicultural society. In other words, a flourishing future multicultural modernity will rather depend upon a modernization of the traditions of al-Andalus, of the House of Osman, of Habsburg Kakanien.

Post-nationalism?

In Western Europe, the postwar period has seen the disappearance of a number of previous national conflicts. Conflicts have evaporated between Norway and Denmark over Greenland, between Belgium and the Netherlands over the Scheldt waterways, and between France and Germany over Alsace-Lorraine. The issue of the partition of Ireland was laid to rest for a couple of decades. The originally dispersed and occupied lands of Western Germany and of Austria were soon re-unified in both cases with little friction.

The return of the Saarland to West Germany and the Italian retention of South Tyrol were, in the end, peacefully settled.

Nation-state conflicts were transcended. While a quarter to a third of Frenchmen had a 'bad or very bad' opinion of their German neighbours in the mid-1950s, by the 1980s polls both in France and in Germany revealed that the other was the best friend.[15] Hot national issues were either frozen or melted down by the socio-political polarization between Communism and capitalism. West Germany became the ally of Britain and France, while East Germany was aligned with the USSR. The Cold War froze the old Macedonian question, and indeed all Balkan issues, along the Yalta borders. It also kept German *irredentisme* under cover and control.

In Eastern Europe, the Soviets were suspicious about regional groupings – breaking with Tito's Yugoslavia over a Balkan federation – but they were even more vigilant with regard to any manifestations of nationalism. National hatred – among Hungarians and Romanians, Hungarians and Slovaks, Poles and Germans, Czechs and Germans, among most Eastern Europeans against Russians, etc. – was papered over by 'proletarian internationalism'.

There is little, if anything, which so clearly demonstrates the new post-nationalist era in Europe, the new *Zeitgeist*, as the fact that none of West Germany's new allies supported an amputation of the new Communist states of Poland and Czechoslovakia in favour of the 1937 borders of the Reich. All kinds of subversion of Communism were legitimate, but not boundary revisions.

For all their Western and low-profile national conception, however, the West German Christian Democrats could never bring themselves to accept voluntarily the postwar map of Europe. But they were powerless to redraw it, and it fell upon the Social Democrats (and the Liberals, shed of their nationalist wing), under the leadership of an anti-Fascist *émigré*, Willy Brandt, to recognize explicitly the post-nationalist era of Western and Central Europe.

By 'nationalism' we mean here the *-ism around the nation-state*, ideological affirmations about its necessary creation – if it isn't in existence – its defence, its extension, its power and glory. As such, nationalism is not synonymous with ethnic values, which pertain to issues of ethnic – however defined – homogeneity and heterogeneity and interests within given state borders and powers.

Postwar Europe experienced a socio-political overdetermination of the national manifesting itself in a more modest national pride.

Even allowing for a wide margin of uncertain interpretations, two differences stand out from Table 14.3. There has been a considerable decrease of national pride in the EEC core of Western Europe since 1970. Secondly, there was around 1990 significantly less national pride in Europe than in other parts of the world, except Japan.[16] Between Eastern and Western Europe there is no general difference in the amount of national pride. The low scorers comprise Central Europe, save Austria-Hungary, and

European modernity and beyond

Table 14.3 *National pride in the world, 1970–1990*

Per cent answering 'very proud' to be (respective nationality). Averages unweighted.

Region/Country	1970	1981	1990
Western Europe	*62*[a]	*32*[a]	*35*[a]
	62[b]	*41*[b]	*45*[b]
Austria	n.a.	n.a.	53
Belgium	70	29	31
Britain	n.a.	53	53
Denmark	n.a.	30	42
Finland	n.a.	n.a.	38
France	66	31	35
W. Germany	38	21	17
Greece	n.a.	76[c]	72[d]
Ireland	n.a.	67	77
Italy	62	40	40
Luxemburg	81	51[c]	62[d]
Netherlands	54	20	23
Norway	n.a.	41	45
Portugal	n.a.	33	42
Spain	n.a.	51	45
Sweden	n.a.	30	41
Eastern Europe	n.a.	*67*[e]	*39*
Belorussia	n.a.	n.a.	34
Bulgaria	n.a.	n.a.	39
Czechoslovakia	n.a.	n.a.	25
Estonia	n.a.	n.a.	30
E. Germany	n.a.	n.a.	29
Hungary	n.a.	67	47
Latvia	n.a.	n.a.	49
Lithuania	n.a.	n.a.	41
Poland	n.a.	n.a.	69
Russia	n.a.	n.a.	26
New Worlds	n.a.	*62*[f]	*62*[g]
Ex-Col. Zone	n.a.	n.a.	*71*[h]
EIM[i]	n.a.	*30*[j]	*46*[k]
Japan	n.a.	30	29

Notes: [a] The EEC 6. [b] All the below. [c] 1983. [d] 1985. [e] Hungary only. [f] Argentina, Australia, Canada, Mexico, USA, ranging from 49 (Argentina) to 76 (the USA). [g] Brazil, Canada, Chile, Mexico, the USA, ranging from 53 (Chile) to 75 (the USA). [h] India (74) and Nigeria (68). [i] Countries of Externally Induced Modernization. [j] Japan only. [k] China, Japan, South Korea, Turkey, ranging from 29 in Japan to 67 in Turkey.

Sources: 1990: World Values Survey 1990–1991, variable 322; the rest: R. Inglehart, *Culture Shift in Advanced Industrial Society*, Princeton, Princeton University Press, 1990, p. 411.

Russia. The two proudest stand out from their context, the Irish and the Poles, as they do in their Catholic zeal.

World War II had a strong impact upon the defeated powers. Only a minority of the population says it is prepared to fight for its country in Germany, Italy and Japan. This holds also for Belgium, but in the rest of the world covered by the latest World Values Survey only for Brazil (see Table 14.4).

Table 14.4 *Willingness to fight for one's country*

Per cent of the adult population willing to fight in case of war. Unweighted country averages.

Western Europe	67
4 major countries of WE	53
Eastern Europe	83
New Worlds	68
NW excl. Brazil	76
USA alone	79
Ex-Col. Zone	86
EIM[a] excl. Japan	92
Japan	20

Note: [a] Countries of Externally Induced Modernization: China, South Korea, Turkey.

Source: World Values Survey 1990–1991, variable 263.

Questions and answers take on different meanings in different contexts. The overall Western European average is inflated by the heroic stance of a few small, peaceful nations who have never fought a modern war – Denmark, Iceland and Sweden, with 89, 77 and 89% prepared fighters, respectively. The average, of 53%, for Britain (74%), France (66%), West Germany (42%) and Italy (31%), is more telling.

In Eastern Europe, only the East Germans (53%) and the Czechoslovaks, the compatriots of the 'Good Soldier Svejk' (66%), harboured widespread reservations about fighting. The Poles, the Belorussians and the Bulgarians were all more than 90% for fighting. (The Poles' Western Catholic-nationalist counterpart, the Irish, stick with the Western European pattern this time, with 61% willing to fight in case of war.)

What causes are Europeans committed to? Putting together two *Eurobarometers*, in 1982 and in 1987, we get the following picture. Two-thirds (63%) were prepared to sacrifice something for world peace. Two-fifths could offer something for human rights (43%), the fight against poverty, the protection of nature and individual freedom (36%). One-fifth (20%) only was open to sacrifice something for national defence.[17]

From 1982 we have a *Eurobarometer* survey of the EU countries (Iberia excepted), of youth and of adults, about causes 'sufficiently worthwhile for you to do something about, even if this might involve some risk or giving up other things for'. From a list of ten items, 'world peace' was mentioned by a majority in all countries, except Ireland. A majority of French and Greek interviewees were prepared to do something about 'the struggle against poverty', for 'human rights', and for 'the freedom of the individual'. Luxemburgians committed themselves against poverty and for human rights. The Dutch also rose to the issue of human rights.

No other issue rallied a majority anywhere. No cause on the list had convinced a majority among the Irish, not even their 'religious faith'. Apart from world peace, nothing had gained a majority among Belgians, Britons, Danes, Germans and Italians. In all countries, concern with poverty and environmental protection was significantly stronger than to national defence.[18] It will be remembered that Reagan's Star Wars and missile rearmament programmes were on the political agenda by the time of the survey.

By way of conclusion, there are behavioural as well as attitudinal reasons for characterizing Western Europe as post-nationalist, defining 'Western Europe' as Europe west of the Oder–Neisse rivers and of the Adriatic.[19] Even if arguably not *post*-nationalist, however, in the late twentieth century this area has become the *least nationalist* part of the world.

The postwar transformation of Germany has been central to this process. Therefore, the current re-emergence, in the wake of re-unification, in certain intellectual and political German circles of an explicitly national, proto-nationalist discourse needs to be followed by all concerned about the future of Europe.[20] So does, of course, the official burial of anti-Fascism by the Italian Berlusconi, part-Neo-Fascist government of 1994. However, this is not (yet) an era of nationalism in the West. This writer's Enlightenment opinion is that Europe will peacefully survive both German re-unification and the creeping Italian rehabilitation of Fascism.

Public collectivism and family individualism

Another syndrome of European cultural modernity may be summarized as characterized by a blend of class articulations of political values, public collectivism and family individualism.

Class articulation of values and identities followed from the endogenous, industrial road to modernity. More than anywhere else in the world, collective identities on the basis of complex and heterogeneous sets of economic position, i.e. class identities, self-conscious cultural cleavages and conflicts between such sets, public discourse about them, and collective organization of them, have played a crucial role in European history, East and West, North and South.

The working-class movement was born in Europe, and its class discourse spread from there. Modern political rights, such as the right to vote, were defined, argued for and fought for in terms of class in Europe, more than anywhere else.[21] Governing parties explicitly referring to themselves as class parties and having established themselves as such in competitive elections are confined to Europe, the antipodal settlements of Europeans (in Australia and New Zealand), the former British colony of Jamaica, and, formerly, to Chile.

The endogeneity of European modernity meant that all the battles for and against a perspective of progress *vis-à-vis* one of experience and tradition, for or against popular or divine rights, were fought out among the natives themselves.

Postwar developments have diluted the density of class milieux, with the new suburbs of the boom, with the de-industrialization since the 1970s, with new patterns of consumption and cultural mediation. On the other hand, class perspectives were also extended, by urbanization, by southern and eastern industrialization, with secularization, and a general decline of traditional deference. The Western European labour movement reached its widest political and industrial influence in the years around 1980.[22]

The current of public collectivism, of support for using public institutions and resources for collective purposes, derives both from the early modern state tradition, of absolutism and constitutional monarchies, and from the challenges of class. Public interventionism was spurred by the opponents, like Napoleon III, Bismarck or Leo XIII, as well as by the adherents of the socialist labour movement. Instead of being weakened, or rendered superfluous, by the postwar boom, this interventionist tendency re-asserted itself around 1960, above all with the enormous expansion of the welfare state. Crucial political battles were won by the interventionists, within West German Christian Democracy and by Scandinavian Social Democracy. In both cases the key issue was a public pension system. (Cf. above Chapter 5.)

There are different kinds of individualism and collectivism in this world. Economic and political individualism have usually gone together with patriarchal family collectivism. Europe's -ism-ic history of clashing ideologies has included most conceivable combinations. Nevertheless, for the last hundred years, and in particular for the past half-century, I think it can be argued that Europe has, more than any other part of the world, had a combination of economic and political forms of collectivism with family individualism.

Several forces have interacted here. The Western and Central European early modern family pattern, with late marriages and a considerable number of people never married, manifested a relative family individualism. It implied a relatively long unmarried period of youth, which facilitated associated action generally, and risky, oppositional action, like working-class action, in particular.

The theoreticians and the leaders of the socialist labour movement – Marx, Engels, Bebel et al. – were at least rhetorically explicitly anti-patriarchal, and, together with a few liberal intellectuals, like J.S. Mill, the socialists were from the beginning women's best friends, although seldom very faithful.

The entrenchment of patriarchy in the family and in civil society generally meant that the establishment of individual rights and freedoms for women and children required state intervention. Sometimes, the European interventionist tradition was applied for that purpose.

Above in Chapter 6 we took notice of how an egalitarian individualist conception of marriage was pioneered by the Scandinavian countries in the 1910s and early 1920s and by the Soviet revolutionaries. Something similar happened with the position of *children*, with respect to which the interdependence of personalistic individualism with interventionist public collectivism is very clearly visible.

By the end of the 1920s the paramountcy of 'the best interests of the child' in family disputes had been established in Scandinavia and in Britain (and in most of the USA).

Mid-1920s Soviet legislation pioneered the prohibition of physical punishment of children. Apparently, this kind of humanitarianism survived well into the brutality of the Stalinist 1930s. When defected peasant soldiers of the USSR were interviewed in 1950–1 by US sociologists, the following verdict on Soviet legislation was recorded: 'Children must obey their parents, but in a free state like the USSR this is impossible.'[23] The norm against physical punishment of children had been internalized, and informants were horrified by seeing children being hit in postwar Germany.[24]

Natalist and accommodationist conservative concerns finally came to lay their heavy hands on the family policy of the Stalinist era, in the USSR from 1944 till the new family code of 1968.[25] But on the whole, one may say that its arrangements of gender and generation relations constitute the most enduringly progressive achievements of Leninism, perhaps the only lasting ones. After the war they were bequeathed to the new rulers of Eastern Europe, but without the avant-garde individualism of the Soviet 1920s, and instead draped in sanctimonious normative exhortations of Stalinist provenance.[26]

Scandinavia has continued to be the children's vanguard, however. After having done away with spanking in schools in the early postwar period, in the 1980s Scandinavians legally forbade parents to spank their children, a right which the Spanish Civil Code of 1981 explicitly gave parents (§155). In this respect the Scandinavians have only been followed by the Austrians, so far. The Nordic countries have also adopted the legal presumption of parents' joint custody/responsibility of their children, regardless of parents' civil status or whether or not they are cohabiting. In the Norwegian case this is coupled with the right of children to seek other guardians, but parents cannot escape their legal responsibilities to their children.[27]

'Post-materialism', class voting and public interventionism

The interesting, now famous, thesis developed by Ronald Inglehart,[28] of a 'culture shift' from 'materialist' to 'post-materialist' values, is not only one of value change. It also explicitly argues for the dwindling significance of class with regard to political evaluations and acts, such as voting.

In our context Inglehart's work raises two issues. Is it true that class has lost its character as a specificity of European politics? Secondly, is it correct that 'post-materialism' indicates a historical turn towards a 'value-based political polarization'?

Without denial of the great value of the empirical work by Professor Inglehart – which I am myself making grateful use of – it seems clear to this writer that his basic thesis of the substitution of a 'value-based political polarization', grounded in a conflict of materialist and post-materialist values, for a 'class-based' one is flawed in two respects. (That something is flawed does not mean, of course, that it lacks substance.)

First, Inglehart's picture of class voting derives from the Anglo-Saxon manual–non-manual distinction and the index of class voting invented by Robert Alford, the percentage of manual voters voting left minus the percentage of non-manuals voting for the left. That was once a handy measure, and Inglehart is in considerable company using it. But there are two problems with it. The major one is its questionable usefulness for comparisons over considerable time. Such comparisons presuppose, that the manual–non-manual social distinction today is more or less the same as it was in the 1950s. The changes of the social structure make that assumption very unlikely.

Swedish pollsters have calculated the size of the structural effect (of very broad categorial changes). With the same structure of non-manual occupations in 1985 as in 1956, the Swedish index of class voting would have changed from 51 to 42, instead of to 34 according to a completely unadjusted manual–non-manual division.[29] More sensitive attention to the changed meaning of being 'non-manual' would certainly have diminished the change even more.

Another relevant critique is more technical, and relates to how class voting should be adequately measured. John Goldthorpe and associates in Britain have argued that class voting should be captured by dividing the odds of manuals voting left or right with the odds of non-manuals doing so. That measure of cross-class voting shows no declining trend of class voting as far as Britain is concerned.[30] In brief, to what extent, and if, class voting has secularly declined remain open to controversy.

Secondly, Inglehart's counter-position of materialist–post-materialist values to class alignment is questionable also with regard to his conceptualization of those values. For some reason, he has given his 'materialist' value a partisan, right-wing orientation. In Western democracies, for most of the time, maintaining order, fighting inflation and crime, keeping a strong defence and, to a lesser extent, maintaining high growth or a stable economy[31] have been right-wing priorities. Left-wing 'materialism' instead would be, fighting unemployment and poverty, ensuring economic equality and social security.

The effect of this is, that Inglehart's 'post-materialist'–'materialist' dichotomy cannot be used as an alternative to class in predicting political alignment, because it is itself to a large extent a traditional left–right opposition. That a left-wing ideology is more likely than working-class membership to be expressed in left voting is little surprising. Nor is the operationalization of the distinction very apt for distinguishing what is usually meant by materialist and non-materialist values.

Because of the partisan operationalization of materialism–postmaterialism, it is not paradoxical, as it should have been, that the most clear-cut 'materialist' political option in the EC, according to Inglehart's own data, is Christian Democracy.[32]

Be that as it may, let us look at the empirical record of manual–nonmanual class voting. Thanks to Ronald Inglehart, we have a large set of presumably comparable cross-national data available, the pooled political polls of the *Eurobarometer* for the period of 1980 to 1987.

For each country we shall calculate the ratio of the proportions that someone from the manual class and someone from the non-manuals will vote for the largest left-wing and for the largest right-wing party. This gives us a measure of relative class support for the two sets of parties, irrespective of their relative size. The overall significance of class voting will be indicated by the odds of manuals voting for the more left-wing rather than the more right-wing of the two largest parties divided by the same odds among non-manuals. The odds ratio indicates how strongly the chances for choosing one or the other of the two major political alternatives of the country is affected by manual or non-manual class belonging.

In both cases, *the longer the distance from 1.0, the more class-specific the voting*. A percentage ratio less than 1.0 means that more manuals than non-manuals are supporting a right-wing party, or vice versa. An odds ratio less than unity means that the more right-wing party has more support than the other in both classes (see Table 14.5).

Class voting is still a distinctive characteristic of Europe in the 1980s. Greece is an exception, close to the USA in the relative class distribution of voting. But the intra-European differences are very large. Denmark, and Scandinavia more generally,[33] have the most clear-cut class cleavages. In the 1991 Swedish election, for instance, the manual to non-manual ratio of people voting left (Social Democracy or left party) was 2.14.[34] After Scandinavia, Britain, Italy, Spain and Portugal have most class politics. It is worth noting that France differs from the other Latin countries, and aligns itself in this respect with a West-Central European cluster of more blurred class cleavages of voting.

The Southern European Socialist parties have a considerably broader or more heterogeneous social base than their Northern counterparts.[35] The Italian Communist Party (the largest left-wing party in Italy, now the Party of the Democratic Left and member of the Socialist International), on the other hand, is more similar to the Northern Social Democracies.

Table 14.5 *Class voting in Western Europe and the USA, 1980–1987*

Columns 2 and 3: Percentage ratios of manual/non-manual voters for the largest left-wing[a] party, non-manual/manual voters for the largest right-wing[b] party. Column 4: Ratios of the odds of manual voters supporting the more left-wing over the more right-wing of the two largest parties[c] and the odds of non-manual voters doing the same.

Country	Left party	Right party	2 largest parties
Belgium	1.86	1.0	1.86
Britain	1.92	1.75	3.35
Denmark	1.96	3.0	5.86
France	1.20	1.44	1.73
Germany	1.41	1.22	1.71
Greece	1.10	1.25	1.15
Ireland	2.22	0.91	1.78
Italy	2.06	1.10	2.45
Netherlands	1.76	1.04	1.69
Portugal	1.34	1.48	2.0
Spain	1.29	1.86	2.40
USA[d]	1.18	1.13	0.75

Notes: [a] Left and right are here taken in a broad, ecumenical sense. *De facto*, the largest left-wing party is the party belonging to the Socialist International, except in Italy, where the then Communist Party is the largest (now a member of the SI as PDS). [b] The largest party to the right of parties belonging to the Socialist International. [c] Except in Ireland, the two largest parties are the same as the largest left and right parties in the previous columns. In Eire the two biggest parties are the two nationalist ones, Fiánna Fáil and Fine Gael. [d] The left is Mondale and the right is Reagan in the 1984 Presidential election.

Source: Calculations from Inglehart, *Cultural Shift*, pp. 458–60.

The cross-national differences in the electoral base of right-wing parties are much larger than those between left-wing parties, however. The successful supra-class appeal of Christian Democracy is expressed in non-manual to manual ratios of unity or close to it in Belgium, the Netherlands, Italy and, slightly less so, in Germany. The Irish Nationalist Fiánna Fáil actually has more manual than non-manual support. The contrast to the Scandinavian right is brought out starkly in the overwhelmingly non-manual support for the Danish Conservatives, also a successful party in the 1980s, leading Denmark's government.

The varying political significance of class – which, it should not be forgotten, is here only very crudely touched upon by the manual/non-manual distinction – does not exhibit any clear economic pattern, say, of economic development or of economic inequality. Rather, the variations seem to manifest historically evolved national cultures, themselves amenable to structural-cultural analysis, however.

From a scanning and re-analysis of a large number of electoral studies by Paul Nieuwbeerta and Wout Uitee, three conclusions may be drawn. First, throughout the whole postwar period the Nordic countries have had by far the most class-divided pattern of voting. Secondly, there is a secular but cross-nationally uneven trend of declining class voting, defined in manual versus non-manual terms. Thirdly, general explanations for variations are wanting. The only hypothesis left standing was that the larger the manual working class, the more class voting.[36]

The old European orientation towards public intervention and collective social arrangements are maintained as specific values of the continent also in the early 1990s (see Table 14.6).

Table 4.6 *World support for government provision*

Per cent agreeing that the government should provide the following. National surveys in 1991.

	Min. standard of living	Upper limits on income	Jobs for everyone	Index of support[a]
E. Europe[b]	91	45	88	1.97
W. Europe[c]	85	34	64	2.53
USA	56	17	50	3.26
Japan	83	36	86	2.08

Notes: [a] The index ranges from 1 (strong agreement) to 5 (strong disagreement), at the individual level. [b] Unweighted averages from national surveys of Bulgaria, Czechoslovakia, Eastern Germany, Estonia, Hungary, Poland, Russia and Slovenia. [c] Unweighted averages from the Netherlands, the UK and Western Germany.

Source: Calculated from data from the International Social Justice Project, kindly supplied by Professor David S. Mason at Butler University, Indianapolis.

The strong support of government provision in post-Communist Eastern Europe, even before the effects of capitalist 'shock therapy' had become discernible (except in Poland), is noticeable. Least support was found in Czechoslovakia, but the Czechoslovak index score of 2.22 is still considerably more supportive than that of the most positive Western European country, West Germany, at 2.42. Strongest support for government provision was mustered in East Germany (1.68), Hungary (1.73) and Slovenia (1.87).

Europe as a whole differs clearly from the USA, but not, in this respect, from Japan.

Similar results were found by the International Social Survey in 1990. Considerably less support for governmental redistribution of incomes was found in the New World (USA and Australia) than in any of six European countries (including, this time, Switzerland). In his analysis of the survey Geoffrey Evans found a clearer class identity in Europe but no systematic difference in the amount of class polarization around the issue of governmental redistribution.[37]

Public collectivism also implies that the management of business enterprises should not belong to the owners only, but that the employees and/or the state also should have a say. And here again, a European value pattern is discernible, albeit not a unique one (see Table 14.7).

Table 14.7 *World opinion on the running of business and industry*

Per cent agreeing that the owners should run the business or appoint the managers, without further qualification. Unweighted averages of national samples.

Eastern Europe	28
Western Europe	41
North America	55
Latin America	34
Ex-Col. Zone	
India	22
Nigeria	53
Japan	44
Other EIM countries[a]	24

Note: [a] China, South Korea, Turkey.

Source: World Values Survey 1990–1991, variable 126.

Here it is North America (Canada 53% unqualified support for owner-running, USA 57%), that stands out from the rest of the world. Not one of the twenty-five European countries in the survey reached the North American level of owner individualism. The East–West divide within Europe is also sharp. Only three of the ten Eastern countries approach the Western average: the Bulgarians (40%), the Estonians (42%) and the Lithuanians (38%).

Individualizations of sexuality, parenthood and childhood

Above, in Chapter 6, we examined the very uneven exits from traditional patriarchy, with regard to the conception of marriage and of married women's rights. Here, our perspective is from another angle. Instead of focusing on legal rights, we shall take some account of other social norms and values concerning sexuality and parenting.

In most parts of the modern world – the migration-created New Worlds, especially their slave-plantations and the latters' successor societies, are the main exception – sexuality and parenthood have been rather strictly normed. Peripheral areas, marginal social strata and migrant sub-populations may have deviated from the central norm, without undermining the latter's legitimate validity. After the initial social dislocations with the capitalization of agriculture, industrialization, urbanization, etc., there ensued in Western Europe a normative stabilization, around marriage and domesticity. Except for wartime peaks, the proportion of births out of wedlock tended to decline in the course of the twentieth century, or was stable.[38]

At least, this was so till the 1970s, or the mid-1960s in some cases. Then, a dramatic change set in. Hard, comparative evidence about the change of general sexual norms and practices is not available. That they changed, anybody with a contact with those times knows. The proportion of extra-marital births is not a very good indicator of the amount of sexual change, particularly not with the revolutionization of contraceptive technology. The contraceptive pill was allowed for general use in the USA in 1960, and spread into Europe in the course of the decade; in West Germany, for instance, since about the mid-1960s, received with stern moral warnings and by Papal condemnation.[39] Non-marriage is also a reflection of secularization, which, as we saw earlier in this chapter, took a new jump at the same time.

Nevertheless, I do think that the share of births out of wedlock is an indicator of a de-regulation of sexual and parental norms in favour of a wider range of individual choice. This holds in particular to the extent that the change is not concentrated within a special ethnic or other social group, which, by and large, is not the case in Europe.

The pattern illustrated in Table 14.8 is very uneven, with a wide range between the two poles of Sweden and Greece. Longer time series show that the current Austrian rate of extra-marital births is about the same as it was in 1919, and clearly below its rate for 1927–35. My guess is that it expresses an alienation from the (Catholic) Church of part of the population, as well as sexual rights. The Nordic countries, on the other hand, and Sweden in particular, exhibit dramatic increases from the 1960s and on. In 1960 extra-marital births accounted for 11.3% of the total of live-born babies in Sweden, whereas the 1990 figure was almost five times higher.

In the Table we can discern a Protestant tendency towards more informal sexuality, with a traditional Austrian and a recent French exception from a more strict Catholic pattern. But there is no discernible Communist effect. (Ex-)Protestant Communist East Germany was close to Capitalist Protestant Denmark, but not to Catholic Communist Czechoslovakia or Hungary, which were more similar to West Germany and to Portugal.

Here we can hardly speak of any all-European pattern in terms of levels. But there is a tendency for a particular rapid change in Europe. (Whereas the rate of divorce, also an indicator of family individualism, tended to increase more in the USA, measured absolutely, than in Western Europe, from a former much higher level.[40]) The Northern European countries represent most clearly a European combination of private individualism and public collectivism. In other countries, tendencies in that direction may be discerned.

Child–parent relations have been significantly affected by three other post-1960 tendencies, all of which tend to weaken family collectivism. One is the entry of mass media, of television, into children's lives, which opens up a whole special world outside that of home and neighbourhood. Whether their main effect is a global media moulding or an extension of individuation

Table 14.8   *Extra-marital births per 100 births,*
1970 and 1990

Country	1970	1990
Austria	12.8	23.6
Belgium	2.8	9.0[a]
Czechoslovakia	5.7	8.2
Denmark	11.0	46.1[b]
E. Germany	13.3	33.6[b]
Finland	5.8	22.9[b]
France	6.8	28.2[b]
Greece	1.1	2.1[b]
Hungary	5.4	13.1
Ireland	2.7	14.5
Italy	2.2	6.3
Netherlands	2.1	11.4
Norway	6.9	38.6
Portugal	7.3	14.6[b]
Spain	1.4	8.3[a]
Sweden	18.4	51.8[b]
Switzerland	3.8	6.1
UK	8.0	27.9
W. Germany	5.5	10.2[b]
Argentina	26.0	33.0[c]
Japan	n.a.	1.0
USA	10.0	21.0[c]

Notes: [a] 1987. [b] 1989. [c] 1985.

Sources: Council of Europe, *Recent Demographic Developments in Europe*, Strasburg, 1991, p. 36; United Nations, *The World's Women*, New York, 1991, p. 16.

remains an open question. The coupling of the opposite alternatives is only yet another manifestation of the dialectics of modernity.

Secondly, there is the development, spearheaded in Eastern Europe and pronounced in Scandinavia after 1970 but much less important elsewhere, of extra-parental daycare, and of pre-primary schooling, in the French, Italian and Belgian 'maternal schools', in the German Kindergarten, etc.[41] The media and daycare/pre-schooling both reverse the parental home-centredness which followed upon the constitution of modern childhood.

Thirdly, the more unstable conjugal life of parents is also beginning to affect child–parent relations. The number of one-parent households has increased, comprising in the early 1980s about one-eighth of all households with children in most countries of Western Europe. The rule is a narrow band of variation, from 10.2% in France to 14.2% in Sweden, with Ireland (and possibly some Southern European country) as a low exception, at 7.1%. With regard to mono-parentalism, Western Europe occupies a middle position between Japan, at 4.1%, and the USA (with its ghetto society, and generally higher divorce rate) at 26%.[42] In the USSR in 1979 14% of all family units were mono-parental.[43]

If we calculate from the children's point of view, about 95% of all children up to 15–16 (or later if still in compulsory education) in Ireland, Italy and Switzerland, around 90% in Czechoslovakia, Finland, France, East and West Germany and the UK, circa 85% in Scandinavia, and little more than 75% in the USA lived in two-parent families in the early 1980s. The Swedish data also allow us to take into account re-made couples, i.e. couples other than the child's parents. In 1984–5 9% of Swedish children and 10.5% of 16- and 17-year-old youths, lived in households with a reshuffled adult set-up.[44]

Finally we shall look at some current world views on parenting, with the usual caveat that the results have to be read in national and historical context, and that there is always a risk that questions are received differently across cultures.

The patterns of parental values do not correspond very well either with continental or with social systemic boundaries. On the other hand, meaningful cultural questions should produce some clustering correspond-ing to known cultural configurations. In Table 14.9, therefore, the countries have been grouped with a regard both for cultural/historical proximity and for the diffusion of parental ideologies. Cases of deviation from the clusters will be noted below.

Table 14.9   *World views on parenting*

Qualities of children to be encouraged, independence or obedience? Parental duty to do their best for their children even at the expense of own wellbeing, or should parents have their own lives and not be asked to sacrifice? *Dominance scores*, i.e. the percentage agreeing with the former of each pair of questions minus that agreeing with the opposite statement. Unweighted national averages.

Region/Country	Independence	Parental sacrifice
North-Central Europe[a]	29	34
South-Western Europe[b]	−9	60
Eastern Europe I[c]	41	26
Eastern Europe II[d]	0	25
North America	15	52
Latin America[e]	−11	64
Ex-Col. Zone[f]	−40	70
East Asian EIM[g]	55	(16)[h]
Turkey	−12	39

Notes: [a] Austria, West Germany, the Netherlands, Denmark, Finland, Iceland, Norway and Sweden. [b] Britain, Northern Ireland, Ireland, France, Italy, Portugal, Spain. [c] Bulgaria, Hungary, East Germany, Estonia, Latvia, Lithuania. [d] Czechoslovakia, Poland, Belorussia, Russia. [e] Brazil, Chile, Mexico. [f] India, Nigeria. [g] East Asian countries of Externally Induced Modernization: China, Japan, South Korea. [h] An average makes little sense here: China score 42, Japan 12 and South Korea − 5.5.

Source: World Values Survey 1990–1991, variables 225, 227, 236.

A consistent family individualism in this context involves an encouragement of both children's and parents' independence, and a consistent family collectivism the opposite. But the other possible combinations are, of course, not to be taken as 'inconsistent'. Rather, we may call them a child-centred or a parents-centred individualism.

There are here clearly two Europes, one more individualist than most of the world, and one not. But it is not the usual line-up. *Central Europe*, except Czechoslovakia and Poland but linking up with Bulgaria, *the Baltic and the North Atlantic areas* embrace child independence and are relatively restrained in demanding parental sacrifices. Denmark and West Germany and, on the eastern fringes, Latvia, Lithuania and Bulgaria have the strongest individualism. Lithuanian respondents were in fact the only ones in Europe where a majority accorded parents priority to their own lives (score above −17). (The South Koreans were the only other people in the world doing that: −5.5.) Sweden comes out as a relatively low scorer in the North-Central European grouping.

The *Southwest of Europe*, from Belgium to Portugal, including the British Isles, has a distinctively collectivist cast of family values. Portugal, France and Northern Ireland, in that order, also have a marked preference for obedience over independence, whereas the others in the country family are split about even (in the Irish Republic, even with a small majority in favour of independence). The marked Franco-German difference, a reversal of old stereotypes, is confirmed also by other, schooling evidence.[45]

The more authoritarian part of Eastern Europe consists of, in particular, Czechoslovakia and Poland, and Belorussia and Russia.

How the stark deviations from Confucian values in East Asia should be interpreted had perhaps better be left out of a book on European modernity. The guess might be ventured that the responses − in China from an urban sample only − express a critical reflection on the past, rather than an institutionalized value system.

With regard to Europe we may conclude that sharp contrasts in family values persist between blocs of countries which for all practical purposes must be regarded as all modern. But that family, or private world, individualism, more than in the New Worlds and probably more than anywhere else on the globe, is clearly held in a strong, central, part of Europe.

Communist acculturation and the unhappy revolution

Still in 1987 and 1988 I believed in the renewal of the [Communist] Party, which would help in reforming the system. In 1990 there remained almost nothing of those hopes. And in 1991 I was convinced that the CPSU had become a force, that was irrevocably hostile to the public interest.[46]

We need not necessarily take Georgi Arbatov's memoirs *ad personal notam*, but he clearly conveys a major value change of recent Europe − the implosion of Communism.

What brought down Eastern European Communism will have to await more historians' time before an answer is clear. However, one remarkable aspect of the end of Communist Europe, which has not been much taken serious notice of, because it does not fit into any ideological schema, was the surrender without fight of a movement steeled in combat and of a system of power well experienced in the art of repression. The Soviet regime had been sapped of its will to survive.

What I want to do here, given both the enormous historical importance of the event and my severely limited competence in the face of it, is to put forward a context of interpretation and to present some evidence for future discussion and investigation.

Available evidence does not allow us to explain satisfactorily the fall of Communism by an acute economic crisis, or even by an obvious economic dead end, as we saw in Chapter 7 above, relying mainly on World Bank studies. It is true, however, that in the last years of Communism there was a pervasive experience of economic inadequacy and failure. There was a willingness to undertake increasingly radical political and social reform, as the emergence and rise to power of Mikhail Gorbachev and of other new leaders testify. Nor is Communism inherently incapable of profound change without falling apart, as the Chinese success so far demonstrates.

The posthumous verdict of their subjects further shows that European Communist regimes cannot just be dismissed as 'states of injustice', as the prevailing West German ideology has it. In October 1992 national samples of the population of eighteen ex-Communist states of Europe, including Armenia and Georgia of the Caucasus, were interviewed by *Eurobarometer/ Gallup*. One question was 'Taking everything into account, do you feel things are better for you now under the present political system, or do you think things were better for you before under the previous political system?' A clear majority answering better now was found only in Albania, the Czech Republic and Romania. Fragile, uncertain majorities appeared in Slovenia, Slovakia and Lithuania.

Clear majorities of the ex-USSR and of Hungary thought their situation was better under the Communist regime. The Bulgarians were split evenly, and so, by and large, were the Poles. But given the predominant Western interpretation of Poland, it is worth mentioning that actually more Poles (39%) thought they were better off under Communism than in the autumn of 1992 (34%).[47]

The question is unfortunately ambiguous, combining personal socio-economic situation, 'things . . . better for you', with 'political system'. But its invocation of the political system should tend to work against an appreciation of once 'actually existing socialism', and the results of nostalgia appear even more remarkable.

One important part of the constellation of forces that brought down the Communist system in Europe was the erosion of Communist ideology, the inner uncertainty of crucial parts of the regime.

In Eastern Europe Communism became defensive in 1968. The last avant-garde formulation, after the ebullient promises of Khrushchev, was the Czechoslovak Richta Report, part of the Prague Spring in the broad sense. It combined a modernist, 'scientific-technological revolution' perspective with a programme of democratic socialist reform.[48] However, the armed invasion of Czechoslovakia put the half-continent in an ideological freezer, with concessions and apologetics. The previous accumulationist orientation was replaced by a nervous catering to mass consumption, from the late 1970s often sustained by foreign loans.

Ideologically, the bold boasts of future triumphant Communism or the self-critical reform programmes were in the 1970s both replaced by the apologetic concept of Brezhnev's chief ideologue, Mikhail Suslov, of 'actually existing socialism', with its explicit denial and implicit recognition of another, better socialism. Alternatively, in Romania Ceaușescu played the Romanian nationalist card, which also gave privileged access to the West.

The next step in the Communist de-escalation was the Polish crisis in 1980–1. This time only the East German leadership was fully prepared to invade, although the Soviets kept up a considerable amount of pressure. The solution, a 'state of war' or martial law, under the auspices of the Polish army, was a Communist retreat behind a national institution. But it was not, as sometimes assumed in the West, the ultimate repressive resort, as the army was a popular Polish institution. In two polls of autumn 1985 between 70 and 81% of the population expressed their confidence in the military. Trust in the army, which had been running the country since December 1981, was not much less than in the Church, between 86 and 80% in the same two polls. A year earlier, a majority of the population held that the declaration of the state of war was more or less justified, against only a quarter holding the contrary opinion.[49]

In March 1985 the Soviet Union got, for the first time since Brezhnev fell ill in December 1974, a fully fit political leader. Mikhail Sergeievich Gorbachev was intent on radical change, on a revolution within the socialist system. Why the Soviet *perestroika* failed, while the Chinese 'modernizations' so far have been eminently successful, both in pushing economic growth and in maintaining the system of political power, still has to be unravelled.

(Two things are, of course, immediately apparent. The Soviet priority of cultural and political change unhinged the economic system but provided no new economic dynamic, which rapidly worsened the crisis. The Chinese reversal of the sequence, meanwhile, unleashed an economic growth which at least maintained the unity of the regime, if not the latter's popular legitimacy. Secondly, the tasks of modernization in China were more elementary, more easy to unite around, than 'economic reform' in Eastern Europe.)

Some insight into how the circle around Gorbachev shrank and how its ideological perspectives peeled off may be gained from the memoirs of his loyal secretary, Anatoly Chernayev, written in retirement from public life and based on a diary.

The reform coalition fell apart as no economic openings materialized, while the old system was functioning worse than before as national and ethnic tensions mounted. Already by December 1986 an economic stalemate was noted in the Politburo, and prompted a stormy session.[50] The only thing that moved was the ideological debate, which became increasingly polarized with the new freedom of expression and with the absence of any concrete criteria of programmatic realism. Gorbachev was in the end almost the only one in the leadership and its apparatus who was both a democratic reformer and a socialist.

'The answer to the question, What is really socialism?, is the central problem for deciding our ideological standpoint', Gorbachev told his aide in August 1988, as he was struggling with preparing three lectures on the issue. The latter never took place, but Mikhail Sergeievich continued to wrestle with the question till the end.[51]

In January 1990, Alexander Yakovlev, Gorbachev's most important supporter in the Politburo, proposed to him a sort of capitalist *coup d'état*, based on Presidential emergency powers.[52] While Gorbachev never could bring himself to a break with the party and the tradition which had formed him, in the summer of 1990 he recognized a 'crisis of socialism', and he began telling all his foreign friends 'We are turning to a market economy'.[53]

A similar inner erosion took place in Hungary, although in different forms and in a different context. In May 1988 an extraordinary party congress voted the old guard out of power, and a new post-revolutionary generation took over. Market economic reforms proceeded, capitalist enterprises were founded, and a stock exchange opened. In February 1989 the Central Committee of the ruling party came round to accepting a multiparty democracy. In October the same year, the radical and the moderate post-Communist reformers formally split.[54]

In Poland, the martial law government amnestied its opponents in the autumn of 1986, and by January 1989 Jaruzelski and his group managed to bring the ruling party to open official negotiations with the opposition. The Polish development was more straightforwardly political, concerned with issues of democracy and the legitimacy of opposition, than socio-economic.[55]

Even in the Balkans, ideological changes were under way, in nationalist form primarily. Ceauşescu had embarked upon an assertively nationalist course already in the mid-1960s, while keeping some Stalinist trappings. In Serbia Milosevic came to power in September 1987 on a nationalist platform. In Bulgaria, repressive pressures on the Turkish minority were stepped up in the second half of the 1980s. But there was also an amazing self-critical speech by the ageing party leader Zhivkov in February 1989, apparently rejecting 'the previous model of socialism, which has exhausted its possibilities', but not proposing a new model of it, instead asking

Bulgarian intellectuals to explain why advanced capitalism was developing so well.[56]

In the Communist parties of the Baltic republics, nationalist and democratic reform-oriented forces gained the upper hand in the course of 1988 – in Estonia in the summer, in Latvia and Lithuania in the autumn.[57]

By spring 1989, the leaders of the USSR, of Poland, Hungary and Yugoslavia were abdicating from their monopoly of power. More or less free elections were taking place (as in the USSR) or were under way. Radical economic changes had been accepted in Hungary, and were no longer anathema in the other states mentioned, nor even in Bulgaria. Only the rulers of Czechoslovakia and the GDR kept their Marxist-Leninist ideology in the freezer till the people on the streets threw it away. The Romanian and the Albanian rulers, meanwhile, were sticking to their particular concoctions of national Stalinism.

Popular dissatisfaction was mounting in the second half of the 1980s. Hungarians had been moderately satisfied with their economic and political situation in 1986, but had come to a quite critical evaluation of their economic situation by the end of 1988.[58] In Poland, the pattern of opinion by March 1988 was dramatic: more than 80% considered the economic situation bad or very bad, and a good 40% thought that it would get worse. Critical opinion had soared since 1986.[59]

From the GDR we have polls of youth opinion since the 1970s, now declassified. They show a gradual distanciation from Marxism-Leninism, although by 1988 almost 60% expressed some amount of identification with it, three-quarters of which 'with qualification', however. But in May 1989 a majority disclaimed any identification with it. The answers to a number of other questions also indicate a markedly weakened support for the regime in 1988–9.[60]

These popular moods were clearly important to the ideological corrosion of the more open Communist parties, and the former should also be expected to have a material basis in the socio-economic structurations of late Communism. On the other hand, how much the latter was due to systemic problems and how much to changed frameworks of comparison and levels of aspiration remains to be clarified. There are also indications that much of the political-economic dissatisfaction resembled the dissatisfaction with a government in a democracy, rather than with a historical social system.

A Polish poll of 1986 showed that two-thirds of all workers wanted an economic system of predominantly public property, and only one tenth preferred private property.[61] In November 1989 86% of East Germans were of the opinion that the future 'road of development' (*Entwicklungsweg*) of the GDR should be 'the road of a better, reformed socialism'. In February 1990, that was still the view of 56%.[62]

An international opinion poll in November 1993–April 1994 gave the systemic preference of Eastern Europeans shown in Table 14.10.

Only the pupils of Professor Klaus had by then learnt to love the market, with a not very impressive majority. In some countries, from Hungary to the semi-periphery of the ex-USSR, the alienation from post-Communist

Table 14.10　*Eastern European preference for socialism or market economy, November 1993–April 1994*

Dominance scores, i.e. the percentage approving 'former Communist' and disapproving 'current system minus the opposite' stance – double negations and approvals excluded.

Belorussia	68
Bulgaria	52
Croatia	7
Czech Republic	24
Hungary	48
Poland	2
Romania	15
Slovakia	42
Slovenia	0
Ukraine	71

Source: Calculated from R. Rose and C. Haerpfer, *New Democracies Barometer III*, Glasgow, Centre for the Study of Public Policy at the University of Strathclyde, 1994, appendix, questions 23–24.

economics was overwhelming. The people concerned had apparently not counted out socialism as a social system.

One of the persistent ideological differences between East and West Germans is, interestingly enough, a different evaluation of the compatibility of socialism and 'libertarian democracy' (*freiheitliche Demokratie*). In December 1993 only a quarter (27%) of 'Wessis' thought they were compatible, but almost twice as many 'Ossis' or ex-East Germans (45%).[63] If Communist socialism had simply been a monstrous failure, the figures should have been the opposite, at least.

A major West German poll institute, Allensbach, is asking the citizens of 'the new federal provinces' (*neue Bundesländer*) about their current experiences in comparison with life before re-unification. We may interpret the answers as referring to advanced, socially conscious capitalism (i.e. current Germany) and to Communist socialism, in other words to systemic comparisons based on firsthand experience of both. The fact that the questions are not formulated in terms of systems or ideologies, but with regard to before and after a nationally defined event ('re-unification'), makes their answers even more interesting (see Table 14.11).

Right or wrong, East Germans are clearly very critical of their new West German existence in a number of respects. On all social policy and educational issues, except possibility of further education (*Weiterausbildungsmöglichkeiten*), life before re-unification is considered to have been better. Moreover, the future looked much better in the past.

Table 14.11 *East German opinion on better and worse under capitalism and socialism, Spring 1994 (per cent)*

Category	Better now	Better in the GDR
Commodity supply	98	1
Choice of papers	96	1
Travel	95	2
Possibility of independence	93	2
Expression of one's opinion	68	6
TV programmes	59	14
Leisure supply	52	26
Possibility of further education	46	23
Food prices	35	43
Health service	32	39
Free to choose education and occupation	30	36
Security of pensions	29	43
Future prospects	24	57
Occupational opportunities	23	60
School education	22	36
Supply of interesting jobs	20	63
Child-raising	8	49
Traffic safety	7	83
Safety in event of crime	3	93
Sense of community	3	87
Rent	2	94

Source: Institut für Demoskopie Allensbach, *Frankfurter Allgemeine Zeitung*, 14.4.94, p 5

Table 14.12 *(Un)happiness in the world, 1990–1991*

Unweighted national averages, except for the world score, which is the world sample average.

Area	Very happy (%)	Happiness score[a]	Life satisfaction[b]
World average	23	2.01	6.95
Western Europe[c]	31	1.80	7.48
Eastern Europe[d]	7	2.37	5.93
North America[e]	35	1.84	7.81
Latin America[f]	27	2.02	7.44
Ex-Col. Zone[g]	33	2.05	6.65
EIM[h]	21	2.03	6.73

Notes: [a] *The lower the value, the more happy.* [b] *The higher the value, the more satisfied with life as a whole.* [c] Austria, Belgium, Britain, Denmark, Finland, France, West Germany, Iceland, Ireland, Italy, the Netherlands, Norway, Portugal, Spain, Sweden. [d] Belorussia, Bulgaria, Czechoslovakia, Estonia, the GDR, Hungary, Latvia, Lithuania, Poland, Russia. [e] Canada, the USA. [f] Brazil, Chile, Mexico. [g] Ex-Colonial Zone: India, Nigeria. [h] Countries of Externally Induced Modernization: China, Japan, South Korea, Turkey.

Source: Calculations from World Values Survey 1990–1991, Variables 18 and 96.

There have been several attempts at interpreting the change in Eastern Europe between 1989 and 1991. Perhaps the most considered opinion is that of Jürgen Habermas, calling it a 'nachholende Revolution', which has been rendered in English as 'the rectifying revolution'.[64]

Anyway, whatever else it may be, it is also an *unhappy revolution*.

In the Italian essay on Western Europe preceding this book I had a section on the uneven distribution in Western Europe of happiness – more concentrated in Northern Europe – and unhappiness, mainly the lot of Latin and other Southern Europeans.[65] However, confronted with the sad Eastern European visage after the anti-Communist revolution, the Western European differences pale into insignificance (see Table 14.12).

Eastern Europeans were in 1990–1 the unhappiest peoples on earth. The regional averages hide few border transgressions. Poles and East Germans were less unhappy than the Portuguese and the South Koreans, and about even with ex-Colonial Indians and Nigerians, but for the rest, the situation was pretty bleak.

It may be argued that the outcome of anti-Communism was then still hanging in the balance in many cases. However, the fact that in October 1992 only Albanians, Slovenes and Czechs clearly thought that their country was moving in the right direction,[66] seems to indicate that the majority of Eastern Europeans would be singularly unhappy also in 1992, when the power game was well settled.

The data in Table 14.12 do not, of course, tell us anything about how (un)happy Eastern Europeans were before their latest revolution. Above we have given evidence strongly indicating very considerable amounts of Communist unhappiness in the late 1980s. But it is a fact that Hungarians were happier and more satisfied with their lives in 1980 than in 1990. In 1980 they were about as satisfied with their lives as the French and Spanish were, and clearly more so than the Greeks and Portuguese. In 1990, the amount of Hungarian unhappiness had no equivalent in Western Europe.[67]

Compared to previous revolutions in modern history, the Eastern European anti-Communist ones took place under extraordinarily favourable circumstances. The powers in existence gave in without any serious resistance. The whole environment was enthusiastic, full of good will, and materially supportive. No armed intervention, no economic boycott, no political ostracism, no organization of a counter-revolution.

Nevertheless, the happiness of liberation has so far remained a Western European celebration. The Eastern European sphinx has still many secrets to be revealed. However, a good reason for unhappiness has been that the restoration of capitalism has so far (early 1994) meant a fall of living standards for the majority of the population. Only in the Czech Republic and in Slovenia have winners and losers so far been at least evenly distributed.[68]

Notes

1 A somewhat anecdotal eye-witness analysis of the early postwar strategy and frantic activity of the Church in Italian politics is given by the political sociologist Gianfranco Poggi, 'The Church in Italian Politics 1945–50', in S.J. Woolf (ed.), *The Rebirth of Italy, 1943–50*, London, Longman, 1972.

2 Cf. F. Fejtö, *Histoire des démocraties populaires: 1. L'ère de Staline*, Paris, Seuil, 1972, pp. 367ff.

3 G. Winkler (ed.), *Sozialreport '90*, Berlin, Die Wirtschaft, 1990, p. 308.

4 *Die Zeit*, 22.4.1994, p. 78.

5 Historical figures in T. Mackie and R. Rose, *International Almanac of Electoral History*, 2nd edn, London, Macmillan, 1982, pp. 269, 273.

6 *Der Fischer Weltalmanach 1990*, Frankfurt, Fischer, 1989, pp. 138, 395, 466. True, in Switzerland, this is due to the overwhelmingly Catholic (mainly Italian) immigrant population: *Statistisches Jahrbuch der Schweiz 1992*, Zurich, Verlag Neue Zürcher Zeitung, 1991, p. 324.

7 See further D. Martin, *A General Theory of Secularization*, Oxford, Basil Blackwell, 1978, esp. Ch. III; idem, 'The Religious Condition of Europe', in S. Giner and M.S. Archer (eds), *Contemporary Europe: Social Structures and Cultural Patterns*, London, Routledge & Kegan Paul, 1978.

8 *Frankfurter Allgemeine Zeitung*, 3.5.1994, p. 5.

9 Cf. P. Bataille, 'L'expérience belge', in M. Wievorka (ed.), *Racisme et xénophobie en Europe*, Paris, La Découverte, 1994; *Frankfurter Allgemeine Zeitung*, 15.1.1992, p. 27; *Die Zeit* 28.1.1994, p. 69.

10 E. Noëlle and E.P. Neumann, *The Germans: Public Opinion Polls, 1947–1966*, Westport, Conn., Greenwood, Press, 1981, pp. 189–91.

11 *Frankfurter Allgemeine Zeitung*, 18.6.1993, p. 12; G. Kepel, *Les banlieues de l'Islam*, Paris, Seuil, 1991, pp. 72–3 and 229, respectively.

12 Kepel, *Les banlieues de l'Islam*, p. 13; *Frankfurter Allegemeine Zeitung*, 18.6.1993, p. 12; CSO, *Social Trends 24*, London, HMSO, 1994, p. 145.

13 I am here indebted to a number of conversations with the distinguished Swedish Islamologist Jan Hjärpe at Lund University.

14 An interesting symptomatic sign, at the level of a serious intellectual argument, is the French Catholic theologician, *inter alia*, J.-C. Barreaur's high-selling confrontational book *De l'Islam*, Paris, Le Pré aux Clercs, 1991. See further B. Lewis and D. Schapper (eds), *Musulmans en Europe*, Poitiers, Actes Sud, 1992; M. Wievorka (ed.), *Racisme et xénophobie en Europe*, Paris, La Découverte, 1994.

15 M. Dogan, 'Comparing the Decline of Nationalism in Western Europe: The Generational Dynamic', *International Social Science Journal* 136 (1993), p. 186.

16 The percentage of 'very proud' nationals was 43 in China, 45 in South Korea, 53 in Chile, 56 in Mexico, 60 in Canada, 64 in Brazil and in South Africa, 67 in Turkey and 68 in Nigeria, according to the World Values Survey 1990–1991 (directed by R. Inglehart), Institute for Social Research, University of Michigan (data file).

17 Commission of the European Communities, *'Eurobaromètre': l'opinion publique et l'Europe* 9 (1989), p. 6.

18 *Eurobarometer* 17, April 1982, question 144 (ICPSR edition, Ann Arbor Mich., 1983) The causes on the list were, sexual equality, protection of the environment, world peace, poverty, national defence, religious faith, the unification of Europe, freedom of the individual, human rights, the revolution.

19 Cf. Dogan 'Comparing the Decline of Nationalism'.

20 The theme is being livelily debated, *pro et contra*, in the German press, while this is being written, in the spring of 1994. It should not be confounded with xenophobia or right-wing extremism.

21 See further G. Therborn, 'The Right to Vote and the Four World Routes to/through Modernity', in R. Torstendahl (ed.), *State Theory and State History*, London, Sage, 1992.

22 See further, G. Therborn, 'The Prospects of Labour and the Transformation of Advanced Capitalism', *New Left Review* 145 (1984). Cf. J. Mooser, *Arbeiterleben in Deutschland, 1900–1970*, Frankfurt, Suhrkamp, 1984; G. Noiriel, *Les ouvriers dans la société française*, Paris, Seuil, 1986; M. Jacques and F. Mulhern (eds), *The Forward March of Labour Halted?*, London, Verso, 1981; W. Korpi, *The Democratic Class Struggle*, London, Routledge, 1983; R. Ebbighausen and F. Tiemann (eds), *Das Ende der Arbeiterbeweung in Deutschland?*, Opladen, Westdeutscher Verlag, 1984.

23 K. Geiger, *The Family in Soviet Russia*, Cambridge, Mass., Harvard University Press, 1968, p. 99; see also on p. 274 another interviewee telling that a beaten child could go to the village soviet and complain, whereupon the father would be fined.

24 Ibid., p. 275.

25 A brief overview of Soviet family legislation is given by D. Lane, *Soviet Economy and Society*, Oxford, Basil Blackwell, 1985, pp. 110ff.

26 See further *Familiengesetze sozialistischer Lander*, East Berlin, Deutsche Zentralverlag, 1959.

27 See further, and for references, G. Therborn, 'The Politics of Childhood: The Rights of Children in Modern Times', in F. Castles (ed.), *Families of Nations*, Aldershot, Dartmouth, 1993.

28 R. Inglehart, *The Silent Revolution*, Princeton, Princeton University Press, 1977, and *Culture Shift in Advanced Industrial Society*, Princeton, Princeton University Press, 1990.

29 S. Holmberg and M. Gilljam, *Väljare och val i Sverige*, Stockholm, Bonniers, 1987, p. 184.

30 For an overview of the debate see A. Heath, 'Class and Political Partisanship', and D. Kavanagh, 'Ideology, Sociology, and the Strategy of the British Labour Party', both in J. Clark et al. (eds), *John H. Goldthorpe*, London, Falmer Press, 1990.

31 Inglehart, Culture Shift, pp. 74–5.

32 Ibid., Table 8–7, p. 280.

33 N. Elvander, *Skandinavisk arbetarrörelse*, Stockholm, Liber, 1980, p. 319; Holmberg and Gilljam, *Väljare*, pp. 178ff.

34 Data kindly supplied by Professor Sören Holmberg. The percentage ratio is higher in 1991 than in the 1980s, similar to that of 1970, 1976 and 1979, but significantly lower than in 1956–60 at 3.32 and 3.04.

35 The Italian Socialist Party, which was then the second largest left party of its country, has a percentage ratio of 1, i.e. the proportion of manual worker supporters is the same as the share of non-manuals.

36 P. Nieuwbeerta and W. Uitee, 'Explaining Differences in the Level of Class Voting in 20 Western Industrial Nations, 1945–1990', Nijmegen, Dept. of Sociology of the Catholic University of Nijmegen, 1992.

37 G. Evans, 'Class Conflict and Inequality', in R. Jowell et al. (eds), *International Social Attitudes: The 10th BSA Report*, Aldershot, Dartmouth, 1993, pp. 126, 134; Cf. also P. Taylor-Gooby, 'What citizens want from the state', in ibid.

38 P. Flora (ed.), *State, Economy, and Society in Western Europe, 1815–1975*, Vol. 2, Frankfurt, Campus, Ch. 2.

39 S. zur Nieden, 'Die Pille', *Emma* 7 (1991), pp.15ff.

40 F. Castles and M. Flood, 'Why Divorce Rates Differ: Law, Religious Belief, and Modernity', in Castles *Families of Nations*, p. 304.

41 Cf. OECD, *Employment Outlook, July 1990*, Paris, 1990, Ch. 5.

42 OECD, *Les familles monoparentales*, Paris, 1990, p. 34.

43 Lane, *Soviet Economy and Society*, p. 113. The figure is a census datum.

44 A.-M. Jensen and A. Saporiti, 'Do Children Count?', *Eurosocial* 36, 17 (1992), pp. 42–3; I. Raton, 'Les jeunes de moins de 15 ans: enfants et jeunes adolescents', *Méthodes* 8 (février 1991), p. 55; J. Gysi 'Familienformen in der DDR', *Jahrbuch für Soziologie und Sozialpolitik*, [East] Berlin: Akademie-Verlag, 1988, p. 519, related to GDR population statistics; *Barns levnadsvillkor*, Stockholm, SCB, 1989, p. 85.

45 H. Kaelble, *Nachbarn am Rhein*, Munich, C.H. Beck, 1991, p. 172.

46 G. Arbatov, *Das System*, Frankfurt, Fischer, 1993, p. 380. Arbatov has been Director of the Institute for US and Canada Studies in Moscow, since 1967, and has been a very important foreign policy adviser of the Soviet government for about a quarter of a century.

47 *Eurobarometer*/Gallup survey conducted in October 1992, annex Figure 13 of the Report. I am indebted to Brigita Zepa, who conducted the Latvian survey, for having made this study available to me.

48 R. Richta, *La civilisation au carrefour*, Paris, Anthropos/Seuil, 1974.

49 A. Sulek, 'Politische Meinungsumfragen in Polen – Träger, gesellschaftlicher Kontext und Zuverlässigkeit empirischer Studien', in G. Meyer and F. Ryszka (eds), *Die politische Kultur Polens*, Tübingen, Francke, 1989, p. 134; K. Jasiewicz, 'Zwischen Einheit und Teilung: Politische Orientierungen der Polen in den 80er Jahren', in ibid., p. 147.

50 A. Chernayev (German transcription Tschernayer), *Die letzten Jahre einer Weltmacht*, Stuttgart, Deutsche Verlags-Anstalt, 1993, pp. 114–5.

51 Ibid., pp. 164–5, 281–2, 393.

52 The story is told by Chernayev, who says he basically agreed with Yakovlev and was in daily contact with him during that time. ibid., pp. 282–3.

53 Ibid., pp. 309–10.

54 See further, e.g. N. Swain, *Hungary: The Rise and Fall of Feasible Socialism*, London, Verso, 1992; and G. Horn, *Freiheit die ich meine*, Hamburg, Hoffmann und Campe, 1991.

55 T. Garton Ash, *The Polish Revolution*, London, Granta Books, 1991, pp. 362ff; W. Jaruzelski, *Mein Leben für Polen*, Munich, Piper, 1993, Ch. 13.

56 D. Selbourne, *Death of the Dark Hero*, London, Jonathan Cape, 1990, pp. 143ff.

57 B. Meissner (ed.), *Die baltischen Nationen*, 2nd edn, Cologne, Markus, 1991, pp. 118ff, 153ff, 232ff.

58 *Journal für Sozialforschung* 28, 4 (1988), supplement.

59 L. Kolarska-Bobinska, 'Die marktwirtschaftliche Reform im gesellschaftlichen Bewusstsein und in der Wirtschaft Polens in den Jahren 1980–1990', *Journal für Sozialforschung* 30, 3 (1990), p. 291.

60 P. Förster and G. Roski, *DDR zwischen Wende und Wahl*, Berlin, Linksdruck, 1990, pp. 41ff.

61 Kolarska-Bobinska, 'Die Marktwirtschaftliche Reform' p. 292n.

62 Förster and Roski, *DDR zwischen Wende und Wahl*, p. 56.

63 *Frankfurter Allgemeine Zeitung*, 14.1.1994, p 5

64 J. Habermas, 'The Rectifying Revolution', *New Left Review* 183 (1990).

65 G. Therborn, 'Modernitá sociale in Europe (1950–1992), in P. Anderson et al. (eds), *Storia d'Europa*, Vol. 1, Turin, Einaudi, 1993.

66 *Eurobarometer*/Gallup poll, October 1992.

67 The Hungarian data are in both cases from the *World Values Surveys*, of 1980, reported in Inglehart, Table 7.1, and of *Culture Shift*, 1990–1991, of which I have been kindly given access to the data file.

68 R. Rose and C. Haerpfer, *New Democracies Barometer III*, Glasgow, Centre for the Study of Public Policy at the University of Strathclyde, 1994, appendix, question 26.

PART V

COLLECTIVE ACTION AND SOCIAL STEERING

People act on the basis of their cultural alignments and of the structuration of their resources and constraints. The latter both patterns their capacity to act and provides them with rational interests of action, with incentives and disincentives. This study focuses primarily on the basic layout of the European social stage, rather than on the plays staged there. This fifth part, therefore, will be in no way comparable in scope with the three previous empirical ones, which would have burst the given format. However, before heading for the exit we shall take a glance at what is, and has recently been, on stage in postwar Europe.

Protest, movement and association

Collective action may be understood as a continuum of joint or at least contiguous actions, with the ephemeral crowd in action at one pole and the enduring association with a professional staff and institutions of decision-making at the other. Crowds and crowd action may be of very different sorts – celebrating, punishing, demanding, protesting, etc. Here, however, we are mainly interested in collective action with a view to changing or defending, radically or moderately, given social conditions. Therefore, 'protest' seems a relatively adequate short designation for the crowd end of the collective action continuum.

'Movement' is, of course, ambiguous in connotation. It is used also with respect to broad-ranged, ambitious and ideologically charged associations, or sets of associations, such as 'the labour movement'. But a 'movement' may also refer to something in-between a crowd and an association, to a rather sustained effort in pursuance of certain values, which is not necessarily organized in a formal association or which is, in any case, much broader than any existing association or set of associations. That is the sense in which 'movement' is referred to in the title of this section. The 'women's movement' is the best illustration.

Between protest and association a negative correlation should be expected, for two reasons. With respect to the powers in existence, the two are likely alternative ways of raising one's voice, either through the loudspeaker of direct crowd action or through the encounter of representatives across a negotiation table. Secondly, although associations may call mass meetings, strikes and boycotts, for example, they have a rational propensity for keeping members and sympathizers under control, in order to avoid provocations, loss of negotiating respectability, or being affected by rival activists. Movements may be seen as leaning either towards protest or towards association.

National political cultures should tend either towards the protest or towards the association side of the spectrum, albeit run through by temporal variations of commitment and quiescence. Different structural and cultural bases of collective action may also favour one form or the other. For instance, gender action has tended more towards protest than class action, though we know both stable autonomous women's associations and class crowds.

Variations of collective action in postwar Europe should be expected first to all to have followed the systemic divide of the continent, between capitalist democracies and Communist dictatorships. (The peripheral capitalist dictatorships are bracketed here.) I do not think it is very fruitful to treat collective action under Communism and under democratic capitalism as each *sui generis* and incomparable. On the contrary, we shall see how some lines of demarcation should be drawn North–South rather than East–West. But the very different structuration of rights, and of other parameters, seem to sometimes make a separate treatment of the two halves of Cold War Europe most practical.

15

CIVIL SOCIETIES AND COLLECTIVE ACTION

Alexis de Tocqueville was one of the first, a hundred and fifty years ago, who emphasized the significance and the social preconditions of associations in modernity. He located the latter in the egalitarian New World and made a perceptive comparative observation: 'Partout où à la tête d'une entreprise nouvelle, vous voyez en France le gouvernement et en Angleterre un grand seigneur, comptez que vous apercevrez aux Etats-Unis une association.'[1] Other things being equal, the more socially – not necessarily incomewise – egalitarian a country, i.e. the more widely spread resources of action and communication among the population, the more associative it should be.

In relation to the New Worlds, Europe was, of course, more status-ridden, but European modernity was long prepared by guilds and corporations, autonomous city organizations, Protestant parishes and other forms of collective popular organization. Among the free, literate peasantry of the North, with their old traditions of local ecclesiastical and judicial co-government, modern associations spread rapidly and vigorously in the second half of the nineteenth century. The legacy has not been squandered. Comparative data from around 1970 put Sweden and the USA, followed by the rest of the Nordic countries, at the top of a list of non-economic voluntary organizations.[2]

In the field of associations it is the Latin worlds, Old and New, that come out most clearly at the low end (see Table 15.1), together with Japan. Even (early) under post-communism (1990–1), the Eastern Europeans are more similar to Germanic than to Latin Western Europe. From EC data we also know that Greece in this context belongs to the Latin world.

Intra-EU data convey the same picture of the underdeveloped civil society in Southern Europe. Or, perhaps we should say, more cautiously, the under-associated society there. Because we do not here take into account other forms of sociability, such as the famous Mediterranean male café society.

The North–South cleavage of associations in Europe is pervasive. With the single exception of Italian party membership by 1990, the five Southern EU countries exhibit a consistent below average membership in political parties, trade unions and professional organizations, religious associations, women's groups, ecological, Third World and human rights organizations, sports clubs and cultural associations.[3]

Table 15.1 *The extension of civil society, 1990–1991 (per cent of the population belonging to a voluntary organization)*

Germanic Western Europe	*70*
Austria	54
Belgium	59
Britain	53
Denmark	81
Finland	78
Iceland	90
Ireland	49
Netherlands	84
Sweden	84
W. Germany	68
Latin Western Europe	*35*
France	39
Italy	36
Portugal	34
Spain	30
Eastern Europe	*67*
Bulgaria	60
Estonia	73
E. Germany	84
Hungary	54
Latvia	68
Lithuania	60
Russia	66
North America	*63*
Canada	65
USA	60
New Latin World	*41*
Brazil	43
Chile	45
Mexico	36
Ex-Col. Zone	
Nigeria	86
EIM	
Japan	36

Source: World Values Survey 1990–1991 (directed by R. Inglehart), Institute for Social Research, University of Michigan (data file).

In this cleavage, Belgium belongs to Northern Europe, a North–South pattern that goes back at least to the founding of the modern labour movement at the end of last century.

The association divide of Western Europe largely corresponds to another manifestation of a civil society, frequent political discussion. About two-thirds of Western Europeans say they discuss politics. Well below average in political interest are the Belgians, the Spanish and the Portuguese (only about half), and, further, the Irish and the Italians (around 60%). The French are also slightly below average. Clearly above average in political discussion are the Finns, the Swiss, the Germans and the Austrians (three-quarters or more). The Dutch, the Luxemburgians and the Greeks are somewhat above the average, and the British are just on it. (Swedes and Norwegians were not counted.) The huge gender gap is particularly important in bringing down the Italian, Greek, Portuguese and Irish figures.[4]

Class organization and class action

Besides by the variable of equality-dependence, the rate of association is also affected by the attractiveness of collective action in relation to individual action. Other things being equal, the anciently institutionalized European industrial class societies have furthered collective action over and above the flux of the New Worlds. The distinctively European pattern of class organization is apparent in the relative success of European parties of labour, which have been in national government office in all European countries and which have headed a government everywhere in Europe except in Ireland, in contrast to never having done so in the USA and Canada and only once and for less than a year in Japan until most recently (1994) when a second spell of a fragile premiership opened.

Trade unions may be organizations of 'trades', occupations, or professions, as well as of class. On the whole, however, the rate of unionization is a good modern indicator of class organization. For, and with the help of, the OECD, the Dutch researcher Dr Jelle Visser has made a major comparative study of unionization, mainly, but not exclusively, based on organizational data (see Table 15.2).

The range of union density in Western Europe – from an overall rate in 1988 of 85% in Sweden to 12% in France – means that all-half-continental figures make only limited sense. However, among the most developed countries, the high unionization of Western Europe does stand out. The average among the four big countries may take on a particular meaning because of the French outlier. The three others range from 33.8% in Germany to 41.5% in the UK via Italy's 39.6%.

It might be surmised, however, that the averaged big four situation is a relatively sensible pointer to the trade union situation in the EC, in particular since comparable data are not available for Greece, Portugal and Spain, although the latter clearly fall in below Germany, with Spain in the vicinity of France. The Belgian and the Irish rates of union organization are the highest in the EC, at 53.0% and 52.4%, respectively. The Dutch unions, on the other hand, appear to have been the biggest losers (probably after the Iberian ones, however) since 1975. In 1988 they organized 25% of all Dutch

Table 15.2 *Patterns of unionization, 1975–1988 (per cent union members among wage- and salary-earners in employment)*

	Big Europe[a]	Nordic countries[b]	USA	Japan[c]
Total 1975	38.7	65.5	22.8	34.4
Total 1988[d]	31.7	71.4	16.4	26.8
Manuf. 1988	35.0	92.0	22.0	32.0
Trade 1988	16[e]	39.0	6.0	9.0
Transp. & comm. 1988	51.0–57.0[f]	71.0[g]	32.0	50.0
Publ. 1988[h]	45.1	78.0	36.7	55.8
Priv. 1988	27.0	64.8	12.9	23.3

Notes: [a] France, Germany, Italy, the UK, unweighted averages. [b] Denmark, Finland, Norway and Sweden, unweighted averages. [c] Whereas the other membership figures are net of retired, unemployed and students, this is not the case for Japan. [d] For the USA, 1989; occasionally one of the averaged data is also from an adjacent year. [e] French unionization here supposed to be 0. For manufacturing the source gives the rate to less than five. [f] No data for France available, but they should be in the range from 0 to 26, the public sector rate of unionization. [g] Excl. Finland; Danish data from 1985. [h] Excl. autonomous, market-operating public enterprises, but incl. public transport.

Source: OECD, *Employment Outlook, July 1991*, Paris 1991, Ch. 4.

workers and employees in employment, down 13 percentage points. (The French are estimated to have lost 11 percentage points.)

The Nordic countries set themselves off from all the rest, a fact again underlined by their post-1975 growth – a trend non-dramatically broken by the end of the 1980s, however – and by their firm grip of manufacturing employment, without the help of any closed shop deals.

Sectorally, the importance of the public sector stands out, by which the high rates in transport and communications are likely to be largely explained. By contrast, the generally low union density in the trade sector (which includes also restaurants and hotels) indicates the significant difference between a service society with overwhelmingly private services and one with a large public service sector.

The World Values Survey 1990–1991 also asked questions about trade union membership. Instead of trying to adapt them to the trade union studies problematic of how large a proportion of the recruitment target of trade unions are organized, i.e. the rate of unionization, we shall here use them as an indicator of the relative weight of unions in society as a whole (see Table 15.3). The margins of error at sample studies should be kept in mind, as well as the urban skewing of the Third World samples.

The Communist pattern of proletarianization-cum-unionization was still characteristic of Eastern Europe in 1990–1, although the Bulgarian datum of 20% was already indicating the direction of change. Russian or East German figures were similar to Swedish ones at, 62, 56 and 59%, respectively.

Differences of organization similar to those of workers pertain also to the other side of class action, to that of employers. Strong, nationally centralized and state-autonomous employers' organizations have developed only in the

Table 15.3 *The weight of unions in the world's societies, 1990–1991 (percentage of the adult population belonging to a trade union)*

Western Germanic Europe[a]	26
Western Latin Europe[b]	4
Eastern Europe[c]	48
North America	10
Latin America[d]	4
Nigeria	14
Japan and South Korea	7
China	2

Notes: [a] Austria, Belgium, Britain, Denmark, Finland, W. Germany, Ireland, Netherlands, Norway, Sweden. [b] France, Italy, Portugal, Spain, [c] Bulgaria, Estonia, E. Germany, Hungary, Latvia, Lithuania, Russia. [d] Brazil, Chile, Mexico.

Source: World Values Survey 1990–1991, variable 22.

Nordic countries. Important but decentralized organizations have been established in West Germany and Switzerland, whereas the central employers' associations of Austria, Belgium, Italy and the Netherlands, and the weaker French one, have risen as imbrications of industrial associations with structures and concerns of the state. Among American employers in particular and among Anglo-Saxon employers generally individual action has been dominant. Japanese employers are nationally organized, but employers' actions are not normally collective.[5]

The alternative patterns of protest and association tend to divide Western Europe again between North and South. Apart from structural differentiation, such as social egalitarianism and rural resources of collective communication and action in the North, there is probably also an important aspect of cultural learning involved. Early modern French history taught later generations of French social activists the efficacy of crowd protest in bringing about social change. That was a lesson of 1789, 1791, 1830, 1848 and 1871. Even though setbacks often followed, brief, militant crowd action in the capital, and locally also in provincial cities, was very powerful.

The dramatic nineteenth- and early twentieth-century history of Italy, Spain and Portugal, under significant French impact and inspiration, tended towards similar conclusions. The Central and Northern European experiences – most clearly the defeats or relative insignificance of 1848, but also the petering out of British Chartism –, on the other hand, tended in the opposite direction. Immediate mass action was ineffective at best, and very costly at worst. Instead, long-term collective action by association held much more promise.

Even though with by no means a good fit, the postwar Western European pattern of industrial conflict and industrial association tends to reflect a pattern of direct conflict on one side and association-cum-negotiation on the other.[6] Greece, Spain, Italy and Portugal have the largest involvement in open industrial protest, while having a low or, in the Italian case, average rate of association. The Nordic countries, on their side, have a high rate of association and a modest amount of conflict involvement, in spite of the fact that when they go on strike or lockout the Nordic class organizations are followed by class members to an enormous extent, because of the extension and depth of the former (see Table 15.4).[7]

Table 15.4 *Industrial conflict, 1946–1990, and union density in 1988*

Number of people involved in strikes and lockouts per 10,000 employees. Arithmetic averages. Union members as percentage of employees.

Country	1946–1976	1986–1990	Density 1988
Austria	145	13	45.7
Belgium	331	n.a.	53.0
Denmark	184	161	73.2
Finland	835	111	71.3
France	1,367	62[a]	12.0
Greece	n.a.	4,845	25.0[b]
Ireland	293	245	52.4
Italy	2,313	2,471	39.6
Netherlands	57	27	25.0
Norway	64	276	57.1
Portugal	n.a.	469[c]	30.0[b]
Spain	n.a.	2,223	16.0[d]
Sweden	36	136	85.3
Switzerland	7	0.5	26.0
UK	432	239	41.5
W. Germany	92	45	33.8
Australia	1,589	1,104	42.0
Canada	314	284	34.6
Japan	450	20	26.8
USA	354	25[e]	16.4

Notes: [a] Generalized strikes, covering several enterprises only. [b] Estimate. [c] 1986 and 1987 only. [d] 1985. [e] Excl. conflicts involving less than 1,000 workers and lasting less than a full day.

Sources: Industrial conflict 1946–76: W. Korpi, *The Democratic Class Struggle*, London, Routledge & Kegan Paul, 1983, p. 165; 1986–90 calculations from ILO, *Yearbook of Labour Statistics 1991*, Geneva, 1991, Tables 31A and 2A (reference year for number of employees, 1989): Swiss employees (in 1987) calculated from OECD, *Employment Outlook, July 1991*, p. 101, from which the data on union density are taken.

The period from the late 1960s up to and including the early 1980s were the 'golden days' of the labour movement, in protest as well as in organization and electoral influence.[8] Continental peaks of class protest were the French May 1968 strikes, the 'hot autumn' of 1969 in Italy, the

1974 British miners' strike, and the 1974–5 workers' revolution in Alentejo and in the Lisbon area of Portugal.

On a smaller scale, noteworthy moments of domestic class history occurred around 1970 also in Germany, the Netherlands, Sweden and Norway. Only Belgium, Denmark and Finland seem to have had other recent high point of class struggle – Belgium, and Wallonia particularly, in the quasi-insurrectionary strike around the turn of 1960–1, and Denmark and Finland in their general strikes of 1956.

Since 1980 there has followed a setback. The lower amount of strike involvement in the late 1980s should be seen as mostly an effect of weakened unions and worker collectives.[9] In their increased militancy, Swedish and Norwegian workers form exceptions, together with the (until recently) stably highly militant Italians. While the current trend is real enough, its shape is sometimes distorted by changes of statistical data collection, for instance in France.

In a longer historical perspective the volume of strike protest is still high in the most developed countries, and even more so in Europe. The average amount of industrial conflict involvement in the late 1980s is higher than in the interwar period and in 1900–13. The (arithmetic) average for Western Europe in the second half of the 1980s was 316 (per 10,000 workers/ employees), excluding the recent democracies of Greece, Portugal and Spain (and 755 including them). For the same group of countries, the corresponding figures are 485 for the 1946–76 period, 300 for 1919–38 and 192 for 1900–13.[10]

The postwar trajectory of social conflict started high, in the late 1940s and early 1950s, after the break-up of the anti-Fascist coalition and the coming of the Cold War. The worst confrontations took place in France in 1947–8, with their centres in Marseilles, among the miners of the Nord and Pas-de-Calais, and among the Parisian metal workers.

The spark was usually economic – in Marseilles a raise of the tram ticket prices by a new right-wing municipal government – but escalated rapidly into political battles, between Communists, on the one side, and the anti-Communist government, on the other. The French Socialist Minister of the Interior, Jules Moch, called out the army with tanks and several people were killed, though not as many in as in East Germany in 1953 or in Poznan in 1956. Thousands of people were arrested. The most militant and massive demonstration in the West also took place in Paris, in May 1952, against the US commander in the Korean War, General Ridgway.

There then ensued a certain lull, till about 1960. The centre now was Wallonia, and the Communists were rather marginal. The years around 1970 took the extension of class and social conflict above the 1947–52 level, but not in intensity or violence.[11]

The protest–association axis in Western Europe is also characteristic of collective action among another class, the farmers. Their strong negotiating organizations in the North, flanked until recently by significant explicitly farmers' parties in the Nordic countries and in Switzerland, contrast strongly with the fragmented organizations and the direct action militancy of, especially, the French farmers.[12]

New protests and new movements

The late 1960s and early 1970s saw both the culmination of industrial society and the birth of post-industrialism. In retrospect, the social convulsions at the time appear rather natural. The coincidence of industrial class concentration, the rise of mass education and the final challenge to Western colonialism burst open the smugness of the postwar boom. What ensued was both the zenith of class conflict and the rise of new or renewed protests and movements. Of the latter, the most dramatic was the action of the *students*.

Students are not new social actors. Their capacity for unruly collective action has been well known in the university towns since the Middle Ages. They were prominent in the nationalist and the national-democratic movements and revolutions of the nineteenth century, and they were strongly mobilized in the national movements of 1914 and in the interwar ideological struggles. It would seem, however, that there were two novel features of 1960s student action.

First, the thrust of the movement was internationalist, and often anti-nationalist. Solidarity with other ethnicities than one's own, was a key, and novel, feature of the student movement of the developed world. It was an identification with the Blacks in the American South, with the Vietnamese and with the Third World in general. This internationalist orientation provided the catalyst for mass radicalization from specific grievances with regard to the strains of mass education and to the erosion of parental authority – and with it of the *in loco parentis* principle of many university authorities.[13] It was crucial in the key cases of the US, the West German and the French student movements, which set the example for the others, many of which also started as international solidarity movements.

In the USA the catalyst was the right to vote of Southern Blacks and the Vietnam War. In Germany, apart from Vietnam, there were also a couple of other potent symbols of Third World repression: the Congolese puppet Tshombe and the Shah of Iran, who, as West German guests, provided crucial targets of mobilization. In France, the international trigger was, again, the Vietnam War, but here inserted into a wider complex of the limited legitimacy of the Gaullist regime, which originated in a quasi-*coup d'état* during another colonial war, that of France against Algeria. The relatively long-lived and militant Italian student movement, however, did start, in Trento in 1966, on the basis of purely intra-academic issues, around a sociology degree.[14]

As a second innovation, the 1960s student movement definitely established a new type of collective action, which we may call *triangular action*. The immediate action was directed against the state, or the university authority – in contrast to the interwar period there were hardly any clashes between students of different alignments – but the main meaning of it, more or less deliberately, was a general message, to be relayed and amplified by the mass media.

The world's foremost expert on collective action, Charles Tilly, has argued that the only significant change in collective action in modern times took place in the nineteenth century, from local patronized to national autonomous actions.[15] Nevertheless, this writer would venture that the advent of the mass media under conditions of mass democracy has created the possibility for various kinds of triangular symbolic action, the effect of which is mainly through their media amplification of public pressure upon elected politicians, and not in enlarging one's own movement and its power. And that this venue of collective action was first used on a large scale by the late 1960s student movement.[16]

The Amsterdam 1965 Provos apart, the young collective rebellion of the 1960s was overwhelmingly a student one, not a youth movement *tout court*, although other youth may have attached themselves to the latter. Rock music, youth fashion, pre-marital sex and a general generational experience of boom children formed the core of a much wider youth culture, which clashed individually and family-wise with an older generation. Usually, however, it did not take the form of collective action.

The new student movement first erupted in the USA in 1964, with the students' support for Blacks' civil rights and then with the opposition to the war. It spread from there to West Germany and, in particular, to West Berlin.

To the older generation, West Berlin was the border post of the Free World, once saved by the American air-lift in 1949. To the young generation, it was the place of left-wing possibilities, where you could go to escape the military service and the anti-Communist political bans of the Federal Republic. The American Vietnam War and the Third World issues brought the European generational clash to a head nowhere more dramatically and bitterly than in West Berlin.

The American war in Vietnam, and the West German extra-parliamentary opposition to the Grand Coalition of the major parties, provided the main galvanizers, on top of local issues of mass education, for the student opposition of Germany, France and Italy, which three became the most influential and massive in Europe.[17] In the other countries of Northwestern and Central Europe, the student movement, although in existence and active, was much less influential, less militant, or both. Less sudden massification of higher education and more legitimate or (in the Belgian case) less unified polities made for more limited, dispersed or contained student movements.

The revolt in November 1973 of the students of the Athens Polytechnic, which was bloodily repressed, was very important in the Greek process of democratization, but for the rest, the students' movement came *post hoc* (in

Portugal) or was relatively secondary (Spain) to the assertion of democracy in Southern Europe.[18] There was also a significant but soon defeated student movement in Eastern Europe in 1968, in Poland (clamped down upon in March), in Yugoslavia (repressed in June), and in Czechoslovakia (crushed in the August invasion).[19]

The collective action of the students was usually called 'the student movement', and there was a linkage of numerous groups, crowds and events. But, by and large, it was mainly a fairly brief series of protests.

From about 1970 the students' protests gave rise to a number of left-wing ideological movements, usually Communist of one variety or other, which petered out in the second half of the decade.[20] Only in some places have massive student protests returned since, most importantly, perhaps, in the actions of French *lycée* students in 1986. As a more vaguely defined generational experience, the 1968 rebellions have had enduring effects, which have fed into many forms of social radicalism and public concern, into feminism and environmentalism, as well as into internationalism, Social Democracy, Eurocommunism and generally into social reform.

Old people, above the economically active age, have become socially important in recent decades. Pensions have become a very sensitive political issue, and old age care is on the way to becoming one too. So far, however, there has been rather little collective action among the old. Trade unions organize pensioners in many countries, and in some countries, e.g. in the Low Countries and in Italy, the former have been major actors on behalf of the latter.[21] In other countries, such as Sweden, there are rather large-scale national associations of pensioners.

Occasionally, in Denmark, Germany and Britain for instance, there have also been protest actions, of which the American Black-inspired Grey Panthers constitute the most self-conscious manifestation. The Danish 'C team', meanwhile, which emerged in late 1991, looks back to the wartime Resistance. But on the whole, collective action by people of 'the Third Age' remains for the future. It seems likely to come. So far, however, old people's protests have been most vigorous and influential in parts of the New Worlds, in Argentina and, above all, in Uruguay (personal observation in 1992).

The *women's issue*, on the other hand, has come to the forefront. The 'second Feminist wave', the first one being around the last turn of the century, started at about the same time as the student protests. Between the two rebellions there have been several kinds of relations. Both had the same core of support, i.e. young educated people, although the Feminist vanguard was often slightly older than the ordinary student activists. Both were, and saw themselves, as left-wing. The student protests opened up a new arena of provocative symbolic action, which the women's movement then made innovative uses of. But male-dominated student activism was also something feminists reacted against and broke loose from. In West Germany, that process of distanciation began already in 1968.

As a movement of continuously linked actions and groups, the women's movement was also rather short-lived. It got going around 1970 – in

Southern, then dictatorial Europe somewhat later – and by the beginning of the 1980s it had dissolved or become seriously weakened in most countries – Portugal being one exception, and Iceland, where the 1980s saw a successful turn to electoral feminism, another. The latter was triumphantly revindicated in early 1994 when the Women's List conquered the mayorship of the capital Reykjavik.

The international wave of women's protest was not as clearly structured around a few internationally spectacular events as the students' movement. A pattern of ideological influence is discernible, which to some extent differs from that of the students. The centres of international feminism were the United States – a nineteenth-century pioneer of women's collective action – for a short time the left-wing Feminist students in West Germany, the UK and, more regionally, Denmark (in Scandinavia) and the Netherlands (in the Low Countries).

The Treaty of Rome article on equal pay provided the rationale for a tough women's strike in Liège in 1966, and the Third Guideline about non-sexist social rights in the EC provided important support for Dutch women in the mid-1980s.

The absence of any French major influence is striking, although de Beauvoir was, of course, widely read. The French women's movement was extremely short-lived and fragmented. It did produce one of the more memorable symbolic acts of the European women's movement, however: the wreath to the women of the unknown soldiers, at the monument of the Unknown Soldier in August 1970. As in most parts of Europe south of Scandinavia, where socio-economic concerns were more in the foreground, abortion was the main focus of collective action.

In spite of more prolonged collective struggles, with divorce as an added focal issue, the Italian movement also seems to have been rather on the receiving end of international communication. There, the mid-1970s saw a turn to French Feminist psychoanalysis. As in the case of the students, the quiescence of Austrian women is noteworthy.

The women's movement in Europe has hardly given rise to new associations. Indeed, occasionally it has led to the dissolution of earlier women's organizations, such as the UDI in Italy. On the other hand, its legacy is much more enduring and tangible than that of the student protest. Extensive abortion rights were gained almost everywhere, save in Ireland, where, on the contrary, in the early 1980s an amendment to the constitution made abortion under any circumstances not only illegal but also unconstitutional. Child daycare services were also extended greatly, above all in Scandinavia.

As we saw in Chapter 6 above, the 1970s and early 1980s were a period of important legal de-patriarchalization, and in most countries the issue of gender equality has been institutionalized into special governmental offices and academic studies. The activities of these offices may not have been very effective, but nor have the gender equality and autonomy issues gone away. Their multi-faceted manifestations have only made it difficult to keep them in focus of continuous, supra-local collective action. The intellectual heritage of Feminist protest is very well maintained and developed, especially, it appears, in the Anglo-Saxon world, in Norway, and in the Nordic countries more generally.[22]

Among the new movements which sprang from the student protests of the late 1960s, there were also territorial ones, i.e. movements claiming to represent the interests of the people of a certain *territory*, other than that of the state. The whole Belgian party system broke up in this period, beginning earlier in 1965 with the first appearance of the Front des Francophones and a significant advance of the Flemish Volksunie, and consummated in 1978, when all the political parties were divided up along ethnic/territorial lines.[23]

Here, however, the coincidence was probably more an encouraging *Zeitgeist* than any strong causal link. The break-up of Belgium has deep cultural roots, and the student protests were generally less militant and pervasive than in many other countries. The Flemish students' successful campaign against the renowned francophone Catholic Louvain University on 'Flemish soil', 'Wallonians Out!' ('Walen Buiten!'), does show a direct link, however, between student protest and ethnic territorialism. In France, in Spain, after the death of Franco, and in Scotland and Wales, university rebellion did clearly stimulate and provide examples for a broad palette of regional nationalisms.[24] After quiescence in the 1980s (outside Belgium), these movements have shown signs of revitalization in the early 1990s, clearly stimulated by the weakening of the national state within the European integration process.

Regionalist movements now have their own international organization, the Free European Alliance.[25] Regions within the EC have established a whole series of organizations for collective action by collective actors, both general ones, beginning with the Conference of local and regional powers of Europe, set up in 1975, and so far peaking in the Assembly of the regions of Europe from 1989, and organizations of regions with particular characteristics.

For example, there are organizations and networks of traditional industrial regions, of cities with 'quartiers en crise' ('neighbourhoods in crisis'), of maritime peripheries, of mountainous regions, of the islands of Europe, and 'the four motors', i.e. Baden-Württemberg, Catalonia, Lombardy and Rhône-Alpes. In Lyons in May 1991, a major event – 'Europanorama' – featuring exhibitions, political and economic debates, and cultural events was organized by the regionalist forces of Europe within the EC.[26]

There is a mounting demand for a regional chamber of the European Parliament. In spring 1994 an official, consultative EU body of 'local collectivities' was established, the national composition of which has been the object of intense wrangling between regions and municipalities.

The collective action touched upon so far has unfolded by appealing to *positional identities* in the social structure, to workers, employers, farmers, students, women, ethnicities or regional inhabitants, while also making more universalistic ideological appeals. Other foci of collective action have started from certain *value commitments*. Two such currents have been particularly significant in Western Europe in recent decades. One is environmentalism, the other has been concerned with peace and disarmament.

Although it has its own specific origins, *environmentalism* also rose around 1970, slightly after the student revolt and after the second feminist wave. Concerned scholars played a noteworthy part in its emergence, as 'prophets of doom'. A key year was 1972, the year of the UN Environment Conference in Stockholm. Then appeared *The Limits to Growth*, by the Italian-initiated International Club of Rome – *de facto* largely American (MIT) – and in Britain *A Blueprint for Survival*.[27] A few years later politicians Erhard Eppler and Herbert Gruhl raised the alarm in Germany.

As collective action, current environmentalism began in the United States in the late 1960s, leading up to a major national manifestation, Earth Day, on 22 April 1970. The American Friends of the Earth spread to Europe, to Britain and France that same year. Like feminism, environmentalism is more a movement than an association, although the latter has associated to a greater extent and more tightly than the former. In the international organization Greenpeace, environmentalism has made symbolic triangular – actor, target, media – action into a professional art. Greenpeace originated by protesting against nuclear testing in the former British Empire. From Western Canada in 1971 it spread to New Zealand, the USA, Australia and Britain, where its international headquarters was based until its move to Amsterdam in the late 1980s.

Two concerns have made environmentalism a focus of mass action. One has been the opposition to nuclear energy, the other autonomous electoral mobilization. The storm-centre of anti-nuclear militancy was West Germany, where a series of massive demonstrations, often leading to clashes with the police, were staged in the late 1970s and early 1980s. The German example also inspired action in the Netherlands, which was involved in a joint nuclear project in Kalkar, and in Denmark. Sweden also had a mass movement against nuclear energy, though this was more peaceful and more peacefully treated.

It was clear that a great deal of left-wing student energy after 1970 was transformed into anti-nuclear activism. But if and how depended upon the national political system and national political cultures. The anti-nuclear movement was spectacularly weak in France, and remarkably late and peaceful in Italy. In the course of the 1980s, the nuclear energy programmes were shelved or stalled in most countries – in Austria, Sweden and Italy after referenda, in the Netherlands after a 'broad societal discussion'.[28]

Environmental issues briefly played an important role in the beginning of the new protests and embryonic movements in Eastern Europe in the mid-1980s, from Estonia – against an extension of phosphate mining – and Latvia – against a new water power station in Daugavpils and the plans for an underground in Riga – and the Ukraine (Chernobyl), to Bulgaria and its Eco-Glasnost, starting in Ruse with objections to Romanian air pollution from the other side of the Danube. But they were soon overshadowed by issues of political rights and powers, and later by socio-economic problems.[29]

Attempts at electoral ecological mobilization have been made all over Western Europe, with very uneven results. The latter largely reflect the national party and electoral systems. To what extent they also express variations of environmental concern is very hazardous to tell. Southern Europe and Ireland lack significant Green parties or otherwise autonomous electoral manifestations of environmentalism.

So do Denmark, the Netherlands and Norway, although for different reasons, as far as a political observer's impressions indicate. The Socialist People's Parties of Denmark and Norway, and the Dutch Green Left/Green Progressive Agreement are pre-existing left-wing political formations, which through a very high environmentalist profile have managed to stave off new Green challengers. While similar pre-emptive tendencies do not seem absent from the politics of Ireland, the Iberian peninsula, Italy and Greece, they do appear weaker.

Green politics does appear more secondary in least developed part of Western Europe, although there are *Eurobarometer* data already from 1986 showing widespread sympathies with ecological, among other social, movements in Spain and, particularly, in Greece.[30] Significant ecological electoral movements can be found in Austria since 1986, in Belgium (both Flemish and francophone) at least since 1981, in Finland since 1987, in Germany since 1982, in Luxemburg since 1986 and in Switzerland at least since 1987, but electing the world's first Green national MP in 1979. 'Significant' here means at least 4–5% of the vote and parliamentary representation. The Swedish Environment Party polled 5.5% in 1988 and entered parliament, but fell below the 4% barrier in 1991; returning in 1994.

European elections have been important to the Green movement ever since the first one of 1979, contested with a small amount of success by British, Flemish and German Greens. These elections provide an escape from a domestic political and electoral system polarized between right and left, important particularly to the British, but also to the French.

French Friends of the Earth pioneered national electoral campaigning by European environmentalists, putting up the famous agronomist René Dumont as their Presidential candidate in 1974. Thereby they provided inspiration not only to francophone Belgians and Swiss (who had started earlier in the cantons of Neuchâtel and Vaud), but also to the German Greens. However, Socialist cooptation and a polarizing electoral system have kept French ecologists marginal as an autonomous political force, polling 10.6% in the European election of 1989. In Britain in the same election the Greens gained 14.9%, at a 37% turnout, but no seat.

Some of the most massive forms of collective action in modern times have been unleashed by the *threat of nuclear war*. A couple of the largest protest meetings ever, in absolute numbers as well as in proportion to the national population, took place in the Netherlands, against the deployment of a new set of nuclear missiles, in November 1981 and in October 1983. Exact, reliable figures of participants in huge demonstrations are difficult to obtain, but something like 400,000 in the first and 500,000 in the second were noted without any serious controversy at the time. That would amount to 3–3.5% of the Dutch nation in one place at one moment. The Dutch peace movement was directed by the Inter-Church Peace Council, in which the officious Calvinist Church (Hervormde Kerk) constituted the vanguard, but in which the – for a time, between the Second Vatican Council and Woytila's assertion of his powers – unusually progressive Dutch Catholic hierarchy also took part.

Initially in the late 1940s and early 1950s, the anti-atomic bomb issue was pushed by the Communist movement, with the worldwide mass petition campaign, 'the Stockholm Appeal', for the prohibition of nuclear weapons launched in March 1950, and the international front, the World Peace Council. After 1956, peace and nuclear disarmament spawned autonomous mass movements.

Nuclear disarmament developed into a movement in Britain in the late 1950s, in a broad coalition of the classical left, concerned clergy and middle-class secular radicalism. As such it gave inspiration to the West German Easter Marches, with a narrower political base, with little contact with middle-class liberalism or with the mainstream of the labour movement, but with a brief moment of mass success in 1968.

The British CND and the Finnish Peace Committee were more or less the only peace movements which managed to develop associations of some significance. Following a long decline after the 1963 Test-ban Treaty, the nuclear disarmament movement re-emerged after the 1979 Nato decision on new missiles deployment. The Netherlands, Germany, Britain and Belgium were the major centres of protest. The French were conspicuous in their support of the armaments race, and the Italians were clearly second to Central-Western Europe.[31] In spite of their size, however, the protests of the 1980s were unsuccessful.

Contours of contemporary Western collective action

In this multitude of events and organizations we may discern certain contours of a pattern of contemporary collective action. There was around 1970 a remarkable coincidence of dramatic collective action by positionally structured collectivities of workers, students and women, and by people committed to ecological values. Above we noted that those years were also the peak of industrialism and its peripetia into post-industrial societies.

Is there any connection between the social drama and the turn of economic epochs? The culmination of industrialism tended to strengthen labour in relation to capital, and should lead to advances by the former, whether dramatically or not being dependent upon resistance and prior acquiescence. The turn towards de-industrialization took place during the post-1974 crisis. From its positions of strength, it could be expected that labour would have resisted lay-offs and factory closures.

The coming of post-industrialism was prepared by the postwar industrial boom, its opening of social options and the rise of mass higher education. The inevitable strains which this implied, both on educational facilities and on traditional forms of social control, provided a sea of discontent in which radical vanguards could swim. The women's vanguard was also largely a product of recently extended higher education, and of a general, and unprecedented, boomtime youth culture, although feminism was ignited with a lag of one or two years compared with male student leftism. Environmentalism was developed by and spread in the post-student generation of the recently highly educated middle-class, and its limits to growth message appeared corroborated almost instantly by the 1973–4 oil squeeze.

In that way, the various movements were all inter-linked. What gave the years around 1970 their particular tenor of outrage and wrath, however, was their overlayering by a conflict of another temporality, the open challenge to the world hegemony of the Western world. The tenacious challenge of US world power by the poor Vietnamese people brought the various anti-colonial, anti-imperialist and anti-racist struggles in the world to a head, and became a crucial generational experience in Western Europe (and the USA itself).[32] To the left-leaning part of the '1968 generation', the Vietnam War had a similar far-reaching radicalization effect to that which the more directly experienced horrors of World War I and of Fascism had on previous cohorts.

West Berlin was the site of the most bitter confrontation, Paris of the largest one. Nowhere was the generational chasm deeper than in West Berlin, between the young radicals, gathered from all over the Federal Republic into the non-conscription city, and the ageing, former more or less loyal citizens of the Reich, grateful to the Americans, who had saved them from the Russians.

Paris concentrated a mass of students, a very sizeable left-wing intelligentsia, a combative and largely Communist suburban working-class, and the political contradictions of a regime which, however democratically institutionalized, did have the widely contested legitimacy of recently deriving from something close to a *coup d'état*. The tenth anniversary of the regime (13 May 1968) brought the simmering ingredients to the boil. In Italy, meanwhile, it was little wonder that the glaring and enduring inadequacy of educational facilities as well as of the politico-administrative system, coexisting with a strong and broad left (mainly Communist) opposition, should give rise to the most protracted and violent manifestations of students' and youth protest.

The events around 1970 took a specific shape and acquired a special significance in Western Europe – which might very well have been similar in Eastern Europe, but for the Soviet tanks, present or reasonably expected – by their relation to and effects upon the working-class and the labour movement. While leftist students clashed with every labour movement in existence, the rebellion of the former did have profound and durable effects on Social Democracies as well as Eurocommunism, in a new, more global, less authoritarian, more socially circumspect radicalism.

On the other hand, the new social movements, in fact second waves of nineteenth-century movements, of students, women and ecologists, derived a large part of their original ideas and of their repertoire of action from North America. In that sense, ironically enough, given the centrality of the opposition to the US war in Vietnam, the new protest was, among many other things, also part of an Americanization of Europe.[33]

Within Europe we have noted some spatial patterns of collective action. In Scandinavia and in Austria, there are strong and large associations, and rather or very little protest action, whereas in Southern Europe, including France, it is more or less the other way around. There was in the early 1980s more French participation than the EC average in petitions, legal demonstrations, wildcat strikes, boycotts and occupations of buildings. More than average demonstrative activity was also reported from Italy and Spain.[34]

Less clearly visible, there seems also to be another pattern. It is most apparent in the distribution of the peace movement, but it might be spotted in that of the ecological and the Feminist movements too. The sustained moral concerns and social dissent of these movements seem to flourish most strongly in predominantly Protestant-cum-secularized cultures. Protestant clergy have played a crucial part in the strong peace movements, and it may be argued that they have provided the example for their fellow Catholic priests insofar as the latter have participated, which they have significantly in the Netherlands and in Britain. Secularized ex-Protestant middle-class dissent too seems to have been an important carrier of progressive movements, for disarmament, women's rights, and for the environment. This is clearly the case in the Anglo-Saxon countries, in the Netherlands and in Scandinavia. Its weakness in Germany and its absence in the Catholic and Orthodox countries might explain something of the relative feebleness of the movements in these nations.

The non-class movements and protests treated here have all been left-wing in some sense. Without any indisputable logical derivation from classical political cleavages, nuclear energy became interpreted very widely as right-wing, and the anti-nuclear protest as the left stance, for instance. But has there been no significant *right-wing collective action*, except for the 'normal' action of employers and of farmers?

There has, although the postwar insight and power of the moderate right have been such that little special collective action has been needed. But when it has, the forces have been successfully mobilized. May 1968 in France, for instance, did not end in left-wing student celebration, but in a gigantic Gaullist, middle-aged demonstration, after the General, having assured himself of the support of the army for an eventual crackdown, went on the air declaring 'I am *not* going to retire!'

The Swedish employers hold probably two records: for the biggest lockout, in 1980, and for the biggest capitalist street demonstration, against the 'wage-earners' funds' proposal in 1982. (The first ended in a defeat, however, and the second did not prevent the new Social Democratic government from dutifully passing a law about a funds system, but with the union teeth of social change taken out.)

We should also take note that the European right has made a recent very important contribution to world policy and ideology, with the principled stance and rigidity typical of European modern political thought. But it was hardly brought about by any broad collective action, rather by factional party capture and by vigorous leadership in an electoral system favouring large, cohesive minorities. The reference is, of course, to Thatcherism, which may crudely be summed up in its most influential core as privatization and populist union-bashing. One precondition of the success of Thatcherism in this sense was, of course, de-industrialization and its ensuing shift of class power.

The new Christian, mainly Protestant, fundamentalism, which has been so important to right-wing movements recently in the USA and in Central America, has been little significant in Western Europe. The only, partial, exception is Ireland, where a combative Catholic reaction developed in the wake of the Papal visit to Ireland in 1979. Generous state financial support for Catholic, 'free', education mobilized large crowds in late 1980s France, but protests against abortion have not.

The turn of Europe from an emigrant to an immigrant continent has provided most of the firewood for a specifically right-wing kind of collective action. The non-European immigrants and refugees have become the Jews and the Gypsies of the contemporary militant right, without fully dispensing with the latter as xenophobic targets. Again, the European elections have been good electoral training and proving grounds.

The French Front National first emerged as a significant force in the European election of 1984, the German Republikaner in that of 1989. These two countries, plus Italy, which in spite of its constitution, has for long had a neo-Fascist party (MSI), and Flanders (Vlaams Blok) are the only ones with significant far right electoral support, although most countries have at least one party of some significance with some dark side to it, like the Austrian and the francophone Belgian 'Liberals'.

The government entry of the Italian Fascists in spring 1994, with the launching of an officious campaign for the rehabilitation of Mussolini, marks the beginning of a new stage in European far right politics. While it clearly marks the end of postwar Europe, it is not likely to bring a return to the period of preparation for war. Mussolini's days of exalting violence, authoritarianism, the state and imperialism, and of uniformed thugs terrorizing the population with the blessing of the Leader, still look fairly distant.

The distinctive classical far right forms of collective action are the pogrom and the lynching. In somewhat milder forms of assaults upon non-Europeans, this has spread rapidly in the early 1990s, in Germany (both sides), Switzerland, Sweden, France and other countries. However ugly it may appear to all Europeans of the Enlightenment tradition, ethnic friction, peaceful or violent, during the historical turn of Western Europe towards multicultural societies is what social analysts should expect. This development is yet another expression of a *rapprochement* between Europe and the New Worlds.

Protests and movements in the associated nations of the East

Eastern Europe under Communism was an *authoritarianly associated society*, rather than a totalitarian one suspended between an omnipotent state and an atomized society. The state was always subordinate to the Communist party apparatus, and the ruling Communist parties were huge organizations. From tiny vanguards right after the war they expanded at vertiginous speed, percentage-wise most rapidly in the cases of Romania and Poland, to absolute levels first of all in Czechoslovakia, where in 1949 about 19% of the total population were card-carrying Communists.[35]

Table 15.5 *Eastern European Communist Party membership as per cent of the population, circa 1970*

Albania	3.6
Bulgaria	7.7
Czechoslovakia	8.4
E. Germany	11.2
Hungary	6.4
Poland	7.0
Romania	11.2
USSR	6.0
Yugoslavia	5.2

Source: Calculations from L. Cohen and J. Shapiro (eds), *Communist Systems in Perspective*, Garden City, NY, Anchor Books, 1974, Tables II and IV.

The figures in Table 15.5 may be compared to total party membership, of all parties, in the EC, which, according to *Eurobarometer* surveys, was 6.4% of the population in 1975.[36] But the Communist parties were not the only associations. In several countries there were also other parties, albeit subordinate shadow bodies, and, above all, there were the so-called mass organizations. The trade unions comprised almost the whole population. There were also youth and women's organizations, international friendship organizations, sports clubs, etc.

East Germany, the GDR, was probably the best-organized of the Communist countries, and is hardly representative of the group. But it may be used as an illustration of an ideal typical Communist society. Most significant in this respect is the large membership of voluntary organizations, i.e. organizations with no overt political affiliations. Sports organizations, for instance, had together, probably with some multiple counting of membership, almost 3.7 million members in 1988, i.e. more than 20% of the total population. (The GDR was the only country I know of which listed its Olympic games participations and achievements in the official statistical yearbook.) A rather non-competitive sport like angling, certainly without any links to international prestige competition, organized 528,000 people in 1988.

The organization of gardeners and breeders of small animals rallied almost a tenth of the total population, 1.488 million. Popular Solidarity (Volkssolidarität), an organization of charity and social work, may have carried some positive political overtones, but was hardly a step on the career ladder. It comprised 2.1 million members, out of a population of 16.7 million, and 200,000 unpaid helpers. The Red Cross had 706,000 members. Urania, the society for the diffusion of scientific knowledge, was primarily, though not exclusively, geared to the natural sciences. It had 417,000 members.[37]

The dissident 'civil society' literature, which developed in Poland, Czechoslovakia and Hungary in the course of the 1980s, understandably and respectably, and post-Communist anti-Communist literature, also understandably but less respectably from a scholarly point of view, have tended to neglect the 'civil society' of gardeners, anglers, voluntary social workers and lay people interested in science. The dissident civil society discourse developed a normative social conception which more fortunately located democrats have every reason to respect, focusing as it does on plurality, privacy, publicity and legality.[38]

But 'civil society' has also become a camouflaged ideological weapon in the struggle for a particular economic system, as when it is argued that 'civil society's activity . . . is visible in . . . stock exchanges'.[39] The civil society deficit is located in Latin Europe, and outside Europe at least in Latin America and Japan, as we saw above.

What was lacking in Eastern Europe is not very well captured by the ambiguous notion of 'civil society'. Rather, it was something that is much better expressed in German than in English – 'eine mündige Öffentlichkeit', i.e. an *autonomous public*, the possibility to express a genuine opinion in public, without material sanctions for heterodox views.

The protests against Communist power had their specific national patterns, which are still little investigated. Their time-course is largely known, but seldom put together. After the instalment of Communist, or *Communisant*, rule there was armed resistance in two countries, in neighbouring Poland and Lithuania. The Communist monopolization of power in 1947- 8 met no serious resistance anywhere. The break-neck industrial accumulation, attempting to catch up with Western capitalist accumulation, led to major working-class protests in the GDR in 1953 and, to a more limited extent, in Polish Poznan in 1956. Elsewhere discontent was contained.

National Communist party radical change succeeded with little commotion outside the party cadres in Yugoslavia in 1948, in Albania in 1960 and in Romania after 1965; and after some brinkmanship with the Soviets also in Poland in October 1956. Internal Communist change was overrun by nationalist protests in Hungary later in October 1956, and then crushed by the Soviets. It was denied its *raison d'être* by the latter in the case of Czechoslovakia in 1968.

Significant working-class economic collective protest established itself only in Poland, where Poznan in 1956 was followed by Gdansk in 1970, by Ursus, Radom and Gdansk in 1976, and again by Gdansk and other places on the Baltic and by Ursus in 1980. While the trigger of the first was raised work norms, the others followed from higher food prices.

The acute problems of Communist power in postwar Europe were all concentrated in East-Central Europe, from Lithuania to Hungary. Three forces were involved in the basic conflicts of power. One was the working-class and its immediate economic interests, most strongly manifested in Poland, initially very strongly also in East Germany. The second was militant nationalism, originally most militant in the former Polish–Lithuanian Confederation, later on in Hungary. The third component was Soviet, and other Communist (East German and Polish) security interests, which decided the fate of Czechoslovak reform Communism.

Militant nationalism derives from national traditions and the recent experience of the latter. Postwar, the strong Balkan anti-Communist nationalism had little chance, militarily defeated during the war in Yugoslavia and Albania, utterly discredited by the war disaster in Romania, never strong and also discredited in Bulgaria. Poland, on the other hand, was part of the winning Allied coalition. Working-class protest was polarized between that of the most settled and experience-rich, the East German, and that of the rawest, most recently proletarianized and urbanized working-class of Central Europe, the Polish.

What pattern of collective action is discernible in the *endgames of Eastern European Communism*? Communism in Eastern Europe ended in three ways – by dissolution, by negotiation and by surrender. Collective action played a significant part in each, in ascending order of importance.

Decisive, however, was the process of dissolution initiated by auto-transformations from above. Systemic change from above as the chosen exit from Communism as a regime was the main road adopted in the USSR and in Yugoslavia, but in both cases a number of side-tracks and side-plots complicated the story. There was no very serious systemic opposition. Rather, opposition was invited or initiated from above. The path of change chosen and held onto by Mikhail Gorbachev was, of course, crucial to the change of all Eastern Europe. Reform was encouraged, and hardliners everywhere knew that no Soviet help could be counted upon in a violent showdown.

By summer 1988 Gorbachev had reached the conclusion that radical political change was top priority, and that he wanted to 'open all sluices'.[40]

In March 1989 semi-free elections took place in the USSR, for the first time since 1917.

The Soviet path was complicated by nationalist demands rising from the peripheries, from the Caucasus and the Baltics in particular, and, fatally, from a split of the top leadership, transposed into a federal–dominant national unit conflict, between Gorbachev and Yeltsin. The fall of Yalta Communism in the autumn of 1989 seems to have had remarkably little direct effect in the Soviet Union, as far as available sources tell. Striking coal miners, of Kuzbass, Donbass and Vorkuta, added very significantly to the strifes of 1989 and of 1991, and their economic weight was certainly felt in the agony of the system. But neither the miners nor any other socio-economic force focalized the conflicts rousing almost everywhere in the last months of the USSR.

What killed off the Union of Socialist Soviet Republics was, most directly at least, top-level conflict, first by Russia setting up a big tent of its own, and then by the bungled farce of August 1991, the operetta coup against Gorbachev. In the week after the putsch, all the European republics left the union. In December Gorbachev's remaining power was abolished, and the USSR dissolved. Already by May 1991 the federal Presidency of Yugoslavia had ceased to function, also the outcome of conflicts among nationalist republican leaders.

The republics of the former USSR and Yugoslavia are all basically examples of auto-transformations from above. Belorussia is, perhaps, an extreme case of serenity, basically moved by external contingencies, little affected by internal challenge. The Baltic republics, with their huge autonomous national manifestations and their short-lived Popular Fronts, on the other hand, had a massive input of crowd action and of movements, running with, and at times outrunning, their new nationalist Communists.

The Hungarian Communists were facing an articulated opposition, from what might perhaps be called an increasingly complex civil society. On the other hand, they – or some of them – took the initiative of political and economic change, as we noted in Chapter 14 above in the section on Communist acculturation. Negotiations and elections provided an orderly exit from the previous regime. Collective action was not insignificant, however. The rehabilitation burial, in June 1989, of Imre Nagy, the reform Communist executed in 1957, galvanized the opposition. In the autumn of 1989, a successful mass petition changed the electoral calendar in a way favourable to the opposition. But by then a constitutional democracy was already functioning.

Poland was the ideal typical case of a negotiated ending. Uniquely among all the Communist countries, Poland developed and sustained an auton-omous mass movement, at its core a working-class trade union movement. In terms of learning experiences it went back at least till 1970, and maybe also to 1956. With regard to direct personal links, of leaders and ideologues, the movement that later became famous as Solidarity went back to the strike movement of 1976. It drew upon a remarkable coalition of intellectual heritage, alongside immediate working-class interests, of prewar nationalist socialism, dissident Communism and, above all, Catholicism, and sustained by most of the contemporary flower of the nation's culture.[41]

The British miners never managed to rally the same scale of allies as the Polish engineers or miners, and Arthur Scargill never became the world's darling, like Lech Walesa. But the East–West irony in looking at the Polish–British mirror is well worth noting. Polish and British workers in the 1960s, 1970s and 1980s fought for basically the same things, certain short-term protective devices in a world where the bosses were not trusted. The workers' mistrust and militancy were perceived by the governments and the economists of both Britain and Poland as a major obstacle to accumulation. Edward Heath and James Callaghan were politically destroyed by the defensive workers' movement, as were Wladyslaw Gomulka and Edward Gierek.

But the Thatcher Tories, working in a parliamentary democracy, albeit largely helped by the peculiarities of the British constitution, finally succeeded where a whole series of Polish Communist General Secretaries with more or less dictatorial powers had failed, even when deploying the army. The British unions were brought to heel, and their most combative sections shoved off onto the dole. The admiration which a number of frustrated Polish officials of the 1980s had for Mrs Thatcher is understandable.

While keeping, and flexing, its industrial muscles, Solidárnosc also became a national Catholic mass movement, with which the Jaruzelski government in the end saw itself forced to negotiate. Hard bargaining on both sides led to a political-economic compromise, which immediately gathered a momentum of its own, given the country's acute economic crisis.

Where the regimes could not bring themselves to take any initiatives of substantial reform, urban crowds, emboldened by the *laissez-faire* signals from Moscow and by the examples of neighbouring countries, became the major force of change.

Urban crowds played the only main part in the Romanian act, first in Timisoara, then, and decisively, in Bucharest – suddenly angry, suddenly revolutionary crowds, bursting through the carapace of fear. There was no movement, there were no negotiations. True, there were a number of silenced, former oppositional Communists, who stepped into the houses of power that had been thrown open. In some accounts that has been called a betrayal or an usurpation of the revolution, as if the power of a crowd could be betrayed or usurped. In any case, the new power-holders soon faced the test of free elections.

The case most approximating Romania was Czechoslovakia, also decided by crowd action, after a few days of negotiations. But with its students' demonstrations, which started the process, its intellectual leader figures and basically peaceful and mass medial ambience, the Czechoslovak November '89 was more similar to French May '68, except for de Gaulle's fighting speech on 30 May.

Albania, Bulgaria and the GDR may be found on the negotiations–surrender line of the triangle of Communist endings. The push for change started with massive public displays of discontent, in the GDR with mass exits from the country in the autumn of 1989, and weekly escalating (but peaceful) demonstrations in Leipzig. In Bulgaria, in the autumn of 1989, and in Albania, in the winter of 1991, crowd action started only after the belated first moves of change had been made in the ruling party leadership.[42]

The collective action involved in the end of Communism was not so much that of civil societies vindicating themselves – neither the actually existing nor the theorized – as the sudden power of crowds and the manifestation of *national societies*.

Commemorations of national history played a crucial part in many of the popular mobilizations in 1988–9. The Baltics mourned the Molotov–Ribbentrop Pact and its ending of interwar Baltic independence, and celebrated their late nineteenth-century traditions of song festivals. In Russia an increasing turn to pre-1917 traditions and symbolism got a significant push from millennium celebrations in June 1988 of the baptism of Prince Vladimir I. Russian state events have thereafter tended to be cast in Orthodox liturgy.

The Serbs remembered the semi-millennium of their defeat at Kossovo Polje in a monster manifestation. Hungarian public opinion moved in 1989 with the official re-evaluation and commemoration of the 'events of 1956'. Even in tightly guarded Czechoslovakia there was a significant demonstration on 21 August 1988, commemorating the invasion twenty years earlier. The opening of the endgame in 1989 was a lawful demonstration by students in memory of a student who had been murdered by the German Nazis fifty years before.

National politics was the most important explosive in detonating the Communist system, not demands for democracy, capitalism or even more consumption. Democratization started from above, in the USSR, in Hungary, in republics of Yugoslavia, and was accepted in Poland and Yugoslavia. Far-reaching economic changes were also embarked upon by the regimes of countries just mentioned, not with a view to restoring capitalism, true, but heading for a mixed socialist market economy.

National politics is not the same as nationalism. The former is a power stratagem, the latter an ideology or value system. Collective action is not necessarily driven by members' -isms, but by leaders' signals. The USSR and Yugoslavia broke up most directly – abstaining from any claim to a 'fundamental' explanation – because a set of political leaders among the dominant national republics chose to play the national card. Slobodan Milosevic and his Serbian team, from 1987, played it aggressively not only against the 'unjust' federal system but also, and most violently, against other nationalities, the Albanians of Kossovo in particular. Once the cork of the bottle of South Slav nationalisms was released, nationalism became trump in Croatia, and in other parts of Yugoslavia too.

Boris Yeltsin played his Russian role primarily against Gorbachev and the federal power of the USSR, which has so far saved European ex-USSR from the wars of ex-Yugoslavia. But the result was similar for the rest: the collapse of Communist socialism and the substitution of a series of nation-states containing firewood for future conflicts within a multinational federation.

National issues were naturally sensitive in the multinational states of the USSR and Yugoslavia. The Russian imperial tradition which Stalin had built into the postwar USSR and largely into postwar Eastern Europe as well provided many reasons for discontent and *ressentiments*. But the decisive issues were not the legitimate ownership of Nagorno-Karabakh, the independence of the Baltic republics or the status of the Serbian minority in Kossovo. Instead, decisive were the Serbian leaders' questioning of the existing Yugoslav federation, and the Russian leaders' felling of the Soviet federation. In the final struggle for power in the USSR, holding the Union responsible for the crisis and appealing to Russian national sentiments became a forceful means of mobilization.[43]

The third key card sharp in the national de-Communization of Europe along with Milosevic and Yeltsin was Helmut Kohl, who was much more important than the former, probably less so than the latter. The West German Federal Chancellor saw earlier and more clearly than most Germans the chance of using the fall of the old Communist regime for a national unification of Germany. Here again, we can gauge the importance of politics in moulding opinion in contexts of social change.

By the end of November 1989, a couple of weeks after the opening of the Wall, East German opinion was divided half-and-half for and against unification, with opposition more intensive than adherence. National unification had emerged as a popular slogan by then – turning from '*We* are the People' to 'We are *one* people' – but the issue was undecided. However, after Kohl had presented his programme for 're-unification' on 28 November, the national train started rolling. By early February 1990 about 80% of the East Germans were in favour.[44]

With the end of the GDR in immediate sight, change in Eastern Europe was no longer a case of a set of nations undergoing democratization and socio-economic reform, but the beginning of the end of a social system, consummated with the break-up of the USSR into nation-states. National politics became systemic revolution. Popular support for the latter was uneven and largely conjunctural, though. In an interview round from November 1993 to April 1994, a majority of Belorussians, Bulgarians, Hungarians, Slovaks, Russians and Ukrainians preferred the previous Communist regime to their current ones, while Croats, Czechs, Poles, Romanians and Slovenes did not.[45]

But nations, East and West, have also been submitted to systemic evolutionary steering.

Notes

1 A. de Tocqueville, *De la démocratie en Amérique*, Vol. II, Paris, Gallimard folio, 1986, p. 155 (1st edn, 1835). Literal translation: 'Wherever, at the head of a new enterprise you would see the government in France and a great Lord in England, you can count on finding an association in the United States.' (English edition, *Democracy in America*, London, Fontana, 1968, 2 vols.)

2 V. Pestoff, 'Voluntary Associations and Nordic Party Systems', Stockholm, Stockholm University Dept. of Pol. Science, Ph.D. thesis, 1977, pp. 166ff.

3 F. Brettschneider et al., 'Materialien zu Gesellschaft, Wirtschaft und Politik in ·den Mitgliedsstaaten der Europäischen Gemeinschaft', in O. Gabriel (ed.), *Die EG-Staaten im Vergleich*, Opladen, Westdeutscher Verlag, 1992, Tables 92, 93, 95, pp. 578–82; G. Mermet, *Euroscopie*, Paris, Larousse, 1991, p. 261. These data all derive from polls.

4 The data are pooled *Eurobarometer* surveys, 1973–85 and, for the non-EC countries, a 1974–6 international Political Action Survey. The calculations above are based on the presentation in R. Inglehart, *Culture Shift in Advanced Industrial Society*, Princeton, Princeton University Press, 1990, p. 348.

5 See further G. Therborn, 'Lessons from "Corporatist" Theorizations', in J. Pekkarinen et al. (eds), *Social Corporatism*, Oxford, Clarendon Press, 1992.

6 In fact, the correlation in Table 15.4 between conflict involvement and union density is only −0.229 for the 1980s, which indicates a weak negative relationship.

7 Before the French May 1968, the Swedish general strike of 1909 was most probably the most extensive industrial conflict in the world. See further, G. Therborn, 'The Coming of Swedish Social Democracy', in E. Collotti (ed.), *L'Internazionale operaia e socialista tra le due guerre*, Milan, Feltrinelli, 1985, p. 549.

8 See further G. Therborn, 'The Prospects of Labour and the Transformation of Advanced Capitalism', *New Left Review* 145 (1984).

9 While the amount of conflict may be independent of the level of organization, we should expect a change in the rate of organization to correlate strongly and positively with a change in the volume of conflict. Conflict and organization are both, in different ways, expressions of collective strength.

10 The data for the comparative calculations are taken from W. Korpi, *The Democratic Class Struggle*, London, Routledge & Kegan Paul, p.165.

11 For the overall quantitative pattern, see W. Bornschier, *Westliche Gesellschaft im Wandel*, Frankfurt, Campus, 1988, pp. 174ff. For an overview of the French mood of the times, I re-read a self-critical memoir by a participant observer, Dominique Desanti, *Les staliniens: Une expérience politique, 1944/1956*, Paris, Fayard, 1975, pp. 87ff, 125ff. On the Belgian strike in 1960–1, see the anonymously collective work *Wat zoudt Gij zonder 't Werkvolk zijn?*, Vol. 1, Leuven, Kritak, 1977 and 1981, 2 vols., Chs 4–6.

12 See further, M. Peterson, *International Interest Organizations and the Transmutation of Postwar Society*, Stockholm, Almqvist & Wiksell, 1979, which in spite of its general title deals mainly with agrarian interest organizations in the EC; S. Berger, *Les paysans contre la politique*, Paris, Seuil, 1975; Therborn, 'The Coming of Swedish Social Democracy', esp. pp. 589ff.

13 In this escalating or, to employ a Feminist term, 'consciousness-raising', part in a subjectively revolutionary process, Third World-ism differed from its classical predecessor of the late eighteenth century, abolitionism or the anti-slavery movement, in Britain, France and the USA. Cf. R. Blackburn, *The Overthrow of Colonial Slavery*, London, Verso, 1988, pp. 120–1, 136ff, 169ff.

14 This conclusion is derived both from a large number of sources, written and oral, and from the recollections of a participant observer. See, for example, J. Newfield, *A Prophetic Minority*, New York, Signet Books, 1967; S. Leibfried, *Die angepasste Universität: Zur Situation der Hochschulen in der Bundesrepublik und den USA*, Frankfurt, Suhrkamp, 1968; *Kursbuch*12 and 13 (1968); U. Bergmann et al., *Rebellion der Studenten oder Die neue Opposition*, Reinbek bei Hamburg, Rowohlt, 1968; Mouvement du 22 mars, *Ce n'est*

qu'un début' continuons le combat, Paris, Maspero, 1968; *Documenti della rivolta universitaria*, Bari, Laterza, 1968, and *Università: l'ipotesi rivoluzionaria*, Vicenza, Marsilio Editori, 1968.

15 C. Tilly, *The Contentious French*, Cambridge, Mass., Belknap Press, 1986, pp. 389–90.

16 It was known before, however. The British suffragettes, for instance, made ample use of it early in this century. But they were a tiny group.

17 On European lines of influence, see Mouvement du 22 mars, *Ce n'est qu'un début*, p. 17; *Quaderni Piacentini* 34 (May 1968).

18 G. O'Donnell et al. (eds), *Transitions from Authoritarian Rule: Southern Europe*, Baltimore, Johns Hopkins University Press, 1986.

19 For a contemporary overview see *Kursbuch* 13 and *Combats étudiants dans le monde*, Paris, Seuil, 1968. The Prague Spring inspired a student movement in the Baltic countries, and in the Estonian university town of Tartu especially (Marju Lauristin, oral communication, February 1992). The Slovenian student movement reached out actively to its Western counterparts, as manifested in the *Students' Quarterly* published in 1969 by the Ljuljana International Students' Committee. Before the Iron Curtain went down again, there were also some, rather stormy, encounters between West German and Czechoslovak student activists.

20 An exception to this rapid evaporation of student Communism is the Norwegian 'Workers' Communist Party – Marxist-Leninist', which in the mid-1990s still appears intact, rallies around 1% of the national vote, and publishes a daily paper, of more general left orientation, 'The Class Struggle' (Klassekampen).

21 It was gigantic demonstrations against pension cuts which in the autumn of 1994 opened the final crisis of the Berlusconi government in Italy.

22 The above overview is based upon, apart from contemporary observations, S. Andresen (ed.), *Frauenbewegungen in der Welt*, Vol. 1, West Berlin, Argument, 1988; D. Dahlerup (ed.), *The New Women's Movement*, London, Sage, 1986; K.W. Brand (ed.), *Neue soziale Bewegungen in Westeuropa und den USA*, Frankfurt, Campus, 1985; B. Beccalli, 'The Modern Women's Movement in Italy', *New Left Review* 204 (1994).

23 T. Mackie and R. Rose, *International Almanac of Electoral History*, 3rd edn, London, Macmillan, 1990, pp. 58–63.

24 C. Leggevie, 'Propheten ohne Macht', in Brand, 1985 *Neue soziale Bewegungen*, pp. 100ff (France); D. Murphy, 'Von Aldermaston nach Greenham Common', in idem pp. 178ff (Scotland and Wales)

25 *Le Monde*, 4.3.1992, p. 10.

26 See further J. Labasse, *L'Europe des régions*, Paris, Flammarion, 1991.

27 D. Meadows et al., *The Limits to Growth: A Report for the Club of Rome's Project on the Predicament of Mankind*, London, Pan/New York, Universe Books, 1972; E. Goldsmith (ed.), *A Blueprint for Survival*, Harmondsworth, Penguin, 1972. A good, but largely Anglo-American overview of the rise of environmentalism is J. McCormick, *Reclaiming Paradise*, Bloomington, Indiana University Press, 1989. See also A. Jamison et al., *The Making of the New Environmental Consciousness*, Edinburgh, Edinburgh University Press, 1990, which covers Denmark, the Netherlands and Sweden.

28 Apart from contemporary observations, I have here used the contributions to Brand, *Neue soziale Bewegungen*; S. Parkin, *Green Parties: An International Guide*, London, Heretic Books, 1989; D. Murphy et al., *Protest: Grüne, Bunte und Steuerrebellen*, Reinbek bei Hamburg, Rowohlt, 1979; H. Kitschelt, *Politik und Energie*, Frankfurt, Campus, 1983.

29 On Baltic environmentalism, see B. Meissner (ed.), *Die baltischen Nationen*, 2nd edn, Cologne, Markus, 1991, pp. 118, 154; on Bulgaria, see J. Bell, 'Bulgaria', in S. White et al. (eds), *Developments in East European Politics*, London, Macmillan, 1993, p. 85.

30 *Eurobarometer* 25, here taken from Inglehart, *Culture Shift*, p. 379. Electoral data from Mackie and Rose, *International Almanac*, 3rd edn. Useful also is J. Lodge (ed.), *The 1989 Election of the European Parliament*, London, Macmillan, 1990.

31 The cataloguish inventory *Peace Movements of the World*, by Alan Day, Harlow, Essex, Longman, n.d., is a useful overview. Cf. *Die Zeit* 5.2.1993. dossier.

32 Cf. G. Therborn, 'From Petrograd to Saigon', *New Left Review* 48 (1968). Its style is symptomatic, its analysis, I would argue, still valid.

33 Cf., with characteristic verve and exaggeration, R. Debray, *Modeste contribution aux discours et cérémonies officielles du dixième anniversaire*, Paris, Maspero, 1978, esp. Ch. 4.

34 World Values Survey 1981–1983, from Brettschneider et al., 'Materialen', Table 97.

35 Calculated from Z. Brzezinski, *The Soviet Bloc*, Cambridge, Mass., Harvard University Press, 1960, p. 86 (Communist membership) and P. Shoup, *The East European and Soviet Data Handbook*, New York, Columbia University Press, 1981, p. 277 (population).

36 Brettschneider et al., 'Materialen', p. 578.

37 *Statistisches Jahrbuch der DDR 1989*, [East] Berlin, Staatsverlag der DDR, 1989, pp. 330, 353, 413ff.

38 J. Cohen and A. Arato, *Civil Society and Political Theory*, Cambridge, Mass., MIT Press, 1992, p. 346. This is a very important treatise.

39 Z. Rau (ed.), *The Reemergence of Civil Society in Eastern Europe and the Soviet Union*, Boulder, Col., Westview Press, 1991, p. 5.

40 A. Chernayev (German transcription Tscherajew), *Die letzen Jahre einer Weltmacht*, Stuttgart, Deutsche-Verlags-Anstalt, 1993.

41 The Polish movement also had a Western chronicler in Timothy Garton Ash, cf. T. Garton Ash, *The Polish Revolution*, London, Granta Books, 1991.

42 Good overviews of the events are T. Schreiber and F. Barry (eds), *Bouleversements à l'Est, 1989–1990*, Paris, La Documentation Française, Notes & Etudes Documentaires, 1990; R. East (ed.), *Revolutions in Eastern Europe*, London, Pinter, 1992. Among the rest of the bulging literature, I would mention M. Glenny, *The Fall of Yugoslavia*, Harmondsworth, Penguin, 1992; new edn, 1993; G. Schabowski, *Das Politbüro*, Reinbek bei Hamburg, Rowohlt, 1990; Chernayev, *Die leteten Jahre*; and T. Garton Ash, *We the People: The Revolution of '89*, Cambridge, Granta Books, 1990.

43 Cf., V. Zaslavsky, 'Russian Nationalism in the Past and Today', in M. Buttino (ed.), *In a Collapsing Empire*, Milan, Feltrinelli, 1993, pp. 120ff. The level of the debate and of opinion in the end is indicated by a survey in Russian cities in early 1991, reported by Radio Liberty in Munich on 11 March 1991, here cited from ibid., p. 122. To the question 'What does the Soviet Union mean for the average Russian?' 65% answered shortages, queues and poverty, 28% arbitrary power and humiliation, 25% a guarantee of peace. An anti-Soviet Russianism appeared only with the agony of the last two years of the USSR, although a traditional Russian nationalism, often with antisemitic ingredients, had been revived earlier.

44 P. Förster and G. Roski, *DDR zwischen Wende unde Wahl*, Berlin, Linksdruck, 1990, p. 530.

45 R. Rose and C. Haerpfer, *New Democracies Barometer III*, Glasgow, Centre for the Study of Public Policy at the University of Strathclyde, 1994, appendix, questions 32 and 33; R. Rose, 'Getting By Without Government: Everyday Life in Russia', *Daedalus*, Summer 1994, p. 56.

16

EASTERN SOCIALISM AND WESTERN UNION: TWO PROCESSES OF SOCIAL STEERING

Social steering is a concept for designating attempts at deliberately directing social processes towards a certain goal over a significant amount of time. Planned social change or directed social development often operate as synonyms. A presupposition is the modern discovery of the future as a new horizon to head for, full of places you have never seen before. Within this open future perspective, the particularity of steering is its focusing on the road between here and there, not only on choosing the right road but also on how to stay on course.[1]

Europe has seen two of the world's grandest attempts at large-scale social steering: building socialism in the East and uniting the nation-states of the West. The two endeavours have not been compared hitherto, and the currently prevailing attitudes to issues of steering in the social sciences are not very helpful.

The programmes, promises and policies of politicians and governments are rarely carried out completely and with exactly their intended consequences. The new social science orientations of policy analysis, implementation research and evaluation studies have been only too happy to point that out. The stagflation and external supply shocks of their formative decade corroborated their message. The result is that the bulk of the existing literature about social steering is about its failures or severe limitations.

While not necessarily incorrect in what it says explicitly, such a view is historically myopic and theoretically looking into a blind alley, because important successful examples of planned or directed social development exist – from Japanese modernization and postwar return to economic power to the eradication of mortal epidemics in Europe – and because systematic theorizing about social steering has to analyse the conditions of its possibility, which may or may not be practically fullfillable in a given case, as well as its limitations. Since many attempts at social steering are being made, currently reinforced by environmental concerns, on levels from the global to the local, and for a great variety of goals, a systematic attention to the problematic of social steering should be a central task of social scientists.

The reason for this theoretical introduction is that the postwar process of European unification is a very important case of social steering on a continental scale, and the concept of steering offers an ideologically non-contaminated framework for thinking about the Eastern European socialist project. My intention is not to write a history of either attempt at directed development. Rather, my aims are to open up a new discussion of former 'actually existing socialism', and briefly to point out some conclusions bearing upon the problematic of social steering which the available historical evidence of the European integration process offers.

A process of social steering has two sets of actors, the directors and the directed – who in self-managed systems may be the same individuals in different roles – and requires four basic components: a goal and goal-setting as a social process; steering media, by which means the goal of the directors is mediated to the directed, and their characteristic functioning; implementation structures, using the steering media to bring the directed to act in the furtherance of the set goal; feedback mechanisms, whereby information about the outcome of the implementation, whether the process is on course or not, is relayed back to the directors. However, in order to grasp actually existing social steering, you also have to take into account the social context of any social steering process. This context may be summarized by the following three elements: the ordinary strivings of the directed in all their walks of life and their reactions to the steering efforts; the reactions of the environment, external to the social system of steering; chance events, external, contingent occurrences affecting the steering system.

How have these variables operated in the Western union and in Eastern socialism since World War II? What conclusions may be drawn therefrom? As was said above, answering these questions will not involve telling a historical narrative. Rather, it will mean reading and interpreting the signals and the indicators of an instrument panel.

The Communist 'road to socialism'

The set of directors of the Eastern European process was, of course, the Communist party leaders. Three aspects of this set seem particularly pertinent. In composition they were men formed by traumatic experiences very different from those of the Western brand of politicians. Most of them were radicalized by the slaughter of World War I and by the virtually chronic interwar depression, against which the October Revolution appeared like the rising sun. The parties and the International of these 'professional revolutionaries' were more like a monastic order of knights than a political organization in the Western European sense. The former were set apart from the rest of the world, embraced by boundless devotion and held together by limitless discipline. Repression and violence had been an everyday experience for a long time.

The Soviets and the Soviet exiles had lived with the Stalinist terror, had seen close friends and family members disappear. The later Polish general and President Jaruzelski, for instance, was deported to Siberia with his parents, where his father died after a stint in the Gulag.[2] The non-exiles, like

Rákosi (the early postwar Hungarian Communist leader) or Honecker, had normally spent many years in right-wing prisons. This was a tragic generation, permanently shadowed by dark secrets.

It may well be argued that this tragedy was self-chosen by people who had opted for an authoritarian politics and remained loyal to it even when it turned terroristic. True, to many the options may have looked rather forced, between Stalinism and Fascism. But all this is beside my point, which is not to try to convey a personal understanding of these ruthless men. The point is that these traumas bound together and set apart the political leaders of Eastern Europe almost throughout the Communist period – till the death of Tito (in 1980) in Yugoslavia, till the ascendancy of Gorbachev in the USSR, till the senility and death of Kádár, and till the very last days of Communism in the other countries. The combination of an imprint of the worst features of the poorer half of Europe before 1945 and a tenacious longevity in power grounded an institutional rigidity, which as the times kept on a-changing was becoming increasingly brittle.

Communist leadership developed a particular way of organizing power which in the long run was dysfunctional to social steering. It may be summarized as very hierarchical and in principle non-bureaucratic. Not being bound by fixed, foreseeable rules could sometimes mean flexibility, but together with the strictly hierarchic principle, the predominant result was arbitrariness at the top and irresponsible ritualism at lower levels. Any crackpot idea of the leader could be turned into a steering directive, as when the Polish leaders in the mid-1950s saw themselves forced to plan for the cultivation of corn in Poland, upon the insistence of Khrushchev.[3]

The hierarchic principle also meant that no procedures for any orderly criticism and ousting of top leaders were institutionalized. Except in Yugoslavia, Albania and perhaps Romania, any change of the top leadership was also perceived to have to have Soviet approval, and could happen only in times of acute crisis, or upon the death of the Number One. The orderly substitution of Dubček for Novotny in January 1968 was an exception, but it was not without its rumours of a putsch.[4] Again, the argument here is not the obvious one that Communist states were not democratic. It is that the rulers among themselves were subject to a particular rigidity, likely to have increasingly detrimental effects on the steering capacity of the regime.

Thirdly, the important role attributed to ritual must have congested the agenda of the top leaders. Apparently, Honecker and another East German Politburo member, Joachim Herrmann, spent time every day discussing how the central party paper and the main television news should be edited.[5] Now, US politicians are probably at least as media-minded as Erich Honecker was. But the difference is that the former have few if any steering ambitions.

Summa summarum, the grand socialist experiment of Europe was not in the best hands, to put it mildly. The directors of the process became increasingly alienated from the postwar world, their mode of organization favoured pet projects of top leaders rather than rational planning, and the preoccupation with ritual severely limited the time and energy available for other matters.

The directed were in part the non-Soviet CPs and states of Eastern Europe, and, secondly, the peoples of the half-continent, taken separately in national units. This twin task of direction augmented the problems of steering. Most directly, it created a trade-off which came to characterize non-Soviet Communism outside the Balkans. As a national Communist leader you could opt for unconditional subordination to the Soviets, which would ingratiate you in Moscow but might ignite your own population against you, something which would not be held in your favour by the Soviets. Alternatively you could try to appease the domestically directed, and you might run into Soviet disapproval and the risk of Soviet intervention. That was the issue in the GDR before the June rebellion in 1953, in Poland and Hungary in late 1956, in Czechoslovakia in 1968, and in Poland in 1980–1.

All the Balkan countries escaped that dilemma, however, but without reaping any decisive advantages. Yugoslavia and Albania, never dependent on and not easily accessible to Soviet troops, left the camp, in different ways and for different reasons. The Romanians got away with an assertive nationalism, in spite of their border with the USSR. The Bulgarian Communists were lucky never having to face the issue, in spite of an extraordinarily sycophantic posture in front of the Soviets, allowing the Soviet ambassador regular access to Politburo meetings.[6]

This difference between Central-Eastern Europe and the Balkans, as well as the overall Soviet weight upon all Eastern Europe, indicates that not only 'socialism' was at issue, but also the geo-politics of the USSR. In the later perspective, Balkan Romania could appear less important than Central European Hungary.

The *goal* of Eastern European long-term political direction, therefore, was not only socialism, arising from intrinsic movements of social change. *De facto*, the fear of external threat played at least as important a part as the classical labour movement end of societal transformation. Indeed, we may distinguish *three central goals* of Eastern European steering, all very important to the rulers, but varying in priority over time, and together bringing about a foreseeable amount of confusion. One was national socio-economic *development*, industrialization, basic literacy and higher education, urbanization. Another was workers' and women's *rights*, class and gender equality, workers' and women's participation in the running of social life. Given the original minority status of workers – and, even more, of Feminist women – it could be argued that over the long haul these two goals were congruent, leading to a socialist society. However, in the shorter term the two were bound to clash, under any circumstances, between accumulation for the future and the gratification of present claims.

On top of this intrinsic dilemma of developmental socialism came the third goal of preserving and guaranteeing the politico-military security of the Soviet set-up, of *the socialist 'camp'*. This was an end which, although rationally arguable in socialist terms – if the USSR was defeated, everything would be lost – could very well, and indeed did, clash both with the goal of national development and with that of working-class rights. It would be overstating to say that the three goals were incompatible. Working-class growth and an augmented modern military potential would both follow from national industrialization, for instance. However, steering towards three different goals, necessarily rivals for priority, made the Eastern steering process very difficult.

The conventional notion of a 'command economy' does not very well capture this triplicity of Eastern European goals under Communism.

The development of discretionary mass consumption and leisure was not foreseen in the classical socialist agenda. Reluctantly, the regimes came to acquiesce in these goals in the 1970s. But the latter always tended to escape a formulation in planning terms. After all, socialism was originally about the satisfaction of basic needs, not about handling options of choice. But the problem was that the satisfaction of those needs tended to generate needs for choice and variety.

The characteristic *steering medium* of Communist rule was the *political directive*, including the more specific political campaign, or temporary political mobilization for a particular sub-goal. Not only were the law and economic incentives subordinated to, although not replaced by, 'the leading role of the party of the working class', which became constitutionally enshrined but never bound by any constitutional rules; so also was the Plan. Typically, the head of the Planning Commission was a second- or third-rank official. No one ever made it as a top powerholder. No chief Eastern European planner ever achieved the same relative power even as a Western Minister of Finance. Whatever game was being played in Eastern Europe, it was not an economist's socialism.

The political directive was never alone, and it pertained in particular to the members of the *apparat*. For the rest of the population, the directives appeared in attempts at conversion of beliefs and values, as economic incentives, as cajoling, as threats, and as sanctions of dissent.

As a steering medium, the political directive is largely dependent on political loyalty, or, in the jargon of sociological theory, upon people acting primarily according to political norms. That might be expected from the party *aktiv*, but not necessarily from the rest of the population. While offering a certain flexibility to the directors, it is likely not to be very effective with the population at large, unless backed up by legitimate party devotion and by significant non-party dependence. Furthermore, any normative pattern of action in differentiated societies is subject to strong tendencies to routinization and corrosion. It therefore needs to be sustained by institutions of sanctions and incentives.

The political and the law-like directives of party rule and state planning never exhausted the *de facto* steering process. Contracts between enterprises and between enterprise managements and their employees played an increasingly important, recognized part, and informal deals of various sorts became a necessary way of getting by. Bargaining skills and social networks became important. The 'economics of shortage' made that imperative.[7] However, the blueprint remained strictly hierarchical, providing for little known contractual litigation,[8] true, but not for any reciprocity of implementation.

The overriding politicism of Communist steering and the persistent arbitrariness of its directives meant that neither law nor licit incentives were accorded an integrity of their own sufficient even to call attention to the need for their coordination. In times of war and revolution, the 'party line' with its directives was often an effective medium of direction. For a long-term steering of increasingly complex societies it was not very apt. And its supremacy over law and licit incentives yielded declining returns, while both cadres and people learnt to bend the law, to hunt illicit incentives, and to ritualize the political directives into ideological liturgy. Thereby, in the end, the political directives became increasingly subverted.

The Cold War concept of 'totalitarianism' is too crude a fit for this an excessive reliance on the political directive as a steering medium and its internal corruption and subversion.

The *implementation structure* of actually existing socialism was always dual – the party apparatus and the state apparatus. From Polish experiences, we know that that involved a smaller state bureaucracy than in Western countries, something which still might appear surprising to not so few Westerners. It also meant a delimited state competence at the higher level, used to depend on the party directives, and a general bureaucratic slackness in implementation.[9]

The particular cadre implementation of Communist rule has been largely ignored by the organizational literature, and often submerged under the completely different category of 'bureaucracy'.[10] The political dynamism of the '*cadre*', or organizer, which derives from the classical labour movement, is an asset when the goal is single and non-technical. Cadre implementation is geared to mobilizing people for one overriding objective. As such it is flexible and energetic. But it is more congenial to winning a war or a campaign for power than to achieving social or economic development over time. For the latter, even the best, the most sensitive, incorruptible party cadre tends to be overburdened with tasks.[11] In other words, the cadre principle is inadequately differentiated to guide a complex society.

The outcome of the Eastern implementation structure was a considerable, albeit not uniquely outstanding, amount of equality, an originally high but in the end greyly low rate of economic growth, and a considerable neglect of reproductive and maintenance work, be it of houses, streets, railways, enterprise investments, or medical and social care patients.

While not optimal, it seems that this dual command structure probably had more of a positive than a negative effect on projects of social steering. Any state bureaucracy would naturally tend towards administration, rather than steering to something new. Party rule without any state institutionalization would tend to be a charge into the future without any baggage train or engineers, i.e. an unsustainable foray. Insofar as it was not absorbed by internal vendettas or carried by complete idiosyncrasies of top leaders, the party-state structure should be expected to possess a certain dynamism.

However, in practice most of its dialectic was suffocated by 'the leading role of the party', which meant that hardly any state procurator could risk acting on his own (without superior party clearance) against a party functionary of the same or higher rank, however criminal.

Feedback mechanisms were always a special problem for Communist regimes, the result of an inbred belief in the infallibility of their judgement. Free elections were not allowed, but public opinion polls did become legitimate, although not always a publication of their results. Usually, the agency most in touch with public opinion was the one most remote from public debate, i.e. the security organs.

The absence of any open socialist feedback prevented a number of issues from coming to the forefront which otherwise should have been expected to do so from a socialist perspective. The most striking was perhaps the absence of any serious debate about *de facto* gender relations, originally an important Communist plank, later to be lost in officialist complacency. Another, also of impeccable socialist pedigree, was any serious discussion about poverty and inequality, often treated as classified data, as we noted in Chapter 7 above. Environmentalism was not part of the core package of classical socialism, but its importance was recognized early by some Communist regimes, e.g. in the GDR. However, no feedback of public information and debate were allowed, and ecology never entered the overriding trinity of Eastern European goals.

The rather principled rejection of feedback insulated the regimes from pertinent information, and intrinsically impaired any steering process.

The *context* of Eastern European socialist steering was always predominantly hostile, not only externally. Collectivization was nowhere the goal of peasants and farmers. The new Eastern European Communist states stuck to Big Brother's blueprint, but, on the whole, had learnt to avoid the brutal full-scale confrontation of the Soviets. The old industrial working-class stood the risk of losing the gains of trade union protection upon the altar of development. The new one stood to gain economically, but the discipline of factory work had to be broken in.

External powers were menacingly hostile, and had been since the Western interventions in the Russian civil war. That hostility was by no means irrational, given the worldwide revolutionary objectives of the Communists. It was to be expected. But it did raise the cost of any Communist attempt at social transformation.

Postwar Communism was also affected by contingent events, positively as well as negatively. On the one hand, de-colonization, always supported by Communists, even under severe repression, widened the field of Soviet operations. On the other, the generosity of the Marshall Plan, the Western integration of the larger and richer part of Germany, the end to the 1970s credit expansion, and the apparently successful vehemence of the Reagan regime all weakened the East relative to the West. However, the former did not favour an Eastern European socialism, while the latter all converged in restraining the social options of the East.

There is, of course, much more to add to this hasty sketch of the steering problems of Eastern European socialism. But I shall stop here. Besides and before any general and abstract arguments about plan and market, one should look into the parameters of the Eastern European experiment that was undertaken. The steering perspective is a fruitful means of doing so.

The conclusion here is that socialism never stood much of a chance, and that abstract economistic models do not provide any very appropriate clues to the comparative history of Eastern and Western Europe. Eastern Europe never provided the conditions for any proper test of socialism, or of planning.

The directors of Eastern steering became increasingly alienated from the directed, who in any case comprised a difficult set. The goals were in fact multiple. The steering medium was overpoliticized – rather than over-rationalistic – and the implementation structure was insufficiently differentiated, although containing a certain element of flexibility and dynamism, unaccounted for in both the apologetic and the denunciatory planning models. The context, in particular the external one, was predominantly and persistently hostile, quite rationally so. Neither their vanguardist self-conception nor their dictatorial form of rule made the Communists very open to feedback information.

Socialist believers have a legitimate right to deny the relevance of what happened in Eastern Europe to any theoretical conclusion about socialism. However, the sociological historian should not forget that however controversial their socialist legitimacy, the USSR and postwar Eastern Europe constituted both the most large-scale and the boldest socialist attempts in Europe. In terms of concrete outcomes – of equality of tasks, rights, means and risks – the achievements of the Nordic Social Democracies do not fall behind those of their revolutionary rivals, rather the reverse. But whether Nordic Social Democracy was ever a realistic option in Eastern Europe is another question.

The theoretical and ethical debates about socialism and capitalism will hopefully continue. However, the verdicts of history have never depended on any fair trial. Clearly, the Eastern European attempt at steering towards socialism and Communism failed, not because of any intrinsic impossibility of socialism – which was never put to any real test – but due to a particular form of overpoliticized and authoritarian steering.

Towards 'an ever closer' Western union[12]

The set of directors of the Western European steering process has never been a single command structure, neither one group of leaders nor a central directing office. Some individuals have played major roles – Jean Monnet, Robert Schuman, Konrad Adenauer and Paul-Henri Spaak in the initial period, for instance. But they were not a group apart, not an inner circle behind the stage. They had different nationalities, political affiliations, offices, different loyalties and ambitions. So had, even more so, the key actors behind the Single European Act and the Maastricht Agreement. Although the stance of the political leaders of France and Germany has always been crucial, the European process has not unfolded as an outcome of bilateral negotiations.

Rather, the successful European set of social development directors resembles that of another eminently successful steering process, the Japanese. In both there is an 'absent centre', an absence of a central leadership typical of modern national states.[13] In both cases, the directors of the social steering form a set of closely interacting networks, in which decisions evolve in elusive forms, in which both informal contacts and protocol have their parts. In recent years the networks of Europeanist directors have widened by the growth of various interregional links.

That successful long-term directed development in two such different cultures as the European and the Japanese has been brought about by such a complex set-up of directors presents some important challenges to conventional theories of politics and organization.

The directed in the Western steering process are primarily the national states, whereby individuals, enterprises, regions, are affected. True, it also involves, secondarily, certain attempts at corporate and agricultural steering, through industrial and farm policies. To a much larger extent than in most cases of social steering, this relationship of directors and directed makes the European process an élite, or rather inter-élite, concern in a much less deferential culture than the Japanese, albeit legitimized by a very broad general popular sympathy in most member states. The small number of the latter facilitates the steering process, though not necessarily in comparison with very large numbers of individuals, the successful steering of which may be gauged by probabilistic statistics. On the other hand, the small number makes the steering fragile, vulnerable to defection by one or two members.

It is difficult to see how the process could have got started with many more than the six original members, with the particular bonds and interdependencies between them. But a remarkable feature of the European Community integration is its successful management of a doubling of directed member states. How the new applications and intended applications for membership, which amount to yet another doubling, can be coped with is hard to tell. However, it should be borne in mind that in 1848 and 1874 the then twenty-odd Swiss cantons were able to bring about a federation.

The overriding *goal* of European steering has consistently been 'an ever closer union among the peoples of Europe', as it is formulated, most recently, in the Maastricht Treaty of December 1991. The underlying rationale is one of the three major reasons for large-scale attempts at social steering so far: *fear of external threats*. (The other two are scientific knowledge about social causes and effects – at first mainly medical, later economic and sociological – and, secondly, movements of social reform.)

Most important was the fear of yet another devastating European war, which made Franco-German integration the centrepiece of the European process. The fear of the Russians was dealt with chiefly in more traditional forms of military alliance, but in the thaw of the Cold War between the superpowers it was a major motive for Adenauer to throw his full weight behind what became the Treaty of Rome.[14]

More significant has been the economic threat of extra-European economic competition from larger, more resourceful units than those of the European nation-states. To Jean Monnet, who then thought of the Americans, the British with their Commonwealth, and the Russians, that perspective was very important from the beginning. In the 'relaunching of Europe' after the European army had been voted down in the French National Assembly, the peaceful competition challenge launched by Khrushchev, taken quite seriously at the time of the Sputnik, formed a generally favourable context. The cost of nuclear competition to the French alone, faced with US hostility to nuclear proliferation, was crucial to France rallying behind the EEC, linked by the others to Euratom.[15]

The experience of 'Eurosclerosis' in the face of the Reagan boom and, even more, a fear of Japanese and future Southeast Asian competition, although by no means the only significant motives, provided a consensual impetus behind the Single European Act. Fear of external threats, more tangible ones, were, of course, the driving force of Japanese directed modernization.

The goal of a European union has a combination of two features which make it a good steering target. It is at the same time vaguely general and clear. Its vague generality means that it may take many different forms and that many different vehicles may be used to reach it. Many were, in fact, tried, before the EEC was settled upon: the Council of Europe, the OEEC, Fritalux/Finebel, i.e. a customs union between Benelux, France and Italy, a Franco-Italian customs union, a European army, a set of sectoral markets. And for the EC many proposals have been made, and many adopted. On the other hand, a European union has a clarity of purpose which is able to furnish a stable lodestar.

Law is the primary *steering medium* of the European Community process, laid down in the treaties, in the guidelines of their interpretation, in detailed normative rules enacted by the Council of Ministers, and in normative decisions by the Commission. It is through law and law-like rules that the common markets of coal, iron ore, steel, agrarian produce, products and, recently, services are created, structured and monitored.[16]

It is characteristic of European steering that law does not confine itself to formulating general expressions of political will.[17] In some areas it provides very specific obligations for national public authorities, most extensively in the agricultural field. Generally, it furnishes individuals and corporations with rights, enforceable against public authorities as well as against other individuals and corporations. In EC legal doctrine, that is the meaning of the concept of direct effect.[18]

Other media of integration are used, but clearly secondary to law. Money is used mainly in the form of compensatory subsidies, rarely directly in the form of incentives. Indirectly, however, the opening up of the markets of Western Europe has, of course, provided important spurs to intra-Community trade, but European steering has been concerned with the creation or extension of markets, rather than with using them. It has also always involved a substantial amount of market regulation, although how much has always been controversial, from the marketeering opposition of Ludwig Erhard to that of Mrs Thatcher and her successor. Administrative discretion is insignificant, and so is cultural socialization, all important media of national integration. Symbolic action is resorted to, from European passports to the securing of the participation of the EC President at G7 summits, but has also been of marginal weight, so far.

The *implementation structure* of European unification is *sui generis*. The EU has no 'field administration' of its own, and depends locally on the national state authorities. On the other hand, it has two specific implementing organs, in a design established already for the ECSC in 1952: an executive, the High Authority, now the Commission, with an attached central staff, and a court. Both are provided with extensive competence. As specialized organs with no other tasks than regulating and adjudicating European integration, both have developed a very strong commitment to the steering target, unhampered by conflicting other goals and by having to cope with the everyday nuisances of 'street-level bureaucrats', frequent causes of implementation problems and failures.

Since Jean Monnet, the first President of the ECSC, the head of the European executive has usually been a forceful personality who has kept a high profile, which has meant a very significant force for keeping the integration process going. Likewise, Community law has developed vigorously through the jurisdiction of the European Court of Justice and has asserted its supremacy over national law. Since September 1989 it has been assisted by a Court of First Instance of the European Communities, dealing with competition and European civil servants' cases. The very extensive Nordic cooperation which has developed since the 1950s has suffered from an absence both of an executive and of a judicial structure.

The legal doctrine of 'direct effect' provides the directors of European unification with a most important and effective *feedback mechanism* – the invocation by wronged individuals, enterprises and organizations of rights under Community law. In November 1991 the European Court took that principle a step further, and ruled in the Francovich case that EC citizens could sue their governments for damage deriving from a government's failure to implement an EC directive.

The Commission also keeps track of national legislation, and publishes reports on how far and how well national legislatures have kept up with Community agreements. Another important source of feedback is provided by statistical data collection. The EC has in recent years become one of the world's major statistics producers. The EC is not directly dependent on national authorities and their possible filtering for information about legislation implementation or statistical knowledge. It is another matter, it seems, with the actual use of EC 'structural' or agricultural subsidies. However, the world market provides the necessary feedback, also independent of the nation-states, about what happens to European competitiveness.

The social context of the European Community process consists, above all, of the strivings of the member states, the everyday life of their citizens and the pursuit of the national interest by the national governments. We have seen above how well the steering process itself has been set up. But even so, it may be said that a decisive precondition for the success of the former has been its compatibility with the rational interests of its members. This does not require that accepting the steering process is the optimal strategy of any single actor, only, since following the steering is voluntary, that the outcome of the latter falls within a range of acceptable alternatives.

Postwar Western Europe has had a particular fixture arising from a combination of a fear of Germany and a need for Germany. After the two world wars, there was a very natural fear of a nationalist, armed Germany. On the other hand, post-World War I experience had taught far-sighted people that a humiliated Germany was likely to become dangerous, and the new fear of the Russians and of Communism created a need for a re-armed and prosperous Germany. On the German side, there was among the post-Fascist politicians – not least among the Rhineland Catholics from Adenuaer to Kohl – also a fear of a return of German/Prussian nationalism, as well as a national interest in regaining international respectability and access to European markets. This double bind between West Germany and its neighbours, i.e. a deep though conflictual interdependence between the directed nation-states, smoothed the road of European steering.

Furthermore, European integration got under way at the same time as the historically unprecedented postwar boom. National economic interests clashed, and without the drive and the skill of politicians and high civil servants, neither the Coal and Steel Community nor the EEC would have come about. But it was important that under boomtime conditions the economic development of Europe was a plus-sum game. It did not matter that much, therefore, who made the larger or the smaller concessions. Nobody got everything they demanded, but everybody got something.

In the crisis decade of the 1970s, planned steps towards more economic integration were stalled.[19] The new Euro-enthusiasm of the late 1980s should also probably be understood as fuelled by the long-awaited new boom. It was also strengthened by the failure of the half-hearted French attempt at an autonomous crisis policy in 1981–2.

Even under these conditions, however, the success of the European Community process has required a great deal of patience, tact and skill in surmounting difficulties and crises. The most serious ones, hitherto, occurred rather early. One concerned the status of Saarland, which the French had detached from Germany after the war and made into their dependency and which they proposed as a separate member of the Coal and Steel Community, but which the Germans claimed was theirs, in the end successfully, with the legitimacy of a referendum. Another was manifested by the French boycott of EEC meetings in the second half of 1965, over agricultural finance, and de Gaulle's forcing of the prominent German EC President Walter Hallstein to retire in 1967.[20]

The extended market interdependencies among the directed, and the institutional build-up of the directors have operated as important stabilizers in times of crisis and conflict, so that the brakes have only occasionally been used, bringing the process to a halt. But so far, no major actor has demanded a reversal, because there has been no loser, and because the range of alternatives open to the EC has narrowed in Europe.

The most important *environment* for the European process was the United States. The Americans worked for Western European market integration as a means to the recovery of an ally. The Schuman Plan and the Treaty of Rome were autonomous European initiatives, but they were supported, with some competing economic interests reservations by the USA. Indeed, as the British came to realize, the Americans, though keeping a special military relationship with nuclear Britain, stood by the EEC rather than the sterling area.[21] The environment that mattered was positive, and has remained so, in spite of occasional trade clashes. In Europe there was no other significant force than the Soviet Union, and its hostility was taken into account from the outset. Few long-term steering projects, and hardly anyone in high politics, have had the clearly supportive environment which the EC has enjoyed.

External contingencies have borne upon European steering, as upon most cases. Global de-colonization was a very important external contingency favouring Western Europe closing in upon itself, as a sub-continent rather than as a set of colonial nation-states, although Algeria and French 'overseas territories' were associated to the EEC. Indeed, it seems that the Franco-British débâcle at Suez tipped the French balance of governing political opinion in favour of the EEC.[22]

The recessions of the 1970s and early 1980s threw gravel into the European machinery, but out of the frustrations came the European Monetary System and, somewhat later, the Single European Act. The collapse of Communist Eastern Europe has rocked the boat of 1992 celebrations, tilted the EC power relations in favour of a re-unified Germany, but has also, so far, given the EC an extra role, as the special guardian of poverty-stricken, strife-ridden post-Communist Eastern Europe. It has also increased the attractiveness of the EC to previous outsiders, to the Cold War neutrals in the West and the Cold War prisoners in the East.

Whether the momentum of 'an ever closer union' can be kept up after the end of the Cold War and of the division of Germany is not certain. However, so far the directors of the European process have proved themselves very able in coping both with unforeseen external occurrences and with internal clashes of interest.

A market is neither the same thing as, nor in itself conducive to, a community. Indeed, as we saw above in Part III on spacing, European market trade patterns have been surprisingly little affected by the union efforts. The project of Western European unification is hardly sustained by economic functionalism.

The backbone of Europeanism is the set of political-juridical institutions established, the rules of the competitive game and their jurisdiction by the European Court of Justice, the permanent and *ad hoc* settings of national bureaucrats and politicians coming together. This structure is fleshed out by considerable subsidies to the countries of the Southern and Western peripheries and garnished with scholarships to students, grants to researchers and travel expenses-cum-fees to lecturing intellectuals.

In times of trouble, this would be a rather brittle construction. But much of the success, in a favourable context, of Western European steering has been to prevent troubles from piling up. In post-postwar Europe and in a considerably widened union the challenges are likely to mount steeply.

Notes

1 At my department of sociology in Göteborg we have a research programme on social steering and actual social development. For a product of it in English, see G. Therborn, 'Social Steering and Household Strategies: The Macropolitics and the Microsociology of Welfare States', *Journal of Public Policy* 9, 3 (1990). In Swedish there are S.E. Olsson and G. Therborn (eds), *Vision möter verklighet*, Stockholm, Allmänna Förlaget, 1991; M. Blomsterberg and G. Therborn (eds), *Vad styr Sverige?*, Göteborg, Dept. of Sociology, 1991.
2 W. Jaruzelski, *Mein Leben für Polen*, Munich, Piper, 1992, Ch. 2.
3 T. Torańska, *Oni*, Swedish edn, *De ansvariga*, Stockholm, Brombergs, 1986, pp. 338ff. This is a very insight-providing book of interviews with retired Polish Communist leaders by a skilful young anti-Communist journalist.
4 A. Dubček, *Leben für die Freiheit*, Munich, Bertelsmann, 1993, Ch. 15.
5 G. Schabowski, *Das Politbüro*, Reinbek bei Hamburg, 1990, p. 188, and passim. Schabowski was a member of Honecker's last Politburo.
6 G. Horn, *Freiheit die ich meine*, Hamburg, Hoffmann und Campe, 1991, p. 149. Horn is the current leader of the post-Communist party of Hungary, he was once a Hungarian diplomat in Sofia. Kádár refused the replaced Soviet ambassador any similar rights in Hungary, and, according to Andrzej Werblan, former Politburo member in Poland, anything similar was inconceivable in Poland, even in the time of the Stalinist rule (Boleslaw Bierut, oral communication, September 1993).
7 J. Kornai, *The Economics of Shortage*, Amsterdam, North-Holland, 1980.
8 See further H. Berman, *Justice in the USSR*, rev. edn, Cambridge, Mass., Harvard University Press, 1963, Ch. 3; K. Zweigert and H. Kötz, *Introduction to Comparative Law*, Vol. 2, 2nd edn, Oxford, Clarendon Press, 1987, Ch. 27.
9 J.J. Hesse (ed.), *Administrative Transformation in Central and Eastern Europe*, Oxford, Blackwell, 1993, p. 243; Jaruzelski, *Mein Leben für Polen*, pp. 244–5, respectively.
10 The classical work to the contrary here is B. Balla, *Kaderverwaltung*, Stuttgart, Deutsche-Verlags-Anstalt, 1972. Cf. further G. Therborn, *What Does the Ruling Class Do When It Rules?*, London, Verso, 1978, pp. 58ff.
11 A good example of this is given by the West German journalist Landolf Scherzer's reportage about one of the very best local cadres of the late GDR, L. Scherzer, *Der Erste*, Cologne, Kiepenheuer & Witsch, 1988.

12 The main sources used for this section are the three multilingual volumes put out by the European Community Liaison Committee of Historians: R. Poidevin (ed.), *Histoire des débuts de la construction européenne*; K. Schwabe (ed.), *Die Anfänge des Schuman-Plans, 1950/51*; E. Serra (ed.), *Il rilancio dell' Europa e i trattati di Roma*, Brussels, Milan, Paris, Baden-Baden, Bruylant, Giuffré, LGDJ, Nomos, 1986, 1988 and 1989, respectively. Further, E. Haas, *The Uniting of Europe*, Stanford, Stanford University Press, 1958; R. Tamames, *La Comunidad Europea*, Madrid, Alianza, 1987; A. Milward, *The European Rescue of the Nation-State*, London, Routledge, 1992. For later years I have largely relied on the ongoing European reporting in the *Financial Times*, *Frankfurter Allgemeine Zeitung*, and *Le Monde*. I have also learnt a lot from talking to one of the prominent 'Eurocrats', now retired, Paolo Cecchini, and to the Brussels correspondent of Radio Sweden, Rolf Gustavsson.

13 Cf. on Japan, K. von. Wolferen, *The Enigma of Japanese Power*, New York, Alfred Knopf, 1989: 'The Japanese prime minister is not expected to show much leadership; . . . the legislature does not in fact legislate; . . . and the ruling Liberal Democratic Party . . . is not really a party and does not in fact rule' (p. 25).

14 H.J. Küsters, 'The Federal Republic of Germany and the EEC-Treaty', in Serra, *Il rilancio dell' Europa*, pp. 498ff. Ludwig Erhard was vehemently against a European customs union as protectionist.

15 P. Gerbet, 'Les origines du Plan Schuman: Le choix de la méthode communautaire par le gouvernment français', in Poidevin, *Histoire des débuts*, pp. 216–17; J.-B. Duroselle, 'La relance européenne 1954–1957', pp. 53ff, and H.J. Küsters, 'The Origins of the EEC Treaty', pp. 222ff, both in Serra, *Il rilancio dell' Europa*.

16 Cf. P. Piscatore, 'Das Zusammenwirken der Gemeinschaftsordnung mit den nationalen Rechtsordnungen', *Europarecht* 4 (1970). Piscatore was at that time judge at the European Court of Justice.

17 By contrast, law plays a minor part in Japanese steering and social life, cf. Wolferen, *The Enigma of Japanese Power*, Ch. 8.

18 See further T.C. Hartley, *The Foundations of European Community Law*, Oxford, Clarendon Press, 1983, Ch. 7.

19 See further the recollections of an insider, H. Schmidt, *Die Deutschen und ihre Nachbarn*, Berlin, Siedler, 1990, pp. 219ff.

20 A good overview of the EEC in the mid-1960s is given by R. Willis, *Italy Chooses Europe*, New York, Oxford University Press, 1971, Ch. 5.

21 See P. Mélandri, 'Le rôle de l'unification européenne dans la politique extérieure des Etats-Unis 1948–1950' and H.J. Schröder, 'Die amerikanische Deutschlandpolitik und das Problem der west-europäischen Kooperation, Poidevin, 1947/48–1950', both in *Histoire des débuts*; E. Di Nolfo, 'Gli Stati Uniti e le origini della Comunità Economica Europea', in Serra, *Il rilancio dell' Europa*, C.J. Bartlett, *A History of Postwar Britain*, 1945–1974, London, Longman, 1977, pp. 187ff.

22 That is the argument of Küsters, 'The Origins of the EEC Treaty', p. 233. It is supported by P. Guillen, 'La France et la négociation des traités de Rome: l'Euratom', in Serra, *Il rilancio dell' Europa*, pp. 519f, and by the testimony of Christian Pineau, then French Minister of Foreign Affairs and the French signatory of the Treaty of Rome, ibid., p. 284. In their Suez adventure, Britain and France were let down by the USA.

PART VI

MODERNITY AND EUROPE: SIX QUESTIONS AND THEIR ANSWERS

This concluding part is meant to be neither a fast food version of the treat offered above, nor the grande finale of a Wagner opera. It is an attempt at translation, of a scholar's treatise into the terse tongue of the ancient Northerners, and thereby at answering in a crude and straightforward manner some simple, important and difficult questions. Like most contemporary editions of ancient texts, this translation is annotated with a bit of more modern discursiveness.

Is the sociological history of postwar Europe one of continuity or discontinuity with the past?

It is, rather, a history of peripety.

The postwar boom issued into an unprecedented prosperity, but for the rest, the five decades from 1945 to 1995 do not constitute a break with Europe before 1945, or 1939, in spite of the political drama in the East and the change of cast in the West. Rather, the outgoing half of the twentieth century provided the ground on which a number of important turns of European history took place. The 'glorious decades' of the spectacular growth of economic means ended by the mid-1970s. True, the economic growth of Europe since the late 1970s is still impressive by historical standards, but it is not far from the German rate of growth between 1870 and 1913 or the Nordic growth between 1870 and 1950, and it is actually significantly lower than Swedish economic growth between 1870 and 1950.[1]

First seen in some countries as a necessary road to reconstruction and prosperity, emigration out of Europe terminated its centuries-old history and turned into immigration. A peak of national homogenization and ethnic cleansing was soon followed by renewed ethnic heterogeneity. Peasant society was put into museums, and industrialism swept and smoked the continent, but in time the silence before the 'copper red howl' of the factory sirens, to quote a dead Swedish poet, started to return.[2]

The leisure class swapped abode, and was overshadowed by the leisured third age. The working-class was spoken of and spoken to in terms more respectful than ever before, before being shoved out of the limelight and bid farewell to by Rive Gauche intellectuals, waving their handkerchiefs as the young female students of May 1968 were waving theirs, singing-marching 'Adieu de Gaulle'.

The socialization of the productive forces, and, with them, of the means of production, reached its historical peak in the beginning of our period. And then the history of property rights turned around towards privatization, first gradually in the West, then more hurriedly in the East.

Women first entered more frequently into married domesticity than for a long time in European herstory, soon to break out of it, more determinedly, more successfully, and with more autonomy than ever before.

Huge, catastrophic risks emerged, of nuclear war and nuclear meltdown, but did not materialize (save in Chernobyl), while smaller and more frequent risks of accidents came to decline.

The continent's ideological history started under the banners of anti-nationalism, be it European Union, proletarian internationalism, or, in the tiny special case of West German intellectuals, of Western union and constitutionalism. Then came a new tide of nations in 1989–90, brought about in the East, applauded and cashed in on in the West, then gathering momentum in the East and consternation in the West. The victims began to pile up. But while ethnic friction is mounting in multicultural Western Europe, nationalism is still in check there.

The ancient Christianity of the continent got a political shot in the arm in the West, as powerful Christian Democracy. But it was soon overburdened with secularization, theological modernization – national liturgy and popular participation after the Second Vatican Council – the ordainment of women in Protestant Churches, and a new turn to social issues. Islam came to return to Europe, beyond its old and long-lost conquests of al-Andalus and Rûm (Byzantium).

The values of socialism, elaborated in nineteenth-century Europe, were raised onto pedestals all over the continent, including the programmes of early postwar Christian Democracy. They conquered the 'commanding heights' only in the East, where they soon were bitten by bunker paranoia and later mouldered with the ageing of the demobilized soldiery of class war. Eastern socialism was shining only in the shrines and mausolea of power. In the West, socialist and *socialisant* ideology and politics peacefully admitted defeats in the 1950s, but returned and reached their highest ever plateau in Western Europe in the 1970s and early 1980s, for a brief moment of triumph. In the mid-1980s a new countdown started, in the West as well as in the East. However, what in 1989–91 looked like a knock-out, according to some commentators not only of socialism but also of history, now appears more like a count of nine after a flooring blow in round eleven of an n-rounds contest.

When did things happen?

There were three crucial moments of history. One was 1946–48, the second were the decades of turns, 1960–80, and the third was 1989–91.

The late 1940s should first of all be remembered for what did not happen then. The awaited postwar depression did not occur, and instead the boom began. They were also the years when the Yalta agreement settled and the postwar political economy of Europe started.

To most people of my generation and slightly younger ' '68' stands out as a beacon – of hope to left-wing people in the West, of despair and disillusion to left-wing people in the East, of a craze to Western right-wingers, of violent brutality to people on the (subdued) right in the East. However, in the cold light of sociological history, the memories of dawn or twilight both appear as moments of a much vaster process.

With some international variation of timing, the period from the early 1960s to the early 1980s was an amazing concentration of social historical turns. Immigration began to outpace out-migration. Secularization jumped forward. Women turned from the married kitchen to the labour market and to individual emancipation. Labour demands expanded and contracted. Industrial employment peaked and descended. The working-class reached its strongest social position ever, and soon lost it. The boom culminated and went into its first crises. Socialist radicalism exploded and imploded. Postwar right-wing liberalism and moderate conservatism were discredited by the left, and re-emerged, invigorated, in a much more militant form.

Eastern Europe's catching up, in economic resources and in health and life chances, with its richer half-sister in the West reached its highest mark of approximation. And then began to slide backwards again, in relative terms. Major internal reforms of Communism into a democratic socialism started, in the Prague Spring and, somewhat later, in the 'High Gierek' period of Poland in the early 1970s. In the former case these were quashed by external invasion, followed by general ideological congealment in the camp, and by 'the years of stagnation'. The Eastern working-class gathered its maximum strength in the Solidarnosc years of 1980–1, then hedged in by martial law. It was not defeated, however, unlike the British workers, but sapped of its class force by an internal ascendancy of nationalist Catholicism and Western liberalism.

In 1989–91 the 'postwar' period in Europe ended. The victories of the Red Army and the defeats of the Wehrmacht were largely, if by no means completely, undone. Germany was re-united and the USSR was broken up. The nationalist spirit of 1914–18 and of 1939–45, afterwards held at bay in both camps, in different ways, was partly rehabilitated. But in the West it remained programmatically subordinate to the union project of '1992'. Meanwhile, the new political and intellectual leaders of the East in these years idealized all things Western.

These years also put an end with a whimper to the kind of revolutionary politics inaugurated by the October Revolution in 1917 as well as to the system of power following from it. Between the Revolutions of 1789 and of 1917 there were a number of links – of traditions of thought, of vocabulary, of symbolism, and of exemplary memory. Whether 1989–91 means an end not only to the tradition of 1917 but also to that of 1789 is still unclear. But heavy bets are being taken that it is.

What 1989–91 in the end will have meant to socialism, one of the great -isms of Europe, is also not clearly decided yet. Many anti-Communist Socialists and Social Democrats discovered to their surprise that in any case it meant quite a lot. Both in the sense of seemingly closing any alternative to capitalism in the eyes of a wide section of opinion, and, most surprisingly, in an existential sense of loss or even mourning. Cain was my brother, after all.[3]

Interestingly enough, the erosion of Communist ideology in the late 1980s coincided with similar processes among Western Social Democrats. The defeat of Gorbachev and the end of the Soviet Union also coincided with the right-wing break-up of the Social Democratic 'Swedish model', in a wave of marketization, privatizations and mass unemployment. Also as in Eastern Europe, public support for the right-wing spree seems to be short-lived. But, on the other hand, the leftest possible outcome of the Swedish September 1994 election was a Social Democracy significantly more moderate than its manifestations in the 1970s and 1980s.

At any rate, by the mid-1990s what seemed to be the most important meaning of the events of 1989–91 to the prevailing ideologues of the day – the end of socialism and the triumph of capitalism – looks uncertain and fragile.

Was there a convergence or a divergence within Europe and/or between Europe and the rest of the world?

There was a parallel development of Eastern and Western Europe. Within Western Europe there was a movement of convergence before the creation of the EEC. Europe's standing as a developed continent was reinforced, demographically and economically. But among the most developed parts of the world Europe lost culturally.

The postwar boom was common to Eastern European socialism as well as to Western European capitalism, and so was the later slowing down of economic growth. So also were the spread of discretionary mass consumption, the decline of mortality and secularization. The view of property had a similar trajectory in the two halves of the continent.

The Eastern regimes fell, not because the distance to the West had grown, but rather because the distance had become more visible and because the hope of overcoming it had gone.

The European Community has not led to any economic convergence among its members. It has not even had much impact on European trade patterns.

Economically and demographically, Europe became more demarcated from its neighbours than before. Europe did better economically than the New Worlds, approaching the richest ones of the latter – North America, Oceania – while leaving Latin America behind.

But the Japanese repeated in a more massive, more frontal, and more peaceful way their defeat of the Russian navy in 1905 and emerged as an economic superpower, equal to Western Europe as a whole, and having its own sort of socio-economic organization, as well as its own, distinctive culture.

The convergence thesis was wrong in two respects: in ignoring the parallelism of capitalist and socialist Europe, and in missing the emergent East Asian alternative.

Culturally, the American dominance of audio-visual communication largely came to muffle and to wash away a good deal of European mass culture. Nevertheless, we can distinguish in the present a particular, European set of values, but not the ones usually referred to in the cultural histories. There appears to be a European scepticism, with regard to God, science and nation, hardly found elsewhere. Europeans have a more collectivistic view of public social intervention and institutions, together with a stronger tendency towards an individualist view of personal social relations.

Why did what happened happen?

Above all, because of the outcome of the war and of the ensuing boom, operating upon persistent national and regional traditions. Trans-systemic social power and politics have also left important traces. The historicity of European modernity and its contingencies appear to have more explanatory muscle than endogenous systemic dynamics.

The way World War II ended radically restructured means, rights and opportunities, reshaped the political, economic and cultural space of the continent, and gave rise to new identities while discrediting others. It also generated grandiose efforts at social steering, East and West. The boom, which owed much to the war, accelerated the social and cultural dynamics of the Western European capitalisms and of the Eastern European socialisms, to the post-industrial, multicultural transformation of the former, to the erosion and dissolution of the latter.

The social destruction of World War II weakened the forces of capital, landed property and nationalism, and opened up new possibilities of large-scale institutional change, in the West as well as in the East. Although it has not been possible to fully clinch the evidence in support of it, I also think that the destruction of the war laid the basis for – was the necessary but not sufficient cause of – the ensuing boom, which united all postwar Europe and Japan. True, postwar growth must also have benefited from the particularly technologically inventive years just before the war.

The war, with the experiences of Depression, Fascism and nationalist *revanchisme* which led up to it, was a crucial formative experience of the politically and socially active after 1945. The background and the outcome of the war set the postwar period on a certain course of social development. Economic *laissez-faire* was discredited, and von Hayek became (for a long while) an intellectual hermit. Social biology and racial discourse on society became almost taboo, when pictures of the corpses and of the half-dead survivors of the Nazi camps made the truth of Fascist racism public in the spring and summer of 1945. Anti-democracy, a core element of all Fascist ideologies, was discredited as well as militarily defeated. The nation-state had become suspect as a supreme value. The process of Western European unification was set in train with the intention of overcoming nationalism. The social or the welfare state could expand, among other reasons, because the nation-state could no longer be opposed to it. Universalist religion, on the other hand, gained a new lease of life.

The impact of the war was most lasting in Eastern Europe, where the war-and-revolution tradition of Communism was cemented. Until its last days, attempts at bringing Communist socialism onto a new stage beyond negating and overcoming the war and its roots in depressions, Fascism and Malthusian capitalism were nipped in the bud as principles and only half-heartedly promoted as pragmatic and shoddy Ersatz consumption.

A long-lived wartime generation of Communist power-holders led to an ironical gerontification of ruling Communism, and expressed a rigidification of the regimes. When finally the ranks of the wartime generation were fatally thinned out and enfeebled, the Communist regimes began to waver, towards radical reform or collapse. What decided that the latter alternative ultimately won out is not yet clear, although national politics was the mechanism and a difficult economic situation the context.

While the war was a major cause of the boom, the latter also had a number of important effects, some, the products of its own dynamics, affecting the economy itself, others creating social repercussions. The outcome of the boom was that industrialism rapidly ran its course, handing over to a post-industrial economy. Further, full employment, which strengthened the labour movement, led to the culmination of the former in the 1970s. Labour scarcity reversed old migration patterns and the ethnic homogenization trend of the first half of the century. It also, albeit very unevenly, attracted women to the labour market. The expansion of education largely grew out of the boom, and the former created the social ecology necessary for the students' and women's movements, and for the reform movements in the East. Thereby, the bell started tolling for old-style patriarchy and for old-style Bolshevism. The new society of mass consumption and mass communication produced by the postwar boom also cracked the ancient structures of institutionalized religion, as well as the more recent ones of embattled Communism.

The war and the boom were no steamrollers flattening the whole continent into one asphalted parking lot. National and regional variations persisted and were (by and large) reproduced, East as well as West, and a considerable amount of effort above has been devoted to finding out and to demonstrating how. Europe's cultural space was found to be constituted by a number of layers, crossing and undercutting current nation-state boundaries.

The sub-continental variations have at least one major discernible pattern, which may be attributed to a postwar cause: the equality, of both outcomes and opportunities, between strata or classes, between genders, and between children and adults. With regard to equality, there is a strong tendency towards a clustering of the Nordic and the Eastern European countries, versus the more inegalitarian and status-marked Southwestern and Southern Europe. Equality has been an explicit aim and the target of a number of policies both by Nordic Social Democracy and Eastern Communism. Both have had power to realize their goals, the former less so but from much better initial conditions than the latter.

This effect of working- and popular-class power has worked across systemic divides of ideology, political regimes and of dominant property forms. Class power, however, is explainable as generated by systemic tendencies of structuration, enculturation and collective action intrinsic to capitalist societies – and inherited by post-capitalist transitions – as theorized by Marx and the Marxian tradition, which taken broadly stretches from Lenin to Schumpeter.[4] We have seen above how the structuration of relative means between enterprises, states and markets affected power relations both within capitalist societies and in their Eastern alternatives. World War II and the postwar boom, on the other hand, are unique historical contingencies. The ways in which they became socially effective may be graspable by sociological reason, in the manner in which they affect the structuring and enculturing processes and the parameters of collective action. But asking why they occurred takes us onto the territory of the historian.

What is the epochal meaning of the history of late twentieth-century Europe?

We have seen the ascent to the peak of European modernity and the start of the descent from it, and therewith the same of working-class socialism.

The question has to be answered in awe, particularly when writing in English. 'The standard Anglo Saxon assumption is that the determination of world-historical significance . . . should be postponed until a century or so after the event in question has taken place', Richard Rorty asserted in a debate with Jean-François Lyotard.[5] In 2094, the second half of the twentieth century in Europe is most likely to look differently from today. But this writer's guess is that a peripety of European modern history will be at least part of the picture then.

We have given modernity an empirical, non-institutional definition here, as a social period turned towards the future as a means of orienting the present, rather than to the past, or as opposed to gyrating in the present without a compass. In contrast to the currently fashionable debate about modernity and post-modernity/ism, which is remarkably confined to one global master narrative, be it modern, high modern or post-modern, we have highlighted different routes or passes to/through modernity – a perspective, it should be added, that also predicts different exits from modernity.

With this definition and with this institutionally pluralistic perspective on modernity, the European way emerges as one of several roads to, through and, perhaps, from modernity. It acquired certain characteristics from being the first to enter modernity, others from the contingencies of European experience.

From its pioneering, endogenous origin European modernity derived its particularly ism-ic features, its clear and rigid divisions into warring, principled camps, slugging out all the issues about and around modernity among themselves, in civil wars. The Cold War was a sort of institutionalization of these centuries-old internal struggles of European modern history.

The Berlin Wall, dividing the capital of the heartland of Europe, was a symbol not only of Communist desperation. It may also be seen as a monument of European modernity, of its wars and truces among Christian religions, of its fighting patriots and Holy Alliances, of its generation of hostile ideologies, warring nations, closed 'pillars' (*zuilen*), and fortified *Lager* (socio-ideological camps).

Like the two industrial wars of the European nation-states, the Cold War was projected onto a world scale. Indeed, one pole of the latter was actually situated outside Europe.

The thaw of the Cold War, the melting or blurring of ideological principles, represents a major change within European modernity. With regard to religion, science and, more uncertainly, nation, Europe – with some delimited exceptions – has become the sceptical continent of the world.

Europe is the only part of the world for which industry and industrial employment have been a major, or at least relatively predominant, experience. That and the road of internal conflict have made class and class conflict more important and more clear-cut in Europe than anywhere else. Industrialism peaked in Western Europe around 1970, in Eastern Europe about 1980, and working-class power at about the same time, strengthened by a postwar attrition of non-class cleavages, religious, regional or other. Class politics, in the sense of economic class organization and of class voting, is still more prevalent in Europe than in the rest of the world. But it is declining, most likely irreversibly. Two new rivals and potential successors have already announced themselves – media politics and ethnic politics.

The aftermath of World War II lacked the modernist enthusiasm and iconoclasm of its predecessor twenty-five years earlier, and nowhere more so than in (Western) Europe. However, the latter half of the twentieth century did unfold under the banner of modernity. The later triple challenge to modernity – aesthetic, ecological/economic and ideological – from the 1970s and on was more direct to Europe than to any other part of the world.

First, the concept of the avant-garde, now called into question, was central to European modern art, fed both by class traditions of aristocracy and by the idiom of contemporary revolutionary politics.

Secondly, the doctrine of growth and development was not stronger in Europe than elsewhere, rather the contrary. But this somewhat uncertain developmentalism met with, and perhaps allowed the rise of, a relatively strong ecological conservationist movement.

Thirdly, the post-modernist attack on the 'grand narratives' of enlightenment, emancipation, progress, liberation, etc. hit Europe harder, because it went directly to the very heart of European modernity, its elaborate, principled ideologies of strivings for the future. The collapse of Communism had most repercussions in Europe, both because it was a European -ism that had foundered, and because it was European Communist power that imploded.

After the exhaustion of socialism and of steeled European neo-liberalism, with much shorter breath, all the classical -isms of Europe, including their late reincarnations, are in crisis. The only necessary qualification of this is the resurgent vitality of nationalism in Eastern Europe. 'Normalcy' and (actually existing Western) 'Europe' were the most frequent slogans of the anti-Communist forces of Eastern Europe in 1989–90.

Progress, development, emancipation, liberation, enlightenment, have (for the time being) lost their appeal to most Europeans. Growth does remain a goal, however, in scientific cognition and in economics. And there is at least one European ideological tradition which has access to contemporary prime-time – the 1789 legacy of human rights.

Whether the dusk of modernity is setting upon Europe, and the world, at the end of the twentieth century, I shall leave open to future historians. The *Zeitgeist* is usually schizophrenic. The previous *fin-de-siècle* was divided among the Decadents, the (Nietzschean and other) dissidents, the legitimated beneficiaries of the Belle Epoque, and the standard bearers of the future, i.e. the forces of the Second International and of natural and medical science. An empirical sociologist or social historian has to think more than once before coming down on either side of the modernist–post-modernist divide.[6] But the (specifically) European road through modernity has begun its descent.

The Cold War and the culmination of industrialization constituted the peak of European modernity. Descent followed from the blurring of the classical cleavages, the questioning of the future within Europe itself, and from the rise of non-European conceptions of a modern society.

What are the lessons, scientific and practical?

The actual sociological history of postwar Europe differs from both Cold War ideologies, including that of capitalist triumph. Comparative research should not be confined to comparing states. Sociology is a servant of Clio, the muse of history, not her master, and sociological theory should more be geared to accounting for the structural-cultural canalizations of contingencies. Socialism and Social Democracy have been worth fighting for for those who believe in human equality. Both have yielded tangible results, and there is no evidence that the latter will arrive without struggle. Social change has a wide range of possibilities, but radical systemic change is costly.

The actual trajectory of European societies after World War II followed the assumptions and assertions neither of Communist nor of anti-Communist ideology. There were many more parallelisms and much more internal variation than either ideology, and scholarship inspired by one or the other, has argued.

Comparative research should reach out of the ghetto of nation-states. On a number of interesting variables data exist for comparing continents or other blocs of states, including travellers of the same route to/through modernity, intra-continental and intra-state regions. In inter-continental comparisons, Europe often protrudes as a specific social entity. But regrouping Western European regions according to economic resources, for instance, bursts open the nation-state demarcations.

The Mertonian emphasis on cross-fertilization between theory and empirical research is very important, and should be approached with open-armed seriousness. For my part, thinking back and forth between the analytical scheme, on one hand, and the empirical issues and materials, on the other, taught me the centrality of rights in social structures, the common temporal dimension of risks and mobility, and the continuing, contemporary relevance of rituals and public commemorations for collective identity. It also hammered home the recurring importance of the unexpectable, i.e. of the limits of social theory.

With regard to the raging sociological debate on history and sociology, the experience of this study underlines the decisive importance of primary historiographic evidence, the value of a sociological approach to such evidence – attention to systematicity, look out for quantitive indicators, awareness of statistical possibilities – and the secondary but significant helpfulness of a theoretical compass.

Sociological theory can offer a sense of orientation, and a set of questions, but is still little developed for purposes of macroscopic explanation and not just interpretation. In this situation basic sociological theorizing if applied with some systematicity may be very useful as building blocks, often more useful than highly original, and idiosyncratic, elaborations.

The capitalism–socialism dichotomy, as it has been usually applied in the Cold War period, has not corresponded very well to the actual occurrences in Eastern and Western European societies, although 'actually existing socialism' did make a difference, for instance in an egalitarian direction.

An analysis of the Eastern European Communist road to socialism from a perspective of social steering shows the very limited relevance of the major theoretical systemic debates of socialism, markets and capitalism. Postwar Eastern Europe simply does not lend itself to a well-designed test of socialism.

Modernization theory might be able to contain both socialism and capitalism, and it posits some evolutionary tendencies which can be observed in the catching up of Southern and Eastern Europe. But it abstains from specifying any variation to/through modernity, which appears as much too crude, both when looking at Europe in isolation, and even more upon seeing Europe in the global context.[7]

On the other hand, world system theory, which claimed to have finished off modernization, did not appear very potent either. Postwar Europe may very well be viewed as located within a world system. It has in any case to be placed in the world, because the changing world location of Europe has clearly borne upon migration streams, ethnic and religious composition, supra-state integration and the communication of mass culture. But I have found little concrete use for a world system dynamics in understanding and explaining the postwar structurations, spacing and enculturations of the continent.

As far as social practice is concerned, one conclusion from this work is that the considerable social variation in time and space shows that social change is possible, that a number of options are conceivable. Prophets of one option only are always to be mistrusted. And power matters, including national power.

Secondly, the internal variations in social outcomes within Communist and capitalist Europe, and the similarity between the Nordic countries and the most egalitarian ones of the former, indicate the elasticity of systemic constraints, the cunning survival capacity of historical traditions, and the possibility of politically directed social change.

Thirdly, long-term social steering is a difficult and uncertain process. However, it is something which does not deserve to be dealt with only negatively, in terms of 'limitations of', 'failures of', etc. Policy analysts and policy-makers have good reasons to discuss social steering also in terms of possibilities and conditions.

Finally, the enormous cost, in human lives and misery, of the most consensually celebrated, the most favoured revolution in history, the anti-Communist one of 1989–91, underlines decisively the great social cost of radical, abrupt systemic change. To the student revolutionaries of 1968, of my generation, that is a chilling experience.

Notes

1 OECD Europe, which includes Turkey but not Eastern Europe, grew from 1979–90 by 1.7% per capita annually. German growth 1870–1913 was 1.6% and Swedish growth 1870–1950 was 2.1%: OECD, *Historical Statistics, 1960–1990*, Paris 1992, Table 3.2; A. Maddison, *Ontwikkelingsfasen van het Kapitalisme*, Utrecht, Het Spectrum, 1982, Table III.1.

2 Artur Lundkvist.

3 The basis of this observation is a number of conversations with anti-Communist Social Democrats and Socialists, mainly intellectuals and/or politicians. But I am making no claim about their majority or minority status.

4 See further J. Schumpeter, *Capitalism, Socialism and Democracy*, London, George Allen & Unwin, 1961 (1943), esp. part I. This great and haughty conservative economist ended his discussion of Marx paying homage to another great man: 'To say that Marx, stripped of phrases, admits of interpretation in a conservative sense is only saying that he can be taken seriously.' (p. 58).

5 R. Rorty, 'Cosmopolitanism without Emancipation: A Response to Lyotard', in S. Lash and J. Friedman (eds), *Modernity and Identity*, Oxford, Blackwell, 1991, pp. 69–70.

6 That is, in terms of diagnosis. With regard to prescriptions, although I want to say something to everybody, left and right, young and old, European or non-European, it should by now be little surprising to the reader that this author has and recognizes his roots in the Enlightenment tradition of modernity.

7 Once discredited modernization theory is neither vacous nor vicious. But what it has to offer is rather limited. Whether its glass should be taken as half-full or half-empty is open to debate. For a more positive evaluation cf. S. Hradil, 'Sozialstruktur und gesellschaftlicher Wandel', in O. Gabriel (ed.), *Die EG-Staaten im Vergleich*, Opladen, Westdeutscher Verlag, 1992, pp. 91–2.

ENVOI: EUROPE AND THE REST OF MODERNITY

The second half of the twentieth century was the time when Europe returned to itself, after half a millennium of outward expansion. The conquests and the protection rackets abroad had reached their limits by the end of the 1930s. Italy's conquest of Abyssinia in 1935 was the last victorious colonial exploit of Europe. Recently before that, the French and the Spanish had consolidated their power in Morocco, and the French and the British had gained control of the ex-Ottoman parts of the Arab world. After World War II came the necessity of retreat, peacefully or under fire. Withdrawal from colonies was universal and, in the end, only the forms of withdrawal differed. The victory of the European Jewish settlers in Palestine was the only exception,[1] but the state of Israel then maintained itself as an American, and not as a European, outpost. The last imperial offensive from Europe, the Franco-British Suez operation, was a fiasco.

The European return home was not a coming back to pre-colonial Europe with all the acquisitions of modernity added. The former rulers of the world now sought protection behind the shield of foreign, American, troops on their soil, against the other new superpower on the periphery of Europe, and American economic aid turned out necessary for the postwar reconstruction of Western Europe. Europe's structural location in the world had changed dramatically. From the 1960s, the Old World of outbound mass migration also became a continent of immigration, making for a novel cultural diversity.

Nevertheless, within a more modest location in the world, the distinctive features of European social modernity continued to unfold after 1945. Indeed, they reached their maturity.

But Europe ceased to be the explicit yardstick of modernity. It was after World War II that 'development economics' and 'modernization' sociology and political science took off. The latter developed in the wake of the former, and development economics started by looking at the postwar reconstruction of Southern and Eastern Europe. From there and the early works of Paul Rosenstein-Rodan, after the war a key World Bank official, and Kurt Mandelbaum, the focus on development became mainly extra-European. The UN Economic Commission for Latin America under the directorship of Raúl Prebisch came to provide intellectual leadership already by the end of the 1940s.[2]

The social context, the social preconditions, of economic development, acquired the label of 'modernization' in the second half of the 1950s. It was meant to be a generalization of previous tags of 'Europeanization' or 'Westernization'. In its unidirectional evolutionism and its amazing blindness to the specificity of European industrialism, 'modernization theory' was a sort of North American theorization of European history, with Europe itself bracketed.[3]

De-colonization and American dependence have not meant a decline of the economic standing of Western Europe in the world. Already in the late nineteenth century the Anglo-Saxon New World surpassed even the UK in GNP per capita. Wartime destruction in Europe had brought the gap between Western Europe and North America to its greatest length, but by 1970 it was narrower than it had ever been before in this century. Moreover, Australia and New Zealand have been overtaken by several Western European countries.[4]

True, Japan has entered the club of the richest countries, and South Korea has recently reached the level of Portugal and Greece.[5] But the countries of the Southern Cone of the Americas – Argentina, Chile and Uruguay – which in 1950 had a per capita income about the same as that of France, Italy and West Germany, respectively, have been left well behind.[6]

By the mid-1990s, the weight of Western Europe's American mortgage is declining, with the disappearance of the other, peripherally European superpower, the USSR. Is this likely to open up a new flourishing of Europe, on the basis of its rather successful post-conquistador development? For the foreseeable future, that is not very likely, for two sets of reasons.

One is economic. While the postwar boom has not been turned into its opposite in Western Europe, growth has become more ordinary, both by historical and by global standards. And unemployment has kept on augmenting, across business cycles, for two decades by now, with no end or solution, other than accommodation and resignation, in sight.

In Eastern Europe, the cost of going from socialism to capitalism has turned out traumatic to the economies as a whole and to the majority of the population, if by no means to all sectors of the latter. According to the OECD, Eastern Europe except the ex-USSR, ex-Yugoslavia and Albania, lost between a fifth and a quarter of its GDP in 1990–3. Russia and the Ukraine lost more than half. This means that only in the most optimistic scenarios of the most hopeful cases would Eastern Europe on the threshold of the year 2000 be back at its GDP of 1989.[7]

The historically poorer part of Europe is becoming impoverished. A division of Europe similar to that of the Americas is clearly in process. Part of the Balkans and the Caucasian border region have become more like parts of Africa than any other part of the world, caught in the ravages of tribal strife and warfare. The symbolic visit in the winter of 1994 of the Prime Ministers of Bangladesh, Pakistan and Turkey to the city of Sarajevo, besieged by a hostile rural tribe, is a sign of a new world standing of Europe.

How widely and how far down this spiral Europe will go are questions to which any answer seems as good as any other for the moment. A belief in life after Communism, even in a better life, does, of course, remain a reasonable hope. But the new Eastern Question will certainly complicate the European integration process and, more generally, cast a shadow over all-European development in the coming years – a shadow lengthened by the fact that Western Europe is not a superpower with a backyard, but a set of medium to small states, many of which have special relations with certain parts of Eastern Europe.

Probably more important, however, is a second reason for the likely modesty of the foreseeable future of Europe. While Europe has grown successfully after the war, and has maintained, and even bettered, its standing in the distribution of the world's resources, its cultural influence upon the rest of modernity has declined.

The end of exporting aspects of European modernity by gunboat is only one aspect. The European sequence of agrarian to industrial society was not followed elsewhere, and since the 1970s Western Europe has entered into post-industrialism.

The elaborate, principled ideologies which modern Europe has produced are currently in little demand. Working-class socialism may not be a dead duck, but its lively manifestations in Brazil, South Africa or in various regions of Asia no longer have much of a European home base, and no longer draw upon European inspiration. Bourgeois liberalism has been more of a European export since the 1970s, but outside some ex-European corners of the former British Empire and, interestingly enough, the loser of the Falklands/Malvinas war, doctrinaire European liberalism is already bogged down in or reined in by extra-European complexities and by more successful East Asian examples of capitalism.

The scientific and scholarly world centrality of Central and Western Europe was lost to the USA by the Fascist and antisemitic persecutions, and has not been regained, in spite of a considerable postwar élan. The USA became the undisputed centre of Nobel science. After World War II, the twentieth century hardly had a capital, but if there was one, it was no longer Paris, but rather New York. At least since the New York School of Abstract Expressionism in the 1940s, what is modern art is no longer decided in Europe unilaterally. Film, television and contemporary music, modern mass culture in general, have their centre in the USA, and to some extent the UK, insofar as they have one. However, the hottest areas of cultural creativity appear to be at the creole interfaces of North Atlantic modernity with experiences of re-formed traditions from Africa, Asia, the Caribbean and Latin America.

The ex-Colonial Zone has offered no challenge, political, economic or ideological, to its former rulers, but the never properly colonized areas of Externally Induced Modernization have. For the first time since the Industrial

Revolution there has emerged in East Asia a kind of rich and developed society owing virtually nothing to Europe.[8] Instead it is being guided by a Japanese vanguard, a common Sinified culture and certain crucial American inputs, while preserving a number of national variants.[9] Since the mid-1970s Europe has been aware of this challenge, even to the point of trying to imitate Japanese methods of management.

What this East Asian alternative modernity will offer and demand in the future still seems unclear. An indication is given by the recent bestseller by Shintaro Ishihara, a prominent Japanese writer and politician. It conveys profound *resentments* against Western racism, American in particular. It proclaims that the 'modern era is over', by which the author seems to mean the Euro-American constructions of 'materialism, science, and progress', while maintaining that economic growth, competitiveness and power will be decisive in the post-modern epoch. Like Northern advisers to the South, or recently Western advisers to Eastern Europe, Ishihara also generously offers an agenda for a competitive America. But readers are left in the dark about how the future will look, apart from being economic and Japanese.[10] Anyway, the intercontinental balance of advice and admonitions is changing.

Other countries of Externally Induced Modernization have also offered chickens to come home to roost. One blow was the OPEC price hike of 1973, engineered in the windfall area of never-colonized Arabia. Another was the Islamic 'Fundamentalist' spectre raised by Khomeini's Iran, yet another survivor of European colonialism.

On the eve of the twenty-first century, Europe is no longer the centre or the vanguard of modernity, and whether it constitutes a major alternative for the future is at least open to doubt. Moreover, Europeans are a small minority of humankind, about one-eighth of the world's population. To the Europeans themselves, the legacy of a specific history remains and will remain important. Its sediments, from Antiquity to the industrial class struggle, are built into the European House. To the rest of the modern world, however, the lights of Europe are growing dim.

However, there is at least one area in which Europe is again making a major contribution to global modernity. That is in supra-national political and economic cooperation and unification. Once Europe was the cradle of nationalism and of the nation-state. Their full force fell upon the continent in the two world wars. Lenin's conception of a Union of Socialist Soviet Republics based on national self-determination, a conception arising from the multinational experiences of the Central and Eastern European labour movement, was the first major practical attempt at a modern supra-national polity. But it was from the very beginning *de facto* overlayered by an authoritarian party dictatorship, and crumbled in the end with the fall of the latter. The post-World War II Western European Community, by contrast, has no real centre at all, and has evolved gradually over an extended period of time.

The European Community has already inspired regional economic cooperation in the other parts of the world, in the Americas from Mercosur to Nafta, in the Asian Pacific, and in the new Central Asia. The increasing integration of international markets, the cross-border mass communication, and the internationalization and globalization of environmental problems call for legal regulations and political interventions beyond the boundaries of nation-states. In spite of its Eastern shadow, and for all its internal controversies, by steering a course of concrete, pluralistic and democratic supra-national development, Europe, 'as a shorthand word for the movement of West European unity and integration',[11] is providing a highly pertinent example to the world of the twenty-first century.

However, the future importance of this example will depend on how two decisive questions are answered. What is the meaning of a European union, once the memories of World War II have faded away and the Cold War polarity has ended? Where does Europe end?

Is the meaning of European unification a single market and a monetary union? Popular enthusiasm for and the world significance of that appear doubtful. Is it the European tradition and European culture? But a key component of European culture was internal conflict and strife, and its classical ideologies are eroding. And the recent cultural diversity of the Western part of the continent means that a re-institutionalization of European cultural history would require an ugly cultural 'cleansing'.

To be successful and important, the European Union needs to be a project of social construction, not just a marketplace nor a museum. In the values of public collectivism and family individualism, and in the experiences, achievements and organizations of the labour movement, of Christian Democracy, and of enlightened conservatism, Europe has the resources for the construction of a European society. Whether they will be used, I am unable to tell.

'Europe' is no longer the most prestigious club in the world. But its boundaries are still important. It is, after all, the most developed club of states. There is, obviously, a practical trade-off between the extension and the erection of the building. On the other hand, after the Cold War and in a post-European world, any reasonable project of a European Union can hardly have as an objective to preserve a division of Europe. That would imply that at least Russia, the Balkans and all the countries west thereof should be invited to join. Whether that will stand any realistic chance of realization will first of all depend on whether the precipitate socio-economic decline of the ex-USSR and the ex-Communist Balkans can be stopped and reversed.

But there are also the border areas, through which any line of demarcation has a certain odour of arbitrariness. The Mediterranean was once a highway of communication, rather than a border of continents and civilizations. And between Mahgreb and Southern Europe there are many links. Morocco indicated its desire to join the European Community a decade ago. Cultural traditions, musical above all, and family reminiscences of al-Andalus have been maintained in Morocco (in Fès in particular) until this day, for half a millennium.

The Ottoman Empire was long a major player in European politics, and Kemalist Turkey was, for all its Turanism, a very Europe-oriented country.[12] Turkey too has an application for EC/EU membership put aside in a Brussels drawer. Now, Europeanized Turkey is facing an Islamic reaction, and the country sees a Central Asian option opening in the wake of the sunk Soviet Union.

Europeans make up the bulk of the so-called Caucasian race. But the fragile mosaic of the Caucasus is an archetypical border area. Currently it is being ripped apart. Does Europe end on this or on that side of the Caucasus?

Central Asia is the fourth significant border area of Europe. In particular Kazakhstan, with a population of a size similar to that of the Netherlands or Australia, and where Kazakhs and Russians each make up a little under 40%.

There are no easy solutions. A significant supra-state social organization would be a major contribution to the twenty-first century. So would the institutionalization of interchanges across the Mediterranean, the Bosporus, the Caucasus and the Kazakh steppe.

Whether Europe's politicians will be level to the challenges facing them is at least open to doubt. But an empirical sociological discourse may very well end at the doorstep of politics.

The future of modernity, however, cannot be left to the politicians. It hinges rather upon dialogues between intellectuals and peoples.

Two issues appear crucial in the current conjuncture. First, are reality, truth, and the search for truth about reality, meaningful conceptions? Only if they are, does any notion of progress, growth, development, or emancipation make sense. Is the occurrence or not of child exploitation, rape, torture, and murder a potentially universal truth, or only one 'local knowledge', or one 'narrative' among many?

Second, can the Enlightenment tradition, of illumination, autonomy, maturity, emancipation, liberation, be separated from its historical economic base, of economic growth and of economic transformation? There are many serious voices now saying that a 'sustainable development' requires self-limitation, particularly on the part of Europe and North America.

If that is at least approximately correct, will economic self-limitation be compatible with collective democracy and with personal and social emancipation? To make them compatible is likely to be a great progressive task of coming years.

The times may have a-changed. But on the barricades of autonomy and maturity (Kant's *Mündigkeit*), of enlightenment and emancipation, of universalistic humaneness, the wheat of intellectuals and social activists are separated from the chaff. Modernity is under siege, or being abandoned. However, there are quite a few of us who think that it, albeit not necessarily the classical European variety, is still worth fighting for.

Scholarship is for everybody and anybody. But the scholar who is looking for truth, in however small currency, had better not forget where the light comes from.

Notes

1 The Falklands War was a special case, as the challenge did not come from people colonized but from an outside local power.
2 See further G. Meier and D. Seers (eds), *Pioneers in Development*, Washington, DC, World Bank/Oxford, Oxford University Press, 1984.
3 D. Lerner, 'Modernization: Social Aspects', J. Coleman, 'Modernization: Political Aspects', both in D. Sills (ed.), *International Encyclopedia of the Social Sciences*, Vol. 10, New York, Macmillan, 1968; T. Parsons, *The System of Modern Societies*, Englewood Cliffs, Prentice-Hall, 1971.
4 P. Bairoch, 'The Main Trends in National Economic Disparities since the Industrial Revolution', in P. Bairoch and M. Lévy-Leboyer (eds), *Disparities in Economic Development since the Industrial Revolution*, London, Macmillan, 1981, p. 12, Table 1.6, and p. 10, Table 1.4.
5 On Japan, see p. 10. On both the recent world location of Japan and Korea, see World Bank, *World Development Report 1991*, Oxford, Oxford University Press, 1991, p. 263.
6 R. Summers and A. Heston, 'Improved International Comparisons of Real Product and its Composition: 1950–1980', *The Review of Income and Wealth* 30 (1984), pp. 220ff.
7 This would happen if Poland had a growth rate of 3%, Hungary of 3.5%, and the Czech Republic about 4.2% a year for 1994–9. The target of a return to 1989 at the end of 1999 is not inconceivably out of reach, though not very likely. It would mean a return to Western European growth rates before 1973. That Russia should be able to return to its not very radiant economic production of resources in 1989 by the end of this millennium is hardly conceivable, on the other hand. It would require an economic growth rate of 10% a year for 1994–9. The GDP data for 1990–3, which are not per capita, are taken from OECD, *Economic Outlook 54*, Paris, December 1993, p. 117. My calculations are based thereon.
8 True, Meiji Japan did borrow legal institutions and various techniques from Europe, but that was a century ago.
9 Cf. G. Hamilton and N.W. Biggart, 'Market, Culture, and Authority: A Comparative Analysis of Management and Organization in the Far East', *American Journal of Sociology*, Supplement Vol. 94 (1988).
10 S. Ishihara, *The Japan That Can Say No*, London, Simon & Schuster, 1991.
11 This meaning of 'Europe' developed in the course of the 1950s, among the six states embarking upon supranational integration: R. Bullen, 'Britain and "Europe", 1950–1957', in E. Serra (ed.), *Il rilancio dell' Europa e i trattati di Roma*, Brussels, Milan, Paris and Baden-Baden, Bruylant, Giuffré, LGDJ and Nomos, 1989, p. 315.
12 Cf. S. Mardin, 'Europe in Turkey', in T. Belge (ed.), *Where Does Europe End?*, Ankara, Mas Matbacilik, 1993.

BIBLIOGRAPHY

Note: International statistical publications are listed by their producers, national (and Nordic) and by their titles. Current newspapers, magazines and periodicals are listed separately, under their titles.

Achten, A., et al. (eds), *Mein Vaterland ist International*, Oberhausen, Asso, 1986.
Addison, P., *The Road to 1945*, London, Quartet Books, 1977.
Alber, J., 'Germany', in P. Flora (ed.), *Growth to Limits*, Vol. 2, Berlin, de Gruyter, 1966.
Albert, M., *Capitalisme contre capitalisme*, Paris, Seuil, 1991.
Alexander, I. and Seidman, S. (eds), *Culture and Society*, Cambridge, Cambridge University Press, 1990.
Ambrosius, G. and Hubbard, W., *A Social and Economic History of Twentieth-Century Europe*, Cambridge, Mass., Harvard University Press, 1989.
Ammerman, N., 'North American Fundamentalism', in M. Marty and S. Appleby (eds), *Fundamentalisms Observed*, Chicago, University of Chicago Press, 1991.
Anderson, B., *Imagined Communities*, London, Verso, 1983.
Anderson, P., *Lineages of the Absolutist State*, London, NLB, 1974.
Anderson, P., *Passages from Antiquity to Feudalism*, London, NLB.
Anderson, P., *English Questions*, London, Verso, 1992.
Andorka, R., et al., *Social Report*, Budapest, Tárki, 1992.
Andresen, S. (ed.), *Frauenbewegungen in der Welt*, Vol. 1, Berlin, Argument, 1988.
Andreucci, F., 'La diffusione e la volgarizzazione del marxismo', in E. Hobsbawm et al. (eds), *Storia del marxismo*, Vol. 2, Turin, Einaudi, 1979.
Annuaire rétrospectif de la France, 1948–1988, Paris, INSEE, 1990.
Annuaire statistique de la Suisse 1990, 1991, Zurich 1989, 1990.
Ara, A. and Magris, C., *Trieste: Une identité de frontière*, Paris, Seuil, 1982.
Arbatov, G., *Das System*, Frankfurt, Fischer, 1993.
Arbetarförsäkringskommittén, *Betänkande*, Stockholm, 1888.
Archer, M.S. and Giner, S. (eds), *Contemporary Europe: Class, Status and Power*, London: Weidenfeld and Nicolson, 1971.
Armstrong, J., *Nations before Nationalism*, Chapel Hill, NC, University of North Carolina Press, 1982.
Arvidsson, B., *Europarådet 40 år*, Stockholm, UD, 1989.
Atkinson, A. and Micklewright, J., *Economic Transformation in Eastern Europe and the Distribution of Income*, Cambridge, Cambridge University Press, 1992.
Austria: Facts and Figures, Vienna Federal Press Service, 1987.
Bade, K., 'Fremde Deutsche: "Republikflüchtige" – Übersiedler – Aussiedler', in K. Bade (ed.), *Deutsche im Ausland – Fremde in Deutschland*, Munich, C. H. Beck, 1992.
Baglioni, G. and Crouch, C. (eds), *European Industrial Relations*, London, Sage, 1990.
Bailey, J. *Social Europe*, London, Longman, 1992.
Bairoch, P., 'The Main Trends in National Economic Disparities since the Industrial Revolution', in P. Bairoch and M. Lévy-Leboyer (eds), *Disparities in Economic Development since the Industrial Revolution*, London, Macmillan, 1981.
Bairoch, P., 'International Industrialization Levels from 1750 to 1980', *Journal of European Economic History* 11, 2 (1982).

Bairoch, P., *Cities and Economic Development*, London, Mansell Publishing, 1988.
Bairoch, P. (ed.), *The Working Population and Its Structure*, Brussels, Editions de l'Institut de Sociologie de l'Université Libre de Bruxelles, 1968.
Balla, B., *Kaderverwaltung*, Stuttgart: Deutsche-Verlags-Anstalt, 1972.
Balle, F., *Médias et sociétés*, 5th edn, Paris: Montchrestien, 1990.
Barbeito, A. and LoVuolo, R., *La modernización excluyente*, Buenos Aires, Unicef/Ciepp/Losada, 1992.
Barns levnadsvillkor, Stockholm, SCB, 1989.
Barreau, J.-C. *De l'Islam*, Paris, Le Pré aux Clercs, 1991.
Barro, R. and Sala-I-Martin, X., 'Convergence across States and Regions', *Brookings Papers on Economic Activity* 1 (1991).
Barth, F. (ed.), *Ethnic Groups and Boundries*, Boston, Little, Brown & Co., 1969.
Bartlett, C.J., *A History of Postwar Britain, 1945–1974*, London, Longman, 1977.
Bataille, P. 'L'expérience belge', in M. Wieworka (ed.), *Racisme et xénophobie en Europe*, Paris, La Découverte, 1994.
Beccalli, B., 'The Modern Women's Movement in Italy', *New Left Review* 204 (1994).
Beck, U., *Risikogesellschaft*, Frankfurt: Suhrkamp, 1986 (English edn: *Risk Society*, London, Sage, 1992).
Beck, U., et al. *Reflexive Modernization*, Cambridge, Polity, 1994.
Bédarida, F., 'Frankreich und Europe – von gestern bis heute', in W. Mommsen (ed.), *Der lange Weg nach Europa*, Berlin, edition q, 1992.
Begeja, K., 'Das Eherecht der Volksrepublik Albanien', in E. Loewenfeld and W. Lauterbach (eds), *Das Eherecht der europäischen und der aussereuropäischer Staaten*, Cologne, Carl Hegmann, 1963.
Belinsky, A. (1982). 'Sozialreht der UdSSR', *Jahrbuch für Ostrecht* XXIII, 1–2.
Bell, J., 'Bulgaria', in S. White et al. (eds), *Developments in East European Politics*, London, Macmillan, 1993.
Benjamin, W. *Illuminationen*, Frankfurt, Suhrkamp, 1969.
Benz, W., 'Fremde in der Heimat: Flucht – Vertreibung – Integration', in K. Bade (ed.), *Deutsche im Ausland – Fremde in Deutschland*, Munich. C.H. Beck, 1992.
Berben, T., et al. 'Stelsels van sociale zekerheid: na-oorlogse regelingen in West-Europa', *Res Publica*, XXVIII,1 (1986).
Berger, P. and Luckmann, T., *The Social Construction of Reality*, Garden City, NY, Anchor Books, 1967 (1st edn. 1966).
Berger, S., *Les paysans contre la politique*, Paris, Seuil, 1975.
Berggren, C. *Det nya bilarbetet*, Lund, Arkiv, 1990.
Bergmann, A. (ed.), *Internationales Ehe- und Kindschaftsrecht*, 1st edn, Berlin, Verlag des Reichsbundes der Standesbeamten Deutschlands, 2 Vols. 1926.
Bergmann, A. (ed.) *Internationales Ehe- und Kindschaftsrecht*, 2 Vols, 2nd edn, Berlin, Verlag für Standeswesen, 1938.
Bergmann, A. and Ferid, M. (eds), *Internationales Ehe- und Kindschaftsrecht*, Frankfurt, Verlag für Standeswesen, 1955, various vols.
Bergmann, U., et al., *Rebellion der Studenten oder Die neue Opposition*, Reinbek bei Hamburg, Rowohlt, 1968.
Berman, H., *Justice in the USSR*, rev. edn, Cambridge, Mass., Harvard University Press, 1963.
Berman, H., *Law and Revolution: The Formation of the Western Legal Tradition*, Cambridge, Mass., Harvard University Press, 1983.
Bernd, C. and Schlatter, E., 'Domestic Violence in Austria: The Institutional Response', in E. Viano (ed.), *Intimate Violence: Interdisciplinary Perspectives*, Washington, DC, Hemisphere Publishing Corporation, 1992.
Berner, R., *Rysk arbetare*, Stockholm, Författarförlaget, 1976.
Beyme, K. von, *Ökonomie und Politik im Sozialismus*, Munich, Piper, 1975.
Beyme, K. von, 'Vergleichende Analyse von Politikfeldern in sozialistischen Ländern', in M. Schmidt (ed.), *Staatstätigkeit*, Opladen, Leske & Budrich, 1989.
Beyme, K. von, 'Reconstruction in the German Democratic Republic', in J. Diefendorf (ed.), *Rebuilding Europe's Bombed Cities*, Basingstoke, Macmillan, 1990.

Birk, R., 'Die Folgewirkungen des europäischen Gemeinschaftsrechts für das nationale Arbeitsrecht', *Europarecht* 25 (1990).

Bjerve, P.J., *Planning in Norway, 1947–1956*, Amsterdam, North-Holland, 1959.

Blackburn, R., *The Overthrow of Colonial Slavery*, London, Verso, 1988.

Blagojevic, B., 'Das Eherecht der Föderativen Volksrepublik Jugoslawien', in E. Loewenfeld an W. Lauterbach (eds), *Das Eherecht der europäischen der aussereuropäischer Staaten*, Cologne, Carl Hegmann, 1963.

Blau, F.D. and Kahn, L.M., *The Gender Earnings Gap: Some International Evidence*, Urbana-Champaign, University of Illinois, 1991.

Blau, P.M. and Duncan, O.D., *The American Occupational Structure*, New York, Wiley, 1967.

Bloch, R., *L'entreprise remise en question*, Paris, Librairie générale de droit et de jurisprudence, 1964.

Blom, I. and Traberg, A. (eds), *Nordiskl lovoversikt*, Copenhagen: Nordisk Ministerråd, 1985.

Blomsterberg, M. and Therborn, G. (eds) *Vad styr Sverige?*, Göteborg, Dept. of Sociology, 1991.

Bloomfield, J. *Passive Revolution*, London, Allison & Busby, 1979.

Boahen, A., *African Perspectives on Colonialism*, Baltimore, Johns Hopkins University Press, 1987.

Bodin, P.-A., 'Karelska Näset som mötesplats för nordiskt och ryskt', in S. Carlsson and N.Å Nilsson (eds), *Sverige och Petersburg*, Stockholm, Almqvist & Wiksell, 1989.

Bodin, P.-A., *Ryssland och Europa*, Stockholm, Natur och Kultur, 1993.

Boeri, T. and Keese, M., 'Labour Markets and the Transition in Central and Eastern Europe', *OECD Economic Studies* 18 (1992).

Bogart, L., *The Age of Television*, 2nd edn, New York, Frederick Ungar, 1958.

Bornschier, W. *Westliche Gesellschaft im Wandel*, Frankfurt, Campus, 1988.

Bosch, G., L'évolution du temps de travail en Allemagne', *Futuribles* 165–6 (1992).

Bosi, M. and Portelli, H (eds), *Les PC espagnol, français et italien face au pouvoir*, Paris, Christian Bourgeois, 1976.

Boujut, M., *Europe–Hollywood et retour*, Paris, Autrement, 1986.

Boulanger, F. 1990. *Droit civil de la famille* Vol. 1, Paris, Economica.

Boulouis, J., *Droit institutionnel des communautés européennes*, Paris, Montchrestien, 1991.

Bourdieu, P., *La Distinction*, Paris, Minuit, 1979.

Boyer, R. (ed.), *La flexibilité du travail en Europe*, Paris, La Découverte, 1986.

Brand, K.-W. (ed.), *Neue soziale Bewegungen in Westeuropa und den USA*, Frankfurt, Campus, 1985.

Braudel F., *Civilisation matérielle, économie et capitalisme XVe–XVIIIe siècle*, 3 Vols, Armand Colin, 1979.

Braudel F., *La Méditerranée et le monde méditerranéen à l'époque de Philippe II*, Vol. 1, Part 1, 5th edn, Paris, Armand Colin, 1982.

Braungart, R., 'Historical Generations and Youth Movements', in R. Ratcliff (ed.), *Research in Social Movement: Conflicts and Change*, Greenwich, Conn. JAI Press, 1984.

Braverman, H., *Labor and Monopoly Capital*, New York, Monthly Review Press, 1974.

Brenner, R. *Merchants and Revolution*, Cambridge, Cambridge University Press, 1993.

Brettschneider, F., et al., 'Materialien zu Gesellschaft, Wirtschaft und Politik in den Mitgliedsstaaten der Europäischen Gemeinschaft', in O. Gabriel (ed.), *Die EG-Staaten im Vergleich*, Opladen, Westdeutscher Verlag, 1992.

Briggs, A., *A Social History of England*. Harmondsworth, Penguin, 1983.

Brinton, W., 'The Helsinki Final Act and Other International Covenants Supporting Freedom and Human Rights', in W. Brinton and A. Rinzler (eds), *Without Force or Lies*, San Francisco, Mercury House, 1990.

Brockmüller, B., 'The National Identity of the Austrians', in M. Teich and R. Porter (eds), *The National Question in Europe in Historical Context*, Cambridge: Cambridge University Press, 1993.

Brubaker, R. (ed.), *Immigration and the Politics of Citizenship in Europe and North America*, New York, University Press of America and German Marshall Fund of the United States, 1989.

Bruto da Costa, A., 'A Despesa Pública em Portugal, 1960–1983', Lisbon, unpublished paper, October 1986.
Brzezinski, Z., *The Soviet Bloc*, Cambridge, Mass., Harvard University Press, 1960.
Bullen, R., 'Britain and "Europe" 1950–1957', in E. Serra (ed.), *Il rilancio dell'Europa e i trattati di Roma*, Brussels, Milan, Paris and Baden-Baden, Bruylant, Giuffré, LGDJ and Nomos, 1989.
Burawoy, M., *The Politics of Production*, London, Verso, 1985.
Burawoy, M. and Lukács, J., *The Radiant Past*, Chicago, University of Chicago Press, 1992.
Carlier, O., 'Aspects des rapports entre mouvement ouvrier émigré et migration maghrébine en France dans l'entre-deux-guerres', in N. Sraïeb (ed.), *Le mouvement ouvrier maghrébin*, Paris, CNRS, 1985.
Carr, E.H. and Davies, R.W. *Foundations of A Planned Economy*, Vol. 1, Harmondsworth, Pelican, 1974.
Castellan, G., 'Histoire des Balkans', Paris, Fayard, 1991.
Castles, F., 'Whatever Happened to the Communist Welfare States?', *Studies in Comparative Communism* XIX, 3/4 (1986).
Castles, F. and Flood, M., 'Why Divorce Rates Differ: Law, Religious Belief, and Modernity', in F. Castles (ed.), *Families of Nations*, Aldershot, Dartmouth, 1993.
Castles, S., *Here for Good*, London, Pluto Press, 1984.
Cecchini, P., *The European Challenge 1992*, Aldershot, Wildwood House, 1988.
Centre for East Asian Cultural Studies, *Meiji Japan through Contemporary Sources*, Tokyo, Centre for East Asian Cultural Studies, 1970.
Champion, A.G., 'Geographical Distribution and Urbanization', in D. Noin and R. Woods (eds), *The Changing Population of Europe*, Oxford, Blackwell, 1993.
Chernayev, A. (German: Tschernajew), *Die letzen Jahre einer Weltmacht*, Stuttgart, Deutsche-Verlags-Anstalt, 1993.
Chernozemski, I., 'Children and the Transition to Market Economy in Bulgaria: "Shock Therapy" with a Difference?' in. G.A. Cornia and S. Sipos (eds), *Children and the Transition to the Market Economy*, Aldershot, Avebury.
Cheshire, P. and Hay, D., *Urban Problems in Western Europe*, London, Unwin Hyman, 1989.
Christaller, W., 'Das Grundgerüst der räumlichen Ordnung in Europa', *Frankfurter Geographische Hefte*, 24,1 (1950).
Christie, N., *Crime Control as Industry*, London, Routledge, 1993.
Clark, C., *The Conditions of Economic Progress*, London: Macmillan, 1957 (originally published 1940).
Clévenot, M. (ed.), *L'Etat des religions dans le monde*, Paris, La Découverte/Le Cerf, 1987.
Cobalti, A., 'Italian Social Mobility in an International Perspective', unpublished paper, Trieste, Dipartimento di scienze dell'uomo, Universitá degli studi di Trieste, 1991.
Cohen, G., 'The German Minority of Prague, 1850–1918', in M. Engman (ed.), *Ethnic Identity in Urban Europe*, Aldershot, Dartmouth, 1992.
Cohen, J. and Arato, A., *Civil Society and Political Theory*, Cambridge, Mass., MIT Press, 1992.
Cohen, L. and Shapiro, J. (eds), *Communist Systems in Perspective*, Garden City, NY, Anchor Books, 1974.
Cole, T. and Winkler, M., ' "Unsere Tage zählen" ', in G. Göckenjan and H.-J. von Kondratowitz, *Alter und Alltag*, Frankfurt, Suhrkamp, 1988.
Coleman J., 'Modernization: Political Aspects', in D. Sills (ed.), *International Encyclopedia of the Social Sciences*, Vol. 10, New York, Macmillan, 1968.
Coleman J., *Foundations of Social Theory*, Cambridge, Mass., Belknap Press, 1990.
Collins, R., *Theoretical Sociology*, San Diego and New York, Harcourt Brace Jovanovich, 1988.
Combats étudiants dans le monde, Paris, Seuil, 1968.
Comisión del Programa 2000, *La sociedad española en transformación*, Madrid, Siglo XXI, 1988.
Commission of the European Communities, *The Regions of the Enlarged Community*, Brussels and Luxemburg, 1987.

Commission of the European Communities, *'Eurobarométre': l'opinion publique et l'Europe* 9 (1989).

Commission of the European Communities, *The Position of Women on the Labour Market*, Women of Europe Supplements, no. 36, 1990.

Commission of the European Communities, *De regio's in de jaren negentig*, Brussels and Luxemburg, 1991.

Commission of the European Communities, *Employment in Europe 1993*, Brussels, 1993.

Commission of the European Communities, *Livre blanc sur la compétitivité, la croissance et l'emploi*, document O/93/355, Brussels, 1993.

Consumer Europe 1989/90, London, Euromonitor, 1989.

Cornia, G.A. and Sipos, S. (eds), *Children and the Transition to the Market Economy*, Aldershot, Avebury, 1991.

Council of Europe, *Household Structures in Europe*, Strasburg, 1990.

Council of Europe, *Recent Demographic Developments in Europe*, Strasburg, 1991.

Council of Europe, *Comparative Tables of Social Security Schemes*, 5th edn, Strasburg, 1992.

Council of Europe, *Human Rights and International Law*, Strasburg, 1992.

Cretney, S.M. and Masson, J.M., *Principles of Family Law*, 5th edn, London: Sweet & Maxwell, 1991.

Crouch, C., *Industrial Relations and European State Tradition*, Oxford, Clarendon Press, 1993.

Cruz Roche, I., et al., *Politica social y crisis ecónimica*, Madrid, Siglo XXI, 1985.

Curtin, P. (ed.), *Africa and the West*, Madison, University of Wisconsin Press, 1972.

Cussack, T., et al., *Political-Economic Aspects of Public Employment*, Berlin, Wissenschaftszentrum FGG/dp 87–2, 1987.

Czaky, M., 'Historische Reflexionen über das Problem einer österreichischen identität', in H. Wolfram and W. Pohl (eds), *Probleme der Geschichte Österreichs und ihrer Darstellung*, Vienna, Verlag der Österreichischen Akademie der Wissenschaften, 1991.

[Czechoslovak] Federal Ministry of Labour and Social Affairs, 'Czechoslovakia', in J. Dixon and D. Macarov (eds), *Social Welfare in Socialist Countries*, London, Routledge, 1992.

Dahlerup, D. (ed.), *The New Women's Movement*, London, Sage, 1986.

Dahrendorf, R., *Life Chances*, Chicago, University of Chicago Press, 1979.

Daniel, J., *L'òre des ruptures*, Paris, Grasset, 1979.

Davies, N., *God's Playground*, Oxford, Clarendon Press, 1981, 2 vols.

Davis, D., *A History of Shopping*, London, Routledge & Kegan Paul, 1966.

Day, A.N.D., *Peace Movements of the World*, Harlow, Essex, Longman.

Deacon, A., 'Unemployment and Politics in Britain since 1945', in B. Showler and A. Sinfield (eds), *The Workless State*, Oxford, Martin Robertson, 1981.

Deacon, B., et al., *The New Eastern Europe*, London, Sage, 1992.

Deák, I., *Beyond Nationalism*, Oxford, Oxford University Press, 1992.

Deaton, A.S., 'The Structure of Demand in Europe, 1920–1970', in C. Cipolla (ed.), *The Fontana Economic History of Europe*, London, Collins/Fontana, 1976.

Debray, R., *Modeste contribution aux discours et cérémonies officielles du dixième anniversaire*, Paris, Maspero, 1978.

Debray, R., *L'Etat séducteur*, Paris, Gallimard, 1993.

Delaisi, R., *Les deux Europes*, Paris, Payot, 1929.

Derbasch, C. (ed.), *Les privatisations en Europe*, Paris, Ed. du CNRS, 1989.

Desanti, D., *Les staliniens: Une expérience politique, 1944/1956*, Paris, Fayard, 1975.

Deutscher, I., *Soviet Trade Unions*, Oxford, Oxford University Press, 1950.

Deveze, G., 'Viol conjugal: comme tous les viols un crime', *Nouvelles questions féministes* 16–18 (1991).

Dhavemas, O., 1978. *Droit des femmes, pouvoir des hommes*, Paris, Seuil, 1978.

Di Nolfo, E., 'Gli Stati Uniti e le origini della Comunità Economica Europea', in E. Serra (ed.), *Il rilancio dell'Europa e i trattati di Roma*, Brussels, Milan, Paris and Baden-Baden, Bruylant, Giuffré, LGDJ and Nomos.

Dixon, J. and Macarov, D. (eds), *Social Welfare in Socialist Countries*, London, Routledge, 1992.

Dobb, M., *Soviet Economic Development since 1917*, 6th edn, London, Routledge, 1966.
Documenti della rivolta universitaria, Bari, Laterza, 1968.
Dogan, M., 'Comparing the Decline of Nationalism in Western Europe: The Generational Dynamic', *International Social Science Journal* 136 (1993).
Dogan, M. and Kasarda, J. (eds), *The Metropolis Era: A World of Giant Cities*, Vol. 1, London, Sage, 1988.
Dohrn, V., *Reise nach Galizien*, Frankfurt, Fischer, 1992.
Dohse, K., et al. (eds), *Statussicherung im Industriebetrieb*, Frankfurt, Campus, 1982.
Données Sociales 1981, 1990, Paris, INSEE, 1981, 1990.
Douglas, M., *Risk Acceptability According to the Social Sciences*, London, Routledge & Kegan Paul, 1986.
Dubček, A., *Leben für die Freiheit*, Munich, Bertelsmann, 1993.
Dübeck, I., 'Hvordan skabtes arbejdsretten i Danmark?', in *Rättsvetenskap och lagstiftning i Norden*, Stockholm, Juristförlaget, 1982.
Duby, G., *Les trois ordres ou l'imaginaire du féodalisme*. Paris: Gallimard, 1978.
Durkheim, E., *De la division du travail social*, Paris, 1st edn, Quadrige/PUF, 1990.
Duroselle, J.-B., 'La relance européenne, 1954–1957' in E. Serra (ed.), *Il rilancio dell'Europa e i trattati di Roma*, Milan, Paris and Baden-Baden, Bruylant, Giuffré, LGDJ and Nomos.
Dyserinck, H. and Syndram, K.U. (eds) *Europa und das nationale Selbstverständnis*, Bonn, Bouvier, 1988.
East, R. (ed.) *Revolutions in Eastern Europe*, London, Pinter, 1992.
Ebbighausen, R. and Tiemann, F. (eds), *Das Ende der Arbeiterbewegnung in Deutscheland?*, Opladen, Westdeutscher, Verlag, 1984.
Edwards, G., *GDR Society and Social Institutions*, London, Macmillan, 1985.
Ellis, M. and Storm, P. (eds), *Business Law in Europe*, Deventer, Kluwer, 1990–.
Elton, G., *Reformation Europe, 1517–1559*, London, Fontana/Collins, 1963.
Elvander, N., *Skandinavisk arbetarrörelse*, Stockholm, Liber, 1980.
Encuesta continua de presupuestos familiares: Año 1988, Madrid, Instituto Nacional de Estadistica, 1989.
Engman, M., 'Finnar och svenskar i St Petersburg', in S. Carlsson and N.-Å. Nilsson (eds), *Sverige och St Petersburg*, Stockholm, Almqvist & Wiksell, 1989.
Eriksson, B., *Samhällsvetenskapens uppkomst* Uppsala, Sociologiska institutionen, 1988.
Eriksson, R. and Goldthorpe, J., 'Are American Rates of Social Mobility Exceptionally High? New Evidence on an Old Issue', *European Sociological Review* 1 (May, 1985).
Eriksson, R. and Goldthorpe, J., *The Constant Flux: A Study of Class Mobility in Industrial Societies*, Oxford, Clarendon Press, 1992.
Eriksson, R. and Jonsson, J., *Ursprung och utbildning*, Stockholm, SOU:1993:85.
Eschenburg, T., *Jahre der Besatzung, 1945–49*, Stuttgart and Wiesbaden, DVA and Brockhaus, 1983.
Esping-Andersen, G. *The Three Worlds of Welfare Capitalism*, Cambridge, Polity Press, 1990.
Eurostat, *Review 1975–1984*, Luxemburg, 1986.
Eurostat, *Employment and Unemployment 1989*, Brussels and Luxemburg, 1989.
Eurostat, *Regions Statistical Yearbook 1988*, Luxemburg, 1989.
Eurostat, *Basic Statistics of the Community*, 27th–30th edns, Luxemburg, 1990–3.
Eurostat, *Demographic Statistics 1990*, Luxemburg, 1990.
Eurostat, *Rapid Reports*, no. 1: *Regions*; no. 6: *Population and Social Conditions* (1993).
Evans, G., 'Class Conflict and Inequality', in R. Jowell et al. (eds), *International Social Attitudes: The 10th BSA Report*, Aldershot, Dartmouth, 1993.
Evans, R., *The Feminists*, London, Croom Helm, 1979.
Ewald, F., *L'Etat de Providence*, Paris, Grasset, 1986.
Eyben, W.E. von, 'Inter-Nordic Legislative Cooperation', *Scandinavian Studies in Law* 6 (1962).
Familiengesetze sozialistischer Länder, East Berlin, Deutsche Zentralverlag, 1959.
Fassmann, H. and Münz, R., Aufnahmefähig aber noch nicht aufnahmebereit', *Die Presse* 15./16.6.1991.
Fejtö, F., *Histoire des démocraties populaires: 1. L'ère de Staline*, Paris, Seuil, 1972.

Ferge, Z., *A Society in the Making*, Harmondsworth, Penguin, 1979.
Ferrara, M., 'Italy', in P. Flora (ed.), *Growth to Limits*, Vol. 2, Berlin, de Gruyter, 1986.
Féron, F. and Thoraval, A., *L'Etat de Europe*, Paris, La Découverte, 1992.
Ferro, M., *La révolution de 1917*, Paris, Aubier, 2 Vols, 1976.
Fierro, A., *L'Europe des différences*, Paris, Bonneton, 1991.
Fischbach, G. (ed.) *DDR-Almanach '90*, Landsberg, Bon-Aktuell, 1990.
Der Fischer Weltalmanach 1990, Frankfurt, Fischer, 1989.
Fitzmaurice, J., *The Politics of Belgium*, London, Hurst & Co, 1983.
Flemming, J., 'Der 1. Mai und die deutsche Arbeiterbewegung', in U. Schultz (ed.), *Das Fest*, Munich, C.H. Beck, 1988.
Flora, P., 'Eine Familie von Modellen für die vergleichende Geschichte Europas', *Zeitschrift für Soziologie* 9 (1980).
Flora, P. (ed.), *State, Economy and Society in Western Europe, 1815–1975*, Vol. 1, Frankfurt, Campus, 1983; Vol. 2, Frankfurt, Campus, 1987.
Flora, P. (ed.), *Growth to Limits*, Berlin, de Gruyter, 1986–, 4 Vols.
Flora, P. and Heidenheimer, A. (eds), *The Development of Welfare States in Europe and America*, New Brunswick, NJ, and London, Transaction Books, 1987.
Foner, P., *May Day*, New York, International Publishers, 1986.
Fordham Law Review, 'Comments' [1936], reprinted in *Selected Essays on Family Law*, compiled and edited by a committee of the Association of American Law Schools, Brooklyn, Foundation Press, 1950.
Forrest, A., *The French Revolution and the Poor*, Oxford, Blackwell, 1981.
Förster, P. and Roski, G., *DDR zwischen Wende und Wahl*, Berlin, Linksdruck, 1990.
Fothergill, S. and Vincent, J., *The State of the Nation*, London, Pan Books, 1985.
Fourastié, J., *Les Trente Glorieuses*, Paris, Fayard, 1979.
Fron, F. and Thoraval, A. (eds), *L'Etat de l'Europe*, Paris, La Découverte, 1992.
Fukuyama, F., *The End of History*, New York, Free Press, 1992.
Gabriel, O. (ed.), *Die EG-Staaten im Vergleich*, Opladen: Westdeutscher Verlag, 1992.
Gallup, G.H., *The Gallup Poll*, Vol. 3, New York, Random House, 1972, 3 Vols.
Ganzeboom, H., et al., 'Intergenerational Class Mobility in Comparative Perspective', *Research on Social Stratification and Mobility* 9 (1989).
Ganzeboom, H., et al., 'Comparative Intergenerational Stratification Research: Three Generations and Beyond', *Annual Review of Sociology* 17 (1991).
Garraty, J., *Unemployment in History*, New York, Harper & Row, 1978.
Garton Ash, T., *The Polish Revolution*, London, Granta Books, 1991 (originally published 1983).
Garton Ash, T., *We the People: The Revolution of '89*, Cambridge, Granta Books, 1990.
Geiger, K., *The Family in Soviet Russia*, Cambridge, Mass., Harvard University Press, 1968.
Gellner, E., *Nations and Nationalism*, Oxford, Basil Blackwell, 1983.
Gephart, W., *Gesellschaftstheorie und Recht*, Frankfurt, Suhrkamp, 1993.
Gerbet, P., 'Les origines du Plan Schuman: Le choix de la méthode communautaire par le gouvernement français', in R. Poidevin (ed.), *Histoire des débuts de la construction européenne*, Brussels, Milan, Paris and Baden-Baden, Bruylant, Giuffré, LGDJ and Nomos.
Gershuny, J., 'Are We Running Out of Time?', *Futures* 24,1 (1992).
Gershuny, J., 'Emplois du temps', in F. Féron and A. Thoraval (eds), *L'Etat de l'Europe*, Paris, La Découverte, 1992.
Gershuny, J., 'La répartition du temps dans les sociétés post-industrielles', *Futuribles* 165–6 (1992).
Getty, J.A., et al., 'Victims of the Soviet Penal System in the Pre-war Years: A First Approach on the Basis of Archival Evidence', *American Historical Review* 58 (1993).
Giddens, A., *Sociology*, Cambridge, Polity Press, 1989.
Giddens, A., *The Consequences of Modernity*, Stanford, Stanford University Press, 1990.
Giddens, A., *Modernity and Self-Identity*, Cambridge, Polity Press, 1991.
Gillis, J., *Youth and History*, Orlando, Fla., Academic Press, 1981.
Giner, S. and Archer, M.S. (eds), *Contemporary Europe: Social Structures and Cultural Patterns*, London, Routledge & Kegan Paul, 1978.

Glendon, M.A., *State, Law and Family*, Amsterdam North-Holland, 1977.

Glenny, M., *The Fall of Yugoslavia*, Harmondsworth, Penguin, 1992; new edn, 1993.

Glettler, M., 'The Slovaks in Budapest and Bratislava, 1850–1914', in M. Engman (ed.), *Ethnic Identity in Urban Europe*, Aldershot, Dartmouth, 1991.

Godwin, G., *Islamic Spain*, London, Viking, 1990.

Goldsmith, E. (ed.), *A Blueprint for Survival*, Harmondsworth, Penguin, 1972.

Goldthorpe, J., 'The Uses of History in Sociology: Reflections on Some Recent Tendencies', *British Journal of Sociology* 42 (1991).

Goody, J., *The Development of the Family and Marriage in Europe*, Cambridge, Cambridge University Press, 1983.

Goody, J., et al. (eds), *Family and Inheritance*, Cambridge, Cambridge University Press, 1976.

Gorz, A., *Adieux au prolétariat*, Paris, Galilée, 1980.

Gramsci A., 'Americanism and Fordism', in Q. Hoare and G. N. Smith (eds), *Selections from the Prison Notebooks*, London, Lawrence & Wishart, 1971.

Graubard, S. (ed.), *Eastern Europe . . . Central Europe . . . Europe*, Boulder, Col., Westview Press, 1991.

Greenfeld, L., *Nationalism*, Cambridge, Mass., Harvard University Press, 1992.

Grtossen, J.M., 'Switzerland: Further Steps Towards Equality', *Journal of Family Law* 25 (1986).

Grzybowski, S.M., 'Das Eherecht der VR Polen', in E. Lowenfeld and W. Lauterbach (eds), *Das Eherecht der europäischen und der aussereuropäischer Staaten*, Cologne: Carl Hegmann, 1963–72.

Guillemard, A. -M, *Le déclin du social*, Paris, PUF, 1986.

Guillen, P., 'La France et la négociation des traités de Rome: l'Euratom', in E. Serra, *Il rilancio dell'Europa e i trattati di Roma*, Brussels, Milan, Paris and Baden-Baden, Bruylant, Giuffré, LGDJ and Nomos, 1989.

Gustafsson, B. and Uusitalo, H., 'Income Distribution and Redistribution during Two Decades: Experiences from Finland and Sweden', in I. Persson (ed.), *Generating Equality in the Welfare State*, Oslo, Norwegian University Press, 1989.

Gutton, J.-P., *Naissance du viellard*, Paris: Aubier, 1988.

Gysi, J., 'Familienformen in der DDR', *Jahrbuch für Soziologie und Soziopolitik*, [East] Berlin, Akademie-Verlag, 1988.

Haas, E., *The Uniting of Europe*, Stanford: Stanford University Press.

Habermas, J., 'The Rectifying Revolution', *New Left Review* 183 (1990).

Habermas, J., *Faktizität und Geltung*, Frankfurt Suhrkamp, 1992.

Habermas, J., *Die Moderne – ein unvollendetes Projekt*, Leipzig, Reclam, 1992.

Hajnal, J., 'European Marriage Patterns in Perspective', in D.V. Glass and D.E.C. Eversley (eds), *Population in History*, London, 1965.

Haller, M., *Klassenstruktur und Mobilität in fortgeschrittenen Gesellschaften*, Frankfurt, Campus, 1989.

Haller, M., et al. 'Soziale Mobilität in Österriech, in der Tschechoslowakei und in Ungarn', *Journal für Sozialforschung* 30 (1990).

Hälsa i Sverige, Stockholm, SCB, 1988.

Hamani, T. and Monat, J. 'Employee Participation in the Workshop, in the Office, and in the Enterprise', in R. Blanpain (ed.), *Comparative Labour Law and Industrial Relations*, 2nd edn, Deventer: Kluwer, 1985.

Hamilton, G. and Biggart, N.W., 'Market, Culture, and Authority: A Comparative Analysis of Management and Organization in the Far East', *American Journal of Sociology*, Supplement Vol. 94 (1988).

Hammar, T., *Democracy and the Nation State*, Aldershot, Avebury, 1990.

Hampden-Turner, C. and Trompenaars, A., 1993. *The Seven Cultures of Capitalism*, New York, Doubleday, 1993.

Hankiss, E., *East European Alternatives*, Oxford, Clarendon Press, 1990.

Harder, H.-D., 'Allgemeiner Kündigungsschutz in ausgewählten europäischen Ländern', *Jahrbuch für Sozialwissenschaft*, 44, 1 (1993).

Harding , S., et al., *Contrasting Values in Western Europe*, London, Macmillan, 1986.

Harris, C., 'The New Russian Minorities: A Statistical Overview', *Post-Soviet Geography* 34, 1 (1993).

Hartley, T.C., *The Foundations of European Community Law*, Oxford, Clarendon Press, 1983.

Hartwich, H-H., *Sozialstaatspostulat und gesellschaftlicher status quo*, 3rd edn, Cologne, Westdeutscher Verlag, 1978.

Hearthfield, E. (ed.), 1992. *Halsbury's Laws of England 1991*, London, Butterworths, 1992.

Heath, A., 'Class and Political Partisanship', in J. Clark et al. (eds), *John H. Goldthorpe*, London, Falmer Press, 1990.

Hedström , P. and Swedberg, R., 'The Power of Working Class Organizations and the Inter-Industrial Wage Structure', *International Journal of Comparative Sociology*, XXVI, 1–2 (1985).

Heidenheimer, A. et al., *Comparative Public Policy*, 2nd edn, New York, St Martin's Press; 3rd edn, New York, St Martin's Press, 1990.

Henke, K.-D. and Woller, H. (eds), *Politische Säuberung in Europa*, Munich, dtv, 1991.

Hennessey, P., *Never Again*, London, Vintage, 1993.

Hepple, B., 'Security of Employment', in R. Blanpain (ed.), *Comparative Labour and Industrial Relations*, 2nd edn, Deventer, Kluwer, 1985.

Herbert, U., *Geschichte der Ausländerbeschäftigung in Deutschland, 1880 bis 1980*, Berlin and Bonn, J.W.H. Dietz Nachf, 1980.

Hernes, G. and Knudsen, K., *Lithuania*, Oslo, Norwegian Trade Union Centre, 1991.

Hesse, J.J. (ed.), *Administrative Transformation in Central and Eastern Europe*, Oxford, Blackwell, 1993.

Hirschman, A., *The Rhetoric of Reaction*, Cambridge, Mass., Harvard University Press, 1991.

Historical Statistics of the United States, Washington DC, US Bureau of the Census, 1975.

Historisk Statistik för Sverige, 2nd edn, Stockholm, SCB, 1969.

Hobsbawm, E., *The Age of Revolution, 1789–1848*, London, Weidenfeld & Nicolson, 1962 and New York, Mentor Books, 1964.

Hobsbawm, E., *The Age of Capital, 1848–1875*, London, Weidenfeld & Nicolson, 1975.

Hobsbawm, E., 'The Forward March of Labour Halted?', in M. Jacques and F. Mulhern (eds), *The Forward March of Labour Halted?*, London, Verso, 1981.

Hobsbawm, E., 'Mass-Producing Traditions: Europe, 1870–1914', in E. Hobsbawm and T. Ranger, *The Invention of Tradition*, Cambridge, Cambridge University Press, 1983.

Hobsbawn, E., *The Age of Empire, 1875–1914*, London, Weidenfeld & Nicolson, 1987.

Hobsbawm, E., *Nations and Nationalism since 1780*, Canto edn, Cambridge, Cambridge University Press, 1991.

Hobsbawm, E., *Age of Extremes*, London, Michael Joseph, 1994.

Hofstede, G., *Culture's Consequences*, London, Sage, 1980.

Hohfeld, W., *Fundamental Legal Conceptions*, New Haven, Yale University Press, 1964 (1st posthumous edn, 1919).

Holland, S., *The European Imperative*, Nottingham, Spokesman, 1993.

Holland, W.W. (ed.), *European Community Atlas of 'Avoidable Death'*, Oxford, Oxford University Press, 1988.

Hollifield, J., *Immigrants, Markets, and States*, Cambridge, Mass., Harvard University Press, 1992.

Holmberg, S. and Gilljam, M., *Väljare och val i Sverige*, Stockholm, Bonniers, 1987.

Holmes, G. (ed.), *The Oxford Illustrated History of Medieval Europe*, Oxford, Oxford University Press, 1988.

Homann, R. and Moll, P.H., 'An Overview of Western Futures Organizations', *Futures* 25 (1993).

Horkheimer, M. and Adorno, T.W., *Dialectic of the Enlightenment*, New York, Herder and Herder, 1972 (1st edn, 1944).

Horn, G., *Freiheit die ich meine*, Hamburg, Hoffmann und Campe, 1991.

Hourani, A., *Arabic Thought in the Liberal Age, 1798–1939*, Cambridge, Cambridge University Press, 1983.

Household Budget Survey, Dublin, Central Statistical Office, 1989.

Hradil, S., Sozialstruktur und gesellschaftlicher wandel', in O. Gabriel (ed.), *Die EG-staaten im Vergleich*, Opladen: Westdeutscher Verlag, 1992.

Huber, E., *System und Geschichte des schweizerischen Privatrechts*, Vol. 1, Basel, Dekoffs Buchhandlung, 2 Vols, 1896.

Human Rights and International Law, Strasburg, Council of Europe Press, 1992.

Hunke, S., *Allahs Sonne über dem Abendland*, Stuttgart: Deutsche-Verlags-Anstalt, 1960.

Hunt E.H., *British Labour History, 1815–1914*, London, Weidenfeld & Nicolson, 1981.

Husbands, R., 'Sexual Harassment Law in Employment: An International Perspective, *International Labour Review*, 131, 6 (1992).

Huster, E.-U. et al., *Determinanten der Westdeutschen Restauration, 1945–1949*, Frankfurt, Suhrkamp, 1972.

Huyssen, A., *After the Great Divide*, Bloomington, Indiana University Press, 1986.

ILO, *International Survey of Social Services*, Geneva, 1933.

ILO, *The Cost of Social Security, 1949–1957*, Geneva, 1961.

ILO, *The Cost of Social Security*, Eleventh and Twelfth International Survey, Geneva, 1985, 1988.

ILO, *Yearbook of Labour Statistics 1984, 1985, 1988, 1991, 1992, 1993*, Geneva, 1984, 1985, 1988, 1991, 1992, 1993.

Inglehart, R., *The Silent Revolution*, Princeton, Princeton University Press, 1977.

Inglehart, R., *Culture Shift in Advanced Industrial Society*, Princeton, Princeton University Press, 1990.

Inquérito ao emprego 4º trimestre de 1989, Lisbon, Instituto Nacional de Estatistica, 1990.

Ipos, S., 'Current and Structural Problems Affecting Children in Central and Eastern Europe', in G.A. Cornia and S. Sipos (eds), *Children and the Transition to the Market Economy*, Aldershot, Avebury, 1991.

Ishida, H., et al., 'Intergenerational Class Mobility in Postwar Japan', *American Journal of Sociology* 96 (1991).

Ishihara, S., *The Japan That Can Say No*, New York, Simon & Schuster, 1991.

Jacobs, D., 'Gereguleerd Staal', Nijmegen, Katholieke Universiteit, Inst. von Politicologie, PhD Thesis, 1988.

Jacques, M., and Mulhern, F. (eds), *The Forward March of Labour Halted?*, London, Verso, 1981.

Jahrbuch für Ostrecht XXIII, 1–2 (1982).

Jamison, A., et al., *The Making of the New Environmental Consciousness*, Edinburgh, Edinburgh University Press, 1990.

Janecková H. and Hnilicová H., 'The Health Status of the Czechoslovak Population: Its Social and Ecological Determinants', *International Journal of Health Sciences* 3 (1992).

Japan Statistical Yearbook 1991, Tokyo, Mainichi Shinbunsha, 1991.

Jaruzelski, W., *Mein Leben für Polen*, Munich, Piper, 1992.

Jasiewicz, K., 'Zwischen Einheit und Teilung: Politische Orientierungen der Polen in der 80en Jahren', in G. Meyer and F. Ryszka (eds), *Die politische kultur Polens*, Tubingen, Francke, 1989.

Jensen, A.-M. and Saporiti, 'Do Children Count?', *Eurosocial* 36, 17 (1992).

Johansen, L.N., 'Denmark', in P. Flora (ed.), *Growth to Limits*, Vol. 4, Berlin, de Gruyter,1986.

July, R., *The Origins of Modern African Thought*, New York, Praeger, 1967.

Kaelble, H., *Auf dem Weg zu einer europäischen Gesellschaft*, Munich, C.H. Beck, 1987.

Kaelble, H., *Nachbarn am Rhein*, Munich, C.H. Beck, 1991.

Kai Yuan Tsui, 'Regional Inequality, 1952–1985', *Journal of Comparative Economies*, 15,1 (1991).

Kangas, O., *The Politics of Social Rights Studies on the Dimensions of Sickness Insurance in OECD Countries*, Stockholm, Swedish Institute for Social Research, 1991.

Kappeler, A., *Russland als Vielvölkerreich*, Munich, C.H. Beck, 1992.

Kaspi, A. and Marès, A., *Le Paris des étrangers*, Paris, Imprimerie nationale, 1989.

Katzenstein, P., *Small States in World Markets*, Ithaca, NY, Cornell University Press, 1985.

Kavanagh, D., 'Ideology, Sociology, and the Strategy of the British Labour Party', in J. Clark et al. (eds), *John H. Goldthorpe*, London, Falmer Press, 1990.

Kepel, G., *Les banlieues de l'Islam*, Paris, Seuil, 1991.

Kern, H. and Schumann, M., *Das Ende der Arbeitsteilung?*, Munich, C.H. Beck, 1984.

Kern, S., *The Culture of Time and Space, 1880–1918*, Cambridge, Mass., Harvard University Press, 1983.

Kirk, M., 'Law and Fertility in Ireland', in M. Kirk et al. (eds), *Law and Fertility in Europe*, Vol. 2, Dolhain, Ordina, 1975.

Kitschelt, H., *Politik und Energie*, Frankfurt, Campus,1983.

Kleinsteuber, H., et al. (eds), *Electronic Media and Politics in Western Europe*, Frankfurt, Campus, 1986.

Klessmann, C. and Wagner, G. (eds), *Das gespaltene Land*, Munich, C.H. Beck, 1993.

Kluegel, J., et al., *Social Justice and Political Change: Public Opinion in Capitalist and Post-Communist Nations*, manuscript (Publication forthcoming).

Knapp, V. and Elis, J., 'Das Eherecht der Tschechoslowakischen sozialistischen Republik', in E. Loewenfeld and W. Lauterbach (eds), *Das Eherecht der europäischen und der aussereuropäischen Staaten*, national reports, Cologne, Carl Hegmann, 1963.

Knight, F., *Risk, Uncertainty, and Profit*, Boston, Houghton Mifflin, 1921.

Kocka, J., *Angestellten zwischen Faschismus und Demokratie*, Göttingen, Vandenhoeck & Ruprecht, 1977.

Köhler, P. and Zacher, H., 'Einleitung', in idem (eds), *Ein Jahrhundert Sozialversicherung*, Berlin, Duncker & Humblot, 1980.

Koike, K., 'Qualifizierung und Arbeitseinsatz in japanischen Grossbetrieben', in K. Dohse et al. (eds), *Statussicherung im Industriebetrieb*, Frankfurt, Campus, 1982.

Kolarska-Bobinska, L., 'Die marktwirtschaftliche Reform im gesellschaftlichen Bewusstsein und in der Wirtschaft Polens in den Jahren 1980–90', *Journal für Sozialforschung* 30, 3 (1990).

Kornai, J., *The Economics of Shortage*, Amsterdam, North-Holland, 1980.

Kornai, J., 'The Hungarian Reform Process: Visions, Hopes, and Reality', in V. Nee and D. Stark (eds), *Remaking the Economic Institutions of Socialism: China and Eastern Europe*, Stanford, Stanford University Press, 1989.

Korpi, W., *The Democratic Class Struggle*, London, Routledge & Kegan Paul, 1983.

Kosellek, R., *Futures Past*, Cambridge, Mass., MIT Press, 1985.

Kotkin, S., *Steeltown USSR*, Berkeley, University of California Press, 1991.

Kozyr-Kowalski, S. and Przestalski, A. (eds), *On Social Differentiation*, Poznan; Adam Mickiewicz University Press, 1992, 3 vols.

Kraus, F., 'The Historical Development of Income Inequality in Western Europe and the United States', in P. Flora and A. Heidenheimer (eds), *The Development of Welfare States in Europe and America*, New Brunswick and London, NJ, Transaction Books, 1981.

Krejčí, J., 'Ethnic Problems in Europe', in S. Giner and M.S. Archer (eds), *Contemporary Europe: Social Structures and Cultural Patterns*, London, Routledge, 1978.

Kruse, A., *Den offentliga sektorns effekter på sysselsätningen*, Stockholm: Nordiska Ministerrådet, 1984.

Kubat, D. (ed.), *The Politics of Migration Policies*, New York, Center for Migration Studies, 1979.

Küsters, H.J. 'The Federal Republic of Germany and the EEC-Treaty', in E. Serra (ed.), *Il rilancio dell'Europa e i trattati di Roma* Brussels, Milan, Paris, Baden-Baden, Bruylant, Giuffré, LGDJ and Nomos, 1989.

Küsters, H.J., 'The Origins of the EC-Treaty', in E. Serra (ed.), *Il rilancio dell'Europa e i trattati di Roma*, Brussels, Milan, Paris and Baden-Baden, Bruylant, Giuffré, LGDJ and Nomos, 1989.

Labasse, J., *L'Europe des régions*, Paris, Flammarion, 1991.

Lach, D., *Asia in the Making of Europe*, Vol. 2, Chicago, University of Chicago Press, 1977, 2 Vols.

Laffont, R., *La nation, l'Etat, les régions*, Paris, Berg International, 1993.

Lagoudis Pinchion, J., *Alexandra Still*, Cairo, American University in Cairo Press, 1989.

Lampert, N., *Whistleblowing in the Soviet Union*, London: Macmillan, 1985.

Lane, C., *The Rites of Rulers*, Cambridge, Cambridge University Press, 1981.

Lane, C., *Management and Labour in Europe*, Aldershot, Edward Elgar, 1989.

Lane, D., *Soviet Economy and Society*, Oxford, Blackwell, 1985.

Lane, J.-E. and Ersson, S., *Politics and Society in Western Europe*, London, Sage, 2nd edn, 1991.

Laroque, P. (ed.), *Les institutions sociales de la France*, Paris, La Documentation Française, 1980.

Lash, S. and Urry, J., *The End of Organized Capitalism*, Cambridge, Polity Press, 1987.

Lavoie, D., *Rivalry and Central Planning*, Cambridge, Cambridge University Press, 1985.

League of Nations, *Statistical Yearbook of the League of Nations 1937/38*, Geneva, 1939.

Leggewie, C., 'Propheten ohne Macht' in K.-W. Brand (ed.), *Neue soziale Bewegungen in Westeuropa' und den USA*, Frankfurt, Campus, 1985.

Lehmann, J.-P., *The Roots of Modern Japan*, Basingstoke, Macmillan, 1982.

Leibfried, S., *Die angepasste Universität: Zur Situation der Hochschulen in der Bundesrepublik und den USA*, Frankfurt, Suhrkamp, 1968.

Lemke, C., *Die Ursachen des Umbruchs 1989*, Opladen, Westdeutscher Verlag, 1991.

Lenoir, R., 'L'invention du troisième âge', *Actes de la recherche en sciences sociales* 26/27 (1979).

Lepenies, W., *Die drei Kulturen*, Munich and Vienna, Carl Hanser, 1985.

Lerner D., 'Modernization: Social Aspects', in D. Sills (ed.), *International Encyclopedia of the Social Sciences*, Vol. 10, New York, Macmillan, 1968.

Levnadsförhållanden Rapport nr 80, Stockholm, SCB, 1992.

Lewis, B., *The Muslim Discovery of Europe*, New York, Norton, 1982.

Lewis, B. and Schapper, D. (eds), *Musulmans en Europe*, Poitiers, Actes Sud, 1992.

Lipgens, W., *Europa-Föderationspläne der Widerstandsbewegungen, 1940–45*, Munich, Oldenbourg, 1968.

Lipschitz, L. and McDonald, D., *German Unification*, Washington, IMF Occasional Paper No. 75, 1990.

Lipset, S.M. and Bendix, R., *Social Mobility in Industrial Society*, Berkeley, University of California Press, 1990.

Lodge, J. (ed.), *The 1989 Election of the European Parliament*, London, Macmillan, 1990.

Loewenfeld, E. and Lauterbach, W. (eds), *Das Eherecht der europäischen und der aussereuropäischen Staaten*, Cologne, Carl Hegmann, 1963–72.

Lohlé-Tart, L., 'Law and Fertility in Belgium', in M. Kirk et al. (eds), *Law and Fertility in Europe*, Vol. 1, Dolhain, Ordina, 1975.

Love, J., *McDonald's*, Stockholm, Svenska Dagbladet, 1987.

Luhmann, N., *Gesellschaftsstruktur und Semantik*, Frankfurt, Suhrkamp, 1981, 2 vols.

Luhmann, N., *Legitimation durch Verfahren*, Frankfurt, Suhrkamp, 1983.

Luhmann, N., *Soziologie des Risikos*, Berlin, de Gruyter, 1991.

Luhmann, N., *Beobachtungen der Moderne*, Opladen, Westdeutscher Verlag, 1992.

Luhmann, N. (ed.), *Soziale Differenzierung: Zur Geschichte einer Idee*, Opladen, Westdeutscher Verlag, 1985.

Lukács, J., *Budapest 1900*, New York, Weidenfeld & Nicolson, 1988.

Lyotard, J.-F., *La condition post-moderne*, Paris, Ed. de Minuit, 1979.

Lyotard, J.-F., *Peregrinations*, New York, Columbia University Press, 1988.

McCarthy, M., *Campaigning for the Poor: CPAG and the Politics of Welfare*, London, Croom Helm, 1986.

McCormick J., *Reclaiming Paradise*, Bloomington, Indiana University Press, 1989.

Mackie, T. and Rose, R., *International Almanac of Electoral History*, 2nd edn, London, Macmillan, 1982; 3rd edn, London, Macmillan, 1990.

Maddison, A., *Economic Growth in Japan and the USSR*, London, George, Allen & Unwin, 1969.

Maddison, A., 'Economic Policy and Performance in Europe, 1913–1970' in C. Cipolla (ed.), *The Fontana Economic History of Europe*, London: Collins/Fontana, 1976.

Maddison, A., *Ontwikkelingsfasen van het kapitalisme*, Utrecht: Het Spectrum, 1982 (English edn: *Phases of Capitalist Development*. Oxford, Oxford University Press, 1982).

Maggiore, M., *Audiovisual Production in the Single Market*, Luxemburg, EC, 1990.

Maier, C., *Recasting Bourgeois Europe*, Princeton, Princeton University Press, 1975.

Maier, C., *In Search of Stability*, Cambridge, Cambridge University Press, 1987.

Marc, G., 'Les étrangers en France', in *Données Sociales 1987*, Paris, INSEE, 1987.

Marchand, O., 'Une comparaison internationale du temps de travail, *Futuribles* 165–6 (1992).

Mardin, S., 'Europe in Turkey' in T. Belge (ed.), *Where Does Europe End?*, Ankara, Mas Matbacilik, 1993.

Marer, P., et al., *Historically Planned Economies: A Guide to the Data*, Washington, DC, World Bank, 1992.

Marmand C. and Vaughan, P. (eds), *Europe without Frontiers: The Implications for Health*, Chichester, John Wiley & Sons, 1993.

Marshall, T.H., *Class, Citizenship and Social Development*, Garden City, NY, Anchor Books, 1965 (originally published 1950).

Martens, J., 'Die rechtsstaatliche Struktur der Europäischen Wirtschaftsgemeinschaft', *Europarecht* 5 (1970).

Martin, D., 'The Religious Condition of Europe', in S. Giner and M.S. Archer (eds), *Contemporary Europe: Social Structures and Cultural Patterns*, London, Routledge & Kegan Paul, 1978.

Martin, D., *A General Theory of Secularization*, Oxford, Blackwell, 1978.

Martin, R., *A System of Rights*, Oxford, Clarendon Press, 1993.

Marx, K., 'Der achtzehnte Brumaire des Louis Bonaparte', in *Marx–Engels Werke*, Vol. 8, Berlin, Dietz, 1972 (originally published 1852).

Matey, M., 'La situation du travailleur en cas de maladie en droit Polonais', in *International Society for Labour Law and Social Security, 9th Congress*, Vol. 11/2, Heidelberg, Verlagsgesellschaft Recht und Wirtschaft, 1978.

Mathews, M., *Poverty in the Soviet Union*, Cambridge, Cambridge University Press, 1986.

Maurice, M., et al., *The Social Foundations of Industrial Power*, London, MIT Press, 1986.

Mayer, K.U. (ed.), *Lebensverläufe und sozialer Wandel*, Kölner Zeitschrift für Soziologie und Sozialpsychologie Sonderheft 31, Opladen, Westdeutscher Verlag, 1990.

Mazey, S. 'European Community Action on Behalf of Women: The Limits of Legislation', *Journal of Common Market Studies* XXVII, 1 (Sept. 1988).

Meadows, D., et al., *The Limits to Growth: A Report for the Club of Rome's Project on the Predicament of Mankind*, London: Pan/New York: Universe Books, 1972.

Meier, G. and Seers, D. (eds), *Pioneers in Development*, Washington, DC, World Bank/Oxford, Oxford University Press, 1984.

Meissner, B. (ed.), *Die baltischen Nationen*, 2nd edn, Cologne, Markus, 1991.

Mélandri, P., 'Le rôle de l'unification européenne dans la politique extérieure des Etats-Unis, 1948–1950, in R. Poidevin (ed.), *Histoire des débuts de la construction européenne*, Brussels, Milan, Paris, Baden-Baden, Bruylant, Giuffré, LGDJ and Nomos, 1986.

Ménière, L. (ed.), *Bilan de la France, 1981–1993*, Paris, Hachette, 1993.

Mermet, G., *Euroscopie*, Paris, Larousse, 1991.

Merton, R., *Social Theory and Social Structure*, rev. and enl. edn, Glencoe, Ill., Free Press, 1957.

Meyers, F., *Ownership of Jobs: A Comparative Study*, Los Angeles, UCLA, Institute of Industrial Relations, 1964.

Mezentseva, E. and Rimachevskaya, N., 'The Health of the Populations in the Republics of the Former Soviet Union', *International Journal of Health Sciences* 3 (1992).

Miklasz, M., 'La famille en Pologne et ses problèmes depuis 1945', in R. Ganghofer (ed.), *Le droit de famille en Europe*, Strasburg, Presses Universitaires de Strasbourg, 1992.

Milkova, F., 'Le droit de famille en Bulgarie contemporaine', in R. Ganghofer (ed.), *Le droit de famille en Europe*, Strasburg, Presses Universitaires de Strasbourg, 1992.

Millar, J., 'Observations Concerning the Distinction of Ranks in Society', 3rd edn, 1771, reprinted in W. Lehmann, *John A Millar of Glasgow*, Cambridge, Cambridge University Press, 1960.

Milward, A., *The European Rescue of the Nation-State*, London, Routledge, 1992.

Mitchell, B.R., *European Historical Statistics, 1750–1988*, 3rd edn, Basingstoke, Macmillan, 1992.

Mitchell, D., 'Comparative Income Transfer Systems: Is Australia the Poor Relation?', in F. Castles (ed.), *Australia Compared*, London, Allen & Unwin, 1991.

Mitchell, D., 'Taxation and Income Redistribution: The "Tax Revolt" of the 1980s Revisited', paper presented to the ISA Research Committee on Welfare Conference in Oxford in September 1993.

Mitchell, J.D.B., 'British Law and British Membership', *Eurparecht*, 6 (1971).

Mitterauer, M., *Sozialgeschichte der Jugend*, Frankfurt, Suhrkamp, 1986.

Miyoshi, M., *As We Saw Them: The First Japanese Embassy to the United States (1860)*, Berkeley, University of California Press, 1979.

Moll, P., 'The Discrete Charm of the Club of Rome', *Futures* 25 (1993).

Molle, W., *Regional Disparity and Economic Development in the European Community*, Farnborough, Saxon House, 1980.

Mooser, J., *Arbeiterleben in Deutschland, 1900–1970*, Frankfurt, Suhrkamp, 1984.

Morzol, I. and Ogórek, M., 'Shadow Justice', in J. Wedel (ed.), *The Unplanned Society*, New York, Columbia University Press, 1992.

Mouvement du 22 mars, *Ce n'est qu un début, continuons le combat*, Paris, Maspero, 1968.

Mouzelis, N., 'In Defence of "Grand" Historical Sociology', *British Journal of Sociology* 45 (1994).

Müller, H.-P., 'Lebensstile: Ein neues Paradigma der Differenzierungs- und Ungleichheitsforschung?', *Kölner Zeitschrift für Soziologie* 41 (1989).

Müller, W., 'Education and Class Position in European Nations', paper presented at the Conference "European Society or European Societies? Social Mobility and Social Structure", Gausdal, Norway, 24–7 November 1991.

Müller, W., et al., 'Class and Education in Industrial Nations', in M. Haller (ed.), *Class Structure in Europe*, Amonk, NY, M.E. Sharpe, 1990.

Murphy, D., 'Von Aldermaston nach Greenham Common', in K.W. Brand (ed.), *Neue soziale Bewegungen in Westeuropa un den USA*, Frankfurt, Campus, 1985.

Murphy, D., et al., *Protest: Grüne, Bunte und Steuerrebellen*, Reinbek bei Hamburg, Rowohlt, 1979.

Myant, M., *Transforming Socialist Economies*, Aldershot, Edward Elgar, 1993.

Namer, G., *La commémoration en France de 1945 à nos jours*, Paris, SPAG, 1983.

Nasjonalrekenskapeme fylkesvis 1986, Oslo, Statistisk, Sentralbyrå, 1989.

N'Diaye, J.-P., et al., 'Les travailleurs noirs en France', *Réalités africaines* 5 (1965).

Nee, V. and Stark, D. (eds), *Remaking the Economic Institutions of Socialism: China and Eastern Europe*, Stanford, Stanford University Press, 1989.

Neundörfer, L., *Atlas sozioökonomischer Regionen Europas*, 17th edn, Frankfurt, Soziogeographisches Institut a.d. J.W. Goethe-Universität, 1973.

Newfield, J., *A Prophetic Minority*, New York, Signet Books, 1967.

Niehoff, J.U., et al., 'Reflections on the Health Policy of the Former German Democratic Republic', *International Journal of Health Sciences* 3 (1992).

Niethammer, L. *Die volkseigene Erfahrung*, Berlin, Rowohlt, 1991.

Nieuwbeereta, P. and Uitee, W., 'Explaining Differences in the Level of Class Voting in 20 Western Industrial Nations', 1945–1990', Nijmegen, Dept. of Sociology of the Catholic University of Nijmegen, 1992.

Noëlle, E. and Neumann, E.P. (eds), *The Germans: Public Opinion Polls, 1947–1966*, Westport, Conn., Greenwood, 1981.

Noiriel, G., *Les ouvriers dans la société française*, Paris, Seuil, 1986.

Nora, P. (ed.), *Les lieux de mémoires*, Paris, Gallimard, 1984–93, 7 vols.

Nordengren, S., *Economic and Social Targets for Postwar France*, Lund, Institute of Economic History, 1972.

Nowotny, H., *Eigenzeit*, Frankfurt, Suhrkamp, 1989.

Nuti, D. M. 'Theses on Poland', *New Left Review* 130 (1981).

Nye, D., 'European Self-Representation at the New York World's Fair of 1939', in R. Kroes et al. (eds) *Cultural Transmissions and Receptions*, Amsterdam, VU University Press, 1993.

O'Donnell, G., et al. (eds), *Transitions from Authoritarian Rule: Southern Europe*, Baltimore, Johns Hopkins University Press, 1986.

OECD, *Policy and Planning for Post-Secondary Education: A European Overview*, Paris, 1971.
OECD, *Demographic Trends, 1950–1990*, Paris, 1979.
OECD, *Social Expenditure, 1960–1985*, Paris, 1985.
OECD, *The Integration of Women Into the Economy*, Paris, 1985.
OECD, *Labour Force Statistics, 1964–1984*, Paris, 1986.
OECD, *Employment Outlook 1986, 1988, 1989, 1990, 1991, 1992, 1993*, Paris, 1986–93.
OECD, *Financing and Delivering Health Care*, Paris, 1987.
OECD, *The Future of Migration*, Paris, 1987.
OECD, *Labour Force Statistics 1965–1985*, Paris, 1987.
OECD, *Ageing Populations*, Paris, 1988.
OECD, *Reforming Public Pensions*, Paris, 1988.
OECD, *Social Expenditure Trends and Demographic Developments*, paper for the meeting of the OECD Manpower and Social Affairs Committee, 6–8 July 1988, Paris (mimeographed).
OECD, *National Accounts, 1960–1987*, Vol. 1, Paris, 1989.
OECD, *Education in the OECD Countries, 1987–88*, Paris, 1990.
OECD, *Les familles monoparentales*, Paris, 1990.
OECD, *Health Care Systems in Transition*, Paris, 1990.
OECD, *Economic Survey of Germany*, Paris, 1991.
OECD, *Historical Statistics, 1960–1989*, Paris, 1991.
OECD, *Labour Force Statistics, 1969–1989*, Paris, 1991.
OECD, *National Accounts, 1960–1989*, Vols 1–2, Paris, 1991.
OECD, *Regional Problems in Switzerland*, Paris, 1991.
OECD, *Historical Statistics, 1960–1990*, Paris, 1992.
OECD, *National Account, 1960–1990*, Vol. 1, Paris, 1992.
OECD, *New Directions of Work Organization*, Paris, 1992.
OECD, *Economic Outlook 54*, Paris, December 1993.
OECD, *Monthly Statistics of Foreign Trade*, October 1993.
OECD Urban Affairs Programme, 'Urban Statistics in OECD Countries', Paris, 1988 (mimeographed).
Okun, A., *Equality and Efficiency*, Washington, DC, Brookings Institution, 1975.
Olson, M., *The Rise and Decline of Nations*, New Haven, Conn., Yale University Press, 1982.
Olsson, S.E. and Therborn, G. (eds), *Vision möter verklighet*, Stockholm: Allmänna Förlaget, 1991.
Padgett, S. and Paterson, W., *A History of Social Democracy in Postwar Europe*, London, Longman, 1991.
Palme, J., *Pension Rights in Welfare Capitalism*, Stockholm, Swedish Institute for Social Research, 1990.
Pålsson, A., 'Economic Policy and the Distribution of Wealth', in I. Persson (ed.), *Generating Equality in the Welfare State*, Oslo, Norwegian University Press, 1990.
Panaccione, A. (ed.), *The Memory of May Day*, Venice, Marsilio, 1989.
Panikkar, K.M., *Asia and Western Dominance*, London, George Allen & Unwin, 1953.
Pap, T., 'Das Eherecht der Ungarischen Volksrepublik', in E. A Loewenfeld & W. Lauterbach (eds), *Das Eherecht der europäischen und der aussereuropäischer Staaten*, Cologne, Carl Hegmann, 1963–72.
Parkin, S., *Green Parties: An International Guide*, London, Heretic Books, 1989.
Parry, R., 'United Kingdom', in P. Flora (ed.), *Growth to Limits*, Vol. 2, Berlin, de Gruyter, 1986.
Parsons, T., *The System of Modern Societies*, Englewood Cliffs, Prentice-Hall, 1971.
Pauninen, H., 'Finskan i Helsingfors', in *Helsingfors' två språk*, Helsinki, Meddelanden from Institutionen für nordiska språk och nordisk litteratur vid Helsingfors Universitet, 1980.
Peschar, J. (ed.), *Social Reproduction in Eastern and Western Europe*, Nijmegen, Institute for Applied Social Sciences, 1990.
Pestoff, V., 'Voluntary Associations and Nordic Party Systems', Stockholm, Stockholm University Dept. of Pol. Science, Ph.D. Thesis, 1977.
Peterson, M., *International Interest Organizations and the Transmutation of Postwar Society*, Stockholm, Almqvist & Wiksell, 1979.

Petersson, O., et al., *Medborgarnas makt*, Stockholm, Carlssons, 1989.

Pettersson, T., *Bakom dubbla lås*, Stockholm, Institutet för framtidsstudier, 1988.

Philips, R., *Untying the Knot*, Canto edn, Cambridge, Cambridge University Press, 1991.

Pieters, D.C.H.M. and Schell, J.L.M., *Inleiding tot Het Sociale Zekerheidsrecht van de landen van de Europese Gemeenschap*, Delft, Commissie Onderzoek Sociale Zekerheid/Ministerie van Sociale Zaken en Werkgelegenheid, 1990.

Piore, M. and Sabel, S., *The Second Industrial Divide*, New York, Basic Books, 1984.

Piscatore, P., 'Das Zusammenwirken der Gemeinschaftsordnung mit den nationalen Rechtsordnungen', *Europarecht* 4 (1970).

Plestina, D., *Regional Development in Communist Yugoslavia*, Boulder, Col., Westview Press, 1992.

Pockney, B.R. (ed), *Soviet Statistics since 1950*, Aldershot, Dartmouth, 1991.

Poggi, G., 'The Church in Italian Politics, 1945–50', in S.J. Woolf (ed.), *The Rebirth of Italy, 1943–1950*, London, Longman, 1972.

Poggioli, R., *The Theory of the Avant-garde*, Cambridge, Mass., The Belknap Press, 1968.

Poidevin, R. (ed.), *Histoire des débuts de l'unification européene*, Brussels, Milan, Paris and Baden-Baden, Bruylant, Giuffré, LGDJ and Nomos.

Popescu, T. and Eliescu, M., 'Das Eherecht der sozialistischen Republik Rumänien', in E. Loewenfeld and W. Lauterbach (eds), *Das Eherecht der europäischen und der aussereuropäischer Staaten*, Cologne, Carl Hegmann, 1963–72.

Poulton, H., *The Balkans*, London, Minority Rights Publications, 1991.

Pound, N.J.G., *An Historical Geography of Europe*, paperback edn, Cambridge, Cambridge University Press, 1988.

Preston, S., et al., *Causes of Death*, New York and London, Sewin Press 1972.

Przeworski, A. and Sprague, J., *Paper Stones*, Chicago, University of Chicago Press, 1986.

Przeworski, A. and Underhill, E., 'The Evolution of Class Structure in France, 1901–1968', Chicago, University of Chicago Dept. of Political Science (mimeographed).

Putnam, B., 'The Political Attitudes of Senior Civil Servants in Britain, Germany, and Italy', in M. Dogan (ed.), *The Mandarins of Western Europe*, Beverly Hills, Sage, 1975.

Quellenec, M., *Analyse structurale de dévéloppment économique des régions françaises, 1864–1970*, Paris, Université de Paris, 1972.

Rabinovitch, A., *The Bolsheviks Come to Power*, New York, Norton, 1976.

Rabinow, P., *French Modern*, Cambridge, Mass., MIT Press, 1989.

Ragionieri, E., 'La storia politica e sociale', in R. Romato and C. Vivanti (eds), *Storia d'Italia*, Vol. 4, Turin, Einaudi, 1976.

Raton, l., 'Les jeunes de moins de 15 ans: enfants et jeunes adolescents', *Méthodes* 8 (1991).

Rau, Z. (ed.), *The Reemergence of Civil Society in Eastern Europe and the Soviet Union*, Boulder, Col., Westview Press, 1991.

Rauch, G. von, *Geschichte der baltischen Staaten*, Stuttgart, Kohlhammer, 1970.

Raun, T., *Estonia and the Estonians*, Stanford, Hoover Institution Press, 1991.

RECLUS/DATAR, *Les Villes 'Européennes'*, Paris: La Documentation Française, 1989.

Regional Trends 28, CSO, London, HMSO, 1993.

Regiones europeas de antigua industrialización, Bilbao, SPRI, 1989.

Reid, A. and Marr, D. (eds), *Perceptions of the Past in Southeast Asia*, Singapore, Heinemann, 1970.

Richta, R., *La civilisation au carrefour*, Paris, Anthropos/Seuil, 1974.

Rieg, A., 'Traits fondamentaux de l'évolution du droit des régimes matrimoniaux dans l'Europe du XXe siècle', in R. Ganghofer (ed.), *Le droit de famille en Europe*, Strasburg, Presses Universitaires de Strasbourg, 1992.

Rilevazione delle forze di lavoro aprile 1990, Rome, Istat, 1990.

Roberts, S. and Bolderson, H., 'How Closed Are Welfare States?', unpublished paper, Brunel University, July 1993.

Robertson, A.H. and Merrills, J.G., *Human Rights in Europe*, 3rd edn, Manchester, Manchester University Press, 1982.

Roemer, J., *A General Theory of Exploitation and Class*, Cambridge, Mass., Harvard University Press, 1982.

Roemer, J., *Free to Lose*, London, Radius, 1988.

Rokkan, S., 'Nation-Building, Cleavage Formation and the Structuring of Mass Politics', in S. Rokkan et al. (eds), *Citizens, Elections and Parties*, Oslo, Universitetsforlaget, 1970.

Rokkan, S., 'Cities, States, and Nations: A Dimensional Model for the Study of Contrasts in Development', in S.N. Eisenstadt and S. Rokkan (eds), *Building States and Nations*, Vol. 1, Beverly Hills and London, Sage, 1973.

Rokkan, S., 'Eine Familie von Modellen für die vergleichende Geschichte Europas', *Zeitschrift für Soziologie 9*, 2 (1980).

Rokkan, S. and Urwin, D., *Economy, Territory, Identity*, London, Sage, 1983.

Romein, J., *The Watershed of Two Eras*, Middletown, Conn., Wesleyan University Press, 1978 (paperback edn, 1982).

Room, G., *'New Poverty' in the European Community*, London, Macmillan, 1990.

Rorty, R., 'Cosmopolitanism without emancipation: A Response to Lyotard', in S. Lash and J. Friedman (eds), *Modernity and Identity*, Oxford, Blackwell, 1992.

Rose, R., 'Getting By Without Government: Everyday Life in Russia', *Daedalus*, Summer 1994.

Rose, R. and Haerpfer, C., *New Democracies Barometer III*, Glasgow, Centre for the Study of Public Policy at the University of Strathclyde, 1994.

Rosén, J., *Det karolinska skedet*, Lund, Gleerups, 1963.

Rosenau, P.M., *Post-modernism and the Social Sciences*, Princeton, Princeton University Press, 1992.

Rosoli, G., 'Italian Migration to European Countries from Political Unification to World War I', in D. Hoerder (ed.), *Labor Migration in the Atlantic Economies*, Westport, Conn., Greenwood Press, 1985.

Ruedy, J., *Modern Algeria*, Bloomington, Indiana University Press, 1992.

Rywkin, M., *Soviet Society Today*, New York, M.E. Sharpe, 1989.

Sachs, A. and Höff Wilson, J., *Sexism and the Law*, Oxford, Martin Robertson, 1978.

Sahlins, P., *Boundaries*, Berkeley, University of California Press, 1989.

Said, E., *Orientalism*, New York, Vintage, 1979.

Said, E., *Culture and Imperialism*, London, Chatto & Windus, 1993.

Samuel, R. (ed.), *Patriotism: The Making and Unmaking of British Identity*, London, Routledge, 3 vols, 1989.

Sartre, J.-P., 'Présentation', *Les Temps Modernes* 1 (October 1945).

Saunders, P. and Klau, F., 'The Role of the Public Sector', *OECD Economic Studies* 4 (1985).

Scardigli, V., *L'Europe des modes de vie*, Paris, Ed. du CNRS, 1987.

Schabowski, G., *Das Politbüro*, Reinbek bei Hamburg, Rowohlt, 1990.

Schaser, A., 'Die Fürstentümer Moldau und Wallachia, 1650–1850', in W. Fischer et al. (eds), *Handbuch der europäischen Wirtschafts- und Sozialgeschichte*, Vol. 4, Stuttgart, Klett-Cotta, 1993.

Scherzer, L., *Der Erste*, Cologne, Kiepenheuer & Witsch, 1988.

Schlau, W., 'Der Wandel in der sozialen Struktur der baltischen Länder', in B. Meissner (ed.), *Die baltischen Nationen*, 2nd edn, Cologne, Markus Verlag, 1991.

Schmidt, F., 'The Prospective Law of Marriage', *Scandinavian Studies in Law* 15 (1971).

Schmidt, F., 'Discrimination because of Sex', in F. Schmidt (ed.), *Discrimination and Employment: A Study of Six Countries by the Comparative Labour Law Group*, Stockholm, Almqvist & Wiksell, 1978.

Schmidt, H., *Die Deutschen und ihre Nachbarn*, Berlin, Siedler, 1990.

Schmidt, M., 'Gendered Labour Force Participation', in F. Castles (ed.), *Families of Nations*, Aldershot, Dartmouth, 1993.

Schmitter, P. and Lehmbruch, G. (eds), *Trends Towards Corporatist Intermediation*, London, Sage, 1979.

Schönfeld, R. (ed.), *Nationalitätenprobleme in Südosteuropa*, Munich, Oldenbourg, 1987.

Schöpflin, G. and Wood, N. (eds), *In Search of Central Europe*, Cambridge, Polity Press, 1989.

Schreiber, T. and Barry, F. (eds), *Bouleversements à l'Est, 1989–1990*, Paris, La Documentation Française, Notes & Etudes Documentaires, 1990.

Schröder, H.J., 'Die amerikanische Deutschlandpolitik und das Problem der west-europäischen Kooperation 1947/48–1950', in R. Poidevin (ed.), *Histoire des débuts de la construction européenne*, Brussels, Milan, Paris and Baden-Baden, Bruylant, Giuffré, LGDJ and Nomos, 1986.

Schulte, B., 'Europäisches und nationales Sozialrecht', *Europarecht* 25 (1990).

Schumpeter, J., *Capitalism, Socialism and Democracy*, London, George Allen & Unwin, 1961 (originally published 1943).

Schwabe, K. (ed.), *Die Anfänge des Schuman Plans, 1950/51*, Brussels, Milan, Paris and Baden-Baden, Bruylant, Giuffré, LGDJ and Nomos, 1988.

Schwarz, H.-P., *Adenauer: Der Aufstieg, 1876–1952*, 3rd edn, Stuttgart, Deutsche-Verlags-Anstalt, 1991.

Schwarz, H.-P., *Adenauer: Der Staatsman, 1952–1967*, Stuttgart, Deutsche-Verlags-Anstalt, 1991.

Schwiedrzik, W., *Träume der ersten Stunde*, Berlin, Siedler, 1991.

Scott, H., *Kan socialismen befria kvinnan?*, Stockholm, Liber, 1978 (orig. edn: *Does Socialism Liberate Women?*, 1974).

Seers, D., 'The Periphery in Europe', in D. Seers et al. (eds), *Underdeveloped Europe*, Brighton, Harvester Press, 1979.

Selbourne, D., *Death of a Dark Hero*, London, Jonathan Cape, 1990.

Serra, E. (ed.), *Il rilancio dell'Europa e i trattati di Roma*, Brussels, Milan, Paris and Baden-Baden, Bruylant, Giuffré, LGDJ and Nomos, 1989.

Sexton, J., 'Bilan de l'émigration irlandaise, de ses causes et de ses conséquences', OECD conference paper GD(93)49, Paris, OECD, 1993.

Sharabi, H., *Arab Intellectuals and the West: The Formative Years, 1875–1914*, Baltimore: John Hopkins University Press, 1970.

Shonfield, A., *Modern Capitalism*, London, Oxford University, 1959.

Shoup, P., *The East European and Soviet Data Handbook*, New York, Columbia University Press, 1981.

Sisson, K., *The Management of Collective Bargaining*, Oxford, Blackwell, 1987.

Siune, K., et al., *Det blev et nei*, Copenhagen, Politiken, 1993.

Skellington, R., *'Race' in Britain Today*, London, Sage, 1992.

Skocpol, T., *Protecting Soldiers and Mothers*, Cambridge, Mass., Belknap Press, 1992.

Slomp, H., *Labor Relations in Europe*, New York, Greenwood Press, 1990.

Smeeding, T., et al., *Poverty, Inequality and Income Distribution, in Comparable Perspective*, Hemel Hempstead, Harvester Wheatsheaf.

Smeeding, T., et al., 'Poverty in Eastern Europe: Lessons for Crossnational Income Comparisons from LIS', in *Poverty Measurement for Economies in Transition in Eastern European Countries*, Warsaw, Polish Statistical Association and Central Statistical Office, 1992.

Smelser, N. (ed.), *Handbook of Sociology*, Newbury Park, Sage, 1988.

Smith, A., *An Inquiry into the Nature and Causes of the Wealth of Nations*, London, Methuen, 1970 (originally published 1776).

Smith, A., *Lectures on Justice, Police, Revenue, and Arms*, ed. E. Cannan, Oxford, 1896.

Smith, Anthony, *The Ethnic Origin of Nations*, Oxford, Blackwell, 1986.

Snare, A., 'Den private volden: om hustrumishandling', in C. Høigård and A. Snare (eds), *Kvinners skyld*, Oslo, Pax, 1983.

Social Trends 21, 24, CSO, London, HMSO, 1991, 1994.

Sombart, W., *Why is There No Socialism in the United States?*, White Plains, NY, M.E. Sharpe, 1976.

SOPEMI, *Trends in International Migration*, Paris, OECD, 1989, 1990, 1992.

Sorokin, P. *Social Mobility*, Glencoe, Ill., Free Press, 1927.

Spadafora, D., *The Idea of Progress in Eighteenth-Century Britain*, New Haven and London, Yale University Press, 1990.

Spence, J., *In Search of Modern China*, New York, Norton, 1990.

Stadsregioner i Europa, Stockholm, SOU, 1990: 34.

Stark, D., 'Coexisting Organizational Forms in Hungary's Emerging Mixed Economy', in V. Nee and D. Stark (eds), *Remaking the Economic Institutions of Socialism: China and Eastern Europe*, Stanford, Stanford University Press, 1989.

Statistical Abstract, 1982–1985, Dublin, 1986.

Statistical Abstract of the United States 1989, 1990, Washington, DC, Dept of Commerce 1989, 1990.

Statistical Handbook of Japan 1988, Tokyo, Statistics Bureau, 1988.

The Statistical History of the United States, ed. B. Wattenberg, New York, Basic Books, 1976.

Statistical Pocket Book of Hungary, Budapest, Statistical Publishing House, 1989.

Statistical Yearbook of Ireland 1990, Dublin, 1990.

Statistical Yearbook of the Netherlands 1991, The Hague, Staatsuitgeverij, 1991.

Statistisches Handbuch für die Republik Österreich 1990, 1991, Vienna, Österreichisches Statistiches Zentralamt, 1990, 1991.

Statistisches Jahrbuch für die Bundesrepublik Deutschland 1990, Stuttgart and Mainz, Statistsches Bundesamt, 1990.

Statistisches Jahrbuch der DDR 1987, 1989, [East] Berlin, Staatsverlag der DDR, 1987, 1989.

Statistisches Jahrbuch der Schweiz 1992, Zurich, Verlag Neue Zürcher Zeitung, 1991.

Statistisk Årbog 1990, Copenhagen, Danmarks Statistisk, 1990.

Statistisk Årbok 1990, Oslo, Statistisk Sentralbyrå, 1990.

Statistisk Årsbok 1989, 1991, 1993, Stockholm, SCB, 1989, 1991, 1993.

Statistisk Årsbok för Finland, 1987, 1989, 1990, Helsinki: Statistiska Centralbyrån, 1987, 1989, 1990.

Stearns, P., *Old Age in European Society*, London, Croom Helm, 1977.

Stein, L., *Der Sozialismus und Communismus des heutigen Frankreichs*, Leipzig, 1842.

Sternberger, D. and Vogel, A. (eds), *Die Wahl der Parlamente und andere Staatsorgane*, Berlin, de Gruyter, 1969.

Strange, S., *States and Markets*, New York, Blackwell, 1988.

Stuurman, S., *Verzuiling, kapitalisme en patriarchaat*, Nijmegen, SUN, 1983.

Sulek, A., 'Politische Meinungsumfragen in Polen – Träger, gessellschaftlicher Kontext und Zuverlässigkeit empirischer Studien', in G. Meyer and F. Ryszka (eds), *Die Politische Kultur Polens*, Tubingen, Francke, 1989.

Summers, R. and Heston, A., 'Improved International Comparisons of Real Product and its Composition: 1950–1980', *The Review of Income and Wealth* 30 (1984).

Summers, R. and Heston, A., 'The Penn World Table (Mark 5): An Expanded Set of International Comparisons: 1950–1988', *The Quarterly Journal of Economics* CVI (May 1991).

Svennilson, I., *Growth and Stagnation in the European Economy*, Geneva, UN Economic Commision for Europe, 1954.

Sveriges Socialdemokratiska Arbetareparti (SAP) *Partistyrelsens Verksamhetsberättelse 1916–1992*, Stockholm, SAP, 1916–92.

Swain, N., *Hungary: The Rise and Fall of Feasible Socialism*, London, Verso, 1992.

Swann, D., *The Retreat of the State*, Hemel Hempstead, Harvester Wheatsheaf, 1988.

Swedberg, S., *Våra grannländers näringsliv*, Stockholm, Rabén & Sjögren, 1959.

Sweezy, P., *The Present as History*, New York: Monthly Review Press, 1953.

Szalai, A. (ed.), *The Use of Time*, The Hague, Mouton, 1972.

Szelenyi, I., *Socialist Entrepreneurs*, Madison, University of Wisconsin Press, 1988.

Szöllösi-Janze, M., ' "Pfeillkreuzler, Landesverräter unde andere Volksfeinde" Generalabrechnung in Ungarn', in K.-D. Henke and H. Woller (eds), *Politische Säuberung in Europa*, Munich, dtv, 1991.

Sztompka, P., *The Sociology of Social Change*, Oxford, Blackwell, 1993.

Szücs, J., *Die drei historischen Regionen Europas*, Frankfurt, Neue Kritik, 1990.

Tamames, R., *La Communidad Europea*, Madrid, Alianza, 1987.

Taylor, C., et al., *Multiculturalism and 'The Politics of Recognition'*, Princeton, Princeton University Press, 1992.

Tapinos, G., *L'immigration étrangére en France*, Paris, Institut national d'études démographiques, 1973.

Taylor-Gooby, P., 'What Citizens Want from the State', in R. Jowell et al. (eds), *International Social Attitudes: The 10th BSA Report*, Aldershot, Dartmouth, 1993.

Teich, M. and Porter, R. (eds), *Fin de Siècle and Its Legacy*, Cambridge, Cambridge University Press, 1990.
Teng, Ssu-yü and Fairbank, J. (eds), *China's Reponse to the West: A Documentary Survey 1839–1923*, Cambridge, Mass., Harvard University Press, 1954.
Teubner, G. (ed.), *Dilemmas of Law in the Welfare State*, Berlin, de Gruyter, 1986.
Teubner, G. (ed.), *Juridification of Social Spheres*, Berlin, de Gruyter, 1987.
Therborn, G., 'From Petrograd to Saigon', *New Left Review* 48 (1968).
Therborn, G., *Science, Class and Society*, London, Verso, 1976.
Therborn, G., 'The Rule of Capital and the Rise of Democracy', *New Left Review* 103 (1977).
Therborn, G., *What Does the Ruling Class Do When It Rules?*, London, Verso, 1978.
Therborn, G., *Klasstrukturen i Sverige, 1930–1980*, Lund, Zenit, 1981.
Therborn, G., 'Why Some Classes Are More Successful Than Others', *New Left Review* 138 (1983).
Therborn, G., 'Classes and States: Welfare State Developments, 1881–1981', *Studies in Pollitical Economy* 13 (Spring 1984) (reprinted in W. Clement and R. Mahon (eds), *Swedish Social Democracy: A Model in Transition*, Toronto, Canadian Scholars' Press, 1994).
Therborn, G., 'The Prospects of Labour and the Transformation of Advanced Capitalism', *New Left Review* 145 (1984).
Therborn, G., 'The Coming of Swedish Social Democracy', in E. Collotti (ed.), *L'Internazionale operaia e socialista tra le due guerre*, Milan: Feltrinelli, 1985.
Therborn, G., 'Class Analysis: History and Defence', in U. Himmelstrand (ed.), *Sociology from Crisis to Science?*, Vol. 1, London, Sage, 1986.
Therborn, G., *Why Some Peoples Are More Unemployed Than Others*, London, Verso, 1986.
Therborn, G., 'Klassernas språk och klasskampens spår', in U. Bergryd (ed.), *Den sociologiska fantasin*, Stockholm, Rabén & Sjögren, 1987.
Therborn, G., 'Migration and Western Europe: The Old World Turning New?', *Science* 237 (4.9.1987).
Therborn, G., 'Tar arbetet slut? och post-fordismens problem', in U. Björnberg and I. Hellberg (eds), *Sociologer ser på arbete*, Stockholm, Arbetslivscentrum, 1987.
Therborn, G., *Borgarklass och byråkrati i Sverige*, Lund, Arkiv.
Therborn, G., 'Revolution and Reform: Reflexions on Their Linkages Through the Great French Revolution', in J. Bohlin et al. (eds), *Samhällsvetenskap, ekonomi, historia*, Göteborg, Daidalos, 1989.
Therborn, G., 'States, Populations and Productivity: Towards a Political Theory of Welfare States', in P. Lassman (ed.), *Politics and Social Theory*, London, Routledge, 1989.
Therborn, G., 'Social Steering and Household Strategies: The Macropolitics and the Microsociology of Welfare States', *Journal of Public Policy* 9, 3 (1990).
Therborn, G., 'Cultural Belonging and Structural Location, and Human Action', *Acta Sociologica* 34, 3 (1991).
Therborn, G., 'Staten och människornas välfärd', in B. Furuhagen (ed.), *Utsikt mot Europa*, Stockholm, Utbildningsradion, 1991.
Therborn, G., 'Swedish Social Democracy and the Transition from Industrial to Postindustrial Politics', in F. Fox Piven (ed.), *Labor Parties in Postindustrial Societies*, Cambridge, Polity Press, 1991.
Therborn, G., 'Class and the Coming of Post-Industrial Society', in S. Kozyr-Kowalski and A. Przestalski (eds), *On Social Differentiation*, Vol. 1, Poznan, Adam Mickiewicz University Press, 1992.
Therborn, G., 'Lessons from "Corporatist" Theorizations', in J. Pekkarinen et al. (eds), *Social Corporatism*, Oxford, Clarendon Press, 1992.
Therborn, G., 'The Right to Vote and the Four World Routes to/through Modernity', in R. Torstendahl (ed.), *State Theory and State History*, London, Sage, 1992.
Therborn, G., 'Modernitá sociale in Europa, 1950–1992', in P. Anderson et al. (eds), *Storia d'Europa*, Vol. 1, Turin, Einaudi, 1993.
Therborn, G., 'The Politics of Childhood', in F. Castles (ed.), *Families of Nations*, Aldershot, Dartmouth, 1993.

Therborn, G., 'Sociology as a Discipline of Disagreements and as a Paradigm of Competing Explanations: Culture, Structure, and the Variability of Actors and Situations', in P. Sztompka (ed.), *Agency and Structure: Re-orienting Social Theory*, Philadelphia, Gordon & Breach, 1994.

Therborn, G., 'Routes to/through Modernity', in M. Featherstone, R. Robertson and S. Lash (eds), *Global Modernities*, London, Sage, 1995.

Therborn, G., 'Dialectics of Modernity: On Critical Theory and the Legacy of 20th-Century Marxism', in B. Turner (ed.), *A Companion to Social Theory*, Oxford, Blackwell, forthcoming.

Therborn, G., 'Exits from Patriarchy and the Politics of Childhood', forthcoming.

Thernstrom, S., 'Working Class Social Mobility in Industrial America', in M. Richter (ed.), *Essays in Theory and History*, Cambridge, Mass., Harvard University Press, 1970.

Tilly, C., *The Contentious French*, Cambridge, Mass., Belknap Press, 1986.

Tilly, C., *Coercion, Capital and European States, AD 990–1990*, rev. paperback edn, Oxford, Blackwell, 1992.

Tilly, C., *European Revolutions 1492–1992*, Oxford: Blackwell, 1993.

Tocqueville, A. de, *De la démocratie en Amérique*, Vol. II, Paris, Gallimard folio, 1986 (1st edn, 1835) (English edn *Democracy in America*, 2 vols, London, Fontana, 1968).

Todd, E., *L'invention de l'Europe*, Paris, Seuil, 1990.

Toranska, T., *Oni*, Warsaw, 1982/1990 (Swedish edn *De ansvariga*, Stockholm, Brombergs, 1986) (English edn *Them*, New York, Harper & Row, 1987).

Touraine, A., *La société post-industrielle*, Paris, Denoël, 1969.

Touraine, A., *L'après-socialisme*, Paris, Grasset, 1980.

Touraine, A., *Critique de la modernité*, Paris, Fayard, 1992.

Trompenaars, F., *Riding the Waves of Culture*, London, Economist Books, 1993.

Turner, B., 'Outline of a Theory of Human Rights', *Sociology* 27, 3 (1993).

Turnock, D., *The Human Geography of Eastern Europe*, London, Routledge, 1989.

Tyomkina, A., 'The Problem of Advancing Industrial Democracy in a Post-Socialist Society', *Economic and Industrial Democracy* 14, Supplement (1993).

Uitee, W., et al., *Sociologie*, Groningen, Wolters-Noordhoff, 1992.

Unemployment in Poland I–III quartor 1993, Warsaw, Główny Urzad Statystyczny, 1993.

Unesco, *Statistical Yearbook 1963, 1973, 1991*, Paris, 1964, 1974, 1991.

Unicef, *Central and Eastern Europe in Transition: Public Policy and Social Conditions*, no. 2, Florence, 1994.

United Nations, *Statistical Yearbook 1951, 1970, 1988/89, 1990*, New York, 1951, 1971, 1990, 1992.

United Nations, *Commodity Trade Statistics*, New York, Series D (1956–1980).

United Nations, *World Economic Survey 1989, 1990*, New York, 1989, 1990.

United Nations, *The World's Women*, New York, 1991.

United Nations Economic Commission for Europe, *Labour Supply and Migration in Europe*, New York, 1979.

Università l'ipotesi rivoluzionaria, Vicenza, Marsilio Editori, 1968.

Uusitalo, H., *Income Distribution in Finland*, Helsinki, Central Statistical Office, 1989.

Veblen, T., *Theory of the Leisure Class*, 1899.

Vecernik, J., 'Earnings Distribution in Czechoslovakia: Intertemporal Changes and International Comparison', *European Sociological Review* 7 (1991).

Veinstein, G. (ed.), *Salonique, 1850–1918*, Paris, Ed. Autrement, 1992.

Veldkamp, G.M.J., et al., *Inleiding tot de sociale zekerheid*, Deventer, Kluwer, 1978, 2 vols.

Venturi, R., et al., *Learning from Las Vegas*, Cambridge, Mass., MIT Press, 1972.

Verhallen, H.J.G., et al. (eds), *Corporatisme in Nederland*, Alphen aan den Rijn, Samson, 1980.

Visser, D., *Flaggen, Wappen, Hymnen*, Augsburg, Battenberg, 1991.

Vogel, A., 'Frauen und Frauenbewegung', in W. Benz (ed.), *Die Geschichte der Bundesrepublik Deutschland*, Vol. 3, Frankfurt, Fischer, 1989.

Vogel, J., et al., *Ojämlikheten i Sverige*, Stockholm, SCB, 1987.

Vogel, W, *Bismarcks Arbeiterversicherung*, Brunswick, G. Westermann, 1951.

Vries, A. de, *Effecten van sociale zekerheid: onderzoek, theorie, methode, Armoede onderzocht*, Tilburg, Katholieke Universitet IVA, 1986.

Wagner, P., *A Sociology of Modernity*, London and New York, Routledge, 1994.

Walker, R. et al. (eds), *Responses to Poverty: Lessons from Europe*, London, Heinemann, 1984.

Wall, R., et al. (eds), *Family Forms in Historic Europe*, Cambridge, Cambridge University Press, 1983.

Wandruska, A. and Urbanitsch P. (eds), *Die Habsburgermonarchie 1848–1918*, Vol. III:1: *Die Völker des Reiches*, Verlag der Österreichischen Akademie der Wissenschaften, 1980.

Wat zoudt gij zonder't werkvolk zijn?, Leuven, Kritak, 2 vols, 1977 and 1981.

Weber, M., 'Die Stadt', *Archiv für Sozialwissenschaft und Sozialpolitik* 61 (1921) (English edn *The City*, New York, Free Press, 1966).

Weber, M., *Wirtschaft und Gesellshaft*, Vol. 1, Cologne, Kiepenheuer & Witsch, 1964 (English edn *Economy and Society*, 3 vols, Totowa N.Y., Bedminster Press, 1968).

Weck, C. de, 'Akademisch frei von kleinauf', *Die Zeit*, 15.1.1993.

Wedderburn, Lord, 'Discrimination in the Right to Organize and the Right to Be a Non-Unionist', in F. Schmidt (ed.), *Discrimination and Employment: A Study of Six Countries by the Comparative Labour Law Group*, Stockholm: Almqvist & Wiksell, 1978.

Wedderburn, Lord, *Employment Rights in Britain and in Europe*, London, Lawrence & Wishart, 1991.

WHO, *Evaluation of the Strategy for Health for All by the Year 2000*, vol. 5, Copenhagen, 1986.

Wievorka, M. (ed.), *Racisme et xénophobie en Europe*, Paris, La Découverte, 1994.

Wiggershaus, R., *Die Frankfurter Schule*, Munich, Carl Hanser, 1986.

Wiktorow, A., 'Soviet Union', in J. Dixon and D. Macarov (eds), *Social Welfare in Socialist Countries*, London, Routledge, 1992.

Wiktorow, A. and Mierzevski, P., 'Promise or Peril? Social Policy for Children during the Transition to the Market Economy in Poland', in G.A. Corniea and S. Sipos (eds), *Children and the Transition to the Market Economy*, Aldershot, Avebury, 1991.

Williamson, J.G., 'Regional Inequality and the Process of National Development: A Description of the Patterns', *Economic Development and Cultural Change*, XIII (1965).

Willis, R., *Italy Chooses Europe*, New York, Oxford University Press, 1971.

Winkler, G. (ed.), *Lexikon der Sozialpolitik*, Berlin, Akademie-Verlag, 1987.

Winkler, G., 'Leistungen der Sozialversicherung europäischer sozialistischer Länder', unpublished paper, East Berlin, Institut für Soziologie und Sozialpolitik der Akademie der Wissenschaften der DDR, March 1988.

Winkler, G. (ed.), *Sozialreport '90* Berlin, Die Wirtschaft, 1990.

Witt, P.-C., 'Die Gründung des Deutschen Reiches von 1871 oder dreimal Kaiserfest', in U. Schultz (ed.), *Das Fest*, Munich, C.H. Beck, 1988.

Wolfe, T., *From Bauhaus to Our House*, New York, Farrar Strauss Giroux, 1981.

Wolferen, K. von, *The Enigma of Japanese Power*, New York, Alfred Knopf, 1989.

Woodruff, W., *Impact of Western Man*, London, Macmillan, 1966.

World Bank, *World Development Report 1987, 1990, 1991, 1993*, Oxford and New York, Oxford University Press, 1987, 1990, 1991, 1993.

World Bank, *World Tables 1992*, Baltimore and London, Johns Hopkins University Press, 1992.

World Bank, *Statistical Handbook 1993: States of the Former USSR*, Washington, DC, 1993.

World Values Survey 1990–1991 (directed by R. Inglehart), Institute for Social Research, University of Michigan (data file).

Wright, E.O., *Classes*, London, Verso, 1985.

Wright, E.O., 'The Comparative Project on Class Structure and Class Consciousness: An Overview', *Acta Sociologica*, 32, 1 (1989).

Wright, G., *The Ordeal of Total War, 1939–1945*, New York, Harper & Row, 1968.

Wuthnow, R. (ed.), *Vocabularies of Public Life*, London, Routledge, 1992.

Yearbook of Nordic Statistics, Copenhagen, Nordic Council of Ministers, 1989.

Yurt Ansklopeditsti, 'İstanbul', Istanbul, Agadolu Yanincilika, 1983.

Zaslavsky, V., 'Russian Nationalism in the Past and Today', in M. Buttino (ed.), *In a Collapsing Empire*, Milan, Feltrinelli, 1993.
zur Nieden, S., 'Die Pille', *Emma* 7 (1991).
Zweigert, K. and Kötz, H., *Introduction to Comparative Law*, 2nd edn, Oxford, Clarendon Press, 1987, 2 Vols.
Zysman, J., *Governments, Markets and Growth*, Ithaca, NY, Cornell University Press, 1983.

Current newspapers, magazines and periodicals

(a) Regularly followed in 1991–4

Dagens Nyheter, Stockholm.
The Economist, London.
Financial Times, London.
Frankfurter Allgemeine Zeitung, Frankfurt.
Le Monde, Paris.
Svenska Dagbladet, Stockholm.
Die Zeit, Hamburg.

(b) Occasionally studied and referred to

Le débat, 78 (janvier–fevrier 1994).
Economie européen, 46 (1990).
The Economist, supplement, 'A Survey of the Music Business', 21.12.1991.
Employment Gazette, London, October 1991.
Eurobarometer 17, 34, 36, 39. Luxemburg, 1982–93.
Eurobarometer, Trend Variables, 1974–1990, March 1991.
Euromonitor, European Consumer Expenditure, London, 1987.
European Economy 47 (1991).
Financial Times, 20.10.1993 'Derivatives' supplement and 21.1.1994 'The FT 500' supplement.
Fortune, 29.7. and 26.8.1991.
Futures, 1, 1 (1968).
Futuribles, 1–2 (1975).
International Herald Tribune, Paris, 3–4.10.1992.
International Journal of Health Sciences, 3 (1992).
Journal für Sozialforschung, 8 (1988) supplement and 30, 1 (1990) Meinungsprofile.
Kursbuch, 12 and 13 (1968).
Nytt Juridiskt Arkiv, 87 (1962).
El País, Madrid, 20.9.1992, 2.10.1993.
Quaderni Piacentini, 34 (May 1968).
Social Indicators Research, 23, 1–2 (1990).
Das sozio-okonomische Panel: Wochenbericht, 37/90 (1990).
Der Spiegel, 10 (1956).
De Standaard, Brussels, 18.12–19.12.1993.
Turkish Daily News, Istanbul, 26.2.1994.

Index